CATHERINE DE MEDICI

Tournament at the French Court. Section from a tapestry. The persons represented are Henri II, Catherine de Medici and probably Henri III.

CATHERINE
DE MEDICI

❧❀❧

JEAN HÉRITIER

TRANSLATED BY CHARLOTTE HALDANE

London
GEORGE ALLEN & UNWIN LTD
RUSKIN HOUSE MUSEUM STREET

PRINTED IN GREAT BRITAIN
in 11 *point Ehrhardt type*
BY SIMSON SHAND LTD
LONDON, HERTFORD AND HARLOW

PRELIMINARY NOTE

In order to avoid any mistaken interpretation, the author wishes to underline the following point. Machiavelli and Machiavellism are very often discussed in this book. The personality of the author of *Il Principe*, and also Machiavellism, are envisaged uniquely from the point of view of the sixteenth century. Here, therefore, Machiavelli is not portrayed according to his legend but as an Italian patriot (the true precursor of the unity of the peninsula) as well as an executive official, who was never at the head of affairs but whom it pleased to jot down, not even maxims, but political recipes, according to the Italy of his time. This also means that at that period Machiavellism was not a doctrine, and even less, a system. It was pragmatic and empirical, having recourse to methods appropriate to the immediate needs of the revolutions and civil wars, as well as the ambitions and vengeances that unfolded themselves on a small stage. Catherine de Medici's political aims—and that was why she was misunderstood—were in advance of a period confined between the limits which inspired the thoughts of the Secretary of the Second Chancellery of Florence, a post that he occupied for fourteen years (1498-1512).

CONTENTS

ILLUSTRATIONS

✥✤❁✤✥

PART I

❧❀❦

YOUTH AND HUMILITY

CHAPTER ONE

NAKED AS A NEW-BORN BABE
(April 1519— November 1533)

◈

Very little is known about the early childhood of Catherine de Medici, born on a Wednesday morning, April 13, 1519, of the marriage of Lorenzo de Medici, Duke of Urbino, and Madeleine de la Tour d'Auvergne. The young Duchess died of puerpural fever fifteen days after the birth of the baby girl who was predestined—although no one could then either have foreseen it or even had a presentiment of it—virtually to become, as the mother of the last of the Valois, ruler of France from 1559–89. Lorenzo died five days after Madeleine. The child, Florentine on her father's side and of Auvergne on her mother's, was orphaned in her cradle.

The cruelly premature death of Lorenzo de Medici finally put an end to French influence in Italy, which had already been more than threatened by the secret treaty, signed on January 17, 1519, between Leo X and Don Carlos, who was to become the Emperor Charles V, and which was to confirm that of 1512. Italy passed over to Spain and later to the Empire. The apparent Machiavellism of this change in papal politics was in fact a piece of Ghibelline trickery. Guicciardini, who was in the confidence of the second Medici Pope, Clement VII, successor to the most Ghibelline pontiff, Adrian VI, the former Provost of Utrecht, preceptor and later minister of Charles V, has revealed the illusions that prompted this rupture with France. It was intended to follow the precepts of Machiavelli. The plan was to make use of the Hispano-Germans to throw the Barbarians, who had arrived there from Gaul, out of Southern Italy, and then to make war, in the kingdom of Naples, on the Imperialists, and to defeat them.

The death of Lorenzo de Medici prepared the way for this return to the policy of Julius II. The sacking of Rome in 1527 was the factual result of this Ghibelline mistake, which had led to the loss of Pavia. In 1519 God alone knew that the weak and puling infant in the orphan's cradle in the Medici palace would one day prove to be the link in the chain of French history between François I and Henri IV. Thus later on, after Richelieu, the Italian, Mazarin, was enabled to complete the great work of conquering the new German Holy Roman Empire, founded on the defeat of the Valois by the Hapsburgs, supporting and suffering the Medici Pope, whose orphaned great-niece, then still a tiny and insignificant babe, would one day make good this error by saving France from becoming a Spanish colony: a political policy based on the principle of princedom, which was to replace the spirit of Christianity. Charles V did not renounce this spirit of Christianity, but the force of circumstances was moving in the opposite direction. Instead of allying himself with the Emperor against the Sultan, François I did the contrary. The dice of iron and of destiny were cast down.

In an elegy Ariosto, who at the time of the deaths of Catherine's parents had been sent to Florence by the Duke of Ferrara, reminded the city of the Red Lily that a few leaves can revive a lone branch. The Florentines remained torn between fear and hope, wondering whether the winter would destroy or leave her to them. For Catherine, so frail and threatened, was the last legitimate heiress of the Medici. Her grandmother, Alfonsina Orsini, widow of Pietro de Medici, died a few months later, on February 7, 1520.[1] The Cardinal Giuliano de Medici, bastard of Giuliano, the nephew of Lorenzo the Magnificent, and cousin to the orphan, was appointed her tutor. Clarice, the sister of Lorenzo II and wife of Filippo Strozzi, was given charge of the child, who already, in October 1519, had been presented to Leo X. Marco Minio, the Venetian ambassador to Rome, had been impressed by the Pope's emotion: '*Recens fert aerumnas Danaum*', Leo X had said to him when he was informed of the arrival of Alfonsina Orsini.

Virgil's melancholy line was quoted in reference to the sad situation of the last legitimate descendant of Lorenzo the Magnificent. Alessandro, and his blood-brother Ippolito, the future Cardinal, grandson of the Magnifico by Giuliano, Duke of Nemours, who died

---

[1] For the reader's convenience we give the dates in thousands according to the calendar in usage today. We know that prior to the edict of Charles IX in 1564, the year began on Holy Saturday and not on January 1st, which means that the contemporary documents referring to the months of January, February, March, and often the beginning and even the major part of April, bear a date in thousands which is one year behind our own. Until the year 1582 (October 5th to 15th) and the Gregorian reform, it is enough to advance every date by ten days, to bring it into line with our own calendar.

in 1516, were bastards. In those days there was no prejudice against bastardy, which did, however, preclude the dynastic succession. The glorious line of the Magnifico was therefore centred in the orphan, the sole legitimate heir to the rulership. She alone barred the way to disruption. At the cradle in which so fragile a hope was in danger of disappearing, the Pope's sadness was easily understandable. As we have seen, the defeat of his alliances had placed the Pope among the adversaries of François I although, according to the immutable tradition of pontifical and Italian diplomacy, which never showed its hand until the very last moment, he had not broken with him. Nevertheless the King of France was refused the orphan's tutelage.

Even Reumont and Baschet, who minutely explored the archives of Florence, Venice, and Rome, are vague and confused regarding the orphan's infancy. Alberi, who collated all the Florentine and Venetian texts, merely states that 'an astrologer was called in to draw up little Catherine's horoscope. It was said that he predicted for her a life full of sorrows, agitation, and storms, a life that was to be a perpetual sacrifice for the sake of French unity.' In his otherwise very conscientious edition of the *Letters* of the mother of the last Valois, Hector de La Ferrière could not quote a single text. Nor is anything to be found in the Italian archives in the Bibliothèque Nationale. It appears that Catherine's earliest years were passed in Rome. The records agree in placing the child's return to Tuscany in June 1525; her tutor having since November 19, 1523 become Pope with the name of Clement VII. With her was also brought back her illegitimate step-brother, Alessandro, 'who had been born to Lorenzo in 1512 by a beautiful and healthy peasant girl of Collavechio (a village in the Roman countryside) a subject or serf of Alfonsina Orsini'.[1]

We know as little about the years that followed their return to Florence, where the brother and sister lived in the Medici palace, only leaving it in the fine weather for the villa of Cajanus, in the environs of the Tuscan capital, as we do about the Roman years. A pastoral letter from Clement VII to François I and dated April 18, 1526, shows how her tutor watched over Catherine's interests. He prevented the Duke of Albany from administering the possessions of Madeleine de la Tour to the detriment of the orphans. He charged the nuncio Roberto Acciaioli to obtain the pension promised her by the King of France. We know nothing else about the years

---

[1] J. H. Mariéjol, *Catherine de Médicis*, p. 9.

B

during which the little girl grew up to the age of discretion under the surveillance of the Strozzi.

The Italian wars had recommenced. The defeat at Pavia revealed the Ghibelline mistake of his predecessors to Clement VII. Italy was becoming Imperial territory. On May 22, 1526, Clement VII joined the new Holy League, that of Cognac, the reverse of the Holy League of Julius II. Now they were banding together against the Empire, re-becoming Guelph. François I, emerging from the prisons of Charles V, Venice, Milan, and most of the small Italian principalities, were uniting with the Pope against the Emperor. The aim of the confederation was 'to put an end to the wars that were desolating Christianity'.

François wanted nothing less than peace. His aim was to escape the treaty of Madrid. On that point Carl Brandi's great book has furnished the proofs. If the King of France was driven by necessity, tradition and the rights of chivalry were on the side of the Emperor. The League appealed to Henry VIII who promised to protect it. Like Machiavelli and Guicciardini, the Pope hoped that once freed from the Imperialists, Italy could also free herself from the ever-threatening hegemony of France. Charles V gave Clement VII the direct riposte. Troops, under the command of a Lutheran, George of Frundsberg, were provided for him by his brother, Ferdinand, Archduke of Austria and King of Bohemia, from whom John Zapolya, an ally of the King of France, was trying to wrest the crown of Hungary. At the beginning of May 1527 Rome was assaulted and afterwards sacked. The Constable of Bourbon, who had passed into Charles V's service, was killed there. Luther was destroying Babylon. And that was made possible by a Catholic king! Such are the bloody games and contradictions of politics.

Almost at the same moment tumult had broken out in Florence against the Medici. The passage of the troops of the Constable of Bourbon through the south of the Arno valley coincided—a normal synchronization—with the beginning of the Florentine uprising. On April 26th, Silvio Passerini, Cardinal of Cortona, to whom Clement VII had entrusted the government of the Republic, and whose unpopularity was equalled by his incapacity, was forced to leave the city. Alessandro and Ippolito de Medici left with him. Little Catherine was now a duchess without a duchy. The Florentines wasted no time. They assaulted the palace, which was defended by those citizens who remained loyal to the Medici. The child of eight years was caught up in revolution. As Louis XIV remembered Paris during the Fronde, so Catherine was always to remember Florence in revolt. She spent a few more years in the midst of these disturbances, until the end of September 1530. The years from eight until eleven are those during which a little girl's intelligence develops a great deal. Those were the years of Catherine de Medici's apprenticeship to politics and war.

Henceforward we have numerous, precise and excellent sources on Catherine de Medici and her initiation into the experimental politics of civil wars, wars that she did not learn about in books but lived through. Her school was life, in the midst of sedition, when the horrifying acts committed by a furious populace were unleashed simultaneously with the disgraceful behaviour of the powerful, who sold themselves to the foreigner and fooled the little man, living by bloody treachery. For, as Lucan so magnificently said in his *Pharsalus*, civil wars, with their useless sacrifices, are the worst of all: '*Bella geri placuit nullos habitura triumphos. . . .*'

In order to safeguard her against the epidemics that had been ravaging Florence for several years, the French ambassador, Monsieur de Velly, obtained the new Council's permission to take Catherine away. 'On the evening of December 7, 1527, he conducted her, heavily veiled, to the convent of the Santissima Annunziata delle Murate, where she was to stay for the time being. The name of this convent, the Murate, was aptly suited to a residence where the young Medici was as closely supervised as a captive.'[1] But her captivity was greatly softened by the affection immediately shown towards her by the nuns of the Order of St Benedict. This is proven by the *Chronicle of the Murate*, by one of the nuns, Sister Justine Niccolini. The warmest sympathies were aroused by the unhappy child's affability, charm and sweetness. Yet the various factions continued to tear Florence to pieces. The Medici always had their partisans. Capponi's *Ottimati* fought violently against the *Arrabiati*, i.e. the Madmen, of Francisco Carducci, who in the spring of 1529 were victorious. The worst kinds of violence, including vandalism, customary in such times of disorder, when nothing any longer impedes the destroying fanatics, fell on the city of the Red Lily. Escutcheons, coats-of-arms and statues were smashed, churches sacked, tombs desecrated. The child in her cloister, to which only the echoes of such furious deeds penetrated, could not have foreknown that the last thirty years of her life would have the same horrible setting; a setting, this time, no

[1] Reumont and Baschet, *La Jeunesse de Catherine de Médicis*, p. 96–97.

longer of an Italian city, but of an entire kingdom, the kingdom of France, whose lilies were to become red with the blood of the citizens as they killed one another by thousands. And that took place because some insisted that others should be forced to go either to mass or to the preacher, according to whether they belonged to the Papist and Roman, or to the Protestant and Genevan confessions.

In few famous lives has there been at their beginning so clear a prefiguration of their maturity and old age as in that of Catherine de Medici. Not to take into account the powerful influence of childhood memories on Catherine, after she had become the queen-mother, with the only aim of saving the nation from civil war, would be to deny the most fundamental laws of psychology. For the horrors of civil war were engraved on her memory at the most impressionable age, that of the last years of her childhood. A monstrous war, Montaigne was to call it. And his adjective is the only exact one.

On these Florentine horrors we are very well documented. By the Treaty of Barcelona, June 29, 1529, Clement VII was reconciled with Charles V. The Emperor promised his natural daughter, Marguerite, born in 1522 at Audenarde of his transient affair with Jeanne van der Gheinst, in marriage to Alessandro, Catherine's natural brother. Bastards were the most convenient matrimonial currency used by those realistic politicians admired by Machiavelli and Guicciardini. Marguerite of Austria was to become Duchess of Parma, Governor of the Low Countries under Philip II, and mother of Alessandro Farnese. Born three years after Catherine, and dying three years before her, Marguerite was to occupy on the tragic scene of the sixteenth century a place that would give her opportunities to reveal the full measure of her genius, comparable in many ways to that of the sister of Alessandro de Medici.

François I and Charles V, meanwhile, were negotiating the second Peace of Cambrai, also known as the Paix des Dames, on account of the preponderating roles played in concluding it by Madame Louise de Savoie, the King's mother, and the glorious daughter of Maximilian of Austria and Marie de Bourgogne, widow of Philibert le Beau, aunt of Charles V, the admirable Marguerite,[1] who was buried in that marvel of flamboyant Gothic, the church of Brou-en-Bresse. The Paix des Dames, signed on August 3, 1529, signified the renunciation by François I of French hegemony beyond the Alps. The bar-

[1] There are two important works on this first Marguerite of Austria, duchess of Savoy, later also Governor of the Netherlands from 1507-30: Max Bruchet, *Marguerite d'Autriche duchesse de Savoie*, and Comte Carton de Wiart, *Marguerite d'Autriche*.

barous Gauls departed and made room, not for the realization of the dream of Machiavelli and Guicciardini, but for the harsh reality of Imperial conquest. François I handed over his Italian allies to Charles V. In Naples and Milan the keys to the peninsula were in the hands of the Hapsburgs. The princes and republics of Italy had only one desire—to flee their threatened embrace. Francisco Sforza saved his Milanese. Venice came to an understanding with the Emperor. Pontifical diplomacy succeeded in excluding Florence from the Paix des Dames. Clement VII had his plan, which was to retake the rebellious city, and the Treaty of Bologna was to enable him to do so. He would crown Charles V Emperor and King of Lombardy, thus recognizing the new Charlemagne. The recapture of Florence was worth the price. In August 1529 Charles V came to an agreement with the Pope; the Prince of Orange was to mete out punishment to the Florentines. On his arrival at Genoa they sent four ambassadors to him, but in vain. The *Arrabiati* knew that thenceforward they could expect no quarter. As they had been told to surrender unconditionally they prepared for battle. It was to be Florentine democracy against the Pope and the Emperor. The laws of history prove that this type of struggle is always of exceptional fury. The enraged city of Florence in the summer of 1529 was one of the most terrible examples of it.

The irresponsible nuns in whose convent Catherine had been placed wished to reinstate in their place of honour the six heraldic balls of her family coat-of-arms, which according to tradition represented symbolically the six pills of the medical profession practised by her ancestors. The little girl thereupon almost vanished in the Florentine tumult. At the beginning of the siege Leonardo Bartolini had suggested putting her in a brothel, for the Pope would not then be able to give in princely marriage a relative who had associated with prostitutes. Battisto Cei had an even better idea: to chain her, naked, to the city walls. And Bernado Castiglioni went still further, proposing that she be raped by the soldiery.

Those who were less savage finally prevailed over these fanatics by pointing out that Catherine was a hostage of too great a price not to be well guarded. In order to prevent her attempted escape, which they had learned was being prepared by Clement VII and François I. Sylvestro Aldobrandini, chancellor and secretary of the Council, was instructed by the Council of Ten for Liberty to transfer Catherine from the Murate to the cloister of Santa Lucia. Savonarola's Christian democracy still maintained its prestige amongst many

Dominicans. Those of San Marco, of which Santa Lucia was a dependency, were of this number. In the midst of threats, cries, groans and tears, this child of eleven years showed noticeable coolness and presence of mind. Her head had been shaven and she wore a nun's habit. She stated categorically to the commissaries that she was vowed to the cloister and refused to leave her venerable mothers of Murate. But on July 20th, she was obliged to obey and to go to Santa Lucia. On August 3, 1530 the defenders of the city of the Red Lily lost the battle of Gavinana, at which the Prince of Orange was killed, as well as Francisco Ferruccio, commanding the troops that had been sent to help the Florentines. The Prince of Orange, Philibert, successor to Bourbon as the head of the Emperor's armies, and to Moncada, as Viceroy of Naples, aspired, it was said, to Catherine's hand in order to become sovereign of Florence. Clement VII was alleged to have promised it to him, with a dowry of 80,000 and a tribute of 150,000 gold écus, to be raised from the conquered city.

The value of the pontifical promises was dubious. Clement VII was too attached to Florence. Nevertheless the *Duchessina* was already an important personage on the political chessboard. And that undoubtedly saved her life by causing the more intelligent of the *Arrabiati* to reject the proposals to send her to a brothel, chain her naked on the ramparts, or cause her to be raped, put forward by the more enraged members of Florentine democracy.

On August 12th, they capitulated, giving the Emperor all freedom to establish the new regime on condition that he would respect their municipal liberties. Florence was bled white; it had lost 14,000 combatants and 8,000 citizens in battle, massacre, torture, misery and sickness. It was ruined, devastated, at the mercy of the worst reprisals, promised by the *Pallesque*, or partisans of the Medici, to their enemies. According to custom the victors quarrelled with one another—Guicciardini against Valori. The latter was appointed Governor of the Romagnas by the Pope. The German, Nicolas von Schomberg, Archbishop of Capua, was appointed administrator of Florentine affairs. This, however, was merely a provisional administration. The Emperor had his eye on Alessandro de Medici. In the following spring Catherine's natural brother received the governorship of the city of the Pennas. Together with the Bishop of Vasoni and the pontifical procurators, he had travelled to Augsburg and Flanders in order to pay homage to his Imperial sovereign. On June 1, 1531, four ambassadors were appointed to Alessandro, who had become Duke of Florence. On July 5th the Emperor's ambassador to Florence, Mussetola, installed Alessandro on his master's behalf. In order that his family might remain in the city of the Red Lily Clement VII had played the Ghibelline card. Thenceforward the Medici were vassals of His Caesarian Majesty.

Catherine remained an instrument of matrimonial politics. Clement VII wished to have her with him. For a long time the marriage of this cousin, who, on account of the difference in their ages (he was born in 1478), he called his niece, had preoccupied him. The first of such marriage plans went back to 1524, as between Catherine de Medici and the second son of the King of France. The latter remained faithful to the diplomatic policy of a Florentine marriage. France had given a wife to Lorenzo II. She offered a husband for the daughter of the defunct Duke of Urbino. An intimate of the Urbino court, of Milanese family and born at Mantua, an exact contemporary of Clement VII, Baldassare Castiglione, was a first-hand witness to this. At the beginning of 1530 there had for some time been talk at the Court of Mantua of a marriage with Catherine, who would have been dowered with the little principality of Carpi, a possession of the Duke of Ferrara's. Clement VII did not encourage this match. Nor did he show himself any more favourable towards the advances of the French Government, which following the revanche of Pavia, was greatly in favour of the Italian alliances, particularly with the Pope, whom it was endeavouring to detach from the Emperor. The coronation had just taken place. Charles V's brother was preparing to become King of the Romans (his election took place on January 5, 1531). Negotiations were proceeding for the liberation of the Sons of France, still captives in Spain, and for the marriage of the Emperor's elder sister, Eleanor of Austria, widow of Emmanuel the Fortunate, King of Portugal, with François I, who for the past six years had been the widower of Queen Claude.

The plans for the Florentine marriage were complementary to the Austrian marriage, which had been under discussion since 1526. The Emperor, having become King of Lombardy, seemed as much a menace to the Italian princes as to the Very Christian King. There was already talk of Imperialist tyranny. Even Henry VIII was disturbed by it. France, therefore, had to play a new hand in Italy.

All this was part of the diplomatic preparation for the breaking-off of the truce sealed by the Paix des Dames. This was the foreign policy of the friend both of the Pope and the Sultan, the rival of

Charles V.[1] This policy remained faithful to the plan of redeeming
Pavia and Madrid and of rectifying Cambrai, which weighed so
heavily on French politics. Thence sprang the attempt to act as
mediator between the Pope and the King of England after his
repudiation of Catherine of Aragon, the aunt of Charles V, and
between him and Clement VII in the matter of the concilium,
desired by the Emperor but feared by the pontiff. François I needed
Clement VII because a reconciliation between France and the Holy
See would put an end to the consequences of the Holy League.
In spite of that terrifying year, 1527, this was still in force. The capture of Florence was a slight compensation for the sacking of Rome.
The Pope hesitated between the Emperor and the King. In his
Storia d'Italia Guicciardini reported that the Emperor 'expressed to
the Pope his strong desire to marry Catherine de Medici, his niece,
to Francisco Sforza, in order to compel Clement to support this
prince in Milan, and even more, to break the alliance proposed by
France'.

François I charged the Duke of Albany, uncle and tutor of Catherine, to go to Rome. The Pope had the little duchess brought from
Florence, and on October 12th, she arrived in the Eternal City.

Months passed, but Clement VII still came to no decision. The
only letter of Catherine de Medici written before 1533 that we
possess is one dated from Florence on March 16, 1529. This unique
letter, addressed to François I, reveals that since the age of ten the
Duchessina had been, in personal contact with the King of France.
In it she alluded to the marks of friendship and the renewed offers of
François I. She took advantage of them in order to ask the Very
Christian King to bestow an abbey or another benefice on Vicente
Ridolfi, the son of Rosso Ridolfi, who for six years had been her first
teacher. Thus, as a child, Catherine corresponded with François I in
very familiar terms, which were authorized by their family relation-
ship.

The envoys François I had appointed to her agreed in praising the
distinguished qualities, both of mind and heart, of the little duchess.
Nicolas Raince spoke of her wisdom and prudence and her self-
control. The Vicomte de Turenne said in September 1528 that he
had never seen 'a person of her age more aware of the good or evil
that is done to her'. This precocious mental maturity left Catherine
in no doubt of the importance attached by European politics to the

---

[1] This term was used by the Duke de Lévis Mirepoix, in his brilliant and profound study
of François I, Book III, Chap. IV.

apparently weak and delicate orphan that she was. How could one imagine that she knew nothing of the numerous proposals of marriage, apart even from those of France and Milan, that were being made all around her? And how, being already so reflective and clear-sighted, could she have remained indifferent to them? It is permissible to suppose that Catherine, child though she still was, but so astute and perspicacious, was not unaware of this general interest in her small self. Yet she remained utterly powerless, having passed from the captivity of the convent into the Pope's tutelage.

Thenceforward she learned through daily experience that to remain in the background was not synonymous with unimportance. Her schooling in misfortune was rounded off by her discovery of the machinations of politicians. In Florence, whilst the princes of Europe were competing for her hand, revolutionaries had tried to seize the little duchess by force. These contradictions in her fate provided her apprenticeship. Whilst other little girls, even the daughters of kings, were playing with their companions, the little recluse of the Murate and Santa Lucia, an orphan imprisoned in a cloister, heard nothing there except the echoes of politics, rebounding from the fighting on the ramparts. Yet the most distant courts as well as the nearest, from Edinburgh to Milan, and from Paris to Nancy, were preoccupied by this child. From her earliest years onwards Catherine de Medici breathed in the subtle and corrupt air of politics. And politics were to become her natural element, as sacred or divine love became that of other girls. At the Murate, at Santa Lucia, in Rome, wherever she resided, politics took first place and could not even be separated from religion. Was there also room there for the love of God? All the evidence is to the contrary. Apart from the pious ritual which was merely automatic, the milieu of the Church, which was Catherine's, did not concern itself with the life spiritual. Such concern was kept in reserve for times of sickness and death. And as for love, which subjugates ordinary mortals to the laws of Aphrodite, Catherine did feel it, for a very short time, for her cousin, the handsome Ippolito de Medici, whom, it will be remembered, Leo X had wished her to marry. It appears, however, that this love remained a platonic one.

The only slightly romantic episode in the long life of this woman, in which politics were to predominate to the extent even of prevailing over maternal love (and this explains her amazing patience as a queen who was openly deserted) belongs to the best documented portion of her history. Amidst all the negotiations that were proceeding with regard to her marriage, it is worth pausing for a moment to consider the frustrated hopes of a love-match which were briefly aroused, between her eleventh and thirteenth years, in the most exclusively political feminine genius of history, beside whom Elizabeth I of England and Catherine of Russia themselves appear as merely frivolous. Only Isabella of Castille was as indifferent to love. But in the case of that great stateswoman her austere faith predominated over her political interests. In Catherine nothing else predominated. She was the incarnation of statesmanship. From this, as soon as she read him, sprang her dominating interest in Machiavelli. He did not influence her. She quite naturally recognized herself in him. The essential genius of Machiavelli was that he desired, searched for, and wanted unity—although in vain. During the course of this study we shall see that unity was also the essential goal for Catherine, upholder of the State, amidst all the factions.

The last years of her childhood were the only ones during which Eros was able to touch this princess, without, however, capturing her heart. Bembo, in his *Letters*, praised the son of Giuliano de Nemours, more beautiful than the loveliest flowers. The famous canvas of Titian in the Pitti Palace in Florence reveals a grand nobleman, of splendid appearance. Archbishop of Avignon at sixteen, a Cardinal at eighteen, 'there was nothing ecclesiastical about him save his habit, and even that he did not wear'.[1] Clement VII had bestowed on him the purple and the hat in order to remove him from Florence, which he was safeguarding for Alessandro. This was the cause of the enmity between the two cousins. Ippolito spread the legend according to which Alessandro's mother had been a black slave. 'Ippolito was ambitious, loving pomp, generous, magnanimous, passionate and restless. He could never become accustomed to his ecclesiastical status. Clement VII knew this and watched him closely but without ever succeeding in altering his inclinations. . . . He was very intimate and very friendly with his cousin Catherine.'[2]

Antonio Suriano, the Venetian ambassador, reported the rumour that the cardinal intended to renounce the hat and to marry the *Duchessina*. He was very much in love. She loved him tenderly, trusted no one but him in everything. It is easily understandable that such a young girl as Catherine should have loved that magnificent cavalier. In Titian's portrait 'his face is gentle and serious and has

[1] Mariéjol, *op. cit.* p. 15.
[2] Reumont et Baschet, *op. cit.* p. 134-5.

the melancholy expression one finds in those destined to a premature death; he wears the rich Hungarian costume of red velvet which he wore when, as legate to Germany, he appeared there escorted by 800 Hungarian horsemen, raised at his expense; he was a poet and musician and had translated the second book of the *Aeniad* into Italian verse; he played the lute, the flute and the organ pleasantly; he loved carousals, tournaments and great hunting parties and always generous, like Leo X, he had in his suite Barbarians from all countries, Tartars skilled at drawing the bow, Ethiopians, trained to battle, Indians, daring divers, Turks to conduct his hunts. ...'[1]

What was the *Duchessina*, compared with this sumptuous prince of the Church? Suriano has left us a brief mental and physical portrait of her: 'The Duchess is in her thirteenth year; she is very lively, shows an affable character and has distinguished manners ... she is short and thin; her features are not delicate and she has protruding eyes, like most of the Medici.' Giorgio Vasari, who painted her portrait when she was about to marry the Duc d'Orléans, spoke of Catherine in dithyrhambic terms in his *Life* of Sebastian del Pombio, and in a letter to Carlo Guasconi: 'Her charm cannot be painted or I would have preserved its memory with my brushes.' How are we to choose between the lyrical praise of Vasari, an enthusiastic painter and shrewd courtier, and the realistic Suriano, a diplomat without illusions? One of the members of the suite of Cardinal de Tournon, who had seen Catherine in Rome in October 1530, found her tall, beautiful, and with a good figure. One of Clement VII's secretaries, writing around the same time to Alessandro de Medici, described her similarly. The Milanese ambassador, Andreasi, also described her to Francisco Sforza at that time, as tall for her age, agreeable in appearance, without a trace of make-up, her skin white, a little greasy, still a little girl, too delicate (*molto tenera* in the original text) to be married.

A painting by Angiolo Bronzino showing her at fourteen reveals that she was no beauty and justifies Suriano—very dark, with marked eyebrows, bulging eyes, a large nose, the upper lip thin, the lower, thick. The face is intelligent, of a meditative and secretive intelligence, joined to melancholy. It is already a surprisingly mature face: almost masculine, very Medici, with an ecclesiastical subtlety and an observing glance; the reflective expression in such a young girl impresses and holds one. It is a face that at an early age had already been modelled by experience of life. But one looks in vain for the

[1] H. de La Ferrière, *Lettres de Catherine de Médicis*, Introduction to Vol. 1, p. XXI.

cruelty that slander imputed to Catherine de Medici and which in this unflattering portrait would not have failed to show. The ugliness of the *Duchessina* does not contradict her charm, which court flatterers transformed into beauty. As a young girl by virtue of her graciousness, her kindness, the art of pleasing, her mental gifts, and tactfulness, Catherine was one of those ugly ones who do have charm. And none of this escaped Suriano's clearsightedness. Like Suriano, Bronzino, who was both poet and painter, understood her character which, at first disconcerting, did not yield itself easily and could yet attract sympathy whilst safeguarding her inner life behind an apparent sociability.

We do not know to what extent the feelings of the *Duchessina* were shared by her cousin. The Pope nevertheless feared a budding idyll. Taking as a pretext the unhealthy air of Rome, he sent Catherine back to Florence in April 1532. A letter from the Bishop of Auxerre to Anne de Montmorency proves that politics and not health were the reason for her return. 'I do not know whether it be to avoid expense, or to give distinction to the affairs of Florence, of which the Government in the coming month (the month of May) will be entrusted to Duke Alessandro, or to remove any suspicion the Emperor may have . . . I know well that he and his people do not trust the Pope, nor does the Pope trust them.'

Nothing was more justified than this mutual mistrust. Whilst Charles V supported the suit of Francisco Sforza, negotiations were continuing between Clement VII and François I. Placed in the care of Maria Salviati, the *Duchessina* was obliged to remain waiting in Florence for over a year whilst her fate was being decided. Her longing for Rome, where she had known her first brief hours of happiness and freedom, can be imagined. There she had a real court —the Bishops of Ferli and Borgo, her uncle Albany, Florentine ladies and pages. The Duchess of Camerino and Maria Salviati never left her side. Clement VII often received her. But the handsome Ippolito was there. She was, nevertheless, not unaware of the unrivalled prestige of a marriage to the second son of the King of France. She was too wise to waste away in vain pinings for love. During the first six months of 1533 the Cardinals de Tournon and de Gramont were concluding the negotiations for the French marriage, while Imperial diplomacy continued uninterruptedly in its endeavour to break them off.

Guicciardini has recorded the game that Clement VII was playing with Charles V.

The Emperor was not duped. Yet he was reassured by his disdain for the low status of nobility of the Medici. He believed in the Pope's intentions but not in those of François I, and he thought that his own plans would be favoured by bringing pressure to bear. He therefor advised Clement VII to ask François I to recall his envoys. This was forthwith done. Charles V was caught in his own trap. By the audience of May 3, 1533, at which the Pope settled everything with the two French Cardinals, the Emperor was faced with the *fait accompli*—a meeting at Nice between Clement VII and François I had been decided upon. Gramont was able to leave for France with the certainty of success. The Pope's voyage to Nice was officially announced on July 17th. The marriage had been arranged.

As was only natural, Charles V opposed the Nice meeting. As Nice belonged to Charles III le Bon, brother of Louisa of Savoy, the King's mother, direct conversations between uncle and nephew were to be feared, to the detriment of the Spanish alliance. Guicciardini, always so well-informed, tells us that the Emperor 'realized with annoyance that the attentions by which the Pope appeared to have honoured him, by travelling twice to Bologna to confer with him, would be cancelled out by His Holiness's journey to Nice'. He threatened to break off the marriage of Marguerite of Austria to Alessandro de Medici. 'Meanwhile the Pope,' Guicciardini continues, 'sent envoys to the Duke of Savoy to request the use of the Castle of Nice, which the Duke, in order not to displease the Emperor, made some difficulty in placing at his disposal. In order to remove all obstacles, Clement chose the City of Marseilles for the meeting, which the King passionately desired, thinking that it would be more glorious for himself to meet the Pope in his own State than anywhere else. Clement, for his part, had no reluctance to come to France, because he was determined to satisfy the King, no longer by illusory hopes or by flattering his vanity, but by definite results.'

An intimate of Clement VII, and possessing perhaps a deeper and more realistically practical intelligence than Machiavelli, the author of *Storia d'Italia* knew what he was saying. The calculating, cold, dissimulating, prudent, self-controlled, laborious, clever and industrious character of the successor to Hadrian VI held no secrets for Guicciardini. The influence of Clement VII on Catherine de Medici should never be forgotten. Her apprenticeship, that had begun during the Florentine quarrels, was completed by the lessons she learned from the Pontiff, whose cleverness at pretence Guicciardini was pleased to stress, and who, as the Bishop of Auxerre wrote to the Duke of Albany, was inclined by nature to retreat. When he left for

Marseilles, Clement VII was only thinking of rounding off, at the expense of François I, his success over Charles V. Master of the art of dissimulation, and when he was not perturbed by fear, in conducting an intrigue—those are the actual terms in which Guicciardini spoke of Clement VII, 'a man of little good faith, greedy for money and miserly of benefits'.

For nearly a month Catherine de Medici waited at Villefranche for the arrival of Clement VII on October 7, 1533. The Pope remained there for two days. He was not in the slightest hurry. He had left Rome on September 9th, but did not embark at Livorno until October 5th. He arrived at Marseille on the 11th. The fiancée was kept waiting until the 23rd, the date of her official reception at Marseilles. Catherine was still travelling slowly towards her Royal and French destiny. This slowness in the march of events was always to accompany her and now was the precursor of greater postponements still. Catherine's true entry into French history was not to occur until twenty-six years after her arrival at Marseilles. Her marriage had been under discussion since 1524. Catherine's third schoolmaster was patience.

Patience and slowness. Clement VII had his reasons for allowing matters to lag. He had been aware since May 1531 of the reciprocal conditions demanded by François I, who signed the marriage contract on the preceding April 24th, at the castle of Anet, belonging to the Grand Senechal of Normandy, Louis de Brézé and his wife, Diane de Poitiers. This was another of those strange meetings that occurred so frequently in Catherine's life—the future mistress of Henri II, who was to cause the Dauphine and the Queen so much unhappiness (all the crueller for being unadmitted) was by her presence on the scene at that time associated with the decision of François I to take the daughter of the Medici into the House of France. Diane, obviously, had no part in that decision. At thirty-two, she was merely the very beautiful and frigid spouse of an old husband, the grandson, through his mother, Charlotte de France, of Charles VII and Agnes Sorel. This nobleman—whose tomb in Rouen Cathedral, a marvel probably due to the collaboration of Jean Goujon and Jean Cousin, confirms his very high and illustrious rank—was born of a redoubtable father. On June 13, 1476, Charlotte de France and Pierre de Lavergne, surprised together like the Lovers of Rimini, were killed by Jacques de Brézé. With such a family tradition a man has no liking for giving his wife to the King, and the novelists must admit to having been romancing by imagining as historically true the story that Diane de Poitiers gave herself to François I in order to save her father, Saint-Vallier. In 1531 Madame Diane was virtuous and good and did not dabble in politics. Six years later, however, the widow of Louis de Brézé, favourite and sovereign mistress of the Dauphin Henri, was to make the little Florentine, whose marriage contract was signed by the King of France in her castle of Anet, her slave, though one that hated her.

The contract named an annual income of 30,000 livres for the Duc d'Orléans, a dowry of 10,000 livres and a furnished castle for the Duchesse. Generous as usual, the hero of Marignan reserved all the rights and possessions inherited from Madeleine de la Tour d'Auvergne to the fiancée, and stated no settled sum for the remainder. But this financial generosity was not unaccompanied by secret political conditions attached to the contract—Pisa, Livorno, Reggio, Modena and Rubiera would be given by the Pope to his niece and in consequence to her future husband. On his side the Pope endowed Catherine with 100,000 écus in gold, whilst excluding from her dowry her possessions in Tuscany. There had been a great deal of discussion with reference to the celebration of the marriage in France. The Pope, who at first was against this proposal, in the end gave way on this matter of precedence.

Whilst Catherine awaited in Nice the command to Marseilles, Clement VII did not remain inactive there. Guicciardini reported that 'as Clement VII was conducting the negotiations personally with the King, and using all his skill in the matter, he very soon gained the confidence and the heart of that very candid prince. In spite of the conclusions drawn by many people and especially the Emperor, they did not conclude any treaty'.

But whatever Guicciardini may have said, the Spanish political spies lived up to their reputation and had kept Charles V very well informed. The plan for a secret treaty exists. It was discovered by Armand Baschet, autographed by François I himself, among the manuscripts in the Bibliothèque Nationale.[1] Guicciardini knew nothing of it. Although this meeting, of which he disapproved, threw him into a bad temper, he accompanied the Pope to Marseilles. He was not present at the conversations, and the planned treaty was never put into effect. François's attempt, however, is worthy of attention. The treaty, containing seven points, included an undeniable threat of war against the Emperor: 'Fifthly: that the conquest of

[1] *Op. cit.* pp. 325-7.

the Duchy of Milan will be for the Duc d'Orléans. . . . Sixthly: that this conquest, having taken place, Our said Holy Father will make no difficulties over Parma or Placenzia. Seventhly: that Our said Holy Father and the King will contribute equally to the conquest of Urbino.'

The *Duchessina* travelled from Nice to Marseilles by road.

François I, accompanied by his sons, the dukes of Orléans and Angoulême, received Catherine in the Pope's house. As evidence of her humility the Florentine maiden prostrated herself before the King of France, kissing his feet as if he had been the Pope himself. After being raised up and embraced by her future father-in-law, her fiancé and the Duc d'Angoulême, Catherine was presented to Eleanor of Austria. Contemporary chronicles report that on the same evening François I gave a great supper-party in honour of Clement VII. The signing of the contract took place on October 26th. On the 28th, the Pope himself performed the nuptial benediction.

A picture by Vasari in the Palazza Vecchio in Florence shows this marriage. Clement VII is placing the hand of Catherine in that of Henri of France. They are surrounded by François I and Eleanor of Austria, Marguerite Tudor, dowager Queen of Scotland, Maria Salviati, the Duchessa de Camerino, the Cardinal Ippolito and other princes of the Church. The large tame lion, a present to François I from Hadrian Barbarossa, and the dwarf Gradasse add a picturesque note to this ceremonial scene.

Eleanor and her ladies escorted the two child-spouses to their room (Henri and Catherine were both the same age, fourteen). If contemporary records can be believed, youth was no impediment to marital consummation. This precocious conjugal activity enchanted Clement VII, who early in the morning came to have news of them and found the young couple very well satisfied with the night they had spent together, which as Sovereign Pontiff he rejoiced to find they had passed in such respectful observance of moral theology. He showed thereat the greatest satisfaction. Let us take their contemporaries' word for it, and let us rejoice with the Holy Father in these early nuptials. According to Paolo Jiovio, 'the malcontents complained of this *mésalliance*, and of the haste with which the marriage had been consummated. For in spite of his extreme youth Henri took his wife that very evening. Although her dowry included the castles of her mother in Auvergne, 100,000 gold écus, pearls and jewels of great price as well as a magnificent trousseau, all this was considered insufficient to bridge the gap in rank between them, and the amount of her dowry as well as the fame of the Medici were called into question, which gave rise to a piquant reply by Philippo Strozzi, at that time ambassador to the King. Whilst the dowry was being counted, the treasurers said that it was a very small one in comparison with the greatness of the Royal House. Strozzi told them that he was greatly astonished that men of such high rank were so little informed of the affairs of the realm, for they appeared to ignore that the Pope, by means of this solemn contract to which he had set his hand, had promised to add three inestimable gems to the dowry, desired madly but in vain by three great Kings. When they asked in surprise what gems these were, Strozzi replied, 'Naples, Milan and Genoa'.

Brantôme, in his *Discours des Dames*, referring to Catherine de Medici, took what was merely Italian boasting quite seriously. Charles V, he said, 'feared that the Pope would help him to lose Naples, Milan and Genoa, as he had promised the King of France he would'. He even particularises: 'He had promised him this in an authentic document.' Bernardo Segni, a contemporary of Paolo Jiovio, held the same opinion. Mariéjol has shown that this was a mere legend. The Egg of Naples, the Point of Milan and the Table of Genoa did not symbolize this triple wedding present; they were bought under Henri II and were so called in remembrance of the French conquests at the time of the Italian wars.

Failing the Egg, the Point and the Table, the presents exchanged were still numerous and of great value.

On November 27th, Clement VII re-embarked, and the Court left for Avignon, 'after reiterated embraces', said Paolo Jiovio. And Guicciardini: 'The Pope and the King were very pleased with one another.' François had shown himself too trusting in this Medici, who under his tiara remained a diplomat of bad faith. Clement VII went home quite determined to keep none of his political promises. The victor of Marignan soon discovered this, but did not attempt to remind the Pope of his promises at Marseilles. The poor father-in-law, whose hopes had been frustrated, merely said, in referring to Catherine, that he had accepted a daughter as naked as a new-born babe.[1]

[1] With reference to the early years of François I, one can no longer dispense with the authoritative work of Mme Paule Henry-Bordeaux, *Louise de Savoie, Régente et Roi de France* (published in 1954). This entirely re-opens the question. In the midst of the kingdom's perils, from Louis XI, to Henri IV, three great women regents upheld the continuity of the public welfare: Anne de Beaujeu, Louise de Savoie, Catherine de Medici. They were worthy of their great model of the thirteenth century—Blanche de Castille, whom Madame Catherine, in particular, studied. Her own misfortune was that none of her sons was a Saint Louis. But Providence gave her as successor a man of genius, her son-in-law, Henri IV, who carried out the policy that the widow of Henri II had with indomitable courage, but without success, attempted to implement.

C

CHAPTER TWO

THE BOW AND THE CRESCENT

(November 1533—July 1559)

❧❀❧

How would France welcome the young Duchesse d'Orléans? According to Marino Giustiniano, in 1535 ambassador of the Most Serene Republic to the Very Christian King, the entire nation was still disgruntled with the Florentine marriage, opining that Clement VII had cheated François I. But on the other hand Catherine seemed dear to the whole Royal Family. François I had wanted the marriage. He was too fair-minded to blame his daughter-in-law for the political disappointment that had followed on it. It was a serious disappointment for this precursor of French hegemony, which was to be based on the deep understanding he already had—apart from general principles, and due to his Italian experiences—of the balance of power in Europe, with which practical politics had replaced the idea of Christianity. The incompetence of his son, Henri II (which he had foreseen), was in fact to postpone for a whole century, through the Treaty of Chateau-Cambrésis, the preponderance of the Kingdom of the Lilies.[1] What did remain of his activities was saved and preserved by Catherine de Medici. Henri IV, Louis XIII and Richelieu, Mazarin, Louis XIV again took up and completed the political policy of François and Catherine. At home, the plan which had been pursued for a lengthy period was to strengthen and develop the power of the Crown. Abroad, the predominant pre-occupation with the Germano-Spanish problem and the interest taken in building up the fleet led to a policy of connections farther afield, with Poland, Turkey, and America. The Florentine marriage was one of the moves in the resistance against Charles V.

Naked as a new-born babe . . . was François I really sure of it? Why should he have treated his daughter-in-law harshly? The

---

[1] On all this cf. the two vols. of the authoritative work by Lucien Romier: *Les origines politiques des guerres de religion.*

Duchesse d'Orléans appeared at court merely as the wife of the Second Son of France and very soon it was said that the political value of this marriage hardly counted any longer. Catherine was to owe to no one but herself the influence that she was to achieve in the Royal Family. Thanks to her precocious mental maturity and her sharp, supple wits, she did not deceive herself on this score.

A phrase penned by Marino Giustiniano arrests and holds our attention: *Pur ella è molto obediente*—'But she is very obedient.' And that was why they liked her. Catherine had understood immediately that she mattered less than nothing and in consequence must be self-effacing and submissive. It is entirely to her own credit thus to have entered the House of France. It was necessary for her to show that she appreciated its greatness. *Molto obediente.* By refraining from drawing attention to herself she avoided appearing to be an intruder. Her task was to make herself liked, yet without attracting too much attention, and never to forget that she had only arrived there by royal favour. In Florence she had learned early in life that to escape danger it is best to avoid attracting attention. At this court, the foremost in the world, she was in danger owing to the relative obscurity of her birth and the weakness of her political position. Her brothers-in-law were not married; after Queen Eléonore, after the Queen of Navarre, after the King's daughters—Madeleine, promised to James V of Scotland, and Marguerite, she was the first in rank of all the women of France. Yet there were many indications to prove to her that she was still regarded as an upstart. She was too tactful to engage in intrigues. *Molto obediente*—that was her demeanour. And the force of circumstances was to impose this role on her for more than twenty-five years, so that in 1544 the nuncio, Dandino, writing to the cardinal of the Papal Court charged with affairs of justice, was to say that he did not think that greater goodness and purity were to be found anywhere than were shown by Catherine de Medici. The gentlest of women, said Michel de L'Hospital, in his Latin epithalamium on the Dauphin François and Mary Stuart.

Thus, discreet and submissive, Madame Catherine, a child-wife, was installed at the Court of France. As an orphan she had been used to pomp and grandeur, whilst herself remaining in the shade. In Rome it had been the shade of the Pope. Would the King's shade protect her equally well? Catherine knew that she had everything to receive but nothing to give. Her intuition did not deceive her. She knew that she had nothing to offer but herself. How would the Royal Family and the Court receive so unimportant a princess, cousin of a defunct Pope who himself was the bastard of a younger Florentine son?

When Catherine entered the Royal Family the favourite, the magnificent Anne d'Heilly, Duchesse d'Étampes, official mistress of François I, was twenty-five, in the full flower of her beauty. The most beautiful of blue-stockings and the greatest blue-stocking among the beauties, as she was nicknamed, held her lover as much by her mind as by her physical charms.

Queen Eléonore, the Emperor's sister, lived very much in retirement. Most of the time Catherine saw the Duchesse d'Étampes in her father-in-law's company. She managed to win favour with her. Apart from his mistress, the woman with the most influence over François I was only fairly rarely at Court—his sister, Marguerite d'Angoulême, Queen of Navarre by her second marriage in 1527 to Henri d'Albret. This Marguerite of Marguerites, this Marguerite among Princesses, was one of the most distinguished women of her time. Catherine was able to please her too, and to be liked by her. Marguerite of France, four years younger than herself, her sister-in-law, was to become Catherine's most intimate friend. She did not marry the Duke of Savoy, Emmanuel-Philibert, until after the peace of Cateau-Cambrésis, on July 9, 1559. Marguerite was then thirty-six. As Duchesse de Berry and a really remarkable woman, she played a considerable part in the life of Madame Catherine.

The Royal Family was well-disposed towards the newcomer, who knew how to behave with discretion and charm.

According to reliable sources, the first intimate relations between Diane de Poitiers and Henri de France, who, as the result of the death of his brother François (on August 15, 1536) had become Dauphin, did not occur until the end of 1536 or the beginning of 1537. Prior to this date they attribute no love affair to Catherine's husband. In default of documentary evidence we must resign ourselves to knowing nothing about the early marital life of Catherine de Medici and Henri II. Exactly three years had passed between the date of their marriage and the beginning of the Dauphin's liaison with Diane de Poitiers; a period equivalent to the years in which the character is formed, the temperament becomes firmer, and a human personality acquires those characteristics which in the course of life grow more marked. Life itself will further modify them until in maturity they become fixed, to be, however, once again re-modelled by the onset of old age. The erosion of time changes the soul no less than the body. It is only through gradual re-touching that the truth of a portrait becomes apparent, a truth that like life itself is constantly altering and changing, and which events silently yet strongly influence.

The court of François I, that of a great prince hailed as the true patron and protector of arts and literature, was the splendid forerunner of that of Louis XIV. Its splendour was less harmonious than that of Versailles, more lively, vibrant and warm to excess. Fontainebleau was the Versailles of the Valois. To evoke it is to describe it, especially in the words of Michelet: 'A harmony of age and of season ... its fantastic shades, arousing dreams before winter, two feet away from the little Seine, between golden grapes. ... A French Italy. ... Thenceforward France parted from Italy, detached herself, and took up the torch. ...'

A French Italy . . . in those words, as so often, the exact image sprang from the mind of that astounding visionary. There the daughter of the Medici was not to feel herself in exile. She was humble because she was weak. She was prudent and never taken by surprise. She knew that in this France, humanist and bright, a Medici would be at home. The door was as yet only ajar. But it was open wide enough to admit among the proud goddesses with whom François I liked to surround himself, the little Florentine from too insignificant lineage, who by her own gifts was to compensate for this inferiority. The only inferiority to which, rightly, she admitted. She would soon efface it whilst hiding the fact that it weighed on her, for she felt the injustice of it.

As a young wife Catherine was as Suriano had described her—of a lively nature and a charming mind. She had self-assurance, wit and subtlety. She was bright and keen to learn; in addition to her own tongue she acquired French, which she grew to know so well that the Venetian ambassador, Giovanni Correro, in 1569 spoke quite as a matter of course of the Queen reading at Carcassonne, on her return from the Bayonne meeting a few years earlier, 'a manuscript chronicle' relating to Blanche of Castille. Catherine continued to study Latin, began to learn Greek, as well as mathematics and natural history, and was keenly interested in astronomy, that supporter of astrology to which, as we know, she was to become fervently addicted. During the early years of her married life she was still a schoolgirl, sharing the lessons of the Daughters of France, Madeleine and Marguerite. François I, who loved nothing more than women who wished to be truly cultured, took an interest in the studies of the little trio.

An Italian, Catherine also belonged to the Church, to convents and pontifical palaces. She was a born diplomat, courtesy incarnate, and secretive to the last degree. Adept at every inflection, it was natural enough that in spite of her ugliness Madame d'Orléans should have won over François I who delighted in every kind of attractiveness, whether of mind or of body. On the other hand she was incapable of retaining her husband's affections. Henri's nature, so different from that of François that he was almost his opposite, was no less antithetic to Catherine's.

The Venetian documents do not refer to Henri before 1542; by then he had been Dauphin for six years and Diane de Poitiers' lover for the same period. Matteo Dandolo was struck by his vigour; one might have thought that the Dauphin was all muscle. In 1546 Marino Cavalli wrote: 'This prince is twenty-eight years old; he has a very robust constitution and his humour is a little melancholy; he is very skilled at all feats of arms; he is not a brilliant conversationalist, but holds his opinions very definitely and very firmly; when he has said anything once he sticks to it to the end. His intelligence is not particularly quick, but it is often such men who succeed best; they are like autumn fruits that ripen late, but which for that very reason are better and more lasting than those of the summer or spring. . . . He spends his money both wisely and honourably. He is not addicted to women; his own wife suffices him; as for conversation, he is satisfied with that of Madame la Sénéchale de Normandie, who is forty-eight. He has a genuine affection for her, but the view taken is that there is nothing lascivious in it, but that they are like mother and son; it is said that this lady has taken on the task of indoctrinating, correcting and advising Monsieur le Dauphin, and encouraging him in all actions worthy of himself; and in fact the role suits her marvellously. Having been vain and a scoffer and very little in love with his wife he has become quite a different man; he has also corrected a few other little youthful faults. He likes to take part in military exercises; and his courage, of which he has already given proofs at Perpignan and in Champagne, is generally praised.'

This is a basically important document. It allows us to see Catherine's young husband at a date prior to its own. It throws light on the incompatabilities in their respective characters. It also sheds light on the origins of his liaison with Diane de Poitiers. Henri was no intellectual. An ugly and intelligent wife did not attract him. The correspondence of this prince, still, unfortunately, almost entirely unpublished, is only of political interest, with the exception of a few notes to Diane, very tender, and to Catherine on their children. When reading the letters of Henri II one cannot help being struck by the mediocrity of the personality they reveal. Henri, Dauphin of France, did not lack culture; the Genoese humanist Theocrenus had been his tutor. He knew Latin, Italian and Spanish. He had a good memory. But his correspondence and politics reveal that in his private as well as his public life he showed little intelligence. He never took any initiative excepting for the navy, in which he took a keen interest and which he greatly developed. His weakness of character is confirmed by all the documents and all the facts.

François I suffered to know how inferior was the son who would become his successor. He had discovered in him a narrowness and hardness of heart in complete contrast to his own generous nature. This narrowness and hardness only disappeared in the case of those people whom Henri loved. He loved them passionately. His letters to Diane de Poitiers, to the Constable de Montmorency, to the Duc de Guise, show him as the utter slave of his loves and his affections. With his favourites he was kind to the point of weakness. It was a superficial kindness which quickly lapsed with absence, although it was immediately revived by the return of those on whom it was lavished. Like most mediocrities, he changed little in the course of time. Yet at the death of his father the melancholy Dauphin appeared, according to Dandolo in 1547, to be 'joyous, rubicund and of an excellent complexion'.

The love life of Diane de Poitiers was exceptionally secretive. This has been of advantage to the novelists' imagination but the despair of historians, for documentary evidence is meagre.

The legend that the daughter of Saint-Vallier gave herself to François I in order to save her father from the scaffold has no substance and can be left to the romancings of Victor Hugo and Le Roi s'amuse. The pardon granted to Saint-Vallier was entirely due to the high standing of Louis de Brézé, Grand Senechal of Normandy. The former had been involved in the conspiracy led by the Constable of Bourbon and owed his survival to the fact that this conspiracy had been made known by his son-in-law, in gratitude to whom the life of the imprudent accomplice was spared. The gossip on this subject in the Journal d'un Bourgeois de Paris has no bearing on this strictly political story. Madame de Brézé only intervened in the matter insofar as a woman of her birth and rank had certain connections and influence at Court. The widow of the Grand Sénéchal, who was both very able and very beautiful, managed to attract the attention of the

Dauphin Henri. At the beginning of their liaison—as the result of which the favourite became the Comtesse de Saint-Vallier and later the Duchesse de Valentinois, the greatest lady in the land—she was thirty-eight.

Her portrait at Chantilly, a Clouet, is that of a lady of sixty, who had undoubtedly been a very great beauty. There is no proof that the numerous Dianes sculpted or painted by the artists at the French Court were portraits of the favourite, but there is also no proof to the contrary. Is the marvellous Diana with the stag and greyhounds sculpted by Jean Goujon, which was transferred from Anet to the Louvre, and in which he remembered both the allegory of the Fountain of Life by Rosso and the Nymph of Benvenuto Cellini, a portrait of the favourite? Does the Venus of Nicolo dell'Abbati, after a drawing by Primatizio, which is in the ballroom at Fontainebleau, represent the Duchesse de Valentinois? And did the favourite pose for the Diana the Huntress on wood, a greyhound on her right side and a bow in her left hand, a work of the school of Fontainebleau in the Louvre? We do not know, and are therefore free to dream in front of these statues and pictures, from which, however, the memory of Diane de Poitiers cannot be disassociated.

There are also the necklace of cameos on shells in the Cabinet des Médailles at the Bibliothèque Nationale and their Artemisian agates, as well as the medallion with the Latin inscription of *Diana dux Valentinorum clarissima.* Everything that survives of Anet seems to speak still of the *Grand'sénéchale.* There are also the glasses by Jean Cousin and the enamels by Léonard Limosin. Are these allegories or portraits? Does the goddess symbolize the woman merely allegorically, or did the woman pose for the goddess? It matters little.

It gives one pleasure to evoke in all the splendour of her late summer the widow of Louis de Brézé at the moment when Henri, Dauphin of France, vowed to be faithful unto death to her beauty and her worship. As nothing either forbids us or compels us to do so, we may identify the lady of Saint-Vallier with the Diana of the artists. Why should the favourite with the crescent not have resembled the goddesses of Anet and Fontainebleau? Here she is—tall, supple, muscular, with long limbs, strong soft arms, a wide chest with well-spaced breasts, her shoulders plump without being too heavy, with an exquisitely pure line, the neckline perfect, with regular features, a skin all lightness, a commanding glance and fine chestnut-coloured hair. She is a horsewoman, used to fresh air. Knowing herself to be exceptionally beautiful, her feminine intelligence made it clear to her that her beauty was the best weapon she possessed for furthering her ambitions. Her culture was more fashionable than deep, but was enough to satisfy a prince who did not care for literature and in the arts was only interested in music. Diane had a calculating mind, a cold heart, and was not at all passionate. The reliable documents that we have compel us to see her as anything but a tragedy queen: her personal position was all that mattered to her. She was a real business woman and in her eyes Henri II was above all the banker whose love for her had given him into her hands. But a business woman who was also very much the politician. The King was entirely under her influence.

We do not know whether that influence was due to sentiment or sensuality. There is a lack of basic sources dealing with the love affair of this famous couple. The lover and the mistress were both equally secretive; on that point the evidence is unanimous.

However secretive they may have been, Catherine was well informed about Henri II's passing fancies. Her first rival was Jean Fleming, a Scotswoman, the natural daughter of James IV, widow of Lord Malcolm Fleming, killed at Pinkie in 1547; she arrived in France in 1548 with Mary Stuart. The Constable de Montmorency had introduced this magnificent Stuart woman to the Royal bed, hoping that her sexual attraction might free the King from his impassioned devotion to Madame de Valentinois. It is known that Henri d'Angoulême was born of their love affair. What is less well-known is the alliance that was formed between Catherine and Diane, which resulted in her dismissal. Catherine knew all about her husband's affairs. Diane de France, Henri's daughter when he was still Dauphin, had been born in 1539, twelve years before Henri d'Angoulême, by Filippa Duci, a very beautiful Piedmontese girl whom, when a soldier, he had raped. Nicole de Savigny, Baroness of Saint-Rémy, was also the mistress of Henri II and bore him a son, Henri. But he only acknowledged the daughter of the Piedmontese and the son of the Scotswoman.

All this was common knowledge. In a letter of June 12, 1582, to her son-in-law, the future Henri IV, Catherine refers to the Duchesse d'Étampes, at the same time as the Duchesse de Valentinois, as having had a perfectly honourable relationship with Henri II. But against this allegedly platonic relationship we can quote another letter, addressed to Bellièvre, dated from Saint-Maur-des-Fosses on April 25, 1584, in which the Queen Mother wrote at length to the treasurer of the royal finances about the behaviour of her daughter Margot and the lessons she should be taught on this subject: 'I was hospitable to Madame de Valentinois; he was the King, yet even so I always let him know that it was to my great regret; for never has a woman who loves her husband liked his whore; for even though this is an ugly word for us to use, one cannot call her anything else.' The word is in complete contradiction to the allegedly honorable relationship mentioned in the letter to (Henri of) Navarre. The context proves that it was not meant as an insult but as a statement of fact. In which letter was Catherine telling the truth?

Henri II's passion for Diane de Poitiers excluded all others. Apart from her he only had short carnal affairs, which have been substantiated. Diane dominated him for more than twenty years. The lover's enslavement was complete. Let us accept these contradictions on Catherine's part. Henri II was handsome; all his portraits prove it and particularly the François Clouet. Diane had the beauty of a goddess. How can it be proved that only chivalrous love held them in its sway?

Let us be as cautious as the ambassadors of the Italian princes and the Venetian Republic, but let us not forget, either, the verses of Diane to Henri II, comparable to Mary Stuart's famous sonnets to Bothwell:

> *Ains, tremblottante et détournant les yeux,*
> *'Nenni! disais-je—Ah! ne soyez déçue!'*
> *Reprit l'amour, et soudain a ma vue*
> *Va présentant un laurier merveilleux.*
> *'Mieux vaut, lui dis-je, être sage que reine.'*
> *Ains, me sentis et frémir et trembler.*
> *Diane faillit, et comprenez sans peine*
> *Duquel matin je prétends reparler . . .*

For the rest, it matters little. Catherine was atrociously jealous of Diane. There is the most definite evidence of that jealousy. From 1537–59 Catherine was a wife whose pride had been outraged, silent but not consenting, beaten but not resigned. We already know her genius for dissimulation. Where did she find the strength and patience to dissimulate for so long? In trying to discover it may we not attempt a deeper analysis of that essentially secretive character?

A queen, first of all, is called upon to have children. Catherine de Medici married the Duc d'Orléans at fourteen and a half. If one may believe a despatch dated October 30, 1533, from Antonio Sacco to the Milanese government, François I, after having himself put the young couple to bed, 'wished to watch them jousting, and each of them jousted valiantly'. But their jousting was sterile. Catherine's sterility continued for more than ten years, and it was torture to her. This may possibly have been one of the main reasons for this princess's predilection for the doctors, diviners and magicians with whom she surrounded herself. 'She used philtres and avoided travelling on muleback because that animal, reputedly infertile, transmitted its sterility to those women who mounted it.' She had recourse to the tarot and to charms, and to the prescriptions of alchemists, such as those of Albert le Grand, Isidore le Physicien, Photius, Tabariensis and de Blérius.

There is a document which clearly reveals the very odd mixture of superstition and Catholic faith to which Catherine resorted. It is a copy of a kind of scapulary on which prayers were inscribed in Latin, French and Hebrew, and which was always worn by the Queen. This is very probably the piece of vellum on which were sewn various figures and which was referred to by Le Laboureur in his annotations to the *Mémoires de Messire Michel de Castelnau*, but the authenticity of which was queried by Mariéjol on the grounds that it was an example of excessive credulity.[1]

To Catherine astrology was inseparable from religious devotion. It would be completely wrong to represent her as unbelieving and superstitious. She was both superstitious and a believer. She was a true Italian, and an Italian of the Renaissance. It is quite certain that the agony of finding herself barren, and the terror of being repudiated for that reason, drove her from the very first years of her marriage to the practice of sorcery. Precise details were given by a sixteenth-century doctor, Nicolas Venette. Added to what Brantôme said about Henri II they give us reason to believe that both husband and wife suffered from malformations; Henri II from hypospadia and Catherine from tortuosity of the vaginal canal. The seer and mathematician Jean Fernal, who had succeeded Louis de Bourges as physician to the King, treated the infertile couple. The Constable de Montmorency also advised remedies with so much zeal that in a letter written in June 1543 Catherine, at last pregnant, particularly

[1] Owing to a lucky chance, during research in the Department of Manuscripts at the Bibliothèque Nationale, we found this document, which seems to have escaped our predecessors, and which must not be confused with Catherine's talismans, which are well-known.

thanked him for it. Catherine's unhappiness was deepened by the birth of the daughter of Filippa Duci, which proved that Henri II's hypospadia did not prevent him from becoming a father. Learning that her repudiation had been decided on, she took the initiative. She offered to retire to a convent or even, if François I wished it, to place herself at the service of whichever princess might be chosen to succeed her as the Dauphin's wife.

This extreme humility could not but please the chivalrous monarch, who consoled his daughter-in-law and assured her that she need have no fears of being unjustly dismissed. By all the signs of affection she had shown him as well as by the charms of her mind Catherine had made herself dear to François I. For her father-in-law she was the living image of Italian culture. And Catherine deliberately chose to remain an Italian. In spite of her learning she always disdained to write French correctly. She remained faithful to Italian fashions and ordered her clothes from dressmakers in Milan and Mantua.

Although he had, in addition to Catherine, his mistress Anne d'Étampes to keep him company, in the midst of all his political problems the King had few close intimates in his household; his son was hostile to him and his wife had become almost a stranger. There was only his daughter, as Marguerite, his beloved sister, was almost always in Navarre. Catherine's charming and attentive presence livened up his domestic solitude.

Catherine was fond of hunting and she also played *palle-mail*. Her skill with the cross-bow astonished the Court. An artist in all things, she enjoyed dancing and ballet as much as hunting and archery. She invented the amazon style of riding which for the first time enabled women to trot and gallop like the cavaliers whom they accompanied at the fastest pace. She also invented dances and games, and was very accomplished at silken embroidery.

François I, himself an artist, thought that the bow would be the most fitting symbol for this young amazon and huntress. He wanted it to be placed in the heavens, remembering that Iris was the messenger of the gods. The Duchesse d'Orléans bore on her Florentine scarf the colours of hope of a French Italy, which he would not give up. To them the King added the motto 'It bears joy and hope before it.' And indeed Catherine was always to be the messenger of peace; a messenger, alas, misunderstood and fought against. An Iris who was rejected in the periods of calm between the storms of the Wars of Religion. Nearly forty years of massacre were to pass before her message of peace, launched as early as 1560 and taken up by Henri IV, was to be accepted with such bad grace by an exhausted France. The scarf of Iris held no attraction for the Florentine princess's husband, who belonged wholly to Diane. The crescent shone in the skies above the royal lover. The shades of night dispelled the bow of seven colours. It faded in its turn before the silver rays of the planet that Theocritus associated with female sensuality. Catherine's conjugal life was darkened by the love life of Diane de Poitiers. The rainbow was a merely ironical symbol. The moonlight over the châteaux of Touraine shone on a pair of lovers who insolently proclaimed their perfect faithfulness to one another, a couple that only death would part. Catherine seemed merely a servant, a serving-wife to whose bed his mistress herself brought the King, so that he might engender the children of France.

Léonard Limosin, who was both an enameller of genius and a clever courtier, portrays both Diane and Catherine in one of his masterpieces. The Queen is shown as Juno, her white shoulders a little too fat; the favourite is Venus, slender and more beautiful. The intention is clear, the loved one was the goddess of love and not the chaste sister of Apollo. Henri was subservient to her in everything and nobody ignored it, either at Court or in the city.

Ronsard, in Pindaric style, led the chorus of court poets who sang the praises of the Artemisian goddess:—

> *Serai-je seul vivant en France de votre âge,*
> *Sans chanter votre nom, si craint et si puissant,*
> *Dirai-je point l'honneur de votre beau croissant,*
> *Ferai-je point pour vous quelque immortel ouvrage?*

During the whole of the twenty-two years during which Diane remained in favour lyres were tuned and resounded in hymns of praise to her. Anet was her poem in stone, that of the crescent. The emblem of Artemis shone in her hair, which with clear-sighted coquetry she refused ever to dye. Diane was sure that her beauty would last, as much under the fine grey ashes of winter as in the golden brown of autumn. As Duchesse de Valentinois she continued to defy the swift course of time.

Not that the splendour of her body was actually immortal. Leaving aside the dithyrhambics of hired flatterers, Diane the woman did age. As with all authentic beauties, even the tarnished mirror of time reflected her exquisite beauty until the end. In the eyes of her lover she would always remain as he had first known her, in the full splendour of her approaching forties. Diane knew it. Proudly she continued to uphold his impassioned illusions. *Sola vivit in illo*, she had engraved on the woodwork at Anet, as well as the motto of the crescent: *Donec totum impleat orbem*; the one being for whom his mistress lived, Henri de France, Dauphin, and later, King. Her whole world, that her love completely filled, lay in a heart that was as much that of a son as of a lover, and which would try vainly to escape her if the impossible were to occur and intriguers were for an instant to separate him from her. In order to capture the prey that is quite close, the javelin is even more effective than the arrow: *Consequitor quoties qui petit.*

Her pride was accepted, known and praised. Olivier de Magny paid his court when he said that:—

> *Ici voit-on un grand croissant*
> *De peu à peu se remplissant,*
> *Et la, en même apparence,*
> *L'Ecusson des armes de France.*

Omnium victorem vici. J'ai vaincu le vainqueur de tous. 'I have conquered the conqueror of all.' Beside the flattery of the adjective and the name to which it referred, the truth was in the verb.

The medallion of Diane on which those three words are engraved commemorates a triumph that no others among our kings' mistresses could wrest from the Duchesse de Valentinois, not even the Marquise de Pompadour. Michelet knew this very well: 'To be moved by nothing, to love nothing, to pity nothing. To feel only enough passion to give a little colour to the blood—pleasure without tempests, the love of gain and the pursuit of wealth.' He was perhaps exaggerating, underlining too heavily, but basically he was right. One need only read the letters of the lovers of Anet and Chenonceaux to realize that in spite of his invectives his intuition had once again served Michelet well. He also added these striking words: 'The Grand' sénechale's best support was her intimacy with the Queen, the young Catherine de Medici, whom she owned completely; Diane held the keys of the alcove and when Henri II slept with his wife it was because Diane had wanted and demanded it.'

The secret of this *ménage à trois* was this—it was necessary to produce Children of France. Could a more complaisant wife than the Florentine girl have been found anywhere among the princesses descended from emperors and kings? A wife who was so submissive that she had offered to wait on her husband's second wife, if on account of the ever empty cradle she were to be repudiated? Catherine's cleverness consisted in having suggested this herself. The orphan from the convents of Tuscany had become the ally of the ambitious châtelaine of Anet. The crescent rises above the terrestial orb. The rainbow disappears from the zenith. . . . Catherine, nevertheless, only effaced herself in order to remain. To remain, to wait, to last out. Her youth in Italy had innured her to doing so. The divinity of the arrogant mistress was merely illusory, since she also was mortal. And on the way to the grave she was by twenty years in the van. Catherine had the advantage of youth. She was too prudent to sacrifice it to useless rebellion.

Catherine strengthened her patience by remaining in an Italian environment. One of her intimates was a diplomat and poet, Luigi Alamanni, whose elegies, sonnets, fables and satires charmed her, and who, twenty-six years older than she and used to political missions, gave her good advice. Her first cousins, the four Strozzi—Lorenzo, Roberto, Leone and Piero, the sons of Clarice de Medici—were her dearest companions. The despatches of the Tuscan ambassador enable us to reconstruct this Italian entourage of François I's daughter-in-law.

Catherine de Medici spent the first twenty-five years of her life in France in the company and under the influence of Florentine exiles, the *fuorusciti*, the enemies of Cosimo de Medici, regarded by them and by her as a usurper. If under François I Catherine played no political role, under Henri II she gradually began to do so. Catherine was then the procurator of those banished Italians who very oddly, under diverse forms, represented the state of mind, the grudges, the confused hopes of the peninsular mosaic, groping towards the still vague longing for national unity. Her interest in Italian affairs was due more to her personal affections than to purely political motives, although her interest in politics, apparently first aroused in this milieu, was to become when applied to France the exclusive passion of the mother of the last of the Valois.[1]

Whilst awaiting important developments in his affairs Ferdinando de San Severino, Prince of Salerno, sang the light and gay songs of his native Naples alternately with the noble psalms of Goudimel,

[1] Thanks to his patient and detailed researches in the Italian archives Lucien Romier was able to throw new light on this *milieu*, on which the French documents, including Catherine's correspondence and unpublished contemporary documents in the French archives, yield next to nothing.

which Catherine, who shared her husband's love for music, that most consoling of the arts, asked the court musicians to perform. Catherine remained all her life the friend of musicians. Under her enlightened influence Charles IX in 1570 granted the charter of an Academy of Music and Poetry to the poet Antoine de Baïf and the musician Gourville, who without knowing themselves to be the precursors of Richelieu called it the Académie Française.

Music, the arts, literature and the sciences—Madame Catherine always loved, understood and protected them. During her early years at the French Court she became adept at them. Thus she provided herself with a shield against the sadness of her married life and the favour of François I, and was able to distract herself from her jealousy of Diane de Poitiers whilst making herself indispensable to her father-in-law. Thus she passed her childless ten years.

On Saturday, January 19, 1544, Catherine gave birth at Fontaine-bleau to her first-born, the Petit Dauphin François, later François II. A year later another child was born, Elisabeth de France, on Friday, April 2, 1545, again at Fontainebleau. Claude de France was also born at Fontainebleau on November 12, 1547. For the past seven months Catherine had been queen. On February 3, 1549, a second son was born to the royal pair, Louis, Duc d'Orléans, who died on October 24, 1550, four months after the birth of the future Charles IX, Charles-Maximilien, born on June 27th, 'one of the most beauti-ful children one could wish to see', Henri wrote to the Duc de Guise. On Saturday, September 20, 1551, Catherine gave birth at Fontaine-bleau to her third son; Henri III, her favourite. He was christened Edouard-Alexandre: the name Henri was not given to him until his confirmation. On May 14, 1553, Marguerite—the famous Queen Margot—was born at Saint-Germain-en-Laye. On March 18, 1555, Hercule was born at Fontainebleau; he was confirmed as François. On June 24, 1556, twin daughters were born, Jeanne and Victoire. The Spanish ambassador, Simon Renard, reported that this double birth nearly cost their mother her life. Victoire 'remained dead in her belly for six hours and one of her legs had to be broken to save the said lady'. Jeanne died in August. These were Catherine's last children.

In twelve years she had had ten children, of which seven survived. Late as was her recovery from her barrenness, it was complete.

François I, ailing, suffered through the open hostility of his son, the friend of the disgraced Montmorency, and of the Lorraine princes, whose wild ambition disturbed him. Since 1545 the Dauphin had refused to attend the Privy Council. The memoirs of the period testify to their undoubted disagreement. They attribute atrocious statements to Henri and the Guises on the dying François I and his third son, Charles, who died on September 8, 1545. One must accept these accounts of domestic enmities with reserve, but as they are on record they do reveal a family conflict. The return of Anne de Montmorency, the favours bestowed on Albon de Saint-André and the Guises immediately on the accession of Henri II, are significant in this respect. Catherine's loyalty to her father-in-law proves that she was against the coterie that dominated her husband, but her unfailing prudence caused her not to fall out with them. Her feelings were on François I's side. She knew only too well of what an important protector his death would deprive her and she was deeply grieved by it. The influence of Diane de Poitiers, strong enough already in 1541 to cause the Dauphin to forbid his wife any relations with the Duchesse d'Étampes, the enemy of the Comtesse de Saint-Vallier, would henceforward be unrestrained. The births of her children were to be the only protection that the abandoned wife would enjoy from now on; Queen Cinderella, as M. Philippe Erlanger so prettily and rightly called her.

As against Diane and her creatures, the Constable de Montmorency and his family, and the Lorraine princes, Madame Catherine was in truth no more than a royal brood-mare. Her domain was the bed in which, for reasons of State, Henri II slept with her. She knew perfectly well that nothing more was asked of her than to bear children. To a being in whom political passion never ceased to grow, to be the legal concubine, whilst the mistress was queen by favour, was a cruel fate. And the illegitimate reign of the Duchesse de Valentinois was even politically legitimized. When Pope Paul III sent the new queen the Golden Rose, he did not forget to present the royal favourite with a pearl necklace.

Henri II gave everything into Diane's hands. He did not even hesitate to present her with the crown jewels, or to give her (as Matteo Dandolo informed the Council of San Marco) 'the right of control over all the offices of the kingdom which are obtained from the new king on payment of a certain sum, and from this she has made 100,000 écus and more'. This fiscal generosity was to cause the dour Montmorency to become Catherine's ally. Everything that fell from the loving hands of the King into the lap of the Sénéchale escaped Montmorency, who had no liking for sharing. The Bonhomme, as Brantôme has said, made no concessions when it came to money and his avarice drew him nearer to Catherine. Soon he was the declared enemy of Madame de Valentinois. The Guises did not care about money. In contrast to Anne de Montmorency they were more ambitious than avaricious. Diane, who preferred wealth to glory, did not stand in their way. As for Saint-André, the third man in the extraordinary triumvirate of Henri's favourites, he was clever enough not to take part in their quarrel and by remaining equally amiable with everyone he was almost the only member of the Royal Council who did not antagonize the Constable.[1] The Spanish Ambassador, Saint-Mauris, said that Montmorency treated Charles de Guise, Archbishop of Rheims and future Cardinal of Lorraine, like a contemptible fool. Such affability was usual among these feudal chiefs, to whom François I's weak successor had handed over the State, as he had given himself into the hands of the Duchesse de Valentinois. Like Hercules spinning at the feet of Omphala, Henri II abandoned his authority to a woman and to his favourites, who were fighting one another. 'Under the reign of Henri II the various factions were solely serving their own private ambitions, which were only impeded by their mutual rivalries.'[2] The advantage of a monarchy is that it should be above all parties. In the case of Henri II it was dominated by them. The Wars of Religion were the result of this bankruptcy of the royal power, of a State which had in fact become republican, and the natural breeding-ground of partisan struggles and sedition.

The Duchesse de Valentinois, châtelaine of Chenonceaux, having at her disposal all the unclaimed parts of the kingdom, also benefited by the confiscated property of the Protestants and the seizure of the goods of the Jewish usurers. To enable her to make certain of the Royal coffers, the titular treasurer, Duval, was obliged to give way to Blondel, who was completely devoted to her interests. Henri II insisted that she be given the place of honour everywhere. At formal visits to Paris, Lyons, Rouen, Diane appeared as queen. From the Emperor and the Pope, to the highest members of the French nobility, the whole world paid court to Diane. Everything was under the sign of the Crescent.

A temple was necessary to this cult of Diane. As François I had had Fontainebleau, as Louis XIV was to have Versailles, so the Duchesse de Valentinois had Anet, the masterpiece of Philibert de l'Orme. Henri II never refused her anything. Catherine's establish-

[1] Lucien Romier: *Jacques d'Albon de Saint-André*, pp. 47–48.
[2] Id.: *Origines politiques*, I, p. 33.

ment could not be compared to the favourite's. We possess the Queen's accounts, kept by Mademoiselle du Goguier, and checked with the care that the Medici always took of their affairs. They give us very exact information. Expenses for hunting figure very prominently in them. But those of the Château of Montceaux-en-Brie bear no comparison, however slight, to those of Anet. The queen's château, under Henri II, was Anet. Montceaux was a fine country house with large orchards and well stocked with game, abundant rather than luxurious. Catherine's highest personal expenditure was not more than 60,000 livres a year, only a little in excess of income. The account book figures prove that the Florentine lady kept her budget balanced like a good housewife and careful bourgeoise.

It was said that the successive births of his children preoccupied Henri II who was anxious to endow them well. An exemplary lover, an unwilling husband, the King was an excellent father. His letters prove it and so do those of Diane. Catherine was rather less anxious about her brood. Her correspondence between 1544 and 1563—for the whole period when her children were still little or adolescents—is revealing on this point, even if we take into account the fact that many letters were certainly lost. One finds no domestic references in it. The whole correspondence is small, less than twenty letters written between December 21, 1546, and October 20, 1563; some of them to Jean d'Humières, administrator of the Maison des Enfants de France and to his wife, others addressed to the Constable de Montmorency, the Duc de Guise, the Duchesse de Savoie, and Guillaume de Villefrançon, provisional representative of Tavannes to the Government of Burgundy. The seventeen letters to her daughter Elisabeth, beginning in November 15, 1560, are written more particularly to the Queen of Spain, for they are essentially political. We thus have about forty letters, spread out over nearly twenty years, during which she might have been concerned about her children—their illnesses and accidents and also the final moments of François II. The tone of the letters to Elisabeth is affectionate. Those referring to François II reveal an anxious mother, but one who has not forgotten politics; a few intimate details, very short, in passing. In such a busy letter-writer, expecially at this time—before 1559—when her political activities were only occasionally diverted from Italian affairs, such paucity is significant. It appears therefore that Catherine did not feel any very deep maternal passions. There is no evidence to show that she was not a good mother, but everything suggests that she was so more by profession than by vocation. She later developed a predilection, surprising in one so politically-minded, for her son Henri, which became positively tyrannical. And in fact Henri III was Catherine de Medici's only love. Thus Eros took a curious revenge, although nothing impure can be discerned in this obsessive affection.

Was she, on the other hand, as has often been claimed, as much in love with Henri II as she was jealous of Madame de Valentinois? Let us consult the letters. There are only five written by the Queen to the King. The first, of September 26, 1551, refers to a political matter, concerning Leo Strozzi, Prior of Capua and commander of the galleys. At the end of May 1552 another strictly political letter, concerning a request made to Catherine de Medici by the English Ambassador, Sir William Pickering, with regard to the capture of some ships by the Bretons, and in which she advises him that the English should be treated gently. The letter of the following June 6th, also deals with the capture of a Florentine ship by the Prior of Lombardy. On January 20, 1558, another letter containing political news, the most interesting of which concerns the pregnancy of Mary Tudor. The superscription is always the same: 'Your very humble and very obedient wife.'

Even when collating the very few letters in which she refers to the King we find almost no comments on the married life of Madame Catherine.

Picked from the huge mass of letters from Catherine, those referring to her marital life, which are unfortunately extremely few, leave us in no doubt that she was always equally attached and submissive to her husband, anxious to please him, afraid of him, and careful not to displease him. But to restrict ourselves to the negative side of Catherine's feelings for Henri II would be a mistake. She loved him. She always suffered from his absence. She worried when she knew him to be threatened by the dangers of war. With that dramatic and Italian streak she often revealed, she made her ladies-in-waiting wear mourning when he was with his armies.

Owing to lack of documentation we cannot know the depth and extent of Catherine's love for her husband. It is certain that she did love him. The gratitude of the Medici to the Valois, who in marrying her had almost committed a misalliance, appears in her letters: 'I had the honour of marrying His Majesty the King', she wrote one day to Henri de Navarre. This honour seemed to her to justify her complaisance with regard to Diane de Poitiers, who in return always treated her well. The letters of Diane and those of the Venetian ambassadors prove it. Henri II was very pleased by the reciprocal friendliness of his mistress and his wife. He showed his thanks to them both by gifts and little kindnesses. He once gave 5,500 livres to the Duchesse de Valentinois to mark his pleasure in the services she had rendered Catherine.

Catherine and Diane were always associated on public occasions such as the entry into Lyons in June 1549; at Rouen in 1550; the celebrations in connection with the bishopric of Paris on June 19, 1549. At these Madame de Valentinois appeared behind the Queen, with the Princesses of the Blood Royal.

If she did detest her, Catherine knew how to dissimulate her feelings, like her confidant, Anne de Montmorency. In spite of the inevitable passing quarrels, 'none of the members of this *ménage à quatre* disturbed the peace. They formed a strange, irregular family, as united as any bourgeois. They shared one and the same preoccupation, the welfare of the royal children. They entrusted their education to mutual friends, Monsieur and Madame d'Humières, themselves the parents of a large family'.[1]

The head of the household was Anne, who shared his authority with Diane, whence sprang the aversion he felt for her, but which only revealed itself in moments of bad temper. Catherine and the Constable manoeuvred secretly against the royal mistress. The bond between the Queen and her confidant was a political one. Montmorency kept watch over the Children of France as if they were his own. If the paternal zeal of the redoubtable Lord of Ecouen was not disinterested it nonetheless appeared to be sincere. Montmorency had chosen to play the part of the lion, and Diane the lioness, and to counteract his influence the Guises had become Diane's allies.

Between them—Henri II, led by the Constable and the favourite, both splendid examples of still flourishing feudalism; Catherine, biting on the bit in silence, but invariably perfectly submissive to the three other members of the ménage—they were acting a comedy in which she wore the most impenetrable mask of them all. She raised it only occasionally and only for her confidant, who was then her principal correspondent. We have about sixty letters dating from 1543-63, from his 'good gossip and friend', as she always signed herself. The letters to Montmorency are as free in style as those to

---

[1] Francis De Crue: *Anne, duc de Montmorency, connétable et pair de France, sous les rois Henri II, François II et Charles IX*, p. 29.

the King were carefully worded. There was a firm alliance between Queen Cinderella and the man who, under Henri II was, in spite of the Guises, the real head of the State. 'Created a duke and peer of France, Montmorency was in charge of the affairs of State from 1547–59. This long rule of twelve years lasted in spite of the rivalry of the Guises, an uninterrupted source of changes in French politics. What were the results of Montmorency's long administration? The tree must be judged by its fruits. Under Henri II Montmorency in the first place contributed to establishing national unity. . . . France and Montmorency was the common cause sustained by the Constable.'[1]

Did Catherine, allied to Montmorency, play a political role under Henri II? Diane de Poitiers undeniably did so and Tavanes's words on the subject have the very ring of truth: 'The Constable was pilot and captain of the ship, of which Madame de Valentinois held the tiller.' The King's two favourites were often compared to the sun and the moon, the sun reigning over the State, the moon over the Prince. At the Spanish Embassy they made fun of this pair in double harness, which dragged the king along without allowing him to drive; the Constable was compared to the donkey and Diane to the she-ass. The courtiers preferred mythology to such disrespectful terms; Diana or Venus was their favourite; the Constable was Mars —Catherine was Juno, and Henri was Jupiter. But she was a Juno who made no scenes with Jupiter. And in spite of this god-like disguise the King was a weakling. He had himself addressed as *Majesté* and not *Sire*, as if he were Caesar in Germany, but in fact he was a mere plaything in the hands of Mars and Venus. Such was the reverse side of that Olympia and the historical truth. The crescent insisted on living up to its motto; Diane on being Venus and having everything in her power. Mars, at the Louvre, was not her lover but her adversary. Thanks to the king, who refused to sacrifice one of them to the other, the two rivals achieved a state of equilibrium. It was in order to disrupt this equilibrium in her own favour that Diane supported the Guises. Madame de Valentinois was the living, active cause of the rivalry between Lorraine and Montmorency.

The Guises against the Montmorencys; their rivalry was to be woven into the Wars of Religion. Diane de Poitiers knew very cleverly how to weave it. She was no less skilful in seeing that neither

---

[1] Id. *ibid.*, p. 487. The two admirable books of Francis De Crue on Montmorency (the first a study of him from his birth until the accession of Henri II) have re-established his true personality.

of the two factions triumphed over the other. This was also Catherine's policy later on, between the Bourbons and the Guises. And this policy of equilibrium was completed by family alliances. Diane never made the mistake of openly opposing Anne's influence over Henri. She signed her letters to the Constable 'your humble and good friend'. Diane and Anne thus formed a politically antagonistic couple between whom the King, whose permanently weak character never offered any resistance to these two dominating personalities, remained captive. François I, in his dealings with his favourites, had always retained his political freedom, whereas Henri II abdicated his. He preferred to play the lute, write verses, keep an eye on his architects, sleep regularly with his wife, and idolize his mistress rather than, in order to reign, quarrel with those whom he found it so convenient to allow to reign in his stead. He concentrated all his serious work on the Navy, with regard to which he genuinely was the precursor of Colbert. His only exercise consisted in hunting or taking part in tourneys or other physical activities, at which he was both vigorous and enduring. Henri had a taste for that submissiveness which Catherine practiced by necessity. The more obedient he was to Anne and Diane the more precious they became to him.

He favoured the Guises for the same reason. They, too, knew how to impose themselves. The despatches of the Venetians, those of the Florentine, Ricasoli, and the Ferrarese, Alvarotti, leave us in no doubt in the matter. The Guises and Montmorencys occasionally insulted one another. Diane stood aside, but without ceasing to act. The King suffered it and only intervened to calm their quarrelling; for Henri II was a man of habit and was not inconstant like his father. His entourage knew this—to last, with Henri II, meant to govern. This was the reason for the caution the rivals showed towards one another, for their comparatively rare disputes, after which they could take refuge under the shelter of politeness and courtesy, which was always available. In spite of his violent nature Anne de Montmorency played his part with skill. The truce of Vaucelles on February 5, 1556, was his work and guaranteed five years of peace between the successors of Louis XI and those of the last Grand Duc d'Occident, nearly a century after the latter's death. Had the fratricidal war between the Valois and the Bourgignons then come to an end? It is to Montmorency's honour that he did sincerely endeavour to make peace between France and the Empire. On May 4, 1557, the marriage of his son, François, to Diane, natural daughter of the King and widow of the Duc de Castro, made him a blood relation of the Royal

Family. His grandchildren were also those of Henri II. Such was the reward of staying the course.

Catherine, however, was still awaiting her reward, a share in political power. It meant nothing to her that in July 1548 she had been made a member of the Council instituted by Henri II at Mâcon, whilst he himself was in Piedmont. Her secret ambition was to be a queen at last, and no longer the woman who was only expected to produce children. In April 1522 Henri II was leading his troops in the Rhine campaign which led to the occupation of the three German but French-speaking Bishoprics, Metz, Toul and Verdun. In spite of the challenge sent to the Emperor by the King of France, 'protector of German liberties', the French government did not attach to this expedition the importance which was later attributed to it owing to an historical illusion, born of the theory of natural frontiers.[1] This theory was quite foreign to the policies of those days, when the struggle for hegemony, the spirit of sovereignship, were paramount. Italy still remained of first importance. The subjects of controversy with Charles V were, since the death of François I, Milan, Sienna, Naples, Sicily, Aragon, Navarre, Artois, the Flanders, in a word, the Treaty of Crépy. The German princes, at war with the Emperor, had summoned the King of France, Vicar of the Empire, to their aid. This is the meaning of the Treaty of Chambord, signed on January 15, 1552, *pro Germaniae patria libertate recuperanda*. Metz, Toul, Verdun were the price paid for French help. It was a meagre price, for it was merely a matter of provisional occupation and not of annexation. The French Court had nothing more in mind than a journey to Germany, undertaken with an expeditionary force. The heroism of François de Guise, besieged in Metz, the set-back to Charles V, who had come in person to attack the place, lent the French intervention a sudden importance which had not been fore-seen. The affairs of Piedmont still remained in the forefront.

Before they left on their military expedition on March 25, 1552, Henri II and the Constable thought it advisable to hand over the regency to the Queen, under the guidance of the Cardinal de Bourbon, Bertrandi, Keeper of the Seals, and Admiral d'Annebaut. Although Lucien Romier was right to contest the legend of the effacement and humiliations of Catherine, and to say that 'the Court had never, since Anne de Bretagne, known a queen whose spirit and behaviour

---

[1] The researches of M. Gaston Zeller confirm those of Lucien Romier, and make it impossible for us to see in this affair, in future, 'a plan of expansion towards the East that had been ripening for a long time'.

was so entirely in accord with her functions', and even if it is undeniable that she undoubtedly held a different place from Queen Claude and Queen Eléonore, the ineffectual wives of François I, it is nevertheless an established fact that she was merely the fourth member of the Royal ménage. She only maintained her rank and the appearance of being queen at the price of her very great discretion. She only avoided insignificance by submission and humiliation by humility. However great the interest she took in Florentine affairs, however passionately she may have cared about them, she always took care never to intervene in them officially. Her correspondence with the Duke and Duchess of Florence always remained within the domain of family relationships. Tuscany only had envoys in France between 1547 and 1548, and between 1550 and 1551. There are no signs that Catherine ever took any particular notice of the two ambassadors, Ricasoli and Capponi.

The documentation, however, incontestably proves Catherine de Medici's constant zeal for the exiled Italians, once she had become Queen of France. Their influence in French society was of long standing and powerful. Ever since the Middle Ages they had counted for a great deal in France, where Dante had taken refuge during his exile. Later they found a particularly favourable atmosphere in that French Italianization which was the result of the wars of Charles VIII, Louis XII, and François I—in the intellectual sphere for artists, writers and scientists; in commerce for Italian traders, particularly at Lyons, in the importance of the Bank of Florence; in the activities of the Italians at Court, diplomats, great noblemen, prelates and soldiers; and even more, perhaps, in the inclusion of Italians in French administration. In France the *fuorusciti* were hardly exiles at all: 'The accession of Henri II gave them the entry at Court; by favour of the Queen they took first place there, associating themselves most often with the ambitions of the Lorraines, and by their own passions adding poison to all the Italian disputes.'[1]

These exiles were chiefly Florentines. Nevertheless the number of Neapolitans and the parts they played were also important. There were also Genoese and Milanese, and refugees from all the Italian principalities, and from Rome.

The Florentines were backed by their banks, for in the economy of the sixteenth century the bankers of Florence had replaced the Jews and the Lombards of the Middle Ages. Certain of the Florentine

[1] Romier, *op. cit.* p. 133.

financiers were also Jews. The two most important banks, the only ones that could hold their own against the Fuggers, those Bavarians of genius and precursors of modern plutocracy, were those of the Salviati, related to the Medici, and of Albisse d'Elbène, the royal banker. Between the Italian and German bankers there was a strong and flexible link. It is not surprising in this connection that Catherine, descended from a commercial dynasty, and who at Court was regarded as a Florentine shopkeeper, should have enjoyed this milieu, which was both familiar and sympathetic to her. Whilst the King, the princes, and the courtiers were only concerned with matters of chivalry or pure politics, Catherine was used to men of finance. Albisse d'Elbène was the husband of one of her ladies-in-waiting, Lucrezia Cavalcanti. They were constantly in touch. The King needed money, more and more, for the Italian wars were ruinous. Albisse d'Elbène and his kind became all-powerful. What is now-a-days known as international capitalism was born and developed at a surprising speed in the sixteenth century. The Jews were brilliant at it; the brothers Nasi of Florence, for instance. Finance and politics were united through the Salviati and the Strozzi. Ricasoli had a significant term for it—'synagogue of the refugees', he called it, as far back as 1547. This synagogue made its domicile with Catherine's favourite poet, Luigi Alamanni, who was her *maître d'hotel* and in her confidence, married to one of her waiting-ladies, a Florentine, Maddalena Bonajusti, whom she had chosen as her confidante.

Such was Catherine's Italian entourage. It throws light on a number of things. In this connection the Queen of France could not act officially, and to this is due the absence of evidence on the subject in her correspondence. But although veiled—and this was not the kind of thing to displease her—her enthusiasm was none the weaker on that account; on the contrary, even stronger. This enthusiasm led her to become the secret but active ally of the Strozzi brothers, promotors of the exiles' revenge. It must never be forgotten that this was the political apprenticeship, both secret and complicated, of which Catherine was to retain the methods and habits during the thirty years of her reign, lasting through the accessions of her four sons. Under François II she was forced into genuine effacement by Mary Stuart and the Guises, though this was less complete than might have at first appeared. From Charles IX onwards she did in fact reign, although under Henri III she suffered periods of eclipse during which she was reduced to resorting to the blundering activities of François d'Anjou. Only in the hour of her death did she renounce politics, which had been her whole life's passion, a passion of which the origin is to be found in the quiet participation, which yet was both as deep as it was obstinate, of the wife of Henri II, apparently withdrawn, voluntarily discreet to the point of humility, in Italian affairs, and by rebound in those of France.

Her abilities were put to the test during this spring regency of 1552. Montmorency was informed that Catherine was dissatisfied with the narrow limits of her power, yet above all she wished to obey the King. 'She would approve of anything whatever, so long as it was the King's wish.' Her letters show that she carried out her task most conscientiously. She travelled to Châlons in order, she said, 'to learn there the business and responsibilities of a commissary'. She was pleased to be politically active. At the end of June Henri II sent for her to join him at Sedan, where, however, she remained only a few days. Catherine's letters to the Marshal de Brissac and the Constable are dated from Châlons on June 14th, 15th, and 17th, and one undated one appears to have been written during the last few days of the month. Brissac was then fighting in Piedmont. From these letters it is clear that Catherine was following the military operations closely, and was also politically and diplomatically active in French affairs. She appears at ease, in her natural element.

She displayed the greatest deference towards Montmorency. Her 'gossip' was prodigal of advice, which she apparently received with gratitude. She was coming and going in the rear of the armies—to and from Châlons, Rethel, Sedan, La Fère—and all this activity delighted her. The slightest incidents aroused her interest. And that is how we shall find her continuously during the course of her royal life—watching over everything, neglecting nothing, the mistress of the household inseparable from the Queen, kind but firm, a woman accustomed to managing her own household.

We shall often catch her in the very act. She was kind and generous. No one hated quarrelling more than Catherine, who was fated to live in the midst of conspiracies and wars. She longed for peace and friendship, liked always to arrange matters, neither to exaggerate nor to dramatize, to drive nothing and nobody to the bitter end. That was the difference between her and Richelieu, whose policy was otherwise similar to hers. She resigned herself to violent measures only in the last resort, when they seemed the lesser evil, but they nonetheless distressed her. She preferred, as she said, more gracious methods. She did use torture when it was justified, but only when she was forced and constrained to do so. And withal she was the most obliging person on earth. The ten volumes of her correspondence contain letter after letter recommending either her own servants or those of her friends. Serviceable, always grateful, never forgetful of kindnesses shown her, contrary to her legend she was much more inclined that way than to revenge. In politics she was vindictive, but not or very little, in private.

The Queen's regency of 1552 was twice renewed by the King before the Truce of Vaucelles. Catherine gained real prestige through it, which showed itself even in her physical appearance. On the whole her health was good, although it did not protect her from very serious illnesses. At the beginning of her first regency she nearly died of scarlatina, scarlet fever as it was then called. She was nursed by Diane de Poitiers. The doctor who was treating her, Guillaume Chrestien, praised the devotion of the King's mistress at the sick-bed of his wife. In a despatch to the Duke of Ferrara, Alvarotti reported the King's anxiety, confirmed by a letter from Diane to Brissac. This anxiety proves that her husband was fond of Catherine; the harmony that existed between the *ménage à quatre* was no fable, but stands out from all the first-hand documents, an ordered harmony that surrounded Diane. The crescent was no satellite but a planet. It filled the entire orb. Diane put up with the hostility of the Queen and the Constable, knowing that it could not come into the open on account of their political interests.

She was nevertheless disturbed by those three brief regencies before Vaucelles. The Constable, for his part, was not the kind of man to admit that a woman could run the State, nor would he have tolerated it. Even the Duchesse de Valentinois took her precautions against appearing in the forefront of the political scene. Henri II abandoned power to his favourites, but on condition that they left him the appearance of authority. Montmorency and the Guises were always careful to respect his susceptibilities, and Catherine no doubt did so more than anyone else.

She took good care never to intervene, except by requests, in the affairs she had most at heart, like those of Italy, arising from the internal as well as external policies of the government of Henri II. The Guises were opposed to the truce of Vaucelles. The intrigues of Cardinal Caraffa, nephew of Pope Paul IV, the bitterest imaginable enemy of Spain, favoured their ambitions on the Kingdom of Naples. Vaucelles had secured to France the Three Bishoprics and Piedmont. The abdication of Charles V, seven months after the truce, seemed to indicate a great weakening of the House of Austria, by the division of the Empire between his brother Ferdinand, King of the Romans, who had become Emperor and Governor of Hungary and Bohemia, as well as of all the German domains, and his son Philip, King of Spain, possessing the Netherlands, Naples and Sicily, to which the English marriage had added the kingdom of Mary Tudor. And in addition there were above all the West Indies, the immense and fabulous empire of the New World. Spain was, as we would say today, a world power, the only one existing at that time. How much was France worth, beside her? Catherine, a realistic politician above all, was never to lose sight of this fact, and from this sprang her constant caution with regard to Madrid.

The intervention of François de Guise in Italy, in the war between Paul IV and Philip II, broke the truce of Vaucelles. In order to forestall an English intervention on behalf of Spain, Coligny, in the first days of January 1557, attempted a surprise attack on Douai, but this failed. At the beginning of April there was fighting around Rocroy. On May 23rd, Coligny captured Lens. General warfare was again breaking out. The failure of Montmorency's policy was complete, and in Italy the military offensive of François de Guise was equally so. The entry of England into the war on June 7, 1557, worsened the situation. The Duke of Savoy, Emmanuel-Philibert, took over the command of the Spanish army, 60,000 strong, in the Netherlands. He was fighting there to save his own fatherland, which had been in French occupation since 1536. A stateless prince, the son of Charles III of Savoy and Beatrix of Portugal was less than thirty years old when, having learnt the art of war in the service of Charles V in the German territories, he revealed himself as a great leader, worthy of his nickname, *Tête de Fer*, given him by his troops and justifying his sublime motto: *Spoliatis arma supersunt*, taken from Juvenal's satire on the nobility, for he was a humanist. He had been despoiled, but arms remained to him.

On St Laurence's Day, August 10, 1557, this great man proved that if one can control it one should never despair of destiny. In less than five hours Henri II's army had been annihilated under the walls of Saint Quentin. There were 3,000 dead, nearly 5,000 wounded, and 6,000 prisoners, including the Constable himself, the Field Marshal de Saint-André, the Duke of Longueville and the Duke of Montpensier. France had not known such a disaster since Pavia. Anne de Montmorency's military failure was complete. On the battlefield his only talent, like that of the feudal lords at Crécy,

Poitiers and Agincourt, consisted in indomitable physical courage. He was only disarmed after having been seriously wounded in the ribs.

The disaster of Saint Quentin was to weigh heavily on the whole of the second half of the sixteenth century. The brilliant feats of arms of the Duc de Guise in recapturing Calais and Guines from the English at the beginning of January 1558, following the plan of Henri II and Coligny, and in taking Thionville in the following May from the Imperialists, saved the honour of the Lilies and laid the foundations of the prodigious fortune of the Lorraine princes under François II and Charles IX. But they had no influence whatever on general European politics. Spain's predominance was based on the victory of the dispossessed Savoyard. On November 7, 1659, in the Ile des Faisans, an Italian from the Abruzzi was to sign, after a whole century had passed, the first pact that would begin to make amends for Saint Quentin; Cardinal Mazarin, continuing the work of Richelieu and Henri IV, which, however, was not finally completed until nineteen years later, when at Nimègue, the Franche-Comté, Cambrésis and Valenciennes were at last united to the French kingdom. Spain—Italy—Savoy—this was the axis of politics during the century-and-a-quarter that it took France to replace it by her own, a long and hard stretch of time.

Nor would this ever have been possible save for the genius of an Italian, Catherine, then still obscure, but which the aftermath of Saint Quentin was to reveal, and who was to hand over France, worn out but not mutilated, exhausted but rescued, to Henri IV.

The discovery of her genius was as sudden as it was complete; no one, excepting the members of her Italian entourage, could have expected it. If one considers the general picture of European politics during the ten first years of Henri II's reign, the secret Italian activities—Catherine's secret activities—in the last resort stand for very little. Catherine was never able to take an open part in public matters, even concerning Italy. The King, under Diane's influence, might occasionally listen to his wife, but could not take her into partnership. Catherine's Florentine interests were after all and above all merely family interests. In her letters during this period individuals and financial matters took the most prominent place. Her most important political letter concerning Italy is the one dated September 29, 1554 (of which a copy in Italian still exists), in which Catherine wrote to her very dear and great friend, the illustrious Captain and Regent of the Republic of Siena, and which is addressed to all the members of the government of that city. She was extremely pre-occupied by the siege of Siena. This letter proves her continued devotion to her Italian homeland (a Machiavellian memory) but does not show her as playing a front-rank role in politics. In it the Queen promised to plead constantly with Henri II on behalf of her dear Siennese and the tone of the letter is warm.

For her the question of Siena was a family matter—Catherine and Philippo Strozzi against Cosimo de Medici. There is no doubt that she was passionately concerned about this war, calling herself Protectress of Siena.

On receiving the news of the disaster at Marciano, which on August 2, 1554, ruined all her Siennese hopes, Catherine fell into one of her Italian rages, which usually she was able to control. She thereafter supported the policy of war to the death, which ended with the siege of Siena and in spite of the heroism of Monluc and the French, with the surrender of April 17, 1555. It was only a long time later that she finally resigned herself to this final blow to French ambitions in Italy. She took refuge by retreating into the background and silence, but without ceasing to act as far as she was able with Diane and the Guises against Montmorency's peaceful policy, which triumphed at Vaucelles. Thus the wife of Henri II had not given up the revenge of the Duchess of Urbino nor had she forgotten that she was Italian by birth. That was the state of mind of the exiles.

Italian as she was, did she in fact ever feel herself to be a French-woman? In reading everything she wrote in 1557, whilst fighting was going on from Flanders to Naples, one notes with surprise the omission of any allusion to Saint Quentin. An indefatigable correspondent, in those days when France was so nearly lost, Catherine wrote nothing worthy of attention. This would be the despair of any historian who might seek at all costs, in her own words, a sign that Catherine was a patriotic Frenchwoman. Yet other documents prove that such a Catherine did exist. The fact that this evidence does not appear in her letters attracts attention. But on the morrow of the disaster the Queen was spurred on by the situation rather than by her emotions. That alone gave her the opportunity to emerge from the political withdrawal into which the collapse of her hopes for Tuscany had forced her. Montmorency was beaten and captured and at Compiègne Henri II was endeavouring to raise new troops; he was said to be completely crushed and overwhelmed by the disaster, with no one at his side and not knowing what to do. Diane appeared delighted by the catastrophe which had ridden her of the despotic leader of the amazing *ménage à quatre*. The three cardinals who were members of the Council—Lorraine, Guise, and Châtillon—were incapable of dealing with the situation. The Court had retired from Compiègne to Saint Germain. The Dauphin had been sent to Touraine. The Parisians were fleeing. There was panic throughout the Ile-de-France. Only Catherine remained, to whom the King, less broken up than was rumoured, immediately turned; having written to François de Guise that it was necessary to remain in good heart and to be surprised at nothing. He sent the secretary Robertet to the Queen, asking her to obtain funds from the Paris municipality in order to carry on the war. This was no more than a purely administrative measure, but a measure that Catherine was to turn into the salvation of the public welfare.[1]

This was Catherine's first appearance on the political scene, which she was immediately to leave, only to reappear on the death of Henri II and to remain for thirty years in the forefront of it. Into the stormy skies of Saint Quentin the bow, herald of peace, had shot the scarf of Iris, entwined about its arrow. The crescent had temporarily disappeared. Catherine's first act of revenge against Diane was a political one—the sweetest, to this careful student of Machiavelli.

The Parisians were furious with the Guises, who had instigated the war and with Anne de Montmorency, who had conducted it so badly. Catherine had better things to do than to waste her time in vain maledictions. The King had ordered her to act; she did not hesitate for an instant. As Brantôme said, the State was in the balance. By August 13th, the Queen had gone to the offices of the City of Paris, i.e. to the Municipal Council. Madame Marguerite, the princes and princesses, the cardinals and ladies-in-waiting accompanied her, for she decided to make her approach in full state. She, the princesses and her ladies were in mourning. Madame Catherine knew what language to use to these Parisian citizens, whose fear had lowered their pride and curbed their avarice. She informed them that the King of France could ask the peasants, who were completely ruined, for no more money, and that therefore he was appealing to his loyal

[1] For the aftermath of Saint Quentin in the threatened capital, we have followed *Les Registres des Délibérations du Bureau de la Ville de Paris*, and listened to Brantôme, ever a faithful witness as regards Catherine, in whose wake he lived, since we have nothing from Catherine herself except her completely banal lines to Montmorency when he was a prisoner. We have also read the despatch from the Venitian, Soranzo, of August 14, 1557.

cities and especially to Paris, foremost of them all. Sincerely moved, she was both eloquent and pathetic, as befitted an Italian familiar with the orators of ancient Rome. She succeeded in conveying her emotion to the entire assembly. She demanded nothing—she implored their help. An adverb—that does not surprise us—fell most naturally from the pen of the town clerk, who had no intention of coining a phrase: 'She humbly asked for money to help the King, in order that he might immediately raise 10,000 infantrymen.' Humbly, Madame Catherine obtained 300,000 livres.

In order to make it quite clear that they were masters in their own house, the Parisian notables requested the Queen to withdraw from the council chamber of the Hôtel de Ville during their brief deliberations. There was no argument. They voted that, in order to raise the 10,000 men 'there would be a levy of the sum required on all the inhabitants of the said city and suburbs with no exceptions or exemptions'. One hundred notables each immediately offered 3,000 francs. Catherine thanked them with tears. Always practical, she promised to recommend these generous citizens to Henri II for special privileges.

They all mingled their tears with hers. She expressed to them her humble gratitude, and aroused their general admiration. The satisfaction of the Parisians was evidence of the Queen's tactfulness. The Florentine had received her naturalization papers as a Frenchwoman from the Parisians. She had given fresh courage to them all.

To the French it was a revelation. On the medallion struck to commemorate the siege of Thionville, Catherine's portrait is next to Henri II's. The King spent more time with his wife, whose only thought was to please him. He paid honour to the Queen's circle by appearing there more frequently. Now the wife began to gain on the mistress. Pietro Aretino had written to her, one day, that she was the only queen, paying tribute to her both as woman and goddess. Such was the importance that Catherine, until then disdained, at that time acquired. Hector de la Ferrière has quite rightly stressed it: 'The poet Habert called her the new Pallas; Roville, the great Lyons printer, dedicated the first edition of Gelli's *Circe*, translated by Denis Sauvage, to her and congratulated her on bearing the excellent character of the great Cosimo I, who had resuscitated literature; Guillaume Postel, the authority on Orientalism, dedicated his *Description de la Terre sainte* to her. She patronized the enamellist Della Robbia, the great artist, Léonard Limosin, who so often modelled her portrait; she had her own painter-in-ordinary, René

E

Tibergeau; her sculptor-in-ordinary, Nicolas Saget; she patronized Jodelle, Mellin de Saint-Gelais, whose play, *Sophonisbe*, translated from Trissino, she caused to be produced; she took as almoner the traveller, Thévet; and appointed Amyot, who had been presented to her by L'Hospital, as tutor to her two sons.'

Brantôme, whose discourse on Catherine is in no way chronological, delighted in describing the magnificence dear to this princess. Catherine's own Court only dates from the last years of Henri II. Its loveliest ornaments were Madame Marguerite, the King's sister, Mesdames Elisabeth and Claude, the sovereigns' daughters, who when the battle of Saint Quentin was fought were thirteen and ten years old; Madame la Dauphine, the adorable little Queen of Scotland who was already sixteen and whose mother-in-law said that she need only smile to turn all French heads. These princesses were as well educated and artistic as they were delicious and beautiful. The more mature ladies formed a blossoming orchard around these budding beauties. The loveliest among these luscious fruits was Anne d'Este, Duchesse de Guise, of whom Ronsard thus sang:—

Vénus la Sainte en ses grâces habite;
Tous les amours logent en ses regards.

The other members of the beauty chorus were led by Madame Diane de France, the King's legitimized daughter and daughter-in-law of the Constable.

Brantôme delighted in recreating this 'lovely troop of ladies and girls, creatures more divine than human'. The historian shares the chronicler's pleasure in them, and joins him in saluting Madame Catherine, who 'appeared as the queen above them all'. As Queen-widow and Queen-mother the splendour of her surroundings was to rival François I's. From the end of the reign of Henri II the bow began to oust the crescent from the sky. The lover was no longer indifferent to the scarf of Iris. His mistress's advancing years gradually transformed his devotion to her into a filial one. Even black and white, the colours which once had been so dear to him, now seemed to him occasionally a little monotonous and austere, and faithfulness no less so. Their relationship was gradually modified. Diane had become the maternal friend, less powerful against his wife than the favourite she had been and of whom Lucien Romier so prettily said that she was 'a kind of dowager goddess'.

Nevertheless the prejudice against Catherine did not disappear from the Court. There is a really frightful letter from the Duchesse de Guise dated April 21, 1558, in which she wrote that the Medici were 'tradesmen who are not fit to call themselves our servants'.[1] Catherine was aware of this contemptuous hostility, and took care not to stress the advantage her behaviour after Saint Quentin had given her. She still pretended to remain indifferent to politics. The situation was deplorable. The States-General, possessing restricted powers since January 5, 1558, had been incapable of remedying the appalling ills that oppressed the kingdom—the State in anarchy owing to the absence of the Constable, which exacerbated the rivalry between the Lorraine and Châtillon factions; financial ruin equalled only by the poverty of the people; the Lutheran heresy, spreading more and more rapidly in its Calvinist form, which quite naturally was encouraged by the disastrous economic situation, a result of the futile Italian wars and the Spanish victory at Saint Quentin. The aim of the Vaucelles truce was to allow the country's finances to be restored, and the breaking of it had led to catastrophe. The letters of Simon Renard, previous to Saint Quentin, allow us to judge of the incapacity of Henri II, giving in to the unrestrained policy of the Guises, who wanted the truce broken in order to eliminate Montmorency from power. France was at the mercy of international finance. Since the Hundred Years War the country's economy had never been so lamentable.

In the midst of this general disorder Protestantism attracted all those hopes blighted by the Catholic Church, which was incapable of reforming itself, and by the Royal State, which had fallen into the hands of the feudalists, fighting one another over their homeland's broken body. The Reformation never ceased to make progress throughout 1556–59, favoured by an infinite number of causes and conditions, both material and moral. The wars of old provided great facilities for contact with foreign countries, owing to the passage of mercenary troops, which now, in France, were for the most part Lutherans, provided by the Germans and the Swiss. These facilities of contact did more for the spreading of the Reformation than either intellectual or moral propaganda, diffused by word of mouth or in print. As Protestantism spread the Guises became stronger, for all their interests were united with the defence of feudal and Catholic privileges. The Spanish affinities of the Guises, stronger than their

[1] Found by Romier in the Archives of Modena. It is an essential document as revealing the private feelings of the House of Guise with regard to the Italian, of too lowly birth,

temporary reasons for the breaking off the truce of Vaucelles, have been well proven by Alvarotti, confidant of the Cardinal de Lorraine. The Cardinal was closely linked with the Jesuits, basically inimica. to the Reformation.

There is one piece of evidence of capital importance, showing the anti-Protestant influence of Diane de Poitiers, contained in the letter of the Nuncio, Lorenzo Lenti, Bishop of Fermo, to Cardinal Caraffa, on October 24, 1557. In Protestant eyes she was the very incarnation of pagan immorality and she constantly feared that scruples of conscience might cause the King to separate from a mistress who was causing him to commit the sin of adultery. Catherine remained quiet and did not take sides. She was keeping herself ready. At this period her correspondence still remained as banal as possible. Her letters in the spring of 1559, when the peace of Cateau-Cambrésis was being negotiated, make not the slightest allusion to this important event.

They contained nothing on Spain, nothing about the Protestants. Nevertheless there is documentary proof that she was interested in the latter. The heads of the New Church mentioned her in their correspondence, together with Madame Marguerite, the King of Navarre, the Duc de Nevers, as favouring their cause, although still timidly. Yet this was the time when Henri II decided to repress heresy by iron and fire, when the Catholic people demonstrated, especially in Paris, against the Huguenots, who were themselves increasingly imprudent and provocative. They exasperated the King. He swore that if he could settle his external affairs he would make the streets run with the blood and the heads of that infamous Lutheran rabble. Their repression was only postponed by the need to make peace with Spain.

Catherine's state of mind is therefore remarkable. Whilst the King had chosen the path whence were to issue the Wars of Religion the Queen was in fact against the policy of persecuting the Huguenots. Henri II preferred to sacrifice his father's tradition—war on the Hapsburgs, on the coalition of Vienna and Madrid—rather than to renounce the extirpation of heresy. Nevertheless, one must not attribute to him any wish to serve the idea of Christianity. After Vaucelles he did nothing to oppose the revival of war against Spain, at the very time when a genuinely Catholic alliance would have been possible. But nor did he choose to seek the help of the German Lutherans or the English heretics in fighting Austria and Spain. Having no part in the government, Catherine was not called upon to choose. She did not do so. History must nevertheless take into account her sympathy for the Protestants, however latent it may have remained. This sympathy revealed a state of mind unusual in those days—Catherine remained indifferent to all fanaticism, all crusading mysticism aimed at the punishment of heretics. Such a state of mind only existed in faraway Poland, of which the French knew nothing, imagining that nation, whose élite was Italianized and Latinized, to be a land of barbarians, peopled only by brutal and uncultured Sarmatians, amongst whom Henri III, king of that republic in spite of himself, refused to remain. In Italy strong political influences were at work to harden a natural scepticism against the Reformation, for both in France and in Rome scepticism only flowered in secret. Scepticism was foreign to the hard and cruel Spaniards. But Poland was as far from the Inquisition as from Geneva or Rome. Only the Sarmatians would have understood the attitude of the daughter of the Medici. That was why, when the Queen Mother later on sent her confidant, Jean de Monluc, Bishop of Valence, to Poland in order to further the candidature of the Duc d'Anjou to the Polish throne, this ironical prelate was so warmly received there.

The Queen also remained apart from the various factions that were intriguing against one another for the State before they fell to arms over it. On his return from captivity Montmorency succeeded in ousting the Lorraines. This was his revenge for Vaucelles, coinciding with the sacrifice of the previous conquests, and leading to the reconciliation of the Catholic dynastics, thenceforward united against the Reformation. Diane de Poitiers was in favour of peace. Catherine continued to remain, apparently, utterly indifferent. But the sudden complete surrender of the Italian conquests threw her at her husband's feet. She vehemently attacked her former confidant, Anne de Montmorency, whom Henri II approved and defended against her. Indifferent as she was to the religious struggles, Catherine was impassioned for Italy. The Siennese dreams had not been blown away by the smoke of the Spanish conflagration; Catherine refused to give way to victorious Spain. And we should never forget that Spanish fanaticism was then and always remained antipathetic to her. The violent scenes which arose in November 1558 between herself and Henri II and Diane revealed why she had acted so energetically after Saint Quentin: to the Medici protectress of the exiles, the friend of the Strozzi and the enemy of the usurper, Cosimo, Spain was the permanent adversary. In this princess, to all appearances so discreet and self-effacing, the policy of peace at any price found an opponent who did not hesitate to say of the Constable that he had never done anything but evil. And if one may believe her contemporaries she threw the worst affront into the teeth of the Duchesse de Valentinois: 'I have read the histories of this kingdom and I have found in them that from time to time at all periods whores have managed the business of kings.' Both at Court and in town the only talk was of the Queen's revolt against the policy of making peace with the victors of Saint Quentin. She did not want. peace because of Italy, for Italy was to be French and not Spanish. And what is remarkable here—and proves that royalty naturalizes even princes of foreign birth—is the fact that in this she was not following Machiavelli, precursor of a united and independant Italy. She preferred a French Italy to an Italian Italy. In this she was two and a half centuries ahead of Napoleon, who put on the iron crown of the Kings of Lombardy, and became the Emperor and King.

Public opinion, however, was for peace at any price, and Catherine once more subsided. The marriage of her daughter Claude to Charles III of Lorraine at that moment tightened her bonds with the Guises. This alliance succeeded those they had already contracted with the House of France—Anne d'Este, grand-daughter of Louis XII, married François de Guise; Mary Stuart, Queen of Scotland, the Dauphin. The Lorraines were nearer to the steps of the throne than the Montmorencys; the Constable was only the father-in-law of a legitimized daughter of the King. The one did not equal the other.

The Italian wars were definitely lost at Cateau-Cambrésis. In that respect Catherine's instinct was not at fault. The marriages of March 1559 symbolized the triumph of Spain—Madame Marguerite and the Duc de Savoie; Madame Elisabeth and Philip II. The Daughters of France were satisfied with their husbands; Emmanuel-Philibert was a hero, the Catholic King the most powerful sovereign in the world. Catherine knew only too well that silence alone enables the vanquished to vanquish their unjust fate. . . . Peace was only obtained by the sacrifice of a whole page of past French glory and even of very recent glory in the reconquest of Calais. On March 12th, the agreement between France, England and Scotland left Calais to Henri II only for eight years, after which it was to be returned to England, unless France paid instead an indemnity of 1,250,000 livres. If this payment were not made, the city recaptured by François de Guise, the name of which was engraved on the heart of Mary Tudor, would have to be surrendered. The clause relating to the return of Calais to France was only to become operative in case of an attempted aggression by England against the Very Christian King or Francis and Marie, co-sovereigns of Scotland. It was hoped that the troubles in Scotland and English intervention in the States of Marie Stuart would enable this clause to operate. England, for her part, planned to ignore it. Philip II, who needed peace as much as his adversary, wrote to Granvelle not on any account to break off negotiations. Nor did the Constable de Montmorency or the Cardinal de Lorraine profit by it. Instead of seeking a compromise they gave way completely. For them the essential point was to end the war in order to throw everything into the struggle against heresy. And it is their fanaticism alone that explains the pro-Spanish *volte-face* of the loser of Saint Quentin.

In reading the Treaty of Cateau-Cambrésis, signed on April 2, 1559, with Elizabeth I of England and on April 3 with Philip II and Emmanuel-Philibert, one can only admire the clearsightedness with which Catherine had opposed her husband and the Constable and peace at any price. In exchange for Saint Quentin, Ham, Le Catelet, Thérouanne, the towns of Marienburg, Thionville, Yvoi, Damvillers and Montmédy were returned to Spain; Bovignes and Bouillon to the Bishop of Liège. Philip II remained at Hesdin. The Duke of Mantua recovered Montferrat, excepting Casal and a few strong-points. Valenza in the district of Milan was returned to Spain; Bonifacio and the Corsican fortresses to the Republic of Genoa. Siena fell into the hands of Cosimo, who shortly afterwards became Grand Duke of Tuscany. The lion's share fell to Emmanuel-Philibert. Apart from Turino, Pignerol, Chieri, Chivasso and Villanueva d'Asti, provisionally reserved to France until the succession to Louise de Savoie was settled by arbitration, and apart from the marquisate of Saluzzo, everything was returned to the victor of Saint Quentin: Piedmont, Nice, Barcelonette, Savoy, Brescia and Bugey. The claims of Jeanne d'Albret and Antoine de Bourbon on Spanish Navarre were annulled. France admitted herself completely defeated. Nearly three-quarters of a century of struggle for Mediterranean hegemony were wiped out.

We know what the Italian Catherine thought of this repudiation of a policy in which she had put all her hopes. We know what Brissac, Monluc, Tavannes, François de Guise, Vieilleville, Brantôme, thought of it; the tears of those who loved France; the signature which in an hour gave everything back, stained and blackened; the sacrifice in one day of something that could not be wiped out in thirty years; the return of those conquered spots for which a sea of French blood had been spilled; the 180 lost places; the loss and the ruin to which miserable France, who once had triumphed over all the nations of Europe had let herself be reduced; the forty million in gold and the hundred thousand men that the Italian wars had cost, wasted in one moment . . . these complaints, this indignation and fury have echoed down the centuries. On the other hand the latest historians and the best informed are not in agreement on Le Cateau-Cambrésis. Henry Lemonnier is resigned to it. Louis Batiffol approves of it without reserve, as did the common people at the time, expressing their joy: 'Cateau-Cambrésis', he wrote, 'turned French policy towards the north and the east, that is, in its normal direction.' The distinguished author of the *Siècle de la Renaissance* is here, it seems to us, the victim of an historical illusion. In the sixteenth century the centre of gravity of Imperial hegemony was to the south-east, south and south-west of France, and not to the north or to the east. Flanders was dangerous because it was Spanish. The Empire was dangerous through the union of the Hapsburgs of Vienna and Madrid, which facilitated and increased the abandonment of Italy. To the east were German princes, in difficulties with the Emperor. No doubt to the legislators and diplomats, when they give themselves over to that French mania for the pleasures of theorizing, the Rhine appears the natural frontier of the French *pré-carré*; an ideal frontier. But nothing, either documentarily or in fact, justifies us in attributing to Ancient France, and in particular France of the sixteenth century, a theory of State according to natural frontiers, a theory that did not appear until it was developed by the ideologists of the French Revolution.

The immediate threat was Hispano-Italian. The Treaty of Cateau-Cambrésis gave the Madrid-Vienna alliance complete freedom of action, since France renounced Italy. The wars in the peninsula, madly entered into by Charles VIII, had become a matter of public safety after the election of Don Carlos as Emperor, since François I was not resigned to his failure in the Imperial election and had chosen to go to war against his successful rival. Thenceforward their aim was basically national and justified according to historical geography. They broke the link of the Empire, the Madrid-Vienna axis. This was to be revealed under Louis XIII, when from 1630–60 it was necessary to fight in Westphalia and the Pyrenees, with the basic aim of freeing the German lands from the Spaniards, in order partly to redress the diplomatic disaster of Cateau-Cambrésis. Spanish hegemony, which lasted for more than a century, dated from that deplorable treaty. The strength of the Empire lay in Spain, and only in Spain. In the German lands the Empire was too pre-occupied by the Protestant princes, the kings of the North, Hungary, and the Turks, to become a danger on the Rhine. Until Germany was united the danger on the Rhine was a mere side issue. In the middle of the sixteenth century this future contingency could never have been foreseen.

To approve of Le Cateau-Cambrésis because of the defence of the Eastern Marches (the north, let us repeat, belonged to Spain since she occupied Flanders; and since she occupied the Franche-Comté the east was also hers) is to project on to the period of Henri II a view that would not begin to be true until Frederick II, and even then only very feebly. In fact the question of the Rhine arose through the wars of the Revolution and the Empire, with the military occupation of its banks, following on the subtle policy of influence of the seventeenth and eighteenth centuries, and finally the treaties of 1815, when thanks to England Prussia, the enemy, was installed on the banks of that river; nor should it be forgotten, either, that the rise to power of that state had its origin in the treaties of Westphalia, which were so favourable to Brandenburg. In the sixteenth century it was non-existent and one of the signs of this was the indifference of both sides to the Three Bishoprics. The Germano-Spanish threat was then basically in the Mediterranean. It was its Mediterranean strength alone that made Spain redoubtable in Flanders and the Franche-Comté, and this situation was confirmed by the abandon-ment of Italy at Le Cateau-Cambrésis. Contemporary observers interpreted the position correctly, as against modern historians, haunted by dread of invasion across the Rhine, to which our fore-fathers, ever since the mid-Middle Ages, no longer gave a thought. In the view of Old France, the threat of invasion lay in the north and the west, but hardly at all in the east. After England the enemy was Spain, in Flanders. The eastern corridor did not assume import-ance until after Spanish hegemony had been achieved. Once Spain was conquered the Rhine was subjugated. Historians of the past took the same view as their contemporaries. They agreed with Catherine, whose instincts in both domestic and political matters were extremely sound. It was not as a theoretician that she had protested against a defeatist peace, but as a Florentine, versed in her

Machiavelli and Guicciardini, who both felt and knew that Italy was the principal stake in the struggle between the Empire and France, and that Italy in Spanish hands was France's greatest danger, since the most powerful and dangerous enemy was in Madrid. We agree with Lucien Romier in maintaining that the opponents of Cateau-Cambrésis were politically right. Vaucelles was a compromise, which left the future open, but Le Cateau-Cambrésis was an abdication that sacrificed it.

Catherine de Medici, with Siena and Florence foremost in mind, chose France's side. The experience of a whole century's history since then proves her to have been right. From Cateau to Nymeghen it was necessary to continue fighting for another 120 years.

For France it was a fool's bargain. Spanish hegemony dominated foreign affairs, and the Religious Wars the policies on the home front. 'Between the southern countries, where heresy had been stifled, and those where it had triumphed, France in 1559 became what Italy had been at the beginning of the century—a European battlefield,' as Henri Hauser very rightly said. That anti-national peace bore within it the seeds both of civil war and war abroad. Henri II, too unintelligent to know anything of this, lived in a world of illusion. The medallion struck to celebrate the treaty shows a heap of weapons on which France is seated, a Victory in her right hand, and holding out the crown and the palm. The exergue at the base of the medallion is *Gallia . . . Optimo principi*, as motto. What an anti-climax! Forty years of French massacres plus a century of Spanish domination over Europe. The work of Charles VII, Louis XII, François I, and even the efforts made during the reign of Henri II, all destroyed; this was what that poor misguided prince was glorifying. As his mistress announced, he imagined that it would enable him to 'purge the kingdom of the infection of heresy'. He was filled with such zeal that he even dreamt of punishing England; misplaced zeal, halted by Philip II, whom religion never blinded to politics and who did not hesitate to defend Elizabeth I to the Pope nor to oppose the French plan for an expedition against Geneva.

Suriano, as an anti-Protestant Venetian, supported Henri II, and the other Italian ambassadors were of the same opinion. In the eyes of all European Catholics with the exception of Poland, the extirpation of heresy was the first duty of princes. Henri II followed this trend, which explains his mistake without, however, excusing it. Catholic Europe, for the anti-Protestant crusade, needed France too badly not to pay the highest price for her collaboration. Without indulging in that most useless of all literary activities, the re-making of history, it is enough to take note of Brissac, Monluc, Guise, Tavannes, Vieilleville, none of whom can be suspected of any tenderness towards the Reformation. The crusade was not in the least irreconcilable with a French peace. Only a few isolated contemporaries here and there might have thought that such a crusade was against sociological and moral laws, according to which all persecution—unless it results in complete extermination, as in the days of the crusade against the Albigensians, which in the half-Protestant Europe of the mid-sixteenth century was impossible—strengthens heresy. Luther and Calvin, like Torquemada and Pius V, were persecutors of heretics and they only differed from one another in their theological definitions of heresy—Protestantism on the one hand, Papism on the other.

Catherine de Medici was one of those isolated individuals, which had caused the Genevese to imagine that she was sympathetic towards them, when in fact she only favoured a policy of compassion, or, as it would be termed in the eighteenth century, of toleration. By God's will this unfanatical Italian was to succeed the fanatical King, whose zeal even bored Philip II. The broken lance of Gabriel Montgomery in the tournament of June 30, 1559, the splinters of which pierced the eye of Henri II, made Catherine the true successor of that prince. When on July 10th, the King died of his wounds, a policy exclusively directed towards the extermination of the heretics was faced by a state of mind inclined to compassion, and by that very fact exceptional—Catherine's. The conflict between this state of affairs and that state of mind was the framework of the Religious Wars. The policy of compassion was constantly to come into conflict with the religious passions, whether Catholic or Protestant, of the sixteenth century. Tiepolo, writing from Ghent to the Venetian Senate on July 10, 1559, expressed the following thoughts, at that time the most natural in the world: 'It is an extraordinary thing that by burning somebody nearly every week, it is not possible to extinguish the fires of heresy, but that, on the contrary, they increase day by day.'

This could not surprise Catherine de Medici. She was too realistic for that, and she had also suffered at first hand from the fanatical fury of the Florentine rebels. No doubt she was indifferent to the principle of freedom of conscience. To her, theological arguments seemed a waste of time, and persecution seemed useless cruelty. As a student of Machiavelli, Catherine never forgot that 'Nevertheless, the Prince must not cause himself to be feared in such manner that should he be unable to gain love, he should be unable to escape hatred, for one can always steer a middle path', and, echoing him, Guicciardini replied: 'There is a great difference between having discontented subjects and having desperate subjects. A man who is discontented may seek to cause damage, but does not lightly endanger himself, for he awaits an opportunity that may never occur. But the desperate man looks for it, hastens it, hopes for a new turn in events and endeavours to create it. It is only rarely, therefore, that one needs to be on guard against the former. But one must always be on guard against the latter.'

'To steer a middle path' was Machiavelli's teaching. The heretics who had been burnt had not done so, neither had those who burned them. How many Protestants had the Queen not seen die by fire, after the first flames had arisen in Paris, at the incident of the Proclamation of the Placards, in 1534? What purpose had it served, since the Cardinal de Lorraine asserted that two-thirds of the French were Lutherans? Catherine's pragmatism rejected everything unpractical. She feared the hardening of hearts that would engender hatred. She knew that nearly half of Europe had passed over to the Reformation. Would it not be wiser to re-read Machiavelli before ordering the fires to be lit again? . . . 'There is no stronger fortress than a people's affection, for a prince hated by his subjects must expect to see the enemy without rush to their assistance as soon as he sees them having recourse to arms. . . . Fortresses can be helpful as well as harmful; but the one thing that never helps and always harms is to cause oneself to be hated.'

If Lorraine was well-informed, what folly it would be to cause oneself to be hated by the partisans of those fanatics who so obstinately insisted on being burnt! Wisdom therefore counselled compassion and not repression.

CHAPTER THREE

THE FLORENTINE SHOPKEEPER
(July 1559—March 1560)

-》❀☙❦-

The ten days that elapsed after Henri II was wounded and until he died at Tournelles on July 10, 1559, were terrible ones for Catherine. She had expected for a long time that her husband would die a violent death. The *Centuries* of Nostradamus, the prophet of Salon-de-Crau, which had been published in March 1555 by a Lyons printer, Macé Bonhomme, had predicted such a death for him. The Queen was obsessed by the fatal quatrain:—

> *Le lion jeune le vieux surmontera,*
> *En champ bellique, par singulier duelle,*
> *Dans cage d'or les yeux lui crèvera,*
> *Deux classes une, puis mourir, mort cruelle.*

Nostradamus's prediction coincided exactly with that of Lucca Gaurico. The Italian bishop-astrologer, who was world-famous, approved by the Popes—by Julius II and Leo X as well as Clement VII and Paul III—had told Henri II, three years before Nostradamus published his *Centuries*, to avoid all single combat, especially in his forties, as at that period of his life he would be in danger of a head wound which might lead to blindness or death. After his prediction Nostradamus was commanded to the Court of France and became physician-astrologer and councillor-in-ordinary to the King. Catherine had the greatest confidence in him. The premonitory dream she herself had on the death of Henri II finally convinced her of the truth of fatal horoscopes. She begged the King in vain not to take part in the tournament. The tragedy affected her so deeply that she fainted and afterwards took to her bed.

On the very day of his father's death François II gave his mother the roll of investitures. He declared that he conferred on her full authority as Governor of France. Barely adolescent, he was aware of his weakness and inexperience, and that in spite of having attained his legal majority nearly two years previously and of his marriage, he remained a child. Catherine knew in advance that her son's legal majority would be exploited by the Guises, uncles of Mary Stuart. Her innate caution advised her to remain in the background, whilst remaining the ally of the Lorraines, against the Montmorencys and Diane de Poitiers, who were responsible for the bad treaty. She arranged very cleverly to avert the Lorraine reprisals against the Montmorencys, and remained true to her conciliatory mission. The mourning widow changed her coat-of-arms. In place of the rainbow there was, palewise on a field of gules, on either side of the shield, the broken lance which had caused the death of Henri II—*Lacrymae hinc, hinc dolor* was the motto. And to this symbolism of mourning was also added a heap of quicklime with the words: *Ardorem exstincta testantur vivere flamma.* 'The doused flame burns in the lime if water is poured upon it.' Watered by tears—the flame extinguished and corroded by eternal widowhood. Whilst the Queens of France wore white for mourning and for this reason were called white queens, Catherine wore black. Her mourning was that of a wife who before becoming queen had loved her husband unto death and beyond the tomb; the ardour of that love was to conquer death. The sincerity of her suffering is beyond doubt, nor was her prudence less so. Her heart and mind both bade her not to deviate from her usual reserve. Thus, in spite of the filial appeals of François II she allowed the young Queen to put her uncles in power. Military control was handed over to Duke François; finance, diplomacy and affairs of the interior to the Cardinal of Lorraine. The letters from the Duke of Alba to Philip II dated July 1559, give us precise information with regard to the very first days of the new reign. Alba and Don Ruy Gomez de Silva, the ambassador-in-ordinary of the Catholic King, were received by the young prince and his Privy Council on the day after Henri II's death. The Constable, his sons and his nephews, the Châtillons, presented them. The Guises informed the Spaniards that they were henceforward in charge of the government. After dinner François II informed the Constable that he was retaining him in the Privy Council, but not in power, and authorized him to relax at home. This was a dismissal, in due and proper form.

François II was not the fool he was alleged to have been according to a tradition as false as it was tenacious, originating in Protestant pamphlets, and the case made out in favour of the Bourbons or the

Montmorencys, such as the famous collection of Louis Régnier de la Planche, on *L'État de France, tant de la République que de la Religion*. Although he was not particularly intelligent, he does not appear to have been stupid, nor did he lack culture. Marie Stuart, with whom he was madly in love, although not yet sufficiently mature to be a real husband to her, dominated him completely. This goddess from the north brought him into the power of the Guises, but she had so much charm that he imagined himself to have the most devoted relatives when in fact they were the most ambitious of protectors. His health was very bad, he was a neurotic, with an exaggerated passion for hunting, and no more than an ailing child who had become king and thought himself a man. His dominant characteristic —which was shared by his brother, Charles IX—was violence, which he imagined to be strength. His otitis and adenoidal infection were so serious that he died of them. His contemporaries were perplexed by his disease, unknown to medical science in his day. There is no doubt that it was of tubercular origin, in view of his frequent attacks of quartian fever, mentioned by members of his entourage, and frenzies of all kinds. He was also impotent, for La Planche could not have invented the story that 'his generative organs were constipated and blocked, incapable of functioning'.

The Court seers agreed in prophesying that he would not outlive his twentieth year. Perrenot de Chantonnay, who was both ambassador and chief of the secret police of Philip II, was a spy of genius. There is no doubt that he was thoroughly informed about the young King's ill-health, of which he sent his master full details. The Court was expecting François II to die very soon. This caused the Duke of Alba anxiety; his successor was still a minor, which made Catherine's regency almost certain, and this was not to the taste of the Catholic King, who was also well-informed regarding the hostility, or, more exactly, the distrust felt by the Queen Mother for Spain. As for the Lorraines, they were in the greatest hurry; their sick nephew was incapable of governing by himself, and they thought only of providing him with distractions, however bad for his health these might be. Catherine did not interfere. It was not that she did not love her son, but she believed him to be the slave of the Scotswoman, towards whom her past affection had turned to enmity, on account of that young woman's frequent rudeness, for being the least submissive of characters she could never hold her tongue nor control her moods. Nevertheless Catherine never failed to pay her the consideration due to a Queen of France.

The original documents make this out to have been a matter of personal antipathy, for under François II Mary Stuart's political role was merely to obey her uncles, and for that reason Catherine had no cause of conflict with her. We know what the Duchesse de Guise thought of the Medici. Nothing is more likely than that her niece referred to the Florentine shopkeeper who was her mother-in-law in so many words. The phrase was current, and Catherine could not have been ignorant of it. Giovanni Michele, who on several occasions represented the Most Serene Republic in France, in his report to the Venetian Senate, after his embassy in 1561, said that that 'the Constable had spoken of the Queen disrespectfully, calling her a shopkeeper's daughter, and the Queen knew of it'. Catherine, a merchant's daughter despised by her daughter-in-law, who boasted of being the daughter of a king, did, as we know, suffer from her lowly birth. But Florentine merchant's daughter though she was, the descendant of the Magnifico knew her own value. She retained a strong grudge against Mary Stuart, yet this grudge did not follow the young Queen to Scotland. All the references to her in Catherine's letters after 1561 prove that she had both forgiven and forgotten. Later she intervened several times in her favour with her mortal enemy, the Queen of England, and in the warmest terms.

Henri II's widow could not fail also to appear as a Florentine shopkeeper to the partisans of Diane, who when she lost her lover lost everything. But those watchful observers were disillusioned. An Italian diary kept at the beginning of the reign of François II proves that the Queen never lost her self-control.[1] She found it sufficient to inform the favourite that she no longer wished to meet her, but assured her that she might nevertheless continue to enjoy her own possessions, as well as those given to her by the late King. In Jacques-Auguste de Thou we can read how the Guises themselves, excepting her son-in-law, the Duc d'Aumale, took it upon themselves to make it clear to Madame de Valentinois that her hour of disgrace had arrived. The Cardinal de Lorraine lectured her very cleverly.

The Guises had indeed lowered themselves by admitting into their family, which claimed descent from Charlemagne, the daughter of a king's mistress, and so they told the lady of the crescent, fallen from the Royal Olympus. These compliments must have delighted Catherine, for they were being conferred on Diane by the Lorraine Princes, and not by herself, in the name of the new King. The Crown Jewels, which Henri II in his weakness had given to the

[1] Discovered by Lucien Romier (Bibliothèque nationale, fonds français, No. 3950).

greedy Duchesse de Valentinois, were returned, not to Catherine, but to François II and Mary Stuart. Her mother-in-law gave the young Queen her own most beautiful jewellery, especially her large pearls. In accordance with the custom at all accessions, an inventory was made of the Royal Jewels in the possession of Diane. Whatever the novelists may say, this was done with no trace of personal revenge. It was purely an administrative formality, but one which nevertheless perturbed the venal duchess.

There was general surprise at the generosity of Madame Catherine towards a woman whom it was said she had called a whore, in a voice loud enough for her husband to hear it. This generosity was according to the usual custom of this princess, who always avoided burning her bridges. She pretended to disdain and to forget Henri II's whore. In the following September, when she was travelling to Rouen, she passed close to Anet without going out of her way to stay there. If it was true, as was told at Court, that one day in a jealous fury Catherine had thought of ordering the Duc de Nemours to throw vitriol at Madame de Valentinois, the days of her anger were long ago over. The Queen preferred to remain faithful to one of her protective talismans, on which on an azure base is seen a star, surrounded by a serpent biting its tail, an emblem of Saturn, with the motto: *Fato prudentia major*. Diane, although in disgrace, remained redoubtable. It was wise not to exasperate her. Did not Machiavelli say: 'To satisfy the people and nurse the powerful is the maxim of those who know how to govern.'?

Whilst waiting until she was in a position to govern, Catherine took her precautions, which were commented upon by the ambassadors of the Italian States and the Catholic King. The Venetians have stressed the attitude she adopted in the Council of François II. She caused to be admitted to it princes and nobles whom she knew to be on her side or to favour it—the Dukes of Savoy, Ferrara and Lorraine; Lansac, the former governor of the young King; La Broche, lieutenant of his men-at-arms, and Sourdis.

The Florentine shopkeeper was thus assuring herself of allies against the Bourbons, the Lorraines, the Montmorencys and the Châtillons. The six Lorraines in particular seemed dangerous, more so than had ever been the master of Ecouen and Chantilly; they were the Duke François, the Cardinal de Lorraine, the Duke of Aumale, the Cardinal de Guise, the Marquis d'Elbeuf, the Grand Prior of Malta. Their mother, Antoinette de Bourbon, was the daughter of

F

François, Count of Vendôme, and of Marie of Luxemburg, Countess of Saint-Pol. Through their father they belonged to the very illustrious House of Lorraine. Their grandfather was René II, Duke of Lorraine, and the Royal geneaology of the Dukes of Lorraine is known from René of Anjou onwards. To Claude, his fifth son, had fallen as his share of the paternal heritage the French fiefs of the Countess of Guise and Aumale, the Baronnies of Joinville, of Sablé, of Mayenne, of la Ferté-Bernard, of Elbeuf, and numerous lands in the Île-de-France, Picardy, Hainault, Flanders and Normandy. The fame of the Lorraine Princes, opposing the last of the Valois, caused their adversaries to call them foreigners, but nothing was more inexact. Both on their paternal and maternal sides the Guises belonged to the Blood of France, being descendants of Saint Louis, in both the male and female lines. Since Henri IV and the steady succession of the Bourbons, and with the progressive disappearance of appanages, it has been too easily forgotten how complex were the laws regulating the feudal inheritances, not excepting those of the House of France. To the nobles of the sixteenth century genealogies were living history and politics, and the Lorraine Princes had the right to consider themselves the equals of the Princes of the Blood. Since the fall of the House of Burgundy, in the person of Charles the Bold, there were no greater nobles than the Guises, feudalists whose illustrious origins ceded nothing to the appanagists. This can never be repeated too often. Both the Lorraine Princes and the Princes of the Blood were equally linked to the Capetine dynasty by multiple and crafty matrimonial alliances and tenures of appanage. The Protestants alleged that the uncles of Mary Stuart were of foreign birth and stressed the fact that Claude was merely a younger son. They evoked no response, except among the personal enemies of the Lorraine Princes. When, conversely, the Lorraines claimed primacy over the Capets as descendants of Charlemagne, all the adversaries of the Valois and the Bourbons agreed with their claim.

Marriages and inheritances frequently altered the Lorraine tenures. From an administrative point of view, as their father, Claude, had become a naturalized Frenchman under letters patent from Louis XII in 1506, the Guises were French, even more so as their mother was a Bourbon. It was perfectly in order that François and Charles should be heads of the Government of François II. Claude had served France magnificently on the battlefields and François I had appointed him Governor of Champagne, then of

Burgundy and Grand Veneur. He was the first great nobleman who was not a Prince of the Blood to become a peer of France.

When one considers the Guises in their own time and place, freeing oneself from the mental habits induced by the anti-feudal monarchy of Louis XIV, a monarchy which, incidentally, deviated from the tradition of the Capets, one can appreciate their power. One understands very well why, in their case, the daughter of the Medici continued to maintain the humble attitude which she had adopted ever since her entry into the House of France. Even although she was Queen she still cut no great figure compared with these authentic descendants of Saint Louis, who did not hesitate to claim Charlemagne as their ancestor. The Montmorencys could not hope to equal the Guises except by favour. When they fell they were no more than powerful barons, descended from Bouchard, no doubt contemporaries of Hugues Capet, but who for five and a half centuries had owed everything to the Kings of France. The Guises on the other hand claimed that their birth entitled them to everything.

The Princes of the Blood, Bourbons-Vendômes and Bourbon-Montpensiers, could, by virtue of the Salic Law and succession by primogeniture, victoriously claim precedence of birth over the Guises, and as far as the legislators were concerned this was self-evident. But the feudalists did not see it that way. Louis I of Naples and Sicily, son of Jean the Good, great-grandfather of the Good King René, was the brother of Charles V of France, of Jean, Duke of Berry, of Philippe the Bold, Duke of Burgundy. In grandeur and dignities appanagism did not count for less than succession according to the Salic Law, that invention of legislators, and the female lineage was worth the male. (This can be seen in the power of the House of Burgundy during the fifteenth century.) Yolande d'Anjou, mother of René II of Lorraine, grandmother of Claude, great-grandmother of the Guises, was the authentic descendant of Jean the Good. The Guises considered themselves as near to the throne of the Valois as those Bourbons, who were also only allied to the Valois through the female line, by the marriage of Henri d'Albret with Marguerite d'Angoulême, and of Jeanne d'Albret with Antoine de Bourbon. And how far back was their relationship with Saint Louis, through Robert de Clermont, his sixth son, who died in 1318! Here, too, the Guises could match themselves against the Bourbons. The legislators despised these feudal genealogies, the masses followed the legislators, venerating the Blood of Louis IX, transmitted from male to male to the exclusion of any female line, down to the King of Navarre, who was according to the Salic Law the legitimate heir of the Valois, if they should become extinct, just as in accordance with this law Philippe VI was the heir of Charles IV the Beautiful.

In the eyes of the legislators, the masses, and all the nobility related to the Bourbons, the Crown Councillors by right of birth were Antoine and his brother Condé. Whilst the Bourbons could claim their rightful place there, the Guises were mere intruders in the French Government. It was in order that François II should make them his ministers, but inadmissable that they should become his masters. Bourbons against Guises, the monarchical tradition against the feudal tradition, the legitimate heirs against the heirs of the appanagists. The Protestants understood this so well that in warring against the Guises they called themselves the Royalists. Royalists against feudalists. This is the deeper explanation of the Wars of Religion. The King's party, after Valois, is Bourbon and not Guise. In this the nation's instinct never faltered. At the time of the League, the masses in the big cities were on the side of the Guises on account of their hatred of the Hugenots; nevertheless, in spite of such deviations due to the religious quarrels, when after thirty years of massacres they had to choose between the Infanta of Spain, grand-daughter through her mother, Elisabeth of France, of Henri II, and the Béarnais, descendant of Saint Louis in the male line, they chose the Béarnais. He was compelled to become a convert to Catholicism because the basic laws of the kindom itself demanded it of him as successor to Henri III. Thanks to the Edict of Nantes, the Huguenots, Royalists in the first instance and Protestants only in the second, consented to it. The members of the League, allied to the feudalists, were not in the Capetian tradition. And by and large the Catholic people, however great their horror of the heretics, in the end refused to follow them. Fanaticism is less strong than tradition.

The consequence of the rise to favour of the Guises was the fall of the Constable de Montmorency and the Marshal de Saint-André. Beside the conqueror of Metz the most important member of the House of Guise was the Cardinal de Lorraine. The Cardinal was thirty-six. His intelligence was both sharp and lively, his memory astonishing, his eloquence remarkable and his appearance both noble and handsome. He was highly educated and knew Italian, Latin and Greek; he was a theologian of unusual ability. His high morality was at that time very exceptional. On the other hand he was excessively avaricious; his duplicity was as great as his readiness to take offence, his character revengeful, envious, selfish, and he had the gift of making himself generally detested by his insolence and violent temper. On this subject the Venetian, Giovanni Michele, may have been influenced by the Ferrarese, Alvarotti, the Cardinal's confident, who saw only his good qualities. Alvarotti did not attempt to attenuate Charles de Lorraine's passionate ambition, which was one of his dominant characteristics, and which was served by his consummate cleverness, of which he was so proud that in praising it the poets compared him to Mercury. All these exceptional gifts caused the Chancellor, Olivier, to call him a born monster and as an anagram of *Carolus Lotaringus* to give him the motto, *Orator Gallicus unus*. Even Théodore de Bèze was not indifferent to the Cardinal's charm. On coming out of a conference one day, he said that were he himself like him, he would hope to convert and give back half the people of France to the Faith. Before the battle of Dreux, Coligny admitted that he was less afraid of all his enemy's weapons than of one sole priest.

That priest was the Archbishop of Rheims. Charles knew brilliantly how to please, whether in speech or in writing. And if he did place religion in the service of politics, like all churchmen during the Renaissance, with the exception of the Saints, he was at least a genuine believer, which was by no means the general rule among the great ecclesiastical nobles. He observed the fasts, mortified his flesh, willingly waited on the poor, sang in the choir, forgot neither blessings nor graces and liked to celebrate mass frequently; all of which activities were far from common among his contemporary prelates. It is proved that he worked in his diocese, arranged synods, instigated reforms, watched over the zeal and morality of his clergy and the education of the children. He had great virtues to balance against his faults. Unfortunately for him, at a time when military valour was prized above everything else, he was a fearful coward, which was regarded as all the more shocking as his brother François was the very incarnation of heroism.

His duplicity, to which all the reliable witnesses refer, was particularly harmful to the Cardinal. Charles de Lorraine deceived in order to conquer. He admitted it by the symbols he had chosen—a pyramid surmounted by a crescent, wreathed with ivy, and the motto: *Te stante virebo*; a lighted chandelier: *Lux publica principis ignis*. He used even his virtues to further his career. They shone in order to draw attention to him. The ivy and the flame; how well Charles de Lorraine knew himself! Clever, marvellously intelligent, yet both his cleverness and intelligence at the service of his pride, a pride that made him hateful, whatever charms he used on those who were not deceived by him. His most pathetic victim was Henri II. Thus he succeeded in beating the Constable, without ever rushing things. This was a far stretch from the Tiger of France, pursued by François Hotman and the Huguenot libellers, and whom even the Spaniards, who knew him to be dangerous, libelled in their reports and letters.

François, Duke de Guise, was very different from his brother. His military genius was unquestionable and he was essentially a great captain. In 1559 François de Guise was forty. Brantôme praised his tall and fine figure, his very handsome appearance and assured manner. François was certainly the great Monsieur de Guise le Grand. Marc-Antonio Barbaro in his Report to the Senate of Venice after his embassy of 1563, said that as regarded good counsel, conduct and military valour, he had few equals anywhere. Monluc deeply admired him, for his powers of endurance were equalled only by his courage. He was always in the front rank, taking his share of the chores and the fatigues that are a soldier's lot. On account of the lance-wound he received full in the face at Boulogne he was known as Le Balafré, a nickname also given to his son, Henri de Guise, who was similarly wounded in the face. On several occasions he received other serious wounds. This magnificent warrior was both generous and affable although a very strict disciplinarian. His Catholic faith was simple and sincere. It was generally agreed that he was ambitious. Monluc said that the motto of Monsieur le Duc was 'Everyone in turn'.

The political position of his brother, the Cardinal, was always higher than his, for in this field the diplomat was superior to the warrior. As early as 1547 the Nuncio, Dandino, wrote that they would be the favourites and pets of Henri II.

Twelve years later it was no longer a question of favouritism—they were the masters. The one dreamed of becoming Pope, the other practised the art of kingship. The most reliable documents prove beyond doubt that they both had these ambitions. When later Henri de Guise, the King of Paris, stretched out his hand towards the Crown of France, he was only following in the family tradition. His father often signed himself by his first name only, like a king, and his handwriting resembled that of François I. He was the son-in-law of Renée de France, Duchesse of Ferrara, daughter of Louis XII. The beauty of his wife, Anne d'Este, whom L'Hospital nicknamed the Holy Venus (and Ronsard also praised) was that of a queen and empress. What majesty! That Greek profile, that neck and those splendid shoulders across which lies a huge pearl necklace . . . a goddess such as Diane de Poitiers had been. Next to her Catherine was a mere bourgeoise.

There are two drawings of Catherine, made in 1555 and 1560, the second by François Clouet. Between thirty-six and forty-one Catherine changed little. Is this the Florentine shopkeeper despised by the husband of a grand-daughter of the House of France, and by a prince of the Church, an aspirant to the throne of St Peter? She was less ugly than in her youth. The expression remained the same, thoughtful and penetrating. She was certainly neither a goddess nor a sovereign, but decidedly a bourgeoise, a very, very high bourgeoise, in spite of her denigrators, and who did have a presence, doubtless not superb but nevertheless dominating; dominating by the consciousness of a sense of power which she both felt and knew to be well-grounded, however much she strove to hide it. The heavy chin rests on the high neck-band, above the piping of the little white collar. Only in the second portrait does she wear mourning, yet both are severe. This woman was not seeking to charm by her physical attraction. Nevertheless she was sure of herself. She knew exactly what she wanted.

Did her contemporaries know this or even have an inkling of it? We have seen how surprised and admiring they were on the day after Saint Quentin. This was forgotten when once again Catherine de Medici withdrew. But as the widowed Queen, mother of a king who was still a child, she inevitably attracted attention. The Venetian ambassadors took no notice of the woman, only of the Queen.

Catherine's prestige lay in her intelligence, not in her beauty. From the moment of her widowhood, when in spite of herself she moved into the foreground, all observers witnessed to her superior intelligence.

François II was entirely submissive to his mother. She might have taken advantage of this to counterbalance the influence of his uncles. She did nothing of the kind. She knew the Guises well enough to know that as between them and herself there could never be either a division of power or equilibrium but only a struggle for influence. This struggle, in view of her experience of the factions at the Court of Henri II and of what had resulted from them, she preferred to avoid. Davila called the Guises a newly arrived family from Lorraine.

Catherine was a new arrival from Tuscany and her blood was not equal to theirs. We can never emphasize too often the importance of this matter of blood to the men of the sixteenth century, whose outlook was still so deeply feudal. Against Catherine was the fact that she was merely a Medici and this was to weigh against her all her life. At the time of Henri II's death this weight was particularly heavy. And when power was offered to her the Queen Mother did not make the mistake of accepting it. Her son's filial deference pleased her but she refused to take advantage of it. As against the mother, the Guises had the wife, Mary Stuart—the radiant daughter of kings against the cunning Florentine shopkeeper.

The Princes of the Blood were kept entirely away from power. But they did not share Catherine's resignation. The differences in character between the Bourbons, their relatives and allies, were great, and weakened their opposition. Antoine, husband of Jeanne d'Albret, born in 1518, eldest son of Charles de Bourbon, Duke of Vendôme, and of Françoise d'Alençon, was a handsome man, brave, liberal, and eloquent, but vain, inconstant and irresponsible. Nobody had any illusions regarding his religion. Protestant fanaticism, which his wife showed in so many instances, was foreign to him. He found in the new religion a force capable of once again giving the Bourbons, who had been suspect and held back since François I and the affair of the Constable, the new political importance which their House refused to renounce. In May 1558 he had been mixed up in the Calvinist demonstrations of the Pré-aux-Clercs. In disgrace at Nérac, he appeared capable of becoming the head of the Reformationists. On the very day of Henri II's death, Alvarotti and Raviglio, writing to the Duke of Ferrara, referred to the rumours according to which the Bourbons would take up arms to assert the rights of the King's blood cousins against the Lorraine Princes, his uncles by marriage. It is probable that Prince Louis de Condé had indulged in certain verbal indiscretions. He was then living at Court, like his brother, the Cardinal Charles de Bourbon, but who, unlike Monsieur le Prince, had not in any way renounced his Catholicism.

The fifth son of Charles de Bourbon, Condé at the age of twenty-nine appeared to be a fortuneless younger son, all the more miserable because he suffered from ill-health and was also a hunchback. In revolt against his unjust fate, Condé, nephew of Anne de Montmorency by his marriage with Eléonore de Roye, was also in disgrace. Although still at Court, in the eyes of the Guises he counted for no more than his brother Antoine. Very brave and belligerent, with as great a passion for politics as for love-making, he was furious at having no means with which to gratify his desires. He threw himself wholeheartedly into the Reformation because this seemed to offer him a method of revenge. His pension of 4,000 livres, added to his wife's income of 6,000 left him, for a prince of his blood, in a state of near penury, already with four children to support.

Antoine had a little kingdom; Charles, Cardinal-Archbishop, rich benefices. This prince of the Church, who was not particularly intelligent, and who was later to be nicknamed Le Bonhomme, and to become the ephemeral Charles X, King of the League, was, at thirty-six, keeping very quiet. The Cardinal had no ambitions. The King of Navarre, in Béarn, was hoping for a change of fortune that would carry him to power in France. The Prince de Condé was only able to achieve such a change by his own efforts. He did not tarry. Already on July 11th, in the Council, he opposed the taking of any decisions until after the arrival of the King of Navarre, the first of the Princes of the Blood, whom he himself had hastily summoned to Paris. Whilst the Queen Mother was refusing combat with the Guises, Condé showed himself determined to claim all the rights of the Bourbons.

Appanagists against favourites; the shelter of monarchical tradition supported the reformer. The reason for the resistance began to appear. Immediately the Lorraines came to power, Louis de Bourbon appeared as the champion of the basic laws of the kingdom. Events were on the side of the Lorraines, tradition on that of the Bourbons. This was the theme of the Wars of Religion. Catherine watched and waited.

The situation of the Protestants was becoming more and more tragic; the edict of Écouen was applied with inexorable rigour, heretics were being burnt week by week, Anne du Bourg, arrested after his defiance of Henri II, on the point of being condemned to death. Condé was for immediate insurrection. Very brave, intelligent but incautious, he thought only of vengeance. Together with the Marshal de Saint-André, the Constable de Montmorency had followed the Queen Mother's line of awaiting events. Novello, the Ferrarese envoy, even communicated to his master the anxiety that this was causing the Lorraines, and of which the Duchess de Guise had told him. Coligny held back because he did not wish to displease the Constable, his uncle, and also because he disapproved a recourse to violence. After long discussions it was decided to negotiate with Catherine, who was known to be in favour of conciliation, on behalf of the supporters of the Religion. It was thought that as Antoinette de Bourbon, their mother, was of the Royal House, family ties might ease matters. Historians of today are too inclined to underestimate the power of these family alliances, which were the happy counter-weights to rivalries and factions. The ramifications of the four branches of the Bourbon tree—Vendôme, Condé, La Rochefoucauld, Montpensier—spread as far as the Guises. By the marriage of François de Montmorency with Diane de France, the feudal dynasty of which Anne, in his retreats of Écouen and Chantilly remained the redoubtable and redoubted head, had also become linked with the Royal Family. It belonged to the House of France by blood alliances. Through their mother Louise de Montmorency, who had become the aunt of Henri II's daughter, the Châtillons were the Constable's nephews. To the great nobles of the past such cousinships offered immediate and practical interests. By force of circumstances resulting from the decisions of the great reformist kings, a Charles VII, a Louis XI, a François I, powers of administration and authority were more and more fully handed over to the legislators and to officers who had sprung from the Tiers. The resistance of the nobility to this taking over of offices by plebeians was, above all, based on family ties, which kept their feudal tenures, the bestowing of favours and charges alive. Thence came that astonishing mutual regard between individuals who in reality detested one another because they realized that in spite of their antagonisms and quarrels they were linked by a mysterious and powerful bond, that of the Blood.

A violent-tempered, embittered man like Louis de Bourbon was apt to forget it. But his brother and companions had good cause not to do the same. Among these princes the Montmorencys were still socially and politically on the upgrade; and the Châtillons, the last among them to have arrived, had an even greater interest in avoiding the dangers inherent in recourse to violence. The three Châtillon brothers owed their high positions to their relationship with the Montmorencys. Odet was a Cardinal, Gaspard an Admiral of France, François Lieutenant-General of the French Infantry. The silver spreadeagle on their armourial bearings symbolized their ambitions, which they did not wish to see endangered by a rash rupture with the Guises, who controlled the distribution of the Royal favours. It was even in the interest of the Religion to temporize. Among the Châtillons, Coligny's position was analogous to that of Monsieur de Guise le Grand among the Lorraines, and even more important, Cardinal Odet did not have the dominating personality of a Cardinal Charles.

Of a very thoughtful nature, his passions were as a rule controlled by his will-power, and he was inclined to compromise rather than to break off relations. His advice now prevailed. The King of Navarre was charged with explaining the point of view of the Princes of the Blood to Catherine, and to ask her to intervene in order to persuade the Lorraine Princes to collaborate with the Government.

In that summer of 1559 Coligny was just forty-two. Few men have aroused greater controversy than this famous victim of Saint Bartholomew's Night, both among his contemporaries and later historians, who for three and a half centuries have been concerned with him. He is the great man of Protestant hagiography, the hero of romantic literature, the traitor of Catholic history.[1]

In times of tumult and trouble there are no impartial contemporaries. However unfanatical they were, even the ambassadors of the Most Serene Republic could feel nothing but antipathy for the man who, ever since the death of Henri II, appeared to be the chosen leader of French Protestantism, naturally opposed to all their own traditions of paganized aristocracy. The rest of the Italian diplomats, the Ferrarese, Mantuese and Tuscans, were all in the service of anti-Protestant States. The position of the nuncios is self-evident. To the Spaniards, Coligny was the enemy *par excellence*. Nor did the English like him, because he was too much Calvin's man, and they had seen in the case of Knox and the Scottish Presbyterians where Calvinism could lead to, once it fell under the control of a fanatic.

The Admiral, who was exactly the same age as François de Guise, was his boyhood friend and companion-in-arms. He did not share the military genius of Monsieur de Guise le Grand, his gifts being essentially those of administration and organization. His career was less brilliant because his talents were lesser. According to the sources, we cannot assume that in the reign of Henri II he was a victim of disfavour. The fact that he was the Constable's nephew would have sufficed to protect him. It was said that Diane de Poitier's opposition prevented him from being nominated Governor of Piedmont in 1550. Nevertheless in 1553 he was at the same time Admiral of

---

[1] Even such serious and well-documented writers as the Comte Delaborde, A. W. Withead, Charles Merki, have been unable to free themselves from their respective religious sympathies, and whilst wishing to portray him truthfully saw him in the light—clearly or shadowed—of the Reformation or Catholicism. Even more than that of the Guises his personality has been distorted by parties and sects. Lucien Romier's remains the most praiseworthy effort at impartiality.

France and Governor of the Île-de-France. The Admiral of France was the King's Lieutenant-General at sea, the commander-in-chief of the fleet.

After the Battle of Renty on August 13, 1554, when owing to the inaction of the Constable the victory over the Imperialists was only incomplete, the Duc de Guise found reason to complain of such inaction, which he considered deliberate, in order to diminish the glory of a younger rival, more fortunate in war. Coligny, who had been envious of Guise since Metz, took his uncle's part in this quarrel. This was the beginning of their intimacy. It was concealed beneath superficial courtesies. Although a lesser nobleman than François, Gaspard was the nephew of the all-powerful favourite; François, the hero of Metz, the most popular of captains. Both of them had good reason to respect one another. When, two years later, the Châtillons were converted to Calvinism, this did nothing to improve their relations with the Guises. But this conversion followed and did not precede the breaking-off of the friendship between the Duke and the Admiral.

Representing France at Vaucelles, ambassador to the Emperor and his son Philip, even although already suspected of heresy (he had not then publicly professed his new faith), Gaspard de Coligny's career was full of appointments and honours. When the Truce of Vaucelles was broken and hostilities were resumed against the Imperialists, the Admiral hoped to find in Saint Quentin his siege of Metz. He did not do so. In spite of his courage and talents, he could only save his honour, his uncle's disaster on Saint Laurence's day 1557 having made surrender inevitable, after seventeen days of magnificent resistance. The *Discours* he drew up at l'Écluse, on December 28, 1557, on his defence of Saint Quentin, was an apologia. The impartial reader is forced to recognize that honour would have been even more brilliantly saved had the leader not surrendered before his subordinates and his soldiers. Emmanuel-Philibert was so taken aback by this that he could not at first believe that it was the Admiral who stood before him. The sacking of Saint Quentin lasted for two days and according to custom was atrocious. It was a serious matter that Coligny had chosen to surrender rather than be buried in the ruins of the town, for he actually surrendered whilst the battle still raged. Coligny's calculating attitude was the very reverse of glory, and showed him up as a theologian and politician. In spite of his valour, which was indubitable, he resembled the Cardinal de Lorraine more than Duc François. The latter was an ambitious hero; the Admiral was a man of ambition in whom military virtues gave place to political interests.

On that bloody night of the capture of Saint Quentin Coligny appears to us as he was always to be—a man whose carefully considered moves at the service of his personal ambitions were not in any way inferior to those of his rivals. He surrendered, not because he was afraid (his courage was flawless) nor to save his own life. . . . He surrendered in order to remain alive and to avenge the glory he had missed. He knew the Bible well enough to believe with Ecclesiastes that a live dog was worth more than a dead lion. He was not the kind of beaten foe to bury himself beneath the ruins and the debris. And in that he resembled Catherine. How well one can understand that the struggle that later took place between her and him was as bereft of frankness on one side as on the other! Coligny, telling his companions, at the moment of his surrender, to point him out to the Spaniards in order to avoid any mistake; coldly stating, in his *Discours*, that he deliberately tried to fall into the hands of a Spaniard, and that the one who captured him took him down through the very breach that he was defending and into which not a single enemy had as yet penetrated, and finally agreeing that his golden chain and his Saint Michael should be shown to the Duke of Savoy in order to complete his identification. Coligny was a clever man. Owing to circumstances he died a martyr's death, and suffered it with the nobility that was inbred in him; every honest person must inevitably pay tribute to the tortured Admiral—and admire the man who despised his executioners. Yet it was at Saint Quentin, when he humiliated himself before Emmanuel-Philibert, raising his helmet to him and telling him that he was not the Admiral, even to replying that it was not so long ago that the Duke of Savoy had met him and should therefore recognize him—it was at that moment of capitulation that Coligny showed his true nature, that of a leader who was more of a politician than a soldier, less religious than political and who only gradually became a fanatic. A fighting Cardinal de Lorraine, but neither a hero nor a saint. The pure incarnation of French Protestantism in the sixteenth century was François de la Noue, the epic and sublime Bras de Fer. The Catholics of the Wars of Religion had no one to pit against him, for they lacked a Bayard.

Coligny's cleverness enabled him to avoid being swept away by the fall of the Montmorencys. The Guises recommended him to François II, who left him his honours, telling him that he hoped to have recourse to his services. Nothing was more natural to him and more in conformity with his interests than the Admiral's opposition to the crazy plan of a civil war, for which Condé was pressing. Psychologically and intellectually Coligny and Catherine were in many ways similar, a similarity that was responsible for the long and slow tragedy that was to last for ten whole years, from the day after Wassy to the morning of Saint Bartholomew's Day. By winning over Charles IX the Admiral thought he had beaten Catherine. By bribing Maurevert, Catherine thought she had rid herself of the Admiral. But circumstances were stronger than they had reckoned with; owing to the murderer's clumsiness Coligny escaped, and Charles IX's incredible weakness permitted the man whom he had called his father to be done to death.

In 1560 Catherine and Coligny were both in favour of what was later to be known as freedom of conscience and which at that period was called 'the policy of pity'. Neither of them conceived it otherwise than being in the interests of the principle of rulership. Both of them loved France and desired her greatness, yet they were unable to sacrifice their personal ambitions to her. In the case of the Sovereign her unbridled passion for rulership was the basic reason for her political errors; for the worst of them all—her crime, and even worse than a crime, her fault—Saint Bartholomew. In the case of the great feudal nobleman it is the only explanation for the unfortunate handing over of Normandy to the English. So long as the Guises were powerful Coligny and Catherine remained allies. They had a common enemy. Compared to such protagonists the Bourbons were small fry and continued to be so until on October 20, 1587, Coutras revealed his own greatness to Henri of Navarre. We ourselves are able to retrace the pattern of history and thus to understand the genesis of events. The worst historical mistake and also, unfortunately, the most common, is to judge past events retrospectively, in the light of all we know to have occurred subsequently, but which at the time could not be known to contemporary observers. Even such masters as Mariéjol and Van Dyke, the Florentine's biographers, made this mistake. Who, in August 1559, twenty-eight years before Coutras, could have foreseen that Antoine de Bourbon's little boy, running about barefoot on the pebbles of Béarn and at the age of six fighting the village lads, was to become the man predestined to realize the common hopes of Coligny and Catherine, destroyed in both their cases by overpowering personal ambition? In putting a brake on Louis de Bourbon's impetuosity, in sending

Antoine to the Queen Mother, the Admiral was the instrument of conciliation, the need for which he understood as well as she did.

Force of circumstances proved his clearsightedness, which shocked Chantonnay, to have been in vain. The Spaniard was so far from imagining that there could be any solution to the religious controversy other than by sword and fire that in his letters to Philip II he accused Coligny of betraying the Constable in the interest of the Lorraines. At that moment the Lorraines themselves were still inclined, not towards tolerance, which was against both their interests and their habits, but towards conciliation. They were to be so until Wassy. But contrariwise, the Catholic and Protestant masses were of the opinion of Chantonnay and Condé, demanding fire and iron. Opposing passions were becoming exacerbated. Tomorrow, Anne du Bourg at the stake; then the plot of Amboise; after that Wassy and, with precarious truces, civil war for thirty-six years. The Florentine shopkeeper and the calculating loser of Saint Quentin, whom Philip II had seated at the bottom of his table without addressing a word to him or even giving him a glance, both thought that politics were ruled by reason. Events were to give the cruellest lie to this view. And in their revolt against the facts Catherine and Coligny both, one day, lost their own reason. For the Admiral, Hampton Court and the pledging of Havre, of which he was the Governor; for Catherine, the Louvre and the Matins of Paris, the strangling of her own subjects—such was life's double answer to the policy of disinterestedness which was the weakness of the author of *Il Principe*. It was not enough to calculate or to bargain and weigh things up. In politics reason can only win if it is wedded to emotion; enthusiasts are stronger than intellectuals. The greatest shrewdness was that of Henri IV. '*Mes paroles ne sont point de deux couleurs: ce que j'ai à la bouche, je l'ai au coeur.*'

Which led to Coutras and the Edict of Nantes; the sacrament of Chartres, and Vervins.

In 1559, when François II had handed over power to them, public opinion was on the side of the Guises. Nobody but the Protestants read the Bible. The clerics influenced Catholic opinion and in the hero of Metz they saw God's chosen, the Judas Maccabaeus who would save Israel. Unity of faith, which was inseparable in the eyes of nearly all Catholics as well as Protestants from national unity, was embodied in the view of the former in Duc François. Later, the Huguenots thought the same of Coligny. Although the two forms of religion were in opposition, their doctrines were of similar structure, based on the principle of One State, One Faith. Both Christianity and Mahommedanism, issued from Judaism, are in essence totalitarian, and this should never be forgotten. To look for freedom of conscience among the Protestants is to ignore both the evidence and the facts. There were among them a few isolated individuals in favour of this new idea, such as Sébastien Castalion, Colinet, Pierre Toussain, Viret, but the remainder were no less shocked by it than were, among the Catholics, Michel de L'Hospital, Montaigne, Guillaume Du Vair. As regards both Catherine and Coligny, their views on freedom of conscience sprang from political and not doctrinal motives. As for Calvin, his Genevese dictatorship proves that in matters of religion he was of the school of Torquemada. If he disassociated himself politically from Knox and his Scottish violence, this was only because his intelligence bade him to do so, but was in no way due to his lack of fanaticism. To Calvin politics were a matter not of ideology but of practice, and this was the balancing factor against his undeniable sectarianism. He resembled Philip II; his mysticism could take into account the complex changes in reality, and when necessary prudence came before zeal. When one compares the letters of Calvin with those of Philip II one is struck by the analogies between these two theocrats, by their suppleness of behaviour, associated with their rigid principles. These inhuman great men resembled one another as Catherine de Medici and Gaspard de Coligny did. And all four met at the crossroads of self-interest, calculation, and cunning, at which Elizabeth I of England joined them. The Biblical concept of monarchy was as much Calvin's as Philip II's and Elizabeth I's; a concept in which nothing exists except by sovereign right, and according to which the monarch is the spiritual as well as temporal judge.[1] The modern concept, which distinguishes between the spiritual and the temporal, was on the contrary Catherine's, always. (Saint Bartholomew was the result of panic, and not at all of a plan to exterminate heresy.) It was also Coligny's until around 1568. At that time, caught up by his role of patriarch of the new Elect, the Admiral came under the sway of the preachers and their proselytizing fanaticism.

After a century of religious wars, both internal and external, the views of Catherine and the earlier Coligny were to prevail under Henri IV, with Richelieu and Mazarin, but for too short a time.

[1] Ref. to the Biblical monarchy in France cf. our studies on *Sully* (July 1938); *Louis XIV et l'état;* and in *Carrefour* (November 1938): *Louis XIV et la tradition capétienne.*

1. FRANÇOIS I. Attributed to Jean Clouet   (*photo:* Giraudon)

NRICVS II FRA[...] REX XRIANI[...]
NO ÆTATIS SV[...] XXXVII · 155[...]

2. HENRI II. School of Clouet   (*photo:* Giraudon)

Twenty-five years after the death of Mazarin, Louis XIV himself was to return to the Biblical concept of monarchy, of royal theocracy, with the revocation of the Edict of Nantes—the only error that can be held against this greatest of kings). The sons of Ignatius, whose practical subtlety merely disguised a theoretical rigidity no whit inferior to that of the sons of Dominic, by the Edict of Fontainebleau exterminated the sons of Calvin; and in the name of the same principle. The Calvinists knew this so well that they reproached the King with his error, which was the persecution of the true faith— their own. They did not reproach him for his tyranny. In those countries where they were masters, they treated the Catholics as the Catholics treated them. And Biblical metaphors flourished in both camps. The vocabulary of the monks in league against Henri III was the same as that of the Calvinist ministers against the Guises. The preacher and the priest complemented one another. The same eloquence proclaimed the fame of the second Balafré, of Henri, King of Paris, as twenty-five years earlier that of the first, François, victor of Dreux.

The immense popularity of Monsieur de Guise le Grand overshadowed the Cardinal de Lorraine, Prime Minister in fact, but far less well-known to the nation. The nation was for the Guises. It felt, confusedly, that things were going from bad to worse, and that saviours were needed. The Guises appeared as those saviours, in whom the people placed all their hopes. In the face of the Protestant peril, the economic and financial peril, the political perils (that very young and ailing King), the peril threatening from without (that Spain, that England, of which after the intoxication of peace at any price, over the prone body of Henri II, the increased strength and growing danger were suddenly discovered) the Lorraine Princes appeared to have been sent by Providence.

Let us take our place among the French during that summer of 1559. Let us look at France. Where did she stand? And what was happening?

During thirty years the French Reformation had been proceeding almost obscurely. The intellectual élite was interested in it; a few clerics, a few men of letters, a few great ladies even passionately so. A powerful emotional leaven was working amongst the common people in favour of Lutheran ideas, but nobody took any notice. From time to time a reformationist of humble origin became too excited and attracted the attention of the police. The flames at the stake burned fast and the smoke soon blew away in the carefree and

G

light air of France. There were a few scandals, the affair of the Placards among others. They were talked about and then forgotten, forgotten with characteristic French frivolity. On the whole, in spite of the indiscretions and clumsiness due to the noisy zeal of new converts filled with enthusiasm for martyrdom, the attitude of the French Protestants under Henri II was conciliatory. Economic difficulties, however, increased the numbers of the discontented and the Reformation seemed a remedy for all ills, both spiritual and temporal.

There were a few raids on hidden weapons; there was repression, but it was occasional and made few victims.. 'According to the total number of victims, among a population of twenty million inhabitants . . . in a third of a century Christian France condemned fewer victims to the stake than Revolutionary France sent to the scaffold in sixteen months'.[1] Nevertheless that repression naturally sowed the seeds of martyrdom, whence germinated the power of propaganda and grew the need for unity, spurred on by Calvin, who had taken refuge in Geneva. The spiritual tyranny of this great theocrat arose from persecution. In order to stifle it methodical massacres, such as those organized by the Duke of Alba in Flanders, would have been necessary. The French Government never resorted to them. Henri II disappeared at the moment when, having signed the peace with Philip II, he was about to adopt Spanish repressive measures in France. In ten years the French Reformation was already organized. It had had enough time to take advantage of the unlucky wars of Henri II, the struggles at Court, the general economic and financial distress, the powerlessness of the Catholic Church to reform itself, the suspensions and interruptions of the Council of Trent, summoned too late after the peace of Crespy in 1545. The perpetual indecision of the Very Christian Monarchy had facilitated the progress of Geneva. Henri II's political incompetence was caught in a dilemma —either to become Protestant and conquer the Empire, or give way to the Empire and uphold Catholicism. There was a way out of that dilemma, that attempted under François II and Charles IX by Catherine de Medici, Coligny, L'Hospital, differing in method but all aiming at the same end—freedom of conscience; but in deciding on a policy of extermination Henri II had closed the door to it. Thanks to the weariness and exhaustion of nearly half a century of murders, Henri IV was at last enabled to open it. Richelieu's victory proved that it was the only way. In safeguarding freedom of con-

[1] Peirre Imbart de la Tour: *Calvin*, p. 362. The figure of sixteen million seems more correct than that of twenty. Cf. *infra*, p. 69.

science the Grand Cardinal ended the Protestant rebellion, and by allying himself to the North German Lutherans whilst maintaining Catholicism as the official religion in France, he weakened Austria. Catherine, Coligny and L'Hospital had understood this: Henri II was too weak-headed even to suspect it. By proclaiming the death penalty for the dissidents, the King drove them into revolt. This was in the spirit of the times; but a great prince would have been in advance of his time. Catherine tried to be so, but she came on the scene both too late and too early. It was through Henri IV that her efforts succeeded; Henri II had condemned them to failure in advance. From the day when two Christian confessions found themselves face to face, the one, official, the other unrecognized, the clash became inevitable. A clash which, alas, was bound to be hastened and intensified by the rivalry of political factions, foreign interventions, and the anarchy engendered by France's economic ruin.

One cannot emphasize too often the extreme complexity of the Reformationist movement in France.

A revolutionary and democratic current ran through the French Reformation, arising from the discontent of the working-classes and propagated by preachers who themselves belonged to those classes,[1] a current that ran counter to Protestant doctrine and against which the founders of the Reformation always fought. For the reformation was based on the authoritarian principle and it is nearly always forgotten that its leaders—a Luther, a Zwingli, a Melanchton, a Calvin, were reared on scholasticism. 'The Reformation did not seek, as has so often been said, to establish a kind of intellectual anarchy in the religious domain. It aimed, on the contrary, at submitting men's minds and consciences to what it regarded as the supreme authority in matters of faith, namely Holy Scripture, to which all personal opinions were to give way. . . . The Reformation was the substitution of one authority, considered as infallible and divine (a paper God, the Catholics jeered, pointing to the Scriptures), for another authority, that of the Pope.'[2] It is historically incontestable that owing to the lack of a supreme arbiter the force of circumstances brought in liberalism, by making of freedom of conscience an end when, to the theologians of the Reformation, it had merely been

[1] On this point, see Henri Hauser, *La Réforme et les classes populaires en France au XVIe siècle*, in *Etudes sur la Réforme française*, pp. 81–103.

[2] Jacques de Missècles: *Les Huguenots et la Royauté au XVIe siècle*, Editions de l'Association Sully, Colmar, 1932, pp. 5–6.

a means. Three centuries of religious experience have proved that Bossuet, historian of the *Variations*, was right, and the literal-minded Protestants are no longer anything but a minority, whose resistance is becoming weaker and weaker, less and less capable of stemming the tide of the future of Protestantism, as it gnaws away and breaks up such islands of resistance as still remain to the increasingly individualistic interpretation of the Gospels. But in the sixteenth century the Calvinist theocracy was too powerful, the Genevan Rome too strong for its authority to be overcome. The French Protestants of the sixteenth century wanted the Very Christian King to be so as a Calvinist, against Rome, against Madrid, against the Pope and against the Catholic King. They wanted this in the name of what, for them, was religious truth. They were royalists, all the more so because a Protestant King would mean the triumph of The Religion.

Royalists, the Huguenots were absolutists, and this so clearly that their controversialists in the following century were to base their struggle on the superiority of the King to the Pope. In the sixteenth century they were insurgents, and not revolutionaries. They rallied around Henri III, behind Henri de Navarre, whilst the Leaguers had only one idea—to dethrone the Valois, on whom they heaped insults, shave his head and shut him up in a monastery. Not having succeeded in doing so, they murdered him and honoured Jacques Clément as if he had been a saint. Heretics in religion, the Protestants were royalists in politics. Led by the Princes of the Blood, they fought to deliver the King, prisoner of the Guises. They were with Condé, against Duke François; with the Béarnais, heir to the throne, against Duke Henri. As soon as Henri III was free of the King of Paris they unhesitatingly recognized him. Whether or not it was a disastrous illusion to dream of a Protestant French monarchy is another question. As a matter of fact, which is the only point at issue here, the Protestants were royalists. Catherine de Medici understood this so well that even after Saint Bartholomew she continued to follow her policy of conciliation. The rebels claimed that they were in arms against the King's bad servants, falsely sheltering under his authority, and that they themselves were fighting to restore it to him. In his *Remontrance à Henri II* Crespin wrote, 'Were the English kings and the German princes obliged to give up their States because they tolerated the Reformation? Everyone knows that the contrary happened, and what honour, obedience and faithfulness those peoples who had accepted the Reformation bore their princes.

... I may even assert that they had not formerly known what it was to be obeyed.'

The king had to be Protestant because to the theorists of the Reformation freedom of conscience was inadmissable. As early as February 1526 Luther himself had written to John of Saxony that a country can have only one form of religion. Zwingli, Calvin and Knox thought the same, and they all acted up to their beliefs. In his *Farrago Rerum Theologicarum*, published in 1526, Lambert d'Avignon was categorical on this point. He declared that kings, princes and magistrates should hunt heretics from their dominions. It was their duty, in order to protect their own families from being seduced and to avert all lapses from Christ and the truth. Freedom of conscience was a matter for nations alien to the Christian faith, but not for the faithful. Anne de Bourg, at the stake, made obeisance to the all-powerful king. The punishment of heretics was taught by Calvin—and we know in what manner he carried it out in Geneva—as well as by Théodore de Bèze in the *Traité de l'Autorité du Magistrat*, by Colladon and all the theoreticians excepting Castalion and a small number of freethinkers. One should not fight against the king but against his religion, which was the false one. They were certain that once his bad servants were removed the king would adopt the true faith. . . . This tradition was so powerful that politically the movement of '89 was directed against absolutism and not against the king. Later, the ideas of '89 caused the movement to deviate. Once there had been a recourse to arms it was no longer a case of prevention but of extermination—in the king's name. Politically Calvin and Bossuet reasoned alike; the difference between them was a political, not a religious one. We know only too well, thanks to an interval of centuries, that the Protestant insurrection put the Crown in mortal danger, but the Protestants of the sixteenth century did not see matters thus. If we are surprised by this it is simply because, having learned tolerance from the philosophers of the eighteenth century, we are nevertheless still projecting our present-day ideas and feelings into the past. Even to its few defenders in the sixteenth century, tolerance was a fact but not a doctrine. It was compassion, a lesser evil, a compromise, like the Edict of Nantes, to which both sides resigned themselves. But 1559 was not a time of resignation, only of war. In the eyes of the Protestants the prince was the prisoner of heretics. In the Catholic view the Calvinists wanted to make the kingdom into another England or Scotland. Coligny, seeking conciliation, still hoped for a change. He counted on Catherine; otherwise a recourse to force would be inevitable. The almost desperate economic and financial situation, the political situation, both interior and exterior, more than precarious as the result of the premature death of Henri II, favoured adventurers, such as Monsieur le Prince.

Until the Guises came to power the movement for reform in France had been religious and not political. Lucien Romier, who with reason recognized that nothing in the religious principles of the Reformation was in opposition to royal policy, considered that had it been more accomodating and less Calvinistic it might have been possible to impose it on the Valois. But it seems that, on the contrary, there was a basic incompatability between the spirit of the Reformation and that of France.[1] The attraction of novelty, the Gallican tradition, the abuses of the Catholic Church, the sufferings of the common people, as always the first victims of economic and financial distress, gave many Frenchmen the impression that salvation would come from Luther. On the other hand, as events gradually developed and Calvinism organized itself, the resistance of the masses became stronger and spread. The revolutionary elements introduced into Protestantism by hotheads among the lower orders frightened the bourgeoisie. Huguenot vandalism very soon turned the country people against the new religion. As soon as it appeared to endanger the social order and the traditions of popular devotion the French Reformation ceased to progress. It is certain that had it not been for the intervention of the Bourbon Princes and the part played by the anti-Guise aristocracy on the one hand, and by the systematic persecution of the new faithful on the other, those Frenchmen attracted by the Reformation would fairly soon have turned away from Protestantism, as did, at the very beginning, the humanism of Erasmus. It is extremely difficult to synthesize a movement so complex in its origins, its evolution and its failure. The refusal of Catholicism to reform itself soon enough brought about the first advances of Protestantism. Although considerably anterior to Luther's intervention, the Catholic will to reform had been neither powerful nor rapid enough to break the resistances against it.[2] The French Reformation

---

[1] On this point cf. Albert Autin: *L'Echec de la Réforme* en France au XVIe siècle.

[2] Ref. all this, cf. Louis Pastor, *Histoire des Papes depuis la fin du Moyen Age*, vols. V and VI from Innocent VIII. to Julius II. From vol. VII (Leo X) the battle is joined, which retarded the interior reforms even longer. Unless one has read Pastor and *L'Allemagne et la Réforme* by Janssen, it is impossible to understand this struggle. (Translator's Note: It will be necessary to ascertain the German titles of these works.) Together with Imbart de la Tour, these masterpieces of German historical science dominate everything that has been published later on this question.

was later transformed into a religious confession, and opposed Church against Church. And finally, from 1560 onwards, politics gradually became involved.

Until then the official documents of the Reformed Church of Paris, which had taken the lead in the movement, did not even demand that the State religion should be changed, only claiming freedom for the new cult. But little by little the anti-Catholicism of the Reformationists became more and more militant, aggressive and intense. Calvin, whose foreign policy was a moderate one—and his actions in France sprang from this policy—was too far away to be obeyed. Thus the excesses of the Protestants impeded their progress. The general body of the French Reformationists remained loyal. Realizing that the resistance of the majority of the people was invincible, the theologians of the Religion only asked for freedom of worship. The Valois were aware of this Catholic resistance. Nor did they ever endeavour, not even Catherine de Medici, who was very little inclined to Romanism, to transform this Gallicanism into a Gallican schism and even less into a Lutheran heresy. The paganized customs of a people steeped in the Gallic as well as the Latin tradition clashed with a return to the Gospels. For paganism had been absorbed into the Roman religion, and it was in this that the French differed from the people of the North, where Catholicism had been merely a veneer over the ancient Scandinavian and Teutonic cults. The Latin predilection for free will clashed with the acceptance of predestination; for works, with the justification through faith alone; for the splendours of Catholic ceremonial with the cold austerity of the pulpit; and the belief in the actuality of the sacraments with that in their purely symbolic significance. The cult of the saints, and in particular that of the Virgin, of Our Lady, who to them was practically a divinity, was too dear to the hearts of the French for them not to have been shocked by the iconoclastic Reformationists. This was a cult that the peoples of the North had never known. As for the Scriptural dogmatism of Calvin, this was unacceptable to the humanists, to whom the Church, so long as they took care not to attack the foundations of orthodox faith, left a great deal of freedom. Erasmus was the most illustrious example of this and we know that this great man never accepted Luther. He died in 1536, the same year in which Calvin published his *Institutes of the Christian Religion*. It is certain that Calvinism would have disgusted him. The French theologians formed a doctrinal college, which Gallicanism itself protected against an imported heresy of German and Genevese origin. Artists and men of letters also resisted it, in the name of beauty, exalted by paganism and accepted by the Catholic Church, which during two centuries had been collaborating with the Renaissance. The hostility of the élite was no whit less than that of the people. Both the one and the other took a long time to reveal themselves because French nonchalance is never disturbed until the danger has become mortal, and it is apparently that nonchalance in particular to which must be charged the advance of Protestantism under François I and Henri II. The Protestants were not stopped because they were not a nuisance, but when they did become a nuisance the reaction set in.

To imagine that the French monarchy might become converted to the Reformation was an illusion. Freedom of conscience and of worship was the only remaining possibility. But to this both Catholics and Protestants were opposed. On both sides foreign intervention surreptitiously began. News of English and German atrocities against Catholics furnished good arguments to the supporters of pitiless repression of the heretics. As we have seen, from 1556–59 Protestantism had progressed uninterruptedly owing to the means of direct propaganda brought in by German and Swiss troops. Increased imports, owing to the drop in French production due to the financial and economic crisis, brought with them a growing number of German, English and Swiss merchants. The constant troop movements made the control of frontiers and roads very difficult, and the pedlars of Lutheran literature took advantage of the situation. Libels and lampoons proliferated, passing from hand to hand, and added fuel to the flames of the new converts' religious emotionalism.

Let us take a glance at the correspondence that was passing during the last years of Henri II. On May 9, 1558, the Reformationist minister Macas wrote to Calvin that 'the fire has been lit in all parts of the realm and all the water in the sea would not suffice to put it out.' At about the same period Alvarotti informed the Court of Ferrara that half of the French adhered to the Reformation. The Cardinal de Lorraine was even more pessimistic—he let the Madrid Government know that two-thirds of the realm were heretical. The nuncios were becoming more and more anxious. The Curia and its representatives abroad were making scientific calculations. It is practically impossible to rely on the statistics of the period. They did not distinguish between the discontented, the misguided, and heretics. Théodore de Bèze, who had as many sources of reliable information as he had reasons not to minimize the figures, reckoned that at the time of Henri II's death there were 400,000 Protestants;

the Venetian ambassador, Michele Suriano, gave the same number
—a low one for a total population of roughly sixteen million souls.
To speak of a half or a third is too much in contradiction with this
400,000. What, then, should we believe? Very probably Bèze and
Suriano did give the exact figures for the true believers, for their
percentage is the same today, when, including Alsace, there are one
million Protestants in forty million Frenchmen. If we take one
million as the total number of believers, sympathisers, and discontented people whom the Reformation was able to attract, we are
certain to have allowed for the maximum number, roughly a sixteenth of the subjects of the Very Christian King. At the end of
thirty years of preaching, with very great facilities for its diffusion,
and of a repression that on the whole was moderate, (the most
severe Edicts, that of November 19, 1549, that of Châteaubriant on
June 27, 1551, that of Compiègne on July 24, 1557, were only applied
sporadically and with restraint, despite the torture chamber and the
zeal both of the ecclesiastical and civil tribunals) the Reformation in
France had not been able to gather even an imposing minority. The
edict of Ecouen of June 2, 1559, which ordered real extermination
and the despatching of commissaries to the provinces in order to
'proceed to the expulsion, questioning, and correction of the said
heretics' met with such resistance from the Huguenots that on June
10th, the famous judicial assembly followed, with the protest by Anne
Du Bourg to the Paris Parliament, in the actual presence of the
King, who ordered his arrest as well as that of his colleague Louis du
Faur.[1] Owing to Henri II's death the edict of Ecouen never even
began to be carried out, which confirms the powerlessness of the
previous repressions. No evidence of France's fundamental hostility
to Protestantism can be stronger than the simple arithmetical fact
that after thirty years of almost unimpeded proselytism only one-
sixteenth of the population had either actually or emotionally gone
over to the Reformation.

This fact explains the popularity of the Guises. For the time
being the great majority of the country was on their side. France was
preoccupied almost to desperation by the economic and financial
situation, far more so than by the Protestant question, which was
mainly of serious concern to those public-spirited individuals who
formed the élite. And that situation was indeed tragic.

[1] The most recent account of the judicial assembly is still that of Pierre Champion, in
Paris au Temps des Guerres de Religion, pp. 34–43.

The gold and silver inflation resulting from the Spanish conquest of America had caused a real crisis in the modern meaning of the term, even in the France of the first half of the sixteenth century, then still almost entirely rural. The commercial rate of gold was moving further and further away from its legal rate, allowing intense speculation on the exchanges, to the greater profit of international finance, in which the Jews were beginning to play a leading role. Our forefathers were not spared phenomena such as a shortage of goods and the high cost of living, although at a pace and on a scale far less intensive than in our time. Between 1501 and 1560 the value of the *livre tournois*, in intrinsic francs of 4 g 5 of fine silver, dropped from 6·64 to 3·34. In more than half a century the *livre*, taking into account its diminished purchasing power, had lost only about 56 per cent of its value. To the French of that day, unused to monetary manipulation (the drop in the *livre* had been extremely slow, declining between 1400 and 1500, in spite of the disasters of the Hundred Years' War, only from 7·53 to 4·64) such a devaluation of more than one half, in sixty years, appeared catastrophic. But during the Wars of Religion this devaluation continued and accelerated, the *livre* dropping to 2·57 after 1580 and remaining at that rate until the end of the century. When Henri II died complaint was general and people declared themselves ruined. They had in fact lost in gradual stages two-thirds of their purchasing power. To them it would have seemed unthinkable that the real value of the currency should be reduced to one-400th part of the *étalon-or*. The rentiers, civil servants and country gentlemen were hit, whilst the producers, merchants, and particularly the financiers were doing well. The victims of the devaluation of the currency and the consequent rise in prices suffered all the more because the reign of François I had seen the social emergence of the bourgeoisie and civil servants, and was also the Golden Age of the rural nobility.[1] The rise in wages of labourers and journeymen that followed according to the ineluctable economic laws was, however, behind the rise in prices, and so was in fact a fall. The mobile capital of the bourgeoisie was in similar case. On the other hand business capitalism and speculation enriched a minority, composed chiefly of Italians, Germans, and Jews. The State was getting deeper and deeper into debt, since the creation of

[1] The term is that of Pierre de Vaissière, in *Gentilshommes campagnards de l'Ancienne France*. The first chapter (pp. 7–174) gives a marvellous picture of that rural nobility in the first half of the sixteenth century, and its relations with the peasants. The atmosphere is one of general happiness.

the first *rentes* on the Hotel de Ville de Paris in 1552, at usurious rates of interest.[1] Spain's financial difficulties also affected France. The moneylenders entered into their Promised Land, from which they have never since been expelled.

The unfortunate wars of Henri II increased the miseries of inflation and of consecutive devaluations. From his accession until his death loans, taxes and other expedients, the usual and ineluctable concomittants of ruin, continued unremittingly to increase.

The situation worsened after Le Cateau-Cambrésis and the death of Henri II. Troubles broke out. The discontent, anxiety and anger of the ruined bourgeoisie and nobility fostered the Reformation. Thanks to the landed gentry the Protestant infection began to spread even in rural circles. As great feudal overlords the Guises were well acquainted with the country people and their natural setting, with the small nobility. They understood the need for swift and energetic action whilst the great mass of the peasants had not yet been affected by Calvinist propaganda. They recognized that the greatest evil was the financial crisis. They at once began to take an inventory, a sinister one. Of the forty million *livres* of the Public Debt, nearly twenty million were due for immediate repayment. Civil and military servants had not been paid for months, sometimes even for years. On paper the various taxes were estimated to bring in about twelve million, but facts gave these estimates the lie. The growing state of anarchy made it easy to evade the tax collectors, but it did not make it possible for the Government to do the same with regard to its bankers, who wielded a mortal weapon—the refusal of any further advances.

The Cardinal de Lorraine called in the President of the Exchequer, and member of the Council, Michel de L'Hospital, to manage the finances. Payment of the forced loan, which in the previous year had been demanded according to the traditional euphemism as a contribution to the happy accession, was now insisted upon. Draconian methods of economy were adopted. In his *Relatio* of 1561, the very well-informed Venetian Giovanni Michele put his finger on the weak spot: 'The final third part of the revenue, over and above that required for annual expenses, was never paid into the Exchequer, partly owing to failure to collect it, partly owing to the deliberate neglect of the ministers, who by trickery themselves appropriated a portion of it and let the remainder lapse. For, as the King gave liberally, now to one and now to another, they acquired the rights of

[1] To the denier 20 (16 per cent) which can be reduced to the denier 12 (8 per cent).

distribution, exploited them to their own profit and thus enriched themselves, to the King's great prejudice.'

Michele was the ambassador and representative of an aristocratic and mercantile Republic and took a passionate interest in financial affairs. His report is full of details on the finances of Henri II. He was struck by the general impoverishment, which was such that in Normandy and Picardy the peasants were emigrating. The Guises imposed a drastic reduction of expenses on the Court, which was obliged to submit to it. The same was not the case of the civil and military servants and pensioners. For most of the officers it was a case of poverty or misery. When they went to Fontainebleau to protest, the Cardinal de Lorraine remained adamant; they were ordered to leave and were threatened with the gallows. There was general and deep indignation in consequence.

The people as a whole approved of the policy of economies, under the eternally illusory hope that they would lead to tax reductions. They approved the vigour of the Guises and had confidence in their policy of financial reform, which the King's youth prevented him from carrying to a successful end. It was known that François II was ailing; it was feared that he would have no child; a Regency was anticipated. As regarded foreign affairs the fame of Monsieur de Guise le Grand reassured those Frenchmen, who were becoming more and more numerous, who were perturbed by the consequences of Cateau-Cambrésis. They remembered that the Duke had told Henri II that he would rather lose his head than agree that the peace had been either an honourable one or to the King's advantage.

The popularity of the Lorraine Princes did not escape the Protestants and redoubled their anxieties. Courteously received at Saint Germain, Antoine de Bourbon was admitted to the Privy Council, but not to the Council of Affairs, by which it was conveyed to him that his prerogatives entitled him to merely formal respect. He was not thereby permitted to discuss matters of moment. Antoine did not demur. His attitude shocked the followers of the The Religion, but in fact Antoine was hoping to conciliate both parties, his own and that of the Guises. Condé was becoming impatient; the Cardinal de Bourbon took care not to compromise himself, the Montmorencys remained neutral and their attitude was backed by the Châtillons. The faithful and the preachers deplored Antoine de Bourbon's ineptitude, his futility. The edict of Ecouen was about to be applied. The trial of Anne Du Bourg, which had begun on June 19th, continued. It was said that Philip II was proposing to send troops to France, to purge her of her heretics, as had been done in Spain for the reconquest of the country from the Moors and their allies the Jews. Cardinal de Tournon, who had passed for a moderate, approved the application of the edict of Ecouen.

The alert was given in the 2,500 Reformed Churches. According to Chantonnay, 2,000 of the country gentry were on the side of Calvin, and cadres were therefore ready for resistance, as well as troops, for the feudal links still held and the vassals were converted along with their sovereign lords. Anvils, cried the preachers, were being forged into hammers. 'All the more so as religious faith was uniting with political and social discontent to create those known as State Huguenots at the same time as the Religious Huguenots.'[1] On September 4, 1559, the edict of Villers-Cotterets ordered that those buildings in which prayer-meetings had been held should be razed and flattened forever. Even allowing for exaggerations, there is no doubt that as from August 1559 persecution had become a fact. Informers were encouraged; house to house investigations multiplied. As regarded heretics there was no appeal from the sentences passed by the Châtelet. Sentences became more numerous and also more severe. Immediately after the death of Henri II at the end of 1559, apart from Anne du Bourg, who was strangled and burnt on December 23rd, there were thirteen cases of death by torture in Paris, one a woman. Catherine de Medici, to whom, trusting to her gentleness and benevolence, the Reformationists appealed, had promised Eléonore de Roye, the Princesse de Condé and Coligny to intervene in their favour. She was written to, reminded of her former sympathy with the Reformation, of the days when she had sung the Psalms. But although her promises had been sincere, she was helpless against the Guises, who had the edicts on their side. During the trial of Anne du Bourg the Reformationists made the mistake of threatening her. They went so far as to say that God, having begun by punishing the late King with sudden death, would, in order to complete his vengeance, raise His arm once again against the Queen Mother and her children. Even worse, they announced that the torturing of the Councillor would involve a great risk of further trouble and inflamed emotions. These threats had an official character, for the Reformed Church of Paris made itself responsible for them. The Religionists had forgotten Catherine's Italian touchiness and she replied that they were trying to frighten her and that Calvin's men had not yet arrived

[1] Henri Hauser: *La prépondérance espagnole*, p. 45.

as far as they seemed to think. The indignation of the friends of Anne du Bourg, their vain attempt to rescue him from the Bastille, the assassination of the President, Minard, by shooting, in the Rue Vieille-du-Temple, on December 12, 1559, were of disservice to the unfortunate man. As the result of his martyrdom, on December 23rd he became a saint of the New Church.

In spite of the annoyance caused her by the Huguenot threats, the Queen Mother persisted in her conciliatory endeavours. She requested the ministers to calm the faithful. Matters could still be arranged. As Régnier de La Planche put it, within the small bounds of her influence she held the reins. But in Reformationist circles the fanatics were still gaining ground, and were aiming at nothing less than the destruction of Papist idolatry. In reply the Parisian Catholics, especially the common people, were ferreting out the heretics. The growing hatred in both camps caused Catherine great anxiety. Repressive edicts followed one after the other. Informing had become general; everyone spied on, suspected, provoked and denounced his neighbour.

The spies in the service of Spain were not without information regarding the plotting of Monsieur le Prince, however secret it may have seemed to be. Philip II had informed the Guises, François II, and Catherine herself, that he was ready to assist them with a military expedition against the Protestants. Thereupon the English, informed of this by their ambassador, Throckmorton, feared a Franco-Spanish alliance against themselves. They knew that François de Guise had it in mind. They therefore favoured the underhand dealings of Condé. When reading these ambassadorial despatches of the two Powers who had been allied against France and who both hated her equally, it is clear that the religious and civil troubles interested Philip II and Elizabeth I politically and socially far more than the defence of the Faith. No doubt Philip II was the enemy of the Reformation and Elizabeth I the enemy of Papism. But primarily, both of them were the enemies of France, and would play either the Catholic or the Protestant hand above all in order to harm her. Religious considerations only came afterwards. Among the great Reformist French nobles the situation was similar. The martyr's zeal of the common people was not theirs. Du Bourg was all the more glorified because this great Parliamentarian was basically religious and for that very reason exceptional. He was therefore a sort of human flag, handed over to the veneration of the faithful people in order to distract the attention of the religious Huguenots from indiscreetly straying to the goings-on of the State Huguenots. There is a sentence worth remembering in the *Mémoires* of Michel de Castelnau de La Mauvissière: 'In the name of religion they were attempting to overthrow the political power of the kingdom. At the Protestant assemblies not only religious matters but affairs of State were discussed.'

To what extent was Catherine informed of all this? Owing to the lack of documentation we do not know. But on the other hand we do know that Coligny, who was on excellent terms with her, followed the plans of Condé very closely and was in touch with Throckmorton, as the Guises, on the other side, were with Chantonnay. The pastors were preparing their faithful flock for action against the Guises, but not under any pretext against the King. The ambitions of the Guises, their alleged foreignness, their usurpation of the positions rightfully belonging to the Princes of the Blood; the minority in fact of the young François II leading to a factual regency, to their advantage, which by right belonged to those Princes; the necessity to have recourse to the States-General; respect for the fundamental laws of the kingdom violated by the uncles of the young Queen—these were the themes of a great deal of preaching backed up by numerous pamphlets, all aimed at justifying the overthrow of the Guises. From Strasbourg, the jurisconsult François Hotman was making active propaganda in favour of resorting to violence, whilst in Geneva Calvin was absolutely condemning such violence, unless all the Princes of the Blood and the Parliaments consented to a revolt against tyranny. François—who signed his letters after the fashion of kings—and Charles, with his hopes of Rome, were much too clever to play the tyrants and thus by idiotic haste to ruin the future promise held out to them by the miserable ill-health of the son of the Florentine shopkeeper.

But their enemies did throw themselves into the fight with such idiotic haste. English help was the principal and incontestable reason for it. Among the officers retired for reasons of economy and thus put into cold storage, England found men whom it was easy to arouse. Throckmorton did so in masterly fashion. The *Complaint to the French People* gave a veneer of idealism—according to the eternal methods of English hypocrisy—to a policy of which in March 1559 Throckmorton's letters to Cecil and Elizabeth cynically revealed the methods and ends: 'Now is the time to spend money and it will never have been better spent.' Where did the money come from? The disgruntled soldiers and excited pastors did not even ask.

They preferred to recite the *Complaint*: 'People of France, the time has now come to prove the faith and loyalty we bear to our good King. The strangers are at our gates, whom they have sent for to be the ministers and instruments of their wicked enterprise. . . . They are bringing down 8,ooo Italians, to put the poor French people to prey and pillage. . . . .' Those Italian phantoms prevented anyone from seeing the couriers of Elizabeth, with their sacks of gold and silver. They justified the raising of men which the British subsidies paid for. The King would be delivered, the Guises would be arrested and judged by the States-General; the basic laws of the kingdom would be restored. Nothing would be done against God, the King, his brothers or the State. Condé, the silent chief of the conspiracy, insisted on it. A Prince of the Blood, he could not personally compromise himself by joining the rebels, who seemed determined to dare everything against the Lorraines. Calvin remained hostile to the conspiracy. The German and Alastian Lutherans did not want the Guises to perish. In those circumstances a front man was needed. He was found in the person of an adventurer from Périgord, who after having been sentenced for forgery by the Dijon Parliament had taken refuge in Geneva and become a Calvinist convert. His name was Jean du Barry, sieur de La Renaudie.

At Court, however great the anxiety may have been, nothing definite was known. There was talk of a demonstration by petitioners, discontented officers and non-commissioned officers, which was sanctioned by the Capet tradition. But as the Court was moving from Blois to Amboise, more precise information arrived. It came from German sources as the Lutherans, like Calvin, disapproved of the conspiracy. The Spanish police informed the brothers Perrenot (Chantonnay and Granvelle) who both told the Guises, warning them that they stood in personal danger. The Cardinal was extremely frightened. His brother remained calm, convinced that it was a case of grievances and not a plot. The revelations made to his secretary by a Parisian lawyer, Pierre des Avenelles, a member of the Reformed confession and in whose house La Renaudie, too confident and talk-ative, had stayed, proved to François de Guise that it was in fact an armed threat. The castle of Amboise was placed in a state of siege. Catherine then intervened (this we know from Régnier de La Planche, confirmed by letters from the Cardinal de Châtillon, the Admiral and Andelot and a despatch from Chantonnay, all written between February 25th, and March 20th). She always held that prevention was better than cure. She sent for the three Châtillon brothers. In

3. DIANE DE POITIERS, Duchesse de Valentinois. School of Clouet   (*photo:* Giraudon)

4. MICHEL DE L'HOSPITAL   (*photo:* Giraudon)

complete accord with the Chancellor Olivier, she asked them for their opinions, and not to abandon either herself or her son. The Admiral said how very great was the discontent no less religious than political; he complained of the Lorraines, those foreigners who were handling the affairs of the kingdom, of the removal of the Princes of the Blood, the disgrace of Montmorency. It would be reasonable to cease pursuing the members of the Religion, as their numbers made it impossible to exterminate them. What was necessary—and the Admiral was quite firm on this point—was an edict in clear terms, permitting the nation to live in peace until a Council was called at which everyone could state his case.

Coligny's boldness was based on the Queen Mother's approval. Knowing of her friendship for him, the Guises were inclined to conciliation, in order that Catherine's sympathy for the Protestants which until then had remained very discreet, should not be officially expressed. The Admiral was gambling, and rightly, on the fact that it was in the Guises' own interest to use consideration towards a woman whose self-effacement although they despised her, they knew, nevertheless, to be due to tactical reasons and not to indifference. Catherine's, Olivier's and Coligny's policy immediately won. On March 2, 1560, the edict of Amboise repealed the most stringent measures of the edicts of Henri II.

In his very recent book, *Le Protestantisme en France au XVIe siècle*,[1] M. Samuel Mours showed very clearly that it was only progressively that the Reformation emerged from the Catholic Church, impelled by the force of circumstances that transformed the prayer meetings into dissident churches, and of this he gave proofs. There was no premeditated will either to schism or heresy. The facts prove that Catherine's policy of compassion would have brought about religious peace, had it not been suppressed by the opposing fanaticism of the two religions. We can never repeat often enough that the source of the ensuing catastrophes was the criminal and mad reaction to that edict, in the form of the Amboise conspiracy, with its sequel of hatreds and mutual reprisals.

Coligny signed the edict of March 2nd, together with the other members of the Council. Each of them hoped to interpret its very loosely worded contents to his own advantage, for it was a document that clearly bore the stamp of Catherine de Medici. It was a forward-looking document, that opened up possible paths. The important thing was to annul the past, and to stop persecution and this the

[1] Paris, 1959.

H

amnesty did, for amnesty is the basic necessity of all forward-looking policies. A distinction was made between the profession of the Calvinist faith and any plot against the safety of the State. Religion was dissociated from politics. In view of the ideas and customs of the times, the innovation that, buried beneath the reticence of formal language, Catherine managed to introduce into the Royal legislation, was striking. For this edict of March 2, 1560, was the forerunner of the edict of Nantes, the edict of Grace, of Henri IV and Richelieu, thirty-eight years before the former and sixty-nine before the latter. In that Europe in which the Pope, Philip II, Calvin, and Elizabeth I were the representatives of theocracy and Biblical monarchy, politics and religion became two separate domains. The pragmatism of Machiavelli had crept into its clauses, of which it has been said that they were a mere trap. Catherine wanted to wipe out the past for the sake of the future: 'Princes, and especially new princes', the Florentine wrote, 'have often found more zeal and devotion in those of their subjects who, at the beginning of their reign appeared suspect, than in those in whom at that time they thought they could have confidence.'

As the protectress of those Protestants who were not enemies of the Crown Catherine gave them her support in those days preceding the tumult of Amboise.[1] The Catholic theologians immediately remarked upon the oddness of the edict, as Nicolas Bruslart, Canon of Notre-Dame de Paris, noted in his *Journal*. The edict meant so much to the Queen Mother that she charged Jacques de Moroges, who bore it to Parliament for registration, to request those gentlemen on her behalf to speed the formalities. Her wish was granted and the edict was registered on March 11, 1560.

Although his subtlety was famous, the Florentine shopkeeper had won a move over the Cardinal de Lorraine. In face of the spirit of rebellion she had made the necessary concessions so that the essential fact was admitted—the distinction between religion and politics; the religious amnesty was granted, and the supremacy of the State affirmed. Sigismond Cavalli, the Venetian ambassador, understood Catherine when he wrote in 1574: 'All her important actions have always been regulated and guided by a very strong passion, which could be discerned in her even during her husband's lifetime—the passion to rule.' This passion was (except in certain hours of panic, as on August 24, 1572) inseparable from the caution which made it all

---

[1] Paul van Dyke has very well shown, in *Catherine, le soutien des huguenots*. Cf. Vol. I of his book, chap. XIII, pp. 206-24.

the more certain for her to be able to satisfy it. In dissociating politics from religion Catherine discovered the method of removing from the Bourbons the pretext for their complaints regarding the sufferings of the faithful, and from the Guises the pretext of saving the State by persecuting heresy. She found herself a path between the two camps.

It is significant that Coligny was at her side. Both of them had taken up a position that no one else had thought of—for freedom of conscience. A younger son of the House of Montmorency, the Admiral, in spite of the important posts he occupied, was still not such a very great nobleman that an alliance with the Florentine shopkeeper was beneath him. The Constable, head of the Bouchard dynasty, to whose protection the Châtillons owed everything, was nearly seventy. The King of Navarre, the Prince de Condé, were not of the stuff of statesmen. As heads of militant Catholicism, on condition that they put politics at the service of religion, the Guises had the future on their side. Coligny's calculating mind and Catherine's passion for power, until then restrained, were drawn together by force of circumstances. The Admiral remembered what the Constable had done. Catherine remembered François I. It was natural that they should understand one another. The edict of March 1560 was their joint work. Lorraine was too subtle not to realize the danger of such collusion between two consummately able personalities, beneath the austere mask of the Admiral and the pretence of discretion of the Florentine shopkeeper, who had entered the bed of the Kings of France. He in his turn gave pledges. On March 15 Alvarotti wrote to the Duke of Ferrara that a new policy was in preparation. He understood that Coligny was not the man of clumsy plots, that in him the Protestant faithful (and was it not to one of them that the Guises had owed their warning?) could find a leader. Amboise was enveloped in an atmosphere of conciliation. A split was on the way between the moderate and political Huguenots and the Huguenots of whom the preachers had made fanatics. It appeared that the time for bargaining had arrived. Why should the Lorraines leave the advantage to be gained to a rather malodorous character, Olivier; to an unlucky soldier, Coligny, and above all to the intriguing daughter of those Tuscan bankers, to that Catherine de Medici whose ambition was to rule the kingdom? A kingdom which they, too, wanted to dominate, at once, but over which her maternity, so slow in maturing yet in the end so productive, had assured the despised Florentine such redoubtable rights.

PART II

❧❀❧

THE ACCESSION

CHAPTER ONE

GOVERNESS OF FRANCE
(March—December 1560)

~❧ ❦❧ ❧~

The removal of the Court to Amboise had disconcerted La Renaudie and his troops. It might have been hoped that this edict of compassion would have nullified his plans, but nothing of the kind occurred. At the very moment when the edict was being rushed through Parliament, La Renaudie was making new decisions. Castelnau and Mazères, two leaders of the conspiracy, would meet him at the Castle of Noizay, near Tours. They would then proceed to Amboise, the main body of the troops joining them by the valley of the Loire. These troops were a mixed lot, horsemen and infantry, recruited both in England and Scotland and in the Germanys, Switzerland, Savoy and France. There was no dearth of money nor of arms. On the other hand, La Renaudie having deliberately not given any precise orders, no one knew exactly what was to be done. They just marched on, in groups of two or four dozen. According to Pierre de La Place, who as a Protestant had reasons for being well informed, La Renaudie disposed of 500 horsemen and some infantry. Régnier de La Planche expressed surprise at the plotters' daring.

Audentes fortuna juvat, on condition that they combine caution with audacity. La Renaudie and his accomplices took not the slightest care. They were very quickly spotted. The Duc de Nemours was able to surprise Castelnau, Mazères, and several officers at Noizay. Investigations and searches were made everywhere in the vicinity. Those groups which had reached the immediate outskirts of Amboise were very easily taken. Renaudie thought, nevertheless, that he still had room to manoeuvre, and a new rallying-point was arranged in the forest of Châteaurenaud. The royal troops soon discovered it, and on March 20th, it was attacked by Pardaillan and his cavalry. There was a short battle. La Renaudie killed Pardaillan by a sword-thrust, and he himself was killed in close combat by a soldier with a musket. His corpse, along with two prisoners, was taken to Amboise. Failure was complete. In opposing this ridiculous plot, Calvin had been right. England had played an important part in promoting it, hoping thereby to hold up the Scottish plans of the Guises.[1] But partisan fury had ruined everything; the common fever of civil wars. Once started, it could not be stopped. As early as March 15th, Alvarotti wrote to tell the Duke of Ferrara what he had learned from the Duke's own daughter, the Duchess de Guise. Some prisoners had boasted that they would put to death François and Charles de Lorraine, and even the Royal Family, their accomplices. Others, less excited, said that they would be satisfied with imprisoning the Queen Mother and François II. There seems to have been a great deal of propaganda directed against Catherine. (It must not be forgotten that printing facilitated the distribution of a large number of libellous pamphlets, which was not possible before the sixteenth century.) She was described therein as a whore who had given birth to a leper. There was a centre for the distribution of such calumnies at Strasbourg, under the direction of François Hotman, who was then preparing his famous *Epitre envoyée au Tigre de la France*, which was probably printed at Strasbourg in the following April and immediately put on sale. This worst kind of libel on the Cardinal de Lorraine gives an idea of the tone of the attacks on the Guises and by extension on Catherine de Medici, François II and Mary Stuart. Hotman was in the pay of the Prince de Condé. He is the best-known of a whole horde of libellers, set to work as soon as the Lorraines came to power.

The climate propitious to conspiracy and insurrection had been created, and in view of it this setback seemed all the worse. The anger of Calvin, who declared that no enterprise had ever been worse conceived or more stupidly carried out, was understandable. The letters granting amnesties and pardons, which had been sent on March 16th, to the civil and religious administrators, had had no effect. Once the conspiratorial machinery was set in motion nothing could stop it except forcible repression. As from March 17th, after the attempt of Bertrand de Chandieu, Condé's lieutenant, against the Royal Castle itself, hangings and drownings had begun. Throckmorton agreed with Chantonnay and Alvarotti in stating that the tortures happened after this abortive attempt. The era of cruelty had returned. It is incontestable that this was due to the stupidity of La Renaudie and the

[1] Cf. Jean Dureng: *La Complicité de l'Angleterre dans le complot d'Amboise*, in *Revue d'Histoire moderne*, Vol. VI, pp. 249–56.

intrigues of Condé, the silent instigator of this lamentable attempt. The Guises had agreed to sign the edict, accepting the will to peace of the Queen Mother. Catherine had the support of the Chancellor, Olivier, and the Châtillons. It was she who had taken the initiative, for she had too much political sense not to know that the only way to stifle the tendencies of French Protestantism towards founding a theocracy similar to that of Geneva, by the voluntary or compulsory conversion of the King, was to withdraw from the Reformationists, thanks to freedom of conscience, any pretext for conquering the State. Freedom of conscience, clearly distinguishing religion from politics—and the edict of March proves it—did forestall such a conquest.

Under François I and Henri II the most active Protestant elements had engaged in public activities which left no doubts as to their intentions, namely to apply, to the advantage of the new faith, the principle, *cujus regio, ejus religio*. Andelot, who did not adopt the temporizing methods of his brother the Admiral, imposed the pulpits on Brittany by force, and this gained him the praises of Bèze. In 1559 the Reformationists had taken by assault the Church of the Cordeliers in Valence. The Lord of Montbrun drove his peasants by beatings to the preacher. These are some examples taken from many, all of them prior to the edict of Ecouen.[1] Catherine was too well-informed not to be convinced that these excesses only arose among a minority of fanatics. Nevertheless the heads of the Protestant movement tolerated them. Having lived through the civil wars in Florence she did not ignore that in the end the most rabid always carry away the rest. And that was why she had insisted on taking the initiative, with the edict of Amboise.

One can imagine her fury at the crazy exploit of La Renaudie, which gave terrible weapons to the supporters of the edict of Ecouen. Was the policy of compassion to fail? In pointing to the tyranny of the Guises the Huguenots declared conspiracy to be justified. This was against the evidence, since the attack had followed on the edict of pacification. Catherine was so angry that she herself demanded severe repression. The moment of justified torture had arrived. She was particularly anxious with regard to the English subvention,

[1] With regard to all this, cf. Jean Guiraud, *Histoire partiale, Histoire vraie, Vol. II, Chapter XVI*, which gives all the relevant references. In comparing the various accounts with one another, Protestant and Catholic sources and works respectively, and in a detailed examination of them, impartiality obliges the historian to write off both groups of fanatics equally, as well as the politicians. In addition read also the volume dealing with the sixteenth century in *L'Avenir du Christianisme* by Albert Dufourcq.

which the captured mercenaries had revealed. This was not any longer a matter of religion but of politics, and in that domain Catherine could not admit that anyone but the sovereign might have the last word. 'When it is a question of keeping one's subjects in order', wrote Machiavelli, 'one should not lay oneself open to charges of cruelty, all the more so as in the end the Prince will, by making a small number of necessary examples, have been more humane than those who by their weakness encourage disorders which bring with them murder and banditry. For such upheavals can shake the State, whereas the sentences inflicted by the Prince are only aimed at a few individuals.'

On re-reading the original documents dealing with the Amboise repression, one finds a striking difference between the despatches of the ambassadors and the accounts of the memorialists. And having done so one always returns, in this connection, to the eminently correct statement of Père Daniel, at the beginning of his *Histoire de France*: 'The historian who makes use of them must exercise particular caution with regard to the memoirs which contain accounts of civil wars. For such memoirs are particularly liable to partiality and animosity.' Alvarotti, Michele, Chantonnay, even Throckmorton, are unemotional. There is neither prolixity nor vehemence in La Place. La Planche, on the other hand, spreads himself and is full of indignation. The tone changes according to whether the witness was a Catholic or a Protestant. Yet La Place was a Huguenot. His lack of emotion is significant. It appears that the avengers of the victims of Amboise were inclined to be more literary than historical. In this instance Michel de Castelnau de la Mauvissière, a great servant of France and the least fanatical of men, appears to be the most accurate. The first volume of his *Mémoires* contains no material for romantic invective. This honest and temperate writer does not mention the pastime of the ladies who with cruel voluptuousness watched the executioner beheading young and handsome noblemen, a performance arranged by the Queen Mother. It is certain that they were present, but this appeared too usual an occurrence to be dwelt upon, and it would be beyond reason to read into it signs of hatred and revenge. Those who did so, like Agrippa d'Aubigné, were implacable partisans and therefore highly suspect. Anne d'Este's tears seem very touching, but did she shed them for those who had wanted to kill her husband? Let us admit our scepticism and quote Castelnau: 'It is certain that the King's Queen Mother, who wished to be known as a Princess full of pity and kindness, cancelled many executions which were to be carried out on the conspirators, a considerable number of whom were released and sent away on Her Majesty's advice.' This is infinitely more in line with Catherine's point of view than the Neroism attributed to her by the Protestant hagiographers, true to the polemical tradition, of whom even Jacques-Auguste de Thou became the echo. From political necessity she had to make a few examples, but according to Machiavelli's advice, only small in number. The Prince 'must above all seek to make himself feared without making himself hated'.

Catherine de Medici considered that the defeated should not be driven to desperation; a rule applied by all political realists. Contemporary documents prove the Queen's wish to be merciful. She resigned herself to sternness, but she did not do so with pleasure, for killing was a political mistake. 'When I had to govern', wrote Guicciardini, 'I was never in favour of cruelty and overmuch punishment; nor are they necessary, for apart from certain cases when examples have to be made, in order to maintain respect, it is enough to inflict lower sentences than might have been earned, so long as one makes it a rule to punish all those who deserve it.'

In spite of the tumult and the massacres, on March 31st, the edict of compassion was confirmed. The Huguenots retained the right to petition. The address which they shortly afterwards presented to the King proved that the larger majority of them were not supporters of the Amboise conspirators. Théodore de Bèze praised the Royal clemency. On formal orders which in several places had to be reaffirmed, those imprisoned on religious grounds were freed. At Valence, where the troubles had been serious, there was an amnesty. Nowhere were the Reformationists required to abjure their faith. The detailed instructions were so precise that the officials charged with carrying out the edict were forbidden to interfere in matters of conscience. It was Catherine who introduced this distinction between politics and religion, that principle of the modern State which has always been, is, and always will be violated by affronted sectarians. In spite of the tumult of Amboise she was determined that it should be respected.

Circumstances were particularly difficult. Apart from the hundred executions there had been massacres. Did the dead number 1,200, as the enemies of the Guises claimed? This is unverifiable. The Chancellor, François Olivier, was so deeply affected by the outbreak of violence and the repression of it that it hastened his end; he died on March 30th. With the old minister passed an excellent defender of the policy of moderation. His place was filled in the interim by Charles de Marillac, Bishop of Vienne, and Jean de Morvillier, Bishop of Orléans, who, being only Keepers of the Seals, played no other part than to deal with current affairs. Catherine stood alone in opposition to the Guises, who were exasperated by the riots of Amboise, and she lacked the support of the Châtillons. She remained in contact with the Admiral, who had been charged to carry out an investigation in Normandy on the origins of the conspiracy, of which the results proved that the policy of the Guises had convinced the Protestants that their only hope of salvation lay in revolt. Catherine did not hesitate to tell the two brothers so. She intervened to ensure that the edict of March was put into operation. The Huguenots addressed petitions to her. She openly became their protectress. She would not permit current religious matters to be confused with the Amboise Affair.

The Guises were intent on discovering the real instigators of the plot. The Prince de Condé, whom everyone suspected and whose papers were seized, affected indignation, declaring that he had had nothing to do with the revolt and knew nothing at all of its origins. He abandoned his accomplices, holding himself in reserve for better days. His two henchmen, the brothers Maligny, Jean and Edmé de Ferrières, had managed to escape, taking the most compromising papers with them. A Prince of the Blood could not be prosecuted without established proofs.

Did Condé inspire the mass of libels against the Guises that then appeared? In view of the fact that they were distributed everywhere by a methodical means of propaganda, this seems more than likely. Of all these libels the most famous, published anonymously, was *Le Tigre* by Hotman. Now Hotman had been for a long time in the service of the Bourbons and in particular of Condé, on whose behalf he had been one of the instigators of the Amboise plot. Hotman's power of invective is a delight to a man of letters; all the clichés of revolutionary literature stem from it. The Cardinal was a mad tiger, a venomous viper, a sepulchre of abomination, a miserable spectacle. Recollections of the *Catilinaires* predominate. This furious diatribe amused Catherine, who as a shrewd woman never took written insults tragically, judging that the noise they made was greater than the damage they did and that their very excesses soon bored the reader.

Propaganda was answered by counter-propaganda. The scribes in the payment of the Lorraines replied with less acerbity—the poet,

Guillaume des Autels, and Jean du Tillet, clerk of the Paris Parliament. Whether erudite or men of law, they were not polemicists in Hotman's class. It was gradually learned that the Queen Mother was interested in this literature. She was sent placards, requests and petitions were even offered to her personally. The traditional easy access to a prince by his subjects made it possible to introduce as many libels at Court as was considered desirable, to the extreme anger of the Guises. The agitation against them grew and spread; even their castles, for which they secured military protection, were attacked. There were caricatures and posters; threats of death abounded. The Government sent spies amongst all the Huguenots who might have been involved in the uprising, seeking to obtain proof of a plot against the safety of the State, which would make it possible to attaint the Bourbons. In this effort to re-establish order, Montmorency, in spite of his enmity towards the Guises, did not withold his support from them. The Châtillons themselves gave an ear to their rivals' advances. The revolutionary trend was becoming more serious and causing anxiety to all these great feudalists, afraid of being overthrown by the leaders in the pay of England or Monsieur le Prince, by all those furious people to whom the Reformation was an excuse for rioting. They remembered the War of the German Peasants. Calvin loathed and hated sedition no less than Luther.

But sedition did not deter Condé, drunk with hatred and eager for revenge, and who was seeking to be forgiven by the faithful for the betrayal of Amboise of which they accused him. As for the King of Navarre, he went even further than before in his policy of consideration for the Lorraine Princes. It was thought that his tendency to moderation was due to the agitation among the Protestants in his States, encouraged by the fanaticism of the Queen, Jeanne d'Albret. Like the Constable and the Châtillons, Antoine de Bourbon knew very well that under cover of the Reformation and after the troubles at Amboise the old revolutionary current, until then checked and held back, but always latent since the Jacquerie, was growing and threatening to burst its dykes. There were too many Huguenots in Navarre for him not to realize the danger—In 1572 the Venetian ambassador, Contarini, could write of the Protestants that 'the majority of this sect consists of tradesmen such as cobblers, tailors, and similar ignorant people'. This majority was inspired by the unsuccessful assault on Amboise and was not to be stopped by love of the King, any more than were, in the fourteenth and fifteenth centuries, the Jacques, the Ecorcheurs, the Maillotins, or the Cabochiens. Was not the King, still a child, the prisoner of those usurpers, the detested Lorraines? Was it not the task of his faithful people to deliver him? There was Jacquerie in Agenois, not far from Nérac. Antoine, although indifferent to religion, had many reasons to pay attention to the social threats that were combining with the other-worldly claims of the zealots of the new faith. If the policy of the Guises gave the Reformationists leaders,[1] those leaders had a policy which did not ignore their own feudal interests. Feudal solidarity was to be of advantage to the Guises. Although the Bourbons and the Châtillons were Protestants and against the Guises, they also belonged to the same social group as the Lorraine Princes. Common interest was strengthened by common blood. That is why there appeared, after Amboise, to be a spirit of reconciliation, which was only natural. Catherine did everything in her power to tighten and deepen such a reconciliation. The State Huguenots were capable of understanding politics and the Guises were more political than religious. Grounds of agreement must be sought and found. Catherine de Medici was determined to find them. Taking advantage of the anxieties in both camps, she was to devote to this objective her diplomacy, her obstinate patience, her Florentine subtlety as a negotiator, who knew by experience that civil wars—and Amboise had been an incident of civil war—are the most difficult of all to end, and do the greatest damage.

The institutions of the kingdom offered the Queen Mother an instrument whereby she might herself govern it, through the interposition of a second party. This was the post of Chancellor of France. The Chancellor was the representative of civil justice and the King's vicar. He had the right to wear the Royal purple, and also of primacy before all other members of the Government. In the time of Olivier, an elderly, ailing and timid man, this right was not in fact asserted, and the Guises remained the masters. As Minister of Justice the Chancellor was responsible for the application of all orders and edicts. After the King, he took precedence over all others—ministers, secretaries-of-state, and parliamentarians. He bared his head to the King, the Royal Family, the Princes of the Blood, but not to any ministers, even although they might be Cardinals or Lieutenants-General of the kingdom. The man of the *Fleurs de lys* above all, the King's representative when the latter was unable to preside at the

[1] This term used by V. L. Bourrilly, in *Bulletin de l'Histoire du Protestantisme français* (August–September 1898).

Council, unremovable—he might be disgraced or exiled but not deprived of his post except in the case of high treason—he was the supreme judge, part of the eternal system of Capetian justice. He wore the Great Seal around his neck and was responsible only to the King. He was not the latter's servant but his representative, and stood to the King as the King stood to God.

By way of the Chancellorship power could be wrested from the Guises without violence. Olivier's death allowed Catherine to do so. She knew that she needed a man who would be her instrument and had known for a long time whom she would choose for this post. His name was Michel de L'Hospital. He was born in Auvergne, at Aigueperse, not far from Riom. He was therefore her compatriot on her mother's side. He was still relatively young, fifty-three. He was the son of a doctor in attendance on the Constable Charles, and belonged to a family devoted to the Bourbons. Better still, he was accustomed to Italian ways, for as a jurist he had studied law at the University of Padua. He had been an auditor of the rota in Rome. A legislator as well as a cleric, and in both capacities trained in the prudent subtlety of Italy, he formed the natural link between Erasmus and Montaigne. At thirty he became councillor to the Parliament of Paris. He was sent on a mission to the Council of Trent. Henri II's sister, Madame Marguerite, had so high an opinion of this Paris parliamentarian that she appointed him her Master of Petitions, Councillor of State and finally Chancellor of her Duchy of Berry. In 1554 the King appointed him first lay president of the Chamber of Exchequer. His reputation as a legislator was such that Brantôme reported that he was compared to Sir Thomas More, the martyred Chancellor of England. He was a humanist in the great tradition, knowing Latin and Italian as well as French. Cautious and clever, on good terms with the Lorraine Princes, a Court poet who sang of the victories of Monsieur de Guise le Grand, Metz and Calais, and of the Scottish marriage of the Dauphin, he was not one of those to bear a grudge. He was known to be as gentle and humane as he was learned, wise, an enemy of violence, very politically-minded and well-informed. The Duchesse de Montpensier suggested him to Catherine as successor to Olivier, in order that the appointment did not fall into the hands of one of the Guises' creatures. And since the Guises approved of him, what better choice could there be? Catherine did not hesitate for an instant. She proposed his name to the Council, who made no difficulties in accepting him. Nobody thought that there was anything to fear from this high official, erudite, a perfect latinist, a writer of excellent hexameters and an accomplished Court poet. On June 30, 1560, the office of Chancellor was filled—by the will of the Queen Mother, Michel de L'Hospital entered the Government and history. 'He therefore returned from Savoy', said Jules Gassot, 'and arrived at Chinon, where Monsieur le Duc de Guise knighted him.'

Michel de L'Hospital became a subject of polemics. According to those who were on the side of Rome or of Geneva, he was called a knave or a patriarch.[1] In reality, if one studies both the facts and the sources closely, he appears to have been essentially a politician, of great intelligence and a very honest man; a good and admirable Frenchman, who, when it was necessary, placed the King and France before his own fortunes. Very clever at paying his court, and looking after his interests, at cultivating what Béroalde de Verville called the way of success, as a good Auvergnat he stuck closely to his own interests and there was nothing of either the hero or the saint about him.

He understood immediately that Catherine was Queen; a queen who was a prisoner of the various factions and who had to be set free. He thought of nothing else. In spite of the differences in their personalities, his psychological and political outlook was Catherine's own. He was to Catherine what Richelieu was to be to Louis XIII, her partner in the exercise of Royal power. The genius belonged to Catherine, as it did to Richelieu. Louis XIII followed and supported the Great Cardinal. Michel de L'Hospital followed and supported the Florentine shopkeeper, who by force of circumstances became the Governess of France. One can no more separate L'Hospital from Catherine than Louis XIII from Richelieu, or Mazarin from Anne of Austria. Politically-minded as she was, Catherine still had a woman's nerves. Although physically very brave, she lacked the strength of character that would have enabled her always to place power at the service of reason. But L'Hospital also lacked such strength. For that

---

[1] There is a whole hagiography of L'Hospital, which today seems somewhat faded and over-generous, the typical example of which is still the essay by Villemain on *La Vie du Chancelier de L'Hospital*, which comprises the final hundred pages of his *Etudes d'Histoire moderne*. But on being re-read they appear not altogether negligible and it must be admitted that this L'Hospital, the incarnation of virtue, is in the last resort closer to historical exactitude than the dishonest official contemned by Catholic writers. Montaigne's letter to the Chancellor of April 30, 1570, dedicating the Latin poems of Boëtius to him, reveals the sympathy and admiration that L'Hospital was able to arouse in that disillusioned judge of human character. In our *Michel de L'Hospital*, published in 1943, we ourselves attempted to draw a true portrait of the chancellor of Irenism, supplemented a few years later by that of M. François Albert-Buisson.

reason the Queen Mother and her Chancellor were always to confuse compromise and even weakness with compassion. And this was the basic cause of the failure of what we might call the policy of Amboise. In Catherine the woman too often won over the queen. In L'Hospital the administrator, always anxious to arrange matters, won over the statesman, who must never forget that nothing can be arranged unless one has power at one's disposal; the necessary power to see that justice is done. The double mistake made by Catherine and her Chancellor was always to have relied on cunning, and not, whilst they could have done so, relied on power, which in the end brought the Queen to violent measures. In that respect she no longer listened to Machiavelli; Machiavelli who had always been the man never to stop at any effort and effort is power—never discouraged by setbacks, and preferring force to cunning, as has been authoritatively pointed out by M. Georges Mounin, who in order better to describe the illustrious Florentine did not hesitate to use a term unknown before our time—the word activist.

Although it was an apparent paradox yet it was a profound truth that religious freedom could only be achieved by the sword. Henri IV understood this and that was why, at Nantes, he was able to put into practise Catherine's impotent wisdom. From Coutras to Fontaine-Française, Henri IV's victories achieved what Saint Bartholomew succeeded no less in accomplishing than the conference of Poissy. Yet Catherine made Henri IV's success possible. Had it not been for her that great man would have found no France left; a France that, although not freed, had at least been safeguarded by cunning. The entire history of her rulership from 1560–89 proves it.

At the beginning of that summer of 1560 only cunning was possible, and in that Catherine was a master. The nomination of L'Hospital, recalled from Savoy, was so far from displeasing the Guises that the Cardinal himself had written to him to return to France. As soon as he was appointed as arbitrator between the factions, anxious above all to ensure the royal authority, he threw himself into the conciliatory plans of the Queen Mother. He preferred to follow a policy of 'good counsel and reason' rather than to follow in the wake of 'very audacious and very powerful people who always liked to use force'. Catherine knew that everything would take a long time and be very difficult. She summoned the King of Navarre. L'Hospital and Navarre would provide the balance against the two Lorraines; blood and law against privilege. Catherine had instinctively discovered the basic principle of the Capet monarchy. Henri II was the

I

King who abandoned everything to his favourites, his mistress or his friend. The king-judge and king-arbitrator reappeared in Catherine. Her recall of Antoine de Bourbon followed quite naturally and logically on her recourse to L'Hospital.

The Florentine shopkeeper had appeared on the scene noiselessly. As soon as trouble had threatened she had asked that the Privy Council should meet in her own room. Her maternal anxiety made it natural that she should wish to keep her son close to her. Catherine always took advantage of any opportunity that presented itself. The Amboise coup had so shaken the Guises that Spain abandoned them. As Chantonnay noted, Catherine did not make the mistake of adding to their discredit. They were popular with the militant Catholics, and nothing useful could be accomplished either without them or against them. Catherine was a newcomer; she had barely been touched by the fury of the factions. The Châtillons were in agreement with the Guises in putting her in the forefront. On this point Pierre de La Place was quite explicit. There is no doubt at all of the alliance between Catherine and the Admiral. Her authority was already so strong that the Guises did not dare 'to vomit out what they had previously kept down, against the Houses of Montmorency and Châtillon'. The whore, the brothel-keeper, ignobly insulted by Condé's pamphleteers, wasted no time in prosecuting these filthy pen-pushers. It was a much more urgent and important task to secure the loyalty of the three Châtillon brothers, especially Gaspard. The Admiral was a power in Israel, and if he refused to sanction it the faithful would not attempt an armed revolt. Temporarily, Catherine had mastered the Guises. The time had come to bring in the Huguenot leaders, the political Huguenots. In foreign affairs the English were to be treated with consideration and for this reason the intervention in Scotland, sanctioned by France, was stopped by the Treaty of Edinburgh on July 5, 1560. This involved relinquishing the Scottish protectorate, one of the oldest traditions of French diplomacy. Cecil made no mistake about it when he wrote: 'To cover up all that, we prefaced the article with some kind words to which our adversaries were obliged to agree; and *satisfied with the kernel, we left them the shell to play with.*'

The policy of non-intervention in Scotland was the foreign counterpart of non-persecution in France. This was the reversal of the Lorraine policy; Catherine's masterstroke was to induce the Guises to agree to it. La Place saw matters clearly: the submission of the Guises was Catherine's personal achievement. Nothing was so important as that, and as regarded the immediate future, the Bourbon alliance would take care of it.

Coligny had informed the Queen Mother of the results of his investigation in Normandy. He calculated that there were 50,000 Reformationists able to take up arms. The Duc de Guise said that he could dispose of twice that number 'to break their necks'. Such threats of civil war were increasing. Catherine, knowing that since Le Cateau-Cambrésis the Guises were no longer trusted by Spain, continued to remain in touch with Philip II. Her daughter Elisabeth served as her secret agent, sharing this role with Sébastien de L'Aubespine. The Catholic King was following a very complex and subtle policy. He was in negotiation with the Queen of England as well as with the Queen Mother of France. However surprising this may appear to those who see the past in the light of subsequent events, in 1560 Philip II was not on the side of the Lorraines. Quite the contrary was the case. At that moment the Scottish question loomed before everything else in Philip's eyes: to remove Mary Stuart from the English succession, for her accession to the throne of the Tudors would have made the whole of Great Britain a close ally of France. And it was for this reason that he allowed Catherine to imagine that she dominated him through his young wife. Thanks to the unrivalled intelligence service organized in France by the Duke of Alba, during his residence there in the last months of the reign of Henri II, and which was directed by Chantonnay, Philip was extremely well-informed as to the situation. The English spy system was no less active than the Spanish. Letters from Throckmorton, as early as 1559, exist and leave no doubt in the matter. A comparison of these with those of Chantonnay allows us to measure the degree of Catherine's mistaken view of foreign affairs at the time of François II.

François de Guise was even more completely deceived and imagined that Spain would help France against England. And the Protestants also believed in a dream of England against Spain. In Elizabeth I's policy Flanders was even more important than Scotland was to Philip II. On no account must Antwerp fall to the French. On that score she feared even the Spaniards less. The bankers of Antwerp and the wool industry meant far more to the English than revenge for the defeat of Amboise. Although she did not neglect economics, as a good Italian they mattered far less to Catherine. She remained a student of Machiavelli and a Florentine shopkeeper as well, but she was nevertheless, and this must never be forgotten, a queen before a shopkeeper. Economics were already of capital interest to England and essentially so to Spain, for in spite of the galleons of Peru the Spaniards would have died of hunger had it not been for Flanders, which they exploited by force. Catherine, above all a politician, was more keenly interested in the possibilities for negotiation with the Spaniards offered to her by Antoine de Bourbon, who was claiming that part of Navarre which was being held by Philip II. Her letters reveal her aims, and they were confirmed a year later by the mission of Jacques de Montauberon d'Anzances to Philip II. The son of Charles V had the advantage over the Florentine shopkeeper, who was trying to intervene in Spain, of a secret police that kept him informed of her every move. Catherine took a long time to discover this, and to strengthen her own spy system. In that summer of 1560 she thought herself more astute than her son-in-law. As soon as the Treaty of Edinburgh following on the death of Marie de Lorraine, had put his mind at rest regarding Scotland, he secretly drew closer to the Guises. He was no more losing interest in the extermination of the French heretics than in keeping the Very Christian King out of Scotland. Few princes were to play a more complex and complicated diplomatic hand than Philip II, the Cautious King, whose genius was more reflective than active, so much so that it occasionally bordered on confusion; he was the Demon of the South, who created his own Hell in which to imprison heretics.

With very sound political intuition Catherine de Medici had drawn closer to the Bourbons. She nevertheless made the mistake of including Philip II in her plans for Navarre. She applied her desire for conciliation in internal matters to foreign affairs. With regard to the former she had scored an outstanding success when after the Amboise troubles she announced the formation of a National Council for introducing reforms into the Gallican Church; a Council the president of which was to be a prelate who enjoyed her full confidence, Cardinal de Tournon, then in residence at Rome and whom she had chosen instead of Lorraine. In religious as in political affairs, the Florentine Queen promoted her own people. Lorraine accepted Tournon, but obtained from Pius IV the same rank as he held, that of legate of the Holy See in France. Spain and Rome both resisted this Gallican plan. The Queen was so intent on it that L'Hospital's first official appearance was on July 5, 1560, when he addressed the Parliament of Paris on the necessity of reforming the Church in France, the abuses of which were obvious. This intervention by the Chancellor confirmed the edict of Romorantin, of the previous May, 'edict on the residence of bishops and other ecclesiastical prelates'. One must not allow oneself to be impressed by the very severe clauses it contained against the Reformationists, and by the fact that it once again exclusively handed over the repression of heresy to the Church tribunals. These were concessions made to the Cardinal-Inquisitors Lorraine and Tournon, to Rome and to Spain. And in return, whilst the ecclesiastical tribunals were charged with the suppression of illicit assemblies insofar as they were seditious, freedom of belief remained unchallenged. The repression of heresy having been removed from the secular authorities by the edict of Amboise, the Church could no longer have recourse to them when heresy was condemned. On reading the edict of Romorantin it becomes clear that it was deliberately inapplicable. Catherine succeeded in rescuing the Huguenots from the Inquisition which Rome, Spain and the Guises wanted.

By an error that has been almost everywhere repeated, this edict is attributed to Michel de L'Hospital, who, however, did not assume office until May 20th, having been nominated on March 30th. The Chancellor did no more than apply the seals to it. Adminstratively it was, as he said, his law. In reality it was the fruit of Catherine's resistance, as tenacious as it was subtle, to the Cardinal de Lorraine. The Queen Mother had succeeded in withdrawing from the hands of the minister the instrument of torture, which after the tumult of Amboise she had had to resign herself to allowing him. To the Huguenots who complained of the severe measures the edict contained, Michel de L'Hospital rightly pointed out that if his law was a bad one it could later be abrogated. For if the Inquisition had been allowed to establish itself matters would have been far worse. They would never have been able to free themselves of it and both in religion and politics France would have become a second Spain.

The edict of Romorantin is in Catherine's most characteristic manner, which was always to outflank the insurmountable obstacle; to light counterfires in order to stop the fire from spreading. As an artful Auvergnat the Chancellor could not but admire this masterpiece of duplicity—*sembler tout accorder en paroles, pour mieux refuser tout en actes.*[1] To appear by word to agree to everything in order the better to refuse everything in deed. This was so much the Queen's idea that already, on August 6th following, the definition of illicit assemblies was referred by the ecclesiastical to the lay tribunals. Private assemblies were soon to be authorized by the Cardinal de

[1] Tr. Note: This is italicized in original.

Lorraine himself. The administration turned a blind eye to the public assemblies. Madame Catherine's compassion had succeeded, but it was nevertheless inseparable from the determination to punish anyone who might again make trouble. Those responsible for Amboise protested furiously against an edict that was aimed at them by providing for the repression of the propaganda of the preachers, printers and hawkers, as well as for acts of vandalism and attacks against or molestation of individuals. Freedom of conscience was safeguarded, except in the disturbance of public order. Catherine endeavoured to complete and perfect this draft of her religious policy. In the spring of 1560 she had already presented France with the means of avoiding forty years of massacre and ruin.

The fury of the sects, alas, was to prove stronger than the wisdom of the woman who, when the troubles again broke out in the provinces, had shown herself to be the good and watchful Governess of France.

The Protestant attacks against the Catholic churches increased after the Ambroise incident and were to continue for years, apart from certain brief periods of intermission. The researches of Albert Dufourcq, by their very objectivity, put this beyond doubt. The repression of the Amboise tumult was followed by real Huguenot terrorism. In April 1560 there was the sacking of Saint Phébade and the Church of the Jacobins at Agen. In August the Church of Négrepelisse, near Montauban, was made to become a temple. On the preceding July 16th, the Calvinists of Montauban had made an expedition to the neighbouring small town of Saint-Antonin, where they set fire to the churches. On June 19th, there had been iconoclastic incidents at Lectoure. On October 19th, 20th, and 21st, at Montpellier, Catholics were massacred, sixty churches and chapels were pillaged and the victims numbered 1,200. Led by the Lords of Mauvans, in Provence, incidents of vandalism multiplied, including fires and sacrilege and the murder of priests, in the dioceses of Senez, Riez, Glandèves, Fréjus. From Castellane to Forcalquier, around Sisteron and Draguignan, at Aix, Salon, Marseille, a real hunting-out of Catholics was organized. In August 1560 the Mauvans, having joined up with Montbrun, had invaded the Comtat Venaissin, where their iconoclastic bands had a free hand. This went on throughout the year 1561 and spread throughout the region of Valence, Romans and Montélimar, as far as Orange. In Berry in 1561 the recourse to arms led to the sacking of Sancerre and the burning of Lignères. The riot of Bourges, on August 17, 1561, was serious. At Lyons in the Loire Valley, at Tours relics were thrown into the river; at Orléans, where the Huguenots captured the city, the statue of Joan of Arc was broken, and this disclosed the English influence. The Queen of Navarre allowed such violence to develop in her States, where she had imposed the cult of Geneva. At Châteauroux, at Saint-Genou, at Dun-le-Roi near Saint-Armand-Mont-Rond, priests were murdered and churches profaned. At Issoudun, the minister Dorsanne, with the complicity of the magistrates and officials, forbade the Catholic religion. A map of the Protestant attacks during the years 1560 and 1561 makes the cause of the Catholic anxieties and reprisals very clear. From Normandy to Poitou, from Berry to Provence, one can follow the course of this state of anarchy, which was no more spontaneous than that of 1789. Mézeray, who possessed ample archives, of which too many disappeared during the Revolution, has proved that it was all part of a methodical plan—the raising of troops, the formation of cadres, impositions, the help of officials, threats and attacks that were not repressed. The tumult of Amboise had become simultaneously epidemic and endemic.

Ronsard's *Le discours des misères de ce temps à la reine mère du roi* appeared in June 1562. The date is important—three months after Wassy. The poet recalled events prior to Wassy and therefore to the First War of Religion. This had already been going on for two months when in October 1562 there appeared the *Continuation du Discours*, which was followed in December by the *Remonstrance au peuple de France*.

After two such frightful years the great poet gave rein to his indignant sorrow. Faced with the monstrous history of that time, with all those fatal catastrophes, he expressed himself in pathetic lines which if one did not know their date, one might think were written after the First War.[1] During those two years Catherine did her utmost to stop the bloodshed. Even in the face of such Protestant fury the Queen persisted in her policy of moderation which continued until Wassy and—what is almost always forgotten—which explained Wassy as later on the successive Michelades were to explain Saint Bartholomew. Reprisals against reprisals, the grim historical law of civil and religious wars. Nothing deterred Catherine from her carefully thought-out plan. Catholic authors reproach her for having

---

[1] The great political and religious addresses of Ronsard appeared from 1562-3, from *L'Institution pour l'Adolescence du Roi Charles IX* to *Réponse aux Injures et Calomnies de je ne sais quels Prédicantereaux et Ministreaux de Genève.*

been the accomplice of the Protestants; a completely unfair reproach, which the facts disprove. The Queen Mother was not in favour of a form of Gallicanism similar to the Anglicanism of Henry VIII; she loathed theocracy too much to agree to a form of Caesarian Papism. As the niece and cousin of Popes she knew that a clerical government was one of the worst of all. In her view, to transform the King of France into a spiritual and temporal sovereign at one and the same time could only appear sinister or absurd. There was no encouragement to be found in the Anglican example of Henry VIII and Edward VI, followed by Mary Tudor's Papist reaction and ending in Elizabeth I's difficulties with her national clergy. All the Queen Mother was seeking was simply a possibility of allowing two confessions to co-exist simultaneously in the States of the Very Christian King. Beginning with the edict of Romorantin, she went to work to this end with Michel de L'Hospital.

L'Hospital, a courtier of the Lorraine brothers, the issue of Charlemagne, as it pleased him to address them, could be her indispensable representative, without appearing to be a prime minister. He was an expert in both royal and French administration, devoted to the personal policy of the Florentine Queen, whose ambition was to save the kingdom over which by force of circumstances she had been called to rule from civil war, which she now with alarm saw to be increasing and of which, having had a painful experience of it in her childhood, she knew the perils.

The Governess of France wished to see matters for herself and to negotiate personally. She had agreed to read a remonstrance addressed to her on Ascension Day 1560, in which the Guises were accused of being the authors of all the ills of the kingdom. After Mary Stuart had discovered the Queen Mother reading this memorandum, the Guises no longer had any doubt of her Huguenot sympathies. Catherine nevertheless continued to make her own investigations. Régnier de La Planche has reported the audience that she granted him in June 1560. Catherine was less secretive than her legend asserts. Her activities were once again discovered on this occasion, by the Cardinal de Lorraine himself. La Planche, who belonged to the Montmorency party, and was in the parlance of the time a *connétabliste*, considered that the Bourbons should replace the Lorraines in the Government. La Planche's views encouraged Catherine in her attempts to separate the State Huguenots from the Religious Huguenots. Her call to Antoine de Bourbon was a new step in this direction. In agreement with Coligny the Queen Mother considered that an assembly should be called, comprising the Council, the Princes of the Blood, the Grand Officers of the Crown, and the Knights of Saint Michael, and that it should proceed to a detailed examination of the situation. On August 21st, this assembly met at Fontainebleau, in Catherine's own chamber, for she now no longer hesitated to appear in her new role as Governess of France. Anne de Montmorency had responded to her call, but Antoine followed his brother Louis; neither the one nor the other appeared. This was a setback for the Queen Mother.

We are well informed on this assembly, which in the Queen Mother's mind was to take the place of the States-General, by the Venetian despatches, by *L'état de la religion* by La Place and *L'état de France* by Régnier de La Planche, confirmed by the report of Louis de Gonzague. At the first session of the Council, Michel de L'Hospital claimed that there was no need to summon the States. At the second session, on August 23rd, Coligny presented two petitions from the Reformationists of Normandy and Picardy, which were under his authority as Admiral and Governor. Each of these provinces asked for a church in order that members of the Religion might freely worship there, without anxiety. Coligny based himself on the investigation that Catherine had ordered him to make.

After Coligny, Jean de Monluc gave a discourse, in which he stressed the distinction between the faithful of the new religion and the rebels. Jean de Morvillier and Charles de Marillac spoke to the same effect. Pierre de La Place and Régnier de La Planche agree that in this contest of eloquence Marillac took the place of honour. His programme was that there should be religious tolerance, and that the States should prepare administrative and ecclesiastical reforms; this was also the Queen Mother's. In both La Place and La Planche his harangue appears as a masterpiece of Christian wisdom and of political realism. It received unanimous approbation, and as François de Guise and his brother the Cardinal agreed to renounce the forcible extirpation of heresy, Catherine's success seemed complete. The inevitable incidents during the sessions on the following two days, August 24th and 25th, do not lessen this impression. The assembly ended on the 26th, with the Royal decision to convoke the States-General (according to Chantonnay this had to be conceded as the result of a memorandum from the Parliaments, that had been very annoyed at not having had representatives at Fontainebleau) to call a national Council, to renounce the secular arm in matters of religion, and to oblige the chief ecclesiastical and civil officers to remain in residence. At the end of that summer of 1560 Catherine offered the whole of France those two remedies—a general, or alternatively, a national Council for the Reformation of the Church, and the calling together of the States-General. The absent Bourbons had missed the occasion of associating the highest Protestant authorities of the kingdom with that effort at pacification, from which they would have been the first to benefit. Owing to the impossibility of agreement between the Princes, their absence was to lead to a refusal to come to terms by the faithful of the two Churches. The deeper reason for this was that Condé's adventurous demon, taking advantage of the changeability of the King of Navarre, urged him to make use of the troubles that followed on Amboise, to develop them on a wider scale, and to transform them into a rebellion of the nobility, analogous to the Praguerie, the League for the Public Good, and the Crazy War. The troops for such a rebellion were to be provided by the Messianic fervour of the Protestant masses. The Blood of France could call all the more successfully on those masses because they were faithful to the King, and the fact that the Lorraines remained in power would easily give the appearance of truth to the calumnies of the pamphleteers against the comedy played, according to them, by Catherine, in her pretence at inaugurating a new religious policy.

The libellers found all the more eager readers because the prejudice against petticoat rule remained strong, even in sixteenth century France, when women played such an important part in society. In this instance prejudice was reinforced by suspicion of the Italian Queen. Catherine knew this. That was why she chose L'Hospital as her deputy, a legislator whose mind was completely in accordance with the Capet tradition, which had been served by a Guillaume de Nogaret, a Georges d'Amboise, and an Antoine Duprat, whether they were clerics or laymen. He was known not to be a Calvinist. Years of calumny and indiscreet praise were to elapse before he was alleged to have gone over to the Reformation. In 1560 he inspired confidence in the people. They saw him as the defender of the national interests, of which both the élite and the ordinary French people of the sixteenth century had a much clearer notion than is generally supposed; the reputation of a Jean Bodin is a proof of this.

On the Protestant side Coligny was then of the same opinion. But not Condé. The latter's feudalistic aims had a double purpose—to free the King from the Guises and to restore the Faith on the ruins of Papism. As against the politicians, who were beginning to rally to the Queen Mother, the Chancellor and the Admiral, the fanatics formed two camps; the one around the Guises, for Rome; the other, around the Bourbons, for Geneva. Rome and Geneva were only symbols of their passions, as much political and social as religious. Feudal ambitions and democratic claims were the same in both camps. The spirit of the league was as strong among the Protestants as among the Catholics, as was also the crusading sprit. This is the key to the Wars of Religion.

Temporal interests, ideologies and rival mystiques, similar although under opposing symbols, are to be found on both sides. The Reformationists knew themselves to be in the minority. The necessity to resort to force in order to win, the arguments of Amboise, swayed the fanatics, to such effect that at the very moment when the Fontainebleau assembly was adopting officially a policy of concili-ation as a possible basis for national reconciliation, Condé was putting the final touches to a plan for rebellion in the South. His designs were soon discovered; La Place and La Planche leave us in no doubt that they were seditious. He had carried Antoine and all the other Bourbons with him. The Bourbon chroniclers themselves confirm Alvarotti's and Chantonnay's despatches on this point. This recourse to arms in reply to the Queen Mother's attempt to settle matters proves the serious responsibility of the Princes of the Blood in fomenting the Wars of Religion at this early stage.[1]

Thanks to Catherine at the end of 1560 the situation could still have been saved. It would have been enough to have followed the words of the Gospels—'Let the dead past bury its dead'—and to collaborate in a policy of forgetting, forgiving and pitying. Coligny understood this; Condé refused to understand it and the vacillating King of Navarre followed him. The wounds that had nearly healed were re-opened. Catherine's indignation was all the greater because she had hoped to win over the Princes of the Blood to her cause, that of a Royal and French peace. Her habitual caution warned her against making a scene. Instead she immediately began to try to detach the King of Navarre from his brother. She showered him, as well as Jeanne d'Albret, with friendly letters. She insisted on Antoine coming to Court. She did the same with regard to the Constable, however suspicious she may have been that he was in connivance with

---

[1] In Viénot's *L'Histoire de la Réforme française* there is not the slightest allusion to these facts, which would have ruined his case, which was favourable to the Reformation.

the Bourbons. We know through Chantonnay that the master of Chantilly was not fooled by this Florentine amiability.

The Admiral, knowing that only the Queen Mother could save Condé from the vengeneance of the Guises, pleaded that Prince's cause with her. Catherine listened, replied in affable but evasive terms, determined to prevent that enemy of her policy from doing any further harm. To accuse her of perfidy would be absurd, for she could not have done otherwise, placed as she was between the Bourbons, the Guises, the Montmorencys and the Châtillons, all of them with military forces at their command whilst she had none, the Royal troops being under the Guises, as executive ministers. When the Nuncio complained of the irreverant attitude of the Cardinal Odet de Châtillon, at mass on Saint Michael's Day, the Queen Mother defended him. The Nuncio declared that they would have to return to the edicts of Henri II. Catherine explained that repression was a mistake, and in any case impracticable, for she claimed that it would involve the extermination of two-thirds of the subjects of the Very Christian King (her exaggeration was deliberate). She considered that a council, either general or national, was necessary. The Nuncio was scandalized.

Catherine found herself opposed by Philip II. Knowing that he might be asked for military help, he intervened without hesitation in the internal affairs of France. He wished to avoid at any price a return to the foreign policy of François I and Henri II (before Vaucelles) which was based on the alliance with the Lutheran German princes. As Sébastien de L'Aubespine wrote, he feared that 'some understanding might be reached to the detriment of the Low Countries'. Pius IV resigned himself to a general council solely in order to avoid a national council. On November 29, 1560 the pontifical bull appeared, decreeing the re-opening of the council for Easter, at Trent. Once again, after a great deal of trouble, Catherine had won. Monsieur le Prince had been arrested on October 31st.

The investigation lasted two weeks. The procedure was suspended on November 26th. Catherine was so deeply affected by this affair that on the day of his arrest she wept, foreseeing only too clearly the consequences that would ensue on the victory of the Lorraines over the Bourbons, who were responsible for the breakdown of the policy of unity. With her usual adroitness she drew closer to her old companion, Anne de Montmorency; their quarrels and reconciliations had been so many that they had only a superficial effect on their relationship. She needed his help against the Lorraines and she

knew him too well to fear for one moment that he would give way
to his rivals.

Christophe de Thou, president of the Commission appointed to try
the Prince de Condé, regarded him as a thorough rebel. The facts
justified this harsh opinion. When François II declared that the
Prince had wanted to deprive him of his crown and his life he was
mistaken. In fact the plot was aimed at bringing the Bourbons to
power by handing over to them the chief offices of state, once the
Guises were thrown out, even at the price of civil war. Catherine
could not agree that this obvious crime should go unpunished. There
was nothing surprising in her attitude, which was according to her
desire for peace. It is certain that the judges were not ordered to
bring in a verdict of guilty. They investigated the affair methodically.
The Chancellor had left them complete freedom to do so. He pointed
out to François II, who was impatient that it should end, that to keep
the trial in suspense was a powerful method of controlling the discontented. They would remain quiet so long as they feared to hasten
the torture threatening Condé by rebellion, but that in avenging him
they would be terrible and without restraint. How well one recog-
nizes here Catherine's predilection for temporizing! Machiavelli
said: 'Yet a prince must not fear his own shadow and listen too
easily to the frightening reports made to him. He must, on the contrary, be slow to believe and to act, yet without neglecting the laws of
prudence. There is a middle way between a mad sense of security
and reasonable suspicion.'

Between the Guises and the Bourbons, Madame Catherine, already
the Governess of France, kept to the middle path recommended
by Machiavelli's empiricism. The facts prove that she was wise and
foreseeing. François II died of acute mastoiditis on the evening of
December 5th, before the end of Condé's trial. Catherine had been
awaiting this sad end for several days. The politician won over the
mother. Chantonnay's letters to Marguerite of Parma describe the
Queen as having long talks, during her son's illness, with Antoine
de Bourbon. The Spaniard, whom this greatly disquieted, tried in
vain to see Catherine, who managed to avoid receiving him, whilst
showing him great consideration, for Philip II was not to be
offended. Her correspondence at the end of November and the
beginning of December proves, however, that Catherine was intending to counterbalance her son-in-law by means of the Constable de
Montmorency and the Duke of Savoy, without, either, forgetting the

Emperor, as can be seen in her long official letter (countersigned by the Procurator-General, Gilles Bourdin) to the Bishop of Rennes, French ambassador to his Caesarian Majesty. Her son had died on the previous evening, yet Catherine was sufficiently cool-minded to deal with the Emperor and the General Council. So much does a great passion dry up other feelings. Madame Catherine's passionate preoccupation, which at that moment predominated over all other emotions, was whether she would at last come into power, since Charles IX was only ten years old. The moment had arrived for making the decisive move in order to triumph simultaneously over both the Guises and the Bourbons.

The Guises were now expecting to be deposed, as they themselves had deposed the Constable. The Florentine mind was too subtle to be read even by the sharpest of the Lorraines, Cardinal Charles. Catherine needed the Guises in order to protect herself with regard to the Catholics, as she also needed Antoine de Bourbon, to protect herself from the Protestants. For that very reason it was necessary for the enmity between the two Houses to end. Otherwise, according to the basic laws of the kingdom, Antoine would become Regent, when the Guises and the ardent Catholics would oppose him. The kingdom would be running into an Amboise conspiracy in reverse. The Queen Mother's powers of persuasion were able to prevail with that impressionable Prince. She pointed out to him the Spanish, Savoyard, Catholic Swiss and Lorraine perils, as well as the dangerous position of Condé, facing capital punishment. Even before the death of François II Catherine de Medici had taken Antoine de Bourbon in hand, carefully pointing out to him that the young King might still recover, and that it was only his illness that had kept his anger with Condé in check. She was a great reader, familiar with the ancient constitutions of the realm; she reminded Antoine of the precedent of Blanche de Castille, the Spanish Regent, and ancestress of the Bourbons.

Through Chantonnay and Suriano and the Ferrarese ambassadors we can follow this marvellously thought-out approach to the taking-over of power. The Governess of France was no longer satisfied to remain in the wings, but was resolved thenceforward to take the centre of the stage in full limelight. And if she did become Regent, would not Antoine be the Lieutenant-General of the kingdom, and thus master of the armies? As for the Guises, they would remain ministers. The light-minded Bourbon was attracted by the bait, and the Lorraines were haunted by the fear of suffering the same fate as the Montmorencys after the death of Henri II. An expert huntress, the Florentine Queen sang as sweetly as a magic bird. The only obstacles in the way of Antoine's agreement were the petitions of the heads of the Reformed Church. The Queen Mother tenaciously nursed and made use of the remaining ambition of the First Prince of the Blood. Every day he gave way a little more. He finally agreed that the Royal Seal should remain in Catherine's hands and that she would hand it over to him in the event of urgency or necessity. When François II died his mother was already mistress of the land. The difficulty was to remain so, now that she could no longer claim the King's authority, in fact and by right, since Charles IX was still a minor. That François II was so in fact had greatly eased matters. Having lost that trump Madame Catherine decided to play her hand even more firmly.

This time her game was no longer to be crafty but to assert herself and to present everybody with the *fait accompli*. 'The animals whose appearance the Prince must know how to assume are the fox and the lion'—the Queen had reflected on those words of Machiavelli. The time of the fox was past, the hour of the lion had arrived. On the evening of December 6th Madame Catherine summoned the Council around the little Charles IX. She officially informed the King of Navarre, the Lorraine Princes, the Cardinal de Tournon, the Marshals de Brissac and de Saint-André, and her partner L'Hospital, that it was her maternal duty to rule in the name of the Child King. She would do nothing without consulting the Council, and the Council would address itself solely to herself, assisted by Antoine de Bourbon.

That was her will. It was the *Hoc volvo, sic jubeo: sit pro ratione voluntas* of Juvenal. Her tone was that of the sovereign; what reply could be made that would not be an impertinence? Antoine dared not demand more than interim powers if the Queen should fall ill. Catherine looked him up and down. She fall ill? She would never be so ill that she could not fulfil her task. . . . Antoine, impressed, gave way again. The Royal claws had scratched his neck. All were silent. The Constable had not yet arrived and by next day it was too late to protest. He was obliged to be satisfied with the eighth place in the secret Council which was to form the Government of Catherine de Medici. In order to control the Privy Council as well as the four Secretaries of State, she herself confirmed all the members thereof in their posts. With incomparable skill, in order to avoid all parliamentary debate, she did not demand the title of Regent. In Old

France fact was right. Catherine was in fact Regent. That was enough. Such was her realism. On the following December 21st the standing orders of the Council did not refer to her as Regent. The King of Navarre received the minutes and transmitted them to the Queen Mother, to whom they were addressed. Catherine would see everything, control everything, summon the Ministers and Secretaries of State. Even as regarded the army the Lieutenant-General would seek her agreement. 'Princes', said Machiavelli, 'must make the art of war their sole study and sole occupation; this is rightly the science of those who rule. By it they maintain themselves in their power.' As a woman, Catherine could not do without technical advisers with regard to warfare—Antoine, Monsieur de Guise le Grand, the Constable and the Marshals. But supremacy being reserved to the First Prince of the Blood, Catherine was satisfied; the weak Antoine would obey her and the army would safely be in the Queen's hands.

It was as the descendant of Italian dictators that Madame Catherine knew so well how to manoeuvre; being a woman she would use an intermediary to make herself chief of the army and thus head of the people. As regarded purely political matters, they were her domain. She would look into everything alone at first, and only afterwards consult her Council of Regency. Catherine had apportioned to herself the lion's share. But she remained more of a fox than a lion and it was not in her nature only to be a lion. In those last days of 1560 Catherine de Medici's reign began. On examination of the documents and the events in detail, it is clear that a real coup d'Etat had successfully taken place, without either violence or scandal. Was it not merely a case, as she herself said, of a mother refusing to abandon herself to despair, submitting to the Divine will, helping and serving the King, her second son, to the best of her feeble ability, having decided to keep him beside her and to govern the State like an affectionate mother?[1] Affectionate mother, her children's governess, Governess of France.

---

[1] According to the letter of Luigi Gonzaga to his brother, the Duke of Mantua, from Orléans, December 12, 1560, Gonzaga Archives, p.p. Lucien Romier, in *Catholiques et Huguenots à la Cour de Charles IX*, pp. 3–4.

CHAPTER TWO

IMPOTENT WISDOM
(December 1560—July 1562)

❧❀❀❧

Calvin's letter to Sturm of December 16, 1560, referring to the death of François II, reveals that the Protestant religious leaders were utterly opposed to accepting a policy of conciliation. 'God, who struck the father in the eye, has struck the son in the ear.' That was why their contemporaries believed the Protestants to have been responsible for the deaths, one after the other, of Henri II and François II. In fact, there had been no deliberate clumsiness on the part of Montgomery; whatever views Catherine may have continued to hold about it, it was a stupid accident. As for the poison supposedly poured into the ear of François II, that was a ridiculous fairy-tale. His was a case of mastoiditis.

Europe already knew that Catherine had assumed power. In this connection the Venetian ambassadors are particularly worth consulting, both their reports to the Most Serene Republic and their despatches. On December 8th, Giovanni Michele wrote: 'In the Government the Queen Mother is regarded as the person whose will is supreme in everything; it is she who will have the leading hand in negotiation, so much so that authority will only be exercised by Her Majesty and there will be no other head of the Council than herself; it is hoped thus to avoid all rivalries. The offices have been divided among the secretaries in such a manner that one will take charge of Italian affairs, another of Spain, and another of those concerning Flanders. Each will have his separate function, so that in this way matters will be settled much more quickly and without confusion and no reports on the negotiations will have to be made to either the Cardinal de Lorraine or the Constable, as in the past. They will go straight to the Queen, and if she requires the Council to meet she will summon it on her own authority and give the answer.

K

Thus Catherine had arranged to manage foreign affairs, by which she was no less preoccupied than by affairs of the interior. As she wrote to her daughter Elisabeth, she wanted to preserve her authority, not for herself, but to keep the kingdom together: 'God has left me with three little children and a divided kingdom, without one single person on whom I can wholly rely, without some particular passion of his own.'

She expressed the same view to Guillaume de Saulx, the son of Gaspard de Tavannes, Lieutenant-General of Burgundy, of which at that moment he was temporarily in charge: 'Thanks to Our Lord, this kingdom has not been left without legitimate and real successors, of whom I am the mother, who for the good of it will take in hand the duty of supervising the necessary administration of it.' And she said in person to Sébastien de L'Aubespine, that her aim was 'gradually to restore everything in this kingdom that might have been spoiled by the malice of the times'. She had seen too closely, felt too deeply and understood too clearly the damage done both to France and to the monarchy by Henri II's surrender to the parties who fought one another for control of the State. The essential task was to put the State beyond the reach of faction, never to become the tool of coteries of any kind, but to form a third party, that of the French people as a whole, both Catholics and Protestants, who wanted to live in peace. Nor must she ever allow this third party to become feudalized or herself its instrument, for Catherine feared to become dominated by it. She could not foresee the historical law whereby the final victory has always, in France, gone to such a third party—Henri IV, the young Louis XIV, Bonaparte when Consul, Louis XVIII granting the Charter. Her plan was to work through intermediaries, the King remaining the supreme arbiter by birthright according to the Capet tradition, which Catherine had studied and knew well, having during twenty-five years had the leisure to reflect on it. She was as much a student of books and documents as a woman of action.

When she became Governess of France her policy and method were experimental and she was only responsible for their failure in so far as she too greatly underestimated the intellectual and emotional forces which, whatever she believed about them, and whatever may in the event have been said about them, predominated in the Wars of Religion. It was a conflict in which politics were superimposed on the theology of the scholars and the fanaticism of the Protestant or Catholic leaders, around whom all the most violent partisans collected. At that time, when politics and religion were so closely entwined, it was a weakness to be purely political. On the other hand, apart from her Chancellor and, at the beginning, the Admiral, nobody was willing to support the Queen's efforts. Even Coligny's support was precarious because held in reserve; that cunning man was keeping on good terms with the Calvinist ministers, nearly all of whom were extreme fanatics. As the Cardinal de Lorraine was shortly to place himself under the orders of Spain, Coligny would, in return, ally himself with England. When the Admiral no longer supported the policy of compromise, Catherine was left alone in her impotent wisdom to control the excited parties. During a whole year and a half Catherine was able to apply the brake. But the brake was too weak and the destructive surge became stronger and stronger. It nevertheless slowed down the rush into the abyss; the Governess of France would never agree to removing it. After a whole quarter of a century of struggle that only involved two frantic minorities, France, finally deeply wounded, was to bring Catherine belated help by adhering to her policy at the time of the War of the Three Henri's. And Henri IV was faced with ten years of fighting in order to accomplish the result that Catherine, for lack of adhesion to her policy on the part of France as a whole, had been impotent to impose on the country, but which she had endeavoured to bring about from the moment she came to power, namely civil peace through religious peace, based on Royal arbitration.

Because she was a foreigner the mystique attached to the Blood of France, which was so helpful to the Béarnais, did not support the Florentine Queen, struggling with the same task for the public welfare. If one were to misjudge the importance of these imponderable factors one would be unable to understand both her greatness and her failure, for it was these factors that prevented the Governess of France from sparing the country she served so devotedly those eight religious wars. A religious war is a civil war. 'A monstrous war!' as Montaigne cried in the third volume of his *Essays*. Who knew this better than Catherine? Yet she always refused to accept the evil as incurable, never let herself be discouraged from offering a means to put an end to it. Henri IV was to use these same means, benefiting no doubt from the weariness of the people and the exhaustion of the combatants, but even more from this mystique of the Blood of France, the support of which the Lorraines lacked as well as the Florentine.

Antoine and Louis de Bourbon, who could rightfully claim it, merely wasted this treasure through their incurable frivolity allied to their rash adventurousness, thus increasing the fury of the factions.

The Queen, as the King's mother, slept in little Charles IX's room, or in a communicating room. Generally an early riser, she began work as soon as she was dressed. A good housekeeper, she assigned the tasks of each of her servants; a watchful mistress, she saw to it that her orders were strictly obeyed. She appointed the Hellenist Jacques Amyot Grand Almoner, and Gondi, Master of the Royal Wardrobe. This man, Giovanni-Battista de Gondi was an old servant, nearly sixty. She sent for him to come to France when she married, and appointed him her major-domo. He became a naturalized Frenchman and the complete type of the faithful Italian, in whom Catherine confided. Distrusting with good reason the Cardinal de Lorraine's honesty, she withdrew the finances from him and handed them over to Michel de L'Hospital, of whom she was sure. The Duke de Guise remained Commander-in-Chief of the land armies under the nominal authority of the King of Navarre, and Gaspard de Coligny head of the navy. All his titles were returned to the Constable, but in fact the commands were already filled. In order that he should not feel discontented Catherine played on his avarice and sent him more than 90,000 gold écus. In dealing with this enormous sum the Constable would be kept too busy to interfere with the Chancellor, and Catherine would be able to rely on her two cronies, one of whom owed it to her to have re-built his fortune, and the other to be the first power in the State after the king, which in fact meant herself.

So now the Lorraines were held and the Bourbons balanced. The Châtillons figured in the Privy Council in the person of the Cardinal Odet. In the Secret Council the Queen eliminated the Guises and replaced them by the Constable, together with the King of Navarre. To govern, she needed around her only people whom she could control. To the others she gave honours, dignities, appointments, but not the reality of power. That belonged to her alone.

L'Hospital had pointed out to her all the advantages that could be drawn from the States-General. In spite of Tournon's opposition they decided to call them together immediately, at Orléans itself, on December 13th. The news of the elections was good; as usual the peasants voted well, that is, for the official candidates; the Protestants did not make too much trouble and their hostility to the delegates of the clergy was not disquieting; the nobility and the bourgeoisie themselves felt nothing but mistrust for the first faith in the kingdom, which was genuinely discredited by its abuses, and of which the growing ultramontanism offended Gallican tradition. Also, the majority of the representatives of the nobility and the bourgeoisie were anti-Guises. The whole Tiers, formed of deputies elected by the peasants, was for the Government. Nevertheless Protestant and Bourbon influences hostile to the Florentine were to be feared, and the preachers were demanding fresh elections on the pretext that there was a new king. There, too, Catherine made use of legislative tradition—the King of France does not die. L'Hospital succeeded in having the campaign for new elections dismissed by those who had been elected. The revolutionary tendencies of the extreme Calvinist elements shocked the country in general, even those who were favourable to the Reformation, and it was satisfied with the steps taken by Catherine to legalize the measures proclaimed in the edicts of compassion. The average Frenchman, as one would say to-day, longing above all for tanquillity, was only too pleased to follow a government that was anxious to arrange matters. He was becoming more and more dissatisfied with everything, because nothing was getting any better. After having placed his hopes in the Guises, he was now hoping in L'Hospital.

It was known that immediately François II was dead the Queen Mother had ordered Condé's trial to be suspended. The imminent death sentence had not been passed. On the contrary, Catherine restored his freedom to the Prince. If Condé preferred to remain in prison this was by his own choice, for the sake of his honour, which did not allow him to accept his release 'without knowing who was his party, and by whose order he had been made prisoner'. He had agreed to nominal imprisonment in Picardy, at La Fère, which belonged to the King of Navarre. Catherine had seized the opportunity offered to her by Condé's point of honour and was provisionally freed of him. The absence from the States-General of the head of the Protestant civil war faction was a trump which the Queen Mother was careful not to lose. She promised Condé a public exoneration, asking him merely to wait a little longer in order that it should have a greater effect.

Catherine knew that without the Tiers she could do nothing. She pandered to the vanity of the bourgeois members by ordering that they should remain covered and seated, like the nobility and the ecclesiastics. At the official opening session, on Friday December 13th, (was this choice of date dictated by superstition?) in the wooden building that had been erected in the Place de l'Estape, the Chancellor explained in detail the political plans of the Royal Government. L'Hospital, as the spokesman of the Queen Mother, expressed himself in legislative terms. He praised the States-General as an institution of the kingdom.

Like Louis XI, Catherine de Medici was as willingly accessible to her people as she was jealous of her authority. Those who met her found that their prejudice against this Italian Queen disappeared. This was the reason for her constant changes of residence, yet in spite of her keenness to be always in touch, she could not go everywhere, and so was only able to overcome this prejudice in a small number of cases. As we accompany her, live with her, we can see how completely she had absorbed the best of the Capet tradition. That is why the memoirs of the period refer so often in familiar terms to our good mother Catherine, our good Queen Mother, who loved her kingdom, had a noble, generous, and magnanimous character, knowing neither avarice nor a spirit of revenge, as was said by Jules Gassot.

In relying on the support of the Tiers, L'Hospital was carrying out Catherine's wishes. To the deputies of the States-General he praised the familiar ways of kings, which had never harmed them, for there was nothing so pleasing and satisfying to the people as being able to draw close to their ruler. Yet in spite of these amiable words he did not hesitate to criticize the Tiers, along with the two privileged orders; the people were envious, although no door leading to high honours was closed to them and they could attain to the highest posts both in the judiciary and the church and by feats of arms to nobility and other honours; apart from this, to labour was the finest activity of all, and trade created great wealth, which brought men both honour and respect. As for the nobility, let them all, including kings and princes, remember that they were the descendants of serfs, who should all the more become humane and kind, the more power they acquired, but neither hard nor proud. The clergy's cupidity had brought it into disrepute. Discord had been created by the vices of the citizens; religion had become a pretext for civil war, in contradiction to the Gospels, which bade men live together in peace and friendship. Let us therefore remember the maxim of our forefathers: One Faith, One Law, One King. (*Une foi, une loi, un roi*). Let us not make rash innovations.

This might have been written by Montaigne, who at that time had not yet published anything, but as Councillor to the Bordeaux

Parliament stood very well at Court. In February 1558, as a lawyer, he had been included in the royal suite on the occasion of the marriage of Madame Claude de France to Charles III of Lorraine. Now he was getting ready to pay his respects to the little King Charles IX at Saint-Germain-en-Laye. Montaigne was well equipped to understand Catherine and she to understand him. The legislator from Auvergne, the parliamentarian from Périgord, and the reader of Machiavelli spoke the same wise language, and for all three of them facts counted for more than frenzied mysticism. 'Let us', urged the Chancellor, 'substitute for all those diabolical words—faction, sedition, Lutherans, Huguenots, Papists—the beautiful name, Christians.' Christians. The King of France was not Catholic, like the King of Spain; Apostolical, like the King of Hungary; Caesarian, like the Emperor. He was the Very Christian King. The legislator knew his authorities and his traditions, and he also knew his own duty. He was the King's man, and therefore the servant of the Royal arbitrator, the defender of the Third Party. And could this party be formed any better elsewhere than in the Tiers Etat, of which the legislators formed the cadres? The Tiers was the King's side, because the Tiers stood for France as a whole. L'Hospital's address already summed up the programme of the politicals, a programme as old as the defence of the State against the troubles of civil war; that of Charles V and his Marmousets, of Charles VII and his Councillors, of Louis XI and his Compères, a policy that was Royal and Gallican, French and Christian.

This Royal and Christian policy was not in contradiction to Machiavelli. All three were founded on the same realistic attitude to experience. It is too often forgotten that Catherine's favourite author wrote Chapter XI of *The Prince*, entitled *Of ecclesiastical principalities*, in which he said that for princes there was neither happiness nor security except in such States as were 'governed by super-human means, to which our feeble reason cannot attain'. It was this realism that Christian and French policy had in common with Machiavelli's, both of them based on agreement between experience and theory. To a Michel de L'Hospital it came naturally. There was in his case no modern liberalism. Neither was there any implacable realism in the manner of Frederick II of Prussia and his successors, to whom reasons of State were a principle and not an exception. The Capetian realism was very pliable and ready to bow to human nature. In endeavouring to understand Catherine these nuances must never be forgotten, for she was enamoured of the Capetian tradition, which blended with Florentine flexibility.

'The King has not received his crown from ourselves, but from God and the ancient law of the kingdom.' There was neither democracy nor liberalism in Catherine de Medici's mouthpiece; he stood for the union between King and people, the King being essentially the representative of the people, the States expressing what was incidental to this relationship, in the scholastic sense of the term. Here the Chancellor was replying to the Pope of Geneva, who had already professed in *The Christian Institution* that the States-General was the sole legitimate power that might oppose the King. Calvin was a Royalist, but a Royalist to whom the nation was if not the trustee, at any rate the guardian of authority. L'Hospital the legislator was still more of a Royalist than Calvin the theologian, and this was natural. The King being too young to rule had handed over power to his mother, according to the Capetian tradition.

Collaboration, always. Substitution, never. The legislator was for the Queen Mother. The sovereign King, the immortal King, had delegated his powers to her. The States had not to discuss the matter. The Governess of France was truly the King, and the King was France, the soul of France, of which the three estates were the body. This was the essence of French Royalty.

This is also the true sense of the famous harangue of December 13, 1560, when stripped of the false interpretations of the nineteenth century. Tolerance in fact, whilst awaiting tolerance by right. The King is sole judge of the one as of the other. And this tolerance, in which there was nothing theoretical, is, properly called, compassion.

It was, in consequence, no more permissible for the subject to rebel against his prince on religious grounds than for a son to do so against his father, although, as it was no longer possible to deny the general danger as the result of the religious quarrels, and civil war was threatening, a national council was necessary in order to bring the dissidents back into the fold and re-establish the unity of faith in the interests of general peace. Kindness would do this more effectually than severity and thus, according to the Royal will, the Chancellor combined justice and charity.

The clergy cared little for this call to compassion and demanded the extirpation of heresy. The nobility and the Tiers, on the contrary, approved of this tolerance. They were hostile to the Guises and thus benevolently inclined towards the Huguenots. As Catherine de Medici wished, they declared themselves incompetent to decide the question of the Regency and accepted it as a fact. They were frightened by the admitted deficit of forty million livres. They took this as a pretext to demand that the session be suspended in order that they might report back on it to their constituents. According to the rules, the Government's financial difficulties permitted political demands to be made, such as control of the finances and legislative action, which Catherine was anxious to avoid, knowing only too well what disorders would follow parliamentary government by the States-General in the circumstances that prevailed. The orator of the Tiers, Jean de Lange, a Bordeaux lawyer, upheld the traditional principle of the union of the King and the people, founded on the mysticism of the Sacrament and the Blood of France; it was not he who caused Catherine any anxiety. The fanaticism of Jean Quintin, orator for the clergy, who described the Reformationists as criminals who should be excommunicated, rightly seemed to her very dangerous. The demands of the orator for the nobility, Jacques de Silly, Lord of Rochefort, regarding the confirmation of their privileges, had a feudal sound which was not at all reassuring. The majority of the nobles sympathized with the Protestants and Quintin was obliged to apologise, as Coligny considered himself offended by his speech.

On the question of the subsidies that should be granted to the Government, the Government itself decided that the deputies should return to their provinces in order to ask their constituents for precise powers. L'Hospital again urged them to peace. On January 31, 1561, the States broke up. It had been decided that new elections should be held in order to return thirty-nine deputies to Melun on May 1st, who would exclusively examine financial affairs. But in spite of this restiction, what Catherine feared came to pass. The nobility raised the question of the Regency, the Tiers decided that the Guises should be excluded from the Council. The Lorraine Princes, the Marshal de Saint-André and the Duchess de Valentinois would have to render strict accounts. Catherine decreed new assemblies on May 25th, for a meeting of the States at Pontoise on August 1st. She manoeuvred as well as she was able between the parties that were becoming worked up by election fever, which was even arousing the emotions of the masses. She endeavoured to gain time and to distract public attention by the celebrations of the Sacrament on May 15th. Navarre was confirmed in his post as Lieutenant-General of the kingdom, Condé was solemnly rehabilitated, the Protestants were free to practise their religion, which scandalized the zealots of the Catholic party. The Duke de Guise, supported by Don Juan Manrique de Lara, the Ambassador-Extraordinary of Philip II, who had been charged with making Catherine, whom they regarded as almost an heretic, see reason, and by the Nuncio, Sébastian Gualterio, did not hesitate to make a very emphatic scene with the Queen Mother. The Lorraines, whose possessions were threatened by plans for confiscation and restitution, pointed out to the Constable that he would in his turn become the victim of such an inquiry; and the same held good for the Marshal de Saint-André. The latter did not hesitate to write to Philip II, on January 31st, offering him his services and requesting him to honour him with some command.

Philip II took advantage of this offer by threatening the Queen Mother with armed intervention. Such intervention was a permanent anxiety to Catherine, for the Catholic King renewed the threat of it whenever he judged it expedient to do so. This continued throughout the reign of the Florentine Queen and it has been proved that her Spanish son-in-law was her most perfidious and persistent enemy. Had it not been for this enmity the Queen Mother's policy at home would have been far freer. The official intervention of Spain in France's internal affairs dates from that mission of Don Manrique de Lara in January 1561. Philip II, dominated by the principle of sovereignty, which he arbitrarily identified with the spirit of Christianity, was the true representative of the Caesaro-Papism of the Emperors of the Middle Ages, and considered himself responsible for watching over the King of France. He had personally recommended Monsieur de Guise le Grand to Catherine, and had promised the former his support. That was why Saint-André was asking for the same favour. It is easy to imagine the fury of Antoine de Bourbon, which Philip was pleased to exacerbate, by refusing him the title of King of Navarre.

Catherine defended herself by appointing Coligny to the Council, and thus introducing the head of the moderate Protestants into the Government. The fear that his property might be confiscated forbade the Constable to break with the Lorraines and even assured them of his benevolent neutrality. Faced with the Spanish threat, backed up by the reprimands of the Holy See, the Queen Mother favoured the Protestants more and more. She authorized Coligny and Condé, as well as their families, to practise the new religion in the apartments reserved to them at Court. The King's licence was granted to the printers of the Psalms in the Huguenot version.

Letters patent of February 22, 1561, ordered the suspension of all prosecutions on religious grounds until the National Council. The edict of April 19th, confirmed the repression of seditious plots, but on the other hand ordered that religious prisoners should be freed. Catherine replied to Pius IV's complaints with a categorical refusal to take violent action. On February 20th, she wrote to Elizabeth of England that her friendship and alliance were one of the things that she wanted most in this world. She was disquieted by the Catholic resistance to her conciliatory measures and very hostile to the Lorraine Princes, for she could not forget how they had treated her during the reign of François II.

One evening the Duke de Guise reproached the Queen for drinking at two fountains, summoning her to choose between Rome and Geneva, assuring her 'that if he were permitted to use force he would undertake to re-establish religion in very little time, as he was quite ready to sacrifice his life for this purpose'.

That was his tone. Catherine pleaded her cause to the victor of Calais, whose insolence redoubled as he told her that she had only been given power in order to defend Catholicism, otherwise the rights of the Princes of the Blood to exercise it were superior to hers. The rapprochement which had taken place between the Constable on the one hand and Monsieur de Guise le Grand and Jacques d'Albon de Saint-André on the other had given the Catholics resistance leaders who were convinced that they no longer had to fear or to consider anyone. This rapprochement was known as the Triumvirate and was sealed when the three men went together to Easter Communion at the Holy Table. The Triumvirate knew that it had the support of the Parliament and Catholics of Paris, who had been alarmed by the Huguenot provocations during Lent. These provocations had also been supported by Calvinist excesses in Guyenne, Agénois, Languedoc, Provence and the Dauphiné. The national Protestant synod at Poitiers on March 10th had given the Reformationists a consciousness of their power. But in return there were very heavy Catholic reprisals wherever the Protestants were the fewer. Brawls and acts of vandalism were on the increase. Soon there were killings on both sides.

Although desolate, Madame Catherine obstinately refused the indiscreetly offered help of her Spanish son-in-law and in order to proclaim her independence favoured the Bourbons. The reconciliation of the Guises and the Montmorencys revived the feudal danger under the pretext of religion. In the eyes of the Queen Mother the Princes of the Blood, in spite of their Protestantism, were the lesser evil, for since the downfall of the Constable de Bourbon the appanagists could more easily be controlled by the Crown than any of the other feudalists. Owing to the force of circumstances, and in spite of Amboise and the fanaticism of their preachers and leaders, the Protestants were becoming increasingly royalist, although on condition that the good sense of their chiefs remained stronger than the religious passions of the masses.

On that evening of April 6, 1561, the insolence of François de Guise towards the woman whom he still regarded as the Florentine shopkeeper and Governess of France only by usurpation, convinced the Queen that the most pressing danger lay with the feudalist faction. Catherine was completely clear-sighted in the matter but her emotional suffering was due to her knowledge that she could count on help from no quarter whatsoever, and that she stood completely alone, for her Chancellor was merely a high official and his weakness was due to the weakness of the State itself.

If the Pope and Philip II were intervening in the affairs of France Calvin was no more reluctant to do so. In December 1560 he had sent a memorandum to the King of Navarre in favour of the abrogation of the edict of Romorantin, which he considered was too restrictive of the edict of Amboise, which he wanted revived.

To this the Queen Mother had reacted by confirming the edict of Romorantin, whilst at the same time the freeing of the religious prisoners left no doubt of her desire for pacification. The intervention of certain ministers, sent from Geneva, was officially disavowed by the Senate of that city, to which the French Government had protested. Calvin's correspondents had to admit that the policy of repression had been abandoned everywhere. As was to be expected, this forbearance was regarded as a sign of weakness by the fanatics in both camps. When the Cardinal de Lorraine left Orleans, demonstrators had mocked him, crying that the mass had been kicked out.

Catherine, nevertheless, still upheld the distinction between politics and religion. By the edict of Fontainebleau on April 19, 1561, the repression of illegal assemblies was placed within the jurisdiction of lay judges. The Protestants were restless; the Royal arbitrator balanced the scales. Processions had caused trouble and were therefore restricted in number. The faithful then complained that they were being persecuted by the Queen, who had gone over to Calvinism. Ridiculous rumours were spread, alleging the conversion of the little King. Catherine very soon realized that the Guises were spreading such false rumours on behalf of Madrid and Rome. The King of Navarre on the contrary—and Chantonnay informed Philip II of it—had yielded to her and claimed to be no longer a Protestant. In dealing with the history of the Wars of Religion it is always forgotten that, whilst Condé publicly went over to the Reformation, the First Prince of the Blood was never more than a sympathizer, which was the very reason why the Queen Mother held him so much in esteem. He was the living symbol of the policy of peace between the two religions, but, alas, a more than fragile symbol. Catherine wanted peace; Antoine submitted to it, according to the way the wind blew, now on the side of Rome, now on that of Geneva. He was no support to her.

It can never be said too often that Catherine de Medici stood alone, sovereign of a State respected by none because none feared it. This lack of strength left the field wide open to the extremists, to the partisans of Guise and Condé. There were fewer and fewer oases of peace; wisdom was exceptional and becoming more and more powerless. Catherine had wanted to wait and see. But what was coming closer and closer was factionalism, more and more recalcitrant to her peacemaking efforts. The Huguenot proselytisations were becoming agressive and arousing a reaction among the Catholic masses; the troubles they engendered became greater day by day. Already in November 1560 the synod of Clairac, near Marmande, had begun the preparation of the Calvinist organization for the Religious Wars. The Triumvirate was a first outline of the attempts that would be made in 1562, to form Catholic leagues, to counter the Protestant formations, modelled on the lines proposed by the Guyenne conference. Both sides suspected Catherine de Medici of bad faith because she persisted in a policy of arbitration which she had not the power to impose on them. In a very penetrating phrase Augustin Thierry described Henri IV as a Michel de L'Hospital who bore arms. Without the sword in hand justice is a sham. It was the weapon that the Queen Mother was always to lack. When the Wars of Religion broke out the French State had no other arms than a broken blade.

Catherine was a Henri IV without arms. This was so true that the Royalists did not unite until after Coutras, the efforts of the Politicals along the same lines having failed, like those of the Queen Mother. The peacemaker with no power at his disposal is an arbitrator who commands no respect. The State had lost its power under Henri II, when that prince delivered it over to the parties and to Spain. Thus the State was unable to make any successful resistance to the growing power of Protestantism. The League was as much a logical consequence of this as the rebellion of the Huguenots. In order to survive, Madame Catherine's wisdom was to be reduced to perpetual negotiations. Her crowning genius was that she was able to do so and succeeded, in spite of all, in preventing foreign armed intervention from occurring as well as civil war. It was not until 1590, more than a year after the death of the Queen, followed, eight months later, by the assassination of Henri III, that Philip II was able to proclaim himself Protector of the Kingdom of France. Not until February 12, 1591, did the Spaniards and the Neapolitans enter Paris to garrison it. In Catherine de Medici, Governess of France, history must impartially pay homage to the Queen who, by never despairing of her country, postponed for thirty years this shame, which threw the kingdom back into a condition similar to the worst years of Charles VI and the regency of the Duke of Bedford. Impotent to avert civil war, Catherine's wisdom did prevent a foreign war, from which she saved France by never giving Elizabeth I and Philip II an official pretext for open intervention.

The Florentine put into practice Machiavelli's precept: 'The Prince who encourages the rise of another power ruins his own.' Her correspondence exists to prove that her most constant effort was to keep Philip II and Elizabeth I out of France whilst the French, at war with one another, did not cease, according to their eternal habit, to invoke their aid. She cossetted the Englishwoman and the Spaniard. But to explain away this attitude on her part as due to her matrimonial wishes—her sons married in England and her daughter Margot in Spain—is to deny the documentary evidence. In Madame Catherine the mother was inseparable from the Governess of France.

Henri III's sharp mind made no mistake about this. Let us re-read the letter, so very authentic, of the son who was dearest to her and, in spite of his weaknesses and vices the most worthy of her, the one who really understood her. This letter was written after the death of Catherine de Medici to Jean de Vivonne de Saint-Gouard, Marquis de Pisani, who had been her ambassador at Rome: 'The mourning and regret that I suffer by being deprived of (the benefit of) her presence can be compared only to the resentment which naturally follows upon the loss of persons of equal degree, who may rightly be described by the title, Mother of the King and Mother of the Kingdom.' In the Queen's funeral oration, given on February 4, 1589,

Messire Regnault de Beaune, Patriarch of Aquitaine and Archbishop of Bourges, described her not only in the noble phrases usual on such solemn occasions, but in the right terms which posterity, heir to the internal conflicts, has always refused to grant her.

How well he understood Catherine de Medici! Let us inscribe on the threshold of this French reign of an Italian Princess the words of that Bossuet of the sixteenth century, which were placed on her catafalque and which are the very truth of history: 'She was ever ready to offer both her person and her means and all her understanding in order to settle and pacify matters, and undertook several long journeys throughout this Kingdom, at the peril of her life. Even in the great troubles that have lately occurred in this Kingdom, she devoted herself to doing so, in such wise that it was by no fault of hers that all these matters did not have a good outcome.'

A new Penelope, constantly re-weaving her material, which the French undid as soon as she re-wove it, she fully deserved the preacher's praise: 'Her patience was greater than Sarah's, for her life was one long exercise in patience.' By this exercise of patience Catherine de Medici saved the heart of the citadel. Her wisdom was impotent, but by managing to survive in the midst of catastrophe, she safeguarded what was essential. In order to do this she nearly always had to use cunning. She did not prefer cunning to force, for she had a natural taste for grandeur, yet she nevertheless submitted too willingly to the use of cunning. Alone against all, she thought to find in doing so an easier victory. But she was unable to escape her destiny, which was to burn without flame, like the quicklime in her armorial bearings.

The mutual reprisals between Catholics and Huguenots were multiplying, creating in the whole of France a genuine atmosphere of civil war. The most serious was referred to in a despatch from Suriano, dated May 16, 1561—Catholic preachers were beginning to state that in the case of the sovereign's apostasy the oath of allegiance would cease to be valid. This was to be the leading theme of the drama of the League as we see it developing, fourteen months after Amboise. Meanwhile Calvin was endeavouring to curb the fury of the Reformationist mobs, as his letters prove. In contrast to Knox in Scotland, ranged against Mary Stuart, Calvin gave the French Protestants only wise advice. 'Let us', he told them, 'possess ourselves in patience.' Violence could do nothing but harm to the Religion's progress, by provoking reactions which would have greater numbers on their side.

Catherine de Medici understood that in both camps only the leaders were capable of exerting a restraining influence. The most urgent task, therefore, was to win them back. Without them religion, politics, the country's finances, would fall into the hands of the furious factions. Catherine was convinced that the religious as well as the financial crisis could be settled by political methods. In her eyes religion still appeared as a matter of politics. In that, as we have said, she was mistaken. Everything to do with faith (belief in a revealed religion or ideological mysticism) escapes political calculations. Force alone can clinch the arguments engendered by fanaticism. But the Queen Mother disposed of insufficient forces, due, as one is constantly obliged to realize, to the bankrupt condition in which Henri II had left the State. Catherine's dominating idea was a National Council, to include the Protestants, whom the Fathers of the Council of Trent had refused to admit. She showered attentions on Pius IV whom she knew to be mistrustful and hostile towards her. Above all she was worried by the rapprochement between the Triumvirate and Spain. She noted the growing popularity in Paris of François de Guise. This double danger, the Spanish and the feudal, caused her constant anxiety. The best method of countering it seemed to her to be the disassociation of politics from religion; on the one hand there was to be a political assembly and on the other a religious one, successively, not simultaneously. A restricted political assembly, which was to take place before the meeting of the new States-General on August 1st; and a similar religious assembly, before the end of the Council of Trent.

The Queen Mother arranged matters so that as the result of the national synod at Poitiers the Protestants sent representatives who, on June 9th, presented a petition to Charles IX, asking for permission to build their own temples. The Reformationist profession of faith was presented at the same time, but separately. The distinction between politics (the right to build was an administrative matter) and religion was officially accepted by the envoys, elected in the name of all the churches in the kingdom. Calvin's will to peace had prevailed. Catherine could assume that her Huguenot subjects were loyal. In spite of the triple opposition of Rome, Madrid and the Sorbonne, the National Council was summoned three days later, for July 20th. The *fait accompli* would compel the Triumvirate to give way; they could not do otherwise than accept a discussion of policy relating to a plan for building cultural edifices. As for the bishops, they were obliged to obey an order to meet, according to custom.

The political assembly and the religious assembly appeared to be practical possibilities.

The foxiness of this was wonderful. The success of this plan was due to the loyalty of the Huguenots. Enemy of Catherine though he was, Calvin was too politically-minded to neglect the advantage his collaboration with her would bring. The Queen Mother's letter of April 22, 1561, to Bernadin Bochetel, Bishop of Rennes, her ambassador at Vienna, does not allow us to doubt her will—in her own words—'to decide matters regarding the reformation of the churches of this kingdom in order to provide for the complete pacification of the troubles and the uniting of this people in one sole religion, for to think that they could be kept in obedience and concord whilst their minds are so disturbed and preoccupied with such diverse opinions and doctrines no one in this world would consider to be possible, and I feel too deeply the harm and danger resulting from it to leave this situation any longer without remedy or provision'.

Those were the words and the thoughts of the Queen Mother, magnificently French and humanitarian. Her intention was to confront the inimical divines with one another on the theological plane after having first settled the political question. Reasonable individuals, too few in number, approved of it. Madame Catherine naturally inclined to benevolence, considered that gentle methods were far better than violence; and these were also in accordance with wisdom and the interest of the country. But the Parliament of Paris resisted and even suspended publication of the edict of April 19th. The fanaticism of the parliaments was no whit less than that of the synods. The parliamentary prejudice against the coexistence of two religions in one and the same State was so strong that La Boétie even caused Montaigne to share it. After the edict of January 1562 he was to propose that Parliament and not the King should be the arbitrator on the reform of clerical abuses and the reconciliation of the parties. This was a misunderstanding of the fact that the conflict went much deeper than the mere reform of such abuses and was a matter of faith itself. Catherine understood this. Coexistence was the only possible reasonable solution to the conflict. In order to subdue the parliamentarians, on June 18th, she went to the Paris Palace of Justice, accompanied by her son and the Privy Council, 'in order to consider the matter of religious differences as far as they concerned the State'. L'Hospital's harangue dwelt on the needs of those troubled times. It sufficed to follow 'the example of the captain of a ship, who hauls in sail and tacks here or there, according to the wind'.

L

The legislator denounced the ill-will of parliamentarians and officials of all ranks, whose important positions enabled them to bind their kings hand and foot. He emphasized the distinction between political facts and the value of religion.

The parliamentarians were obliged to hold an assembly, from June 23, to July 11, 1561, jointly with the Royal Council. Complete freedom of discussion was granted. The Triumvirate posed as the champions of the true faith. The Cardinal de Lorraine, though in moderate terms, demanded repression. His brother, François, was vehement and called for the sword. Coligny replied to him in the same tones. As the Protestant leader he stood against the Catholic leader, but affirmed his submission to the King of France. Antoine de Bourbon declared himself true to the Roman faith. Coligny demanded freedom of worship, both *de jure* and *de facto*. The Triumvirate recommended a return, purely and simply, to the edict of Ecouen. In the end they accepted a sentence of banishment instead of the death sentence in cases of heresy, the latter being reserved for attempts against the public peace. This proposal was voted for, but Catherine did not hesitate to have the official report on it burnt, and to forbid its duplication. She did not wish to be bound by a document that condemned her policy. In every instance when cunning became obvious trickery Catherine had recourse to Royal prerogative, to reasons of State. On July 12, 1561, she resorted to reasons of State against the Triumvirate, the parliamentarians, and to the people of Paris, who were rejoicing in the anti-Protestant vote. In her opposition to a policy of violence Catherine was unshakable.

Having taken this precaution she pretended to allow matters to take their course. Her play-acting at this point is indubitable. Given the frame of mind of the Catholics, she was unable to do otherwise. For there was one insurmountable obstacle—the anti-Protestantism of the constitutional bodies and of the majority of the people, especially in Paris. Catherine never forgot that Machiavelli had written that 'the animals whose forms the Prince must know how to adopt are the fox and the lion. The former defends himself badly against the wolf, and the latter easily falls into the traps set for him. The Prince will learn from the one to be skilful, and from the other to be strong. Those who despise the role of the fox have not learned their business'. She also remembered the advice that 'The Prince must sometimes dodge and duck, mingle caution with justice, and, as it is said, if the lion's skin does not suffice, sew the fox's skin on to it.'

Sixteenth-century realism readily admitted that 'a prudent prince neither can nor should keep his word unless the circumstances in which he gave it still exist, and he can do so without harming himself'. Machiavelli's view was founded on his experience of human dishonesty, men being 'always prepared to break their word; the Prince must therefore not make a point of being truer to his; and such lack of faith is always easily justified. I could prove this ten times over and show how many engagements and treaties have been broken by the faithlessness of princes, the most fortunate of whom is always the one who best knows how to put on the fox's coat. The point is to be able to play one's part well and to know how to pretend and dissimulate at the right moment'.

Chapter XVIII of *Il Principe* is the one that Catherine de Medici most often followed: *Should Princes remain faithful to their obligations.* Let us free ourselves from the artificial morality of the eighteenth century as well as from democratic hypocrisy and reflect on the manners and customs of Catherine's time and her political needs. The point, according to Machiavelli, was to uphold one's authority. The whole of France acclaimed François I when he violated the Treaty of Madrid. In his book, *De la sagesse*, Pierre Charron, an exemplary Christian and a friend of Montaigne's, approved of Machiavelli. By that very fact he justified Catherine. Politics are apart from morality but should obey it; no Christian would contest this. Nevertheless there are occasions when, confronted by abuses of power or by the bad faith of an opponent, to sacrifice one's policy to morality would be a form of stupidity that would ensure the triumph of the greater evil. In such a case it is the lesser evil to have recourse to reasons of State. The first aim of any policy, even though it were a Christian one, must be to ensure the safety of the Citadel. Its guiding principle must be that of the Roman Law of the XII Tables: *Salus populi suprema lex esto.* 'To do under cover what cannot be done openly', wrote Charron, 'to join caution and courage, to bring contrivance and intelligence to bear where nature and an open hand are insufficient; to be, as Pindar said, a lion in battle and a fox in council, a dove and a serpent, as is said in Holy Writ.'

Dove and serpent—no words apply more aptly to Madame Catherine. Her impotent wisdom sought the supreme good—peace; the triple peace, abroad, at home, and in religion. She was obliged to slip between fists that were clenched for warfare. Her mind was made up. The dove of the ark, bringing back the green olive branch, brought the promise of the rainbow. She was rejected by all. Why, then, should she forget that Moses had fashioned a serpent of brass to cure the children of God, bitten by the serpents of fire sent by Divine wrath? When she is considered as she should be, in her own period, her environment, and the prevailing circumstances, Catherine de Medici deserves praise for having been such a clever actress. The immorality of the means was justified by the morality of the end. Thus, Ferdinard the Catholic had earned the praise of Machiavelli: 'A prince who still reigns, but whom it does not suit me to name, never preaches anything but peace and good faith. But had he kept one and the other, he would more than once have lost his reputation and his States.'

Even Jean Bodin, enemy of Machiavelli though he declared himself, considered François I to have been right when he broke the truce he had sworn to Charles V. This theorist on monarchy, author of *La République*, was compelled to recognize that there exist situations in which the methods advised by Machiavelli are the only possible ones. Faced with growing anarchy Catherine had no choice in the matter. Like the Prince, she had to bear herself in such manner that 'on seeing and hearing *her*, one *thought her* to be full of sweetness, sincerity, humanity, honour, and particularly of religion'. This was a French and royal necessity, imposed by the public welfare and reasons of State. The Queen Mother could not do otherwise, and that was enough to justify her. Reasons of State were no theoretical matter to her, for she never indulged in theorizing, any more than Machiavelli did. She was empirical and practical, responding to the immediate necessity. The vote of the parliamentary assembly explains at one and the same time both the edict of July 30, 1561, and Catherine's personal intention to twist and in due course to abrogate the anti-Protestant clauses as soon as she was able.

Catherine remained firm in her policy of pacification. That part of the edict which was aimed against the Reformationists was merely so in appearance, an attempt to mislead the Triumvirate, the Catholic party, Rome and Madrid. The Protestants understood this at once. They took no notice of these sham interdictions. The Catholic masses were taken in by them. Having by this means gained a more or less tranquil respite, the Queen Mother was negotiating with the religious and lay Protestant leaders. Chantonnay was uneasy with regard to the proposed conference. On July 5th the Pope had sent a pastoral letter to the King, desiring that the universal council should be the sole competent authority. Coligny, in whom Catherine had complete confidence, was preparing the organization of the conference. Thus the reformed religion was being given official status. Catherine was clinging to the *fait accompli*, namely two religions, two faiths, under one law and one king. But the doctrine remained immutable—one faith—and preachers were given safe-conducts, like foreigners or accused persons.

Catherine was taking care that the representatives of the Reformation at the conference should be persons of distinction; she herself endorsed and corrected the list of names, including Théodore de Bèze, and Pierre Martyr, but not Calvin; the Pope of Geneva was both too dangerous and too obvious. Catherine cautiously removed his name and Coligny approved her action. Her masterstroke was to flatter the vanity of the Cardinal de Lorraine so that he should be favourably inclined towards an argument or controversy, in which his eloquence would wipe out that of the Calvinist theologians. All this was arranged by Madame Catherine and the Admiral. The latter was anticipating the victory of the new theologians. The Queen was hoping for an entente, for she could not take these theological quarrels tragically—which was her permanent mistake. The lesson of Luther before Leo X was a dead letter to her. Her dogmatic indifference was too strong for her. Her view was: let us all pray to God as we please. Catholic both by habit and predilection, she yet saw no reason why others should not go to the Protestant churches. She might well have said, before Montaigne: 'It is an unfortunate affliction to think oneself so strong as to convince oneself that no one else can think otherwise,' which was then an unusual attitude. Even an Etienne Pasquier, Gallican and political adversary of the Jesuits and enemy of the Leaguers though he was, said that the practice of two different religions in one and the same town was a form of debauchery or vice, and this was the view of a moderate legislator. Catherine and L'Hospital were too far in advance of their own time to understand its passions fully. They thought that the fever was a religious one, but of political origin, whereas in reality it was a political one due to religious origins. If that is not understood the whole basis of the Wars of Religion is falsified.

Whilst the assembly of the clergy was taking place at Poissy on July 30, 1561, in the neighbouring town of Pontoise the new reduced States were about to open. They were composed of thirteen noble deputies and thirteen from the Tiers. Their first session took place on August 1st. Whilst these twenty-six members, all of whom were opposed to female government, were discussing the regency, Cathetine had some emotional moments. Antoine de Bourbon behaved perfectly, however, and was entirely on the side of the Queen. They finally agreed on a motion honouring the Salic Law and on a scheme whereby the Governess of France and the Princes of the Blood would swear an oath of fidelity to the little King. They then discussed the delay in the promulgation of the grand ordinance of Orleans, subsequent to the States-General of December to January. As this was a matter of legislation and administration Catherine left it to the jurists. She encouraged reforms so long as her personal power was not in question. She broke the resistance of the Parliament by her personal intervention, closing her door to Gilles Le Maistre, the first president and persecutor of the Huguenots. The registration took place on September 12, 1561.

Catherine was in fact too politically-minded to take no interest in ordinances, which were the principal instruments of Capet legislation. In drawing up this ordinance of Orleans, the Chancellor and the King's Council had based themselves on the memorandum-books presented by the States. The list of the 150 articles of this ordinance which was drawn up by Georges Picot, when compared with the memoranda of remonstrances and/or complaints, proves that most of those articles were taken from the Tiers. The edict concerning the police and justice of 1563, also called the ordinace of Roussillon, thirty-nine articles, of which half were due to the initiative of the Government, and the ordinance of Moulins, of 1566, in eighty-six articles, completed that of Orleans, as well as a multitude of edicts concerning matters of detail, letters patent and circulars. Michel de L'Hospital had composed a noble motto for the new reign—*Pietate et justitia*. By re-establishing the canonical elections, by insisting on a respect for discipline on the part of the clergy, by enjoining religious teaching and the supervision of schools, the Chancellor had paid tribute to piety. Royal justice was professionalized by the abolition of venal appointments to judiciary offices, the definition of juridical provinces, the imposition of law graduates as judges, instead of churchmen or soldiers, to the benefit of centralized authority and the sovereign's arbitral powers.

We like to think that the sceptre supported by two columns, those expressive arms of the new regime, under the motto of piety and justice, symbolized the sceptre of the Very Christian King upheld by Catherine de Medici and the Chancellor L'Hospital; by the descendant of apothecaries whose destiny was that of the city of the Appenines, and by the son of the doctor to the Bourbons, both of them of plebeian blood, Auvergnat blood, and by that fact very close to the perennial interests of the humble French people. In reading those ordinances and edicts it becomes very easy to understand that Madame Catherine, Governess of France, despite the proud feudalists and encroaching appanagists, remained the good housekeeper, the good mother, who, together with the methodical and even timid clerk who was her servant, worked to build and repair France as she rebuilt and repaired her own farms in Auvergne, her castles and palaces in Paris, the Ile-de-France and Touraine, as she maintained her parks and hunting lands, cultivated her kitchen-gardens and orchards, like a shrewd property owner.

She may have been a Florentine shopkeeper, but she was much more of a French housewife, who was keeping the Royal household with scrupulous care—the House of France of which she was Governess. Machiavelli was her favourite political author, whilst the clerks and Michel de L'Hospital, the greatest of them all, were her administrative colleagues. Hers was the work of a good mother and a valiant Frenchwoman, which, alas, was constantly menaced by the resistance of all the privileged groups, the rage of the parties and sects, the indifference of a nation that has always been bored by the subject of public welfare, always will be bored by it and never takes any interest in it until it finds itself on the edge of or even at the bottom of the abyss. This is, alas, a sad lesson of French political history, and which in the course of time has become even more marked.

The nobility and bourgeoisie of Pontoise, the bishops of Poissy, all met together at Saint-Germain-en-Laye on August 27th. The *de facto* although not *de juro* regency was admitted and ratified. The deputy for Autun, Bretaigne, orator of the Tiers and a Calvinist, made a definitely anti-clerical speech demanding that church property should be used to make good the deficit. The nobility, for the greater part ruined, agreed. Catherine and L'Hospital knew what they were doing when they separated the clerical deputies from those of the nobility and the Tiers, who were placed together. This encouraged an understanding between the two lay orders against the religious order, the only one then rich enough to pay the State debts. The clergy resigned itself to the situation, and voted for a contribution to lighten these by the sum of sixteen million livres. But in matters of religion as such their resistance remained firm. The Queen Mother discharged only the lay deputies. She retained the clerics at Poissy for the conference, convinced that she would still succeed in her policy of reconciliation. She, as well as the Chancellor, had been deeply impressed by the example of the Germanies, where a *modus vivendi* between Catholics and Reformationists had gradually taken place. Their plan was not to give way at all on matters of dogma, but to give way, and very liberally, as regarded the forms of discipline and the ceremonies connected with the cult, and thus to constitute a third religious party corresponding to the third political party, the assembling of which would be speeded up by such reforms. That had been Catherine's intention, and her entourage of enlightened and liberal-minded clerics, such as Jean de Monluc and moderate legislators like L'Hospital, had given her the impression that it could be realized, all the more easily because this confirmed her own wishes.

The active complexity of the German character, its constant development under the Empire, enabled certain contacts to be made between Augsburg and Rome, however precarious they may have been; but the logical minds of the French prevented any similar contacts from being made between Rome and Geneva. Catherine's Italian pliancy was much closer to this German capacity for development, this German plasticity than to the hereditary French predilection for the rational and its deductive processes. Force of circumstance was able to impose both religious and political peace on the French, although always precariously and for short periods, but ideologically the Frenchman enjoys civil war. Once it has broken out, his love of pleasure soon reasserts itself and he longs for peace, but only, as soon as it is re-established, to relapse into his previous quarrelsome behaviour: the Edict of Nantes, then, again, the Protestant war; the Edict of Grace, after that the Fronde, which was only political . . . then the Camisards. The descendants of the Gauls do not enjoy a peaceful life. Even in our time very few Protestants are resigned to the fact that France has remained Catholic; very few Catholics do not consider Protestantism to be an affront to reason. This spirit of intolerance is inseparable from that rationalizing mania which is in essence a French one. Whilst in the ordinary way of life the Frenchman is conciliatory and easy-going, as soon as he discusses politics or religion he becomes fanatical.

Where there was only a deplorable and deep-seated urge, the subtle and sceptical Florentine could merely discover malice. She wrote to the Pope that it was possible to receive the Protestants into the Church on condition that certain concessions were made as regarded ritual. She was, for instance, in favour of utraquism. An

agreement such as the *compactum* of the Council of Basle, which at
the time of the Hussite quarrels had, under certain conditions,
permitted Communion of both kinds, seemed to her easy to arrange,
as also the holding of services in French. In order that they might
have accepted this, all the French bishops would have had to be like
Jean de Monluc, all the Cardinals like Odet de Châtillon, and all the
intellectuals like Montaigne. Calvin would have had to be a precursor
of Georges Callisen, himself a precursor of Leibniz, an Irenist who
accepted the fundamental community of the various Christian
confessions, existing side by side, fraternally, irrespective of their
differences in practice. But the Pope of Geneva was the exact
opposite of an Irenist. Able, no doubt, and politically subtle, but
rejecting any doctrinal compromise with horror. He had authorized
the conference from motives of policy, as it gave civil rights (*droit de
cité*) to the Reformationist theologians. Alvarotti wrote to the Duke
of Ferrara on August 29th, how furious François de Guise was about
this assembly of prelates, saying that it would be made into a '*couil-
lonnerie*'.[1] It is clear that the atmosphere was anything but Irenian.

And as religion was still the major preoccupation of the parties
confronting one another, Catherine had nearly everyone against her.
Even in the Empire the *interim* of Augsburg attempted by Charles
V, and which the Cardinal de Granvelle had endeavoured to defend
to Paul III, failed as the result of the advance of Lutherism, which it
had facilitated. Catherine thought herself cleverer than Charles V
and repeated the experiment. She had a religious policy but her
contemporaries, both Catholics and Protestants, with the exceptions
that we have mentioned, did not have one. When Catherine de
Medici argued from facts they argued from ideas, that intellectual
sore of France. The theological attitude of the Protestants pleased
Catherine in so far as they were agreeable to accepting the King as
arbitrator. The Catholic theologians, on the contrary, expressed
their views in the words of the Cardinal de Lorraine at the conference
of Poissy; the King is not the judge here, 'for in matters of faith the
Bishops judge the Emperors, and not the Emperors the Bishops'.

Here Catherine was closer to the Protestants than to the Catholics.
So long as the King remained the supreme arbiter in his kingdom
she was indifferent to the distinction between the two powers. Thus,
without meaning to do so or even suspecting it, although she was so
naturally anti-theocratic, she was advancing Gallicanism in the
direction taken by Henry VIII in England. And that was why she

[1] Tr. Note: this word is untranslatable into polite English.

wanted to establish a French church in the Rome of the Popes; a church which, when she founded it, this admirer of Blanche de Castille dedicated to Louis IX—Saint-Louis-des-Français.

At the beginning of Catherine's reign the threat of schism was obvious; none of the theologians had any misapprehensions about it; the conference was to the interests of the Reformationist doctors, but just as naturally it was to be expected that the Sorbonne and the Cardinal de Tournon would remain inflexibly hostile to it.

Although she was a relative of sovereign Popes, Catherine was so broadminded that in her eyes, and with her love of history, her religious policy was justified by the precedent created by Philippe le Bel: 'If', she said to Chantonnay, 'an assembly of prelates expressed in disputation divergent opinions, it would not be the first time that this had happened in France.' She overlooked the fact that the first time this had been the case, the disputations had been between Catholics, whilst this time the conference she had demanded brought face to face with one another theologians, of whom some were still Catholics and others were no longer so. Nor did she foresee that the Protestant doctors, basing themselves on the Royal arbitration, were confronted not by adversaries but by judges who had consented to listen to the heretics not in order to arrive at some agreement, but quite on the contrary, in order to confound and condemn them. Whilst Catherine thought that she herself and the Royal Family who were present at the refectory of the Dominican sisters at Poissy— where the conference opened on Tuesday, September 9, 1561— were there as arbiters, the Catholic doctors considered that in matters of faith such arbitration was null and void. It is undeniable that theology was on their side, for it is not, as Catherine imagined, capable as is philosophy of adjusting itself to freedom of thought. A Catholic in practice, and a most sincere one at that, the Queen Mother was not so as regarded doctrine. To her, faith and morals depended on Royal authority on the same grounds as politics, and she introduced a doctrinal freedom into the religious domain which was theologically indefensible. Without even realizing it she passed from freedom of conscience in fact, which force of circumstances finally did impose on the various Christian Churches, to freedom of conscience of right, which short of being ruined by it none of these Churches could accept. And that is why after four centuries, in spite of the progress of toleration, Oecumenism still remains unrealizable. The ambiguity between royal authority and religious authority was at the very heart of the discussions at Poissy. With the most laudable intentions, in order to preserve peace, Catherine intensified by this ambiguity the religious causes of the civil war.

Pierre de La Place, Michel de Castelnau, the *Histoire ecclésiastique*, and especially the *Diaire de l'Assemblée des Evêques*,[1] as well as the reports of Claude d'Espence, Rector of the University of Paris, allow us to follow this famous conference in detail and to understand why Castelnau was right, as against Catherine, when he remarked with good sense—and here his good sense was superior to all Florentine subtlety—that such a disputation was of necessity useless; something that Catherine had not foreseen. After the tourneys of sacerdotal eloquence, as vain as they were brilliant, between Théodore de Bèze and Charles de Lorraine, the conference increased the anxiety of the religious authorities, both Protestant and Catholic. Catherine, who was intellectually interested in everything, was extremely interested in these controversies. To her surprise, the theologians took them tragically. She saw the Cardinal de Lorraine, Bèze, Pierre Martyr, privately. She gave an amiable welcome to the Papal legate, the Cardinal Ippolyto of Ferrara, who arrived at Saint Germain on September 20, 1561, and took advantage of his quarrels with the French cardinals to draw him into her own game, leading him on to preside at a restricted and private conference of twelve ministers of the Religion and twelve Catholic theologians. It was useless. The Spanish intransigeance of the General of the Jesuits, Lainez, whom Cardinal Ippolyto had brought with him from Rome, finally poisoned the atmosphere. Lainez referred to the pastors as wolves, foxes and serpents. He reprimanded the Queen Mother with unlimited violence, accusing her of violating the law of the Church by these conversations between Catholics and those who had been excommunicated, reminding her that she had no enlightenment in matters of faith and was without any authority whatever in the matter. Catherine wept. But with her usual energy she made a quick recovery. She narrowed down the conference still further, this time to five theologians on either side, in order to discuss the Eucharist and Transubstantiation; they began their argument on the eve of Saint-Michael and continued it for a fortnight. Catherine herself saw to it that both sides maintained the necessary courtesies towards one another, but refrained from appearing in person in order not to give the impression that she was presiding at the debate.

[1] Documentation in *Le Colloque de Poissy* by Ruble. The *Diaire* was published for the first time by Mgr Joseph Roserot de Melin in Rome and Poissy, which entirely re-opens the question.

The conference of Poissy ended on October 14th. The theological cleavage between Catholics and Protestants was now all the deeper because their discussions had made the differences that separated them even clearer than heretofore. Both sides were confirmed in their intention to exterminate heresy, whether Roman or Genevan. Catherine de Medici was thinking of her policy of compassion; the theologians were only concerned with the true faith. She could not induce these men, to whom the theoretical priority of matters spiritual was of the first importance, to admit the pragmatical priority of a political policy. The Calvinist theologians would only accept royal arbitration as an instrument of such spiritual priority; the Prince would decide that those theologians who were in error were in the wrong; on this occasion, the Papists. The Protestants defined royal arbitration in the same sense as the Catholics accepted pontifical sovereignty. In Catholic opinion such sovereignty was confined to matters of faith and morality; the Protestants demanded that royal arbitration should be extended to include them. It was impossible to find grounds for agreement. The Queen Mother who, in this as in so many other questions, was ahead of her time, considered that as a matter purely of policy the two confessions should be allowed to co-exist side by side, leaving each individual free to practice whichever he decided was the true one.

She favoured the Protestant leaders because, in contrast to the theologians, they admitted that in certain cases matters spiritual might be disassociated from matters temporal, whilst Catholic doctrine distinguished between them without separating them. Because the moderates in the Catholic party thought the same Catherine de Medici assumed that her personal influence over Coligny would finally bring the Admiral to calming down the zeal of the theologians. Amongst them Théodore de Bèze was inclined to wisdom. But quite to the contrary, all that the Cardinals de Tournon and de Lorraine and the Triumvirate desired was the extermination of the heretics. Catherine's choice was in accordance with her character and plans. She was impervious to the theological scandal involved and therefore the advance of Calvinism did not disturb her so long as the members of the new faith remained good and loyal subjects. There lay the danger, revealed by the excesses committed by furious preachers or their followers, to which the Catholics responded similarly, driven to desperation by insults, sacrileges, provocations and ill-treatment. The Catholic nobles left the Court, regarding it as infected by heresy. Michel de L'Hospital, when he addressed the Parliament of Paris on November 11, 1561, was rightly severe in condemning these desertions.

The Lorraines and their allies resolved to take extreme measures to bring to surrender a princess who was in favour of religious peace. In agreement with Rome, Madrid, the Princes of Savoy and Tuscany, the Triumvirs were determined on civil war.

In accordance with his customary caution, Philip II was much less enthusiastic for this anti-Protestant crusade. Catherine de Medici was informed of his attitude, which explains her epistolatory expressions of devotion with regard to her son-in-law during the summer and autumn of 1561, when she was overwhelming him with maternal affection. Spanish intervention must at all costs be prevented. Rome was pressing Philip. The latter finally threatened Catherine that he would invade France if she were to become a Huguenot. He hoped thus to force her to give way to the Triumvirs, for he had no confidence in her protestations of affection. Chantonnay was harassing her. Whilst her kind phrases grew ever warmer, the Queen Mother never lost sight of her aim—an entente with the Calvinist leaders. Politically this was the lesser evil. She held on to it in spite of the fact that the demands of the Reformationists were causing her anxiety because, threatened by the double danger of both feudal and foreign intervention, by a Catholic crusade, which once again as in the Hundred Years' War would have turned France into a battlefield, the French Calvinists appeared to be the natural allies of the Crown. Force of circumstances dominated the Queen Mother's policy as well as the Admiral's.

It is an historical illusion to imagine that the possibility of English intervention on the side of the French Huguenots was as big a danger as Italo-Spanish help for the Catholics. In 1561 England still counted for little on the chessboard of European politics, dominated by Spain. And the Treaty of Cateau-Cambrésis had disarmed France as Spain's adversary, France being closely encircled by Italy, the Imperial alliance, the Franche-Comté, the Netherlands and Artois. In order to dismiss from our minds all the literary interpretations transmitted to us as the legacy of the Wars of Religion, it is only necessary to look at a map of France in 1559. The Princes of the Blood—and the relatively small numbers of Calvinists in proportion to the whole of the realm matters little, for they had lands and troops—owned half of the Pyrenees region and the whole of the Massif Central—Navarre, Béarn, Albret, Armagnac and Foix, Rouergue, Périgord, Limousin, Marche, Bourbonnais, Forez, Auvergne. Brittany was unsure. Spain was at the gates, from Bayonne to Perpignan; her ally, Savoy, from Nice to Bourg; from Bourg to the Three Bishoprics (Imperial islets in France, precariously held) still Spain and the Empire. Then Luxemburg, then the Netherlands and Artois. And through the Brenner and the Valteline, the strategical passes between the Empire and Italy were easy of access. Always Spain. She was mistress of the Mediterranean. She could manoeuvre her troops and those of her allies from Nice to Calais, without discontinuity. Historical geography makes nonsense of the Queen's critics. War had to be avoided at all costs; to have entered into a new armed conflict with Spain would have been France's death warrant; Catherine felt and understood this. Internal anarchy, financial ruin, the general misery as the result of economic exhaustion, Protestant militarism due to the disbanding of the Royal troops after Le Cateau-Cambrésis, all this justified the Queen Mother's wish for peace. Peace at any price, it may be said; no doubt. There are times when humiliation is the height of wisdom, as the dismemberment of a country is the sole irreparable evil, and when to gain time makes it possible to prepare for future revenge and victory. The honour of a people is not as clear-cut as that of one man. *Primum vivere*. A man who has vanished can be replaced, but not a people. The Florentine understood that as well, she who knew that her Italian homeland had been destroyed by the Barbarian and Imperial invasions. Now she had at all costs to prevent the same happening to her country of France. The religious agitation required rapid measures to be taken. Catholics and Protestants in arms were fighting more or less everywhere. Riots were threatening to become warfare. Both sides carried their dead around, crying out for divine and human vengeance. The masses were still more or less indifferent, yet the epidemic was spreading, from one to another. Protestant iconoclasticism and vandalism were raging, and their excesses gave rise to punitive measures.

Théodore de Bèze was head of the Church of France. His authority was acknowledged by Condé, Jeanne d'Albret and the Châtillons. Apart from the Cardinal de Tournon, the Chancellor and the secretaries of State there would only have been Huguenots on the Council, Bourbons and Châtillons, had not Antoine turned towards the Catholics in order to please Philip II in the hope that he might be recognized as King of Navarre. Catherine knew that she could rely on Coligny and Bèze; with L'Hospital they were the Queen's men. A Royal Triumvirate under Catherine's direction was thus formed against the feudal Triumvirate. The facts prove the goodwill at that time of the Admiral and Théodore de Bèze, who agreed to the evacuation of the Catholic churches that had been illegally occupied by their co-religionists. They also agreed to the departure of the French bishops for Trent. They intervened to ensure that the evacuation that had been ordered took place without trouble. Catherine granted permission to the Reformed religion to occupy premises for worship on condition that the meetings never included more than 500 persons and passed off quietly. She was preparing to give official recognition to freedom of worship.

Bèze feared only one thing, the fanaticism of the preachers and the faithful. On November 4, 1561, he admitted it to Calvin: 'I dread that impatience may snatch a certain victory from our hands.' Bèze was highly intelligent. Rigid doctrinaire though he was, he bowed down, like Calvin, to the necessary concessions—the practice of the cult outside the towns and the limitation of the numbers of worshippers at each temple, in order not to shock the zealots. In proportion to the numbers of the faithful and the frame of mind of the population he considered that such measures should be taken. He intervened both at Paris and at Lyons to calm the ardour of new converts. Almost as much as L'Hospital, he became the conciliator. Gaspard de Coligny approved. Madame Catherine saw herself nearing the haven of grace of religious peace which was the pre-condition for civil peace.

She continued along the road leading to this unprecedented innovation, which filled her mind and was her creation—the co-existence of two religions in one State. It was now necessary to substitute for the confused edict of July an edict that would define the new situation unambiguously. The delegates of the Parliaments (one president and one councillor) were commanded to Saint Germain on December 20th, and L'Hospital saw to it that they were Politicals. Administrative measures for pacification were taken. Catherine went very far; Antoine Caracciolo, Bishop of Troyes, having been compelled to resign his cure after having been converted to Calvinism, received a pension of 2,000 livres in compensation. Cardinal Ippolyto encouraged Catherine's Irenism. One can imagine the indignation of the Catholics on hearing that the Papal legate had been to hear the minister Jean de La Tour preach. Here as always the logical minds of the French were shocked by Italian subtlety. Uncompromising Spain protested; Rome was obliged to call the imprudent Cardinal to order. Catherine was impervious. She had fifteen Huguenots or Politicals named for the order of Saint-Michael, which ensured a majority in favour of her plans. She ordered the Royal administrators in the provinces to collaborate with the Protestant aristocracy on whom Coligny was bringing his moderating influence to bear. Nevertheless, the fanatics belonging to the Religion were provoking very serious incidents, such as the murder of the former ambassador to the Porte, the Baron de Fumel, by peasants at Agenois on November 24th. Catherine, who sinned through optimism, thought that Condé would pacify the South and gave him his instructions. What would he have done? No one knows, for illness prevented his departure. These troubles revealed the need for decisive measures and their urgency. Would they be taken in time? Catherine and the Royal Triumvirate hoped so.

Were Spain, Savoy, Venice, Florence, the Holy See, in fact preparing to launch a crusade against calvinized France? Documentary evidence makes it difficult to decide precisely how successfully such a plan could have been carried out. The fact remains that the French Catholics were expecting foreign intervention, to punish the Huguenots, favoured by the Italian Queen's betrayal. It was necessary to free France from the Genevese heresy. Calvin was highly perturbed. And the Protestants did remain too few in numbers. This could not be denied if one only counted as such those who professed the Reformed religion and did not also include those who for various reasons were discontented, and who later, at the time of the Fourth War of Religion, after Saint Bartholomew, were to form the faction of Catherine's youngest son, the future Monsieur, the party known as the Malcontents, which too often has been wrongly confused with that of the Politicals. An inquiry conducted by the Nuncio's office established that the maximum number of Huguenots was four per cent, which for the whole of France would have meant fewer than 700,000, a figure that a little later would be increased to one million, made up of Protestants and sympathizers. It is probable that the Nuncio's figures applied to practising Protestants and not to sympathizers as well. In the event of a religious war it would have had to be reckoned that about a quarter of the population would have ended by following the Reformation leaders, a whole discontented section taking up arms for the King and the Princes of the Blood, against the Lorraines and the Cardinals, roughly, four million souls. That would have allowed for a levee of 100,000 men over the whole of France, a very serious situation, and one that Catherine, who was well informed, was aware of.

In December there were a large number of massacres of heretics, at Grenade in Toulousain, at Cahors, Carcassonne, Amiens. A memorandum dated February 4, 1562, from the Cardinal de Tournon to the Cardinal Charles Borromeus, informs us that the Catholic party had decided to make use of the weak Antoine de Bourbon and to set him up against the Queen Mother, so that the Blood of France could be claimed to be on the Catholic side; a very clever manoeuvre, an Amboise plot in reverse. Chantonnay announced with satisfaction to Madrid that civil war was drawing near. Catherine informed Philip II that the Very Christian King intended to remain master in his own realm. She was awaiting the Spanish invasion. As she was sure of the loyalty of the Protestant chiefs, for whom Philip II, was the enemy above all others, she did not hesitate to ask the Admiral what strength he disposed of. Coligny replied that more than 2,150 churches were ready to serve the King, offering him their lives and their property. Whilst the Triumvirs were appealing to the foreigner Catherine turned to the French Protestants, whom she considered as Royalists: twenty-seven years later Henri III was to do the same. Catherine had no intention, obviously, of being converted to Calvinism. She was acting politically and her policy was a national one. She knew the formidable military might of Spain. She knew instinctively what would be the policy of the Béarnais; to prevent France from falling under Spanish domination on religious pretexts. The Protestants were organized on a military basis. The Queen Mother intended to use them as the kernel of French resistance against the foreigner.

Contrary to Lucien Romier, we do not think that in this respect she made a grave political error, or committed an act of folly. That would be to imagine that the people as a whole were ready to follow the Triumvirs in their anti-Protestant crusade. The very duration of the Wars of Religion seems to us against this view—five hundred thousand to one million Protestants were able for forty whole years to gather around them sufficient forces to compel the Catholic armies to capitulate in the end. The reunion of the nation took place around Henri IV and before his conversion, not around the League. The Catholic masses endured civil war, but did not want it.

Catherine de Medici was following events very closely, as her correspondence proves. She understood the need for peace of an exhausted country. Faced with the Catholics who wanted civil war, she appealed to the Protestants who had given her pledges of loyalty. The massacres were the work of fanatics belonging to both parties.

M

There is another fact also—the Protestant chiefs were against the over-enthusiastic members of their own confession; the Catholic chiefs were on the side of theirs. Catherine chose the former against the latter because she considered that with the Protestants religious peace might be possible, but impossible with the Catholics. No, Catherine did not lose her head. She was undoubtedly playing a very risky game, a game which, however, she could play without giving up the policy which in her wisdom she had decided upon—religious freedom under Royal authorization. Bèze, the Admiral, Calvin himself, accepted that policy. The Triumvirs rejected it. In 1561 it was they who were the rebels. The letter of December 26, 1561, from Charles IX to Philip II is explicit and clear: 'It is not for a subject, when his master commands him to be reasonable, to complain or to seek other aid in order to stray from the obedience which he owes to him.' The child King signed those magnificent words expressing the Royal concept of the State, which was his mother's, as it was that of Philippe le Bel, Charles V, Charles VII, Louis XI and François I— the King must be master in his own house. This was the House of France, containing several dwellings for the French, Catholics or not, since as a result of the evils of the time some Frenchmen had ceased to be Catholics. Did they remain Royalists? That was the whole question.

Catherine's choice was according to her policy. And her mouthpiece Michel de L'Hospital was to express it in non-equivocal terms, affirming the unity of the Royal State, over and above the diversity of religions. As against the Biblical monarchy, in which the State confounds policy with dogma, the Florentine was beginning to build along the very lines of the Capet tradition the modern monarchy, that which Henri IV was to found, which Richelieu was to respect, in spite of his spirit of principality and his taste for dictatorship, and which to the disaster of France and the dynasty, Louis XIV destroyed by the edict of Fontainebleau. For the Biblical form of monarchy carries in its bosom the monster destined to devour it—Jacobin totalitarianism. Two and a half centuries of history have justified Catherine de Medici, who could only think according to her own period; but a century after her day Louis XIV's rupture with the Capet tradition (Henri V was to call him the first of the Bonapartes) proved her, *a contrario*, to have been right, for to a large extent 1793 was the result of 1685, when the State re-asserted its tyranny over the private minds of the citizens. Her pragmatism made it possible for the Florentine shopkeeper to see the situation more clearly than did the theoreticians concerned with unity of faith, who were to reduce the State to becoming the stake in the struggle between the various sects and parties. We will never cease to stress the fact that Catherine, in her desire to disassociate French unity from religious unity, was following no theory and no system. She detested theories and systems, as her whole correspondence proves. She had understood that, as factionalism was taking on more and more of a religious character the only means of saving the State was to maintain it above religious faction in the same way as the Capet tradition, which she understood perfectly, had always succeeded in maintaining it above political faction. The new situation demanded a new policy, but towards the same end. Catherine de Medici's genius consisted in her capacity for adaptation to any given situation, in order never to be caught unawares. Machiavelli had said it: 'Every mutation provides stepping-stones towards another.' The Queen Mother's calling on the Protestants in those last days of 1561 was in conformity with her character and with political necessity.

The assembly of the parliamentarians did not open until January 3rd, at the Castle of Saint-Germain-en-Laye. Since it had not been possible to abolish the religious divergences, which were an evil, and since persecution was a much greater evil, since the Poissy conference had failed and the fanatics in both camps were murdering one another, a new policy had to be found. In his harangue preliminary to the activities of the assembly, the Chancellor explained it.

'It is not here a question of *de constituenda religione, sed de constituenda republica*, and many may be *cives, qui non erunt christiani*.' The boldness of these words, and the shock of their import, cannot be fully appreciated unless one understands the state of mind of the men of the sixteenth century, all of whom, both Catholics and Protestants, were imbued with the Biblical tradition; all except the legislators. Imbued with the Imperial Roman tradition, the legislators proclaimed that the King was Emperor in his domains. He was the sole judge as to whether or not he should accept religious freedom within them. *Quod placuit principi legis habet vigorem*. It pleased the King to inaugurate a new form of monarchy. The legislator explained the legal aspect of it, but the feudalists did not accept it. Catherine's tragedy lay in the fact that she was unable to compel them by force to do so.

The majority of the forty-eight members of the assembly was in favour of freedom of conscience and equality as between the two cults. The Queen Mother affirmed her personal Catholicism. François d'Andelot, with his customary fanaticism, demanded the closing of the Catholic Churches. Montmorency and Saint-André were still upholding the edicts of Henri II. Antoine de Bourbon supported a policy of repression. There was great indignation among the adherents of the Religion.

Catherine was not displeased by the attitude of the King of Navarre, since it weakened the Huguenots, who by that very fact were obliged to show her still greater consideration. On January 17, 1562, at Saint-Germain-en-Laye, she caused her son to sign a new edict, which was essentially a form of *modus vivendi*. 'To keep our subjects in peace until by God's grace we may be able to reunite them in one fold.' Certain measures were to be taken whilst the council's decisions were awaited. Catholic buildings and property were to be restored by the Protestants. The latter would not be allowed the right of meeting either in public or in private in the cities. On the other hand, daily meetings outside the towns were permitted for sermons, prayer-meetings and other activities of the new cult. Even in the cities, private practice of the cult, consistories and propositions —as defined in the speech of Michel de L'Hospital—would be legally authorized. The Government authorized synods, of which the Reformed ministers would have to give notice. The ministers would be officially recognized; officials would have the right to attend the sermons.

The French monarchy recognized the Protestant religion, both *de jure* and *de facto*. All administrative details would be settled between the Royal Government and the delegates of the Churches. Bèze and Coligny had served Catherine de Medici well. Their wisdom was to be seen here. Their illusion—which was to have sinister consequences —was to hope for the conversion of the little King, to see in him a new Josiah, as Bèze wrote on April 12, 1562, to the pastors of Zurich. If Catherine had no religious afterthoughts even the most reasonable Protestant leaders had. What appeared to her as a practical politician to be solely a service to the State, to the disciples of Calvin remained a concession which had to be made on the hard road that led to the evangelization of France, which the country as a whole did not want. Rome, with the usual suppleness of pontifical diplomacy, was resigned to compromise. Geneva saw the situation as a means towards the further progess of the Religion. The Triumvirs and the French bishops, determined on the policy of repression, prepared to resist the edict of January. Royal wisdom could not close the gap between the Protestants who were seeking to outwit Catherine, and the Catholics resolved to return to the days of repression. The particular gravity of the situation was due to the fact that both sides disposed of arms. Only the Queen was almost without them, possessing only very few reliable troops.

She thought that for the moment all would be well. Lansac, whom she had sent to Rome, informed Pius IV that the edict of January was a political necessity and asked him to authorize the sale of church property as well as utraquism and the suppression of images. The French Government begged the Holy See 'not to impose on the General Council the decisions of Rome, as was done in the time of Paul III'. It pledged itself to maintain the kingdom in the Catholic faith and to send its representatives to the Council. In spite of the failure of Poissy, Catherine persisted in hoping that Trent would bring about the reunion of the Churches. Oecumenism was the fundamental basis of her religious views, and in that direction she went very far. Jean de Monluc and Michel de L'Hospital were working for it under her guidance. Theological conferences between representatives of the two cults continued at Saint-Germain from January 28, until February 11, 1562. The Queen Mother was still envisaging the sacrifice to the Protestants of the rites that displeased them—worship of images, communion under one kind, the exclusive use of Latin for the liturgy. She even admitted the equal validity of baptism, whether administered by a pastor or a priest. The conferences naturally failed. Rome was prepared to accept the Protestant theologians at Trent, on condition that they pledged themselves to accept the decisions of the Council. In spite of all Catherine's efforts Geneva refused.

Calvin's doctrinal intransigeance was equalled by the suppleness of his political attitude. But at this stage only doctrine was at issue. The Pope of Geneva would not give way to the Council. This Calvinist infallibility was inconceivable to a mind like the Florentine's, who accepted the supremacy of the Council and had obtained from Rome the concession to allow the Reformationists to attend it. The religious and lay leaders of French Protestantism followed Geneva's intransigence. Nevertheless, Calvin did not oppose negotiations, which Bèze and Coligny were encouraging. Both at Geneva and at Saint Germain it was considered a good thing to gain time, and Rome thought the same.

The Triumvirs and the ardent Catholics on the one hand, Condé and the zealots of the Religion on the other, thought precisely the reverse. To them a recourse to violence seemed the only way out. They all thought themselves sufficiently strong to defeat their adversaries. The Catholics, supported by Philip II, became indignant, remonstrated, threatened. Paris, the Sorbonne and the Parliament, were the soul of the opposition to the religious policy of the Queen Mother. The Parliament could not admit that the unity of faith, the bond that held States together, might be broken. Catherine loudly affirmed that she was only thinking of averting trouble: 'No one detests the severity of the penalties inflicted on the dissidents more than I do.' Her conciliatory policy was in accordance with the kindness of her heart. To kill men for the sake of religion was, in her eyes, the greatest of evils. On this the documentary evidence is categorical; her aim was to deal gently in religious matters, and she did not admit any other method. On February 18th, the Parliament replied by a refusal to confirm and register the edict. According to its tradition, it opposed the monarchy's will to introduce reforms, partly through ordinary pride, partly through narrow conservatism and caste spirit. The populace of Paris, filled only with rancour against the Huguenots on account of the excesses they had committed, was for the Parliamentarians. In the same way it would later be for the League, for the Fronde, and against the liberating Triumvirate of 1770, Aiguillon, Maupéou, Terray. The strength of the Parliament was tremendous, for it rested on the support of Paris, where the preachers openly denounced Catherine as a Jezebel and her advisers as the prophets of Baal. The Paris Commune was already rising against the nobles, who had gone over to Anti-Christ. The spirit of the League had come into being; the permanent revolutionary spirit of Paris, changing direction now to the Right, now to the Left, for or against the Church, for or against the King, according to the winds of passion that swept it along. Paris was against Catherine. In the provinces matters could still be arranged; but not in Paris.

In her attempt to conciliate the Protestants the Queen Mother made the mistake of introducing Andelot to the Council and of allowing Coligny to supervise the education of Charles IX. When this became known it increased the general indignation. The Queen retreated, forbade sermons at Court, stressed her personal devotions, and took measures against the iconoclasts. Catherine's position was further imperilled when Antoine de Bourbon joined the Catholic party. This Julian the Apostate, as he was denounced by the faithful, was now in opposition to the Châtillons, and was insisting on his claim to the Regency. The Governess of France could not on any conditions tolerate this. The Constable was on the side of the Navarrese; Catherine, exasperated, sent him back to Chantilly. Her exasperation was due to the fact that she realized her danger and at the same time her weakness. The First of the Princes of the Blood having passed over to the Catholics, how could the Queen Mother continue to maintain her own Regency? The mystique of the Blood of France would now no longer be on the side of those members of the Royal Family in favour of the Reformation, but on that of the intransigent Catholic feudalists.

The grandson of Saint Louis had joined the Lorraines and the Montmorencys. The Catholics were becoming the masters of France. Condé was ill and could not help her. Had the hour of violence against the Lutheran sectarians struck? What remained to Catherine? L'Hospital was a legislator and one cannot reply to guns with documents. But the Queen Mother no longer had guns. The Triumvirs had them, and so did Coligny. Catherine turned to the Protestant soldier for help. Antoine de Bourbon, backed by Spain (that had a hold over him by promising him Navarre), immediately demanded the dismissal of the Châtillons. Chantonnay's ultimatum left her no choice between war or the dismissal of the Admiral. Catherine refused to accept the ultimatum.

Coligny then behaved as he had done at Saint Quentin. Rather than be faced with the responsibility of defying Philip II he preferred to resign, becoming once again the man who surrendered his sword to the victor before the capitulation of the city. In spite of Catherine, he left the Court on February 22nd. The letter from the Cardinal de Tournon to St Carlo Borromeo on February 22nd places this fact beyond discussion; Tournon had witnessed and spoke about Catherine's anger at the resignation of the only man who could have put the sword at the service of reason. The Admiral had given way to Navarre. For was it not now necessary to treat the latter, the Regent by right, with consideration? And was the Governess not now opposed by the mystique of the Blood of France? Coligny had carefully weighed up the situation and come to the conclusion that a man of sound judgment should not become involved in it. He retired to his country seat; a retreat dictated by caution. Catherine was too experienced politically not to realize immediately the danger his defection placed her in. Condé was a mere adventurer of the Blood Royal; like his brother Antoine, he had no sense of continuity, his only interest was in his personal affairs and he was completely indifferent to the country's welfare. Once the Admiral had left, Catherine could no longer count on the Royalists. She was the prisoner of the feudalists, whose determination to exterminate the heretics could no longer be delayed.

She was not a resigned prisoner and continued to fight. As she was no longer able to play the part of the fox, she became once again the lioness. A lioness, alas, who would have to face singlehandedly a desperate struggle against the Parliament, Paris and Spain. Coligny found the gardens of Châtillon more to his taste than the apartments of Saint Germain, especially as there he was not compromising himself in the eyes of the man who would almost certainly become Regent tomorrow, that Antoine de Bourbon whom he nevertheless despised. An admiral must be able to calculate the force of the winds and navigate between the shoals. Whilst Catherine was still trying to save France for peace, in his dreams he followed the expedition he had sent from Le Havre on February 18th, under Jean Ribaut, to colonize Florida. The Admiral loved the sea and was a colonizer; an Evangelical colonizer who used intermediaries, leaving to others the struggles of a Cortez, a Pizarro and an Almagro, keeping the honours for himself. In the reign of Henri II he had been much concerned over Brazil, where the Portuguese explorers were unsuccessful. In 1555 Durand de Villegagnon had sailed from Honfleur, and on the banks of the Rio de Janeiro this servant of the faith had built a Fort Coligny and a Henryville. There was a Protestant empire to be founded in those distant lands. Gaspard de Coligny gave the plan his full support. In the year 1557, whilst Monsieur de Coligny was surrendering to Emmanuel-Philibert under the ramparts of Saint Quentin, Reformationists and ministers swarmed out there. The expedition even included a man of letters, a friend of the noble savages, Jean de Léry. Noble savages and good Christians—according to Geneva. Calvin was full of enthusiasm for this mission, which, however, was too theological. There were quarrels and disputes. In 1560 the Portuguese recaptured the lands of these latter-day saints.

A Papist America gave the Admiral sleepness nights. After the Brazilian failure circumstances made it possible to make another attempt. A Florentine navigator, Verazzano, had landed in Florida. Catherine was interested in this region, which was associated with memories of her home. She encouraged Coligny. The Admiral's thoughts were following Ribaut and his Dieppe men with the little troop of Huguenots to the Gulf of Mexico, carrying the flag of the

Very Christian King beyond the Antilles, to those lands that had seemed to have fallen to the Catholic King. With René de Landonnière and Jacques Le Moyne de Morgues, Protestant France had perhaps reached its Promised Land. '*Si Dieu m'aide, j'irai à fin*'— why did not Coligny in that hour when he abandoned Catherine to come to grips all alone with the fanaticism of the sectarians, himself follow out that noble motto of the pioneers of the Franciscan coast? Was the ideal of Ribaut and Landonnière not the same as the Florentine's? The stele that they erected on the captured coast bore the arms of France, 'adorned by a portrait of Peace, carrying no iron lance but an olive branch'.

In the capital the parties confronting one another rejected the olive branch. Condé, who had recovered, placed himself at the head of 25,000 Parisian Huguenots, who demonstrated against the Parliament. The Queen Mother was obliged to send troops to guard and to hold Paris. Five or six thousand armed Reformationists immediately proceeded there. On Government orders and threatened by the mob, the Parliamentarians registered the edict on March 6, 1562. Catherine rightly considered herself to be no longer safe at Saint-Germain-en-Laye. The Court removed to Montceaux-en-Brie. A letter from the Queen Mother of March 14th, from Crécy-en-Brie, to the Gentlemen holding the Court of Parliament in Paris, informs us that the Cardinal de Bourbon had been appointed Lieutenant-General for Paris. The Marshals de Brissac and de Termes were his adjutants. In her anguish Madame Catherine sent four pathetic letters—from the 16th to the 26th—to the Prince de Condé, since Coligny was resting, begging him 'to keep in mind the state of this kingdom, the King's life and his own, and to defend them against its enemies'. She assured the Prince that she felt towards him as a mother.

Later on she was to explain this correspondence by annotating it and also in her letters to Christina of Denmark, dowager Duchess of Lorraine, of December 5, 1562, and to the Bishop of Rennes, on December 15th. Examination of the texts reveals that Catherine was counting on Condé's loyalty and on his collaboration in her policy of peace, as well as on the value of the example he would set by being the first to lay down his arms and placing himself at the King's service: 'Honour', she said, 'would go to him who would be the first to obey, and not to him who would be the last to remain armed.'

What had happened to make Catherine discover in Condé, in spite of her only too well justified mistrust of him, the last support of the Throne? At this point chronology is indispensable in giving us an insight into the thoughts, the intentions, and the role of the Queen on this eve of appalling conflict, a conflict which was to last for thirty-six whole years, until the Treaty of Vervins of May 2, 1598, which was a reversion to Cateau-Cambrésis. Thirty-six years of massacres to such an end! Catherine's greatness consisted in holding out for twenty-seven years, nearly always giving way, but without ever sacrificing an inch of French territory or the principle of the authority of the monarchy. She handed over to her successor a France that was exhausted but not mutilated, divided but not carved up: a France for which her Governess struggled and fought to the death, never at any moment of this incessant battle despairing of the public good. *Impavidam ferient ruinae.* Let us consider Catherine de Medici, who did not hide any of the dangers from herself. Determined to confront them, she addressed a final appeal for peace to the French, stubbornly resolved to hate and destroy one another, in the person of Condé.

Coligny having retired to his domains, Antoine de Bourbon parading his enthusiasm for Spain with all the ardour of a neophyte (which delighted the Inquisition), the only hope left lay in his brother. The Guises had already entered the tumult of battle by the massacre of Wassy, of which the Queen Mother learned as soon as she arrived at Montceaux, on March 8, 1562. The Lorraines had forced the pace, and the militant Catholics, bent on civil war, with them. It was necessary at all costs to prevent Protestant reprisal. For this there was only one means, which was to associate Condé with the King's justice, thus diverting him from partisan revenge. Catherine was obliged by force of circumstance to turn to the instigator of the conspiracy of Amboise in order to arrest the advance of the Catholics towards another attack, of which Wassy had been the prelude. She had no embarrassment of choice, and time was pressing.

It appears that when they had withdrawn from Court, the Lorraine Princes, like Coligny, were waiting on events. There was nothing to delight them in the sudden zeal of the King of Navarre for Rome and Madrid. The Guises, the Montmorencys, the Châtillons, none of those powerful vassals had any great liking for that wavering appanagist. His constant and too close *volte-faces* were a source of anxiety to them. They were willing to allow the Florentine shopkeeper to disentagle the skein of the Bourbon betrayals to the best of her ability. And they were not above enjoying the discomfiture of the Constable, whom Chantonnay was harrying in the service of Spain. Monsieur de Guise le Grand occupied his time with his household, his divine spouse, his hunting, his dogs and his birds, of which he wrote to Anne de Montmorency, asking him for sakers, those very large falcons which were so difficult to procure. But Monsieur the Archbishop of Rheims was unable to keep quiet. He was intriguing so that Philip II should grant him the dukedom of Brabant. He had not lost sight of his pontifical ambitions. He transformed Catherine's French Irenism into Imperial Irenism, negotating with the Lutheran German Princes, notably Duke Christopher of Wurtemburg, a companion-in-arms in Italy of François de Guise, and a warrior interested in theology. This was at the same time a way of countering the maoeuvres of Condé in the direction of the Empire, which had been going on for some time.

The conferences of Saverno began on Sunday, February 15, 1562. The plan of Cardinal Charles to oppose Augsburg to Geneva, the spirit of Melanchton to that of Calvin, had been ripening for a long time. The discussions lasted three days. His brother and he may have requested that they should become Princes of the Empire and even Electors. This would have been in accordance with the Carolingian ambitions of their family—to become Pope or Emperor. From the height of our modern prejudices we should not look down on them, for although younger sons by birth, François and Charles were more illustrious than the elder branch of Lorraine. Rheims and Metz shone far more brightly than Nancy and Vaudemont.

The Cardinal and his brother went rather far along the road of conciliation with the Lutherans. It appears that their desire to please the German princes inclined them towards no longer opposing a policy of compassion with regard to the French Calvinists. To what degree were they sincere? The documents do not enlighten us precisely on this point, for in their profusion they contradict one another, and thus lend themselves to political interpretations. The game the Guises were playing worried the Queen, who ordered François to rejoin her at Montceaux. The Duke left Joinville-en-Vallage, his mother's residence, three leagues to the south of Wassy, where he arrived on the morning of March 1st. Antoinette de Bourbon, although she was anything but a fanatic, had on several occasions complained of the zeal of the Wassy Huguenots. Like all the French Reformationists they had been encouraged by the edict of January, and interpreted the clauses of this edict in the broadest sense, as allowing them openly to practice their religion; an interpretation which had shocked the Catholic religious authorities everywhere.

On February 22nd, Duke François had written to the Queen Mother, reproaching her for not supporting the Bishop of Chalons, who was having trouble with the Protestants of Wassy. The refusal, opposed by the King's Council, to give him permission to support the Bishop had angered him. It is possible, more or less, to disentangle from among the enormous number of Protestant and Catholic documents that for nearly four centuries have given contradictory versions of the matter, the following facts: the victor of Metz and Calais regarded himself as disowned by the Queen Mother and defied by the followers of the Religion, who, to the number of about 3,000, and with the support of the local authorities, were daring to behave as if they were the masters of the district of Wassy. As Catherine de Medici was recalling him to Court, he made a point of looking into the situation himself, and at close quarters. He decided to halt at Wassy on March 1, 1562, which was a Sunday and a day of worship.

One can easily understand that a warrior like François de Guise did not read the edicts engrossed by long-robed clerks, whom he detested and whose anti-feudalist authority he despised. To him the matter appeared a very simple one—preaching in cities was forbidden, yet sermons were being given at Wassy. Subtle distinctions between assemblies in the towns, outside the walls if they were of a public nature, but inside the walls if they were held in private, were of no interest to this great nobleman used to the rough language of camps. The preachers, theologians as they were, interpreted the clauses of January with great skill. The sixteenth-century map of Wassy shows that the barn in which the Huguenots met was well outside the town, and the Royal representatives on the spot had no objection to it. Duke François considered himself on his own ground at Wassy. He did not admit that Catherine de Medici had any right to extend her protection to subjects who were his, not hers. We should never forget that Duke François thought and felt as a great feudalist. He went to Wassy in order to re-establish his authority, which had been scoffed at alike by the Huguenots and the King's officials. At Wassy he was particularly concerned with his own subjects, who had come from the domain of Joinville. He would not allow his vassals to make a mockery of him by holding illicit assemblies, under the pretext that Wassy was a Royal town, under the rule of the Duke de Nevers.

So Monsieur de Guise le Grand came to see his own people, who were listening to the sermon at Wassy. He was preceded by his officers and pages. They discovered about 1,200 assembled Reformationists. An experience of public meetings makes it unnecessary for the historian to indulge in any histrionics at this point. The Lorraine prince's men and the King's subjects, among whom were also his own subjects, met, insulted one another and fought. The Duke arrived. Before attending Mass he went to the barn and found people already killing one another, as two of his German pages had fired on the crowd. He did not bother to hold an investigation; he intended to restore order, instantly. He saw that the Huguenots were erecting barricades, and reacting immediately as a military man, he gave the order to storm them. He thought this so natural that in his own account of the Wassy affair we may read that with his little troop (about 200 men) he intended to take the place. But in his fury with the insolent defenders he merely forgot one thing, that only his men were armed, with muskets and pistols. The others had nothing but stones and logs. In breaking up a meeting under such conditions massacre was inevitable; but in the heat of the assault this did not for one moment occur to François de Guise. He was hit by several stones; his men saw that he was in danger. The trumpets were blown, the soldiers charged, fired, and put to the sword. Then, as women and children were being slaughtered the Duke became alarmed at the seriousness of the riot; but it was too late.

Whoever has seen or lived through such bloody riots knows that the lust to kill does not quickly disappear. At Wassy it lasted an hour. A detailed examination of the list of victims allows one to establish that the dead numbered sixty-eight men and six women, and the wounded eighty men and twenty-four women. The lists do not state whether they were adults or children; we find the terms son or daughter, but no reference to age. The total came to nearly 180 Protestant victims out of the 1,200 who had attended the prayer-meeting. The percentage of dead reveals the violence of the attack; they included nearly half the victims, whilst on the side of the Guisards there were only a few wounded and one killed. It definitely was a massacre. But the Lorraine prince had seen plenty of others, on all his battlefields. In his opinion this was a mere riot, a fight that had involved a certain number of deaths.

What did he say of Wassy on his death-bed, after his assassination by Poltrot de Méré? As was reported by the Bishop of Riez, he begged his attendants to 'believe that the inconvenience that happened at Wassy happened against his will, for he had gone there with no intention to do them any harm'. He was sincere, for one does not lie before God. He was so sincere that he called the massacre an inconvenience. In the sixteenth century the word no doubt had a stronger meaning than today, yet it meant no more than vexatious, regrettable. Wassy was an incident, nothing more; of this Duke François was convinced even on his death-bed. Yet from this incident, exploited by the Reformationists—who themselves had others on their consciences, some of them even more serious—civil war was to arise. As soon as she received the news, on March 8th, the Queen Mother realized the frightful consequences that could ensue. The torch of civil war had been lit; it must be seized and extinguished. She immediately set about doing so.[1]

The Huguenots immediately flaunted their dead against the butcher of Wassy. The most zealous Catholics replied by praising their Moses, their Jehu who by spilling the blood of the infidels had consecrated his hands and avenged the Lord. Whilst the libels were being written this was the tone of the quarrel. Théodore de Bèze went to ask the Queen Mother for justice and reparation. She received him courteously, even affectionately. Catherine promised him that she would take careful cognizance of the matter. 'Provided that we control ourselves we will be able to attend to everything.'

François de Guise took no notice of Catherine's order to present himself immediately at Montceaux. He replied that he was expecting friends at his château of Nanteuil-le-Haudoin. The fact that the two seats were so near to one another underlined the effrontery of his refusal. Paris was for the Guises and the Duke knew it. He reckoned that he could do as he liked with regard to the Queen Mother, allied to the Calvinists. The Marshal François de Montmorency, eldest son of the Constable, son-in-law of Henri II, Governor of Paris and Lieutenant-General of the Ile-de-France since 1556, who was devoted to Catherine, was facing both the exasperation of the Parisians and the intransigence of the ministers. The latter refused to refrain from preaching, to which the edict of January had given them the right. Condé was contemplating a rising, but Bèze advised against it. Whilst he accepted the measures that were being taken by the religious head of the French Protestants, Condé (and La Noue in his *Discours* is categorical on this point) did not hesitate to send notice to the Reformed Churches of the kingdom on March 10th,

[1] Among the mass of contemporaneous and subsequent accounts of the massacre of Wassy, we consider that of the Rev Charles Serfass, in spite of his hostility to the Duc de Guise, to be the most objective and reliable with regard to the documentation—*Histoire de l'Eglise réformée de Wassy-en-Champagne*, Paris, 1928.

warning them to be prepared to take up arms. As was to be expected they did so without a moment's loss: 'The noble adherents of the Religion in the provinces', La Noue reported, 'were wonderfully aroused by this call and prompt to provide themselves with arms and horses.'

Once again Condé's rash adventurousness was to ruin the patient efforts of the Queen Mother. The fanatical preachers followed that prince, and not Théodore de Bèze, who was endeavouring to temporize. On March 13th, the minister La Rivière wrote a circular letter to the Churches, confirming Condé's. The faithful remembered the massacres that had occurred before Wassy, without, of course, in the least taking into account those for which the new believers had been responsible—Béziers no more than Lectoure, Montauban than Montpelier—which had continued throughout the year 1561. Nothing was in question but Cahors, Grenade, Wassy—Wassy, the abomination of desolation, which was pictured as the most appalling of deliberate attacks. Biblical references, the eloquence and hyperbolism of the preachers, the comments upon them of their flocks, all combined to heighten the tension. Condé and the ministers only overlooked the fact that the forces at the disposal of the Triumvirs were much greater than their own. But Catherine knew it, and she also knew that civil war would give certain victory to the Catholic feudalists. Théodore de Bèze was too intelligent not to have known it too. And so he did his very best to help the Queen to direct the demands of the Protestants, who were still underequipped from a military point of view, on to the judicial plane.

It was in vain. Guise arrived at Nanteuil on March 12th. The very next day he was joined by Anne de Montmorency and Jacques d'Albon de Saint-André. In complete agreement with Antoine de Bourbon they prevailed on him to go beyond Catherine's interdiction. Paris awaited him as a saviour. On the 16th, amidst popular enthusiasm, the Triumvirs entered the city, accompanied by 2,000 cavaliers in procession. The Porte Saint-Denis, the Royal gate, was chosen for this entrance. The defender of the faith was received by Marle de Versigny, Provost of the Merchant's Guild, who offered him two million in gold and twenty thousand men. Guise resisted the temptation—to which a quarter of a century later his son Henri succumbed—to allow himself thus to be proclaimed King of Paris. He wanted Condé publicly to take the initiative in beginning the conflict. He retreated behind the Queen Mother and the King of Navarre. He behaved with perfect courtesy towards Condé, whom he met, accompanied by only 500 horsemen, returning from service at Saint-Jacques. If he wished to have all Frenchmen who would call for a defender and not a challenger, on his side, he must avoid a Parisian Wassy. In order to defy the Royal Government it was above all necessary not to appear to be a rebel. The Duke had enough experience of power and parties to recognize this. He knew Monsieur le Prince well enough to anticipate that he would shortly embark on some adventure or another. At Wassy it had only been a case of his own subjects but the Parisians were the subjects of the King. He did not confuse them but controlled himself and waited. Paris was on his side and he was certain of success, which too great haste would only imperil. Moreover, the fact that in spite of the Queen, Condé was in arms in Paris was enough to justify his own disobedience. He had come there to protect the King's subjects from the Huguenot threat.

Catherine was too subtle to allow herself to be taken in by this play-acting. If the Triumvirs were to be victorious they would have the King at their mercy. Divided, the Protestants and the King's men were too weak to beat the Triumvirs. But if they united it would be another matter. Hence the letters to Condé; let him disarm and come to Court. The Triumvirs would then appear to be the rebels. The first letter was dated March 16th. On the 17th the Triumvirs and Condé were bidden to leave Paris, where only the King's mandatories would keep order: the Cardinal de Bourbon, the Marshals de Brissac and de Termes, Jean d'Avanson and Odet de Selve, members of the Privy Council.

The Triumvirs, speculating on Condé's rashness, were only playing for time. They requested that the Lieutenant-General, Antoine de Bourbon, should come in person to look into matters. Catherine, more and more anxious, removed the Court to Fontaine-bleau. Navarre was unable to get to Paris until the 21st. Next day, on Palm Sunday, he took part with the Triumvirs in the procession of the palms. Would Condé's refusal to co-operate and his obstinate insistence on remaining in Paris deliver Catherine into the hands of the Triumvirs? We have her letters to Monsieur le Prince. What verbal messages, transmitted by Jean de Hangest d'Ivoy, Condé's agent, accompanied them? We do not know. The Nuncio's letters and those of Jeanne d'Albret written during this period show that Catherine was entirely on the Protestant side, which was the least dangerous and for that reason the lesser evil which it is the aim of political wisdom always to seek. Unlike the Triumvirs, Condé could do nothing without her nor against her. Théodore de Bèze was com-

5. GASPARD DE COLIGNY. Contemporary drawing. School of Clouet.

(*Bibliothèque Ste. Geneviève*)

6. FRANÇOIS II, by François Clouet   (*photo:* Giraudon)

pletely loyal. He informed Calvin of his annoyance at the taking
hither and thither of Monsieur le Prince. In spite of all appeals the
Admiral did not emerge from his rural isolation. He was obviously
afraid to involve himself. This loss of time was profitable only to the
Triumvirs, who were in correspondence with the Spanish Ambassador. Catherine asked for support from Elizabeth of England, who
was in contact with Coligny.

In London and Madrid the foreigners were watching for the
moment to intervene. The impotent wisdom of Madame Catherine
can be clearly seen during this second fortnight of March 1562. She
had been advised to leave Fontainebleau for Orleans. She pointed out
what an advantage this would give the Triumvirs. They would go to
war to deliver the State, fallen into the heretics' hands. The Protestants then began to realize the overwhelming superiority of the forces
of the Triumvirs: 'A little fly against a large elephant,' La Noue said
later, with amusing hyperbole. On March 23rd, Condé, accompanied
by Bèze and an escort of 1,000 men left Paris, not for Fontainebleau
but for La Ferté-sous-Jouarre; a few days later he established himself at Meaux. Without taking further heed of counsels of wisdom he
suddenly gave the signal for the armed rising of the Reformationists
in the whole of France. If La Noue is to be believed he was obsessed
with the memory of Caesar—the Rubicon, Rome, the standards
beginning to fly through the countryside, thus he wrote to the
Admiral. But not everybody who would like to be one is a Caesar.
And Louis de Bourbon, with all his audacity, lacked genius and even
common sense.

Catherine, on the contrary, took good care not to rush matters. In spite
of Antoine de Bourbon's insistence she remained at Fontainebleau.
The Triumvirs raised troops. Anne de Montmorency, together with
the King of Navarre, marched on Fontainebleau at the head of three
or four thousand cavaliers. Was it not a matter of protecting the King?
Catherine knew what such protection signified. The clever princess
had no intention of being lured into the Paris mouse-trap and once
again managed to impose her will on Antoine. She would not go to
Paris; it was too dangerous. Monsieur de Guise le Grand hastily
arrived. On the 31st she was obliged to give way. Condé had found
nothing better to do than to depart from the region. On the first stage
of the journey to Paris the Queen Mother sought refuge at the Castle
of Melun, but having no troops she was obliged to leave it. On April
6th she arrived at Paris. The little King was a hostage in the hands of
the Triumvirs. We know from the Nuncio, Prosper de Saint-Croix,

N

and from Chantonnay that the Catholic chiefs had threatened to dethrone him. She had to choose between submitting and resigning. A Catherine de Medici always has enough wisdom to refuse to fight a battle lost in advance. In this case she was absolutely right; she knew that she was alone and could only manoeuvre between the fanatics confronting one another. So she submitted, all the more as there was no lack of threats of physical violence against her person. After studying the character of the Marshal de Saint-André one is not surprised to read in Brantôme that 'he had debated whether or not she should be pushed into a sack and drowned'. The Triumvirs were not the kind of men who would have refrained from doing so. The Queen Mother was haunted by memories of Florence. In spite of her cries of protest, the Child King had been removed from her room at Fontainebleau. It was an Amboise plot in reverse and a successful one.

It would have been impossible without Navarre. The mystique of the Blood of France licensed this attack and justified it in the eyes of the people. Monsieur le Prince made not a single move to come to her aid.

Coligny, who had decided to lie low, and Condé, urged on by ambition, with one accord abandoned Catherine de Medici. Neither the one nor the other realized what an irreparable mistake they were making—freedom of conscience, as well as the Queen Mother, was held prisoner. Centuries were to elapse before the hatred unleashed by the Wars of Religion was appeased—the edict of Nantes, the edict of Grace were merely a truce. With the edict of Fontainebleau, in 1685, Louis XIV himself was to return to the policy of Henri II, which Catherine's wisdom had reversed.

This wisdom had been rendered impotent by the wilful defaulting of the only people who could have benefited from it. In order to show her that she no longer counted for anything, her former companion the Constable, now her enemy, under her very eyes sacked the meeting-places that had been authorized by the edict of January. '*Brise-bancs*' Aubigny called him; and Brantôme, '*Brûle-bancs*'. Whether broken or burnt, the destruction was symbolic. What was in fact broken, burnt, destroyed, was the admirable effort of a woman of genius to create a modern monarchy by avoiding a Biblical form of monarchy which was as much after the heart of Geneva as of Madrid and Rome.

Two confessions under one king—no thank you! War, God willing, would lead to the triumph of one sole faith under one king. Each side thought that it would win; victory was a matter of strength. Condé's mistake was not to have compared forces, to have counted on England, the German Lutheran Princes, the Swiss Cantons, with whom he had for months past been negotiating. Coligny was aware of it. But the tears, supplications, and invective of his wife, Charlotte de Laval, were stronger than the fears he felt as an experienced martial man. He very soon joined in with the *alea jacta est* of the presumptuous student of Caesar. Had he held Condé back, thereby taking away from the Triumvirs their excuse for civil war, he could still have saved everything. He left it to God. Catherine never left anything to God until after all human resources were exhausted. Even when she was held prisoner in the Louvre she gave way but did not despair. She had retreated in order to fight on with the only weapons she possessed—subtle cunning, inexhaustible patience, weapons of weakness—and Catherine knew her own.

Coligny was completely responsible. He knew all about Condé's plans, for he had already joined him at Meaux on March 27th. He reassured Catherine with regard to Monsieur le Prince's call to arms. The latter was defying Paris from Saint-Cloud. Did Bèze lose his head? On March 30th he advised them to undertake a *coup de main*. The military leaders were sure that it would fail. They decided to fall back on Orleans, where the little Huguenot army—2,500 horsemen—arrived on April 2nd. Andelot had occupied the city some days previously. The Queen of Navarre, who had come to Meaux at the same time as Coligny, had insisted that they should take Orleans and Catherine de Medici had been invited to go there, but in vain. Their plan was to make Orleans the capital of Protestant France; Orleans against Paris, like Bourges under Charles VII.

> *Non potuit caput esse Aurelia regni,*
> *Ergo quod reliquum cor animusque fuit?*

asked Scaliger. In this bourgeois city the great Protestant feudalists could without difficulty play the same part as the great Catholic feudalists did in Paris. From Orleans Condé could reply to his brother Navarre as well as to the Triumvirs, the Rohans, the La Trémoilles, the La Rochefoucaulds, the Duras, the Gramonts. Jeanne d'Albret was at Vendôme, having taken away this fief from her husband. There was a shortage of money and the troops were limited by it; there was no infantry to support the cavalry.

Louis de Bourbon, impecunious as ever, had only 1,600 écus. Bèze was only rich in eloquence. According to Monsieur le Prince's usual behaviour, the whole situation was a mere adventure. But this did not prevent the proclamations from following one upon the other. On April 7th, there was an appeal to the Churches for the deliverance of the Sovereigns, who were calling for help, as Catherine's letters proved; on the 8th a manifesto against the Triumvirs appeared; as soon as they laid down their arms the Royalists would do the same. One can see how clear-sighted Catherine had been; had Condé obeyed her, the Protestants would have been rallying to the help of the Government, but at Orleans they were Royalists only in name. France was where the King was and the King was in Paris, the hostage of the Triumvirs. In the eyes of the French masses (and since the Jacquerie history has made it sufficiently plain that they count in France) the Triumvirs were with the King; the Huguenots, at Orleans, were against him. Condé's literary efforts did not move anyone but the adherents of the Religion. On April 11th the Act of Association of the Protestant nobles was drawn up; 4,000 of them signed it. It contained a very clear invitation to Catherine: 'To maintain', it said, 'the honour of God, the estate and freedom of the King, under the Government of the Queen, his mother.' Condé was recognized as Lieutenant-General of the realm in place of his brother.

Theoretically it all held together, but in practice it was totally inefficacious. Catherine had lost her freedom of action. Whilst the Calvinist gentry were indulging in all this wordiness, the Queen, on April 10th, wrote at very great length to the Cardinal Odet de Châtillon: 'I think I may truthfully and to my great regret say that those who are advising Monsieur le Prince to do what he is doing will bring about the ruin of this kingdom, and they say that Monsieur the Admiral is his only adviser.' She urged Odet that Gaspard should intervene in favour of disarmament. Note the date: April 10, 1562. It was too late, and by the fault of Condé and Coligny. Catherine's postscript was without the slightest illusion: 'I can see quite clearly the ruin of this whole monarchy.' Let us weigh her own words, as they reveal her deepest thoughts and feelings: 'And now, as you have always claimed to be a good patriot, make it clear at this moment that you and your brothers do not want to bring about the ruin of your country, but on the contrary, to preserve it.'

'Patriot'—'your country'—that was what Madame Catherine wrote in 1562. Patriot and subject, country and king, are but one. And God? The Mother of the kingdom, unconcerned with theological quarrels, invoked Him on behalf of France, the whole of France. 'I would give my life to see everything at such peace as I long for, and pray God to give it to us.' Nobody except the legislators was willing to echo the wholly national and Christian terms of this letter to Cardinal de Châtillon. Catherine's was the voice crying in the wilderness—*vox clamantis in deserto*. Let us take her letter of April 11th to her ambassador to Spain. It was one long cry of distress at the homicidal fury of the French. It is touchingly sincere. When reading this confession of Catherine's to an old servant whose faithfulness she knew, one can appreciate all her disgust, her weakness, her anger with the Protestants who, by their stupidity and their fanaticism, had reduced her to her position at that time. Catherine was prepared to attempt any measures to heal that partisan rancour, the wounds of which France eternally bore. The recourse to arms by the Calvinists constituted a rebellion. The Queen still hoped it possible that everything might go off 'along a gentle and friendly path'. Otherwise—and it was the first time that she spoke thus and Sébastien de L'Aubespine was instructed to make this known to Philip II: 'I have the final remedies at hand and shall promptly apply them.' Realistically Madame Catherine was turning away from those rash men doomed to defeat by their own disobedience. Coligny, Condé, Bèze, had lost their ally. Were they going to drive her into alliance with their enemies?

The Protestant leaders were resigned to this extremity. Like the Triumvirs they had chosen civil war and an appeal for foreign aid. On April 2nd Briquemault left for London; on the 7th, the German Princes were petitioned for help; on the 8th, the Senate of Geneva; on the 20th, the Prince Palatine and the Emperor Ferdinand. Condé was willing to accept aid from anyone interested in the French troubles; he sent Théligny to Emmanuel-Philibert of Savoy; he even wrote to the King of Spain.[1] As a Prince of the Blood, Condé imagined that he had the right to do so and he called himself Protector of the House and Crown of France.

In spite of the facts he refused to recognize his own responsibility for the war. The traditional call for the deliverance of the King caused the Huguenot risings. Blois, Tours, Le Mans, Rouen, Le Havre, Dieppe, Caen, Bourges, Lyons and Poitiers went over to

[1] The documents are incontrovertible. They are in the department of manuscripts of the Bibliothèque Nationale, *fonds français* No. 10190 and in the portfolios of Simancas which are no longer in the Archives of France, having been returned to Spain; the index number was K. 1500 B. 27. Also, the *Calendars of State Papers* of England contain the letter from Coligny to Cecil of April 11, 1562.

Condé; Dauphiné, Provence and Gascogne rose in part. Almost the whole of Languedoc was for the Religion. In Brittany the Duc de Rohan was recruiting troops. It is noteworthy that in the towns these risings were in the main supported by the people, and in the countryside by the gentility. The peasantry, weighed down by economic distress, remained almost everywhere indifferent. The result of this was the acute lack of infantry in the Protestant armies. These armies were frequently reduced to small numbers that were never sufficiently equipped either with the necessary forces or material to form large manoeuvrable corps, and were therefore only suitable for piecemeal warfare and not for co-ordinated operations. In order to swell their ranks they recruited pickpockets and other criminals completely indifferent to God and the King. That was the reason for the need to appeal to the Protestant States; they alone could furnish the infantry and artillery that were lacking. What a fine beginning to this First War!

After the *coup de force* of Fontainebleau, however, the Triumvirs were able to amalgamate the resources in men and material of the Catholic party and the Government. They could officially ask for aid from Spain, Savoy, and the Empire. They were France, and the Protestants the rebels. The Triumvirs were only in appearance legally in the right, but they exploited this political fiction with which, like it or not, the Queen Mother was associated. She never ceased to point out to François de Guise, the least fanatical of the Triumvirs, what a disaster civil war would be, involving the intervention of Spain, England, the Germans, the Swiss, Savoy and the Italian Princes. This was meant to touch on the great soldier's most sensitive spot, for he who had beaten Charles V and Mary Stuart, disliked his brother's idea of appealing for foreign aid. 'It appeared', the Nuncio informed the Curia 'as if the Duke had become timid and almost repented of having joined the ball.' Catherine's chains were loosened and she was able to negotiate with Condé. He, however, wanted to shuffle the cards, and published the letters that the Queen had written to him. This was a certain means of handing her over to the vengeance of the Triumvirs. Thenceforward Catherine was in their power and no more than a mere signature. Coligny could not but be aware of Monsieur le Prince's folly and wrote to the Queen. He was hoping that an interview might be arranged.

The Huguenot excesses in the South and the Dauphiné, where the Baron des Adrets began his famous and appalling career, did not ease matters. The Protestant chiefs were overridden and the Catholic leaders no less so by the reprisals of the mobs whipped up by priests and monks. The massacre of the Huguenots at Sens on Sunday April 12, 1562, was even greater than that of Wassy. There were at least one hundred dead; strangling, drowning, innumerable rapings and sacking of houses. The revolutionary risings spread throughout the kingdom, with their train of atrocities and iconoclasticism. Compared with what happened from one end of France to the other, after the killings at Sens and the sacriligeous scenes at Orleans on April 21st, which neither Condé nor the Admiral were able to halt, the disorders of the previous year seemed almost idyllic. The atrocities on both sides followed one another inexhorably, according to the social laws that govern civil war. One is struck by the destructive frenzy of the Huguenots twelve years before Saint Bartholomew, which Protestant history shockingly makes out to have been an isolated massacre. It was clear that the leaders no longer had any authority over the multitudes who were led away by preachers who were fanatical to the point of madness. Calvin's letters are a constant and vain protest against this terrorism, which was throwing the French masses, who until then had remained indifferent, into the arms of the Catholics involved in the civil war. On their side the Protestant evidence lists the horrors committed by the Catholics and it is certain that the Royal authorities were as impotent as the Reformationist leaders. The fear of the leaders on both sides of anarchy, which was spreading like wildfire, was the reason for the negotiations that took place at the end of that April of 1562, and for the fact that the Triumvirs restored comparative liberty to Catherine. On May 6th, Coligny wrote to the Constable with the aim of separating him from the Guises and Saint-André. The reply he received on the 12th was that of a man resigned to the inevitable without concealing from himself that they were running into 'the universal ruin of the kingdom'.

Nevertheless, the Triumvirs permitted the Queen to take up residence once again at Montceaux-en-Brie whilst they themselves remained in Paris. They no doubt thought that her impotence would nullify her last attempts to achieve peace. They had solemnly proclaimed that religious diversity was inadmissible, thereby burning the bridges. In reading the documents between April 11, and May 31, 1562, in detail, one gains the impression that the leaders on both sides were under the attraction of this fatal war, and that the only point in their negotiating was their need to repudiate their own personal responsibility in the matter in the eyes of the country. If ever men were led on by events it was in that spring of 1562. Catherine de Medici alone, with a strength born of despair, attempted to dominate them. On May 13th she was at Montceaux. She sent Villars and Vieilleville to Orleans. She placed some hope in Coligny's patriotism, as she had in François de Guise's. She knew the Admiral's dislike of admitting the English and the Germans into France. Had he not declared that he would rather die than agree to the adherents of the Religion being the first to summon foreign forces to France? She trusted him and went very far, saying that the Protestant troops would not be disbanded until after the Triumvirs had departed from Court; Antoine de Bourbon would be the sole Commander of the Catholic and Royal Army.

Condé's irresponsibility saw a trap in the Queen Mother's obvious sincerity. He refused to make any concessions with regard to the freedom of worship. On May 20th he published a declaration in which he denounced Anne de Montmorency, François de Guise and Jacques d'Albon de Saint-André as public and private enemies; emphasizing the fact that the Chancellor L'Hospital, the Prince de La Roche-sur-Yon and even the son of the Constable had fallen from favour because they were suspected of moderation. This was throwing oil on the flames that Catherine was only trying to put out, as she had written to the Bishop of Limoges: 'To put out this fire, which has been lit with such violence that I do not know whether, even if one wished to do so, one could put it out.' When Condé denounced the Triumvirs as servants of Spain and the Holy See, when he threw into their faces his contempt for a foreigner and his two little companions who were daring to lay down the law to a Prince of the Blood, he was deliberately treating his brother, the King of Navarre, as a negligible quantity, which exasperated him. In reply Antoine at the beginning of June chased the Huguenots from Paris and had a few of them burnt.

It was true that the Triumvirs had appealed to Philip II, the Pope, Emmanuel-Philibert and the Duke of Florence for troops and money. They were doing no more than Condé himself. Their behaviour was so similar that the Protestants did not hesitate to address themselves to the Spaniard and the Savoyard, nor the Catholics to the English and the Swiss. We have the letters written by Chantonnay, the Cardinal of Ferrara, the Nuncio, Antoine de Bourbon, Condé, Coligny, Throckmorton. Among all those diplomats, those great noblemen, those warriors, there was only one person who was thinking of the country—Catherine. There again the Florentine shopkeeper was ahead of her time; just as she stood for religious freedom, so did she also stand for the independence of the State with regard to the foreigner. All her letters to Sébastien de L'Aubespine, to her daughter of Spain, her sister-in-law of Savoy, prove that she never abdicated from that attitude of sovereignty. Through force of circumstances she had had to relinquish that sovereignty, at home, to the Triumvirs, yet however much Condé had annoyed her she still offered him a last chance to come to terms. A chance that Monsieur Le Prince threw back with studied insolence when he contemptuously boxed the ears of the three men whose prisoner Catherine was.

A prisoner! As he re-conducted her to Vincennes on May 30th Antoine de Bourbon gave her to understand, by the guard with which he surrounded her, that the time for diplomacy was past and for war had come. Catherine had no more illusions; her letters to Elisabeth of Spain, the Bishop of Limoges, to Antoine de Bourbon, during that month of May 1562, prove it. The memorandum on the disorders at Rouen, dated from Montceaux on the 24th, is characteristic of her. In it the need for obedience to the edict of January is re-affirmed, without qualifications. As she wrote to the King of Navarre, it was necessary 'to settle matters at Rouen with some kindness, whilst waiting for God to give us the means to deal with them at greater leisure'. She admitted to Marguerite of Savoy, 'our pitiful condition, which is certainly miserable, and if it were not for my hope in God, who has helped me so many times, I do not know how I could bear the ills and anxieties that I have and for which I have occasion'.

Catherine had put herself in God's hands. She was one of those souls that never give up so long as a hope of salvation remains to them. *Sperans contra spem.* As this time war seemed inevitable she prepared for it. She had resigned herself to accepting aid from Spain whilst ordering Marshal de Tavannes to raise troops in Burgundy. She refused to go to Paris, for she knew that they hated her there and that they would be glad to see her dead. She saw to it that neither harm nor injury was inflicted on the persons or property of the Protestants who were being evacuated from the capital in order that there should be no pretexts for riots and massacres. She obtained from Condé the promise of a personal interview at Toury, a village in Beauce, near Janville. The Cardinal of Ferrara was impressed by her joy at this: 'She thought', he said, 'that peace was already in her hands.' In her relief she instructed Throckmorton to inform the Queen of England of it. The interview took place on June 6th in open country. Antoine accompanied Catherine to it. As she was no longer free she was able only to guarantee that there would be liberty of conscience, but not freedom of worship. The gentlemen who formed the two escorts kept the anguished silence of a vigil on the eve of battle. The Catholic troops were encamped near Montlhéry; Catherine spent a few days at Etampes. She sent the provinces instructions in preparation for the war. She understood only too well the uselessness of those feminine prayers and tears of which Hubert Languet spoke in his *Arcanes du XVIe siècle*.

Condé hesitated, nevertheless, to break off the negotiations begun at Toury. On June 17th the Queen Mother set out again from Vincennes, where she had returned on the 15th, in a litter (having been injured in a fall from her horse) for Arthenay. Counting on Elizabeth as mediator she had asked the English Ambassador to accompany her. A few days later, whilst she was travelling though the Orleans district, Chantonnay intervened. As the result of his intervention with the King of Navarre her new attempt also failed. Catherine took it upon herself to send the Marshal de Montmorency to Condé's army, where he was received with battle-cries.

It is necessary here once again to pin down the responsibility for what followed. On June 27th the Triumvirs agreed to leave the camp of Talcy in the Blésois district, where the Catholic army was assembled, and to withdraw to Châteaudun, as the result of which the Queen Mother was enabled to see Condé on three more occasions, on June 27th, 28th, and 29th, at the Abbey of Saint-Simon near Talcy. Catherine there gave a methodical account of the situation, striking in its extraordinary lucidity, for in it she foretold how matters would develop in future exactly as they did; she urged that the Protestants should be satisfied with freedom of conscience whilst waiting for Charles IX to attain his majority, for as their forces were so very inferior to those of the Catholics they had no hope of victory; it was both in the interests of the Calvinists as well as of patriotism that they should temporize at this point. Condé was at the end so completely won over that he agreed to retire with his troops. Like his brother he was extremely impressionable. Catherine's sweetness had touched him. But the Triumvirs imagined that it was trickery on her part towards the Protestants and that she was playing their game. The documents prove, on the contrary, that the Queen was perfectly sincere: her letters to Tavannes, of June 30th and to the Duc d'Etampes of July 1st. It is enough to read them to be convinced of it.

Catherine sincerely wanted to gain time, which in a period of revolution and civil war is essential, and to hold France back from the edge of the abyss. The gentlemen of the Huguenot army refused to accept the concessions made by their chiefs. We learn from the Venetian ambassadors that Philip II's promises to Antoine de Bourbon, as a token of thanks for his activities against heresy, became known at that moment. It is certain that this news—and it later appeared clearly enough to have been false—was circulated by Chantonnay, kept informed hour by hour by his spies. Did the Admiral fall a victim to this manoeuvre? Or was he making one of those twisted calculations that were a habit of his? We do not know. We only know that he protested against sacrificing freedom of worship and that he consulted the army on this point. La Noue reported the general indignation at what appeared as a betrayal to people who only dreamed of fighting. They all cried out that these shameful parleys must cease, that the soil of France had given birth to them and would serve as their tomb!

Here the responsibility of Gaspard de Coligny is once again irrefutable. If we do not know the deeper reasons for his conduct, contradicting his previous attitude, the facts are there—Condé had agreed to temporize; at the last moment he had retreated in face of the horror of making war against his own nation, preferring to give way rather than to put France to fire and blood. Jean de Monluc, who had seen him privately on Catherine's behalf, had given him guarantees. Did Coligny see those guarantees as a trap? What oral messages did he receive? La Noue states that the Admiral 'explained to Monsieur Le Prince that although he thought that the Queen, when she accepted his offer, had done so with no wrong intentions and that in addition her desire to save the State from disaster made her seek out every expedient, he thought nevertheless that those who were under arms would circumvent her in order to circumvent him'. Condé immediately changed his mind. In his vacillating character the noble impulse of the Blood of France, which had carried him over to Catherine and peace, was stopped dead. Théodore de Bèze agreed with Coligny, encouraged Condé, and pronounced for war.

According to Mariéjol, Catherine had been playing an Italian game. No, the outburst of anger that followed when she heard of the breakdown in negotiations was not that of a fox but of a lioness at bay, for the lives of her young.

The schemers had united with the fanatics to wreck the wisdom of the Governess of France. Condé refused Catherine de Medici's conditions, 'contrary to the glory of God'. Robertet, whom she had entrusted with a last but useless mission to endeavour at least to postpone the rupture, returned to tell her that the Protestants refused to strike camp, 'and that more than paper would be needed to turn them out'.

What were needed were gunpowder and bullets. On the morning of July 2, 1562, before La Ferté-Alais, the smoke and crackling of the forerunners of war was already arising. Catherine went to Châteaudun to join the Triumvirs. Since the Admiral and Théodore de Bèze had succeeded in urging Monsieur Le Prince to make war, the Queen could no longer avoid an alliance with Guise, Montmorency and Saint-André. As she wrote on July 3rd to the Gentlemen holding the Court of Parliment at Paris with regard to the Calvinists of Meaux, she now only thought of 'seizing the instigators of the sedition; the which, if they do not, I shall employ a powerful force thereto, to punish them in good earnest'.

The Protestants had wished it so. In her impotent wisdom Madame Catherine did not forgive them for their partisan fury, which had thrown her back into the camp of her worst enemies and reduced her to becoming an ally of the Triumvirs who had made her their prisoner.

This was the true origin of the First War of Religion.[1]

---

[1] In his essay *Catherine de Médicis et la Saint-Barthélémy* (*Le Correspondent*, January 1883) Régis Chantelauze explains very well how the Queen Mother has always tried to resist the Guises, who attempted to force her to choose between themselves and the Huguenots; a choice that Condé's weakness obliged her to make in favour of the Triumvirs. This weakness put her at the mercy of the Lorraine's and their allies. By their political ineptitude the Protestants forced her on to the side of their adversaries, who were also hers. As early as February 1562 the preachers attending the synod of Languedoc under the presidency of Viret, had demanded the conversion of Catholics to the new faith, on pain of death. This was well before Wassy and must have been known to the Lorraine's. As Albert Dufourcq recalls, in August 1562, a few months after Wassy, 'nearly 120 priests were killed at Caylus; and 194, with 313 laymen, at Lauzerte; as well as two thousand to three thousand religious, to which the Cardinal de Lorraine himself bore witness. And the tortures inflicted on those martyrs were so terrible that in 1563 Condé forbade the *Discours* of Claude de Sainctes and the *Histoire* by Georges Bosquet on the *Troubles de Toulouse*'. The continuation, containing many documents and facts, may be read in Dufourcq's volume in *Histoire moderne de l'Englise*, VIII pp. 306-16, which stresses the fact that in 1562 more than 20,000 churches were sacked or destroyed throughout the kingdom. Wassy was a link in the Catholic massacres, but on the other hand we must not overlook the chain of Huguenot terrorism between Wassy and Saint-Bartholomew: Nîmes (1562) Saint-Gilles (1562) Coutances (1562) Sully (1563) Nîmes (1567) Orthez (1570). As we shall see, Saint-Bartholomew was an improvised massacre. Catholic contemporaries regarded it as an act of defence, a reply and a reprisal. As for the anit-Catholic atrocities in England, Scotland, Ireland, Sweden, Switzerland and the Empire, they were innumerable.

PART III

❧ ❀❀ ❧

THE ROYAL TRAGEDY

CHAPTER ONE

TOWARDS THE MATINS OF PARIS
(July 1562—August 1570)

❧ ✤ ❧

The Protestant leaders reopened the dams through which French blood was to flow. This was the country's opinion, which we can follow nowhere better, perhaps, than in the *Mémoires* of Claude Haton, curé of Mériot, near Nogent-sur-Seine, in Champagne, a witness of the civil wars. Haton described them from 1562 until 1582, on which date his account ends, without having taken any prominent part in them which might have inclined him to dress up his report. The curé's mind was made up; he was against Catherine, against L'Hospital, against the Montmorencys, against the Politicals, and as anti-Huguenot as one could wish. But he knew how to observe, he could read, and he was well-informed. He might be said to have been a commentator, which he no doubt was; but first of all he watched, listened, and recorded.

We shall frequently resort to these unpretentious memoirs which, in their exact recording of small details can claim to provide historical evidence, and which prompted Fustel de Coulanges to state that 'there is no truth except in details'. Their narrator also shows an exemplary care for accuracy: 'I did not know the truth of it;' 'If I have remembered it correctly;' 'I know nothing of this;'— such phrases constantly recur. Haton had a horror of inventing, interpreting, falsifying or lying. He was highly educated, intelligent, shrewd, interested in everything and as much a soldier as a priest. Inclined as he was to be a Leaguer, he showed no trace of fanaticism or cruelty. He was an excellent citizen who detested civil war, and to him the Huguenots were 'debauched Frenchmen of the Catholic religion'. This shows that he knew little of them, but on the other hand he saw them at work, and he had good eyes. The historian, who knows a thousand things that were hidden from Claude Haton, has no need to share his anger with 'that nest of false vipers', but his anger was nevertheless significant, for it was the reaction of one Frenchman among millions of others to those men who did not hesitate to unleash the religious war even after Catherine, in defiance of contemporary prejudices, had legally recognized them. The very invectives of the curé Haton against Catherine de Medici and her Chancellor prove how greatly the Queen Mother had favoured the members of the Religion. They put beyond discussion the sincerity with which the Queen longed for peace among men through freedom of conscience.

The Protestant atrocities immediately multiplied as the result of war, to such an extent that one cannot help asking oneself whether Coligny and Bèze did not join the party that was demanding war in order to allow all the Calvinist hatred which until then had been contained with such difficulty to quench itself. It would be but human. Tortorel and Périssan, the *Mémoires* of Haton, the *Discours* of Claude de Sainctes, of Gabriel de Saconnay, the *Actes* of Erasmus Fend, and the book by Richard Verstegan, the *Theatrum Crudelitatum Haereticorum nostri Temporis*, which did not appear until 1587, provide sufficient reply, very precisely enumerating all the horrors perpetrated by the Huguenots. They confirm, once and for all, the massacres that took place on both sides, as in all civil wars. They enable us to dispense with futile denunciations of one or the other, illustrating to perfection as they do the eternal ferocity of man, the invincible power over him of fanaticism and the will to destroy, his taste for blood and ruins, his permanent need to kill, violate, burn and pillage, in the name of a religious or political ideal. Blaise de Monluc and the Baron des Adrets were the living symbols of the dual fury of the sectarians. It is to the eternal honour of Catherine de Medici that she had tried, in the face of and against them all, to spare France this fury.

On July 3, 1562, this fury was unleashed. It was to rise to the paroxysmic heights of the Michelades and Saint Bartholomew. It was a decennial crescendo during which the pauses were merely ephemeral. Such truces were, as we shall see, either obtained or imposed by the Queen, who refused to despair of human wisdom and who by so doing rallied all the frenzied haters in the kingdom against herself. Under the influence of their cries of rage the peaceful citizens finally declared, like Claude Haton, that 'the craftiness and malice of the said lady was so great that she delighted in causing division and hatred among the princes, setting them against one another in order that she might reign and thereby remain sole

7. THE EXECUTION OF AMBOISE. March 1, 1560.   (*photo: Giraudon*)

8 THE MASSACRE OF WASSY, March 1 1562 (photo Giraudon)

governess of her son and of the kingdom'. Catherine, who was only seeking to unite the country, was thus accused of deliberately dividing it. Her legend was in fact created by the Wars of Religion, for it was impossible for those men of her period whose passions she did not share to understand the truth about her. Having failed to unite them she resigned herself to opposing the parties whom she had been unable to reconcile, in order to break them. 'The affection of his people', said Machiavelli, 'is the sole resource that a Prince may find in adversity.'

Catherine was never able to win such affection from the French, except from those who came into personal contact with her. But she was too deeply imbued with the teachings of Machiavelli not to continue to strive for it. This was her wheel of Ixion. They held it against her that she was an Italian, a foreigner, and French prejudice was the insurmountable obstacle that confronted her. All this woman lacked, who had it in her to be a great ruler, was the mystique of the Blood of France. Henri III shared this handicap. Successor to François I though he was, and also of the stuff of distinguished princes, his ways were those of an Italian, and a decadent Italian at that. At heart both mother and son belonged entirely to France, yet the France of the sixteenth century never recognized nor even apprehended their true natures, hidden behind a foreign-seeming façade. Both were profoundly and completely misunderstood, and neither the mother's genius not the son's intelligence and talents were ever able to overcome this misunderstanding.

In the eyes of the great and powerful she remained the Florentine shopkeeper; to the people she was simply 'the Italian'. Her origin was the Queen Mother's greatest weakness.

Marco-Antonio Barbaro, Ambassador of the Most Serene Republic, in the year 1563 described Catherine de Medici as follows: 'Forty-four years of age, of a warm and humid temperament, drawn to peace, fond of hunting and activity. As regards her physical appearance she is beautiful and young, of pale complexion, with rather gracious features, a fine presence, beautiful and gracious manners. I can assure you that her mind is very sharp and truly Florentine. This Queen is very clever, very prudent, and very magnanimous; she has knowledge and experience. She has endured the misfortunes caused by the religious dissensions with constancy. She holds to the Catholic faith and claims that she will defend it and bring up the King and her other children in it, following in the footsteps of their princely predecessors. . . . She likes to manage matters

O

and it pleases her to make one believe that everything stems from her authority, both in the Government and in the education of the Princes.'

The subtle Venetian was not misled. When he drew up his report Barbaro knew very well that Madame Catherine had in fact no longer any power. Her desperate attempts to make peace were ridiculed and were referred to as 'the Parliaments'; the futile 'Parliament of Toury' was laughed at. Barbaro knew the Queen's state of mind. In a letter to the Doge of Venice, after the failure of Toury, he spoke of her tears.

Catherine wept for her children, for France, and for herself. Coligny, however, imagined that the country would follow the victors, and that a forced offensive would bring victory to the Protestants. He mistook his own wishful thinking for reality, but the Queen Mother saw matters realistically. Paris seemed especially threatening to her. We know from Throckmorton that the Court had in fact taken refuge at Vincennes and that even Michel de L'Hospital had provided himself with Swiss guards, for Paris and the suburbs were in arms and the common people extremely menacing. He was hated by them and held responsible for the Huguenot excesses. Catherine was particularly troubled by the news from Normandy, where the English were disembarking. Throckmorton was in a state of incessant activity, advising Cecil to take Dieppe by surprise, to occupy Le Havre, and to finance the Protestant revolt. In order to thwart this British intervention, at the end of July the Queen Mother resigned herself to a long interview with Chantonnay, whom she informed (although we can be sure that the Spaniard had nothing to learn from her on the subject) of the appeal of the Calvinists to England and the Lutheran German princes. The Admiral had dared to write to her that he would 'give entry into this kingdom of as many Germans and Englishmen as he could, in the service of the King'.

The Reformationists had not changed their theme-song since Amboise—to deliver Charles IX, the prisoner of the Triumvirs. As regards his captivity, the documents prove them to have been right. But on the other hand, to unleash civil war was a remedy worse than the disease. Catherine had replied to Coligny that he was not required to serve the King thus, by introducing foreigners into France. She requested Philip II to intervene with Elizabeth I and to send reinforcements to the Royal army. Chantonnay, who was under orders to work for the development of anarchy in France, did not commit himself. His letters to Marguerite of Austria, Duchess of Parma, Governess of the Low Countries, revealed the Spanish game, and the anguish of Catherine, whom the English peril, momentarily the most pressing, caused to neglect the Spanish peril, which remained mortal. One has the impression that towards the end of that month of July 1562 the Queen Mother had lost the self-control which she had until then so magnificently retained. What a revenge for Chantonnay—Catherine reduced to imploring the despatch of Spanish troops from the Low Countries into France! He enjoyed this defeat of his enemy and allowed her to recriminate, complain and threaten him that if Spain delayed sending her help she would treat with the Huguenots. He promised her Italian and Spanish reinforcements. But in the end he realized that to trifle with a woman in such a state of exasperation might be dangerous; a treaty at any price with Condé might result from Spain's deliberate procrastination. He wrote to that effect to Marguerite of Austria.

Meanwhile the Triumvirs were beating the Protestants. They had taken Blois and marched on Bourges, taking the Queen Mother, of whom they continued to be suspicious, with them by force. Elizabeth's game was no less subtle than Philip II's. Her Gracious Majesty, like His Catholic Majesty, was above all interested in maintaining and prolonging the French troubles. Catherine strongly reproached the ambassador for this, whereupon his government recalled him to England, under the pretext that he had been insulted by the Parisian populace. She left Vincennes on August 5th. Anne de Montmorency had written to her as if he were her master, sending his son, the Marshal, with his orders to her. Catherine had been forced to obey, and with her children, the Court, and the officials to travel towards the army of the Triumvirs. A letter that she wrote on the way, on August 6th, to Jean Ebrard de Saint-Sulpice—successor at Madrid to the Bishop of Limoges, Sébastien de L'Aubespine—was a pressing demand for help, both for men and money, and gives us the measure of her powerlessness. The monarchy had once again fallen under the yoke of the favourites of Henri II. Three whole years of efforts to re-establish it as the arbiter of the nation were wiped out.

Condé's troops, few in numbers, were soon joined by all those whom hunger and despair threw on the side of the enemies of the government—the unemployed, despoiled peasantry, out-of-work servants and beggars. They were roused by the revolutionary harangues of preachers from the artisan classes, with no theological learning, or apostate and illiterate monks. The contagion inevitably accompanying iconoclasticism, the violation of tombs, profanation and sacrilege, spread like a fever. Both religious and political leaders became increasingly perturbed by it. In November 1561 Théodore de Bèze had already written that he feared his own adherents more than his adversaries. In spite of the Admiral's efforts, apart from the gentlemen who had joined it, the Protestant army was an army merely in name, a mere banding together of the rabble. This was demonstrated at the assault of Beaugency, when the Calvinists themselves were mishandled by the soldiery. The combatants had been fitted out with white cassocks, in order to make it clear that they were Royalist, and that they held the decree of the Paris Parliament, by which, on July 27th, they had been stated to be rebels, as null and void. Théodore de Bèze had provided prayers, some of which, such as that said at the evening meal of the guard, were profoundly moving, both patriotic and Christian.

To Coligny and Condé the King's deliverance was no meaningless formula. They had no intention of capturing the State against the King. Their sole objective was to drive out the Triumvirs and to serve the King. Their mistake was to have recourse to war. In this respect their sincerity and good faith were indubitable.

The Triumvirs, who controlled the State, needed infantry reinforcements; foot-soldiery from the Rhine and German cavalry, as well as Swiss and 4,000 Spaniards. Savoy, Ferrara, Florence, were to furnish troops as well. In order to gain the help of Emmanuel-Philibert the occupied sites in Piedmont were evacuated. The Pope had promised 100,000 gold écus, and in addition to guarantee the pay of 6,000 men. As the Spaniards provided the main force of infantry, the Triumvirs chose the red scarf of Spain, on which a white cross was embroidered, for the whole army. The colours of the Catholic army were therefore those of Spain, whilst those of the Protestant army were of France; mantles, scarves, plumes, standards, were all of them white, which was to be the colour of Henri IV and to become that of the flag of the Bourbons, whose original colours were blue and red.

Elizabeth I, who according to English tradition declared herself to be Queen of France as the result of the Treaty of Troyes of 1420, claimed Calais from her good Huguenot subjects, who, however, in return for a guarantee of military and financial assistance, only offered her Le Havre. But she had need of the Fuggers, Philip II's bankers, who were against the intervention on behalf of the Protestants. She was also in need of the merchants of the Low Countries, who were for the intervention out of hatred for Spain. Credit and commerce held together and she was held by them. In spite of her hesitations, however, she was to intervene, hoping thereby to gain Calais, which Philip II preferred should belong to England rather than France, as his rival preferred that Antwerp should go to the Catholic King rather than the Very Christian King.

The Protestants negotiated with her, whilst the Catholics did so with Philip II. Meanwhile both the English and the Spaniards kept each other reciprocally informed with regard to their dealings with the French. For it is a fact that as regards the principle of kingship politics take precedence over religion. The Protestant leaders demanded 300,000 crowns and 10,000 men from England. They were only given 100,000 crowns and 6,000 men. Le Havre was pledged by them in return, and Calais promised. The documents are incontestable on this point and one need only read them.

No other interpretation can be put upon the Treaty of Hampton Court of September 20, 1562, by which Le Havre was ceded. This port was to be evacuated by the English in return for Calais, which the Treaty of Le Cateau-Cambrésis had given back to France for only eight years.

In this, Coligny's tortuous scheming is clearly recognizable. The Admiral reckoned that the King, once he was delivered from the Triumvirs, would bring into play the clause in the Treaty of Cateau-Cambrésis according to which the cession of Calais would become void in the event of renewed aggression by England against the Very Christian King. Coligny was cheating, or thought that he was cheating, Elizabeth (a bird in hand is worth two in the bush and England held Le Havre), by giving her a pledge that would not be redeemed, since by virtue of the Treaty of Cateau-Cambrésis the non-restitution of Calais would make such a pledge invalid. He was still the same Coligny who at Saint Quentin had surrendered to the Duke of Savoy before the end of the street fighting in the city that he had been charged to defend! To Le Havre the negotiators added Dieppe and promised to add Rouen. Throckmorton noted that neither Condé nor Coligny could hide their shame as they accepted the conditions imposed by Cecil. Elizabeth's Prime Minister had them in his power; if they gave no pledges they would receive neither subsidies nor reinforcements. The Admiral surrendered the port as Governor of Le Havre. It has been alleged that the Vidamus of Chartres, a minor nobleman who was the principlal negotiator of the Treaty, had taken it upon himself to sign it without precise instructions, but this is a mockery since Coligny was in the habit of attending to his own affairs. Elizabeth lost no time; the Treaty of Hampton Court was dated September 20th, but the English had entered Le Havre on August 29th. According to his usual habits, Condé had given way, for the Admiral persuaded him that the Treaty was invalid and he himself imagined it to be so. But Throckmorton was not taken in by Coligny's machinations, of which he warned his sovereign. He knew the facts, for he himself had already begun the negotiations with regard to Le Havre on July 12th.

Catherine de Medici ignored nothing of the matter and thence sprang her vehement protests to Throckmorton, her despatch of Vieilleville to Elizabeth and the instructions she gave Paul de Foix, her ambassador to London. Catherine was working to save Le Havre whilst Coligny was intriguing to surrender it and this is sufficient answer to the Admiral's hagiographers, and to the calumnies directed at the Governess of France. Elizabeth's proclamation of September 27th, which confirmed the Treaty of Hampton Court and broke that of Cateau-Cambrésis, at a moment when France and England were completely at peace with one another, was a dialectical masterpiece, in every way worthy of Coligny. His conscience, however, was clear; he was convinced of the justice of his cause, and according to the teachings of Machiavelli, dishonest means should only be employed when the end, being a just one, justified them. In the eyes of the Calvinists their own cause was both a just and a good one, since it was the cause of the King, who had to be delivered from the Triumvirs, and the cause of France, which had to be rescued from Papist idolatry. It was 'with good and sincere intentions towards the King our good brother', declared Elizabeth, that she had occupied the Norman ports (and with perfect hypocrisy, since she was not in the least taken in). It was merely a matter of saving the King of France's Protestant subjects from annihilation, and 'to procure for them by all good means repose, peace, freedom, and deliverance from the violence of the said House of Guise or any adherents of the same'.

On reading the report made to Catherine de Medici by Beauvoir la Nocle, commander of the fortress of Le Havre on behalf of the Admiral-Governor, which he sent her in order to justify his handing over of it to the English, it appears quite certain that Coligny inspired the above casuistical declaration. Beauvoir invoked the glory of God and the deliverance and safety of the King during his minority. There is a striking similarity between the two documents, to which we may also add the jeremiads of the Vidamus of Chartres, who with Briquemault was the first signatory of the Treaty, writing to Cecil that he was his very humble and afflicted and sad *usque ad mortem*. Nothing was lacking.

Behind Condé, Coligny, the Vidamus, Briquemault and Beauvoir we can hear the theologians, adept at special pleading, as well as the pastors, as internationally-minded at Geneva as were the secretaries of the Curia at Rome, and ceding nothing to the Jesuits. What did France matter? Was this not God's concern? The theologians owed allegiance to no country: they burned both John Huss and Joan of Arc. A man like Coligny obeyed them; a Catherine de Medici resisted them. For her France came first and she knew that God would always recognize His children. Her concern was to save France, and to that she sacrificed everything. She made the little King write a friendly letter to Beauvoir, exhorting him to become faithful once more. Beauvoir's reply was along the lines of Elizabeth's proclamation: 'He regretted to do anything on behalf of his freedom of conscience to displease His Majesty.' He regretted. . . . The needs of the times obliged him to do so, and Le Havre remained in English hands!

The outcry was so great that the Governor of Rouen, Louis de Lannoy de Morvilliers, although he had Protestant sympathies, passed over to the Royal army and on Catherine's orders went to Dieppe as early as mid-August, to oppose the entry of the English there. Other Calvinists refused to follow Coligny, including the Lieutenant-General of the Government of Picardy, Sénarpont, and his sons, Claude de Halluin de Piennes, and François du Fou du Vigean. Catherine's letters of August and September 1562 refer constantly to this handing-over of Normandy to England. Meanwhile Throckmorton, having taken refuge in Orleans, was lodged in the Admiral's own house. The Queen Mother was at the end of her patience and magnanimity: 'To begin with', she wrote on September 20th to her ambassador to the Emperor, 'I shall use all gentle means that are open to me and if they fail I shall resolve myself to using sharp and hard ones in order to have the right of the matter.'

From the capture of Poitiers on May 31st to that of Bourges on August 31st victory succeeded victory for the Triumvirs. Catherine made a point of being present herself at the siege of Rouen, which it was necessary to occupy before the English. Her bravery won general admiration. She had become embittered against the Huguenots since

they had refused the offer of peace made to Condé, in order to stop
the English invasion, by the Duke de Guise, whose military sense of
honour was greater than either his feudal ambitions or his anti-
Calvinist zeal. Louis Madelin has rightly emphasized it: 'a favourable
and immediate peace if he would consent to join with him in order
to expulse these ancient enemies of the Crown. Condé's refusal
authorized the Triumvirs to proclaim themselves the living pillars
and supports of the realm, and sole upholders of the national
religion'.[1]

When reading the documentation one cannot at this point forbear
to admire Monsieur de Guise le Grand. What he was in fact offering
was the free exercise of the abhorred religion. In order to save
Calais the victor of Calais was renouncing his religious policy.
Catherine had admitted to Tavannes that 'I clearly see that I have
wasted my time in endeavouring to settle matters by kindness.'
Thenceforward she was all for war, all the more so as Rouen was
commanded by Montgomery, whom she hated for having mortally
wounded Henri II, and Briquemault, the odious negotiator of the
Treaty of Hampton Court.

The hereditary fighting spirit of the daughter of the Medici, the
spirit of Cosimo, Father of Florence, was now aroused in the Governess of France, her country, which owing to his criminal irresponsibility Condé was rending apart and delivering to the enemy at the
very moment when Guise himself was in favour of peace. Like a true
King of France, Catherine was at her action station. In front of the
16,000 foot soldiery, the 2,000 cavalrymen of the army, to the sound
of the forty-five pieces of artillery, Madame Catherine was determined to prove to the Triumvirs that she had not the heart of a captive but that of an Amazon. Her psychological intuition rarely
deceived her, and she now succeeded in making the impression she
had planned. Anne de Montmorency, who knew all there was to be
known about courage, admired her: 'Madame', he wrote to the
Duchess de Guise, 'I assure you that the Queen has become a very
good captain.' Would the Constable, the Lorraine Prince, the King
of Navarre still treat her as if she were a Florentine shopkeeper, or

[1] John Viénot (*Réforme française*, Vol. I, p. 382) and Henri Hauser (*Prépondérance
espagnole*, p. 60) take good care not to make the slightest allusion to this gesture, so
nobly French; thus does prejudice, behind the mask of objectivity, betray itself by its
deliberate omissions. Neither do Hector de la Ferrière nor Mariéjol refer to it. But C.
Martin, in *L'Histoire générale Lavisse et Rambaud* (t. V, p. 131) mentions the fact in one
line, which obviously seemed sufficient to him—Forneron, on the contrary, stresses it.
(*Les Ducs de Guise et leur Epoque*, Vol. I, p. 410–11).

had she not, at their side under fire, won her right to be Governess of France?

The death of Antoine de Bourbon, killed by a musket shot as he was taking off his trousers as a Rabelaisian gesture of disdain towards the defenders of the ramparts, came at that moment as if to support the recognition of Catherine's right. There was no longer a Lieutenant-General of the realm nor a co-regent. The First Prince of the Blood was now Condé, who had refused to make peace. The capital of Normandy was taken on October 26, 1562.

After the town had been sacked during a whole week, despite efforts to prevent this by Catherine and the Triumvirs, Throckmorton, the former ambassador, and Smith, his successor, fought relentlessly against the vacillations of Monsieur le Prince, who at last appeared willing to talk peace. The Parliament of Paris had decreed the arrest of the Châtillons, but excepted Condé, whom they declared to be the prisoner of the rebels. Catherine, who never despaired of winning him back, handled the volatile Prince carefully. Although it had been reinforced by Andelot's Germans, the Protestant army only disposed of 8,000 foot-soldiers and 6,000 horsemen. Catherine hoped that Condé would listen to reason. She had received satisfactory news from the Council of Trent; the Cardinal de Lorraine was fulfilling the mission on which she had sent him, and was upholding the programme of reforms, although it was so audacious, that she had drawn up. This included utraquism, the use of French for the psalms and prayers, the renouncing of such abuses as frequent excommunications, too great a number of pilgrimages and brotherhoods, the reform of commendums and resignations in favour of third parties as well as pensions subject to no control, and finally the holding of annual diocesan synods, triannual provincial synods, and councils every ten years.

This Gallican and Irenist programme could not fail to facilitate the reconciliation of the French. Condé was tempted. In November Catherine sent Gonnor to him, offering to make him Antoine's successor. Would Monsieur le Prince yield? At the very end of the month meetings took place over which the Queen Mother presided, happy as usual to be involved in diplomatic activities, for loving France as an Auvergnat miser loved his money, she also possessed a Florentine liking for political discussion. Venoimous Italy it was called by the French, still new to the arts of intrigue; Louis XI himself was merely a sharp-witted, cunning, artful peasant. In any matter of bargaining the Florentine shopkeeper was in her element, for negotiation was merely another form of haggling, was it not? She did not fear to face bullets and cannon-balls, but she much preferred to confer. She was delighted when the moment came again to play the fox, which reposed her from the role of the lioness. If Condé were willing to make peace Elizabeth would be obliged to evacuate Normandy and there would be no more *raison d'être* to accept the dangerous assistance of Spain and Savoy. Religious peace would restore freedom of action to French foreign policy; for the maintenance and strengthening of French unity Catherine de Medici had adapted to it the Florentine dream of Machiavelli, which was also her own—that of Italian unity.

England, the Empire, Spain. . . . Why could the Protestants and Catholics in their mutual antagonism not understand what the Queen Mother understood so well? It was these jealous neighbours who were France's permanent and mortal danger.

And indeed she found the handing-over of Le Havre to England intolerable. Monsieur le Prince, embarrassed, refrained from appearing at the meetings, which took place in the environs of Paris. Those on the Catholic side who were present were the Constable, the Cardinal de Bourbon, the Prince de la Roche-sur-Yon, the Secretary of State Claude de L'Aubespine, and Gonnor; on the Protestant side were the Admiral and his brother, Andelot, La Rochefoucauld, Genlis, Gramont and Esternay. But these meetings were abortive. According to Throckmorton, the reason for this was the refusal to consider Condé's army as Royal, and to pay the Germans under his orders. Condé, by denying that Le Havre had been handed over, was lying, which brought him the threat from the English that they would abandon him. Paris, meanwhile, received the Spanish troops on December 7th. Condé caused the negotiations to be broken off and directed his troops towards Normandy, where they were to receive the British reinforcements. Elizabeth's ambassador complained of his dishonesty. The documentary evidence is overwhelmingly against Monsieur le Prince, whose lack of character was responsible for the resumption of hostilities. On December 17th Catherine ordered Montmorency 'to cut short this war, for we no longer have the means to keep it going indefinitely'. Two days later the Huguenots were defeated at Dreux. The triumphant news was immediately brought to her at the castle of Rambouillet, where she had taken up residence in order to be closer to the theatre of operations.

Catherine was only too well aware that this victory belonged to the

Triumvirs and not to herself, and she was deeply worried by the fact that the Spaniards had taken part in the battle. She confided her real views on the matter to Smith, who, as a typical Englishman anxious to keep on good terms with the victor, congratulated her. She considered that 'such victories were calamitous for the King, her son, that she had done everything to avoid it, conceding all that they had asked for in religious matters, but that they had a different aim and other plans'. The capture of Condé, the death of the Marshal de Saint-André, were insufficient compensation for the triumph of Anne de Montmorency and François de Guise. There would now be no counterweight to balance the power of these Duumvirs; the Protestants were completely defeated and Elizabeth decided not to engage herself any more deeply in favour of such uncertain allies. The Admiral's clever retreat made it possible for him to prolong the war, which, however, could have no successful issue for him without English help. It was therefore important to take advantage of the situation to come to terms with him before the victors of Dreux were able to exploit all the advantages they now held. Although a prisoner, Condé was too proud to give way. Catherine made preparations to carry the war to the bitter end. In order that all efforts should be directed against Orleans she established her headquarters at Chartres. Her letters reveal her intense activity. She wrote several every day—political, administrative, diplomatic, even military. The Constable and the Duc de Guise, engaged in military activities, were unable to intervene in government affairs, which Catherine had again taken in hand. She did not despair of bringing the Admiral to repentance. 'Peace is necessary to us to drive out the foreigner'—these words in one of her letters to Gonnor reveal her constant preoccupation.

A comparison between the correspondence of the Queen Mother and that of the Admiral during the last days of 1562, January 1563, and the first two weeks of February, removes all doubt on one point —Catherine was thinking only of France, Coligny had no thought in his mind save the interests of his party. On January 24th he dared to write to the Queen of England that after God he expected her to afford him his principal aid and succour, knowing her to possess divine virtues and powers, for God had chosen and preserved her at this time and presented her with the opportunity to lift up and re-establish His pure worship, abolishing idolatry in all Christendom and even in France. Catherine, on the contrary, was for the nation and wanted national peace. Henceforward Coligny sacrificed his patriotism to his religious passions; a strange reversal of the Christian spirit, for which he had mistaken Calvinist mysticism. Catherine remained solely preoccupied by the aim of expelling the foreigner from France.

The case was clear. Catherine was French and Guise himself had made the honorable gesture of offering peace to Condé in order to deliver Normandy, but Coligny threw himself at the feet of Elizabeth, whom he praised for having 'everywhere so clearly proved that she had no other aim but the advancement of the glory of God'. Since 1562 Coligny's outlook had become that of a Leaguer, a Leaguer of Geneva, and thus he was to remain until his death. This was the origin of the conflict which caused Catherine to oppose him during ten years, after having until then placed all her hopes in him. As the result of a slowly developing fanaticism, of which he himself was for a long time unaware, but which led to the Treaty of Hampton Court, the Admiral had become England's man: to a lesser degree, no doubt, than Henri de Guise was later to become Spain's. Coligny was not the Queen of England's agent, but her ally, and occasionally even her accomplice. Châtillon and Lorraine both renounced their freedom in favour of the foreigner. Both may have known momentary revolts and even repentances. But the chain was too heavy to be broken by these prisoners. Only the hunting-pole of Janowitz, the daggers of the Forty-Five, were to break it, horribly. *Tristem fortunae vicem.* This was the sad fate of the great feudalists who were nevertheless of the stuff to make splendid servants of France. For in their day they alone understood that the nation needed to secure its northern and eastern military frontiers, as Louis XI had wished, and in which Catherine herself, always too much inclined to forming carefully planned diplomatic alliances, and constantly obsessed by the danger of Spanish Mediterranean power, took no interest, whilst they judged the situation above all as military men. The documents do in fact prove that Coligny wanted the barrier of Flanders, and Henri de Guise that of the Rhine. And how ironical this situation was! Coligny, the friend of Elizabeth, was in favour of the occupation of Flanders, which England would never, in any circumstances, have allowed to pass under French domination. The loss of Calais made it even more desirable that Antwerp should be free of Frenchmen. Henri de Guise, the agent of Philip II, preoccupied only by the German Lutheran mercenaries, failed to realize that had the Rhine become French, Germany would escape Spain and that 'King of France, Vicar of the Holy Empire and Protector of German freedom' was a formula that in such an event might ultimately become a fact. The exergue on the famous medallion that Louis le Grand ordered to be struck after the reunion of Strasbourg with Alsace on September 30, 1681—*Clausa Germanis Gallia*—did not mark the end of an imaginary German hegemony, but symbolized that of Spanish preponderance, the strength of which had lain in its reservoir of men drawn from the German States. It was only the defeat of Spain that allowed the Rhine to become French, that Spain at whose service the son of the Emperor's victor was to place himself!

During the last days of January 1563, at Catherine's request, Monsieur de Guise le Grand met Monsieur le Prince at Blois. Coligny, who was becoming more and more anxious over Elizabeth's procrastinations, was willing to enter into new negotiations. He wrote to Condé that nothing was more sought after nor desirable than peace. Yet nevertheless, regaining hopes of England, at the last moment he avoided attending the meeting.

The Queen Mother, lacking funds, was in haste to end the war, but Coligny insisted on prolonging it. The siege of Orleans under François de Guise was progressing most favourably when, in the evening of February 18, 1563, Poltrot de Méré assassinated the hero of Metz and Calais. A minute examination of the documents referring to this crime, committed on the very eve of the day when the main fortress of the Reformationists was expected by everyone to fall, forces us to conclude that the Admiral was the instigator of a deed that freed him from his most redoubtable enemy. Catholic opinion unanimously accused him of it. Looking at the matter objectively, the historian here finds himself faced with contradictory indictments and apologias, supported on both sides by a mass of arguments which prevent him from drawing any categorical conclusion on the subject.

Coligny's approval of Poltrot de Méré's act was definite: 'This death is the greatest good that could have happened to this kingdom and to the Church of God and in particular to myself and all my House.' He said it, proclaimed it, whilst Condé, proud and inconstant yet incapable of baseness, immediately wrote to the Queen Mother expressing his horror at such a crime. The most serious aspect of the matter was that Théodore de Bèze joined in with Coligny's approval. And we have the letter written by Smith from Blois on February 26th to Elizabeth of England. The ambassador was implacable towards his own country's ally: 'The assassin is aged nineteen, a native of Saintonge; he came with the intention of killing the Duke at the instigation of Soubise, at present at Lyons. It was Soubise who sent him to the Admiral, before he passed into Normandy; the Admiral gave him 300 écus. It is also said that he was encouraged in his plan by Théodore de Bèze.' The contradictory statements of Poltrot de Méré, in the course of his interrogation, trial and torture, the Admiral's denials regarding the material issue of having hired him to commit this murder, all contribute to complicating and obscurring the tragedy of Orleans. Let us retain only Coligny's cynical admission: 'I did not dissuade him from it', an admission in writing, contained in the memorandum drawn up by Coligny himself on March 12th, at Caen, countersigned by Bèze and La Rochefoucauld and forwarded to the Queen Mother, and which puts and end to all quibbling to the contrary. The Amiral's active complicity may always remain a matter for discussion, but his moral complicity was crystal clear. Catherine underlined his hypocrisy in her letter of February 25th to Marguerite of Savoy, in which she told her of her suspicions that he wanted to have her assassinated, 'for he hates me infinitely. . . . That, Madame, is how this good man, who claims that he does nothing except in the cause of religion, wishes to despatch us'. The Lorraines were and remained convinced that the Admiral was indeed the instigator of the murder. They did not rest until he was duly punished. Jacques Bainville was completely right in saying that 'this crime added the vendetta to the civil and religious wars'. Nor was the thirst for vengeance to be slaked until nine and a half years later, on Saint Bartholomew's Night.

The death of François de Guise left Catherine in an uncertain position, between the undeniable personal advantage she had gained through the disappearance of one of the Duumvirs and the enormous loss to the State of its greatest military figure. Wounded on February 18th, the Duke died on the 24th. The Queen came from Blois to visit him, having left as soon as the news of the attack on him had reached her. Her letters on the death of Monsieur de Guise are remarkably cold; it is clear that she did not grieve for him. It was a political crime which she considered only from the point of view of her political interests. Does this give us the right to assume that she as well as the Admiral was an accomplice to this deed? Her contemporaries thought so. It is an established fact that Catherine considered Duke François her most dangerous rival on the Catholic side, on account of his unchallenged prestige, which Anne de Montmorency lacked. In public opinion the Constable was regarded as responsible for the defeat of Saint Quentin, nor did anyone ignore the fact that he would have lost the battle of Dreux had it not been for the victor of Metz. Also, he was seventy years of age, whilst Guise was the Queen's contemporary. Montmorency, who was intensely jealous of him, was in favour of peace because war could only contribute to the glory of the Lorraine Prince. Catherine had every reason to believe that she could make use of the Constable, whereas the Duke would always have stood in her way to power.

The Marshal Gaspard de Saulx de Tavannes reported that the Court attributed the very opportune death of Monsieur de Guise le Grand to the Queen Mother. Tavannes is a somewhat suspect source, since his memoirs were not written by himself but by his son, Jean, and recorded more than forty years after the events. There is the Latin letter of Albanus, supposedly Pierre d'Elbène, an intimate of the Queen Mother's. According to Albanus, Catherine had a Machiavellian plan, namely to exploit the hatred of Poltrot and of the Admiral, for personal reasons, and at one and the same time of the Lorraine Prince, as head of the Catholics. Thus Catherine had supposedly incited Poltrot 'to commit the crime, by persuading him to accuse the Admiral, after it was done, of having driven him to it'.

Albanus's letter is completely in the Italian tradition of shady transactions; sixteenth century sources contain many such documents. Its authenticity is not established. Even if it were authentic nothing proves that this accusation rests on solid grounds. But the text of the assassin's interrogations and trial do coincide with certain passages in Albanus. There is in addition, and especially, Catherine's extraordinary display of emotion when, on sprinkling holy water over François de Guise's coffin she almost fainted, as Alvarotti noted in his letter of March 2, 1563. Nor should we forget here, either, that on questioning Poltrot de Méré nothing seemed to surprise her, and that according to the *Mémoires* of Gaspard de Tavannes she admitted that those de Guises planned to seize the throne, which she had well and truly prevented them from doing at Orleans. Finally, in a letter to Philip II from Amboise on April 12, 1563, Chantonnay reported that she had said to the Savoyard ambassador: 'Such are the works of God; those who sought to destroy me are dead.' The Venetian ambassador confirmed his Spanish colleague. In a despatch from Marco Antonio Barbaro of April 12th we may read that Madame Catherine said that if Monsieur de Guise had perished sooner, peace would have been made more quickly. As early as March 30th Middlemore, one of the heads of the English spy system, informed Elizabeth that the Queen Mother had said to Condé, when he was set free, that 'the death of the Duke of Guise had no less freed her from prison than it had set the Prince at liberty, and that, just as the Prince was the Duke's captive, so she, owing to the forces with which he had surrounded the King and herself, was no less his prisoner and deprived by him of her freedom'.

Nothing was truer. Nevertheless Catherine de Medici was too realistic not to know that the dead can be as dangerous and even more dangerous than the living, and Monsieur de Guise le Grand was such a man. Did she think that as far as she was concerned the danger would now be less than her own impotence in dealing with the victor of Metz, and the near-victor of Orleans? The documents at our disposal do not allow us to answer the question one way or another. Coligny's moral complicity in the assassination of the Lorraine prince is proven; his actual complicity, however, remains doubtful. Both factually and morally the Queen Mother's complicity remains in doubt. But the satisfaction that she felt at being freed from the man who was her master as well as master of the kingdom is obvious. First Navarre, then Saint-André, then François de Guise had gone. Of the six men who had been competing with her for supreme power three remained—Anne de Montmorency, in his seventies and ailing; Condé, lacking will-power; and Coligny, lacking character. The sky was brightening. Catherine thought herself able either to make use of or to overcome these survivors. Time was pressing, for the death of the Lorraine prince had exacerbated the rival passions—the scandalous rejoicing of the Protestants and the desperate fury of the Catholics. Libellers and songsters, exciting the factions, proclaimed Poltrot de Méré as avenger and saint, or François de Guise as the martyr whom God had taken unto his glory.

Catherine speeded up the trial and torture of Poltrot, who was condemned to suffer the death of regicides, by quartering, on March 18th, the eve of the truly royal obsequies of his victim. The scaffold on the Place de la Grève, the catafalque and the processions at Notre-Dame, pacified the Parisians slightly. That was the moment to make terms with the Protestants; the edict of pacification was signed at Amboise on March 12, 1563, and was published on the 19th—the very day on which Paris was thinking of nothing but the parricide torn to pieces between four horses and his victim, who was receiving royal honours—and was registered by the Parliament on the 27th. This second edict of Amboise was drawn up by Catherine and L'Hospital immediately on the death of François de Guise. On

February 25th, after an interview with the Prince de La Roche-sur-Yon, Condé had written to his wife saying how much he himself longed for peace 'so necessary to this poor kingdom'. On March 1st the Princesse de Condé had met the Queen Mother. On the 6th, at the Ile-aux-Boeufs, below Orleans, Monsieur le Prince was in *tête-à-tête* conference with the Constable, and on the following day in Catherine's presence. In order to make it clear that he was no longer a prisoner the Queen had had Condé's sword returned to him. She diplomatically used all her powers of seduction and won Monsieur le Prince over. Chantonnay reported that she laughed and danced for joy. Coligny had just captured Caen, and the Emperor took advantage of the situation to demand the evacuation of the Three Bishoprics.

The English at Le Havre and the Imperialists at Metz—it was really too much! If the fanatics of both parties, entirely given over to their fratricidal hatred, did not care, Catherine de Medici could not bear it. Her letter to Gonnor, written from the camp of Saint-Mesmin on March 12th, shows that her only concern was for the public welfare: 'To free this kingdom from all those leeches who are draining its life's-blood from it unto death. By this peace the King, Monsieur my son, remains the master and the forces and the foreigners empty his kingdom.' Chantonnay, as he followed the progress of the negotiations, was highly displeased. In the Constable's case, patriotism finally overcame feudalism, whilst Monsieur le Prince remembered that he was a Son of France. He stood his ground against the fanatical preachers, of whom seventy-two had gathered together and who, not satisfied with refusing to make a single concession, were demanding vengeance against the Catholics, scaffolds for the atheists and also for those heretics who contradicted the dogmas of Calvin. That was their conception of freedom of conscience. The nobility, however, adhered to the party of reason. On the 13th, Montmorency was able to write to Gonnor: 'Peace is concluded and I am sure that you will consider this to be a very good thing in view of the poverty of this realm. I inform you that from here to Bayonne all are shouting '*Vive la France!*'

Vive la France! That was what Catherine wanted to hear, and not Long Live the Pope! or Long Live Calvin! The Constable was a soldier. In his case patriotism finally prevailed, as it had done with François de Guise. The edict of Amboise of March 1563 was a declaration of patriotism and union. But, alas, a precarious declara-

P

tion if it is compared to the first edict of the same name, that of March 1560. Complete and immediate pacification was rendered impossible by rancour nourished on blood. The Queen Mother was unable to conceal the fact from herself. 'It was a case of *reculer pour mieux sauter*' she later admitted. She was counting on gaining time; time that would bring forgetfulness and appeasement, as well as the majority of Charles IX and reforms agreed to by the Council, an amnesty and restricted but legal freedom of worship. The first edict of Amboise had placed the two forms of worship on an equal footing, and this had been confirmed by the edict of Saint Germain of January 1562. But now it was no longer a matter of more than freedom of conscience, a sad set-back after a mere three years! And who was to blame for it but those responsible for the religious war, the Reformationists themselves?

Nevertheless, Coligny remained under Elizabeth's orders, as is proven by Middlemore's correspondence. The Englishman reproached the Queen Mother for the execution of Poltrot de Méré in spite of the fact that he had requested her to prolong his imprisonment until the investigation had been completed. He reproached and argued with her. On March 23rd he was at Orleans and his interviews with the Queen Mother, who received him amiably, led to concessions in favour of his co-religionists. But Catherine remained intractable with regard to Le Havre and Calais and Middlemore complained of the lack of zeal on behalf of England's case shown by both Coligny and Condé. To Smith, Elizabeth's envoy, she replied that the continued occupation of Le Havre would constitute a case for war. She was delighted by the difficulties that were now setting the signatories to the Hampton Court Treaty against one another and took good care not to intervene, leaving the English and the Huguenots at their quarrelling. Coligny was extremely embarrassed by the religious peace which had been made much sooner than he had expected. In reading the details of the discussions that were taking place between the plotters of Hampton Court, as they appear in the *Calendars* of 1563, one can understand Catherine's pleasure and, in spite of the gap of centuries, share it. Coligny was caught in his own trap; he tried to shelter behind the Queen Mother, but she refrained from protecting him.

Théodore de Bèze chose to leave France the day after the Lord's Supper at Orleans on March 28th, at which 6,000 of the faithful were present. Coligny was quibbling over the clauses of the Hampton Court Treaty; Le Havre and Calais were becoming a nightmare to him. The discussions were degenerating into quarrels. Smith accused the French Protestants of bad faith and threatened them with war. Coligny moaned and dared to say that the time to surrender Calais had not yet arrived but that Elizabeth would certainly gain possession of that town later on. Having so good a guarantee, could she not therefore wait for it? The peace that Catherine desired and that had been accepted by Monsieur le Prince was extremely embarrassing to the Admiral's plans. When Catherine had received the first news of the Battle of Dreux, which was bad, she had said that the price to be paid merely meant that in future they would pray to God in French. France, in her estimation, came before everything else. But Coligny, on the contrary, having at first shown signs of patriotism had arrived at the point of subordinating every other consideration to the religious dispute. In dealing with Smith he lowered himself to the extent of admitting to him that if the Queen of England had sent the money she had promised to the Huguenots a few days earlier, they would have been the victors and would then have been able to carry out in full the clauses of the Hampton Court Treaty. His enemy. Monsieur de Guise le Grand, had given way in religious matters in order to save Calais, but the Admiral excused himself, on the grounds of *force majeure*, for not having handed over this stronghold to the English. Even lacking any other documents—and unfortunately there is no lack of them!—Smith's letters to Elizabeth would be sufficient to enable Coligny to be judged, and to be overwhelmingly condemned.

Catherine's honour is vindicated by the condition, for her a *sine qua non*, that was included in the peace that had been signed at Amboise, namely that all foreigners should be driven from the kingdom of France. *All*, claimed the Queen—Spaniards, Italians, English, Germans, whether at the service of Rome or Geneva, of Madrid or London. The Governess of France was thinking only in terms of a France that had again become French.

It is incontestable that the peace of Amboise saved France from being shared out between the Empire, Spain and England. The Queen Mother knew this better than anyone. Let us read her long letter of March 25, 1563, to the Cardinal de Lorraine, in which everything is considered from the point of view of the national interests: 'And also, having seen so much evil being prepared for the utter ruin of this kingdom, the opposing levies being raised for the others in Germany, the threats of those of the Empire regarding the restitution of Metz, the outcome of which we do not as yet know, the

English plans so far advanced that already the whole of Lower
Normandy is more or less in their hands, the Castle of Caen lost,
our kingdom impoverished on all sides and even more exhausted,
of which you may have had news, our friends so cold and whose
designs are also to be feared, to say the least . . . it has been decided
that it were better to protect the King and the kingdom in its
entirety, as it stands, than to expose it to apparent and real danger
by the introduction of so many foreigners.'

The Italian who had become Queen of France placed both her
intellect and her heart wholly at the service of her second country.
The Florentine patriot had invited the Medici to deliver Italy from
the foreigner. He prayed Heaven to produce a prince who would
free Italy from the humiliating and odious foreign yoke. Madame
Catherine had adapted the words of the final Chapter of *Il Principe*
to France. She could also have sung with Petrarch:

> *Virtù contra furore*
> *Prendera l'arme, e fia'l combatter corto,*
> *Che l'antico valore*
> *Negl'italici cuor non é ancor morto.*

Courage in arms against fury, for a brief combat; the ancient
valour and heart of Italy are not yet dead. Madame Catherine
substituted 'the French heart' as a variant on the song of Petrarch
with which Machiavelli ended his book. She thought of France as
he did of Italy when in Chapter XXVI of *Il Principe* he wrote: 'So
that, bereft of life, she awaits whomever may staunch her wounds
and put an end to pillage . . . and cure her of her sores that have
been for a long time running in fistulas. We can see how she prays to
God that He may send someone to rescue her from these barbaric
cruelties and tyrannies.' Catherine wanted to be that rescuer. She
herself failed, but she opened a path for the deliverer, who was to be
Henri IV. Had it not been for the incessant strivings of the Florentine, the Béarnais would have been unable to grasp the standard of
which Machiavelli said so magnificently that 'it offered itself to one
who would brandish in his fist'. The day after the Peace of Amboise,
'her' Peace, Madame Catherine was very close to grasping it. What
the secretary of the Florentine chancellery longed for with all his
soul for Italy she thought she had, this time, won for France.
Catherine believed that through the Peace Treaty of Amboise she
could bring about in France what Machiavelli had so ardently

hoped for Italy, and that the French nation would as the result of this reconciliation unite to follow her, in remembrance of Joan of Arc, in throwing the English out of France.

Both the pastors and Coligny were dissatisfied with the peace. The latter heaped reproaches on Condé for having offered the lesser portion to God and for having destroyed more churches, 'by this stroke of the pen than the entire forces of the enemy could have razed in ten years'. On April 5, 1563, Calvin had written to the Prince de Soubise that Condé was a wretch. From the strictly religious point of view his anger was justified, since the objective of the Reformationists was not freedom of conscience but the domination of the State, in order that the King of France should serve the true faith. In actual fact the peace of Amboise confined the practice of the cult to the nobility, which aroused bitter discontent in the faithful among the common people.

The Queen Mother was too clever not to have taken this into account. She had studied the lessons of history well enough and was too deeply steeped in Machiavelli and Guicciardini to forget, in spite of the failure of her constant efforts to achieve unity, the practical usefulness of the precept *Divide ut regnes*, thanks to which the small city of Rome had become mistress of the ancient world. Since the Protestant leaders had used their religion as an instrument of civil war it was necessary to dry it up at the source; to destroy their control of the masses who had followed them by reducing a movement which had threatened to become a national and popular one to a mere *Praguerie*. Since whole provinces had risen in support of them the danger was a very great one, but the *Praguerie*, the *Ligue du Bien publique*, the insane war, had all failed because the nobility had had no popular support. It was therefore now necessary to isolate the nobility from the Protestant masses.

The edict of Amboise provided for such a move. Coligny, in whom the religious leader was becoming more and more dominant over the politician, made no mistake about it. With Calvin he was against the peace. Henceforward there was no other possible solution to the conflict between him and Catherine de Medici than by force. The Queen knew that in numbers and resources Catholic France was stronger than Protestant France. Her choice was dictated by political realism. So long as it remained impracticable to put the two cults on an equal footing the Reformationists would remain a tolerated minority. Wisdom lay in refraining from recognizing them *de jure* whilst doing so *de facto*, at least until religious passion had calmed down. But the Admiral was exasperated by his defeat and thought only of making it good. Henceforward he would subordinate everything to the conquest of the State in order to re-establish the unity of Protestantism which Catherine was attempting to break. He would oppose Protestant unity to national unity. Still Royalist in principle, the Huguenots would provisionally cease to be so in fact, for necessity compelled them to it. On the morrow of the peace of Amboise the ineluctable chain of historical causality was to bring back war. Catherine, whose clearsightedness had never been dimmed, called it *reculer pour mieux sauter*. But the jump forward could only lead to war. The best method for postponing the evil moment was a diversionary war, for which the English occupation of Normandy offered a cause of which Catherine hastened to avail herself.

On April 1st the Queen Mother made her entry into Orleans, between Monsieur le Prince and his brother, the Cardinal de Bourbon, preceded by the Constable and the Duc de Montpensier, followed by the Admiral and the Chancellor. She compelled the Parliaments to enregister the edict of Amboise. Her instructions to her ambassadors and her letters show her anxiety that the Council of Trent should lead to spiritual peace, and she demanded that it be transferred to Baden or Spires, 'in a place to which the Germans, the first and principal people responsible for the present divisions, should be able to come in all security'. Important as the Council was, the absence of the Lutherans deprived it of the universal status it required.

Madame Catherine wrote to her daughter of Spain that once the foreigners were ejected from the kingdom, the State having regained its calm, she alone would be in command. In her correspondence of April 1563 she referred constantly to the misfortunes of France, resulting from 'the pillaging and execrable evil done by the Reiters' (German horse-soldiery) and said that she was sick to death of it, suffering because she had not the necessary forces at her disposal to punish them. She reproached the Protestants for having destroyed the edict of Saint Germain by war, and blamed those men who aspired to be king-makers. 'This', she wrote to Gonnor on April 19th, 'is the truth, spoken by the King's mother, who loves but him and the preservation of the kingdom and his subjects.'

She had no personal army, since the Constable was head of the armed forces. She had no money; the coffers were empty and the taxes were not coming in. English and Germans, Spaniards and

Italians, behaved as if France were a vanquished country. Coligny was continuing his negotiations with Elizabeth, which were becoming more and more difficult. The signatories to the Hampton Court Treaty were placed in an impasse by the Anglo-Spanish alliance, which the two States had maintained even after the death of Mary Tudor and in spite of the anti-Catholic reaction which had followed on it; both Philip II and Elizabeth I were equally in favour of it, and neither one nor the other had the least intention either of breaking or even of weakening it. Philip would not under any pretext intervene in the matter of Le Havre and Calais. Elizabeth therefore had every latitude to establish herself at Calais without running any risk of Spain coming to the aid of France, and this was the reason for her intransigeance in dealing with Coligny. Here the documents allow us to follow in detail Catherine's policy as she took advantage of the conflict, becoming more and more bitter, between the Queen of England and Monsieur le Prince and the Admiral. It was all to her interest that it should be long drawn-out, thus enabling her to prepare for war on a national scale. She played such a skilful game with Elizabeth's two representatives, Middlemore and Smith, that Coligny was reduced to making the shameful confession that he had had no right to sign the Treaty of Hampton Court and that he ratified it, at Caen, without even having read it. In this way he threw the responsibility for it on to the Vidamus of Chartres. How typical this was, once again, of Coligny and his habit of dodging the facts in order to exonerate himself!

From now on the Admiral, who did not want to go to war against the English but was unable to justify the validity of the occupation of Normandy, was in Catherine's power. In order to avoid having to take sides Andelot let it be known that he was ill. English tenacity was the strongest trump against the Protestants held by the Florentine Queen, whom Elizabeth cursed for not allowing herself to be drawn into the argument.

Little Charles IX had become an adolescent; he was thirteen. Highly intelligent and completely obedient to his mother, the young King played his part in this very Italian comedy. At the Royal sessions of May 27, 1563, he enchanted the Parliament of Paris, and Michel de L'Hospital obtained 100,000 écus, non-redeemable, on the revenues of the Church, paid solely by the bishops and the higher stipendiaries; those were the Chancellor's own terms. The national debt had reached the astronomical figure of fifty million and it was no use pretending that the sum agreed upon was anything but a small beginning, but it was accepted resignedly and everyone bowed to Catherine's will.

Philip II prudently refrained from stating his views on the peace of Amboise. The Fathers of the Council expressed their disapproval of it. Pius IV denounced this shameful peace, the responsibility for which was entirely Catherine's, owing to the favours she had shown towards the Huguenot gang, whom she had made the masters of France. The whole of Europe saw the lovely prey that civil war would have offered it escaping. But the fanaticism of the contending parties did not decrease and a war against England was an immediate necessity to the public welfare. The Queen made it known everywhere that the English saw in Le Havre their revenge for Calais, and that Elizabeth I had personally asserted this to the French envoy, the Sieur d'Alluye, assistant to Paul de Foix. She pressed the pace and on June 25th she took the Court to Normandy. For the past three months she had been assembling her troops; she wrote to her sister-in-law, Marguerite de Valois, that she disposed of forty cannon, could fire 20,000 shots, and had 40,000 infantrymen. 'So that I think that if Queen Elizabeth does not return Le Havre to us willingly, God will enable us to take it by force.'

In the reconquest of Le Havre Anne de Montmorency saw an opportunity for glory analogous to that offered to François de Guise in bygone days by Calais. Condé was thinking of the recapture of Rouen and of his brother Antoine. He was annoyed with Elizabeth, who had just refused to surrender Le Havre in return for a promise to carry out the clause in the Treaty of Le Cateau-Cambrésis with reference to Calais, in spite of its occupation. The wily Tudor Queen had sniffed the poisoned bait; once Catherine was in Le Havre she would disavow Monsieur le Prince. The Florentine had played a safe hand, for the pride of Henry VIII's daughter was clashing with that of the First Prince of the Blood; the offer of Calais had no other end. As soon as this was attained, and Middlemore was dismissed by Condé whilst the Admiral at Châtillon-sur-Loing was caught in the trap of his own intrigues, the way was clear. The Queen Mother immediately entered upon it.

The siege was a short one. The town capitulated on July 28, 1563. The young King was at Criquetot. A sonnet by Jodelle celebrated this victory.

There was general rejoicing. Elizabeth of England had been defeated. On July 31st the Queen Mother wrote to the Bishop of Rennes that it was a 'good thing that had happened in this kingdom by the grace of God, contrary to the opinion of many people; in which He showed His justice and equity, revealing to us by many other graces that He held this kingdom in His holy care and protection'. The allusion was clearly to Coligny, remaining at Châtillon-sur-Loing, where he had never ceased to correspond and to negotiate with Elizabeth's agents. Triumphant, on August 5th Catherine ordered that Throckmorton, then resident in Rouen, should be confined to his house under supervision. Charles IX and the Queen entered Rouen on the 12th. By the 18th a proclamation of the King's majority was issued. Charles IX confirmed his mother in the government of the kingdom. L'Hospital announced that, owing to provocation, the English had forfeited the right to Calais that they had held under the Treaty of Cateau-Cambrésis. Smith's protests were severely rejected by the Queen Mother.

The orders for disarmament and the confirmation of the new edict of Amboise sent by Catherine de Medici were badly received in Paris. The Parliament did not enregister it until September 28th. On arrival at Mantes the Queen had a bad accident when she fell from her horse. But those who hoped for her death were disappointed; her physical resistance was as great as her patience, which seemed truly invincible.

Having vanquished Elizabeth, Catherine immediately began to soften towards her, for both of them were equally interested in preventing Mary Stuart from coming under Spanish suzerainty by marrying Don Carlos. The implacable hatred felt for one another by the Lorraines and the Châtillons since the assassination of Monsieur de Guise le Grand made the renewal of civil war an ever-present danger. Owing to the emptiness of the treasury, the decline of the Navy, which was already serious, although the rebuilding of it had been Henri II's sole claim to glory, and unemployment, peace with England was indispensable. Catherine had seen Coligny again, had re-installed him at the Louvre and re-admitted him to the Council, for she did not despair of using him in negotiating with the English government. The Admiral needed the Queen Mother, for he was deeply harassed by the proceedings which the widow and children of François de Guise had begun against him and which were whipping up the frenzy of the zealots, both Protestant and Catholic. Knowing that time is an incomparable weapon of suffocation, she endeavoured to have matters dragged out as long as possible. On the grounds of feudal solidarity Anne de Montmorency was supporting Coligny, for whose cause Renée de France, Duchess of Ferrara, was pleading with her daughter, Anne d'Este, widow of the Lorraine Prince.

On reading Coligny's three apologias, it is not possible to consider that his case was a good one. Catherine was certainly not taken in. She endeavoured to liquidate the affair by dismissing both the accused and the accusers alike. She had the case postponed for three years or more, according to circumstances, 'forbidding both parties any attempt at coming to blows with one another'. In spite of all the efforts of the Guises Catherine, to rid herself of a problem that threatened to become more and more dangerous, ordered in February 1564 that Coligny should be declared 'purged, discharged, and innocent of' the assassination of Duke François, and further, that the case should be closed. A mock reconciliation then took place in which Henri de Guise refused to take part. Apart from the Government, nobody wanted peace. Pastors and monks were still calling for recourse to the sword in the service of God. The murders that were perpetrated by both sides showed the influence of these clerics only too clearly, as they worked themselves up by reading the Bible, whether it was in a Latin translation, for the Romans, or a French one for the followers of Geneva. In the provinces massacres were taking place more or less everywhere. The whole country was in opposition to the edict of Amboise, in spite of the Government's reminders that it was to be 'inviolably observed, without passion, and excepting neither individuals nor religion'.

Catherine at last obtained the recall to Madrid of Chantonnay, who had been spying on her ever more closely. She hoped to find a more discreet and less perfidious ambassador in Francès de Alava. Knowing very well that in spite of his careful silence Philip II disapproved of it, she attempted to justify the peace of Amboise to him. She had chosen the Royal Council in such a way that the two religions were represented on it according to their numerical importance. She kept a constant watch on it from 1563–7; the lists name sixteen fighting Catholics, led by the Cardinals de Lorraine and de Guise; six Calvinists, including Condé and the Châtillons, and twenty King's men—i.e. the Queen Mother's—so that the latter would always be in the majority. They were those who were loyal to Catherine; L'Hospital, Gonnor, superintendent of finances, Morvillier and Monluc, two Bishops who were devoted to her; the other clerks were politically moderates. The Constable was favourably inclined to this group in the Council, who were also supported by the Cardinal de

Bourbon. The legislators and the Gallicans being at full strength, Catherine de Medici relied on them and thus, also, she was enabled never to accept the decrees of the Council of Trent, in which she discovered, as she wrote to the Bishop of Rennes in February 1564, 'so many things contrary' to Royal authority 'and prejudical to the liberties and privileges of the Gallican Church'.

As the niece and cousin of Popes, she had too much experience of the Curia and its policies, invariably directed towards the establishment of theocracy, to be a Papist. In that respect also she was first and foremost a nationalist, defending Jeanne d'Albret, whom the Holy See wanted to excommunicate and depose, alleging that the Pope had 'no authority or jurisdiction over those who bear the title of king or queen'. She followed the line of Philippe le Bel and Charles VII—France before Rome. The Queen Mother took a very high hand with the ambassadors of the Pope, the Emperor, the Catholic King and the Duke of Savoy, when they made a combined protest at Fontainebleau on February 12, 1564. She had taught the young King his lesson and he very courteously sent the diplomats representing the Catholic powers about their business, reminding them that he had signed the peace with the Protestants in order to drive the foreigners from his kingdom.

The obvious responsibility of the Protestants for the beginning of the first civil war made it necessary to take certain precautions. By the edict of Vincennes of June 14, 1563, the Huguenots were forbidden to keep open shop on Catholic feast days. On December 14th certain restrictions were imposed by declaration and interpretation, relating to places of worship, nocturnal funerals in Paris, and christenings, to be carried out without celebrations in those regions where the restrictions applied. Preaching and communion were forbidden at Court. Catherine de Medici had believed that she would be able to agree to everything as regarded freedom of conscience and of worship. In this she had failed, for which the blame lay on the Calvinists. She had made herself suspect on their behalf, but their reply had been to go to war. She had therefore decided purely and simply to tolerate a minority which had become a seditious one. The preachers, supported by Calvin, Bèze, and Coligny, assailed her with demands, which she opposed simply by the force of inertia. She had Monsieur le Prince in her power owing to his love affair with Isabelle de Limeuil, an enchanting young woman in the suite of the Queen Mother, who, since she had come to power used the beauty of the young women or girls who composed it in order at one and the same time to seduce the great noblemen and to keep an eye on them.

A great deal of nonsense has been both written and said about the Madame Catherine's Flying Squadron. In fact the libellers, and the chroniclers and historians who quoted them, confused the harlots of the Court with the 'very beautiful and honest girls' of whom Brantôme spoke. The archives prove that the harlots, under the direction of a matron—in 1560 her name was Jeanne Lignière—were mercenaries employed in the service of Venus. As soon as she became sovereign Catherine abolished this peripatetic brothel. After the death of François II the Court accounts never refer to any expense of this kind. The maids of honour, on the contrary, were in the personal service of the Queen Mother, and like the pages, they belonged to the nobility. In the *Discours second* of his *Dames galantes* Brantôme showed how severely they were controlled by Catherine. However spicily it may have been dressed up, owing to the prudent anonymity to which his characters were relegated, Brantôme's tale reflects the very severe methods used by the Queen Mother in training her Flying Squadron, who were frequently subjected to corporal punishment. The *Mémoires* of Marguerite de Valois leave us in no doubt concerning the stiff discipline imposed by her mother: 'I did not dare to speak to her', Margot recalled, 'but when she looked at me I trembled with fear of having done something to displease her.'

As head of the Flying Squadron Catherine used it in the interests of her policies. She chose the prettiest of her followers as Armides, in order to disarm the Renauds who were a danger to the State. Louise de Rouhet disarmed the King of Navarre and in the case of Monsieur le Prince this task fell to Mademoiselle de Limeuil. The latter was related to Catherine through the La Tour d'Auvergnes. The diarists have told the tale of the scandal of her pregnancy, her lying-in at Dijon, Catherine's anger, the inquiry opened regarding the careless girl's behaviour, and of the Convent of Aubonne from which she was kidnapped by Condé. She later married Scipion Sardini, a silk merchant who became a financier. In order to make sure of the Duc de Nemours (although he was in love with the widow of François de Guise, whom he married in 1566) the Queen Mother provided him with Françoise de Rohan, a first cousin of Jeanne d'Albret. Mademoiselle de Rohan was infuriated by her lover's marriage, but Catherine was not the woman to be moved by emotional upsets. She herself was completely indifferent to love affairs. We need not for a moment dwell on the polemical allegations of her own involvements with Andelot or the Vidamus of Chartres. A much more despotic passion

held her in thrall, which left her not a moment's leisure nor any
inclination for amorous dalliance—her passion for power. But she
was an expert at provoking and maintaining such emotions in others.
She regretted the fact that the Admiral despised the pleasures of
Eros as much as she herself did.

Monsieur le Prince, like his brother Antoine, was easy prey. The
Protestant literature heaps reproaches and curses on Condé, who was
mad about women, and as Agrippa d'Aubigné put it, allowed himself to be chased by every girl at Court. Monsieur le Prince was
enslaved by Aphrodite to such a degree that, at the same time as
Isabelle de Limeuil, he had as his mistress Marguerite de Lustrac,
widow of the Marshal de Saint-André. His wife, Eléonore de Roye,
had died. To the despair of the adherents of the Religion, he indulged
in wild dreams of fantastic marriages with such women as Mary
Stuart and Anne de Guise, but on November 8, 1565, they succeeded
in marrying him to François de Rothelin, a Longueville, whose
mother was Jacqueline de Rohan. As his love affairs placed him at
the mercy of the Queen Mother, Monsieur le Prince had no authority
whatever. His dealings with the English denigrated Coligny. Protestantism was therefore left without capable leaders and the peace with
Elizabeth was a final blow to it. Catherine even envisaged a matrimonial and political alliance with her in order to have her hands free
to deal with the Empire and Spain, which, owing to the family ties
of the Hapsburgs and the very close alliance that existed between
Madrid and Vienna, in her clearsighted opinion constituted the most
dangerous rivalry to France, for at that period England was only
to be feared as an ally of the Protestants.

As she wished to investigate the political and religious situation of
the kingdom for herself, Catherine de Medici resolved that the young
King should visit his realms. She knew, alas, that they were not
pacified. The curé Haton reveals in his *Mémoires* how great an
interest was taken in the provinces in this journey made by Charles
IX and his mother. Haton used the Julian calendar and dated the
New Year as from Easter 1564. In modern terms the journey lasted
from January 24, 1564, until May 1, 1566.

Nothing was more picturesque nor provided a greater variety of
unexpected incidents than this voyage, spendidly described by Pierre
Champion. During more than two years the Governess of France set
forth to concern herself with her State, travelling through all the
territories over which her authority extended. But this was far more

nominally than actually the case and that is one of the reasons why, like Louis XI, she was so often obliged to have recourse to underhand or brutal methods of government, in the tyrannical tradition of the small Italian principalities. In their pettiness and violence these proceedings were very different from those used by Richelieu and Louis XIV, who could plan and act on the grand scale. The entire Court moved through France, forming a veritable city on the march, with its chariots, shops, innumerable retainers, its soldiers, priests and monks, its 8,000 horses. Like an army it lived off the land, by requisition. In the smallest villages through which it passed it was fêted; in the large towns there were magnificent entries and receptions, carnavals, carrousels, tourneys, games, plays, masques, dances and every kind of entertainment.

At the beginning of this voyage, during a sojourn at Troyes, peace was signed with England, after negotiations which had sometimes been very difficult and during which Catherine had unremittingly dealt with Elizabeth in a high-handed manner. The Queen Mother's imperturbable *sang-froid* was due to the fact that she knew that England's economic situation was very bad. Catherine had even succeeded in winning over Throckmorton, the principle English plenipotentiary. In future, when recommending him to the goodwill of the Parisians, she was to refer to him as the ambassador of peace.

It was a white peace, designed to pave the way for a future alliance, and was signed at Troyes on April 12, 1564. Le Havre had been returned to France and Calais saved. The Treaty of Cateau-Cambrésis was neither confirmed nor annulled. Freedom of Franco-English commerce was established. France would pay 120,000 crowns ransom for the hostages. Her fear of Spain caused Catherine to deal easily with Elizabeth; Ronsard, poet-laureate to the Crown of France, was instructed to address a poetical *Discours* to the Queen of England in honour of the peace and to proclaim the alliance:

> *Le Français semble au saule verdissant,*
> *Plus on le coupe, et plus il est naissant,*
> *Et rejetonne en branches davantage,*
> *Prenant vigueur de son propre dommage.*
> *Pour ce, vivez comme aimables soeurs . . .*
> *Quand vous serez ensemble bien unies,*
> *L'Amour, la Foi, deux belles compagnies,*
> *Viendront ça bas le coeur nous réchauffer,*
> *Puis, sans harnois, sans armes et sans fer,*

Et sans le dos un corselet vous ceindre,
Ferez vos noms par toute Europe craindre,
Et l'Age d'Or verra, de toutes parts,
Fleurir les Lys entre les Léopards.

Ronsard, Catherine's mouthpiece, amplified the modest aims of
his sovereign like a good rhetorician. A century before Mazarin she
had foreseen the necessity of an alliance with England as a counterweight to Spain and the Empire, but without in the least endeavouring to construct a new diplomatic system. To attribute any such
intention to her would be to antedate to the sixteenth century the
Testament of Richelieu, in itself probably apocryphal, and the
theories that arose from French preponderance, which nobody at
that time anticipated. As a trained disciple of the Capétians, she was
working only towards limited objectives. Sufficient to each day was
the evil thereof. She would have laughed at the idea that she fostered
deep plans and long views regarding a policy of natural frontiers,
or the balance of European power, all of them theories that were
non-existent until after the ideological developments of 1789 and
their consequences. She merely tilled her own field. All she wished
to do was to round out and safeguard her bit of land. French security
is a peasant security; one protects one's own field against one's
neighbour's trespassing by putting up hedges and enclosures.
Mazarin was to be the long-term executant of the plans laid by the
Governess of France: the Anglo-French victory of the Dunes paved
the way for the peace of the Pyrenees, and the breakdown of Spanish
hegemony began at Nymeghen. In order to minimize the threat to
Hapsburg power that the Treaty of Troyes might in their view have
implied, the shrewd Florentine Queen instructed the French ambassadors at Madrid and Vienna to impart the news of it 'as moderately
and wisely' as possible, 'in honest and generous terms'. The Queen
Mother also hoped to take advantage of the English alliance against
the Pope. Gonnor definitely said as much to Throckmorton, who
declared that he was delighted to hear it. Catherine de Medici's
Gallicanism was incontestable. In her eyes Catholicism and France
were but one and she refused to admit the theocratic claims of the
Holy See.

Calvin died on May 27, 1564. We do not know what the Governess
of France thought of the Pope of Geneva, since she never referred to
him in writing. No doubt his disappearance from the scene caused
her no distress. The fanaticism of this amazing man, who combined

in his character constructive genius, political subtlety and a will to theocratic power as tenacious as it was violent, was the complete opposite of everything for which Catherine stood. When he disappeared from the scene Calvin left French Protestantism in the hands of Théodore de Bèze and Gaspard de Coligny. The Queen Mother knew them both well enough to hope, with her innate optimism, that she would once again be able to win them over. The enormous service that she had rendered to the Queen of Navarre by defending her against the Pope (in the sixteenth century excommunication still counted for something) had brought about a rapprochement between her and this princess, who was venerated by all members of the Religion. At the interview which they had at Macon Catherine advised Jeanne d'Albret to be more compassionate towards her Catholic subjects, who were suffering conditions of persecution in the typical Calvinist manner, and the Queen of Navarre promised that she would be so.

Their Majesties and the Court were magnificently received at Lyons. Catherine and Charles IX resided with a rich bourgeois, Pierre Teste. The Queen Mother felt really at home in this French Florence. She was pleased to receive there, at the Feast of St John, Lord Hunsdon, Elizabeth's envoy, who bestowed the Order of the Garter on Charles IX. The plague shortened their sojourn in this town that Catherine loved for its commerce, its finances, its arts, its atmosphere, which was simultaneously one of mystery and pride, for its closeness to Italy and the German countries. She learned a great deal at Lyons about conditions in the south of France, and of the spread of anarchy there. Shortly after her departure from the metropolis of the Gauls, at the castle of Roussillon near Crémieux in the Dauphiné, belonging to the Count de Tournon, she drew up the statute called after this place. This statute reveals how closely her mind was in tune with those of the legislators, but with this difference, that her bent was of an entirely practical nature, never toppling over into the divagations to which those enthusiasts for ancient Roman law were naturally prone, into Caesarism or Imperialistic tendencies; she was too much the daughter of merchants for that. It was ordained that in every town, thenceforward, two lists would be drawn up of mayors, sheriffs, consuls and jurists, and the Government could thus select those whom it considered the most useful and acceptable. Paris was for the time being exempted from this just and beneficent measure, which strengthened the central power.

At the same time Catherine was pursuing her foreign policy. She received the Duke and Duchess of Savoy and the Duke of Ferrara. As the result of the death of the Emperor Ferdinand there was a risk of a change of direction in German diplomacy. Catherine's letters show that all this was engaging her attention. Ferdinand I had been a liberal-minded monarch, artistic and cultured. How would Maximilian II turn out? In due course he was to prove himself even more tolerant than his father, but at that moment he appeared to be strongly Spanish. Catherine decided to discard some ballast. On August 4th, by the edict of Roussillon, restrictive measures were adopted against the Huguenots, who were in particular forbidden to call new synods, to open new schools and to make collections for purposes of propaganda or worship. Married priests were ordered on pain of banishment to part from their wives, who according to Roman ecclesiastical law were nothing but concubines. Preachers were forbidden to undertake missionary work outside their own parishes and the nobility to receive, either at prayer-meetings or communion, members of the faithful other than their own vassals. Quite clearly the plan was to restrict Protestant proselytism. The Queen had written so to Coligny, on April 17, 1564. She agreed that 'those of the so-called reformed religion' should be left in peace. But in return she demanded that 'they do no other than live in tranquillity and patience, in obedience to the King, my said liege and son, and to his edict, which will be inviolably observed towards them'. In the event of any attempt to stir up renewed troubles, 'from whichever quarter it may arise, I shall leave no stone unturned, without regard to religion, persons, or any other consideration than the keeping of the peace of this State'.

'From whichever quarter it may arise,' she stated, in the terms of Royal arbitration. To restrict Reformationist proselytism was necessary in order to ensure the public welfare, for the recourse to arms two years previously had revealed the political ambitions of the Religionists. Catherine's intransigence was only concerned with this, but in this respect it was absolute. Nevertheless she would not refrain, either from resorting to force in order to compel the Catholic zealots to respect the religious convictions of those Huguenots, who behaved peaceably.

The journey continued via Valence, Montélimar and Avignon, where the Queen defended the Protestants against the severity of the Pontifical administration, causing their confiscated property to

Q

be returned to them; Salons, where she met her beloved Nostradamus once again; Aix-en-Provence, Marseilles. Indefatigably she wrote, received in audience, presided, negotiated, and quarrelled with the Spanish ambassador; she also thought of marrying Charles IX to Elizabeth, although this princess was seventeen years older than he was. On November 13th they left Marseilles for Arles. Their tour of France took them through the smallest villages, as well as to the large towns. The sovereign was auscultating her people. At Nîmes and also at Montpellier the Huguenots were extremely restless. The representatives of both religions assailed the King and his mother with complaints, which put Charles IX into a bad temper, but Catherine, patient as ever, listened, appeased, and made promises. Béziers, Narbonne, Carcassonne . . . where the roads around the city were snowbound. Whilst her son played at snowballing, the Queen, studious as usual, read fifteenth-century manuscripts, from which she learned that Marie d'Anjou, the wife of Charles VII, had been imprisoned by similar snowstorms behind the ramparts of the high-lying city.

Everything interested and amused her. Nevertheless she was perturbed by the news from Paris, where the Lorraine princes were claiming the right to go about in arms and creating serious incidents. Castelnaudary, Toulouse. . . . On February 2, 1565, news was brought to the city of the Capitouls that the King of Spain had agreed to a meeting which it was proposed to hold at Bayonne. Philip II's evasiveness had made the task of Saint-Sulpice, the French ambassador at Madrid, who was charged by Catherine to arrange such an interview, which she regarded as essential, very difficult. To neutralize Spain was an indispensable condition for settling France's religious quarrels, in which Philip II was constantly intervening on the side of the Catholics. Catherine's daughter, Elisabeth, unreservedly supported her husband's policy and advised her mother to make an alliance with Spain, to which Catherine replied that the Guises were raising France against them. An alliance with Spain might prove a sound policy. But the rivalry between the Houses of France and Austria, lasting for more than a century and a half (from Pavia to Nymeghen), suggests that the alternative path might have been a better one. Catherine, however, pressed ahead as fast as possible; the party of the Guises was the party of Spain and presented an immediate danger.

In spite of the amiable tone of their correspondence Madame Catherine and her son-in-law detested one another. Spain's redoubtable infantry was Philip's strongest argument against his mother-in-law, for, her army being in no way comparable to his, she dared not allow herself to challenge the victors of Saint Quentin. It was obvious that the Catholic King desired to make the Very Christian King his vassal. Chantonnay's letters reveal the very basis of Spanish diplomacy, which had but one aim in view—the ruin of France, thanks to her troubles. The rivalries at Court, the unemployment of the military, the economic and financial difficulties that were becoming more and more serious, provided exceptionally favourable soil for Spain's work of corruption. The method Chantonnay had recommended, in order that the whole of the southern part of the kingdom should fall defencelessly to the Spaniards, was to push France towards the Rhine, against the Germans, by encouraging the legislators in their inclination towards rivalry between the King and the Emperor. The religious peace was an obstacle to this plan, since it removed any further justification for the occupation of the south-west by the troops of Don Diego de Carbajas. Nor had Philip II ever had any liking for François de Guise, whose patriotism had been an embarrassment to him. He would have been satisfied had the Cardinal de Bourbon, who was not very intelligent (although not such an imbecile as he was made out to be) and extremely vain and weak, been appointed Lieutenant-General of the kingdom. Philip had been annoyed by the recapture of Le Havre and the safeguarding of Calais. The principal reason for his hesitation in resuming the war against France was lack of money due to the devaluation of his currency, consequent on the gold and silver inflation, which itself was the result of the enormous quantity of precious metals brought by his galleons from Peru and Mexico.

Since the death of his brother the Cardinal de Lorraine had passed over to Spain, whose influence in the Council of Trent he no longer attempted to thwart. Catherine, who had provided herself with reliable sources of information, knew all about the progressive hispanization of the French Catholics. Those who remained nationalists were regarded by Philip II as heretics and accomplices of the Calvinists. At the end of 1563 and beginning of 1564 the conspiracy of Monluc had revealed the extent of this evil. The hero of Sienna had reached the point of declaring to Jean and Philippe Bardaxi, the agents of Philip II, that France was lost and the situation was worsening day by day: 'If the King of Spain does not put his hands to the oar, in less than a year France will have become heretical,' and he was willing to command the partisans in Gascony on Philip II's behalf.[1] In possession of such trumps, the Catholic King refused to commit himself at Bayonne. He had written to the Cardinal de Granvelle that the meeting would have no political outcome: 'I gave way to the insistance of the two Queens.' It was to be a family reunion and not the diplomatic conference desired by Catherine. Had she known of her son-in-law's mental reservations the Queen's joy on receiving the news of his acceptance would have been greatly mitigated. On March 27th, at Agen, she covered Monluc with attentions and compliments. The Gascon was taken in, but not Francès de Alava, who protested ceaselessly against the favours shown by Catherine to the heretics. The arrival at Bordeaux at the end of May 1565 of a Turkish ambassador revealed that the intention of the Queen Mother—who had not forgotten François I and Suleiman II—was to bring pressure to bear on Spain. The expedition of the French Protestants to Florida, a colony which he regarded as one of his Crown possessions, set the seal on Philip II's annoyance.

Meanwhile the plans for an English marriage for Charles IX were continuing. A detailed study of the documentation reveals that Catherine de Medici was trying to surround Spain with a network of intrigues in order that Philip II should be led to believe that French policy was both freer and stronger than it actually was. From London to Constantinople, via Venice and Vienna, she was weaving the net in which she hoped to enmesh him. On May 21st, at Mont-de-Marsan, she called together the Council, as well as the Princes of the Blood and the Knights of Saint Michael, in order that they should officially confirm the validity of the peace of Amboise. At the moment when she most needed security in order to be free to negotiate with Spain she did not want to run the risk of another uprising. Philip II announced that he would not accompany his wife to Bayonne, but that the Duke of Alba would represent him there. The cautious Lord of the Escorial distrusted the Florentine shopkeeper, so clever that she might have won him over, which he did not wish at any price to happen. According to his usual methods he would give his instructions to Queen Elisabeth and the Duke in the privacy of his study, out of reach of the perfidious amiability of his mother-in-law, who arrived at Bayonne on May 31st, to be greeted

---

[1] On all this, see documents and references in Henri Forneron, *Histoire de Philippe II*, Vol. I Chapters III to X, this great work in four volumes, so unfairly ignored, which on certain points has been completed and corrected, but has never been superseded, even by Spanish historians.

by the bitter complaints of Alava regarding the Ottoman Embassy, the embassy of Satan, as he called it.

Catherine moaned and wept but failed to make any impression on the Spaniard, who replied that it would be scandalous to receive the Turk at such a moment. The family reunion was off to a bad start and Catherine's distress would have been even greater had she known of the instructions given to Alba. Whilst she was only thinking of France, Spain was solely concerned with the welfare, defence, and increase of the Catholic and Apostolic religion. It was a matter of 'mutually promising to promote . . . the honour of God and to uphold the Holy and Catholic religion'. The sovereigns would undertake to 'employ their own goods, forces, and means and those of their subjects' in its defence. The Spanish proposals meant a return to Cateau-Cambrésis and Ecouen—expulsion of the ministers, interdiction of the Reformed religion, and judiciary and other posts to be held only by the Catholics. Spain was shamelessly intervening in French politics. She demanded the publication of the decrees of the Council of Trent. She could not have been more insolent. Philip had decided to speak at Bayonne as the master. He had deliberately chosen the Duke of Alba as his mouthpiece, knowing his diplomatic ability, wholly at the service of his religious intransigeance, his Castilian pride and his hard-heartedness. To the Queen Mother was assigned the role of petitioner, not to say the accused. Philip II was taking advantage of the nervousness—however well she usually controlled her nerves she was, after all, a woman—to which his silences had reduced her. Alba was instructed to question her, wait, investigate, and force her to reveal her hand, and finally to wrest from her everything she had hitherto, through her ambassadors and personal letters, refused to concede. Spain was going to take advantage of this Bayonne meeting, which the Queen had so much—too much—longed for, to compel the Queen Mother to renounce her Italian subtleties.

The Duke of Alba was not subtle. His genius was essentially aggressive and harsh and he went straight to the point. Nevertheless, he was also adaptable and if the obstacle before him was too great he did not obstinately insist on making a frontal attack but went around it. Catholic, and as intolerant as Philip II could have wished, like his master he was the very opposite of a Papist. In the service of Spain he had made war on the Pope. The least clerically-minded of men, he went as far as Caesaro-Papism, but on the side of the Catholic King: 'I would worship with very bad grace', he said, 'all idols made by the hand of man; but the King, made by God, gladly.' This was the basic theory of Biblical monarchy, a theory that did not make its appearance in France until Louis XIV and of which Catherine could have had no idea.

Spain first, against France, first. . . . The talks between Alba and Catherine continued. The Florentine, who would have prayed to God in French, and the Castilian—who in Flanders two years later was to massacre as heretics nearly 20,000 unfortunates—however different and opposed to one another their minds, characters, and temperaments may have been, agreed on one thing—politics before religion. Both were highly intelligent; Alba, reticent and dogmatic, Catherine, lively and inclined to scepticism. Alba was a Spanish Calvin, whilst Catherine was an Italian Montaigne. A fine duel was about to begin between them; scholasticism, theocracy (the King as theocrat, not the Pope) against the novelty of the Renaissance, against the attempt at dictatorship (but the King's, a purely political and national dictatorship). They were almost contemporaries; Alba was eleven years older than Catherine, and both of them were imbued with the same spirit of principality, the same genius for patience and cunning, the same fervour for the greatness of the State. Philip II knew men and the Demon of the South had certainly chosen the right one to confront the Governess of France.

Neither Charles nor Elisabeth, the brother or the sister, counted at all. They were children; the young Queen was twenty, the young King fifteen. They were delighted to meet again and to participate in the celebrations, which in spite of the financial distress their mother had ordered to be splendid ones, to impress the Spaniards. Philip II had decided that when she made her official entry into Bayonne on June 15th his wife's appearance would be second to none in magnificence. He presented her with the trappings of the white palfrey that the King of France had given to the Queen of Spain, the value of the harness being estimated at 400,000 ducats. This rivalry in sumptuousness was a symbol of their rivalry for power, as had been the case with François I and Henry VIII on the Field of the Cloth of Gold, forty-three years previously.

There were compliments and accolades, but Catherine had taken her precautions. When the Duke of Alba questioned him the young King replied that he would under no pretext re-open the religious war. And to show Spain that France was not at her beck and call, it was decided to receive the ambassador of the Sublime Porte. The scandal Alava had predicted became a fact. Philip II knew that the

Moslem galleons were cruising around the coast of Sicily. Catherine had nevertheless summoned the most zealous Catholics to Bayonne, for their speeches would make the Spaniards believe that France was resolved to exterminate the Huguenots. Alba was too cunning to swallow the bait, for he had observed how carefully the Queen avoided committing herself.

The results were disappointing. In her talks with Alba Catherine was vague and made no definite promises. As he received reports of them in his study the Catholic King made discontented note of them. Catherine remained as secretive as in the past and carefully abstained from any declaration by which she might have been bound. There was a striking contrast between her attitude towards Spain and that she had adopted only a short time previously towards England. She wanted an alliance with Elizabeth and tried to avoid a rupture with Philip II. She had chosen between London and Madrid in favour of the Protestant alliance against Spain, but for peace, not for war. Philip was still Elizabeth's ally; with his political realism he had been careful not to sacrifice the advantages of his union with Mary Tudor to religious unity. Catherine wanted to reverse these alliances but she took redoubled precautions in order not to draw her son-in-law's attention to the fact, for he had been the husband of Henry VIII's elder daughter and remained Elizabeth's brother-in-law.

The feasting continued, for it helped to conceal the indispensable silences. Catherine excelled at arranging the pomp and circumstance of all these banquets, balls, tournaments and joustings. She called on Ronsard for more decasyllabic verses, complementary to the ode on the occasion of peace with England:

> *O Siècle heureux, et digne qu'on l'appelle*
> *Le Siècle d'Or, si oncque en fut aucun,*
> *Où l'Espagnol, d'une amitié fidèle,*
> *Aime la France, et les deux ne font qu'un.*

Madame Catherine, who was a great match-maker, and who still hoped that Elizabeth of England would accept Charles IX, was now dreaming of a Spanish alliance. Little Marguerite, the adorable Margot, who was twelve, was paired off with Don Carlos, heir to the crowns of Philip II; and Henri, Duke of Anjou, who was fourteen, would marry the Catholic King's sister, Queen Joanna of Portugal. Their ages and personal inclinations were of no account; princes were used matrimonially as ambassadors were diplomatically, and were sent where the welfare of the State required them to go.[1] But Alba refused to associate himself with Catherine's matrimonial plans. He had not come to Bayonne to arrange marriages. His role was to endeavour to bring France to submission by means of an anti-Protestant crusade, which would be a double gain, both religious and political. But Madame Catherine would not on any account join in this crusade. She was friendly with the Turks, so why should she not also be so with the Huguenots, who at least were Christians?

There was no common ground on which the Queen of France and the representative of Spain could meet. In his disappointment Alba blamed L'Hospital's bad influence for this. Catherine stood by her chancellor. Alba pressed his point—everything came down to the question of religion, to obedience to the decrees of the Council. Did the Spaniard lie or was he ignorant of the fact that Philip II like the Gallican Queen, would in due course refuse to accept these decrees? Catherine certainly knew of her son-in-law's intentions through Saint-Sulpice. She declared to the Duke of Alba and to her daughter, who denied it, that Philip II (and this was the literal truth) was no more submissive to the Council than she was. The conversations had now taken this theological turn, which ever since the failure of the Poissy conference, exasperated her. As Alba wrote on the 29th to the Secretary of State, Franco Erasso, 'things are not going well here but on the contrary, very badly'. One can understand his irritation. He had advised Catherine to resort to Sicilian Vespers to purge France of heresy: 'The head of a salmon,' he said, 'is worth a hundred frogs.' But Catherine turned a deaf ear to him.

The little twelve-year-old Prince of Béarn, whose presence at these interviews had disturbed no one, informed his mother of Alba's intentions. Jeanne d'Albret immediately informed Coligny of all that she had learned of them. This was the origin of the legend that Saint Bartholomew had been planned in advance. But on the contrary, Alba, Alava, Granvelle, were complaining of the Queen's constant evasions and of her clear determination to avoid anything that might lead to a resumption of the armed conflict, according to Granvelle's actual words. As for Alava, he already saw her falling back into the arms of the 'heresiarchs and others who are so, if not in name', who would take advantage of her indecision to

[1] Catherine the match-maker, as Van Dyke rightly called her.

'make her very uneasy'. ('*Lui mettre martel en tête.*')[1]

The Spaniards left Bayonne on July 2nd without having obtained anything from Catherine but vague proposals, either with regard to the punishment of the rebels or a conference of prelates to examine the decrees of the Council of Trent. They hid their stinging sense of failure beneath the usual exchange of Court compliments. Even the Constable de Montmorency realized that a new war for the extermination of the heretics was impossible. The Duke of Alba wrote on July 8th: 'I fear that the heretics who are at Court and those who will come there may make the Queen change her mind.' On July 2nd Suriano had already informed the Venetian Senate that the Bayonne conference had been unable to reach any agreement with regard to the religious question. In a detailed despatch three weeks later he reported that on the advice of the Nuncio in France an assembly of prelates had been convened to which the Huguenots would not be admitted, when no questions of dogma would be raised.

At Bayonne Catherine de Medici had upheld her policy. Nevertheless, the alert given by the Queen of Navarre, as the result of what she had learned from her son, aroused the whole Protestant party. They believed quite sincerely that the Queen Mother had adhered to the point of view of Spain and the Holy See, which demanded the extermination of the heretics. In spite of all her cleverness she had not foreseen that the Spaniards would never accept a compromise. She had gone to Bayonne in order to reach a compromise. But she came away in a state of terrible uncertainty, which rumour immediately interpreted as a premeditated plan for a general massacre of the French Huguenots. Thenceforward they were to consider themselves legitimately on the defensive, free to plot, revolt, resume the war and in their turn to massacre the Catholics. France was once again to be weighed down by an atmosphere that recalled the days of the conspiracy of Amboise, but this time it was even heavier, more dangerous, to the point of deadliness.

The Queen Mother's optimism had driven her into the impasse from which there was to be no issue save the Matins of Paris on August 24, 1572. She had imagined that her personal charm would win over the Spaniards as it had the French. She knew practically

[1] Discussion of the documents duly examined by Philippson, La Ferrière and Mariéjol, and which we also have re-examined, proves that the Protestant historian Combes made a mistake in translating Alava's Spanish despatch containing the word *martillar*. It was not a matter of *marteler* (hammering, tormenting) the Huguenots, but of *se mettre martel en tête* on their account (*martillar*).

nothing of Spain, that sister of Italy who was not in any way similar to her. She had only the vaguest idea of Spain's self-centredness, cruelty and unremitting hatred of the infidel and the heretic, her contempt for France, her Royal theocracy, spirit of principality and unshakeable conviction that she was Western Catholicism's sole rampart against both the Protestants and the Turks. To the Italians of the sixteenth century the uncultured conquerors of the Indies were barbarians. During the middle of the sixteenth century Italy's intellectual influence on Spanish art and letters was still a very weak one. Politically Italy remained a Spanish colony, and despised her fierce conqueror, whom she had not yet overcome. The sixteenth century was not Spain's Golden Age, as has too often been stated under an historically incorrect impression, which fails to take into account the lateness with which this great people was drawn into the stream of the Renaissance. The Golden Age did not flower there until the beginning of the seventeenth century. The great Spanish writers of this Golden Age—Lope de Vega, Tirso de Molina, Calderon, Cervantes—were all born in the second half of the sixteenth.[1] The painters emerged even later; El Greco arrived at Toledo towards 1575, Ribera was born in 1588, Zurbaran in 1598, Velasquez in 1599, Murillo in 1617, and he did not die until 1682, a year after Calderon. In passing we may note that these dates and the fame of these masters are enough to disprove the cliché alleging that thanks to Philip II Spain had become decadent. The Golden Age came after Philip II and did not precede him. When the Golden Age dawned he whose genius had brought it into being after the epic of the Conquistadores was mouldering in the Escorial. Such was the mystery of Spain and of her grandeur, inseparable from death. The Golden Age lasted approximately until 1680 and disappeared in the ruins of Spanish hegemony, after having given birth to the century of Louis XIV.

To a Florentine of 1560 the Spaniards were half-breeds between Arabs and Jews, mercenaries, explorers, torturers of Indians, slayers of women, treasure-robbers, inquisitors and scaffold-builders, about as civilized as Borussians or Muscovites. As yet Spanish intellect had only flowered on the highest spiritual plane, in which the daughter of the Medici took no interest—a Vivès, a Luis de Leon, a Montano, a Luis of Granada, why should she have been interested in such obscure monks? And during her youth

[1] Cervantes, the oldest, was born in 1547; Calderon, the youngest, in 1600; Lope in 1562, Tirso in 1571.

Ignatius Loyala was no more to her than a political agent of Rome. And what interest could she have taken, also, in those Carmelite reformers and mystics who flourished towards the end of the century, in the great Saint Theresa and Saint John of the Cross? Yet Philip II's Spain was also their Spain, in which fundamentally Catholicism and warlike Imperialism were but one. It was with that Spain, as different from herself as could be imagined, that the humanist Florentine Queen, the Gallican Frenchwoman, moderate, sceptical, fond of good living, bred on Machiavelli, Guicciardini, Erasmus, Rabelais and Montaigne, had come into conflict. No contact was possible between them. The inevitable mistake made by the French Protestants was to believe that the Queen of France had become an ally of the Inquisitors, but a mistake for which Catherine, without in the least intending to do so, had made herself responsible. Until Bayonne the Medici had been regarded by the Reformationists, as by the majority of Frenchmen, as merely an Italian. After Bayonne she became in the eyes of all the French people an accomplice of Spain, and in France not only the Huguenots detested Spain and her soldiers, religious, haughty noblemen, and proud, mystically-minded masses; the Spain that had beaten France at Pavia and Saint Quentin, those two disastrous battles. . . .

Catherine did not suspect to what an extent Bayonne and her futile conversations there had isolated her and through her the French State, from the people—forever. The nationalist policy that she continued unceasingly to pursue appeared to them simply as an anti-Protestant one. This was no doubt entirely contrary to fact but appearances were nevertheless against the Queen Mother, and were never to change. The wall of fire lit by the Holy Office of the Inquisition, of which Philippe of Meneses sang in his *Lumière de l'Ame*, remained an insuperable barrier as far as Catherine de Medici was concerned, but in public opinion its crimson light fell on her, nevertheless. The legend of flames and blood which had already begun to build up around her appeared to be confirmed by the meeting at Bayonne. Historians know that the Governess of France had not sold her soul to the Demon of the South. But polemical history, which is built on lies, calumny, spite and absurdities of all kinds, and belief in which to all partisans is an act of faith, was to represent her as his pawn. Nothing whatever could prevail against it. By holding those conversations at Bayonne Catherine de Medici had barred her own way to a moderate policy. Thenceforward no one in France outside her immediate entourage was to believe in her sincerity—

those who stood for Spain and Rome, because they had obtained
nothing from her; those who were for Geneva because they were
convinced that she had gone over to the enemy. The campaign of
libels and caricatures was intensified and the Queen Mother's
affection for her beloved Chenonceaux was ridiculed. Satirical pieces
were published about the parties that she held there. An engraving
by Nicolo Nelli shows her banqueting there, with the legend, as
defamatory as it was outrageous: '*La venerabile poltroneria regina di
Cucugna.*'

The French Catholic zealots were no less keen to exterminate the
heretics than the Spaniards. The Duc de Montpensier's confessor
had told the Duke of Alba that the quickest means to do so would be
to cut off the heads of Condé, the Admiral, Andelot, and La Rochefoucauld. As soon as he returned to Madrid, Alba was ordered by the
prudent Philip II to reassure Saint-Sulpice and to tell him that he
had never envisaged 'taking up arms against those of the other religion'. This diplomatic repentance is too flagrantly contradictory of
the facts to do more than reveal the need in which Philip stood not to
oppose the Queen Mother's religious policy officially, in order not to
force her into the English alliance. He was also highly suspicious of a
proposal Catherine made to him, that they should form a league
against the infidels, which, coming from an ally of the Great Turk,
seemed to him more than suspect. He rightly saw in it 'insidious
views and projects hostile to the Empire', as he wrote to Chantonnay,
whom he had appointed as his ambassador to Vienna. There was a
plan to marry Charles IX to one of the daughters of the Emperor
Maximilian, and Margot to one of his sons, the Archduke Rudolph.
Chantonnay intervened strongly against these suggested matrimonial
alliances. During this summer of 1565 the Queen Mother's correspondence reveals her difficulties. Both in the Empire and in France,
in Italy as well as Spain, she was accused of duplicity, and the worst
was that Elizabeth of England had refused to marry Charles IX. She
had lost at Bayonne the solid ground she had gained at Amboise.

The Court continued its journey very pleasantly, through the
Queen of Navarre's states, Angoumois, Saintonge and Aunis. All
went off well at La Rochelle, which since the loss of Orleans had
become the centre of French Calvinist resistance. The local municipality even agreed to cease persecuting the Catholics and to allow
them to celebrate Mass. The most fanatical Huguenot leaders were
obliged to quit the city. But we know from one of Alava's letters that

as soon as the Court had left the persecutions were resumed. On both sides the sectarians were gaining the upper hand. Catherine, however, pretended to be pleased and was gracious everywhere; in Poitevin, at the beginning of October, and in Brittany, where the Constable was holidaying at his manor of Châteaubriant, and where they celebrated All Saints' Day. At Angers the municipal official charged to make the speech of welcome praised Madame Catherine, 'so wise, such a careful mother, so experienced in the management of affairs'. The Angevin Academy paid tribute to Michel de L'Hospital and his burning zeal to preserve the nation. A large baby had been taught to recite this compliment, dressed up as Justice, complete with sword and scales, which delighted everyone. The Queen Mother was recovering her *joie de vivre*, and her letters reflected her good temper. But at Tours their tone was to change, once the glad welcome of the inhabitants was over and Ronsard's verses had flown away:

> *Le roi s'en va en son Plessis ébattre,*
> *Pour voir le cerf et la biche courir,*
> *Mais il a vu son royaume débattre,*
> *Il le veut voir maintenant refleurir.*

The news from Paris was bad. On November 30, 1565, Catherine wrote a very cold letter to the Governor, François de Montmorency, ordering him to watch over the disarmament of the Parisians, whether Protestant or Catholic. The Châtillons were becoming insolent again; the Cardinal Odet was quarrelling with the Nuncio, Prosper de Sainte-Croix. His uncle, the Constable, threatened the representative of the Holy See: 'If the Pope and his agents wish once again to disturb this realm, then my sword will become Huguenot.' This, coming from Anne de Montmorency, was a particularly serious threat, and the Châtillons, counting on such support, imagined that they could permit themselves everything. They saw themselves as the successors of the Guises, and future masters of the palace.

Catherine de Medici's weakness was that she was a woman. Her correspondence at the end of 1565 with Fourquevaux, who had succeeded Saint-Sulpice at Madrid, and with her daughter Elisabeth, shows that at this time she was, above all, preoccupied with her children's marriages. Philip II pretended to take the matter seriously, but Fourquevaux soon discovered that he was play-acting

and making fun of Catherine. Whilst these discussions were continuing, the Catholic King was working behind the scenes to block
the dangerous plan of Charles IX's marriage to one of the Austrian
Archduchesses. Catherine was wasting her own time and that of
France as well. Her letters give the impression that she was only a
bourgeoise, trying to set up her son. The Florentine shopkeeper,
whom the King of Spain was very cleverly keeping in uncertainty,
had taken the place of the Governess of France. Louis XI had never
behaved in such a way, nor would Richelieu and Mazarin ever do so.

Meanwhile the Court had arrived at Blois on December 5, 1565,
via Chenonceaux and Amboise. The Protestant leaders rushed to
join it, for they were anxious to learn for themselves precisely what
had happened at Bayonne. All of them, even Montgomery, were
made heartily welcome. Yet certain police measures ordered by the
Queen Mother prove her disquietude in face of a concourse that
reminded her of the conspiracy of Amboise. On December 12th she
resumed her tour of France. The Court proceeded to Moulins,
where it arrived on the 21st. Catherine told Suriano the reason for
choosing Moulins—the harvest in Auvergne had been good and
there was an abundance of everything. It was possible to live cheaply
in the Bourbonnais. As a careful housewife Madame Catherine was
always keeping an eye on expenses, and as she found Moulins so
comfortable she decided to remain there for three months; three
months that were to be fruitful for France.

At the Council held on January 12, 1566, Catherine de Medici
declared that it was impossible to deal with the affairs of the kingdom
until the private feuds had been settled. She made it clear that she
was referring to the double quarrel between the Montmorencys and
the Guises (the troubles in Paris) and between the Châtillons and
the Guises (the assassination of Duke François). The decree absol-
ving the Admiral was published on the 31st. The Cardinal de Lorraine and the Chancellor Michel de L'Hospital were becoming more
and more violently inimical and one of their bitterest scenes was
concerned with the ministrations of the Calvinist pastors to sick and
dying members of the Religion. Supported by the Queen Mother,
the Chancellor was contemptuous of the attacks of the Lorraines.
He was entirely concerned with preparing the decree which was to
supplement those of Orleans and Roussillon, and which appeared in
the following February. The decree of Moulins, in eighty-five articles,
dealt basically with the reform of the judiciary. It aimed to strengthen

the central power by establishing grand sessions to be held periodically in the provinces, to be presided over by the Masters of Petitions of the Hôtel du Roi. Leagues, both Protestant and Catholic, were increasing in number all over France. The decree of Moulins forbade all confraternities 'among the common people, under religious pretexts'. These confraternities were strikingly well organized. Their political aims were disguised under professional appearances. The guilds provided their cadres and they were equipped and armed for war, secretly under the command of retired officers. The Catholic confraternities of the Holy Ghost were undisguised provincial associations for the defence of the Faith; among the Protestants, since the synods of Clairac in November 1560 and of Sainte-Foy of November 1561, the conferences fulfilled the same purpose. Thanks to the First War, during the past five years these organizations for civil war had been brought up to strength. In order to break them up the government itself would have had to go to war; the restrictions aimed at them in the decree of Moulins remained a dead letter. The adherents of the two religions continued to massacre one another; at Foix, in June 1566, the Huguenots killed 120 Catholics. A few days later, when repressing the riots at Pamiers , Monluc murdered nearly 700 Calvinists, sparing neither women n or children.

The Florida affair, meanwhile, made matters still worse between France and Spain, whose relationship had continued to deteriorate since Bayonne. Madame Catherine called Francès de Alava to order, reminding him that 'the Kings of France were not accustomed to allowing themselves to be threatened'. She was protecting Coligny's colonial policy up to the hilt. She already had a grasp of economic affairs, a rare thing in those days, and was interested in the colonies; the importance of establishing French outposts in the West Indies was one of her constant preoccupations, and when she learned that the Spaniards had massacred the French colonists in Florida she was extremely indignant and angry. 'I am beside myself', she wrote to Fourquevaux on March 17th. Three days previously she had already found Alava's intervention in French internal affairs insupportable. The collusion between the Cardinal de Lorraine and Philip II, which was public knowledge by then, confirmed her view that Spain was in fact the enemy-in-chief. Disarmed and without a navy—it was impossible to replace that of Henri II, which had become out-of-date—France was obliged to endure fresh humiliations. In revenge, Catherine considered increasing the number of places where sermons would be permitted; she made Madame de Crussol a duchess, and gave up her matrimonial schemes, realizing the mistake she had made at Bayonne. She turned towards Poland, whose king, being childless, could designate one of the Sons of France as his successor, as is proved by her letter of December 1566 to the Cardinal de Tournon. Nothing that was going on or that was in preparation in Europe escaped the Queen Mother's perpetual curiosity. Could not the setback of Madrid be made good at Cracow? Always cautious, she instructed the head of her mission to Poland, Sieur Blaise de Vigenaire, to mention these matters 'as if they were his own ideas, in the course of conversation, without allowing it in any way to transpire that he was charged by ourselves to do so'. At the same time she was concerning herself with the marriage of Charles IX to the Archduchess Elizabeth of Austria, the Emperor's younger daughter, an enchanting little girl of eleven.

During those three months at Moulins Catherine de Medici became certain that she could expect nothing whatever to her advantage from Philip II. In the February decree she affirmed her intention of governing above the parties. As she and L'Hospital remembered their dear and near Auvergne, at the beginning of April 1566 the Court removed to Clermont and to Riom. France's Governess completed her tour of the country via the Bourbonnais, the Nivernais, the Auxerrois and the Sénonais, Champagne and Brie. On May 1st she returned to Paris, whence she had set out more than two years previously.

Arguments between the Queen Mother and the Spanish ambassador became more and more frequent. In spite of the haughty manner in which she received the indiscreet complaints of Don Francès, Catherine took care not to break with him. She was even studying (the mission of L'Aubespine the younger of May 1567) the possibilities of an alliance with a view to peace between the Catholic and Very Christian Kings. This enabled her to refuse to surrender Calais to Elizabeth. The Queen of England based herself on the clauses of the Treaty of Cateau-Cambrésis; eight years had elapsed, whilst France had not paid the 500,000 écus in gold that had been promised, therefore Calais should be returned to its former conquerors. Catherine justified her refusal on the grounds of the Treaty of Hampton Court. As Le Havre had been occupied, this act of enmity had rendered viod the Treaty of Cateau-Cambrésis. The troubles at Pamiers, meanwhile, proved that both Protestants and Catholics were again determined on civil war. 'The Turks could not do worse,' she wrote in a moment of discouragement to the Marshal de Montmorency. From Scotland, where the Presbyterians, led by John Knox, were threatening the crown of Mary Stuart and the French alliance, to the troubles in the Spanish Flanders and the agitation in Picardy—on all sides the threats against the Queen Mother's policy of peace were becoming graver. The new Pope, Pius V, was as friendly towards Philip II as he was hostile to Catherine de Medici, who revealed her anxiety in her important letter of October 20, 1566, to Count Juste de Tournon, her envoy at Rome.

The Queen was then at Montceaux-en-Brie. In the peacefulness of the autumnal countryside she reviewed the seven years of her reign, examined her policy, and in profoundly moving terms justified it. She said that she was obliged to render account of herself only to God, 'all the more as there is no one capable of bringing pressure to bear on my will and my opinions, nevertheless throughout my life I have had only one aim in sight, to do good, and without respect to anything else ensure everything that I thought could be of help and service to the preservation of this realm, which I saw being plunged into obvious ruin and total desolation by religious divisions, accompanied by a great deal of ambition and partisanship, on one side and another, and that God so graciously gave me the means to save and preserve'. And she added: 'Had I done otherwise I would have thought myself to have been a very bad mother, and very neglectful of the honour that I received from the King [Henri II] and the obligation that I owe to this kingdom.'

Madame Catherine dictated this apologia for her past in her library, a rightful apologia (for she had made only one bad mistake, Bayonne) and in accents of simple and melancholy sincerity that ring completely true. She was the kingdom's humble servant, a good and devoted mother, who fully realized the duty laid upon her by the honour she had of governing France. She contrasted her achievement with the calumnies that were spread about her, distorting and caricaturing it, to the lies and deceits of which she herself had been the victim. 'Furthermore', she wrote proudly, 'there is need of no other justification to refute all that than the course of my life and actions. . . . ' She explains to the Count de Tournon what were her plans and intentions in order that he might 'close the mouths of the miserable liars with words of truth' and she pitied those liars more than she despised them. Then, all of a sudden, without transition, the artistic side of the sovereign's nature reappears. A Roman doctor had an Adonis, 'which is so beautiful', for sale. And as well as the

R

artist, the business woman, who does not intend to be over-charged: 'How much would one have to pay for it?' she asked as she instructed Tournon to deal with the matter. This very personal letter reveals the true Catherine de Medici, the woman who was at one and the same time a politician, the mother of a family, and artistic. And, impatient to acquire this beautiful antique statue, she said: 'Inform me of it with all possible despatch.' There was also a touch of the Florentine shopkeeper; it was not to be made known that the purchaser was the Queen of France, for princes were always robbed. Tournon was to approach the doctor who owned this coveted marvel as if on his own behalf: 'As I am informed that he wishes to make some profit on it, find out how much he wants without letting him known that it is for us.'

Alas, if only she had nothing else to do but to collect Adonises! On December 24th, Alava came to ask her to allow the passage through France of the Spanish troops that were being sent to the Netherlands. Fourquevaux was ordered to make Philip II abandon this plan. As ever, Spain claimed the right to treat France as if it were a protectorate. The Flanders troubles came as a handy reason for resisting such insolence. Once again Madame Catherine's robust health induced in her a sense of well-being that events would soon destroy. The Beggars' Revolt, dangerous to Spain, would be even more so to France, as the fever that was flaring up in the Low Countries spread to the Protestants, whipped up, in spite of all the Queen Mother's efforts to control it, by the fanatical preachers and unemployed soldiery. Spain protested against the military measures taken by France to protect her northern and eastern frontiers, highly vulnerable since they remained those of the Four Rivers. The French Huguenots saw in those measures a chance to intervene in favour of their brethren who were being massacred by the Duke of Alba. Catherine de Medici had decided on non-intervention, which was wisdom itself, for neither the French army nor navy were sufficiently strong to take part in a war which, through both religious and political alliances and interests, would have immediately become a European one, but this was to rouse the dual fanaticism of the Catholics, in favour of aiding Spain, and the Protestants, wanting to support the Netherlands. Events prove the wisdom of the course chosen by the Queen, since it avoided another European conflagration until the Thirty Years' War.

But, with the exception of the small group of politicals who were supporting the government and such isolated Reformationist pastors or laymen as Sébastien Castalion—whose death in 1563 had left a gap that no one else had filled—nobody could understand this policy, least of all the Huguenots. Seeing their co-religionists beaten and terrorized, they were clamouring for intervention and organizing an active campaign in favour of it. By force of circumstances, although the internal problems were not in themselves insoluble, Catherine and the Calvinists were from now on to become more and more strongly opposed to one another. It was only on foreign policy that there was no possibility of coming to an agreement. Catherine was for neutrality; the Protestants for intervention. 'Her good sense made her a pacifist; their proselytism made them belligerent,' as Mariéjol very rightly said. The Huguenots countered the Queen's 'France, first,' with 'Religion, first,' and the Catholics, demanding the Spanish alliance, did the same. Religious passions were contravening the nation's permanent interests. Their brethren's danger was to hasten action on the part of the French Protestants . . . and on September 26, 1567, it led to the madness of Meaux.

What was the brutal and apparently unexpected thing that happened, that caused Catherine herself to write of it to the Marshal de Matignon: 'What has recurred here, by which we are dumbfounded, since we neither know nor understand any occasion for it'? During the first nine months of the year the Queen Mother had been busy manoeuvring between Spain, England and the Empire, between the Catholics and the Protestants. She had been no less preoccupied by England's claims on Calais than by those of Spain to have the right to keep an eye on French internal policy. The Calais question had compelled her to take a much less firm line with Philip II than she would have liked. The Montmorencys were extremely hostile to Spain and it was necessary to cool them down. In order to keep the Protestants quiet the Queen Mother had given back the government of Picardy to Monsieur le Prince, and had raised the county of Nogent-le-Rotrou, the favourite residence of the Bourbons-Condés, to the Duchy of Enghien. Charles IX had agreed to stand godfather to the child which had just been born of Monsieur le Prince's second marriage. Nevertheless the Queen and her son were rightly suspicious of the movement of troops in his pay. The King's younger brother, the young Duc d'Anjou, who was sixteen, had been given command of the Royal armies, which had been assembled on account of the troubles in Flanders, whereupon Condé, whose pride had been deeply wounded by the fact, once again launched out on new adventures. He left the Court abruptly, declaring that he had nothing more to do there. The quarrels between the great Catholic and Huguenot noblemen were breaking out again; Andelot retired to Brittany, whilst Coligny and Henri de Guise were provoking and threatening one another. Rumours were spread accusing Catherine of being in league with Spain against the Beggars. The atmosphere was becoming more and more thunderous, yet the Queen Mother, whose weakness it always was to assume that others had as much good sense as herself, did not believe the situation to be serious. As she wrote to the Marshal de Cossé from La Fère on September 4th, she thought that she merely heard 'the sounds of a slight restlessness' instead of real threats of a resumption of hostilities between the *Papegots* and *Parpaillots*, as those on either side called one another.

On her return to Montceaux on September 16, 1567, she continued to have confidence in the common sense of the Protestant leaders, for she was unable to imagine that they would unleash a Second War solely to come to the aid of the Reformationists of the Low Countries. On September 18th she wrote to Fourquevaux: 'There has been some pointless talk about those of the Religion wanting to take up arms; but they were merely a little afraid, so it is said, and it has all died down.'

She believed in peace because she considered that peace was primarily essential in the interests of the whole French nation, and she was right. But what account have sectarianism and pride ever taken of reason? This state of mind was so incomprehensible to Catherine that even after she had ruled the country for seven years she had still not taken the measure of the violent emotion that swayed the Huguenots, ready on the instant to risk everything the moment the Religion seemed to them to be in danger. In the case of the French Catholics, their political interests often counterbalanced their religious ones, as was shown by the behaviour of the Guises and the Montmorencys. But religious interests invariably prevailed in the case of the Protestants. Catherine deceived herself with regard to Condé and Coligny; she saw them primarily as the appanagist and the feudalist, whereas the real masters of French Protestantism were always the preachers, whom the aristocratic Huguenots had never been able to control, and who had the faithful on their side. Neither Monsieur le Prince nor the Admiral had the necessary strength of character to resist them. Not until Henri de Navarre did a Calvinist leader hold his own against the preachers and pass beyond their Biblical fervour.

Catherine misunderstood the Huguenots as completely as the Spaniards. A humanist, and too feminine to be able wholeheartedly to accept an objective that she found personally distasteful, in spite of her genius the sectarianism of the former and the sombre will to power of the latter, their joint and furious dogmatism, were beyond her understanding. The differences between them and herself were too deep. Catherine's wonderful intelligence could easily have made the necessary effort to understand them; she did not make it because she never saw the necessity for doing so. Her entourage consisted of men of liberal mind, such as L'Hospital, Morvillier, Jean de Monluc, and the Italians who were her particular intimates were sceptics. At a time when men full of fury were the popular spokesmen, Catherine believed in wisdom and reason. She believed in life at a time when from Geneva to Madrid men were only passionately concerned with death. She knew that whilst Divine truth is one, to human beings truth has a hundred different faces. She forgot that to the uneducated monks and preachers beyond control there was only one form of truth—their own—and that whoever refused to submit to it was only fit to mount the scaffold of Anne du Bourg or Michel Servet.

Whilst Catherine de Medici, misled by her own good sense, was writing to Monsieur de Gordes that everything was 'thank God, as peaceable as we could wish', the Calvinist leaders were meeting at the Admiral's, at Châtillon, and at Monsieur le Prince's, at Vallery. Coligny's point of view prevailed; they would await events; 6,000 Swiss mercenaries had entered France in the King's pay. A new gathering was held at Vallery on the pretext that they constituted a menace and that the Court intended to abrogate the edict of pacification. The most absurd stories found credence there—that Condé and Coligny were to be assassinated or arrested and the faithful persecuted. As usual Monsieur le Prince and the Admiral gave way to the hotheads. They voted to take up arms. Even the place and the date were decided upon; Rosoy-en-Brie, at the end of September, for a new rising on the lines of the Amboise tumults. At Montceaux they would capture the Queen, her children, and the great Catholic noblemen. In due course the Ventian ambassador, Correro, informed his government of precautions taken by the conspirators to keep their plans secret. Castelnau de la Mauvissière has told in his *Mémoires* how, on returning from Brussels, where he had been sent on a mission, he learned from certain gentlemen he met on the road that the Huguenots 'were all ready, armed, and prepared to be the first to go to war and to seize the King's person, the Queen his mother, his brothers and their Council, who wanted to destroy the so-called Reformed religion and those who supported it'. Castelnau admitted that he thought it more likely to be a fable than the truth, which shows how far the Court was from feeling any anxiety. He mentioned it, nevertheless, but no one took the news seriously. The Constable said that no army could be raised that he would not know about. The Chancellor complained in bitter terms that anyone should raise a false alarm. 'So that', Castelnau said, 'all were very ill satisfied with me for the warning I had given'.

But it was a sound warning.[1] The Queen Mother was still ordering 'that all subjects shall live in all gentleness and tranquillity, observing the edicts' when on the evening of September 24th, her Huguenot subjects occupied Rosoy-en-Brie near Coulommiers and began to descend into the valley of the Grand Morin in order to march against Montceaux. Monsieur le Prince, the Admiral, Andelot, La Rochefoucauld, advanced at the head of 600 cavaliers, wearing breast-plates. The alarm was given by Castelnau and his brothers, who met the advance guard at the bridge of Trilbardou, on the Marne, less than four miles from Montceaux. In the middle of the night the Court, panic-stricken, took refuge at Meaux. The Swiss, garrisoned at Château-Thierry, were summoned. Catherine nevertheless had enough presence of mind to send the Marshal de Montmorency to treat with Monsieur le Prince, and appeal to reason, an appeal which was in vain. But the time that had thus been won was not; the Swiss were able to reach Meaux before Condé was able to begin to attack it. The Constable and the Chancellor advised that it would be best to remain in the capital of Brie and the Queen Mother agreed; from Meaux, under the protection of the Swiss, it would be possible to negotiate. The Guises were against it and for returning to Paris, raising arms, and war. The Swiss Colonel, Louis Pfyffer, guaranteed that they would be victorious. The young King, beside himself at Condé's and Coligny's treachery, insisted on fighting. Catherine gave way and their departure was decided upon. At three o'clock in the morning the Swiss, surrounding the sovereigns and the Court, formed a square, and they set out. The King's Swiss mountaineers, armed with pikes, were vulnerable only to very powerful cavalry charges, as had been seen at Marignan. Condé and his 500

---

[1] On all this, Castelnau de la Mauvissière, as witness and participant is of the first importance (Vol. VI of his *Mémoires*, Chapters IV to VIII). In comparing him with La Noue (Chapter XII), there can be no doubt that the Second War of Religion was premeditated by the Protestants. Coligny and Condé were even more clearly responsible for it than for the first one.

horsemen were helpless against Pfyffer's 6,000 infantrymen. As a military man La Noue could not conceal his admiration for this march from Meaux to Paris, those eleven miles completed at one stage, as far as Bourget: 'I heard it said that this big battalion made an appearance worthy of the Swiss; for, without ever showing surprise, they remained firm for a time, retreating afterwards in close formation, always turning their heads, as does a furious wild boar pursued by the hounds, until they were left alone, seeing that there was no possiblity of pressing them.'

First Amboise, then Fontainebleau, afterwards Meaux. These alternating surprise attacks—Huguenots, Catholic, Huguenot—aimed at seizing the Queen Mother and the King, make it quite clear that the stake for which the parties were contending was the Crown of France. At Fontainebleau she had had to give way to the Triumvirs, with rage in her heart. This time, as the Protestants had so wished it, and fate had so decided at Meaux, and as she had the protection of the Swiss Guards, Catherine de Medici was determined to punish Coligny and Condé for their crime. She determined to have their heads, and so she would. A fews days later the Catholics were finally infuriated by the outrages of the armed Protestants, at Montereau, at Orleans, and at the Michelade of Nimes, on September 30, 1567, when without any provocation eighty religious and priests were massacred. There was a general demand that Coligny should be outlawed, although Condé was still protected by the mystique of the Blood of France.

The Queen Mother expressed her indignation in her letter to Fourquevaux, written immediately after her return to Paris: 'You will hear of this infamous enterprise, which is of a kind from which God preserve us.' The deeper reason for her indignation was that, as Coligny and Condé were preparing to besiege Paris, she was forced to ask Spain for help. In actual numbers they disposed of fewer men than the Constable, but although their cavalry force was small numerically it was extremely well trained, which enabled it to pursue the convoys on the outskirts of Paris. So Catherine once more resigned herself to negotiating, but Michel de L'Hospital encountered the greatest ill-will on the part of the Admiral and Monsieur le Prince. They demanded the expulsion of the Italians from Court, 'those leeches that are sucking the substance from us all'. In doing so they provoked the Queen Mother, protectress by birth of the Italians in France, and whose anger now turned on the Chancellor for considering that it was necessary to give way all along the line.

She blamed his big talk about moderation and justice for the state in which the Government now found itself, but in doing so she was condemning her own policy, which gives the measure of her confusion and anguish. She blamed her own failure—and nothing was more feminine—on L'Hospital, who had done nothing but carry out her orders.

She was beside herself, and to such an extent that she dictated letters to her son in which it was stated that those who 'were all a-quiver to go to the aid of those of the new religion' should be carved up, cut into pieces, without sparing a single one of them. She gave way to her Italian anger to the degree of causing the King to write: 'So many more dead, so many fewer enemies.' She could not forgive the Protestants for the bitter disappointment their ingratitude had caused her, 'the greatest wickedness in this world,' she said to Emmanuel-Philibert of Savoy. The Admiral and Monsieur le Prince had succeeded in exasperating their best friend. Such were the political abilities of those two heroes of partisan interpretations of history.

When at the time during which the Guises had been all-powerful the Protestants had proclaimed themselves Royalists they had spoken the truth. But during that autumn of 1567 in the case of nearly all the leaders, and especially Condé and Coligny, this claim was no longer anything but a cover for their personal ambitions; the one wanted to be king, the other master of the Palace. Monsieur le Prince was already being called the King of the Faithful. Already in March 1564, the correspondence of Renée de France, Duchess of Ferrara, alludes to the preachers and to their desire to see Charles IX, referred to as 'that minor' and in other charming terms, exterminated. Protestant though she had become, the daughter of Louis XII could not approve of such criminal plans. Three or four years previously, a short time before his death, she had informed Calvin of them. It was said that gold medals had been struck, on which were the shield of France and the portrait of Louis de Bourbon. *Ludovicus XIII, Dei gratia Francorum rex primus christianus*, ran the legend. Brantôme's evidence should be remembered here, for it is a matter of eye-witnesses. In *La Vie du Prince de Condé* he reports that Anne de Montmorency showed this medal to the Council on October 7, 1567.[1] The Admiral, always shadowy and cautious,

[1] Leblanc refers to it in his *Traité des Monnaies de France*, p. 270 and Secousse in Vol. XVII, p. 107, of the *Mémoires de l'Académie des inscriptions*. The Protestant historians claim that it was invented by the Catholics, and that the medal was apochryphal. We

allowed the thoughtless Bourbon to compromise himself, even among the Huguenots, for this ambition to become king revealed in Monsieur le Prince a contempt for the Salic Law sufficient to shock almost everyone. The Bourbon heir, on the basis of primogeniture, was the son of Antoine, the young Prince of Navarre, Henri de Béarn. When Catherine had sent investigators to Châtillon-sur-Loing during the previous summer, the Admiral was busying himself with his fields and vineyards. He was adept at providing himself with alibis and escape routes in the case of failure, as had been clearly seen at the time of the Treaty of Hampton Court. Monsieur le Prince, on the contrary, was always willing to be defiant.

At the interview of La Chapelle-Saint-Denis, when he stated that duality of religion was unacceptable to the State, the Constable broke off negotiations. Paris was about to rise against the Huguenots. The two armies met at Saint-Denis on November 10, 1567. The Protestants, who were beaten, were saved from annihilation by the mortal wound received there by Montmorency at the beginning of the afternoon, when the action had lasted barely an hour. The result of the battle was undecided; they all returned to camp proclaiming that they were the victors. Vieilleville described the situation correctly: 'The King of Spain won the battle.' On November 12th the Constable died, nearly seventy-five years of age. Catherine was thus delivered of the last of the Triumvirs; she managed to conceal her joy but did not succeed at pretending to feel sorrow.

As soon as the *Compère* disappeared, the *Commère* took advantage of the situation to tighten her grip on the army by having Henri d'Anjou made Lieutenant-General; Charles IX had refused to give him the post of Constable, which remained vacant. For the first time the King resisted his mother. He was very jealous of his younger brother and wanted to free himself from Catherine's tutelage, for everyone knew of her preference for the Duc d'Anjou. The Venetian ambassadors were very good judges of Charles IX, whom an uncritical literature, the result of Saint Bartholomew, transformed into a monster. Giovanni Michele described him at the age of eleven as 'an

---

ourselves consider that it was authentic. Failing the mystique of the Sacrament, which they rejected, the mystery of the Blood of France, to which they remained attached, was recognized by the Huguenots, which allowed the more fanatical among them to defend as legitimate the dethronement of the Valois, who, having prostituted themselves to Babylon, had become unworthy of reigning. This should never be forgotten and Condé hoped to take advantage of it.

admirable child, and in talent, intelligence, affability, liberality and courage, everything might be hoped for from him as a king. He is handsome, with particularly fine eyes, like his father. His movements and manners are full of ease and gracefulness. But he is not very strong; he eats and drinks very little and as regards physical exercise it will be necessary to handle him carefully. Yet he enjoys the *jeu de paume*, riding, arms, all exercises no doubt worthy of a king but too strenuous; and as soon as he tires himself he needs a long rest for he is weak and very short of breath'. Michele had very well observed this weakness of the little King's, especially of the lungs (from which he died).

He stressed the King's laziness and reluctance to study, for which he had little taste, but which was forced on him by his mother, who was strongly in favour of culture. What young Charles liked was war. He had inherited his father's violence and not the patient genius of his mother. Suriano was no less favourably impressed than his predecessor by young Charles as an adolescent, nor did his sharpness miss any of his faults and qualities, both mental and physical: 'One may hope for much from him if he lives, provided that he is not spoiled.' He emphasized the paleness of his complexion and his education, that did not suit his temperament. Like Michele, Suriano was very worried about the future of this prince, on account of Nostradamus's prediction, 'the astrologer who since a great number of years has always correctly foretold the calamities of France'. Nostradamus had told the Queen Mother that she would see all her children enthroned, which was true of all of them excepting her last-born son, François. The Venetian's political experience taught him that the premature deaths of the last Valois would be the cause of 'the total destruction of the kingdom. Proceeding always thus, from child to child, whilst others governed the kingdom, one would have to wait far too long for a king with supreme powers, honoured by his subjects, respected by his neighbours, feared by all, and who by some signal action would re-establish the greatness and the glory of the monarchy'. Although he reigned for fifteen years and on his accession to the throne was already a man, Henri III, full of talents but as unbalanced as his brother, did not succeed in being that man. It was necessary to wait for Henri IV, son and nephew of those wretched Bourbons, whom the mystique of the Blood of France caused the Protestants to take seriously, and who by a dynastic miracle disappeared before they could succeed to the Crown, a miracle that allowed the Governess of France to preserve his heritage for the great prince worthy to succeed her and thanks to God so different from his father and uncle.

Charles IX was worth more than they. In 1563 Marco-Antonio Barbaro confirmed the opinions of Michele and Suriano. He added that the young King was artistic, a painter and sculptor. He praised his piety, his morality, and saw him as 'magnanimous, affable, frank, of lively intelligence, a student of history and languages, principally Latin and Italian'. Charles had studied in order to please his mother; the documents all reveal his filial devotion, his personal letters as well as contemporary correspondence.

But as his congenital tuberculosis gradually developed, the unfortunate young prince became more and more neuropathic, unbalanced, with recurring crises of near-insanity.[1] In 1567 he was still in sufficiently good health for his personality to remain as the Venetians described it, and also Brantôme, who called him 'the *gentil* King Charles, the brave King, gentle, benign, and gracious'. But however docile he showed himself towards his mother, his opposition to his brother should not be forgotten. It explained many difficulties during the following years, domestic difficulties that accumulated, together with all the religious, political and social difficulties, becoming an ever greater burden to the Governess of France. At the Sessions of Justice of March 13, 1571, Charles IX appropriately rendered the greatest homage to his mother, expressing his gratitude towards her to whom he very well knew that he owed everything: 'After God the Queen, my mother, is the one to whom I have the greatest number of obligations; her tenderness towards me and my people, her industry, zeal, and prudence have so well conducted the affairs of this State at a time when my age did not permit me to apply myself to them, that all the tempests of civil war were unable to damage my kingdom.' Eighteen years later, at the bier of the great sovereign, Henri III was to render her the same homage.

It was the very truth. The family tragedy that, from the day when Henri d'Anjou was appointed to the Lieutenant-Generalcy, was to pit Catherine's three sons one against the other (François d'Alençon, the youngest, hated both his brothers equally, whilst they detested

[1] On Charles IX the best balanced and documented are the pages by Gaston Dodu, *Les Valois*, Part IV, Chapter I, pp. 365–74. They contain a multitude of duly documented references. In *Charles IX* Pierre Champion, however, re-told the story of this prince, whom his correspondence, unfortunately unpublished, reveals as far more unfortunate than guilty. Cf. footnote, *infra.*, pp. 377–8. We must also refer to the subtle and finely shaded account by Baron André de Maricourt in *Les Valois*.

each other) perhaps contributed as much as the fury of the parties to the breakdown of the Queen Mother's policy of pacification. When, on the day after the death of Anne de Montmorency, the young King dared for the first time reply to his mother with a refusal, we should not overlook the clue contained in his answer: 'Young as I am, Madame, I feel that I am strong enough to bear my own sword, and if it were not so, would my brother, who is younger than I, be any more suitable?'

Let us note the date and content. Until then Catherine had only had to fight the appanagists and the feudalists, the monks and preachers filled with the sacred fire that was making her subjects flare up. But from now on her sons were to destroy one another. This was a new problem and one which Machiavelli had not studied. Madame Catherine had to face it alone, with no previous experience to guide her, since during the past seven and a half years of her reign she had been the *genetrix*, the mother-figure before whom all her young had bowed down and trembled. Along the dark and narrow path full of pitfalls which led to the Matins of August 1572, the Florentine Queen for the first time met an unforeseen obstacle—her own sons. The consequences of Saint Bartholomew's Night were to strengthen it and it would not cease to grow. Catherine de Medici's hard and unjust fate conjured up this conflict between Machiavellism and maternal love in the very hour when, the Constable having gone to his grave along with Jacques de Saint-André and François de Guise, she no longer had to contend on the Catholic side with influential men able to contravene her policy. She thought she would only have to struggle against a Coligny and a Condé. But now—although she did not yet realize it, for she was a mother and too authoritarian to notice it so soon—her sons' mutual antagonism would cause new dangers to threaten her. And she had no means of defence or protection against these dangers. This was her personal tragedy.

The Duke of Anjou was still too young to be Commander-in-Chief in fact. The Queen Mother formed a Council of War, consisting of the Dukes de Nemours and Montpensier, and the superintendant of finances, Arthur de Cossé, whom she made a Marshal of France and who belonged to her group of politicals. Her aim was to achieve peace as quickly as possible .The Protestants took advantage of the negotiations to safeguard their troops and to ask for German reinforcements from John-Casimir, son of Frederick III, Elector Palatinate of the Rhine, the hope of all the Calvinists of France and the

Empire, without whose aid nothing decisive could be expected by those of the Religion.

At Châlons, on January 4, 1568, Catherine conferred in person with the Cardinal Odet de Châtillon. On the 15th she returned to Paris, which she found on the point of rising, clamouring for war to the end, offering 600,000 livres towards it, whilst for his part Philip II was offering one million in gold. In spite of this Catherine continued to negotiate with Châtillon, who was demanding that the edict of pacification should be continued in perpetuity and irrevocably, and the payment of the German troops by the King. On this it was impossible to come to an agreement. Condé and Coligny were marching their armies through France, where they were guilty of the worst excesses. Charles IX re-issued the edict, promising to pardon all those Protestants who disarmed, but it was a wasted effort. The *Parpaillots* were no less committed to war than the *Papegots*. After her feminine loss of temper with Michel de L'Hospital, following on the events at Meaux, the Queen Mother had taken him back into her confidence, which won both of them, as well as the Marshal de Montmorency, said Haton, 'the reputation of being Huguenots and heretics; at least it is certain that they were the mainstay and support of the Huguenot rebels'. Catholic opinion was wholly against the Chancellor, 'A Calvinist and Huguenot heretic', affirmed Haton, to whom the Queen and Montmorency appeared no better, 'however often they went to Mass'. L'Hospital was held responsible for all the evils of the times.

To the Catholic zealots he was as much an object of popular execration as the Cardinal de Lorraine was to the Protestants. Catherine retained him in office, nevertheless, for in spite of her increased touchiness she had enough good sense to recognize that the worst of all evils was civil war. She now regarded the Protestants with horror, but unlike her subjects she did not understand that they could never be quelled except by force of arms. Unless she was prepared to submit to Spain peace with the Protestants was a necessity. But the preachers in the churches of Paris, caught up in Lenten fever, who compared the King to the impious Achab and his mother to Jezebel, had no inkling of this. The complacency with which the curé Haton echoed their sentiments is proof of the war-like passions of the masses, who in their ignorance of foreign affairs had not the same reasons as Catherine de Medici for wanting to end hostilities. The doctors of the Sorbonne provided the supporters of war to the end with theological arguments. Holding her own against

Catholic opinion the Queen Mother, who rightly preferred the realism of *Il Principe* to Biblical imprecations, and was equally indifferent to both true and false prophets, insulting one another in sermons and preachings, continued to negotiate. She had to persuade Charles IX, who wanted to punish his enemies, to give way; at seventeen he could not yet realize that one cannot inflict punishment unless one is the stronger party. And Catherine knew that without Spain they could not be so. In Florence they knew their Horace and his epistle:

Cervus equum pugna melior communibus herbis . . .

Rather than submit to Philip II, Catherine preferred to renounce her revenge:

Sed postquam victor violens discessit ab hoste,
Non equitem dorso, non frenum depulit ore.

The mysterious death of Don Carlos would facilitate a rapprochement between France and the Empire, since it put an end to Philip II's former plan to marry the Infant to one of the Archduchesses. The French, in general, were unconcerned with such diplomatic matters, but Catherine knew their great importance with regard to foreign policy, which was always in the forefront of her mind, as is proven by her letters to Fourquevaux. Caring above all for France, her outlook had remained a cosmopolitan one; it was not for nothing that she had been brought up in papal palaces and she was concerned for Christianity, a term she often employed. The spirit of principality, which governed Philip II and Elizabeth I of England and would also govern Richelieu and Louis XIV, was foreign to Catherine, who had not forgotten where it had led François I, the rejected aspirant to the Empire. 'Our affairs', she wrote, 'require it'—the Austrian marriage—'and it is necessary to the good of the whole of Christianity, the safety of which depends on the union of these three princes, without whom everything would collapse.'

Those three princes were their Caesarian, Very Christian and Catholic Majesties. Historians may well be astonished by the realism and insight of Catherine's foreign policy. She wanted a union between France, the Empire and Spain. The English alliance had been secured by the recent Treaty of Troyes, and the difficult question of Calais had been happily settled. Catherine was seeking an entente between the four Great Powers and peace outside France that would lead to peace within. She did not despair of achieving it. We can see her through her admirable letters—a friend of the Humanists, faithful to the conception of Christianity, of a Christian Republic, unlike Louis XI, who was not interested in Europe, and François I, who had given way to the imperialistic temptation to achieve hegemony over it. It was this temptation that had led him to Pavia. Meanwhile the Guises, the Châtillons, the nobles, the clerks of both Rome and Geneva, the bourgeoisie and the masses were thinking only of killing one another, to the greater profit of Philip II, Elizabeth and Maximilian, whose eyes were fixed on that lovely and tempting prey —France delivered over to the factions.

On March 12, 1568 Catherine was able to inform Elizabeth, who had proposed to intervene with Coligny and Condé, that peace was 'well on the way'. Ten days later, with no money, his troops demoralized by their defeat at Chartres, Coligny was forced to make peace and sent his brother Odet to sign it at Longjumeau on March 27th. The edict of pacification was restored unaltered; the Royal treasury would pay the wages of the Reiters that had been sent to Monsieur le Prince; the free exercise of the Reformed religion was extended to Provence; La Rochelle was left to the Huguenots. This peace was entirely due to Catherine, who had imposed it on them all—on her son, the Protestants and the Catholics. It aroused general fury and discontent. It was called, first the Underhand and later the Little Peace. As La Noue said, on the Protestant side they had been drawn into a whirlwind, into the hazards of peace, owing to the ill-will of the German mercenaries. To Catherine the essential matter was that Condé was dismissing his troops whilst she retained her own, those of France. The blindness of the sects and factions was such that they were unable to see the enormous advantage that this gave the Royal State. Coligny knew very well that the Peace of Longjumeau was Catherine's victory. In order the better to prepare his revenge he heaped flowers of speech on the Queen, writing to her that he congratulated himself 'with all right thinking people that it had pleased God, in giving them peace, to deliver this poor kingdom from all the miseries and calamities brought upon them by war'. In reality he considered it 'full of faithlessness', called it the Bloody Peace, 'a long series of assassinations'. But the protests against it of Madrid and Rome prove that, on the contrary, the peace was in the interests of France and the King. Madame Catherine was as well aware of the difficulties as of the benefits it would bring. The poet Etienne Jodelle was instructed to say so in a sonnet, the formal lyricism of which reveals the importance attached by the Queen Mother to the peace which similarly to Amboise, she had wanted:

> *Si ta paix est honnête, et juste, et sainte et bonne,*
> *Qu'elle ait heureuse entrée, accroissance et sûrté:*
> *Si ton discord n'est pas, comme il faut, garrotté,*
> *Que te couronne on voie orner autre couronne,*
>
> *Qui son rond d'or d'un rond de laurier environne,*
> *Non d'olive, qui donne et loisir et fierté,*
> *Et confort au discord, que plus grand'loyauté*
> *Dieu, pour jamais, envers ton beau sceptre nous donne:*
>
> *Qu'il donne a ton Conseil l'adresse et le bon coeur,*
> *A tes beaux ans la joie, et l'heur, et la longueur,*
> *Sur tous à tes faits gloire, à ta gloire mémoire.*
>
> *A moi, qui suis ton tien, grand pouvoir, grand effort,*
> *Tant pour aider qu'orner ta Paix, ou ton discord.*
> *Ton sceptre, ton conseil, tes ans, tes faits, ta gloire.*[1]

Catherine was the only one who desired this peace of which the Court poet sang. The rest of them endured it; La Popelinière said very rightly that they had concluded it 'to catch their breath'. Spurred on by the monks, the Catholic masses, already imbued with the spirit of the League, were massacring the Huguenots in Paris, Rouen, Orleans, Bourges and Auxerre. In spite of his safe-conduct, the Parliament of Tours beheaded Rapin, Monsieur le Prince's maître d'hôtel. On their side, the Reformationists did not carry out the clauses of the peace of Longjumeau with regard to the surrender of strongholds. Everywhere they were pillaging and burning churches, strangling or torturing the priests and the religious. Catherine was helpless against all those maniacs. As always she remained the weaponless arbitrator, ridiculed, and nobody observed the edict of pacification. Lacking the forces to compel the law to be obeyed, the Queen Mother's letters were written in vain. The situation had done nothing but worsen ever since the beginning of her reign. Owing to lack of money, and to relieve the towns of the

[1] There are seven admirable sonnets by Jodelle in honour of Catherine de Medici.

9. QUEEN MARGUERITE OF NAVARRE at the age of seventeen, by François Clouet
(*photo*: Giraudon)

10. TWO SCENES FROM THE WARS OF RELIGION

a). Siege of Chartres by the Prince de Condé 1568
   (G=M. de Piles; H=d'Andelot)

b). Battle of Jarnac, 1569 (A=Coligny and d'Andelot; C=Montgomery;
   D=Briquemault; H=La Rochefoucauld)   (*Bibliothèque Nationale*)

burden of maintaining garrisons, a number of those serving in the
Royal army had to be discharged. Even the faithful Scottish Guard
had been provisionally disbanded. The discharged military went their
separate ways; some to the rebels in the Low Countries, others into
Spanish service. Those who found no employment became bandits.
In the Council itself the insolvency of the State was revealed by the
Duc d'Anjou's opposition to Charles IX. By a letter that she had
intercepted, Catherine knew that Philip II was encouraging his
brother-in-law Charles IX to free himself from the Queen Mother's
tutelage. The members of the Council were split into politicals and
zealots, the latter true Leaguers before the advent of the League.
Carnavalet, Morveillier, Amyot and L'Hospital were on Catherine's
side and were supported by the Cardinal de Bourbon, the Montmorency brothers and Vieilleville. But the Cardinal de Lorraine had
become the leader of the more violent faction. His followers included
Lansac, Nicolas de Pellevé, Archbishop of Sens, and the Duc
d'Anjou. The young Prince used a phrase which in the circumstances
was cruelly comical and naive: 'Let the King remain strong to
preserve those who are good, and punish the wicked.' In the absence
of his mother, who was ill, Charles IX sided with the politicals.[1]

There were alarming reports from the provincial governors and
officials. Condé was making homicidal threats against the Cardinal
de Lorraine, whose purple robes he would dye in his own blood.
Coligny did not threaten, but accused and pleaded. Near Auxerre
the carrier of the money that the Protestants had to contribute
towards the pay of the Reiters was attacked and robbed; there were
dead and wounded. Catherine's illness made the situation worse.
'Political life has been, as it were, suspended,' the Venetian ambassador, Correro, wrote during this illness, which lasted throughout
the month of May 1568. As ever brave and mistress of herself,
Catherine wrote to Coligny from her sick-bed, promising him justice.
What an illusion! The massacres were spreading like an epidemic.
The documents recording the Catholic atrocities alternate with those

---

[1] Documentation in La Ferrière:—*Lettres de Catherine de Médicis*, Vol. III *Introduction*,
P. XXIV, sqq. According to the manuscript of the minutes of proceedings of the session
of the Council of March 1, 1568, *B.N. fonds français*, No. 15546. There are a great
number of quotations and references in Champion's *Charles IX*, largely based on the
fonds Simancas, which was then still in the *Archives nationales*, *série* K., Nos. 1505 et seq.
The *fonds* Simanca is indispensable for the study of Catherine de Medici's policy. Since
the monumental publication of her correspondence there are only a few of her unpublished manuscripts in the B.N. For all this the reader is referred to the bibliography of
the original edition of the present work, revised and corrected in 1942, comprising the
final forty pages of the book (691–731).

S

recording the Protestant atrocities. The victory over Mary Stuart won by the Scottish Presbyterians contributed to the exaltation of the French Calvinists.[1] Catherine was still living in hopes: 'The peace was concluded solely as a matter of necessity,' she told Correro on June 11th. 'There are circumstances when one is obliged to do oneself violence in order to avoid greater evils, and to submit to what one would not have liked. Still, I hope for good results from it.' She did not in the least deceive herself regarding the 'miserable state'—her own words—in which she found herself. She was counting only on Providence to escape assassination.

She knew that the government was incapable of carrying out a surprise attack on the Protestants, but that nonetheless there was no other way of restoring the situation. The correspondence (unfortunately still unpublished) of Charles IX, hers, that of the diplomatic and military agents in the course of the spring and summer of 1568, especially Correro's despatches (particularly those of March and April) reveal the constant hesitations of a feeble government. Like Ovid's Medea, Catherine could have summed up the situation perfectly by exclaiming:

Video meliora proboque; deteriora sequor.

She was obliged to follow them. The country's anarchy was only equalled by the weakness of the State. Correro was not duped by the apparent favour shown to the Cardinal de Lorraine: 'It is by accident

---

[1] There was a genuine Masonic bond between the Calvinists and the Presbyterians. On this subject, which is only just beginning to be investigated and on which important discoveries are already being made, see the important work of William Thomas Walsh on Philip II, the most important among the most recent, together with that by Louis Pfandl, apart, needless to say, from those by Spanish experts engaged in reconstructing the true character of this prince, one of the greatest in history. See also, the very remarkable article by René de Laboulaye, *Calvin et la Maçonnerie*, in the *Revue des Questions historiques* of January 1939, with an interesting bibliography of sources and works; amongst these note in particular Gould and Murray Lyon on the Scottish ramifications of Mediaeval Masonry, through Knox and the Presbyterians under the Regency of Marie de Lorraine and under Mary Stuart. All this, which is only just beginning, will clear up many things. It appears that in the sixteenth century the Protestants, like the aristocracy, the big bourgeoisie and the clergy in the eighteenth, were, without realizing it, used by the secret societies. There is here a new mine to be opened up and explored on the origins of the revolutionary spirit. Without being aware of it, the Huguenot conventicles, like the *Sociétés de Pensée*, were infiltrated by Masonic theory and practices. Another similitude is found in the role of the Jesuits, a genuine Catholic secret society—whatever the sons of Ignatius may claim—against anti-Catholic secret societies. It seems that the Genevese plot was far less of a legend than has been indignantly maintained by Protestant historians.

or necessity.' The popularity of the Lorraines in Paris might make it possible to obtain subsidies from the municipality, which was hostile to the government. Catherine thought that the Archbishop of Rheims' weakness of character would make it easy for her to dominate him, but she forgot that he was not alone; the Duchesse de Nemours, widow of François de Guise, and his son, Henri, were still determined on vengeance against Coligny and the Protestants. It was they who prevented the Cardinal from giving way to the wiles of the Florentine, who would have to accept an anti-Protestant policy although all she wanted to follow was a policy 'of union and friendship' as Amyot said. Correro, a supporter of the Lorraines, saw very well that Charles de Guise was 'completely engaged in this matter of the Huguenots'. It was a question of his own salvation: 'He must do all within his power to extirpate their sect,' and the Venetian added; 'Thus, in this case his own interest is to the advantage of the realm, and even of the whole Christian universe.' Coming from such a thoughtful diplomat these words are significant. The Second War of Religion and the troubles in Flanders had brought grist to Philip II's mill. The Catholic governments were more and more coming round to the idea of an anti-Protestant crusade. Catherine was soon to be compelled by force of circumstances to submit to it, for financial stress and the lack of troops made it impossible for her to pursue her policy of compassion in isolation.

The Jesuits, who had at last been recognized by the French State, had put their exceptionally powerful organization at the service of the Counter-Reformation. Father Edmond Auger, a direct disciple of Saint Ignatius Loyola, was a man of first-rate ability. As the result of his eloquence he became known as the French Chrysostom. He was as great a leader as a preacher. During the ten years that he had lived in France, under his direction and that of the Fathers trained in the school of Ignatius, the Company of Jesus, a genuine Catholic International, powerfully supported by Saint Pius V, had given the adversaries of Protestantism the intellectual cadres they had hitherto lacked, and of which the doctrinal foundations were established and reinforced by Saint Peter Canisius. The results of this counter-offensive soon became manifest; sermons, catechisms and colleges provided the most fanatical monks with theological arguments. Thanks to the Jesuits, anti-Protestant fanaticism now received the same backing as anti-Catholic fanaticism; reason was enlisted in the service of violence although claiming that violence was at its service, owing to the necessity of fighting heresy. A core of anti-Calvinist doctrine was established and diffused and was accepted more readily by the French masses than the opposing doctrine, which they found repugnant to their feelings in too many ways. The Jesuits left it to the curés and the monks to rouse the masses and to force them out of their political and religious indifference, which had allowed heresy to spread. They themselves took charge of the élite—preachers, professors, confessors; their field of action lay among the nobility, the high and big bourgeoisie, and the higher officials.

Edmond Auger, adviser to the Cardinal de Lorraine, introduced to France with increasing success the methods by which Saint Peter Canisius had succeeded in the Empire.[1] The French Protestants felt the first blows of the Counter-Reformation twenty years after the first intervention, in Bavaria, by Saint Peter Canisius, who with Salmeron and Lejay installed himself on November 13, 1549, at the University of Ingolstadt, where he began the theological struggle against Wittenberg, the Saxon citadel of Lutheran thought. Catherine had watched all this with great indifference, for the failure of the Poissy conference had finally destroyed her interest in religious controversy. She had thus allowed herself to be out-distanced by the Jesuits. In 1568 the French Catholic party became their party. The Cardinal de Lorraine's strength was thenceforward based on religion: religion directed the politics of the Counter-Reformation.

Catherine was still thinking in the Italian and limited terms of Machiavelli and Guicciardini, i.e. in terms of pure politics and the insufficiently broad concept of politics first and foremost, when the Jesuits had already synthesized politics and religion, a synthesis which was to be the cause of the defeat of the Protestants. In this defeat lay the origin of persecutions which were not to cease until the day when on the one hand the excesses of the democratic leagues and on the other the military power of Henri IV would hand over to the politicals the victory that Catherine de Medici had prepared, without having herself been able to achieve it. One of the causes of her failure was her mistaken lack of interest in theology, by which she left to the Jesuits the dangers and hardships but also the advantages and honour that accrued to them with the Catholic resurgence. Another no less important cause was her lack of material means. For these two reasons freedom of conscience had become irreconcilable with the re-establishment of Catholicism. Thus the force of circum-

[1] On Saint Peter Canisius, cf. the essential book by J. Brodrick, remembering the previous work by Evennett on the Cardinal de Lorraine.

stances was to compel the princess who was most deeply drawn to a policy of compassion to accept the repressive policy of the Jesuits, the ultramontane and Spanish policy that she loathed above all.

And so, from 1569–89, from the Third War of Religion until her death, Catherine de Medici could do no more than struggle for twenty whole years to preserve and save what was left of the old Capetian, patriarchal and feudal, legislative and Gallican State, in the midst of the ruins piled up by the Spaniards and the ultramontanes, taking advantage of the Calvinist excesses in order to undermine its foundations in the name of the defence of Catholicism. In this she succeeded; but she none the less never succeeded, in spite of her genius, her patience, her tenacity, her exceptional skill at taking advantage of circumstances, in restoring the State to its office as arbiter and judge, nor in re-affirming its power and dignity. Catherine's positive creation collapsed in the turmoil of the Third War. In future the Queen Mother's success would be merely on a negative plane, which was, however still sufficiently great to win her immortal fame. In the face of Roman theocracy and Spanish hegemony she preserved the State from servitude and paved the way for Henri IV, and by his too tardy submission to the mystery of the Sacrament, the salvation of France, a salvation for which she had prepared the ground. But having sown the seeds she did not live to reap the harvest.

Towards August 20, 1568, in conditions that have remained mysterious, Coligny and Condé were informed of the dire peril that had threatened them when, it was said, the Queen Mother had thought of having them carried off in a bold surprise attack from Noyers-sur-Serain, not far from Tonnerre, on the mountainous slopes of Morvan, where they had established themselves.[1] They were certainly informed of the Catholic plans to forbid the practice of the Protestant cult; plans which culminated in the drawing-up of an edict, on August 27th, that practically put an end to the policy of compassion. The surprise attack on Meaux had filled the Queen Mother with a strong desire to avenge herself on the Huguenots, of which their enemies took advantage. Monsieur le Prince and the

---

[1] The account of this affair in the *Mémoires* of Gaspard de Saulx-Tavannes remains highly dubious. Did Catherine in fact give the order for such a surprise attack? Cf. the discussion of this question in *La Troisième Guerre de Religion* by Gigon, and by Mariéjol, in his *Catherine de Médicis*. Examination of the documents reveals that they contradict one another. It only remains certain that according to a despatch from Correro, Condé and Coligny had already decided by August 15th to take refuge at La Rochelle.

Admiral left Noyers secretly for La Rochelle on the 23rd. We do not know exactly when the Queen Mother was informed of this, for her correspondence does not refer to it until September 8th, at the beginning of a long letter to Fourquevaux. It seems that—granting that she had intended to do so—she had not carried out her plan of kidnapping the two Calvinist leaders; the style and tone of her letter are those of a woman surprised and alarmed, but not furious or disappointed.

Unlucky peacemaker as she was, she was now tied to the Ixion's wheel of civil war. It is certain that this time again it was the Protestants who re-opened hostilities. The Cardinal de Lorraine, supported unanimously by the Catholics, demanded that the seals be withdrawn from Michel de L'Hospital. The Chancellor was extremely unpopular and was accused of connivance with the Huguenots. The intervention of the Holy See forced him to offer his resignation to the Queen Mother, not as Chancellor—for in that post he was immovable and did not resign it—but as Keeper of the Seals. It was—the documents clearly emphasize the difference—a compulsory resignation, but he was not dismissed in disgrace. He had in fact occupied the office of Prime Minister and his resignation publicly and officially represented the failure of the policy of moderation. It is wrong to state that Catherine de Medici had demanded it; it was forced upon her. She did not disgrace L'Hospital, who was sacrificed to the demands of the Curia, that had been asked for funds: 'His fall was one of the conditions imposed by Pius V for allowing certain Church properties to be transferred, for which the French Government had obtained permission through the offices of Annibal Rucellai and Charles d'Angennes, Bishop of Mans, the successor of the Cardinal de Tournon as French ambassador. In approving such a transfer amounting to an annual contribution of 150,000 francs in his Bull of August 1, 1568, the Pope laid it down that this money should be used only in defence of the King and the Catholic religion, and that until it should be needed for such a purpose it should be deposited in the hands of a reliable person.'[1]

As Michel de L'Hospital had protested against the terms of this Bull, his retention at the head of the French Government would have entailed breaking with Rome. He understood this better than anyone and requested that his freedom be restored to him. The Catholic zealots were denouncing him as a rebellious creature, the last Anti-Christ. Catherine saved appearances; the Chancellor returned

[1] Louis Pastor, *Op. cit.*, Vol. XVIII of the French edition, p. 39.

the Seals on the grounds of 'advanced age and ill-health', said Jules Gassot. 'Monsieur Bruslart was sent to him, at Vigny, to bring them back, and they were conferred on Monsieur de Morvillier.' This choice reveals that the Queen Mother had changed her minister without having renounced her previous policy. The Bishop of Orleans was also a moderate[1] completely devoted to Madame Catherine. He accepted the office of Keeper of the Seals only from a sense of duty, knowing full well the terrible difficulties he would have to face in carrying out the peace policy that was dear to him. A letter from Morvillier to L'Hospital of September 21, 1568, is of capital importance since it completely disposes of the subsequent statements regarding what we would now-a-days call the fall of the L'Hospital ministry. Jean de Morvillier had not yet received the Seals. The Government was hesitating between four candidates: the First President of the Paris Parliament, the First President of Toulouse, Morvillier himself, and Birague. The Bishop of Orleans wrote as a friend: 'I conveyed to the Queen what you wrote to me about a month ago; at which she told me that to her great regret she knew several things by which she could well understand the means taken to harm you, which she considered proceeded from the hatred certain people feel for you, and the ambition of others; but that you can rest assured that neither she nor the King will ever withdraw their protection from you.' The choice of a new Keeper of the Seals was a laborious business; by October 22nd the nomination had not yet been made.

After having considered René de Biragues, one of her faithful Italians, Catherine thought that it would be better to appoint L'Hospital's friend, Jean de Morvillier, who was not expecting it. The Chancellor had surrendered the Seals on October 7th, after the publication on September 28th, of the edict of August 27th, which he had opposed at the same time as the sale of church property authorized by the Pope. Morvillier's nomination dates from the beginning of 1569. Michel de L'Hospital himself recognized that he left of his own free will. In his testament he wrote: 'Seeing that my labours were not pleasing to the King nor to the Queen, and that the King was so hard pressed that he no longer had any power, in fact dared not say what he thought of it, I considered that it would be

[1] In the sixteenth century this word had none of the pejorative undertones that it carries today when applied to certain spineless individuals of the Centre or Right. But Moderates such as Catherine, L'Hospital, Morvillier or Jean de Monluc were devoid of any kind of nineteenth century Liberalism.

more expedient for me to give way voluntarily to necessity and to the new rulers than to fight with them, as I could no longer remain with them.'

The Chancellor, beaten by that faction among the Catholics who were for civil war, left, as he said, 'with the greatest sadness'. He knew that he was leaving Catherine their prisoner. In appointing Morvillier, the Queen was trying to preserve the essential basis of L'Hospital's policy, which was her own. In spite of her affection for her Italians, Birague and Gondi, she did not hand over power to them. She was compelled and forced to make war on the Protestants but she refused to commit herself as far as the future was concerned by playing into the hands of the Catholic zealots. The proof of this lies in the fact that at the last moment there was some hesitation in deciding between Morvillier, Nicolas de Pellevé, Archbishop of Sens, Sébastien de l'Aubespine, Bishop of Limoges, all of whom were attached to the Chancellory and moderates. L'Hospital, tired of fighting in vain, gave way to despair and was for peace at any price; Catherine stood with indomitable energy for peace through Royal victory. What has wrongly been described as L'Hospital's disgrace was merely a retirement forced upon him by the fact that on this point of capital importance the Chancellor differed from her. Subsequent events proved Catherine to have been right, for once Coligny and Condé were at La Rochelle peace at any price would have meant the rising of the Catholics against the monarchy, fallen into the hands of the Protestants; the League twenty years earlier. The memorandum written by Monsieur le Prince to Charles IX from Noyers on August 22, 1568, leaves us in no doubt on the subject.

Despite its violent terms, there is a great deal of truth in the Bourbon's indictment of the Lorraines, who had become the servants of the King of Spain. Nevertheless the great majority of Frenchmen were on their side. Catherine's extremely reliable political intuition saved her from the mistake made by her Chancellor, which would have been a deadly one; for to have taken sides with the Protestants would have led to deadly defeat—with the Lorraines and Spain overthrowing the Valois monarchy, France would have been dismembered. Once again war against the Protestants was the lesser evil. This is the true explanation of the Chancellor's fall and of his replacement by a politically-minded bishop, who accepted the war as the only possible way out, but without giving up his freedom of conscience. It was for this reason that Morvillier was given preference over Birague, although the day would come when it would be necessary to call in Birague. But the Queen Mother, not yet despairing of a victory which would allow her to exercise clemency, did not consider that day to have arrived as yet. Her letters of September 8th to Fourquevaux and September 9th to the Bishop of Rennes, complement each other: 'The King', she told the latter, 'does not wish for either a judge, an arbiter, or a mediator between himself and his subjects.' This was an allusion to her refusal to accept the mediation suggested by Elizabeth of England; a refusal which had exasperated the English Queen, but which was in accordance with Catherine's constant decision to avert foreign intervention, of which the most sinister and deadly dangerous would have been a Spanish attempt. On September 30th she ordered Fourquevaux to decline the help Philip II had offered her, 'hoping that in a short while one will perceive the methods that we possess for punishing and chastising those who have so far forgotten themselves as to rise against this Crown'.

She would go to war herself; settle her accounts herself. And in order to demonstrate it, on October 18th she informed Philip II that in spite of the Protestant revolt Charles IX was sending the Duke of Alba, in need of reinforcements, 'up to 1,000 men-at-horse and 2,000 good musketeers on foot'. In her own distress she was upholding her prestige. All Catherine de Medici's national pride is evinced in—her own words—'returning the courtesy recently received from the Catholic King'. She did not accept help; she gave it.

On that very day, October 18, 1568, news reached Paris of the death in childbirth of her daughter, Queen Elisabeth of Spain, which Charles IX withheld from her until the following day. The greatness of soul of the Governess of France stood up to the severest tests. In spite of her deep distress, for Elisabeth was her favourite daughter, she met this new blow of fate with invincible courage. And she announced that this loss would never break the bond that united the two Crowns of France and Spain. The Protestants need not hurry to rejoice at this death. In Catherine de Medici all emotions were secondary to her political passion, which she identified with a passion for France, for its power and freedom, and to achieve which she would devote all her energy. As Monsieur le Prince and the Admiral wanted war they should have it, and more than they wanted. As from September 28th all public worship by the Reformed church was forbidden on pain of death; the ministers were banned, within a fortnight, and during the same period all Huguenots were to resign from judicial and financial office under the penalty of a fine; parliamentarians and university officials were compelled to swear fidelity to Catholicism. On the other hand, in spite of the zealots, freedom of conscience was maintained; the freedom of conscience that Catherine had introduced and which even the edict of Fontainebleau of 1685, revoking the edict of Nantes, dared not suppress, although it did suppress freedom of worship. It was forbidden to hunt out those Protestants who remained peaceably at home. They retained the right to 'live in freedom in all the towns and places of the realm, without being investigated, vexed, and molested, nor compelled to do anything against their conscience in the matter of religion . . . '. The Royal Government was always to retain and respect these sections of the edict of Saint Germain. Catherine was making war but she had not on that account sided with the persecutors. She was the enemy only of those Protestants who had gone to civil war, and in order to beat them she had separated the State from the Reformation; no more and no less.

At that time the Queen Mother, contrary to her usual custom, was in favour of civil war, and even complained that the Council was for peace. She admitted so to the Spanish ambassador. She was very tired, her nerves were giving way, she had attacks of weeping and subsequent exasperation. Her impotent wisdom had turned to irritability. Matters were made worse by the quarrels between members of the Council. Embittered by her inability to impose her authority on anyone, Catherine had become bellicose, and feeling for once got the better of reason. She was no longer anything but an exhausted woman, begging for money and reduced to pledging her jewels in order to raise a loan in Florence. The affairs of Flanders, the obvious bad faith of Philip II, who was only trying to make France his man-at-arms in the Netherlands, everything contributed to depress Catherine and to undermine her vigorous health. The end of the winter of 1569 was a very bad time for the Queen, who was obliged to take to her bed during her journey to Metz, where she had gone in order to bar the way to the German reinforcements awaited by the Huguenots. She was comforted by the victory of the Catholic army at Jarnac on March 13, 1569, when her dear son Anjou covered himself with glory. Condé was killed. The young Prince, with one of those furious impulses that, like his brothers, he had inherited from Henri II, profaned the respect due to the dead. To the frenzied joy of his troops, who were by dint of outrages avenging the deaths of

François de Guise and Anne de Montmorency, he ordered Louis de Bourbon's body to be trotted around on a donkey. In both camps bloodthirstiness was only matched by their desire to insult one another. Death was no more respected than life. They lived only for hatred, without being able to satisfy it, according to the atrocious laws of civil war.

This treatment inflicted by the future Henri III on the First Prince of the Blood, who died in combat, was in conformity with the customs of such troublous times, when all moral values are destroyed by the fury of factions and sects. The Catholic profanations were the reply to the sacrileges committed by the Huguenots. Nothing was lacking because there was no criterion other than vengeance over the enemy. If Alava is to be believed the Protestants themselves rejoiced at the death of Condé, accused by them, and especially by Coligny, of having prevented the Religion from spreading, and growing in the kingdom. As a rule the Spanish ambassador was extremely well-informed. There is nothing surprising in the satisfaction Coligny was alleged by him to have felt; with Monsieur le Prince eliminated, the sole representatives of the Blood of France among the Huguenots were a child of fifteen, Henri de Béarn, the son of Antoine, and an adolescent of seventeen, Henri whose father was killed at Jarnac, stalks that were too frail to bear the Lilies. The Admiral did in fact become—and for a considerable time—sole leader of the Reformation. Although Jeanne d'Albret ordered a gold medal to be struck, bearing her own effigy and that of the young Prince, with the motto *Pax certa, victoria integra, mors honesta*, these words merely represented Navarrese pride and meant nothing more, compared to the power which Gaspard de Coligny was thenceforward to hold. Politically it was a disaster—a feudalist had taken the place of a Prince of the Blood. Whatever may have been Monsieur le Prince's faults, he did at least have a certain magnanimity, which on some occasions impelled him to put France before sectarianism. For a long time, alas, there had been no sign in Coligny of any similar attitude.

For Coligny had gradually become a complete sectarian and was no longer the man of destiny for whom France had hoped and waited. His personal duel with Catherine de Medici was now to begin—partly against nation, without any hope of compromise, for which Monsieur le Prince had generally ended by settling, and which is the lesser evil when, for the lack of a strong and independent State, it is no longer possible to discriminate between truth and error, between the nation's permanent interests and sectarian passions. Jeanne d'Albret's fanaticism placed the Admiral unreservedly under the protection of the Blood of France. Until Saint Bartholomew, Jarnac thus became the most important land-mark in the Wars of Religion; in the person of Coligny the Calvinist zealots became the spearhead of the movement. Thenceforward Catherine's policy of moderation found no more support among the Protestants than among the Catholics; the extermination of one party by the other appeared to be the sole solution. It was the superiority of the Catholic forces alone, and not the malice of which the Florentine was accused, that brought about the defeat of the Protestant party.

Catherine was forced in spite of herself to make common cause with the exterminators; she was compelled to countenance massacre as she had been to agree to war to the end. Such is the force of circumstances, which becomes insurmountable owing to human passions. As she ordered a *Te Deum* to be sung in honour of the victory of Jarnac the Queen Mother was so far from foreseeing the consequences of Condé's death that she imagined that the Huguenots would be willing to negotiate. She still despised the Admiral, the man who had surrendered to Emmanuel-Philibert. 'He is', she said to Alava, 'more cowardly than a woman.' What a mistake! For she mistook calculation for cowardice. As leader of the Protestant party Coligny was convinced that with English as well as German help victory would be his. On May 7, 1569, his brother Andelot died. Catherine was under such illusions that she rejoiced at this, as she wrote to Fourqueaux on the 19th. As the result of her joy it was assumed that she had caused his death. Did she have Andelot poisoned? It is impossible to know the answer, but what is absolutely certain is that the disappearance of Coligny's brother was of no political importance; François de Châtillon had always been under Gaspard's thumb. Catherine's joy makes it clear how far she was from realizing that in Coligny the cold and tenacious ambition of the most calculating of men gave the Calvinists the determination to fight to the death, which they had hitherto lacked. She was so pleased that she ordered Fourquevaux to buy two dozen Spanish fans. Although she was so politically-minded, Catherine remained wholly feminine. This was her weakness, from which no woman can escape, even were she a genius of the first rank—Catherine no more than Elizabeth I of England or Catherinee II of Russia, although they were the most virile of Queens. And Coligny, in his supreme attempt to gain control of France, knowing Catherine very well, also knew how to take advantage of having a woman as his foremost adversary.

Jeanne d'Albret and the Admiral kept up what was now no more than a mere pretence—the Protestant insurgents were in arms for the deliverance of the King. Henri de Navarre and his cousin Henri de Bourbon were the official heads of the rebel army, which was called the Army of the Princes under obedience to the King. The masses and the common soldiery might still take this seriously, but no well-informed person believed it any longer. Coligny was an authentic rebel, sheltering behind the prestige of the Blood of France, in the persons of two very young lads. As an experienced military man Coligny took advantage of the fact that through her son, Anjou, Catherine de Medici was in control of the Royal armies which were dispersed as well as divided. The Germans under the Duke of Zweibrucken, who died in the course of the campaign and was replaced by the Count von Mansfeld, succeeded in joining up with the Huguenots in the Limousin at the beginning of June 1569. A little later the Duc d'Aumale, who had been unable to bar their way, joined up with the Duc d'Anjou. The forces on both sides were more or less equal; 30,000 Catholics to 25,000 Protestants. The Catholic army was partly composed of Germans, Spaniards and Italians. Mansfeld's Germans formed about half of the Admiral's troops; *reiters* against foot-soldiery. This was the most sinister aspect of the civil war—roughly 20,000 foreigners were fighting on French soil, the very thing that the Queen Mother had wanted at any price to avoid. In spite of the victory of Jarnac the King's army was in a worse state than the adversary. Madame Catherine travelled to Limoges and accompanied the troops to Berry. She thought, rightly, that the presence of foreigners would make the outcome of a battle most uncertain. She was particularly worried by the fact that there were Germans in both camps, which favoured both desertions and betrayal. She feared defeat, for the King himself, and its most dangerous consequence in bringing the English into Guyenne.

Various small and indecisive actions succeeded one another, together with massacres. Tavannes advised destroying everything in Poitou, but Catherine refused to do so; she was too humanitarian to resort to a burnt earth policy; humanitarian, it cannot too often be said, because she was a humanist. The Royal army was worn out by useless sieges at Niort and La Charité: The Queen Mother returned to Paris. Catholic atrocities and Huguenot atrocities followed one another reciprocally, at La Roche-Abeille, Orleans. Coligny did not despair of wearing down the enemy first; he thought that he could last out longer. His brother Odet never ceased to badger the Queen of England, from whom he obtained money with great difficulty. after pledging the jewels donated by the great Protestant ladies. The French ambassador in London, La Mothe-Fénelon, protested in vain. The Admiral's aim was to march on Paris, but he made the mistake, admitted by La Noue, of besieging Poitiers, where he failed, which gave the Royal army time to regroup. Correro has stressed the energy shown by Catherine de Medici during those interminable months that passed after the useless victory of Jarnac.

Like his predecessors, Correro is a witness of rare political and psychological insight. He watched the unfortunate Catherine attracting the anger of the partisans to herself.[1] The Queen Mother might have said with Montaigne: 'I suffered the inconveniences that moderation entails in such sicknesses; I was assailed on every hand; to the Ghibellines I was a Guelph; to the Guelphs a Ghibelline.' Her Italian origin was always being brought up against her; although she had been reigning for ten years and had sacrificed everything to the public welfare, to the French, who were fighting one another, she was still the Florentine shopkeeper. She was denied the right to govern, but govern she did, and consequently no reproach was spared her.

Nothing escaped Correro's sagacity. He depicts the Queen Mother as 'a foreign woman without friends, weighed down under the general terror, who never hears the truth spoken around her'. In contrast to the libellers (whom so many writers, either superficial or ill-intentioned, have echoed, and of whom the most recent are the worst, unworthy even of being mentioned) who invented the calumnies that surround Catherine de Medici's legend, the ambassador of the Republic of the Doges was only concerned with sending truthful reports to his government. He caught in all truthfulness the picture of that princess, at what was perhaps the most discouraging moment of her life, when she saw her ceaseless and hard labours for

[1] The despatches of the Venetian ambassador are no less important than his reports. They have not yet been published (1959) and are in the Venetian Archives. In his *Charles IX*, Pierre Champion quoted many passages from them. A short time before his premature death he showed us his sumptuously bound collection of all the letters of Henri III which he had had copied. He was planning to do the same with those of Charles IX. We were as much amazed by this rich source as depressed to learn that the State refused to make the same financial grant in the case of her two sons as it had done for Catherine, thus permitting, until 1909, the magnificent edition of her manuscripts by Hector de la Ferrière and G. Baguenault de Puchesse. This was fifty years ago and these treasures still remain among the dusty original manuscripts.

French peace during the past ten years crumbling around her. 'I was often surprised', he said, 'that she did not completely lose control and go over to one or the other of the two parties, which for the kingdom would have been the final calamity. It was she who preserved at Court those remains of Royal majesty that still exist there. That is why I have always said that she was to be pitied rather than blamed. I told her so herself one day and she has often reminded me of it, when telling me of her distress and the misfortunes of France.' In spite of his professional calm the Venetian diplomat could not hide his emotion with regard to Madame Catherine's unshakeable valour: 'I know that she was more than once found weeping in her study; but suddenly she would wipe her tears away, hide her sorrow, and in order to deceive those who judged the state of affairs by the expression on her face, would appear in public, calm and joyous.'

And Correro saw her with her nerves exhausted in spite of all her will-power, for she was a woman, a widow and mother of five children, the eldest of whom, Charles IX, was not yet twenty. She gave way to the contradictory advice of her entourage. He put his finger on the spot: 'The considerations that must govern Her Majesty are innumerable, and she receives very little obedience from her subjects.'

The parties were constantly pursuing Catherine de Medici with their claims, whilst she lacked the power which alone would have permitted her to arbitrate between them. One of the worst historical illusions is to imagine that in past times men saw the events that were happening under their eyes from the same point of view as their descendants. The latter know how it all ended and can draw the right conclusions. What to us often appears to have been most obvious, to them appeared without importance, and vice versa. We know, for instance, that in the last resort the Protestants and the Spaniards as well had fewer resources than the Royal French State. Catherine, facing the empty coffers and confronting hatreds in France, the enormous Empire of the Hapsburgs, at one and the same time bicephalic yet one, despite the division of Charles V's heritage between Madrid and Vienna, could not help but think that war was the worst evil. In a striking metaphor Correro reveals how the political facts appeared to the most experienced minds at that time: 'I could not better describe the state of this kingdom than by comparing it to a leg, an arm, or any other member attacked by gangrene; when the doctor, having cauterized a wound, thinks that his task is finished, he sees another one opening beside it. It is the same with France.'

The Governess of France could not know that despite everything these wounds were superficial and that a hot iron should have been applied to them at once, without fear of seeing England, Spain, the Empire, still under the impression of the victory of Jarnac, profiting by such a cruel operation to invade France and dismember it. The very audacity of such an action would have stopped them. We know this, because the archives have delivered to us the secrets of their weaknesses, which the shrewdest observers at that time might have suspected without, however, having proof of them. What, the Queen Mother asked herself with constant anxiety, would Spain do, or England, or the Empire? That is why she temporized, even after Jarnac, instead of risking all for all. Given the appearances, which hid and distorted reality even in the eyes of her most intelligent contemporaries, there was nothing else she could have done. Like Penelope, she was obliged and compelled to weave and unpick her work in order to gain time, awaiting the day when her sons should have grown up.

At that moment her anger with the rebels was the stronger emotion. She had countered with a plea to bar the peace overtures they had made through the Marshal de Montmorency after the indecisive battle of La Roche-Abeille; she had no intention of being tricked again, as at Longjumeau. The canting tone of these proposals was typical of Coligny's style and it was impossible to know how far to trust his declarations and promises. On July 20th Montmorency had informed the Admiral that the war would continue. Catherine's intuition had not deceived her, for the Huguenot's failure at the siege of Poitiers had shown that a Catholic victory could be won. She understood so well that Coligny was the enemy who must be struck down that she was preparing his chastisement on a legal basis.

The handing over of Normandy to the English by an Admiral of France came within the juridical category of high treason, and so, also, was the appeal for German troops, since only the King had the right to raise foreign mercenaries in his service. According to the customs of the day, however, which were still to a large extent feudalistic, it was possible to close one's eyes to the Protestant appeal for foreign aid, and this Catherine had done. There were nevertheless laws according to which it was a capital offence. Since Coligny had broken the peace of Longjumeau, Catherine availed herself of the regular judicial procedure to have him condemned to death by the Parliament of Paris, executed in effigy on September 13, 1569, and to have a price put upon his head. In order to stress the

11. THE MASSACRE OF SAINT BARTHOLOMEW

12. CATHERINE DE MEDICI. School of Clouet   (*Musée de Louvre*)

infamy of his crime he was ordered to be hanged and not beheaded, whilst his coat-of-arms was broken and dragged in the gutter, and his possessions were confiscated. Claude Haton described the Admiral's execution in effigy. As a good Frenchman he rejoiced at the publication of the edict according to which, 'To all persons, of whatever quality they may be, who may take and apprehend the body of the said Admiral alive, His Majesty would give 10,000 gold *écus au soleil* . . . and to whom did not take him alive but would put him to death, His said Majesty would promise to give 2,000 *écus au soleil*.' And Haton revealed to us the name of one of the men who took it on themselves to carry out these clauses of the edict, 'the sire de Maurevert, a Huguenot gentleman, who was at the camp and in the suite of the said Admiral'. We learn through Haton how and why it happened that the Lord de Mouy was killed by Maurevert when he was in Coligny's company, by the bullet that had been meant for the latter. The evidence of Haton, simpler and more spontaneous than the accounts of Thou and d'Aubigné, seems to us to explain the murder of Mouy. In political assassinations it happens frequently that the wrong person is killed.

Coligny's murder was perfectly legitimate and legal. To denounce Maurevert, the King's killer, is to ignore all the customs of the past and to scorn the documentary evidence. For the King's killer was an executioner-extraordinary, under orders according to the laws and usages following on a published edict, additional to the Paris executioner, who only tortured 'a man of straw dressed in linen dyed the same colour as the uniform worn by the said Admiral', Haton reports 'both on his body and legs, the head fashioned according to his portrait'. This execution in effigy did not, however, calm down the clear-sighted but anxious Spaniards. Don Francès de Alava declared that the Admiral was clever enough to obtain, later on, his rehabilitation in good and proper form, and this did in fact occur.

It is the moralist's right and duty to condemn human cruelty. But historically speaking we are not here concerned with morality— *Scribitur ad narrandum non probandum.* In our forefather's eyes nothing was more natural, normal, or legal than this tracking-down of Coligny. As from September 1569, the Admiral was a condemned man, to be captured, according to a published decree, alive or dead. Placed in its contemporary setting Charles IX's letter to the Duc d'Alençon, conferring the chain of Saint Michael on Maurevert, does not appear in the least shocking. The King's killer had missed

T

the Admiral, but his decision to obey the edict was manifest, and he therefore had a right to be rewarded. The person in question, a great intriguer, received the decoration of Saint Michael; the favour bestowed on him may appear excessive, but the reason for giving it revolted nobody. And in their indignation the Huguenot libellers revealed their bad faith, for among them the King's killers had just as much a regular, customary, and legal position as among the Catholics. It was not until the time of Louis XIV, who was sufficiently confident in his power, that France gave up the King's killers, and gradually the other European sovereigns also did so. With the French Revolution one step further was taken; the State legalized political assassination. After the regicide of January 21st, the list of these is a long one. What we now-a-days call assassination was in those times a just form of execution that was not actually carried out by the executioner himself. Elizabeth of England, Knox and Bèze, made no bones about it, any more than the princes of Italy, Philip II, or Catherine de Medici. To understand this and to remember it will enable us to understand the origins of Saint Bartholomew a little more clearly.[1]

Dear curé Haton was reflecting the views of his day; Maurevert, accusing himself of his error, asked for grace and was forgiven by the Duc d'Anjou, who 'sent him to the King, his brother, to confirm his grace and give him the 2,000 écus as promised, although it was known that the Admiral was unhurt. The said Maurevert was kindly received and paid the said sum by the King. He made his oath, at the King's hands, to serve him faithfully in all matters, and never to do nor to undertake anything against his will'. For a man of the sixteenth century such an incident was the most natural in the world. Claude Haton narrated it in passing, with the same good humour and simplicity as he described the numerous executions of which he was a spectator, or of which he was told. The King's killer was an official, the intermediary who carried out his high designs, and every judicial overlord continued to have the same rights as the sovereign. That is why the frankness with which Coligny approved of Poltrot de Méré

---

[1] In this connection it is astonishing to find such an eminent historian of the sixteenth century as the late Pierre de Vaissière applying the outlook and standards of a modern man of integrity to condemning actions which to contemporaneous opinion at that time seemed perfectly natural and legitimate. Half a century later, in 1617, Louis XIII treated Concini in exactly the same way.... J. H. Mariéjol made the same mistake in perspective, and Pierre Champion did not dare to correct it. In the service and for the honour of Clio, and faithful to the precepts of Quintilian, we are prepared to meet any indignation we may arouse which is due to a point of view contrary to historical truth.

is no more surprising than the phrase used by Charles IX in his letter—the authenticity of which, by the way, is not established—to his brother François, from Plessis-lez-Tours on October 10, 1569, on 'Charles de Louviers . . . being he that killed Mouy in the manner of which he will tell you. . . .' The 'manner' referred to his having killed the wrong man, but this did not in any way attenuate the zeal of the good citizen, anxious to receive his payment for having conformed to the orders of the edict officially promulgated against 'Gaspard de Coligny, so-called Admiral of France.' And to moralize on the subject is merely to gossip.

Andelot's property had been confiscated and in March the Cardinal de Châtillon had been stripped of all his dignities and ordered to give an account of his actions to the Archbishop of Rheims, the Cardinal de Lorraine; the Vidamus of Chartres and Montgomery had been condemned with Coligny. The sentences were announced to the whole of Europe, and thus Madame Catherine, whose wisdom had proved impotent, proclaimed herself inflexible in meting out justice. She excluded from all her repressive measures, however, Jeanne d'Albret and the Princes of the Blood, who had had no part in the Treaty of Hampton Court and whom she did not despair of bringing back into the Royal fold, as well as the Protestant part of the nation. In striking at the Châtillons, the Vidamus and Montgomery, she aimed at the spearheads of the rebellion. The victory of the Duc d'Anjou at Montcontour near Loudun, on September 30, 1569, was a disaster for Coligny, who lost nearly his whole army there, as well as 10,000 killed or wounded, and his German foot-soldiery, as well as his artillery and baggage, eleven pieces and 3,000 chariots, whilst the Royal army only had 200 dead. Monsieur had distinguished himself there like a hero and Catherine's pride in him consoled her for all her trials. Her beloved son was like the Angel of Vengeance, who took pity on the crimes of men and stayed the massacre of the defeated, proclaiming that the French must be forgiven. This prince was sufficiently intelligent to realize when he thought it over, how shameful had been his fury against the corpse of Monsieur le Prince on the evening of Jarnac. He saved La Noue and Crussol, the latter in spite of Pius V's orders to his troops, commanded by the Count of Santa-Fiore, into whose hands he had fallen. The Pope had only sent reinforcements to Catherine de Medici on condition that no prisoners would be taken: 'You must use every effort,' he had written to the Queen on April 13, 1569, 'to

see that these very wicked men are delivered over to deserved tortures.' The doctrine of Saint Pius V was a simple one: 'In no way
and for no reason must one spare the enemies of God.' This Biblical
ferocity appealed no more to Catherine than to her son, Anjou. The
Protestant wounded were cared for, and this was an act of merit,
since La Popelinière reported—and the admission from his Calvinist
pen is valuable—that most of them recovered, whilst most of the
Catholic wounded died. If contemporaries are to be believed, the
Huguenots used poisoned bullets; the outlook of the ministers of
Geneva was precisely similar to the Pope's, and with Coligny at
their service such cruelty may very possibly have been practised.
On the other hand the magnanimity of the victor of Montcontour is
proven. The French were forgiven. Even in war to the end the King
could not forget that the rebels were his children and that, if he was
pitiless towards the leaders, he should show the led the clemency of a
father.

The Royal army was unable to take advantage of its victory,
losing precious time at various sieges in Poitou, of which Coligny,
always excellent at manoeuvring in retreat, knew how to take advantage, whilst Ronsard sang the praises of the Duc d'Anjou, 'like a
powerful little eagle'. Coligny more or less retrieved his situation.
Catherine returned to thoughts of peace, addressing herself to
Jeanne d'Albret, who was established at La Rochelle. But the Queen
of Navarre refused to treat with her unless the King broke off his
alliances with Spain and the Holy See. We know from the despatches
of Contarini and those of Petrucci that they did negotiate, but military operations were resumed, nevertheless, in the spring of 1570.
They were accompanied by the usual atrocities that Coligny, resolved
to avenge himself for the price of 50,000 écus that had been placed on
his head, carried out methodically, in the Toulousain and the Céven-
nes, and which were not merely perpetrated by the military. At
Nîmes, on November 15, 1569, the Huguenots renewed the
Michelade of September 30, 1567. This time there were again one
hundred dead. The Catholic reprisals in the course of the year were
on a larger scale; at Orleans 280 Protestants were burned alive in the
Tour des Quatre-Coins. At the Ponts-de-Cé Strozzi drowned 800
soldiers' wives in the Loire. At Rabastens Monluc amused himself
by forcing around 60 Huguenots prisoners to jump from the tops of
the battlements into the moats, an entertainment for which he
shared a taste with the Baron des Adrets, who inflicted the same fate
on his Catholic prisoners. The chronological record proves, by the

way, that Des Adrets had begun devastating, sacking, and blowing-up buildings in the Lyonnais, the Dauphiné, the Forez, as early as 1562.[1]

The Admiral's plan was to move up on Paris by following the valley of the Loire. But at Saint-Etienne he fell so seriously ill that he nearly died. The Queen Mother had charged the Marshal de Biron and the Councillor of State Malassise to negotiate directly with him. The victory of Montcontour, without a sequel, had left her no alternative to a negotiated peace. Had it been thoroughly followed up it would have enabled a dictated peace to ensue.

The principal reason why that victory had not been exploited was the King's hostility to Monsieur, heightened by envy and jealousy. Although he was not yet twenty Charles's violence frightened his mother. She feared that the brothers might come to blows in a brawl. This latent domestic tragedy was becoming an ever greater obstacle to the exercise of her authority. Coligny and Jeanne d'Albret both knew this; they decided to take advantage of it, judging, in spite of all their own difficulties, that the prolongation of the war would be more harmful to the Catholics and the Court than to themselves. When he recovered, the Admiral (he insisted on retaining this title although the Marquis de Villars had replaced him in his post) continued his march northwards. The Marshal de Cossé, who favoured peace, arranged not to beat him at Arnay-le-Duc on June 13, 1570, thus allowing him to reach the Nivernais without being harassed. On July 7th the Huguenots occupied La Charité-sur-Loire. The perpetual interventions of the Nuncio and the Spanish ambassador against any agreement with the Protestants had their usual result—Catherine inclined resolutely to peace, preferring to compromise with her rebellious subjects rather than to submit to the wishes, the orders even, of the foreigner. The Cardinal de Lorraine was dissatisfied with Philip II, whose determination to keep France's troubles alive had not escaped his notice. He was thinking of marrying the young Duc de Guise to Charles IX's sister, the adorable Margot, who at seventeen was dazzling the court and the city. Now he too was for peace. He also planned a marriage between Henri de Navarre and the eldest daughter of the Duc de Lorraine. The Lorraine princes would thus strengthen their ties with the House of France, both Valois and Bourbon. It can be imagined how greatly

---

[1] On the Baron des Adrets, cf. Pierre de Vaissière's very thorough and well-documented book. The facts are clear; the Protestants have no right to claim that only they were massacred; they themselves massacred with as much fervour as the Catholics. As always occurs, the reprisals alternated ever since Amboise, in 1560.

all this appealed to that inveterate match-maker, Catherine; and she longed all the more for peace.

The Admiral, always well-informed, decided to take advantage of the situation. He had also learned that at the diet of Spier the Catholic majority had won, which meant that the leaders of French Protestantism would no longer be able to draw on the reservoir of German troops. Immediately on entering La Charité he accepted a truce. Cossé furnished him with supplies and through the offices of the leader of the Royal army the Calvinist troops were provided with 60,000 loaves. For some time Catherine had been thinking that a marriage between her daughter and Jeanne d'Albret's son would this time finally put an end to the civil wars, and the Spanish despatches allude to it from the end of November 1569. She had made a violent scene with Marguerite on account of her intimacy with Henri de Guise, the consequence of which had been to throw the Cardinal de Lorraine back on to the side that was for war. Lorraine was in fact entirely Spain's man, as his letters of that year 1569 prove.[1] On November 15, 1568, he had dared to write to Philip II: 'There is no family in this kingdom more devoted and dedicated to Your Majesty's service than ours.' Alava had informed the Catholic King that the Cardinal had offered to hand over the frontier territories to him if the last Valois should die without heirs. By virtue of the rights of his wife, Elisabeth, Philip II would become King of France. This plan met with the Spaniard's approval. The Lorraines had always claimed to disdain the Salic Law. Unlike his brother François, the Archbishop showed no concern for the French nation and merely followed his own personal and family policy, which explains his tergiversations. Henri de Guise's jealousy of the Duc d'Anjou, victor of Jarnac and Montcontour, the desire to avenge himself for the breaking-off of his nephew's love affair with Margot, finally placed the Cardinal and his brothers under Spain's tutelage at the beginning of the summer of 1570.

[1] Based on the Simancas collection and published by Joseph de Croze among the appendices to Vol. I of his book *Les Guises, les Valois et Philippe II*. This book, published in 1866, remains a basic source, as it brings together manuscript documents that are scattered among various French archives. In his *Charles IX* Pierre Champion used hardly any French sources except the note-books of Villeroy, which are in the *Fonds français des Manuscrits de la Nationale*, ref. 27.518. Francis De Crue, who gives several references, made a thorough use of the rich French sources in his three volumes on the Constable de Montmorency and on the Politicals. In our own case the restricted size of this present book has obliged us to use the larger part of these unpublished manuscripts in the *Nationale*, which are chiefly important for a detailed treatment, in a much shorter form than we would have liked.

The Admiral seized this favourable opportunity, when the Queen Mother indignantly gave up any further hope of a happy outcome from the rapprochement she had attempted with the Lorraines and the Spaniards. In his despatches to Philip, Alava complained of these frequent and sudden changes in French policy. The Pope wrote to Charles IX, expressing his horror at the thought of making peace with abominable heretics. As usual, as soon as any foreigner, whether Rome, Madrid, or London, claimed to dictate her line of action, Catherine de Medici preferred to sacrifice her personal feelings to national unity. She decided on making peace, however costly it might prove, and the Admiral immediately took advantage of this decision. The Cardinal de Lorraine retired to his Abbey of Saint-Denis, refraining from taking part in the negotiations, which led to the peace of Saint Germain on August 8, 1570—the Shameful Peace, as Philip II called it. The right of public worship was restored to the Reformed cult, as in the past, and to this was added the right to practice it in two cities of each government department in which it had hitherto not been authorized. Freedom of conscience was generally sanctioned. The Reformationists regained the right to enter universities, schools and hospitals; they were allowed separate cemeteries; there was a general amnesty, prisoners were freed, confiscations cancelled, offices and dignities were restored, and the right of the Protestants to challenge legal decisions before the Parliaments was recognized; during two years they were granted four places of safety—La Rochelle, Montauban, Cognac, La Charité; the latter two instead of the towns of Angoulême and Sancerre, which they had first been promised; the King would be represented there by a commissioner. In return the Huguenots undertook to send back the Germans and to disarm their own troops. It was also stipulated that in Béarn freedom of worship would be restored to the Catholics.

The declaration made by Charles IX after reading of the treaty reveals that the latter was in accordance with the Queen Mother's constant desires. The King recognized the impossibility of putting an end by warfare to France's troubles. He hoped that in future he would be better obeyed and his orders more punctiliously carried out. He did not conceal the fact, either, that he was making peace with a view to ridding himself of the treacheries of the Cardinal de Lorraine. Like his mother, he was as much against the Guises as against the Spaniards. Catherine de Medici confirmed her son's words, declaring that she would assist him with her counsel and with all her might, helping him to see that the concessions granted by the treaty were put into effect, as she had always desired the kingdom to return to the same conditions as had prevailed during the lifetime of Charles IX's predecessors. She particularly wanted to have her hands free in order to mediate, as she was trying to do, between France's two allies who were at enmity with one another, Venice and Turkey.

Suppressing her own resentments, the Governess of France thus for the fourth time since the death of Henri II re-affirmed her desire for national unity and European peace. She restored to the Calvinists everything they had lost by taking up arms. After eight and a half years the peace of Saint Germain confirmed the edict of January 1562. This, also, was truly the Queen's Peace, the work of that indefatigable peace-maker who, although too weak in arms, regarded freedom of conscience as an immutable law, and gave the Protestants the necessary guarantees to uphold it. According to Contarini 3,000 parishes were authorized in the kingdom, which represented the same number of ministers of the new cult. This caused the Venetian anxiety, and the Nuncio, Frangipani, indignation. The zealots of the Catholic party were outraged by the Queen's Peace. The Holy See and Spain protested against it without delay. As the King's representatives in the negotiations had been the Marshal de Biron and the Councillor Malassise, the pun was immediately perpetrated—*la paix boiteuse* (after Biron's infirmity) *et mal assise*. The angrier factions referred to it only as the Accursed Peace; the Devil's Peace, wrote the Duke of Alba, and Alava called them infernal edicts. The preachers of Paris fumed.

But the politicals approved of it. Catherine was trying to persuade everyone to accept this costly peace, a political necessity. She was feeling her way, and the adminstrative documents drawn up to carry out the Queen's Peace were contradictory. Certain of them stated that only the conversion of the King's Calvinist subjects would restore the kingdom's power and stability, and that discord and civil war would never cease in a State where there was a diversity of religions. Others demanded strict execution of the clauses of the Treaty of Saint Germain and of the edict which had followed it on the part of the Catholics, who continued to ill-treat the Reformationists. From his retreat L'Hospital remained the accepted adviser of Jean de Morvillier, who regarded himself merely as his intermediary.

Coligny gained an enormous personal advantage from the Treaty of Saint Germain—he was pardoned, amnestied, re-integrated and thus rehabilitated, as Alava had foretold. Catherine had realistically preferred to forget her sense of injury rather than to avenge herself.

Always an optimist, she did not doubt that his pardon would bring the Admiral back into the King's service, and all of the Huguenots with him. She replied thus to a wish that had been expressed to her by the wise Jean de Monluc, in a report drawn up shortly before the third recourse to warfare: 'And when Her Majesty will have decided to go to war (which will nevertheless be to the regret of many good people) I would beg her to do so with some care and for the relief of her poor people.' She had wanted to prosecute the war vigorously, but in spite of the brilliant victory of Moncontour, after eighteen months no decisive result had been attained. Rather than drag out the conflict, which was only serving the interests of the foreigners, the Queen Mother had sacrificed her personal hatred of Coligny to the need to relieve her poor people.

But she had decided this time no longer to be the dupe of the Admiral's promises or oaths, to keep him under constant supervision and to intervene immediately if that ambitious and deceitful character should try to take advantage of the peace in order to gain the power that had escaped his attempt to do so by force of arms. In that sense the pun was correct; neither Catherine nor Coligny were truly reconciled with one another—limping and badly settled, their peace was at the mercy of any serious incident that might arise. It did not suspend the duel between the Queen and the Admiral, which had merely been transferred from the terrain of war to that of diplomacy. Coligny's new objective was the conquest of the King's person by intrigue, and as soon as Catherine became aware of it the Admiral's suppression was decided on. During two whole years a dreadful and silent struggle was to take place in the study of Charles IX, more and more impatient of his mother's yoke, and seeking a mentor in the Admiral.

In order to defeat this extremely dangerous adversary Catherine was to resign herself to murder, this time forgetting Machiavelli's lessons, herself tearing up her peace and returning to her previous plans, treating her private enemy, who had been rehabilitated, as the public enemy. This was to be a second appeal to the King's killer, with its unforeseen and horrible morrow, Saint Bartholomew. An inexorable fate was to sweep Madame Catherine, who thought herself in possession of internal peace, towards the Matins of Paris, whilst in the shadows the Admiral was preparing to go to war against Spain on religious grounds, thus making the Queen's renouncing the prosecution of civil war on nationalist grounds useless and vain. Such a civil war could only lead to victory over the Protestants by the submission of France to Spanish interests. Catherine signed the the triumph of Henri IV, internal and external policy were to form an inextricable labyrinth.]

In default of a France that was prepared, strong, and independent, i.e. an absolute Power, such as Louis XIII and Richelieu would achieve and Mazarin and Anne of Austria would succeed in preserving in spite of the Fronde, and that under Louis XIV would finally become totalitarian, which would permit him to hold his own against the European coalition for an entire half-century, such a war could only have been carried on in the midst of the troubles with any chance of success by submitting to English interests. On both sides, civil war was dependent on the foreign enemies of France.

Coligny knew this and accepted it. From now on all his efforts were engaged in substituting a pro-English policy for the pro-Spanish policy, whilst Catherine wanted and was attempting to achieve an exclusively French policy and would only agree to an alliance with England on condition that it involved no subjection on the part of France. As between the Admiral and the Archbishop of Rheims, the Queen's policy was unfortunately rendered impossible owing to her domestic tragedy, the mutual enmity of her three sons. Although a Machiavellian, Catherine was a mother; she had not a free hand and she lacked power. With consummate cleverness Coligny was to use the conflict between the royal children against his enemy. From the King's study to the embassies, the most acute struggle was to take place between them. Until the end of the Wars of Religion, due to the triumph of Henri IV, internal and external policy were to form an inextricable labyrinth.[1]

---

[1] In August 1569, at Orthez, the Huguenots massacred nearly 3,000 Catholics, who on capitulation had been assured that their lives would be spared. The result of examining the original documents is incontrovertible—before Saint Bartholomew there had on the whole been more Protestant than Catholic atrocities.

CHAPTER TWO

MACHIAVELLISM AND MATERNAL LOVE
(August 1570—September 1577)

⟿⟼❀❀⟻⟾

Peace having at last been re-established, Madame Catherine was all agog to concentrate again on one of her chief interests—the marriages and future establishments of her children. In her case politics invariably predominated over maternal love but when she was able to combine the two she was delighted. When politics appeared to allow her some respite she turned back to the foremost of her family interests, and in doing so revealed her tidy bourgeoise mind. This was to arrange brilliant marriages and provide splendid establishments for her children. A bourgeoise who had become a queen, her ambitions were worthy of the first throne of Christianity, awarded her by destiny. She intended her sons to marry queens or else princesses of the purest blood royal; her daughters to become queens or at the very least reigning princesses, and her sons to be kings. Her deceased daughter Elisabeth had been Queen of Spain; her daughter Claude was Duchesse de Lorraine; the deceased François II was King of France, husband of the Queen of Scotland, that impertinent Mary Stuart, yet so beautiful and so intelligent, whose misfortunes after having returned to her country, well-deserved as Catherine may have thought them, for she was a severe judge, did not leave her unmoved, since through the broken Scottish alliance they affected France and Catholicism. The Emperor had just given his daughter Elisabeth in marriage to Charles IX and as the result of this match Maximilian would no longer reclaim the Three Bishoprics. Also, Vienna could redress the balance with Madrid, for the Emperor was favourably inclined to a policy of compassion. Anjou, Alençon and Margot remained to be married off.

The Queen Mother was now faced with an absorbing task, far more to her liking than going to war. Madame Catherine liked nothing better than simultaneously serving France and her family interests by means of astute matrimonial diplomacy, which without danger permitted the Governess of France to be the Florentine shopkeeper; the authoritarian Queen to be a provident mother; the woman of affairs to manage her family concerns without neglecting those of the State. To be able freely to devote herself to them, it was well worth while giving up the thoughts she had once entertained of avenging herself on Coligny. It pleased Catherine to apply to the kingdom of France, whose wounds she would nurse and heal, the two Latin verses attributed to Matthew Corvinius, King of Hungary, legislator, humanist, and warrior:

Bella gerant fortes: tu, felix Austria, nube;
Nam quae Mars aliis, dat tibi regna Venus.

The power of the Hapsburgs was founded on brilliant matrimonial alliances; could not similar alliances re-establish France's greatness? Immediately after the peace of Saint Germain Catherine de Medici set to work to achieve them. Would not Don Sebastian of Portugal or Henri de Navarre be a suitable match for Margot? And Elizabeth of England for Monsieur, her dear Anjou, victor of Jarnac and Moncontour? As soon as the marriage of Charles IX to the gentle and exquisite princess—whose portrait by Clouet is one of the gems of the Louvre—had been celebrated on November 26, 1570, the Queen Mother, her position strengthened by this family alliance with Austria, was able more advantageously to negotiate on Marguerite's behalf with Philip II, since the Portuguese match could not be made without Spain's acquiescence, and with Elizabeth for Monsieur. Living in retirement at Villers-Cotterets from the beginning of December 1570 until the end of January 1571, she was wholly concerned with these plans, writing and sending presents to her son-in-law of Spain, notably palfreys, with which the bureaucrat of the Escorial was delighted; for he was as artistic as he was literary and appreciated beauty, and she knew how to please him. Her letters to Fourquevaux are charming; the lioness became as gentle and cajoling as a cat towards her redoubtable colleague, whom the ambassador was instructed to melt.

If the Portuguese match did not come off, however, there was still the eligible Béarnais, and her letters to her good sister of Navarre were equally amiable. Catherine had recourse to Marguerite of Savoy as an intermediary in order to reassure Pius V regarding the Treaty of Saint Germain, against which the Nuncio never ceased to protest; for this ignoble peace was one of the principal anxieties of the Pope, tormented by the advances of that pestilential disease, the Reformation. Since it had been signed the Cardinal Odet de Châtillon and the Vidamus of Chartes were taking advantage of their English refuge to make proposals for the marriage of Elizabeth and the hero of Moncontour. Catherine was closely following every move, and in addition to La Mothe-Fénelon, her ambassador at London, employed a personal agent, Guido Cavalcanti, one of her Italians. From Portugal to England via Spain, from France to Rome via Savoy, Florence and Venice, the Queen Mother's couriers and those of her diplomats and princely correspondents were travelling hither and thither. On reading them it is clear how delighted she was with all these intrigues; she had recovered all her good humour, her mind was sharper than ever, her caution on guard, and her natural graciousness fully evident.

There were two crowns to be captured! In Madame Catherine's view her children's possessions were her own. She imagined that as they became European kings or queens she would have the same right to peer into their States as into their households. With regard to her son-in-law, Philip II, she had to resign herself to failure. But Don Sebastian and Elizabeth might prove more amenable. To this cousin and niece of Popes, Europe was no less attractive than France. As soon as France left her a little peace she became passionately interested in Europe; but as a woman and a mother and not, as Richelieu would be, in building up the balance of power in order that France should preponderate. Let us again repeat it—Catherine lacked any spirit of principality; her tendency was always towards the spirit of Christianity, even if no doubt vaguely, for she was above all a patriot, as she liked to describe herself. She never saw very far ahead; she saw only the immediate situation, although correctly. No doubt she had wider interests than Louis XI, but she was not concerned with the situation as a whole, a concept which only the genius of the great Cardinal was to introduce into French diplomacy— after Sully's dream of the reorganization of Europe—owing to his ambition to transfer European hegemony from the Hapsburgs to the Bourbons. He was to achieve it—and after him, Mazarin and Louis XIV also—by substituting the imperialism of adherence for Germano-Spanish imperialist domination. This marvellous harmony, supple, living, yet restrained—for the Great King's good sense in the final resort always outweighed his imperialist ambitions, led to the security of the Square Field, and by the division of the Germanies to the balance of power in the West, in fact to a French Europe. But nothing was farther from Catherine than this long-considered and mature imperialist scheme which was to motivate the policies of the *Grand Siècle*. Catherine's policy, like Machiavelli's, did not go beyond national unity. She did not view Europe as a field to be dominated by France, but as her letters reveal and prove, a concourse of splendid family establishments. Those of her diplomats and the princes who corresponded with her show how well-informed and invariably inquisitive she was; so inquisitive, in fact, that they were on guard against her indiscretion and her tricks. She wanted to be the mother-in-law of Europe.

It is clear that in London as in Madrid they wanted her to confine her interests to Paris, absorbed by sectarian quarrels. She was making a nuisance of herself, and so unselfconsciously that she never realized that she was being laughed at. Not that this mattered to her in the least. Anjou obstinately refused to marry the Queen of England, whom he described as a whore; Margot sulked when the Portuguese prince was mentioned. Her mother did not press her, finally deciding that the Béarnais would be a better match, since through him peace with the Protestants would be secured. Anjou's refusal, on the other hand, caused her great distress and, however much in love he was with the beautiful Renée de Châteauneuf, she finally persuaded him to give way, at least to all appearances. Elizabeth pretended to lend a favourable ear to his suit. This comedy was to continue for years, during which the Florentine's matrimonial ardour never abated, so that when Anjou finally rebelled against her plans she proposed the last of her sons, François, to Elizabeth, only to meet with similar failure.

For it was one of the basic tenets of Catherine de Medici's policy to secure an alliance with England. The peace of Saint Germain, having infuriated the Catholic zealots, had only rendered the Huguenots defiant and discontented owing to the restrictions imposed by public opinion on the government, in the application of those clauses most favourable to the Reformationists. Coligny was constantly arguing, complaining and protesting. In order to reassure him Catherine instructed Cossé to inform him of her plan for a marriage between Henri de Navarre and Marguerite de Valois, and even of the possibility of an intervention in Flanders against Spain. As Agrippa d'Aubigné said, this was juicy bait for the Admiral, who expressed his satisfaction at it but took good care nonetheless not to leave La Rochelle, for he remembered the King's killer. He had all the more reason to take precautions as Morvillier, owing to illness, had returned the Seals at the end of Febuary 1571. We know through Cavriana, the Florentine ambassador, that financial difficulties had made it necessary to impose taxation on the nobility and that Morvillier, who was only temporary official, was not in a position to deal with their resistance to this decision. As no one else wished to succeed in this unenviable post, Catherine, after the refusal of Paul de Foix, whom she would have preferred, had the Seals conferred on one of her Italians, Birague, whom, in spite of his devotion to her own person, she did not favour, as he was too deeply involved with the Catholic zealots. Although L'Hospital was still Chancellor he could not be recalled, for instead of abating, the hatred felt for him had only increased since the limping and badly set peace which had resulted from the victory of his policy.

Although he was no longer Keeper of the Seals, Morvillier, doyen of the Council, still held a predominant position in it. Without concealing from herself how delicate and difficult a matter this would prove to be, Madame Catherine was determined to see that the Treaty of Saint Germain was implemented. She was deprived of an ally on the Protestant side by the death of the Cardinal Odet de Châtillon on March 2, 1571. Coligny was continuing with his plans against Spain. The politicals were gaining more and more influence at Court. The country as a whole remained very anti-Protestant, and the Huguenots a restless and anxious minority. Spain, very well-informed, threatened to go to war if France allowed Coligny to intervene in Flanders, and if a diversion were attempted in Italy, where Catherine de Medici was intriguing with her cousin, Cosimo, who had become Grand Duke of Tuscany, in spite of Philip II. In order to keep an eye on the Admiral at closer range, Catherine invited him back to Court, where he finally returned on September 12, 1571. Having been showered with presents by the Royal munificence (150,000 livres, and, Calvinist though he was, presented with the revenues of an abbey amounting to 20,000 livres) he appeared sincerely anxious to be reconciled with her.

Although the proposed marriage of Henri de Navarre and Marguerite suited the Admiral, Catherine judged his foreign policy to be a dangerous one. History has proved that the Queen Mother was right. Even if France was much more able to oppose Spain than the Queen thought, she still could not by any means have carried out a strong political offensive against Philip II. Coligny's plan was a reckless one. In spite of her religious sympathies, England would have

opposed France moving into Antwerp, in accordance with the poli-
tico-economic line she had unwaveringly followed since the beginning of the fourteenth century. Catherine was right to oppose
Coligny's plan to intervene in the Low Countries. She thought that
a hidden asset, resulting from the English marriage of one of her
sons, as well as the Béarnais match of her daughter, would give
better results. She preferred a subtle matrimonial diplomacy, that
would at one and the same time serve the kingdom's and her family
interests, to Coligny's adventurous designs. She also understood that
the Catholics would never have tolerated France taking the lead in a
Protestant crusade, which would inevitably have lead to a new civil
war.

Since the second Huguenot rising the Catholic reaction had
grown stronger. Brotherhoods of the Holy Cross and the Holy
Ghost were increasing in numbers throughout the kingdom.
Although leagues had been prohibited by the peace of Longjumeau,
this remained a dead letter, nor did the peace of Saint Germain make
any difference in this respect.[1] The Holy See encouraged and heightened the anti-Protestant crusading spirit. On January 1, 1571, in a
letter to the Duchess of Savoy, Catherine complained in very strong
terms of Pius V's policy: 'I greatly fear that that old boy, the Pope
[ce bonhomme de pape], will in the end, by his actions, stir up Christianity, which God forbid.' As we know from the reports of the Nuncio,
Frangipani, and Alava, she was on bad terms with the Curia which
accused her of atheism. During the Third War of Religion she had
been compelled and forced to accept Papal help in money and men,
as well as Spanish, and she was all the more hostile to Philip II and
Pius V for having had to endure their aid. She was exasperated by the
Pope's letters against the peace of Saint Germain, calling down
divine vengeance on the Valois. As is written in the *Instruction à
Monsieur de La Bourdaisière allant à Rome, touchant l'édit de pacification, le 20 septembre 1571*, she knew 'that certain people watching
from the window were very pleased to see the game being played at
His Majesty's expense'.

And Catherine always did prefer to take 'the gentle path'. Nearly a
century before Richelieu she favoured the Protestant alliances as a
counterweight to the intervention of Madrid and Rome in French
politics. But she did not admit that she should be dragged by such
alliances into the service of Protestantism, nor that they should cause
the rising of her Catholic subjects, comprising almost the whole

[1] Documentation cf. Pastor, *op. cit.* Vol. XVIII, pp. 29–55.

population of the kingdom—a point that Coligny's apologists invariably forget. Remembering what trouble Richelieu had, what resistances he had to break down, before he was able to intervene on the side of the Lutheran princes in the Thirty Years' War, it is readily understandable that in 1571 official intervention in Flanders would have led to the rising of all those Frenchmen who were not Calvinists.[1] The victory of Lepanto on October 7, 1571, finally gave Spain her appearance of hegemony. When the Turk, that ally of the Very Christian King, was beaten by the Catholic King, with the exception of the Huguenots the whole of France enthusiastically applauded Spain for having liberated the West. That was the hour chosen by Coligny to exercise his influence over Charles IX in favour of taking his revenge on Philip II, not only in the Low Countries but also in Turkey, with the help of England, disturbed by Spain's maritime preponderance. There is a despatch of May 11, 1572, from Charles IX to François de Noailles, Bishop of Dax and ambassador to the Porte, which proves to what extent the young King had entered into the Admiral's foreign policy plans: 'All my inclinations unite to set me against the grandeur of Spain, and I am deliberating how to conduct this matter as dexterously as possible.' And the despatch reveals the whole plan—with the aid of the Grand Seigneur, the Queen of England, the Princes of Germany, 'to keep the King of Spain in suspense, and embolden those Beggars of the Low Countries'. This is what might be described as putting the Spaniards in a fine state of umbrage.

Catherine, as usual, waited and watched to see what would happen. The French Huguenots sent to Mons and Valenciennes under the command of Ludovic de Nassau and de Genlis, accredited by the King of France, were defeated. This proved that intervention in Flanders was a senseless adventure, and in addition to their umbrage the Spaniards now also had victory on their side. In her wisdom Catherine was strongly against Coligny's rashiness; fanaticism, in his case, was a cover for everything. Yet his fanaticism combined with his genius for intrigue always to coincide with his personal interests and ambitions as a great feudalist (nothing is more false—as the documentation proves—than the rigid austerity

[1] On Richelieu and his struggle against what he so well described as *les oppressions d'Espagne* (let us never forget that in the seventeenth century the Empire was still as always Spain) the fairest and most exact account is that of Georges Pagès, published in 1939, and which now, after twenty-one years, appears as the definitive one: *La Guerre de Trente Ans*, 1618–84.

U

attributed to him by Protestant hagiography). All the original texts and narratives are steeped in the Utopian atmosphere that prevailed in French Calvinist circles during the second half of the sixteenth century—the heads of the French Reformation were solely concerned with the anti-Catholic crusade. With this end in view they supported the matrimonial aims of the Queen Mother and her ambitions to see all her children carrying the sceptre. Jean de Ferrières encouraged Monsieur to marry Elizabeth and to reign in Flanders; Charles IX, to become a candidate for the Empire; Alençon, to become King of Naples or Duke of Genoa. For the same reason the Protestants were ardent supporters of Monsieur's condidature to the throne of Poland; Protestantism was powerful on the banks of the Vistula. All this was to culminate in the dreams of d'Aubigné and de Sully regarding Henri IV's Grand Design. But on June 16, 1572, Catherine, who was a realist, demanded of the King that he should disavow Ludovic de Nassau. A few days later she herself wrote to the Pope that Charles IX would never begin a war against Philip II unless he were obliged by force to do so.

Jeanne d'Albret, who had come to Paris for her son's marriage, died on June 9th, either from cancer or tuberculosis. (The stories of her having been poisoned are absurd, since Catherine de Medici was the last person to have wished to deprive herself of the ally her daughter's mother-in-law would have been.) After having wavered for a long time, as Tavannes said, on the Flanders question, the Queen Mother had decided on official non-intervention, but on secret aid, combined with an English alliance and a rapprochement with the Huguenots. She thought that in her future son-in-law, the young King of Navarre, she had found a leader to replace the ageing Coligny, whom she had once again protected from the Lorraines by officially putting and end to the proceedings they had started with reference to his alleged complicity in the murder committed by Poltrot de Méré. She was chiefly, and cruelly, preoccupied by Charles IX's submission to the Admiral, and by the intensified enmity between her sons. Through their mistresses, who were her confidants, she spied on them closely. In the case of the Duc d'Anjou this was Renée de Rieux de Châteauneuf. In the Duc d'Alençon's case it was Madame de Sauves, the famous Charlotte de Beaune, the loveliest of the amazons of the Flying Squadron, who as the great-granddaughter of Jacques de Semblançay, niece of the Archbishop of Bourges, and wife of the Secretary of State Simon de Fizes, at twenty-one knew all there was to know about politics.

Madame Catherine had made a happy choice, for Charlotte de Sauves was a born intriguer but nevertheless wholly devoted to the Queen. The Queen herself kept an eye on Charles, with whom she was almost constantly in touch on matters of State. On Coligny's advice the King tried to avoid her, but without success, since he dared not openly defy her. Alava was spying on the Queen, who knew it, and demanded his recall. On November 13, 1571, the Spaniard, whose life she had made impossible by continuous and sometimes very violent scenes, left voluntarily. The memorandum that Don Francès left for his successor is a document of the first importance with regard to Catherine's tragedy, simultaneously political and domestic, after the peace of Saint Germain, when she was obliged powerlessly to watch the development of the hatreds that were setting her three sons against one another, all the more frightful for being dissimulated.

Charles IX, whose mistress, the very lovely Marie Touchet, was a Huguenot, was leaning further and further towards the Reformationists, having forgotten how angry he had been with them at the time of their surprise attack on Montceaux-en-Brie. Coligny dominated this violent-tempered man who, like nearly all such characters, was a weakling. At the beginning of the summer of 1572 the Admiral was completely in control and claimed to direct the Council as he did the King. There were lively altercations at the Council meetings, notably between Coligny and Tavannes on the subject of war against Spain; the Admiral cried out that whoever should prevent such a war was not a good Frenchman, and the Marshal replied that those were the words of a traitor. Pierre de L'Estoile reported that Charles IX was against all his Councillors with the sole exception of Coligny.

In spite of the opposition of the Council, in which the politicals joined the Catholics against the Admiral, preparations for war went on. Venice, whose links with France were so close that her maritime policy would have been ruined by a Franco-Spanish war, was extremely perturbed. Giovanni Michele was charged, as ambassador-in-extraordinary, to intervene and attempt to deter France from embarking on such a wild and lunatic adventure. Michele arrived at Paris a few days after the defeat of Genlis at Quiévrain in mid-July 1572, when Charles IX's letters were seized by the Spaniards, giving them a perfect *casus belli*. Nevertheless, Elizabeth of England negotiated with Philip II, offering to occupy Flushing in order to hand over that port to the Duke of Alba. Catherine was aware of everything, the seized letters and the Anglo-Spanish negotiations. A war against Spain without allies—that was the situation into which Coligny's fanaticism had led France. She received Michele with joyful relief. Charles IX was obliged to make a public declaration of his desire for peace with all his neighbours. Reassured (a natural optimist, she was always quickly reassured), the Queen Mother left for Châlons-sur-Marne, where her daughter Claude had fallen ill. The Admiral regained all his influence over Charles IX, who put up with his mother but who, in all the irresponsibility of his twenty-two years, wanted war, imagining that he would thus win himself immortal glory and obliterate the fame of that brave young eaglet, his brother Anjou. The Venetians were thunderstruck. Cavalli said that the Admiral was becoming as all-powerful as the Constable de Montmorency had been.

Retz and Birague informed Catherine, who was at Paris on August 4th. At this point Tavannes' *Mémoires* contain a passage which is too close to Catherine's political outlook to be regarded as otherwise than reliable. In moving terms the Queen reminded her son of all she had done to safeguard his crown, which both Catholics and Protestants wanted, equally, to wrest from him. She reproached him for seeking the advice of his enemies and for throwing himself without further ado into a war which would in the end hand the State over to the Huguenots. Rather than see that happen she begged him to be allowed to return to Florence. With her usual lucidity she made Coligny's aims clear—he did not want a war with Spain but a war with France.

Catherine was right. Later events prove that civl war would in fact have broken out with a Catholic rising, that as early as 1572 the whole of France would have become one League, and that the Catholics, in order to tear the State from the hands of the Huguenots, would have handed it over to the Spaniards. Those are the facts. No denominational interpretation can controvert them; the French of 1572 placed their religious hatreds before the permanent interests of the kingdom. The third party, which fifteen years later was to become the largest, was as yet only a tiny minority. Any attempt to project Henri IV's policy back into the year 1572 reveals a point of view that is one of those historical illusions that fascinate novelists who adventure in the realm of Clio, but which entirely falsifies history as regards the reign of Catherine de Medici. With the King in his power Coligny imagined himself to hold all France. The ten years it took Henri IV to conquer his kingdom with the support of the third party, are enough to prove that if Coligny possessed a genius for intrigue, he had none as regarded politics and was swayed only by his mysticism and personal ambitions. Catherine faced facts —profoundly anti-Spanish though she was, she was against war because war would in all certainty finally lead, this time, to the subversion of the kingdom. The English documents at our disposal place any further discussion of the matter out of bounds. Elizabeth, who had not forgotten Coligny's bad faith towards her after Hampton Court, had decided to allow France to break herself against Spain and to sell her own benevolent neutrality to Philip II at the highest price.

In order to regain Charles IX's support, Coligny arranged that a remarkable report in favour of intervention should be drawn up by Duplessis-Mornay, the future leader of Huguenot thought, in spite of his youth already at that time very influential among members of the Religion, and who had recently returned from the Low Countries. This report was remarkable for its cleverness although not for its prescience. Its sophistry is striking, recommending a war abroad in order to avoid civil war, that old and erroneous theory of the Cardinal de Lorraine, but this time against Spain. This was Duplessis-Mornay's leading theme. Such a war abroad, he claimed, would be an extremely easy matter, for the Flemish towns would open their gates to the French; it would be both a profitable and a very short war. A century of European history, from Saint Bartholomew to the peace of Nymeghem, proves the utter emptiness of such chimeras, on which the minds of Coligny, Duplessis-Mornay, and those Utopian pilgrims the French Protestants had become were feeding ever since Calvin's realistic genius had ceased to be available to deter them from such dreams. Easy, profitable and rapid—we know what in fact happened even when Richelieu, Mazarin and the young Louis XIV had the whole of France behind them. To hold forth on Duplessis-Mornay's and Coligny's patriotism may be a literary entertainment but historically nothing remains to be remembered of this plan of 1572 except its dire illusions.

On the other hand, Jean de Morvillier's reply to Duplessis-Mornay was justified by events. The statesmen of ancient France lived on solid ground, realistically, which was why they and Catherine de Medici understood one another perfectly. To Duplessis-Mornay, holding forth on the annual sum of one million in gold that France would obtain from the Low Countries, which implied the annexation of those provinces that he claimed France would liberate,

Morvillier replied that in Flanders England, on account of her commerce, was for Spain, and that the Emperor would inevitably come to the aid of Philip II, in order to prevent the Low Countries from becoming a French province. A comparison between these two memoranda—of Duplessis-Mornay and Morvillier—makes it clear that the opinion of Catherine and her legislators was the correct one and that the Protestant visions were of mortal peril to France. It remains to be added that Coligny was only a good general when it came to retreating, that his incapacity in carrying out any offensive was proven by a series of defeats, and that the first French operations in Flanders had ended in failure at Quiévrain. We know through Michele how dramatically the debate ended. By a unanimous vote the Council reproved Coligny, who did not hide his fury. Turning to the Queen Mother: 'Madame', he said, 'the King renounces going to war; God grant that he may not find himself confronted by another one which he will no doubt not be able to renounce so easily.'

There has been a great deal of quibbling aimed at proving that this sentence did not contain a threat of civil war. But instead of quibbling it is enough to read and compare the documents. The basic argument set forth by Duplessis-Mornay's memorandum was that a foreign war would prevent civil war. As there was to be no foreign war there would be civil war instead. In reply to the Queen Mother's will to peace the Admiral admitted thus that there would be a fourth recourse to arms, even more criminal than the preceding ones, since the Treaty of Saint Germain was entirely favourable to the Protestant minority. Coligny, seeing that he would not become master of the palace, generalissimo and avenger of the Flemish massacred by the Duke of Alba, was no longer able to contain himself. His fury was stronger than his caution and he admitted it.

His admission was all the more serious because it preceded a gathering of the Huguenots to go to the help of the Prince of Orange. If it is not isolated from its context the sentence addressed by the Admiral to Catherine can only be interpreted in one possible way—he would take up arms in spite of the Royal government; he would go even further and regarded the consequences of doing so, another civil war, without dismay. 'I cannot oppose what Your Majesty has done', he said to Charles IX, 'but I am certain that you will have reason to repent of it.' Catherine de Medici understood and everyone else also understood. At the very moment when the Béarnais marriage appeared to be about to consolidate the peace of Saint

Germain, the Admiral's frustrated ambition and extremist fanaticism were leading him to the direst ends. In his embittered pride he rose against a government that had forgiven him his entire past, conferring on him powers which he was furiously determined to abuse. Now the Admiral was announcing that with his own hands he would destroy the peace that had been so dearly bought. Was Catherine then to be shipwrecked in sight of harbour? No one who knew her could for one moment suppose so. She would do everything to save the peace of Saint Germain, the Queen's Peace, that limping and ill-set peace that only the marriage of Marguerite and the King of Navarre could place on a less precarious basis. But a Coligny dared to attempt to destroy this fragile edifice. 'When it is a case of keeping one's subjects in the line of duty one must not place oneself in danger of being accused of cruelty, all the more so as in the end the Prince will be found to have been more humane in making a small number of necessary examples than those who through too much indulgence encourage disorders bringing murder and banditry in their wake. For such tumults overthrow the State, whilst the penalties inflicted by the Prince only attain certain individuals.' How could one expect the Florentine Queen not to have remembered this admirable page of Machiavelli's at the moment when the Admiral was threatening her? Certain individuals . . . Coligny had completely relapsed into disloyalty. He had been amnestied, pardoned and restored to his former position, only to proclaim his new rebellion. As he so desired it, his sentence of September 1569 would once again become operative. It had been suspended for a period of three years.

It was necessary for Coligny to die in order that the Protestants should once more become faithful subjects and the kingdom remain at peace. So Coligny would die. He had condemned himself by showing his hand. Patient as ever, Catherine waited for the first signs that he was about to carry out his threats. Hasty action was so contrary to her nature that after her victory in the Council she left for Montceaux, where she spent a few days resting with her daughter Claude. The Admiral immediately took advantage of her absence to act. At this point chronology is of prime importance. On August 11th Charles IX fell back under the influence of Coligny, whom he called his father, and in his despatch to La Mothe-Fénelon ordered the ambassador to work on Elizabeth, as far as he was able, to declare herself openly against the King of Spain. On the same date Morillon wrote to the Cardinal de Granvelle that the Admiral was daily with Charles IX and that 'there is only one lodging between that of the said Admiral and the Court'. On August 13th, the Venetian ambassador informed his government that 3,000 Huguenots were assembled at the French frontier in order to relieve the siege of Mons and that Coligny had had interviews with the English ambassador. On August 11th, the Prince of Orange had written to his brother, John of Nassau, that the Admiral had informed him that he would shortly arrive at the head of 12,000 musketeers and 2,000 horsemen.

The Queen Mother returned to Paris. On August 15th, Gonnicourt, an envoy from the Duke of Alba, asked to be given an official explanation of these troop movements. In order to gain more time Catherine referred to the preparations for Marguerite's wedding. Her mind was now made up. Charles IX was slipping away from her; Coligny had been the stronger. Either he would have to disappear or she would lose her power. As her tyrannical passion for power coincided with the interests of the kingdom she would hesitate no longer. She would have Coligny killed, but how could this be done without causing the rising that she feared? It was then that her genius for cunning came to her rescue; she would arrange for an attempt to be made on the Admiral's life that she could subsequently disavow. To this end she immediately set to work.

There is a limit to a policy of compassion and to respect for the ideas and lives of individuals—the public good. Catherine de Medici had too good a head on her shoulders to forget it. To the end she would defend freedom of conscience—not in theory—for her intelligence was intensely pragmatical and by that fact political and highly disciplined to the changing complexities of the lives of nations—but in practice. As the Calvinists refused to enter into the bosom of the Church, to which almost the whole French nation remained faithful, it was politically wise to allow them to attend their sermons and to treat them in all other respects similarly to the remainder of the kingdom's subjects. But the right to hold prayer-meetings did not include the right to rebellion, since in the domain of conscience these heretical subjects had been justly dealt with, the freedom that they had demanded having been granted, confirmed and guaranteed. As an insurgent Coligny was a criminal of State, and for reasons of State, on higher grounds, namely those of the public welfare.

Madame Catherine was too deeply imbued with the legal tradition not to realize how irregular it would be to have recourse a second time to the King's killer in order to strike down Coligny, without trial, after he had been amnestied, pardoned and re-established in all his posts and honours. Charles IX was under the Admiral's influence and would never allow him to be re-arraigned. It was therefore necessary that Coligny should die at the hand of a murderer. The Queen Mother was not cruel, as she had proved time and time again. Historians may leave to her libellers the legend of an imaginary Medici who delighted in availing herself of poison. But if she was not cruel neither was Catherine tender-hearted. She could be hard, and could watch torturings as calmly as she was prepared to risk her own life in the trenches of Rouen and Le Havre. She had studied Machiavelli sufficiently closely to agree with him that cruelty could be ill or well used: 'It can be said to be well employed (if one may call evil, good) when it is used on one occasion only, dictated by the necessity of retaining power, and on condition that one has no further recourse to it except in the interests of the nation.'

In the present case there was no doubt where the interests of the nation lay. Coligny was ready to unleash a disastrous war. By temperament, character, predilection and necessity Madame Catherine was for compromise. But Coligny would not compromise; the completely free debates in the Council proved his use of intimidation. To endow the Governess of France with any form of modern liberalism is as contrary to historical fact as to psychological and ethical truth, but it is equally contrary to both to represent her as a second Agrippina. Her passion for power was as one with her love for the Crown of France. In his astonishing essay on Catherine de Medici, in which romanticism often goes hand in hand with an extraordinary intuition, leading in its essence to historical truth, Balzac put into this princess's mouth a phrase which expresses her completely: 'You are all inclined to weep over a couple of hundred clodhoppers, sacrificed incidentally, those tears that you refuse to shed for the misfortunes of a whole generation, a century, or a world.'

Reasons of State justified the death of the impenitent rebel, but it was not to be known that it was Catherine who struck the blow. Catherine cunningly gave thought to that revenge being everywhere demanded by the Guises for the assassination of François, ordered by Coligny. Let the Admiral be killed by the Lorraines and Protestant fury turn on them, whose ambition was no less a threat to the State than Coligny's fanaticism. The Guises against the Châtillons— what did it concern the Queen? The revenge of the Lorraines would surprise her at a moment when she herself was entirely taken up with the Béarnais wedding. Once again the royal wisdom would have been impotent, but this time only in appearance. In reality, with Coligny out of the way and the Guises massacred as a reprisal, the field would be clear for the King, freed from the dangerous leaders of both factions, to proceed with his task of pacification.[1]

The documents do not leave any doubt that this was Catherine's plan against Coligny. And when sixty-seven years later Richelieu's librarian, the erudite Gabriel Naudé, published his *Considérations politiques sur les Coups d'Etat*, he deplored the fact that Saint Bartholomew was never rounded off, because the Guises survived the Châtillons. Thus, during the reign of Louis XIII a faithful servant of the king, far from being indignant at the Admiral's murder, considered the police action to have been incomplete, as the Lorraine Princes escaped it. *Et nunc reges intelligite; erudimini, qui judicatis terram....*

The very decor of Marguerite's wedding celebrations was to facilitate the setting, worked out with an art that Caesar Borgia would have enjoyed. Catherine was counting on her daughter's marvellous beauty to enchant the King of Navarre, leader of the Huguenots. She reckoned that this wedding, which she was bringing about in opposition to the Pope and to Spain, would convince French Protestantism of the royal determination to impose on the country the legality of the co-existence in one State of the two religions as symbolized by this mixed marriage. She was also counting on the frivolity of the Parisians, in whose memories the superb pageantry of the wedding festivities would obliterate the bloody incident during which the friends of the Châtillons and the Lorraines would be reciprocally murdering one another. Were they not in any case used to such killings among the nobility, with their retinues of gentlemen and hired assassins? But as Sigismond Cavalli said, the Admiral was an old fox, and it would be extremely difficult to take him by surprise. Killing him would be a very complicated affair, the timing of which might be as ticklish as the consequences might be dangerous. Yet time was pressing. 'For a statesman as for the head of an army it is one of the most important characteristics to be able to review a situation in cold blood, without dwelling on sterile regrets. Catherine possessed this characteristic to the highest degree; with her vivid realism she could consider any problem accurately,

[1] In his authoritative work, in which the objective historian as a rule gets the better of the moralizing Protestant, Van Dyke dealt in some interesting and comprehensive pages with *Catherine et la Saint-Barthélemy.*

discover its solution and carry it out with complete imperturbability.'[1] The greatest danger, obviously, would lie in the presence in Paris of the Protestant nobility, who would be there for the marriage of the King of Navarre, and of the seven to eight thousand men-at-arms assembled by the Admiral for the expedition to the Low Countries.

As we know from a letter written by Cuniga, the Spanish ambassador, on August 20, 1572, Catherine consulted Giovanni Michele. The plan they devised was of truly Italian ingenuity, as Cuniga stressed. The Admiral having been killed by a man of the House of Guise, with regard to the Huguenots, the Queen of England and the Lutheran German prince, all previous knowledge of such an attempt would be disavowed. For nine years Duke François's family had been proclaiming their intention to avenge his murder. The English ambassador, Smith, had informed his government of it, stating that a day would come when Coligny would be assassinated in reprisal for the Orleans attack. The despatches from the ambassadors of Florence and Venice, Petrucci and Michele, and those of the Spanish ambassador and the Nuncio, Salviati, Frangipani's successor, enable us to follow the genesis of the murder of Coligny. Already on July 23rd, i.e. immediately after the news of the disaster of Quiévrain was received, the Queen Mother conferred with the window of Mosieur de Guise le Grand, who had become Duchess de Nemours. She gave her consent to the Lorraine revenge, which she had hitherto withheld, but which after Coligny's threats in the Council she encouraged. Is it a fact that for a long time the Cardinal de Lorraine had been thinking not only of eliminating the Admiral but also of instigating the massacre of the Calvinist noblemen? This question remains unsolved.[2]

But on the other hand the documents are conclusive regarding the extrajudicial punishment of Coligny, which the Guises had only postponed on account of the Queen Mother's opposition. As she

---

[1] François Renié: *La Politique de Catherine de Médicis*. This remarkable essay was published in the Etudes sociales et politiques of the *Cercle Joseph de Maistre*, first year, February-March 1907.

[2] Cf. the very curious study by Lucien Romier on Saint-Bartholomew, in *Revue du XVIe siècle*, Vol. I, of the year 1913. One should also bear in mind Mariéjol's discussion of it. Having ourselves re-examined the documents we cannot commit ourselves in the matter. After Saint-Bartholomew the Cardinal de Lorraine wished to appear as the saviour of Catholicism which had carried out the plan of Pius V to exterminate the heretics. But the documents quoted by Pastor definitely established that Saint Pius V was in favour of legal extermination and not a conspiracy. The Cardinal de Lorraine was too ultramontane to have gone beyond the pontifical intentions. That he should have premeditated a massacre seems, to say the least, more than surprising.

had now withdrawn it, the Guises threw themselves on their prey. With her usual sharpness Catherine had foreseen the situation correctly. Maurevert, the King's killer, had taken up service with the Lorraine princes. A former tutor of the Duke Henri de Guise put his house at his disposal, in the Rue des Fossés-Saint-Germain, which lay directly on the route Coligny took every day on his way to and from the Louvre. It would be easy to shoot the Admiral from a window on the ground floor, and the house had two exits, so that the murderer would be able to escape immediately. Henri de Guise's superintendant was ordered to organize it all; his name was François de Villiers, Lord of Chailly. It was decided not to act until after Queen Margot's wedding and the festivities in connection with it, which took place from August 16th (the day of the engagement) until the 21st (when there was a great tournament in front of the Louvre). The Duc d'Anjou was enjoined by his mother to supervise the arrangements for the attempt. The day and time appointed were the Friday, August 22nd, in mid-morning, when Coligny would be returning from the Council held at the Louvre and presided over by Monsieur, as Charles IX would be at Mass in the chapel of the Hôtel de Bourbon. The secret had been perfectly kept.[1]

It was not only Michele who initially advised that Coligny should be eliminated. A letter from the Archbishop of Rossano, Nuncio in Spain, to the Cardinal of Como, dated from Madrid on August 5, 1572, proves that Philip II was also encouraging such an attempt. He was not at all anxious to have a war with France on his hands, as well as the one he was fighting against the rebels in the Low Countries.[2] Whilst with the complicity of the Guises Catherine de Medici was protecting herself against the indignation and fury of the Huguenots, she knew that Venice, Madrid and Rome approved. The death of the Admiral seemed more than ever to her the most efficient measure to safeguard peace, both internal and external. And she proceeded to carry out this measure with a minute care for details

---

[1] There is an almost infinite number of accounts of Maurevert's attempt. The most complete and carefully documented is that of Pierre de Vaissière (in his essays: *De quelques assassins*). One must however maintain certain reserves with regard to his interpretations of the documents, in which this authority occasionally confuses history with morality. In this case we should not pass judgment on but try to understand the spirit and manners of the period.

[2] Letter quoted by Edgar Boutaric in his essay on *La Saint-Barthélemy, d'après les archives du Vatican*. This essay, which should be compared with that by Lucien Romier, is of the very highest interest. Unfortunately it is barely known of and is to be found in the *Bibliothèque de l'Ecole des Chartes*, twenty-third year, Vol. III, fifth series, Paris, MDCCCLXII, coll. in-8o, pp. 1–27.

such as might be bestowed on a surgical operation. Her royal prerogative of administering direct justice relieved her of any pangs of conscience in the matter. An ascetic priest such as Saint Pius V surprised his contemporaries—as was reported by Çuniga, then ambassador at Rome, on May 19, 1568—by refusing to approve a plan to assassinate Coligny and Condé. He stood for public execution and that alone, and that was why Gregory XIII ordered the medal *Ugonotorum Strages* to be struck in celebration of the Matins of Paris and commissioned Vasari to paint a picture illustrating them.

Neither the Scottish Presbyterians opposed to Mary Stuart under the protection of that holy man John Knox, nor Coligny, confronted with the corpse of Duke François de Guise, nor Philip II, any more than Catherine de Medici, challenged the right to commit a murder in order to ensure what they thought to be the salvation of their religion or their State. And that is why the historian should abstain from all condemnation of a deed which appeared in the eyes of the men of the sixteenth century as perfectly legitimate, and to reject which one would have to be a saint as well as an inquisitor who would prefer the legal extermination of a whole sect to the lawless suppression of rebel leaders. Catherine, who was exclusively politically-minded, preferred the latter method. Philip II, at one and the same time a politician and a mystic, combined both—the assassination of Escovedo, the terrifying tragedy of the death of Don Carlos, the repressions in Andalusia and Flanders, the gigantic *autodafés* of relapsed Jews, the terror in Portugal, offer us a rich selection of atrocities, so that in comparison to him Madame Catherine appears a timid little woman. And it never occurred to anyone, either in Spain or elsewhere, that the Catholic King was going beyond reasons of State. Historical experience has proved only too clearly to what disorder and ruin such a point of view finally leads for us any longer to admit the possibility of distinguishing between ethics and politics and we know that any attempt to do so must inevitably lead to barbarism. We know this and we believe it. But, forgetting the example of Saint Louis and the teachings of Saint Thomas Aquinas, the men of the sixteenth century neither knew this any longer nor did they think so. It is not for us at this point to reproach them for it, for otherwise the whole perspective of history would be falsified.

Excellently organized as the plot had been, it failed utterly because Maurevert missed the Admiral. The King's killer did not have a steady hand and it is surprising that on two occasions his incompetent services should have been utilized. The first time he had killed

Mouy instead of Coligny; the second, he wounded his victim, but only slightly. He fled, and so fast that nobody saw him and it was thought that the musket-shot had been fired by a Florentine, Pietro-Paolo Tosinghi, a creature of the Queen's and Monsieur's favourite. Michele considered that it was he and not Maurevert who drew on the Admiral; possibly they were both there.

The old fox, brave as usual, and completely in command of himself, was not for one moment in doubt as to the instigators of the attack, Catherine and the Guises, all the more so as the musket, abandoned by Maurevert, belonged to one of Monsieur's bodyguards. As soon as he received the news, Charles IX burst into a rage. The Queen Mother instantly summed up the extent and seriousness of the consequences of this abortive attack. The Admiral would demand and obtain from Charles IX without any difficulty an inquiry and a trial which would reveal the truth. Catherine knew her son too well not to be sure that whilst he would not dare to touch her in one of his usual rages, he would kill his brother, the Duc d'Anjou, with his own hand. As for herself, the Admiral would be sufficiently persuasive to obtain her exile. If Coligny were dead no one in the world would have been capable of turning Charles IX against his mother, and she, playing on his hatred of Henri de Guise, could easily have directed his anger towards him. But living, Coligny would turn it on Catherine and Anjou. How to divert that fury from themselves? This was the question that the Queen Mother now asked herself in the greatest anguish. For the first time in her life she panicked.

She immediately shut herself away in her chamber, with the Duc d'Anjou, in order that together they might find a means of staving off the danger—death for the son and banishment for his mother. The first thing to do was to join Charles IX in demanding that the criminals should be found and brought to justice. Although this would only give them a respite of a few hours, those few hours would nevertheless allow them to find a means of countering the steps the King would immediately take. To her son-in-law Navarre and the Prince de Condé Catherine declared that the murder of the Admiral was a grievous insult to Charles IX and that if that kind of thing was tolerated today, tomorrow they would be bold enough to do the same to her son, in the Louvre, either in his own bed or within her own bosom and in her arms. She was too intelligent an actress to imagine that she was taking anyone in, but by adopting this pose she was obliging them at least to wait a little while before accusing her. That was why she accompanied the King on a visit to the Admiral, who had sent to tell him that he would like to see him. At the wounded victim's bedside she expressed her sympathy and indignation, nor did she fail to recall the crime of Orleans, saying how happy she was that the bullet had not remained in Coligny's body, as Poltrot's had done in the case of Monsieur de Guise.

All the first-hand documents agree in stating that as from Saturday, the 23rd, the Calvinist leaders had not the slightest doubt that the instigator of the attack was the Queen Mother herself. Unless justice were immediately done they decided to punish the guilty. The King was for the Protestants and they knew it. Nothing would stop them; Téligny's and La Rochefoucauld's threats were unequivocal. As yet the King was only aware of the fact that the Guises were involved, but he would discover the whole truth from one moment to the next, as he had ordered an inquiry to be held and when he had visited him Coligny had talked to him in secret. Catherine was convinced that her old enemy had spoken against her. The Huguenots were prepared to do everything to avenge Coligny. Catherine remembered the attacks of Amboise and Montceaux and the successive risings. All the leaders and nearly 10,000 armed men were in Paris. What a temptation there was then for them to seize power, with Charles IX's approval! Catherine and the monarchy had never been in greater danger, since it was proved that the King was no longer anything but the Admiral's plaything. Charles IX's letters of August 22nd to La Mothe-Fénelon and Schomberg denounced the instigators of the attack, as far as he was then aware the Guises, with exceptional violence.

Later on there was a romanticized version of all this, based on the *Stratagème* of Capilupi, gaps in the correspondence of the Nuncio, Salviati, and the views of Çuniga, Petrucci, Cavriana, and Cavalli; a collection of all the different opinions contained in contemporary memoirs. Some of them spoke of premeditation on the part of the Queen Mother, and even—which is absurd—attributed a monstrous kind of Machiavellism to Charles IX, quite contrary to his impulsive character and attacks of rage. Others claimed that there was a Protestant plot. But we should not, after all, forget that the documents only reveal fragments of the truth. Even the most considered of them only report a small part of what was said and done and they reflect the ideas, feelings and wishes of their authors. In reading the thousands of pages written around the attack on Coligny and Marguerite's wedding, which became known as the Ruddy Wedding, one would become giddy did one not remember the essential point—Catherine was Queen; she was also a woman and a mother.

As Queen she had proved her devotion to France, her understanding of the permanent interests of the State, her constant determination to sacrifice everything to the public welfare. As a woman she had a passion for power, as others have for love; she was filled entirely with what the Venetians so happily call *l'affetto di signoreggiare*. As a mother she saw that her son Charles had shaken off her tutelage, and that her son Anjou, her favourite, an accomplice in the attack that had failed, stood in danger of death owing to his elder brother's hatred. Her nerves had given way and she was distraught. But we know that in Catherine de Medici the instinct of self-preservation quickly overcame her fears. This instinct of self-preservation now showed her what line to take; she must re-assert her authority over the King and there was only one means of doing so, by terror, in order to forestall the inevitable terrorism of the Admiral's avengers and the counter-terrorism of the Guisards. Knowing that the Huguenots were determined on revenge, Paris was about to rise, for the agents of the Guises were busily spreading their propaganda. What decision should she take? In her gardens of the Tuileries the Queen consulted her Italians—Nevers, Gondi, Birague, on whose personal devotion she could completely rely, and Tavannes, who seemed strong enough to rally the Parisians round the throne. But as the day advanced her danger grew and Catherine was still seeking a solution. She really was like a trapped fox now and in these circumstances Machiavelli could provide her neither with guidance nor help.

But suddenly circumstances brought the Queen Mother this help, which had seemed so completely beyond reach that on that Saturday evening of August 23rd at her supper-table a gentleman from Gascony, Pardaillan, dared to shout in her face that if the King did not do so the Huguenots would furnish their own justice. Two Calvinist noblemen, Bouchavannes, who had always remained loyal to her, and Gramont, during the course of the day, came to tell her that at the Admiral's lodgings there had been a meeting resulting in the decision to attempt a *coup de force*, that the Queen and her children were to be killed, and even the King of Navarre as well, because he was suspected of only being a lukewarm adherent of the Religion. Bouchavannes' and Gramont's accusation is a fact, confirmed by all the despatches of the ambassadors. But was this accusation based on

firm grounds or was it the work of *agents-provocateurs?* Did Catherine genuinely believe in the existence of this plot? Or did she use
it as an excuse? God alone knows.

Thanks to the revelations of Bouchavannes and Gramont, whether
they were true or false, Catherine now had a means of influencing
Charles IX in order to obtain an order from him without which nothing
could be done—the order to massacre the leaders of a new Amboise
conspiracy before they would have time to act. This time they were
too strong to be put down. It was a question of timing—the Huguenots must at all costs be forestalled. If the accusations were true it
was a matter of saving the realm; if they were imaginary, then by the
annihilation of the admiral's avengers and the Admiral himself
Catherine would be saved. From every point of view the Huguenots
were preparing to punish her, either with the King as the result of
the inquiry, or without the King by a sudden attack. Catherine saw
only too clearly that she was lost and that she could only break the
iron bonds of destiny by a third means, by massacring the men
against whom she knew herself in either case to be defenceless. 'If
the sovereigns', Çuniga wrote on August 24th, 'after the Admiral
had been wounded, had allowed two days to pass, what they themselves did would have been done to them.' As the threatened Calvinist Vespers remain merely hypothetical this cannot be confirmed
historically. But we do know that the inquiry had been opened, that
Coligny was the King's master and that, in consequence, had she
not struck first, Catherine would have been lost and France given
over to civil war by the revolt of the Catholics against the King, who
was allied to the Protestants. Catherine staged a killing in order not
to be killed herself. Apart from this, which is certain, everything else
is mere supposition and history cannot concern itself with suppo-
sitions but can only take events into account, which is the only way
to try to understand what happened. The cause of Saint Bartholomew
was fortuitous—Maurevert's clumsiness. On that point the opinions
of the diplomats are unanimous and Çuniga summed it up: 'As the
musket-shot was badly aimed and as the Admiral knew whence it
came, they determined to do what they did.'

This was the true cause of the Matins of Paris. The commentaries
that can be quoted on them stem from moralizing and apologetics,
but not from history. Saint Bartholomew, like Wassy, like the two
Michelades, was an unpremeditated massacre. We do not say a
spontaneous massacre—spontaneity does not occur in history any
more than in biology. Catherine de Medici decided on Saint Bar-

X

tholomew because she could not do otherwise. She considered herself to be acting on grounds of legitimate defence. According to the spirit and customs of the period her right to put the Admiral to death is beyond discussion. It also included the right to kill the Admiral's avengers, since they were the accomplices of a State criminal. Catherine de Medici decided on the massacre of his accomplices because she had failed to murder their leader. In one case as in the other it was an execution of rebels, but an execution that required the King's authority. It was exclusively aimed at the great noblemen —Coligny, La Rochefoucauld, Téligny, Caumont La Force, Montgomery, and a few others. With Paris under arms such a surprise attack, by depriving the Huguenots of their chiefs, would render them impotent. But in this, Catherine's reasoning was at fault, and did not show her usual clarity of mind. Bloodshed provokes bloodshed and all preventative terrorism is a worse remedy than the evil it is designed to cure. Terrorism is only efficacious as a means of repression. Given the state of over-excitement of the Parisian masses, the massacre of the leaders would inevitably lead to general carnage. Catherine, however, trusted in the security measures taken by the Hôtel de Ville and in the peaceful behaviour of the majority of the bourgeoisie.

Accompanied by her son Anjou, she visited Charles IX on the Saturday evening (and not on the Friday as Michele mistakenly wrote). She informed him of the discovery of the plot. The Admiral was a traitor. That was why they had taken the initiative against him, to save the King, France, and the Church. She called her witnesses to appear before the dumbfounded King—Nevers, Gondi, Birague, Tavannes. On the previous evening she herself had been broken, in despair, but they had given her new courage, 'showing her once more', said Tavannes, 'the peril in which she and her children stood, and the resolution only to kill the leaders.' They were confident of being able to convince Charles IX and to drag the order of execution from him.

During two whole hours this mother, terrified of the consequences of the abortive attack on Coligny, and those Italians, implacable towards the Huguenots, Tavannes, who believed in the plot revealed by Bouchavannes and Gramont, the Duc d'Anjou, who knew that if Charles IX did not give way he himself would perish, assailed the unfortunate prince, weakly vacillating between fury and exhaustion. Charles IX invoked his honour, his obligations towards Coligny. Were they certain of his treason? In view of his resistance Catherine and Anjou realized that they would have to act without him, in spite of him. The Queen Mother then said that she and her son would take their leave of him. And, with infallible intuition, Catherine asked Charles IX if he was afraid? That question was an insult; Catherine had touched on a vulnerable spot—would Charles be a coward when Anjou was arrayed in the glory of Jarnac and Mont-contour? The Florentine's Machiavellism was marvellously served by her maternal instinct. With Anjou, her favourite, the victor, she would go, asking for her dismissal, and would accompany her heroic son, leaving behind the son without courage. Instantly, Charles IX was thrown into a state of murderous intoxication by his bitter jealousy; he had a definite attack of mania. He cursed and fled, and as he did so, like an exhausted boar, he shouted at his mother, his brother, and the four men who had forced his hand, the famous invective: 'Kill the lot! Kill the lot!'

He had given way; he had agreed. It was necessary that the legislators on the Council should be informed of Charles IX's agreement, in order to make sure that they would not intervene against the massacre. The King had said 'Yes'. The legislators were covered and would remain the mute spectators of the drama. That was why Catherine was so concerned that Charles IX himself should give the order—she could then no longer be held personally responsible for the massacre, which had become a State execution. There is a revealing sentence in the *Mémoires* of Tavannes: 'A king is more freely permitted to move against his subjects by extra-legal measures than they are permitted to move against him.'

By having made Charles IX give way the Queen Mother legalized the massacre. She was saved. But at what a price!

To feel herself secure, at least for the time being, gave her back all her freedom of thought. When the King had disappeared she held a Council. Birague, her creature, was Keeper of the Seals. Administratively, all would be done in correct order. The King's justice had resigned itself to extra-legal measures because no others were available. They quietly examined the situation and discussed it; whom would they execute, who would be pardoned? Does not a leader on the eve of a battle hold millions of lives in his hand? At the Louvre on that hot evening, vigil of Saint Bartholomew, Catherine de Medici and her five companions, rid of a maniacal king, counted the heads that would be falling. Since they could not make use of the executioner's axe they would have recourse to the assassins' daggers.

The greatest calm reigned at the Council, a real council of war, presided over in the King's absence by the Queen, mother of the King.

It was agreed not to strike at the Princes of the Blood of France— the King of Navarre, Catherine's son-in-law; the Prince de Condé, brother-in-law of the Duc de Nevers by his marriage to Marie of Cleves, an adorable young woman of nineteen, whom Monsieur, who was madly in love with her, would himself have married had she been willing to abjure Calvinism. Like Charles IX with Marie Touchet, he hoped to make her his mistress and he hated his cousin for having become his successful rival. Nevertheless, reasons of State remained the stronger and Anjou accepted the decision to save Henri de Bourbon. A list was drawn up, headed by the Admiral, his son-in-law Téligny and other noblemen. Catherine was later to admit to five or six deaths on her own account. A second list was drawn up also, that of the executioners. Henri de Guise and his brother Aumale, the bastard of Angoulême, were given charge of the Admiral. One executioner was assigned to each of the condemned. To men of the sixteenth century it was all the most natural thing in the world. And the historian remains somewhat sceptical with regard to the uneasiness alleged to have prevailed after the Council among those in the secret of the death sentences. This may be due to an arrangement of the facts posterior to the facts, when the planned executions had developed into a general massacre throughout the city, from the Louvre killings to stranglings in the streets. The accounts by Michele and Cavalli, compared with the registers of the Hôtel de Ville show, on the contrary, that the whole matter was envisaged at one and the same time as a police operation and a capital execution by those who were confident of their rights. None of them had foreseen that the maintenance of public order, for which Marcel, the former provost of the merchants and his successor Le Charron were responsible, would break down on account of the political and religious passions that were in full blast. They thought that they were mobilizing the Parisians in order to resist the Protestants who, it was feared, would rise when the news of the executions became known. In fact they mobilized ferocious murderers as well as benign citizens. As everywhere and always in such circumstances a bloodbath ensued.

Catherine de Medici and her Italians did not know Paris very well, with its impulsiveness and feverishness. Tavannes was a military man who knew nothing about the bourgeois militia and the populace of a capital. Charles IX, sombre and rigid in his weakling's pride, wanting to prove to his mother and brother than he was not afraid of the Huguenots, was in command under Catherine's directions. He did not concern himself with the consequences; he was the master and he would show them that he was. At three o'clock in the morning the bell of the Palace of Justice would give the signal for the executions. Everything had been foreseen for the maintenance of order— the closing of the gates, with the Huguenots' troops encamped in the suburbs; the bourgeois militia was to occupy the squares, cross-roads and quays; the artillery was stationed on the Place de Grève. . . . Everything had been foreseen except one thing—Claude Marcel was not going to use his thugs to reinforce the bourgeois militia of Le Charron, but to exterminate all the Protestants of Paris. Claude Marcel was the Guise's man, a fanatical Catholic, and at the same time enjoyed the Queen Mother's confidence. As others were to kill the great noblemen he would take it on himself to kill the rest of the heretics. He was not concerned with Machiavellism. He was a gold-smith who had become a municipal magistrate but there was nothing of the Benvenuto Cellini about him and he did not go into Florentine sublteies. He ordered his men to make certain that not one blas-phemer be spared. *Le Roi le veut.* Those were the King's orders.

Thus were extra-legal executions to be transformed into the Matins of Paris.

Michelet's account, his superlative genius, discourage one from attempting to re-tell the story of Saint Bartholomew after this great seer. Towards one o'clock in the morning the Queen Mother, who was thinking over the consequences of the decision that had been taken, according to her custom most carefully weighing the *pros* and *cons*, realized that once the Guises and the people of Paris were unleashed, she would no longer be able to control them. She at once discussed the matter with the Duc d'Anjou. The famous *Discours du Roi Henri IIIe à un personnage d'honneur et de qualité*, given by this prince after he had newly arrived at Cracow as King of Poland in February 1574 to his doctor, Miron, whether it be authentic or not, contains statements and admissions which were obviously made by him and which coincide with the account of the Marshal de Tav-annes.[1] 'We were considering', Henri said, 'the events and the con-sequences of so great an enterprise (of which, truth to tell, we had

[1] On this *Discours* and its authenticity, cf. Henri Hauser: *Les Sources de l'Histoire de France au XVIe siècle*, Vol. III, pp. 240–1, and J. H. Mariéjol, *Marguerite de Valois*, pp. 47–49. In our opinion it is an apocrypha and not a forgery, i.e. a fabricated document,

not until then been thinking) when at that very moment we heard a pistol shot.' This explosion in the nocturnal silence suddenly brought home to mother and son, 'stricken with terror and apprehension', what 'great disorders were shortly to be committed'. Catherine and Anjou at last realized that the remedy would be worse than the disease, that they would commit a useless crime, and for that very reason a fatal one. 'To obviate it we immediately sent a gentleman in all haste to Monsieur de Guise to tell and expressly command him to retire to his lodgings and to take good care to undertake nothing against the Admiral, and this order would cancel all the rest. But soon afterwards the gentleman returning informed us that Monsieur de Guise had replied to him that the order had come too late and that the Admiral was dead.' Tavannes simply said of Catherine that she would gladly have retracted. But the inexhorable chain of circumstances did not allow her to do so. The tocsin of Saint-Germain-l'Auxerrois was an hour and a half in advance of the bell of the Palace of Justice, ringing for the Matins of Paris.

Even had the Queen regretted nothing, she could not fail to realize nonetheless, that she had only escaped one danger to fall into another. Jean Yanowitz, known as Besme, the hired assassin of Henri de Guise, having killed the Admiral, was regarded by the Parisians as the avenger of the Catholic religion. It must have been clear to Catherine and Henri d'Anjou, in that dawn of Saint Bartholomew 1572, that in order to rid themselves of a master of the palace they had created a king of Paris. Faced with the massacre they had let loose they vaguely realized that, unleashed in their name, linked to that of the Lorraines, it had become a destructive force beyond their control.

Charles IX had given himself up to the bloody excesses of a madman. His mother and brother, both perfectly clear-sighted, could only find new sources of anxiety in this appalling spectacle of a king shooting down his own subjects.[1] The butchery in the Louvre, the

---

based on true oral or written documentation, in aid of a cause (in this case, we agree with Mariéjol, that of the Gondi). The *Discours entier* is strikingly accurate, both in detail and in its psychological and moral atmosphere. It was certainly forged but it was not an invention, excepting as concerned the part attributed to Gondi, in complete disagreement with the most reliable sources.

[1] There has been a great deal of discussion on the part the King took in the shooting. On objectively examining the documentation we find that the evidence in the despatches of the Duke of Alba seems the most reliable. From which window did Charles IX shoot? This is unknown, but it is known that he did shoot. This unfortunate prince's love of bloodshed is, alas, proved by numerous papers in the archives (indemnities paid for butchered animals, etc.).

man-hunts in the streets, houses, courtyards, gardens, and on the roof-tops, the drownings, all the horrors that occur at all times and in all countries as soon as power has been seized by murderous factions—those were the results of the extra-judical executions demanded by Catherine de Medici. Saint Bartholomew thus took its place in the long series of atrocities, both Catholic and Protestant, that for twelve years had devastated the realm, and in magnitude surpassed them all. Those Matins of Paris were the proof of the failure of the Queen Mother's policy. She had no doubts whatever of her right to condemn Coligny and the other leading rebel noblemen to death. But events proved that she had deluded herself when she had endeavoured to prevent a possible Huguenot retaliation for the abortive attack on the Admiral. There are times when it is preferable to endure an attack instead of launching one.

On August 24, 1572, Paris proved to Catherine that she had made a mistake. What she had always tried to avoid, what Spain and the Holy See had in vain urged her to do, to exterminate the Huguenots, had now been done by her own fault. And as the result of that extermination she had become the prisoner of the Catholic party, of Philip II and the Pope. The anti-Protestant organizations in Paris had drawn up lists of heretics and these provided the grounds for a methodical massacre such as occurs in all revolutionary riots—an appalling law of history and one in which there is, alas, no exception, to whatever ideological or mystical creeds the rival camps may belong. There is no such thing as spontaneous terrorism or anarchy. With the aid of carefully drawn-up lists of suspects such matters are always prepared in advance by agitators. In fact Catherine de Medici had handed Paris over to Catholic democracy. The Matins of Paris were the distant forerunner of the League.[1]

According to whether they are Catholic or Protestant the historians, like the pamphleteers, give greater or lesser numbers of the victims of Saint Bartholomew in Paris and the provinces, for the vengeance on the Huguenots gradually spread throughout the kingdom. In view of the conflicting figures, from the 10,000 given by Papyre Masson to the 100,000 of Péréfixe (the odd thing being that Péréfixe was Archbishop of Paris after having been the tutor of Louis XIV and that his *Vie de Henri le Grand* was written for the young king

---

[1] Read with reservations, on account of the author's prejudices and deliberate omissions, Chapter V of *L'Histoire de la Réforme française* (Vol. I), by John Viénot, concerning Saint-Bartholomew, is of the greatest interest. It proves to the hilt that on that day Catholic extremism was more powerful than the monarchy.

and appeared in 1661) it is objectively impossible to give any exact number of the victims. The English archives contain accounts from witnesses who favoured the Protestants; they agree with Papyre Masson in his short *Historia Vitae Caroli Valesii* and this agreement is worthy of note since Masson was the King's historian and had sources at his disposal which today have disappeared. He mentioned 2,000 victims in Paris and 10,000 in the provinces. In comparing the *Martyrologe* of Crespin and the very detailed examination made in his *Dissertation sur la Saint-Barthélemy*, published in 1758, by the Abbé Jean Novi de Caveirac, the famous eighteenth-century controversialist and apologist for the revocation of the edict of Nantes, we find that out of an alleged total of 15,168 martyrs, the Protestant authors were able only to name 786. The number of those mentioned by name is astonishingly low in relation to the whole in view of the fact that the lists included the most humble names.[1]

But whatever may be the case with regard to the number of dead, it was a fact that Royalty was once again reduced to impotence. Impotent wisdom was succeeded by mad impotence; the situation was infinitely more serious, for the sovereign had destroyed his own powers of arbitration.

Catherine, Gallican and anti-Spanish, was faced with the ruin and wreckage of her policy of public welfare. The Emperor and Elizabeth of England, on whom she had based such splendid hopes of an alliance, were against her. Switzerland, the Northern monarchies, Poland, Turkey, understood at once that the King of France had lost control of his subjects and no longer counted. All the diplomatic despatches, those sent by the French Government after the Matins of Paris, in which the contradictions and lies are obvious, as well as those it received, in which the diplomatic style in usage barely concealed their underlying contempt, expose the confusion of the

[1] On all this cf. the book by the Abbé Lefortier: La Saint-Barthélemy, as one-sided in the opposite sense, as that of Viénot, but equally rich in documentation and facts. When the impartial historian compares the claims of the Protestant hagiographers with the Catholic case, he notes once again that the only way to discover the truth regarding these sectarian quarrels is to revert to the sources and the works of both camps. Should one, as certain authors have suggested, stop at 1,000 victims classified by name, or with the Calvinist La Popelinière, at roughly 2,000? On our part we attach the greatest importance to the *Histoire de France depuis 1550 jusqu'en 1577*, published in 1581 by the Companion de La Noue, who having always remained both a Royalist and a Protestant, both perfectly honest and a moderate, with Jacques-Auguste Thou on the whole provides the best source. We admit that our preference for them both derives from the fact that Rome condemned the latter's book, and the synod of La Rochelle that of the former. This twofold partisan condemnation is a guarantee of the impartiality of both authors.

Queen Mother and her legislators. Just as, in spite of her repeated orders, she had been unable to stop the massacre, so now she was unable to delude anyone. The Huguenots threw over the fiction in which they had sincerely believed, of the rebellion being linked with loyalty to the King. The correspondence, letters and libels on the Protestant side no longer distinguished between the King and the enemies of the Religion. As Hauser said very well, Saint Bartholomew 'had given an impetus to all the democratic possibilities inherent in Calvinism in spite of itself and against Calvin's will. What John Knox did in Scotland, what the Netherlands ministers were doing under William the Silent, was happening in France and in French circles in Geneva.... And, a natural reversal of values, at the moment when Protestant polemics became republican (or at any rate *patriotic* according to the meaning of this word in the Low Countries) Catholic polemics withdrew from opposing and began to confuse the rights of the Prince and the right of God. That is how France, the scene of the most tragic episodes in the religious war, became the centre of European political ideology and of irreconcilable conflicts.'

The battle on which Catherine had insisted had ended in disaster. Indomitable fighter that she was, she first of all covered her retreat. She had gambled and lost; now she paid up, without arguing. She went over to the victors. Machiavellism had failed her because she was a woman and a mother before she was a politician. Faced with the domestic tragedy of her sons' mutual hatred and the submission of the elder to Coligny, the Queen had given way to the woman. Yet Machiavellism was an instrument that should not be discarded. Since violence adopted for reasons of State had only made the situation worse it were better to resort to perfidy. Catherine pulled herself together with her usual will-power. She would lie to everyone and she would not be believed—that she knew. Nevertheless, behind this smoke-screen of lies that she would spread over the battlefield on which she had been beaten, the Florentine Queen would be able to retreat in order to prepare her rehabilitation.

Her genius for dissimulation and deceit was now to be given full rein. From a moral point of view it was a sorry spectacle, but for the historian and politician one more fascinating than ever. 'Princes who adapt their behaviour to a given situation,' said Machiavelli, 'are seldom unlucky and Fortune only changes for those who do not know how to conform to their times. . . . Also, circumstances determine whether or not a prince had behaved well or badly on such an occasion. There are times when extreme caution is necessary, others when the prince must be prepared to take a chance, but nothing is more difficult than to change one's conduct or character at the right moment, either because we are unable to give up our habits and inclinations or else because we cannot decide to give up a course that has always served us well.'

The moment had come to give up the course of the policy of compassion and to howl with those wolves whom one had made the mistake of unleashing. After the shock of the Matins of Paris, the Huguenots were for a time routed, of no account, lacking cadres and reduced to sterile fury and threats. And for the time being also the Catholics, now Guisards, Spaniards and Papists, could not be brought back to obedience. Madame Catherine would follow the same line; she too would also become a fine and thorough exterminator of heretics. By having forced him into taking on the responsibility of signing the order for the executions, she had Charles IX under her thumb, and also Anjou through his complicity in carrying them out. Alençon was still a child; Margot, after her Ruddy Wedding, no longer counted; and the Princes of the Blood had been forcibly converted. It was only necessary to play out the comedy for Spain, Rome, the Guises, Paris, drunk with blood, and the Catholic brotherhoods that controlled the provinces. The people were acclaiming her as Mother of the realm and Guardian of Christianity. Her role was ready for her to step into—Madame Catherine would become the defender of the true faith against the insurgent heretics.

A zealous champion, naturally. Rome, the Escorial, Paris would see to it that the Queen Mother would not stop half-way on such an excellent road. They remembered that barely a fortnight had passed since in her joy at the Béarnais marriage she had ordered medallions to be struck, bearing the monograms of Henri and Marguerite surrounded by a symbolic knot with the legend *Constricta hoc discordia vinclo*. On the reverse side was the Pascal Lamb with *Vobis annuntio pacem*. People were delighted by Madame Catherine's conversion but thought it wiser, nevertheless, to keep an eye on her, for this sudden change had made them suspicious. In order to blot out the memory of Margot's wedding medallion the Queen had three more struck, in honour of the Matins of Paris. One of them resuscitated the motto chosen in the past for Charles IX by the Chancellor L'Hospital, at this moment in his retirement at Vignay weeping for the homicidal madness of men: *Pietas excitavit justitiam*. Another ran *Virtus in rebelles*, and the third, *Ne ferrum temnat simul ignibus obsto*. The use of fire to temper the iron—this delicate allegory was sure to please Philip II, who was fond of the purifying flames, more efficacious than iron. The French ambassador at Madrid was instructed to flatter the Catholic King and to proclaim Charles IX's and his mother's zeal for the true faith. Catherine was also breathing more freely for having escaped the Admiral's avengers. This was even visibly so. The Duke of Savoy's envoy, the Sieur d'Elbène, noticed it; he found her rejuvenated, like someone recovering from a serious illness. She had been dreadfully frightened. Fear had caused her to enter into a desperate battle, a battle which she had lost. But if not her honour, at least her life was saved. For Catherine, who was never embarrassed by scruples or false sentiments, this was the essential thing.

In her interviews and letters she redoubled her promises. The Nuncio Salviati was delighted; the peace of Saint Germain was wiped out and there would no longer be two religions in France. But it was not to be enough for Gregory XIII. On November 20th, the new pontiff, faithful to the policy of Pius V, demanded the complete extermination of the Huguenots through his legate, Orsini. Whatever the over-zealous Catholic apologists may say, claiming for the Holy See in the middle of the sixteenth century a purely imaginary horror of bloodshed, the documents confirm it. Like Calvin, Pope of Geneva, like Henry VIII and Elizabeth I, like Philip II, the sovereign pontiffs belonged to their own period. The heretic, that is whoever holds beliefs contrary to the faith professed by the prince, must perish. The fact that after Saint Bartholomew Catherine was reduced to denying the entirely contrary opinions she held with regard to the relations between the State and the Churches, which are her abiding glory and caused her to be a disciple of Erasmus in thought as much as of Machiavelli in action, allows us to measure the depth of her defeat.

Behind a mask of zeal for the extermination of the Huguenots she lost no time in regaining lost ground. Her task was a hard one but nothing discouraged Catherine. The instructions given to the ambassadors to the Protestant sovereigns allow us to follow the Queen Mother's efforts—(Charles IX obeyed her in everything, crushed by his memories of the massacres he had authorized in the unwitting intoxication of his fury)—to pick up the threads of her traditional diplomacy. We know from a passage in her letter of October 1, 1572, to Du Ferrier, her ambassador at Venice, that her enmity towards Spain was unchanged. Speaking of Philip II, 'he who caused my daughter to die', she underlined that 'in the then state of his kingdom the King my son could not avenge himself, but now that it is all of one piece he will have enough means and strength to resent it.' As early as September 1st she had declared to Walsingham, the English ambassador, that the edict of pacification would be upheld and freedom of conscience respected. Negotiations with the German Lutheran princes were not in any way broken off. On the contrary the documents prove that after Saint Bartholomew there was a redoubling of the French diplomatic activity that had been kept up with regard to these princes from the beginning of the reign of Charles IX. Schomberg on the French side and Languet on the German were the eager intermediaries in these relations.

Meanwhile Catherine covered herself as regarded the Catholics by letting the Admiral's body be dragged to Montfaucon, by attending the execution of Briquemault and Cavaignes, condemned for being involved in the plot—whether true or false—which had been the cause of the massacre, and by ordering the Parliament to resume the proceedings of 1569. The Protestants' conspiracy was confirmed and the execution of the conspirators authorized by the highest jurisdiction of the kingdom. In this way Saint Bartholomew became a slaughter for which the Guises and the people of Paris were made responsible, quite distinct, with all its excesses, from the legal execution of Coligny and his accomplices. After the King, the Parliament of Paris gave legal sanction to the Queen's destruction of her enemy. Thenceforward she was able to dissociate her policy towards the Protestants who remained faithful subjects from the implacable repression that she had been obliged to exercise in the case of the Protestant conspirators. After the Matins of Paris it appeared much more difficult to bring about a return to the policy that had followed the Tumult of Amboise, but it was not an impossiblity and Catherine was an expert at restoring matters in that way. The marvel is that she succeeded in doing so in less than a year, whilst she bestowed the Crown of Poland on her son and ended the Fourth War of Religion.

This war had begun in very different circumstances from the first three. A large number of Huguenots had emigrated immediately after Saint Bartholomew, taking refuge in Switzerland, Germany and England. They belonged mostly to the small and middle bourgeoisie and to the educated classes. The nobility of sword or of robe, by and large, the big and higher bourgeoisie, as well as the peasants, mostly remained, the former having too many important interests to safeguard in France, and the latter attached to their soil above all else. During Saint Bartholomew's Night the nobility had been decapitated and the greatest noblemen had either disappeared or abjured their religion. The new cadres were provided by the country gentry, very close to the people, or by officers, whose sole reason for existence, ever since Amboise, was fighting. The Fourth Religious War, therefore, was a rising of lower-class people, led by those noblemen who were closest to them, and of professional fighters in civil wars. It was a precedent of the Camisards, a kind of Calvinist Vendée and even Chouannerie, in which the faithful, incited by the ministers, fought with extreme ferocity, fighting commune by commune, without any general organization, throughout the kingdom.

La Rochelle was the principal urban centre of the resistance and appealed for help to England. In addition there were two others—Sancerre in Berry, and Sommières in Languedoc. The extreme gravity of the rising was much less on the military than on the political plane; for the first time the Huguenots were fighting against the King and no longer had a Prince of the Blood as their leader; the rabid democracy of the extremist elements in the party spread from man to man. A Protestant form of republicanism was being born, a curious mixture of feudal or communal survivals and Biblical theocracy in the form of new cadres led by the small nobility and the preachers. Catherine's intelligence immediately discovered the point of danger, La Rochelle, a powerful maritime and commercial city, an English invasion base manned by regular troops. Six days after the Matins of Paris she sent reassurances to the townspeople. The massacre at Bordeaux, one of the most terrible after that of Paris, had made a deep impression on those local leaders who were inclined to come to terms with the Court, and drew them towards the resistance party. The Queen Mother, deeply engaged in her Polish negotiations for having her son Henri elected king, needed to proceed carefully with the Huguenots, as many members of the Diet were Calvinists or Lutherans.

The Protestant Bayard, La Noue, remained a royalist, prepared to sacrifice everything to national unity. He agreed to negotiate with La Rochelle and the city gave him the command of its troops. Catherine de Medici, still without an army capable of striking a decisive blow, was having no success whatever in repressing the local revolts. If La Rochelle gave in it would be possible to stamp out the little centres of incendiarism scattered throughout France.

La Noue, outwitted by the preachers who were in control of the city, could do nothing with the citizens, who were determined on war. It was necessary to send the Dukes of Anjou and Alençon to besiege the stronghold, on February 11, 1573. Despite La Noue's efforts a compromise was impossible. The fanaticism of the ministers of the Religion roused the masses against him.

This admirable man, a rarer and rarer exception in times of civil war, persisted in placing France before any faction, and finally retired in discouragement to the royal camp on March 14th. His gesture was the first isolated and astonishing affirmation, which was however to be fruitful, of Huguenot adherence to the apparently new policy of the politicals, that of the union of all Frenchmen, whether belonging to one or the other religion, around the throne. In reality this policy, that of Catherine de Medici and the Chancellor, L'Hospital, was already twelve years old. By a moving coincidence, one of those mysterious supernatural events by which, unknown to contemporaries, the resurrection of a nation is adumbrated, L'Hospital died at Vignay on March 15th, at the very moment when La Noue, without bearing arms against his co-religionists, went over to the King for the sake of peace. After Saint Bartholomew the Chancellor had written a sublime letter to the King, which ended thus: 'Sire, I pray to God to grant you His grace, and to lead you by His hand to the government of this great and beautiful realm, with all gentleness and clemency towards your subjects, in imitation of Him who is good and patient in bearing with our offences and prompt to raise us up and forgive our faults.' That great man, who had been accused of heresy, died a devout Catholic. In his retirement at Vignay he had never failed to practice his religion. The evidence of the Cardinal d'Este, showing him attending mass, confession and communion, is irrefutable.

L'Hospital died a Catholic—La Noue, a Calvinist, withdrew from La Rochelle in order to be nothing else but a royalist, but without in any way renouncing his Protestant allegiance. By a temporal coincidence, and in spite of spatial separation, without knowing what they were doing, so these two just men were handing on the torch of patriotism over and above all parties, a torch that was to be upheld often by feeble and at times even by unworthy hands, and the flame of which Catherine would preserve throughout another sixteen years of trials, vicissitudes and errors. Yet the Matins of Paris would never recur. Never again would the Governess of France become the prisoner of any party. During those sixteen years, which were to include three more wars, she was to resume her policy of 1561, which Michel de L'Hospital had carried out so flawlessly, and even although she was occasionally to fail she would never again renounce it.

The Fourth War of Religion occurred simultaneously with the founding of the party of the Politicals. This party had existed, virtually, since the edict of January 1562, and although they did not at that time form a definite group it included the guardians of that edict. At the same time there was also the party of the Discontented (Malcontents), the name of which is a good description of the characteristic state of mind of Frenchmen throughout the centuries, and which in the end the former party was to absorb. The political party brought together moderate Catholics and realistic Protestants. In his essential and irreplaceable book on *Le Parti des Politiques au lendemain de la Saint-Barthélemy*, Francis de Crue stressed this word, then a new term, *réaliste*, which he assumed to be 'derived, no doubt, from the first syllable of the word "Republic" (*res*). There were numerous names given to the guardians of the public welfare. In addition to the names of *Politiques*, *Malcontents*, *Realistes*, in Poitou they called themselves *Publicains* and in Languedoc, *Fronts d'airain*. They were all for reforms of the same kind—for good order in finance and justice and for religious and civil liberty. They flattered themselves that they had found the solution for the social problems in the convocation of the States-General and of a National Council, both of them working for religious reconciliation. The party's main objective was civil peace. That was why, in warlike France, it acquired a bad reputation'.

The politicals revived L'Hospital's line of thought as well as the best ideas of Anne de Montmorency and that was why the Constable's sons played such an important part in the formation of this party, a party that was also in conformity with Catherine de Medici's real wishes. The domestic tragedy which had set her sons against one another prevented her from leading it, to the greater misfortune of France. The ambitions of the youngest of them, François, transformed this group, of which the *raison d'être* had been the search for peace, into another element of civil war.

The diplomacy of Jean de Monluc, the marvellously intelligent and able collaborator of the Queen Mother, enabled her to bring to a successful issue the very delicate negotiations as the result of which the Duc d'Anjou was elected King of Poland on May 9, 1573. This affair, in which she was delighted to be able to combine politics and maternal love, was Catherine's own work. Thus the Queen of France gained an ally in the distant east, whose importance no one at that time suspected except the Queen Mother, who possessed quite unusual knowledge, not only of Europe, but also of countries like Poland and Muscovy, which, to her contemporaries appeared still to lie in the shadows, and by acquiring this ally she rounded off the Turkish alliance and contained the Empire, drawing Poland into the French orbit and away from Spain. In Catherine's mind there was an even more magnificent alliance to be won and placed side by side with Henri d'Anjou's accession to the Polish throne, namely the marriage of François d'Alençon with Elizabeth I of England. As the son-in-law of the Emperor, brother of the King of Poland, and brother-in-law of the Queen of England, Charles IX would stand in the centre of the network of political and diplomatic matrimonial alliances ranged against the ambitions of Philip II.

None of her three sons were interested in their mother's farsighted schemes. Anjou did not want to go to Poland, because by doing so he would forever lose the Princesse de Condé, that Marie de Clèves whom he hoped to marry, thanks to an annulment of her former marriage, and whose lover he had become. Alençon refused to marry Elizabeth; he was appalled by the age and the legendary sexual reputation of that princess (he was twenty-one years younger than she, who was just forty). Charles IX was debauching himself, hunting, splitting donkeys in half, strangling sheep and pigs, and making love with Marie Touchet in a state of tuberculous frenzy, in an endeavour to forget Saint Bartholomew. Catherine preferred to see him thus degraded to the opposition he had shown her at the time of the Admiral's influence. She found no support at all in this unfortunate wearer of the crown. Owing to her wily intrigues, both in London and in Cracow, she was dubbed Madame la Serpente by her son Alençon's agent, a Huguenot adventurer by name of Maison-fleur, at one and the same time a swordsman, a courtier, and a man letters, who helped his master to deceive her in that incredible comedy of the dupes that the English marriage remained until the end, but to which she clung with her usual tenacity.

In spite of the war of the Protestant libels, all kinds of intrigues, the risings and the interminable siege of La Rochelle, Madame Catherine succeeded in Poland, was gaining ground in England, refused to enter the universal League against the Grand Turk, or to accept the decrees of the Council of Trent. Little by little she returned, at the price of the most prodigious deceits of her career (to

XXIII MEN XI DIES III REGNAVIT AN
MEN V DIES XXIIII OBIIT AN D M
IXXIIIIII KAL IVNII

13. CHARLES IX. School of Clouet   (*Musée de Louvre*)

14a. HENRI, PRINCE DE CONDÉ. Contemporary drawing
(*Musée de Louvre*)

14b. HENRI, DUC DE GUISE (*Bibliothèque Nationale*)

follow them would require a whole book, which would be captivating[1] but which it is impossible to reduce to a synthesis of a few pages) to her policy of compassion, her Gallican policy, directed towards the Moslem, Lutheran, and English alliances, faithful to her alliance with Venice and always very careful in her attitude towards Spain and the Empire. She did not even hesitate to state in public, after the useless visit of the Cardinal-legate Orsini—'In future I shall not allow the Pope to meddle in the affairs of France.' On that day she threw away her mask. She was delivered from the weight of the Catholic consequences of Saint Bartholomew. Elizabeth, godmother to Charles IX's daughter, was only feeding fine words to the people of La Rochelle, as the wise La Noue had foreseen. It was an empty meal, which could not put an end to the increasing threat of famine, in spite of the unusual abundance of shellfish, according to the pastors new manna from Heaven.

It was a favourable moment, what with the Polish success and Elizabeth's friendly attitude. . . . Madame Catherine could negotiate with the Huguenots. By her masterly diplomacy she had wiped out the immediate consequences of her political mistake of August 24, 1572. It had taken her two years to do so.[2]

The fact that in those days there was no newspaper press certainly favoured secrecy, the *sine qua non* of all diplomacy, but on the other hand it made it impossible for the government to direct public opinion according to its needs by press campaigns inspired from above. No doubt our ancestors were far more and better informed than we generally assume, as Lucien Febvre has shown. There were relatively few false rumours, which were the speciality of hawkers, whom the police pursued. But there was almost perfect secrecy regarding those matters that their rulers wished to conceal from their subjects, thanks to the loyalty of confidential agents who when required preserved an obstinate and admirable silence. When we compare the official despatches and the memoirs of even the most important contemporary diarists it is astonishing to see how little the latter knew, unless they were members of the Council, secretaries

---

[1] This book was published by Pierre Champion whilst we were finishing the first draft of our own, twenty years ago. Nothing remains to be added to it. Once and for all, as regards the last two years of Charles IX we refer the reader to this authority. There are only very few points on which we disagree with him.

[2] A complementary volume could be written on the *Diplomatie de Catherine de Médicis*. There is an incomparable wealth of material on the subject in the archives, partly published but which still contain vast unexplored gaps. Our investigations lead us to think that Catherine's diplomatic achievements equalled her political ones.

of State, confidential clerks or ambassadors, of the facts contained in the dusty archives, which for that very reason are so moving and exciting. This was why Madame Catherine was able so freely to dissimulate her schemes until they bore fruit, to a degree that today is almost unimaginable, and it also explains the very great importance attached to the espionage services of the embassies. Since the Revolution and the Empire, espionage has been more or less confined to military matters. At the time of the Valois it was almost entirely concerned with diplomacy; resources, mobilization, strategy, being of very little import. After Saint Bartholomew, French Protestantism was a blind Argus, for there was no longer anyone left in the Councils who could pass on information to it. The obstacles to the Queen Mother's stratagems had practically all disappeared. This was the deeper reason for the complete and apparently so surprising recovery of her foreign policy after the Matins of Paris. But she was to lose the exceptionally advantageous position in which this placed her when the Duc d'Alençon and the Princes of the Blood took over the leadership of the Political party. We can therefore understand why Madame Catherine tried to keep them captive with the ferociousness of a Cerberus.

In order to acquire the approval of Poland Catherine needed religious peace in France. On June 24, 1573, the Treaty of La Rochelle ended the Fourth War, by restoring to the Protestants the rights they had obtained under the peace of Saint Germain—freedom of practice for all those noblemen under the higher judiciary; christenings and marriages to be recognized as valid. The edict of Poitiers confirmed and laid down in detail the clauses and the execution of this Treaty, which made the Catholic defeat clear by exempting La Rochelle, Nîmes and Montauban from occupation as Royal garrisons, and by allowing assemblies in these two latter cities. The Huguenots immediately took advantage of these concessions to demand new guarantees—the rehabilitation of the victims of Saint Bartholomew as well as prosecution of the murderers; restitution of their property, offices, and dignities; admission to schools on terms of complete equality with the Catholics; the maintenance at the King's expense of the ministers of the new religion and of the militia guarding the Protestant cities; the granting of two strongholds; the establishment of a Reformed chamber in the Parliaments.

At the time when they were under the orders of the Princes of the Blood and the great noblemen the Huguenots had never dared to formulate such demands. It was now a matter of creating a genuine

Protestant Union in France. In December 1573 and July 1574 the assemblies of Millau worked out the new organization, based on municipal autonomy. At La Rochelle and Montauban real republics were founded and were followed by a federal system with general districts which were to send delegates to the States-General of the Union. In this manner the Protestant League came into being, threatening a state of separatism, for the system which until then had been merely local now became a national one. A Protestant nation was being born in the Kingdom of France. Such was the poisoned fruit of Saint Bartholomew. Catherine had gained an unequalled degree of diplomatic freedom, but at what a price! The political unity of the kingdom was in danger of being destroyed by religious division. After the peace of La Rochelle the Huguenots ceased to be royalists in fact (*de facto*).

The tremendous danger of the country's political situation could not escape the Queen Mother's notice, and to this was added a lamentable economic and health situation.

Things were no better in the Royal Family itself. The Duc d'Anjou refused to leave for Poland, perhaps as much on account of his fears that his brother Alençon would take over the leadership of the discontented with a view to succeeding Charles IX, whose health was steadily worsening, as in despair at the thought of leaving the Princess de Condé and being lost in the lands of the Sarmatians. He had fallen under the influence of the Jesuits when Father Edmond Auger—to his mother's considerable annoyance—had become his confessor and inclined him to follow the advice of the Cardinal de Lorraine, who was supporting a national and international League of Catholic Union to carry on the anti-Protestant crusade. The *Cause commune* of the Huguenots had aroused in the minds of the Jesuits, and their protector the Cardinal, the view that it was necessary to oppose 'League against League'. Tavannes said it: 'Prudence may as well provide men of goodwill with the means to secure their safety as wickedness may give rebels the incentive to offend them.' The Queen Mother had succeeded in re-establishing French diplomacy on its former level, but against this her return to her previous policy of freedom of conscience was being opposed by Huguenot federalism and Catholic Leaguers. Alençon was taking up an increasingly hostile attitude to Anjou, whilst Anjou was exasperating Charles IX by his grand airs as the head of the Catholic party.

Madame Catherine's marked preference for Anjou—which she was unable to hide—did not help to resolve this domestic tragedy, which was only held in check by the very complexity and antagonisms of the interests involved. Only the departure of the new King of Poland for his States would give back her freedom of action to the Queen Mother, the unfortunate Charles IX and the puerile Alençon being obliged to put up with or give way to her, whilst Anjou was playing on her maternal weakness towards him to resist her. Charles IX had only one desire—that his brother should leave for Poland.

Deeply saddened by these family quarrels, grieved (the actual term she used) by the political necessity in which she was placed to part from the King of Poland ('For otherwise I think that I would prevent it', she wrote to the Duc de Nevers), Catherine was indignant at the demands of the Huguenots: 'What these wretched creatures have the insolence to suggest to us!' she cried. But this insolence arose from the fact that the Court was unable to exact obedience from them and was obliged to negotiate with these insolent wretches. At the same time it was necessary to urge Monsieur[1] to leave France and to keep an eye on the Duc d'Alençon, who was preparing to escape to England with the intention of becoming head of the Politicals, allied to the Protestants, and who had been requested by the Flemish to take over the command of their troops against Spain. The Montmorencys were in favour of Alençon's dealings, which both upset and interested Catherine at one and the same time; to have a Son of France as King of the Low Countries would make a fine pendant to the Polish success! The Queen Mother's taste for subtle intrigues was always so keen that she even considered intervening in the Low Countries with the help of the German Lutheran princes. In order to have a free hand she refused to give the Duc d'Alençon the succession to his brother Anjou as Lieutenant-General of the Realm. The hatred this irresponsible, vain and mediocre prince thereupon conceived for his mother was shortly to precipitate him into the direst adventures.

Charles IX, seeing what were François' ambitions, took a strong interest in the English marriage proposals, which would have set him free of him, as the Polish crown had delivered him from Henri. His loathing for his brothers became a sick man's fixed idea. In order to prove to his mother that he was no longer a child, in an interval

---

[1] This title (which was to continue to be used until the end of the legitimate monarchy) given to the younger brother of the King of France first appeared in contemporary documents at this period.

between two relapses he set seriously to work.[1] A few months before his premature end, when he no longer possessed either the strength, the time, or the means, Charles IX suddenly wished to exercise his kingly profession. This was another source of anxiety for Catherine, who arranged to be always informed of the orders he gave and regularly received the ambassadors. Thus she learned through Alamanni of the relations between the Cardinal de Lorraine, the Catholic King and the Emperor, to counteract her efforts at religious pacification. The Guises on the one side, Alençon and the Montmorencys on the other, Protestant democracy beginning to develop under the indifferent eyes of the Politicals, who were only preoccupied by the Lorraines, the State's obvious impotence, the financial distress joined with economic ruin, on which speculators and the new rich battened—all this, with the general misery of the population and universal discontent, combined to favour the ambitions of François d'Alençon, who was taking on the part of redresser of rights and saviour of the realm.

The Protestant agitation was spreading throughout France and simultaneously, also, that of the Guises. Catherine tried in vain to bring the Lorraines and the Montmorencys together. On January 16, 1574, in the Louvre itself, the Duc de Guise wounded with a sword-thrust one of the gentlemen-in-waiting of the Duc d'Alençon, by name of Ventanbran, whom he accused of having been hired by the Montmorencys to assassinate him. Catherine re-lived those past days when the Lorraine princes and the Princes of the Blood had been at grips with one another, but now the situation was even more serious, for a Son of France was the declared leader of the enemies of the House of Guise and thus the party of the Politicals had gone over to those people who instead of serving the State were endeavouring to master it. Never, in the past fourteen years, had the Queen Mother found herself isolated to such a degree. She lacked the support of Anjou, who with his cunning mind, similar to her own, would have given her good advice and great comfort. Even the loyalty of the Swiss Guard, that last military bulwark of the monarchy, was doubtful, owing to the fact that their wages were either unpaid or when paid had been owing for long periods. On all the roads armed bands were committing murders and robberies. The

---

[1] The contents of his correspondence at present in the fonds français of the Manuscript department of the Nationale leaves us in no doubt of this. As far as the weakness caused by the progressive development of his illness allowed him to do so he was working seriously.

peace of La Rochelle and the edict of Poitiers had been shown to be completely illusory. The Royal authority was in fact non-existent, as in the time of the madness of Charles VI.

The Duc d'Alençon was able to pose as the leader of an opposition that was both Royal and feudal thanks to the Montmorencys, of whom the elder, the Marshal, husband of Diane de France, chief of the Privy Council and commander of the Royal armies, enjoyed great prestige with the discontented and with the third party that was coming into being, and who was more anxious to consolidate the State than to serve one or the other religion. (He was called an armed L'Hospital.) The Protestant noblemen and bourgeois had made an alliance with him, of which the Gallican and legislative members of the Parliaments were also in favour. He was assured of the support of the King of Navarre. An armed rising was agreed upon, to take place on March 14, 1574.

The time set for their escape by the two princes was a little before Lent and that was why the affair, when the plan was revealed, became known as the pre-Lenten plot (*complot des jours gras*). At the last moment the whole scheme collapsed as the result of the cowardice of the Duc d'Alençon. He was too much in fear of his mother to go through with it. Catherine, warned by the clumsiness of the conspirators, and informed of it by Marguerite de Navarre, who was frightened by the prospect of another Tumult of Amboise, was on guard. Alençon was aware of it. His favourite, Joseph de Boniface de La Molle, a younger son from Provence, who at forty-four still remained very handsome and as irresponsible as a court jester, a more fitting champion of Venus than of Mars, and a butt for the mockery of Pierre de L'Estoile, advised him to reveal the whole story in order to obtain the Queen Mother's pardon. On Saturday evening, February 27, 1574, in Charles IX's private apartment at the castle of Saint Germain, he confessed everything. Catherine threatened her sorry son with the fate of Don Carlos. Appalled, the Duc d'Alençon begged Charles IX to forgive him. Such was the hero of the Politicals. For ten whole years Catherine was to be opposed by this snivelling puppet, who dragged himself on his knees in front of a brother whom he detested, allowed himself to be terrorized by his mother, and was as incorrigibly addicted to intrigues as he was incapable of carrying them through. When he was challenged, in his turn Henri de Béarn retained all his self-control, very cleverly claiming that he had been seeking nothing but an opportunity to regain his kingdom. He was forgiven. Condé was acquitted on the grounds of having been no more than an accessory and not a conspirator. Whilst the entire Court fled, believing that there would be a Saint Bartholomew of the Catholics, which caused those days to be known as the Panic of Saint Germain, Catherine de Medici, perfectly in command of herself, returned to Paris, keeping Alençon and Navarre under her own eye, the only one on which she could rely. A few days later the Court was installed at the castle of Vincennes, which was easily defended. The disembarkation in Normandy on March 11th of Montgomery, arriving from England, heralded a new attempt. The escape of the two princes was arranged by using as go-betweens La Molle and his friend, the Piedmontese Count Annibal de Coconat, a splendid ruffian, who was the captain of François d'Alençon's bodyguard. The affair was well organized. They even managed to enlist the help of Madame Catherine's astrologer, Nostradamus' successor, Cosimo Ruggieri. The date fixed upon was April 8th. The Queen Mother was kept fully informed of every move, thanks to the spying of Charlotte de Sauves, who whilst still the mistress of the Duc d'Alençon had taken the King of Navarre as her lover in order to keep an eye on both princes, and who detested La Molle and Coconat. Although the former was the lover of her own daughter Marguerite and the latter of the Duchesse de Nevers, Catherine had both gentlemen arrested.

This political and amorous conspiracy, outwardly apparently frivolous, had a serious side to it which did not escape Catherine's attention. If Navarre and Alençon were at liberty the rebellion might have claimed royal participation and thus have rallied around it a large number of those who were still hesitating whether to join it, not only among the Huguenots but also among the Politicals. The princes, the Marshals de Montmorency and Cossé and even the favourite necromancer were arrested. The affair ended with the beheading of La Molle and Coconat, and the ladies of the Court, when they watched them mount the scaffold, were so moved by their handsomeness that they regarded them as martyrs. If the diarists are to be believed, their decapitated heads were carried away in the hands of their mistresses. But they were only false martyrs, in reality mere adventurers, who had become extremely dangerous owing to their intimacy with the Royal Family. Ruggieri was only condemned to the galleys and was soon pardoned. As at Saint Germain, Alençon had confessed everything. Navarre had claimed to be in fear of murder by the Guises. He never lost his presence of mind and defended himself skilfully.

The imprisonment of the marshals and the disgracing of Mont-morency-Damville, Governor of Languedoc, were inefficacious. In spite of the capture of Montgomery at Domfront on May 25th and his beheading on the following June 26th, in the presence of Catherine herself, prosecuting with implacable hatred to the very end the man who had caused the death of Henri II, the Protestant forces were considerably strengthened by the truce of seven months' duration that Montmorency-Damville signed with them four days later. The Politicals and the Huguenots were in spite of everything drawing more closely together. The sinister consequences of the Matins of Paris had not yet come to an end. With all her energy and subtlety Catherine de Medici could not succeed in restoring the political situation at home, as she had done abroad. The cause of this failure lay in her family struggles. In these she sacrificed reason to sentiment, Machiavellism to maternal love of the most tyrannical and short-sighted kind, her preference for Anjou, and added to this she pursued the Marshal de Montmorency, who was an enemy of the new King of Poland, with typically feminine spite.

'My dear eyes,' she called the victor of Moncontour. Those eyes this woman who had never had a love affair idolized with all the passion of a maternal love that had awakened late in life, the reason for it being that she believed in her adored son's genius and imagined him to be an heroic figure. She worshipped him all the more as the progress of Charles IX's disease made it clear that he would soon die, when the King of Poland would become King of France. What a marvellous collaborator he would then become for her! Catherine was determined without further delay to break the Montmorencys, the assured rivals of Charles IX's successor. Her passion blinded her to the fact that the Politicals, from being the natural supporters of the State, would become her enemies and that a prince of no account like the Duc d'Alençon would serve them as a royal figurehead.

Behind the façade provided by d'Alençon, feudalism under cover of apanagism would obtain control of the party of the Politicals and become on that account even more threatening. It would renew the alliance with Protestantism, the democratic elements in which would this time be unequivocally controlled by the pretence that they were fighting for the King. Alençon was a Son of France. This was enough to legalize the revolt, and even better than the claims of lesser Princes of the Blood, of which in any case there was no lack since Navarre and Condé were supporting him. His mother did not realize this; she, although so suspicious, was taken in by François' medio-

crity, by the youth and apparently easy-going nature of Henri de
Navarre and the weakness of Monsieur le Prince. She was all the
more inclined to do so after the death, after terrible agony, of Charles
IX at the castle of Vincennes on May 30, 1574, as the result of which
she became for months the sole ruler of the kingdom. Whilst the
King of Poland was travelling towards France his mother could
meanwhile arrage everything according to her fancy with a view to
the closest political collaboration between them. That, at least, was
what she imagined; everything seemed perfect to her. But although
she was not in the least aware of it her power was never on a more
fragile basis. Events were soon to prove it to her cruelly.

Madame Catherine, however deeply she may in her heart have
mourned the death of her second son, was immensely consoled by
the knowledge that her beloved one was returning from Poland. As a
result, in her exaltation she committed the very great and essentially
feminine political mistake—surprising in this princess who had been
brought up on Machiavelli and Guicciardini—of recalling him
hurriedly. This time she was Regent by right as well as in fact. In
letters in which tenderness was blended with cleverness (she wrote to
Henri III that if she were to lose him she would have herself buried
alive with him, but at the same time described the situation in such
a manner as to reassure him) she showed herself basically anxious
for the pacification of France. Henri III who had been forcibly—the
term is no exaggeration—sent to Poland, fled from his kingdom in
the night of June 18–19, 1574, as soon as the news of his brother's
death reached him. Once he was beyond the pursuit of his subjects
he no longer hurried. At twenty-three, Catherine's hero behaved like
a schoolboy on holiday. Whilst his mother was busily evolving
great political plans, on his journey through Austria, Venice and
Savoy, Henri gave himself up wholeheartedly to all the most frivolous
amusements. Whilst during those three months she was carefully
composing schemes for their joint government, the son with those
'dear eyes' was whiling away his time in extravagant entertainments
and wild dissipation, refusing to pay the slightest attention to anything serious whatever.

Henri III returned to the stage of French history in the character
of a comic king, the *Roi malgré lui* of Emmanuel Chabrier's musical
comedy. Whatever his charms may have been, we are not concerned
with them, for here they count for nothiug. The French ambassador
at Venice, Du Ferrier, who was a good courtier, wrote the Queen

Mother dithyrambic despatches on Henri, complimenting Catherine de Medici on the young King's greatness, on the excellent teaching and education she had given her son. The realistic and independent Venetian ambassadors give us an entirely different picture. Already in 1569 Correro had stressed Monsieur's exclusive predilection for feminine society: 'He delights in the domestic chase, the palace chase.' In 1572 Michele showed him as given over to idleness and voluptuousness, spending all his time in the company of women. In 1574 Morosini, who saw him in Paris, and Lippomano in Cracow, drew a similar portrait of him. It was that of an androgyne, passing from Gomorrha to Sodom.

The most outstanding characteristic of the new King, whose bravery, intelligence, culture, good address, handsome and agreeable appearance, gentle and affable manners everyone agreed in praising, was an unparalleled frivolity. Events were to show that this extraordinary and disconcerting individual, who for fifteen years was to reign over France, freeing himself more and more completely from his mother's tutelage, neither altogether justified some of the praise lavished on him by Du Ferrier, the critical portraits the Venetians drew of him, nor even the caricatures of the libellers or the strange stories of the chroniclers.

Protean, a higher kind of degenerate, an astonishing blend of royal grandeur and personal unworthiness, Henri III escapes the historian for the psychologist, and at that a psychiatrist concerned with mental pathology. His character included one extreme and another, his ambivalence the best and the worst, both in turn and at one and the same time. He was both a legislator and a dancer, according to his mood as wildly active in the ballroom as at his desk; a military man and a player at cup-and-ball; a breeder of pet apes and little dogs; founder of academies, for his culture was immense; as much in love with female as with male beauty; an exemplary husband, although an unfaithful one; now a self-flagellating monk and anon a subtle and serious politician. As we study the constantly changing, infinitely complex moods of his mind, his character and his temperament, seen through his letters and speeches and compared with the widest range of evidence, Henri III appears above all else as a clinical case. His contemporaries really could not understand him at all. Henri III might have stemmed from the imagination of a novelist and a pervert—had Péladan and Proust been historians he would have been their favourite hero—as well as having inherited some of his mother's genius, both worthy of being admired by those historians who admire Machiavalli and Guicciardini and condemned by the successors of the satirical authors of *L'Ile des Hermaphrodites*. The Henri III of Paul de Saint-Victor and his 'twofold sacred and profane orgy', the Heliogabalus of the Renaissance, is almost as close to the truth as the man described by Pierre Champion, 'remaining calm, legislating, reorganizing his Council, working with his servants', or the man depicted by Pierre Lafue and Philippe Erlanger, who rightly pay homage to the King who died for France.

Whilst he was so slowly returning to his kingdom, Henri III was no more than a decadent Caesar on holiday, who did not even trouble to write to his mother, who finally grew anxious. The Huguenots were threatening; England, the Protestant Swiss cantons and the Palatinate were drawing closer to them. Madame Catherine left for Lyons, at the same time sending Henri III a memorandum by Cheverny. Taking her precautions as usual, she took her son-in-law Navarre and her son Alençon along with her, never leaving them alone for a moment. This memorandum reveals that she was in full possession of her powers, in the plenitude of her genius. It is the very essence of intelligence, in which the woman of superior political gifts appears once more to have triumphed over the impassioned mother. In fewer than 200 lines, closely written, precise and pellucid in their firm realism, based on her experience of fifteen years of power, she drew up a programme of government which is an authentic masterpiece. Had it been carried out it would have brought salvation to France.[1]

Whatever illusions she may have had regarding the greatness and the talents of her son, Madame Catherine knew only too well how inclined he was to surround himself with favourites, and did not fail to put him on guard against them. Let him choose his servants according to their merits and not by favouritism, and 'provide for his estates, not for individuals, for it is of damage to one's service if in order to recompense a person one bestows on him a post of which he is unworthy'. She particularly warned him against keeping an all-powerful favourite: 'Let one man not hold all.' As examples she cited Louis XI and François I, who knew how to select their ministers and clerks. She advised the same regarding the bishops. Let the King

---

[1] The autographed copy of this memorandum, an incomparable document, was discovered by La Ferrière in the fonds français of the Manuscript department of the Bibliothèque Nationale, No. 6525, fo. 49. It is included in the fifth volume of the *Lettres*, pp. 73–75.

first control himself, in order to be able to control everything else. Let him go into everything, deal with everything himself, seeing and verifying all documents, receiving people personally. Let him guard his own secrets and himself hold the key to his cipher. Let him waste no time in carrying out his Royal office: 'Let him begin to do all these things immediately on arrival, for if he were not to do so at the beginning, he would never do so and would see again as much disorder as he has seen, and this must not be, I beg him of it.'

Ever faithful to the Capetian tradition, the Queen Mother recommended him firstly to administer justice, to be firm, and not to pardon too easily. With Machiavelli and Guicciardini, the Governess of France taught her son to hate no one and to love all his subjects, providing that they were obedient. As a provident bourgeoise and a Florentine expert at dealing with financial matters she stressed this point: 'Let the treasurer of the Exchequer bring to him every morning the sum that he ordered on the previous day, and a weekly statement of all his expenses.' The Council of Finance should be abolished. Let the new King reign and govern. He will find faithful servants 'when it is seen that he intends to restore matters as they were during the time of his father and grandfather, for everyone will hope to see the good times return'.

And Madame Catherine—who never deluded herself when in the solitude of her study, with a sheet of fresh paper on her desk, all feminine weakness removed, her mind solely that of a statesman—recalled her own previous failures, in such marked contrast to her advice. 'One may say, as she knows so well how to say and write all this, why did she herself not do it sooner? Had I been in the position in which I am now I would have done so, and since I have been, one does know how everything is going, thank God.' She was in fact delivered from all the masters of the palace, and the only one of them who was still living, the Cardinal de Lorraine, was too much of a coward to be dangerous. By the Cardinal's death on December 26, 1574, even this last opponent disappeared. The way was open. Let Henri III realize it: 'He will soon see that, if it please him, on arriving from there and with so high a reputation he can do everything; but let him desire to do so. . . .'

But let him desire to do so. . . . That was the last thing the Prince was worrying about whilst he was amusing himself in Italy, and in order to please his aunt of Savoy presented her with the French stronghold in Piedmont, giving her those citadels as if they were

rings, with thoughtless gallantry dipping into the contents of the
kingdom as if it were his private jewel-case. Whilst his mother was
governing France from Lyons, he was mutilating it in the midst of
the festivities of Turin. When he at last arrived on September 5th in
the metropolis of the Gauls, after the maternal and filial effusions of
their meeting at Bourgoin, Madame Catherine, much more worried
by her son's incurable flightiness than she appeared to be, set about
the immediate reform of the Council. This was to include no more
than eight members on whom the Queen Mother could rely—
Birague, Chancellor; Morvillier, Limoges, Foix, Pibrac, Valence,
Cheverny, Bellièvre; bishops or legislators, all of them wholeheartedly in favour of her policy of royal and national unity. In
future the Princes would only attend the Council by invitation.
Bellièvre, superintendent of the Treasury, would in future take
orders only directly from the King, who reserved to himself the right
of signature which for so long had been usurped by ministers and
secretaries of State.

Catherine had imposed on Henri III the programme of the memorandum she had sent him by Cheverny. She imposed it and her son
endured it. Very quickly he returned to his pleasures, his caprices,
his extravagances, which he exaggerated by adopting the attitude of
an Oriental despot, a completely artificial one since by nature he was
debonair. This pose made him appear like a Sarmatian with tyrannical leanings, both ridiculous and intolerable, and caused people to
forget that on the other hand he remained easy of access and gracious.
The changes in court appointments which he made in order to
wreak his spite on the entourage of Charles IX finally discredited
him. When Jacques-Auguste de Thou asked the Lieutenant-
General of the Limousin, Simon Dubois, what he predicted of the
new King, he replied: 'Nothing good . . . it is with the deepest sorrow
that I have to tell you so, but events will only too soon prove me
right.' In a few weeks everyone was agreeing with Dubois and at
court nobody took Henri III's fancies seriously. The young King
permitted everything to those of his friends who had gone with him
to Poland and despised his mother's wise advice.

All this became known very quickly. The Huguenots, encouraged
by the spectacle of the *Roi malgré lui* of Poland, who had become the
comic King of France, and the Politicals, shocked by a King who
apparently refused to take France seriously, tightened their alliance.
Catherine persisted in believing that the hero of Jarnac and Moncontour still survived in Henri III. She neglected to deal with the

gathering revolt to a degree that was soon to be punished. The war of the libellers against the King and his mother was reaching a climax. The very exaggeration of their calumnies amused Catherine and prevented her from seeing how serious was the position behind all this frenzied literature.

Firstly there was the offensive against the Italians. The Queen Mother was accused of having handed over France to Ausonian favourites—to the Milanese Chancellor, René de Birague; to the Florentine, Filippo Strozzi, Colonel-General of the Infantry; to the Gondi tribe—Alberto, the Marshal, Giovanni-Battista, Farmer of the Revenue; to Zametti, Ajjacetti and Sardini and all the Italian leeches; the Duc de Nevers was a Mantuan. It was effective, for the French had never liked seeing foreigners employed by the State. Like Catherine, Mazarin was also to experience it, in spite of the immense services he rendered to the country.[1] Another attack was launched against the policy to which Catherine was addicted— *divide ut regnes*, taken from ancient Rome—setting the Guises against the Montmorencys and the Châtillons, the Huguenots against the Catholics. If one does not enjoy such power as was wielded by the Senate of Rome, one thus fosters civil war. She was a poisoner, a necromancer, a monster of hypocrisy—no insult was lacking. Were the French to resign themselves to such tyranny? There was an infinite number of such libels. The vilest collection of them, perhaps, is the *Discours merveilleux de la Vie, actions et Déportements de Catherine de Médicis*, an *in-octavo* volume that appeared in 1575, brought out during the Regency, after the death of Charles IX. It is a very clever pamphlet. That it was inspired by the Montmorencys is clear from the praise it contains of François d'Alençon, whose hatred for his maternal gaoler was well-known. It is uncertain who was the author of this *Discours*. Was it Henri Estienne or Jean de Serres? According to Lenient it was the latter. The historical sympathies of the author are obvious. We ourselves are inclined to think that it was by Régnier de la Planche, on account of its similarities in form and content to *Le Livre des Marchands*, which appeared in 1565 under the title *Du grand et loyal devoir, fidélité et obéissance de Messieurs de Paris envers le Roi et Couronne de France*, which was certainly by him. The extreme danger-point of the attack lay in the

---

[1] The very curious book of Nicolas Froumenteau, *Le Secret des Finances de France*, is extremely important for understanding the point of view of the taxpayers at that period, robbed to the profit of the '*deux cent soixante et quatorze familles*' who were exploiting the kingdom to the point of exhaustion.

publicly acknowledged alliance of the Huguenots and the Politicals, and the intention to spare the Lorraines in order to achieve the sacred union against the criminal Medici and her accomplice Henri III. This theme of a sacred anti-Florentine union had already appeared in the *Réveille-Matin*, in which the letter addressed to the Duc de Guise, dated from Rheims on January 1, 1574, proposed that the Huguenots and Lorraines should unite. Nicolas Barnaud, who was very probably the author of the *Réveille-Matin*, was, like La Planche, a Protestant Political, but Politicals though they were they were nonetheless violent for that. Barnaud went as far as recommending tyrannicide, insurrection, federalism. Hotman's influence is indisputable in this campaign in which the monarchy itself is attacked in the person of Catherine de Medici, accused of the worst crimes, of being an enemy to the good name of France, the jailor of princes and marshals.

These political denunciations had an enormous success. They expressed the aspirations of all those Frenchmen—their numbers were growing day by day—who took an interest in politics and whose patience was exhausted by the government's impotence in restoring civil and religious peace, and prosperity, as well as the honour and greatness of the realm. The nation was being utterly ruined by the anarchy that existed in the exchequer, favouring the worst financial excesses by profiteers. Misery was widespread, to the most scandalous advantage of the Gondi, the Sardini, the Zametti and the Ajjacetti. As the majority of these oppressors of the French people were Italians, among them the Gondi, the favourites of the Queen Mother, this inevitably made her appear to be their accomplice. In fact she was obliged to put up with them, for the emptiness of the treasury gave these operators and business men the chance to squeeze the State dry.

As the official financial system had entirely collapsed, it was only possible to obtain help from them. Catherine de Medici had received a ruined kingdom from Henri II and the civil wars had made it impossible to carry out the judicious reforms that, together with Michel de L'Hospital, she had worked out. Birague impoverished himself in the service of France; the Strozzis died for her; the Gondis compensated for their extortions by eminent abilities and were more Lyonnais than Florentine. In any case, Italian intervention in French affairs and politics, which increased under Charles VIII, dated from the Middle Ages. As usual, the truth was infinitely more complex than either the libellers or an ill-informed public opinion imagined.

Catherine, who seized their point because she had at her disposal sources of information that are also available to modern historical criticism, was contemptuous of all these invectives. Unfortunately she was convinced that her son's military genius, the lightning flashing from those dear eyes, would strike all that rabble dead in the brilliance of a second Moncontour. Forgetful of the wisdom to be found in the pages of *Il Principe*, she persisted in this maternal blindness. The diplomats and even the military men, who had not the same reasons as she to indulge in such dangerous self-deception, thought it necessary to avert without delay the Fifth War of Religion that was coming nearer and nearer. Contrary to her usual habit Catherine clung to her mistaken views. She thought that she would have four armies at her disposal and be in a position to beat the rebels in the South as well as in the West.

But as the result of the news of the death of the Princesse de Condé, which he received at Avignon at the end of November 1574 when he was about to march against Montmorency-Damville, Henri III was suddenly seized by a fit of religious mania, which wrecked the southern campaign. The prospective hero of a second Moncontour became a flagellant, beating himself, with a chaplet made of little skulls, his head hidden in a hood, a monk's cloak over his shirt, walking barefoot and carrying a lighted candle. Catherine took fright and attempted to negotiate, but it was too late. Mariéjol has described the situation very well: 'A republic was constituted within the monarchy, under the command of Damville and the supreme authority of Condé, the only Prince of the Blood at liberty, with its own assemblies, armies, courts of justice, customs offices, finances, taxes, police and hospitals' (January 10, 1575).

It was necessary to accept the *fait accompli*, but this did not appear to perturb Henri III. Whilst his mother was trying to find him a wife in Sweden and endeavouring to appease the Poles so that they should not proceed to elect a new King, the unhappy lover of Marie de Clèves discovered that the pretty and gentle Louise de Vaudemont, who resembled the dear departed, would be able to console him. This marriage, not being of the slightest political interest, was another setback for Madame Catherine. It was followed a few months later by another extravagant gesture in his Turin manner on the King's part—as a sign of rejoicing he renounced French sovereignty over the *Barrois mouvant* in favour of the Duc de Lorraine. The Queen Mother began to ask herself whether, for the sake of the dear eyes of Henri III, it was sensible to allow public policy to be controlled by the alternating moods of a spoilt child? The dyarchy for which Catherine had prepared the way had become nothing else but her personal rule, impeded by the ruinous caprices of a boy of twenty-four, more frivolous than a girl of sixteen, whose sharp mind, when it tired of intellectual activities, was bent only on idle pleasures, inventing entertainments entirely opposed to the public welfare and completely neglecting the duties of a king.

The Union of Calvinists and peaceable Catholics took advantage of the situation. On April 11, 1575, it demanded at one and the same time complete freedom for the Reformed Church, the establishment of two-party parliament houses, the strongholds, the liberation of the marshals, the punishment of those guilty of Saint Bartholomew, the States-General. Madame Catherine's anger was as vain as it was violent, and Henri III's cries of indignation a ridiculous echo of it. Montmorency-Damville had force on his side. A little later Catherine received another blow, this time from Poland. On July 15, 1575, the deposition of the fugitive king had been decided on by vote. She only managed to have the new election postponed until the following December. Everything she had succeeded in rebuilding after Saint Bartholomew appeared to be crumbling. At the same moment the assembly of Montpellier confirmed its intention of allowing no discussion of freedom of worship or of the release of the marshals. Although so closely kept a prisoner, the Duc d'Alençon was able to intrigue with Damville, Condé and La Noue, thanks to several accomplices, mostly feminine and in particular his sister, the Queen of Navarre.

By his agreement with a Son of France the Protestant Bayard considered his loyalty safeguarded and had returned to the service of the rebellion which had re-become royalist. In their mutual hatred Monsieur and the King were rivalling one another in ingeniousness. Both brothers were trying to win over Henri de Navarre. He, however, was a good pupil of Machiavelli, whom possibly he had never read but whom he had nevertheless studied in the person of his mother-in-law, and he took good care not to commit himself. One day when he was ill, Henri III advised him, in the event of his own death, to seize power against Monsieur. The Béarnais did not forget this piece of advice, and thenceforward considered that Henri IV would do better on the throne of the Lilies than François III. This had been anticipated by Jeanne d'Albret, a very astute politician, when she had turned down the suggestion that had been under consideration for a short time after the Third War, that her son

z

should marry Elizabeth of England. The King of Navarre was in a highly delicate position—as the friend of Monsieur and as Margot's husband he was involved with Henri III's most deadly enemies, yet the latter did not hide his liking for him. And the friendship between Monsieur and his cousin did not in fact endure. Charlotte de Sauves, whose coquetry and beauty were equally at the Queen Mother's service, by very cleverly playing on the love that both princes bore her, managed to turn them into rivals. Catherine and her son Henri both played very ably on the love affairs and enmities of members of the court, the Queen in order to govern, the King merely for the sake of intrigue. Henri never looked any further than his immediate circle and remained quite indifferent to royal policy in general. The result was that little by little a new phenomenon in French history developed, which had not been seen even under Henri II, who passed from one coterie to the other—the King's party. This party gave no less trouble to Catherine de Medici than all the rest—those of Monsieur, the Montmorencys, the Guises and the Huguenots.

The hatred these parties bore one another led not only to duels and assassinations but also to brawling and fighting throughout the kingdom, from the court to the towns and villages. 'There were nothing but traps, surprises, imprisonments and executions of party men, both for the King and for the rebels, each of them claiming to defend the public good.' Those words of Claude Haton have the very ring of truth. The frightening instability of Henri III earned him nothing but contempt. Catherine, whose intelligence was well-known, was regarded as responsible for an almost desperate situation. Giovanni Michele, in the *Relation* of his embassy of 1575 even repeats the accusations of the *Discours merveilleux*, calling her a fomentor of discord, a mother who played on her sons' nerves in order to reign in their stead. 'Her aim', he wrote, 'is always to remain in power and to retain her authority even were the Royal succession to go to her son-in-law, as if she believed that she would never die.'

The Queen Mother's policy was hindered by her sons' mutual enmity. The principle of dividing in order to rule could not be applied to her own family, since as their mother she was obliged constantly to intervene in order to restore peace, a fragile peace indeed, which she was forever having to waste her time in making up again. Catherine was finding out that being a mother does not favour Machiavellism. Monsieur, whilst he was lying to his mother, was awaiting an opportunity to escape. He found it on September 15,

1575, when he was able to leave Paris without discovery and arrived at Dreux. François' flight was an absolute catastrophe. The appearance of the King's only brother at the head of the rebels gave them an air of legitimacy, according to the fundamental laws of the kingdom, against the Queen Mother, the accomplice of the Italians, and Henri III, surrounded by them. At this period Catherine's letters were simply cries of distress. Yet according to her custom she very quickly plucked up courage again. The important thing was to halt the German army that was coming to the help of Monsieur's followers. On September 29th Catherine was at Chambord, where she saw her son François, granted him the liberation of Montmorency and Cossé and obliged Henri III to agree to it. In reading her letters to the King, it is clear how strongly he resisted her. His was the obstinate resistance of a weakling who would not give way to a brother whom he loathed. His mother cajoled him, flattered him, called him *mon tout*, overflowed with affection and compliments, used every weapon of seduction to bring him to treat with Monsieur without neglecting to reinforce his army.

Disgusted with the world and with himself, his sickly pride blended with vanity turned to sulking, the King deliberately delayed his reply, which was an evasive one. Whilst his mother, in spite of everything more deeply perturbed by the arrival of the Germans and the national danger than by the claims of Monsieur and the Politicals (and she was right), was in a hurry to end this rebellion from which once again the foreigner alone would benefit, he prevaricated, merely remembering his grievances. The victory of Henri de Guise over the Reiters at Dormans, on October 10th, only delivered France from them to invest the victor with the most dangerous glory. Henri le Balafré (on account of the facial wound he received at Dormans, he was given the same nickname as his father) was going to become a Catholic hero. The Marshal de Montmorency, released from the Bastille, understood this as well as the Queen Mother and favoured negotiating with a view to a truce, which was concluded on November 9th.

In order to take the offensive against Navarre and Condé, Madame Catherine now again resorted to her Flying Squadron, for they surrendered more easily to pretty women than to hard-faced negotiators. We know that the Queen Mother excelled at taking political advantage of such amorous dalliance, all the more so as she was well informed on the sexual passions of that decadent society which had become incapable of drawing a distinction between its pleasures and its advantages. In this respect Machiavelli was avenged, for Catherine used this sensuality to her own ends. She herself, owing to her age, her temperament and her character, was immune from temptation. With completely cold detachment she made use of those men who were unable to control their lechery, and those women whom she controlled were completely devoted to her, for they could make love under the pretext of serving the Queen's policies.

At Champigny, on November 21, 1575, Monsieur agreed to a six month's armistice. There were grave difficulties on account of the resistance the inhabitants of the towns that had been pledged to the rebels put up against being occupied by them; Angoulême, Niort, Saumur, Bourges, La Charité, Cosne, Mézières. In spite of this resistance, and also the escape from the court on February 5, 1576, of Henri de Navarre, which enabled him to retreat to his own kingdom, the Queen Mother succeeded in persuading Henri III that peace at any price was the lesser evil. Disarmed, he was forced to accept the very harsh terms of Monsieur, who now revenged himself, backed as he was by the 30,000 troops at his disposal. Accompanied by Margot, Catherine went to Etigny, near Sens, where she signed a peace of defeat, to the advantage of her least-loved son. One can imagine Monsieur's delight. Public opinion made it clear by calling the Treaty of Etigny the Peace of Monsieur; it was confirmed on May 7th by the edict of Beaulieu, near Loches. By its seventy-three articles the Royal government completely capitulated to the Politicals, allied to the Huguenots. Owing to a paradox, the roots of which lay in the major mistake of the Matins of Paris, Catherine, beaten and humiliated, signed a treaty that in spirit conformed to her policy of compassion, but in a large number of its clauses was against her policy of national unity. The Peace of Monsieur established the freedom of the Reformed religion only in association with certain Protestant demands which went against royal sovereignty—the two-party parliaments, the eight strongholds, the disavowal of Saint Bartholomew, the rehabilitation of Coligny, Montgomery, de La Molle and Coconat.

It was a concession without value that the Reformed religion remained forbidden in Paris and at Court. In return enormous apanages were restored in favour of Monsieur—Anjou, Touraine, Berry, the government of Picardy granted to the Prince de Condé, and that of Guyenne to the King of Navarre, who, having returned to the meeting-house was nonetheless proclaimed Protector of the associated Reformed and Catholic Churches. All this taken together was most disturbing. The King undertook to convoke the States-General within six months. Henri III was obliged to submit to the programme of the Protestant Republic with rage in his heart and tears in his eyes, impotent and in despair. In addition 300,000 livres had to be paid to the Count Palatinate, who had obtained a promise of nearly 4,000,000 florins, and refused to withdraw his Reiters unless he received something on account. And the coffers were empty! Like an angry child, Henri III sulked with his mother. She did not despair however of teaching him his kingly duties, thought him still capable of mending his ways and in spite of everything did not lose confidence in him.

She proved it by her instructions on the art of governing, which she dictated to the Sieur François Montaigne, her secretary, and namesake of the famous author of the *Essais*. Administrator of the Abbey of Chaise-Dieu in Auvergne, François Montaigne enjoyed Madame Catherine's special trust, and she usually made him counter-sign her letters. Often immobilized by illness, due to over-eating or lack of caution, for with her robust constitution she thought that she could take any risks, she provided herself with distraction by giving way to her familiar demon, her passion for politics. These instructions of 1576 supplement those of the previous year, and are no less admir-able. Madame Catherine did not renounce the sensible method of political realism. She knew that her failures were not so much due to her own mistakes as to the constant lack of support which made it impossible for her to correct them or to consolidate her successes.

To re-establish all things in good order and good reason, to replace all things according to God and good sense, those were her own words. She drew up a methodical plan for work, recreation and exercise. The nobles were to engage in tournaments in order to distract them and to turn them from war. The Queen recalled the customs of the Court of Henri II and advised her son to follow them. She emphasized that 'One of the most necessary things to make your subjects love you is that they should know that you care for them in all things, as much for those who are close to your person as for those who are at a distance.' Every day the King should read the despatches, question his envoys, work in constant collaboration with the Chancellor, regularly hold his Council, verify everything him-self, know what was going on in his kingdom and talk with his officials and servants about everything that was of interest and concern to them, even their households. She held up Louis XII, François I, and Henri

II as examples to Henri III. This Florentine Queen had adapted herself marvellously well to the domestic and patriarchal tradition of Capetian royalty, friendly and simple. As she taught it she neither omitted nor neglected anything: 'I have forgotten another point, which it is very necessary that you take the trouble to do and which can easily be done if you think it a good thing to do, namely that in all the principal towns of your realm you win over three or four of the leading citizens, who have most power in the city, and the same number of principal merchants, who enjoy good standing among their fellow-citizens. . . .'

In the most natural way in the world Catherine de Medici carried on the tradition of Louis XI. Balzac, in his prodigious essay on Catherine de Medici, made no mistake about it. Catherine was a modern monarch. The main lines of the policy she laid down for her son when she dictated it to the Sieur Montaigne were nothing less than the political methods of Richelieu. A more human and pliable, even although a less detached and authoritative Richelieu. For she was also a woman and a mother and never ceased to be one, often at her own expense as well as that of the State.

All this mattered very little to Henri III. Just as Monsieur had wanted to revenge himself on him, so he now wanted to revenge himself on Monsieur. He was also too intelligent to fail to realize that feudalism, even more than Protestantism, would benefit by the edict of Beaulieu and that the Guisards would avail themselves of it to cry out that the State was betraying France. His mother realized it just as clearly. Already in 1575 she had drawn the King's attention to the birth of the League. After Beaulieu it made rapid progress, thanks to the fury of all the Catholic zealots. The reply to the Protestant Union was the Catholic Union, a combination of all the local leagues that had been proliferating for twelve years. Henri de Guise made himself the leader of this Union. The royal political police was soon informed of the as yet secret plans of the Lorraine prince to dethrone the Valois and to re-establish the succession of Charlemagne with the aid of the Catholic King and the Pope. Under-cover pamphlets were passed around in which could be read that 'the race of the Capets was abandoned by all' but that, on the contrary, 'the young shoots of Charlemagne were verdant, loving virtue'. The clergy actively supported these claims. The Catholic zealots were everywhere taking up arms. Some of them went as far back as the Merovingian liberties, to 'restore to the provinces of the realm the rights, pre-eminences, franchises and liberties as they were at the time of King Clovis and even better and more profitable, if such can be discovered'.

Thus the League adopted the federalism of the Huguenots. Henri de Guise opposed Monsieur and in consequence the Queen Mother and the King, his accomplices since Beaulieu. Whilst a large number of cities, suspicious of the feudal complexion of this movement, remained undecided, the peasants, informed by clever agents that the new regime would abolish taxes, which had first been invented by the Capets, willingly followed the stream. On the one side there were peasants, nobles, Paris, under the Cross of Lorraine; on the other, peasants, nobles, La Rochelle, under the white scarf. Henri de Guise was against Henri de Navarre and both of them were against Henri III. François, having become Duc d'Anjou, was allied to the King of Navarre. There would no longer be a province in the realm that was not in a state of religious and civil war. Only the bourgeoisie as a whole was still faithful to the government, although even then conditionally.

Catherine decided to strike against the weakest of her enemies, her son François. She detached him from Navarre by proving to him that the alliance of the Politicals and the Huguenots was playing into the hands of the Lorraines. She then reconciled him with Henri III. Her infallible gift for measuring up a situation, when it was necessary to set peoples' interests and feelings against one another, caused her to foresee that once Monsieur had been detached from the coalition of the Reformationists and the Politicals the former would lose their appearance of loyalty to the Royal Family and would be confined to the Republic. Thanks to this manoeuvre, the States-General, when they met at Blois on December 6, 1576, were almost exclusively composed of Catholics, both moderates and zealots. Henri III declared himself a Leaguer and his mother immediately pretended to approve of it.

Her instructions to Biron, who was charged with the negotiations with the King of Navarre, revealed what she really thought. She drew them up by her own hand in that month of December when the King thought it a clever move to pass over to the Leaguers. When reading them one sees that she had not changed with regard to the principle of the coexistence of the two religions.

No, contrary to what was repeated ever since the *Discours merveilleux*, Catherine had not changed her political direction. Circumstances, the force of things, the passions of her entourage, the fury of the sects, her own mistakes obliged her, too often for her taste, to modify her plans. Nothing shook her in her horror of persecutions and her will to religious peace. In December 1576 she was still the Governess who remained faithful to the gentlest methods. During the Matins of Paris she had lost her head, and had to suffer the consequences, but she never gave up trying to free herself from them. She still hoped for the propitious moment to do so, but this moment did not arrive. She deplored the fact that her son declared that he would not tolerate more than one faith in his kingdom. She did not hide it from Nevers and Villequier, to whom she said on January 14, 1577, that Henri III 'should never have expressed himself in so absolute a manner'. To the Cardinal de Bourbon she confirmed the need for religious peace.

One day, at the young Queen's, she began to weep, regretting the fact that her son found everything she did wrong, and followed bad advisers. She was more inclined towards her son-in-law Navarre, not that she liked him—quite the contrary—but because she found in him that spirit of national reconciliation which she refused to renounce. She was also worried by the exaggerated devotions of Henri III and by seeing him too much under the influence of the Jesuits. As a protest against the spread of bigotry she had plays performed during Lent. She remained Gallican and free in spirit. She could not breathe in the atmosphere of the League. She was with Jean Bodin and the moderate representatives in the States, who proposed a union by gentle and pacific methods and without war against Versoris and the Guisards, and who asked that the best and most holy methods and means the King could find should be adopted.

Henri III, who was very eloquent, having passed over to the Leaguers, spoke in their favour, through enmity towards his brother and the Montmorencys. By a majority the States voted for the abolition of the Peace of Monsieur, the suppression of the alleged Reformed religion, and the banishment of its ministers. It was a declaration of war. For the first time since 1560, royalty deliberately took the initiative in a civil war and took sides. Henri III was breaking with the Capet tradition of the King as law-giver and the supreme arbiter. One can understand the sorrow of his mother, who had remained inflexibly faithful to that tradition, for although she had occasionally been forced by necessity to abandon it, she had never renounced nor misunderstood it. The States took advantage of the King's weakness and were about to refuse to vote for the credits unless they themselves had control of them. Madame Catherine thereupon declared herself. She personally addressed the deputies, reminding them that she was a Catholic, with as good a conscience as any other. In the days of Charles IX she had often risked her life against the Huguenots. She still did not fear them. At the age of fifty-eight she was ready to die and hoped to go to heaven. Nevertheless she wished to record her disapproval of the new policy.

Nation before parties. The States-General and Henri III himself were so incapable of understanding this principle that on January 1, 1577, the unity of faith was re-established by proclamation. This time the Huguenots were not fighting for the conquest of the State but for their existence. They no longer, as in the Fifth War, had the Politicals on their side. The King having been captured by the Guisards, backing the Princes of the Blood, the Leaguers called themselves Royalists again, and so they were, since the King of France, having become head of a party, had abandoned the tradition of Capetian unity to the Bourbons. Objective historians must not fail to stress the fact that this Sixth War of Religion had been imposed on the Reformationists by the King, captive of the Leaguers. What in the previous wars had been merely fiction had become a fact. The King of Navarre now appeared and was more and more clearly to appear as the appointed champion of the Lilies.

The weakness of the Protestants lay less in their small numbers than in their divisions. La Rochelle decided to remain on the defensive. The King of Navarre, like his mother-in-law, considered that this recourse to arms was doomed to failure. Monsieur le Prince, envious of his cousin's obvious superiority, was a blunderer, as his father had been. Months went by and were lost. Monsieur, having entirely gone over to his brother, took La Charité on May 1st but left to Henri de Guise the honour of preventing the sacking of that city. To show his satisfaction, on May 15, 1577, the King gave a celebration in honour of Monsieur at Plessis-lez-Tours, worthy of *l'Ile des Hermaphrodites*, at which the women were dressed as men and the men dressed as women, all of them in green, the queen's colour at the time of Henri II and also the colour of joyous folly and renewed hope. On June 9th, to celebrate the reconciliation of her sons, Madame Catherine in her turn gave on the terrace of Chenonceaux an astonishing banquet, of Roman decadence, at which her Medici love of luxury indulged in astounding splendours, which amazed her contemporaries although she had accustomed them to the most magnificent entertainments.

The green and hermaphrodisiac symphony of Plessis was surpassed. An enemy of those lordlings whose ambiguous charms delighted her son, and without ever having personally approved of them, preferring Gomorrha to Sodom, this time Madame Catherine staged the apotheosis of Woman. She arranged this inimitable entertainment with the help of Charlotte de Sauves. Henri III wanted to appear that night as a member of the opposite sex. Wearing a dress of pink and silver damask, covered in jewels, he was attended by his mother's ladies and maids-of-honour, naked nymphs under their transparent veils. As the Hebes of this Olympus in Tourange, their golden tresses floating around them, these laughing goddesses poured nectar and served ambrosia. Their snowy white and pink bodies shone in the gentle light of the torches set among the spring green foliage. The Medici's deep-seated paganism had been unable to resist the temptation of providing this feast of Heliogabalus, hoping thereby to reconquer the affection of her son with the dear eyes.

Three days later Monsieur took Issoire by assault and was present at the massacres that followed. What madness on the part of a claimant to the throne! And especially so soon after Saint Bartholomew!

Catherine and Henri III realized this immediately; owing to his complicity in this massacre Monsieur was now in their power. Through Issoire he was chained to Saint Bartholomew. The Huguenots would never again be able to claim the protection of this Son of France, bespattered with the Blood of their faithful followers. The greatest danger from future rebellions was thus removed, averted. The Protestant defeats continued. Montmorency-Damville had been fighting them since the beginning of May. He besieged Montpellier at the head of a royal army. This made it very easy to end the war, by the treble will of Catherine, Henri III, whom she had persuaded that clemency was the best policy, and Henri de Navarre, who did not hide his view that defeat was turning into disaster.

In spite of the Guises, Spain and the Pope, the peace of Bergerac was signed on September 17, 1577. On reading its clauses it becomes clear that it was a Peace of Monsieur, from which had been removed all the conditions contrary to national unity and the sovereignty of the State. It was promulgated by the second edict of Poitiers. Henri III called it his peace, the King's Peace. Catherine was happy to let his vanity have this satisfaction. She knew that it had only been brought about by her negotiations with Henri of Navarre. The edict of Poitiers conceded to the Catholics the restriction of the Reformed religion to certain definite places and the re-establishment of the Roman Catholic religion over the whole country, even where there was a Calvinist majority, at which the preachers were highly indignant. The policy of compassion was restored with lustre and the rights of both religions were asserted. Catherine's victory was once again complete, for the King dissolved both Leagues of Union simultaneously. Thus he returned to the Capet tradition, taking the Lilies back into his possession. The King of Navarre realized that the hour of his victory had not yet dawned. He had negotiated in order to allow his chances to ripen. The Duc d'Anjou and not he was the one defeated by the Sixth War. And since the Peace of Monsieur the King of Navarre had been in the service of the King of France as Governor of Guyenne. He was to remain so until his rupture with Henri III after the Treaty of Nemours in the summer of 1585.

Freedom of conscience. . . . Royal arbitration. . . . The King as peace-maker, as Saint Louis said, a king who, according to Bodin, the legislator of whom Catherine approved, 'should bring his subjects into accord with one another, and all of them with himself'. This was the whole policy of the Queen Mother. At Bergerac the Governess of France had once again won a victory over the fanaticism of the sects.

CHAPTER THREE

THE STRUGGLE FOR UNITY[1]
(September 1577—June 1584)

❧⟨❀❀⟩❧

Owing to the anarchy into which the State had fallen it was extremely difficult to carry out the terms of the peace of Bergerac. How was unity to be re-established? With her usual practical sense, always based on experience, Madame Catherine decided to leave for the south, where disorders and divisions had reached a climax, in order to look into matters herself. As she became more and more convinced that her son was irresponsible, she did not hesitate to take the major part of the Council with her and to give this journey all the appearances of a national and royal progress. For the same reason she did not wish Henri III, whose entourage she found extremely distasteful and disquieting, to accompany her. The *mignons* (favourites) who were both the members of the King's bodyguard and his partners in his depraved and odious amusements, were the subjects of a great number of entertaining works of literature, but works with regard to which it is necessary to exercise the greatest caution in view of the lack of original documentation. The famous *Ile des Hermaphrodites* did not appear until 1605, and it is almost certain that it was written by Thomas Arthur, Sieur d'Embry, towards 1600, to amuse Henry IV. *Les Tragiques* by Agrippa d'Aubigné was not published until 1616 and the famous satire *Les Mignons* in the book *Les Princes*, whilst a marvel of ironic and sarcastic lyricism, is of no documentary importance; the same applies to the

---

[1] (Translator's Note: As regards the heading of this Chapter, I suggest The Struggle for Unity, although this is not a literal translation of *Le Tourment de l'Unité*. It seems to me, however, the least clumsy version of the various alternatives.) The title of this chapter is the same as that of the very fine book by André Mithouard, which appeared in 1901. We have permitted ourselves to use it because it seemed to us the only one appropriate to the account that follows. Mithouard, an aesthetician, wrote: 'Unity must be created and fought for.' Was that not, historically, the constant effort of Catherine de Médici?

portraits of Charles IX and Henri III, embellished by the most violent insults to Catherine:

> *Une mère douteuse après avoir été*
> *Maquerelle à ses fils....*

In the scales of Clio the genius of Aubigné weighs no more heavily than the quips in the *Hermaphrodites à tous accords* by Tabourot des Accords:

> *Je ne suis mâle ni femelle,*
> *Et si je suis bien en cervelle*
> *Lequel des deux je dois choisir.*
> *Mais qu' importe à qui l'on ressemble.*
> *Il vaut mieux les avoir ensemble.*
> *On en reçoit double plaisir.*

As a man of letters the historian finds all this delightful, but is not fooled by these indigent Juvenals and Martials, living on infamous quarrels.

It is certain that the atmosphere of the Court of Henri III was one of Roman decadence. The idea this prince had had, very sound in itself, to surround himself with servants—the Mignons—who would prove faithful under any tests, very soon led to degeneration. This entourage, which had at first been a purely political one, very soon resolved itself into a group of debauchees who—a natural contradiction at the time of the Renaissance—remained robust warriors, madly brave, and always on the point of fighting. And indeed the short history of the reign of Henri III is an extraordinary mixture of perverse gallantry, duels to the death, assassinations, puerile games and crazy caprices, by which Madame Catherine found herself more and more alienated. For her the feast of Chenonceaux had been one evening's entertainment, to be followed immediately by a return to serious matters. One can imagine with what distress she watched Henri III degenerating in the company of his Mignons.

Monsieur, too, had his Mignons. There were constant fights between the bravos of the two brothers. A civil war in miniature was taking place at the Court of France. The Queen Mother's continual efforts to put an end to it were vain. It was wasting the better part of her time and meanwhile French unity was crumbling, and foreign policy, which continued to gravitate around the question of the Low

Countries, required her immediate attention. Monsieur considered the King's peace to be an insult to his own peace and, owing to all the intrigues it brought with it, his puerile resentment was dangerous. During the pre-Lenten period of 1578 the conflict between the two brothers became intense. The Queen Mother's insistence brought about a sham reconciliation between them and their respective Mignons. On Friday, February 14th, François managed to escape, and reached Angers at the gallop. Madame Catherine, remembering only too well the consequences of her son's first escape, rushed after him on the very next day 'and tried', said L'Estoile, 'to bring him back or appease him'. A few days later the King's Mignons, being no longer able to taunt Monsieur and his followers, turned against the Duc de Guise. The result of this piece of bravado was the terrible duel fought on Sunday, April 27th, at five o'clock in the morning, between three of the King's Mignons—Quélus, Maugiron, and Livarot, and three gentlemen of the party of Lorraine—Entraguet, Ribérac, and Schomberg.

This killing, followed three months later, in the night of July 21st, by the assassination of Saint-Mesgrin by the followers of the Duc de Mayenne, proved, alas, that the habits of the armed bandits who were at grips throughout the kingdom had become those of the Court. Jules Gassot has told the story of the appalling Villequier affair, in September 1577, which was even worse than the others. The husband, claiming that his wife was pregnant by a lover, stabbed her to death in bed. Henri III forbade this murderous husband's prosecution and punishment, for with him favouritism came before everything, and at the same time he even encouraged assassinations that served his own personal vendettas. Such was the case of Bussy d'Amboise. There is no doubt that Henri III and his brother Anjou, for once in agreement, delivered up the lover of his wife to the Comte de Montsoreau and that the murder of Bussy at the castle of La Coutancière in 1579 could not have taken place without their connivance. The customs of Italy at the time of the Borgias had become so well acclimatized in France that nobody was astonished by premeditated or instigated murders which regularly remained unpunished.

The increasing upopularity of Henri III and of Henri de Guise found those Frenchmen who were neither Huguenots nor Leaguers, that is, those of the third party, inclined once again to shelter behind the name of Monsieur in an attempt to save the State. Catherine knew this. She was all the more anxious as she was aware of the indifference of the King, entirely devoted to his Mignons, to her maternal advice. Henri III's favourites and swashbucklers merely despised the hard-working and politically-minded old woman of whom the secretary of Hieronymus Lippomano, Venetian ambassador to France in 1577, in his account of his master's mission praised the courage, caution and clear-mindedness.

Although this Venetian unjustly repeated the contention of the parties that it was she who in the past had fomented the troubles, he nevertheless recorded that as he himself witnessed she was now fighting to save the State. 'A generous, magnanimous and strong woman', he wrote, 'she appears to intend to live for many years yet; which is to be hoped for, for the good of France and all Christian nations.'

Henri III, in spite of his intelligence unbalanced and neurotic, feigned to allow his mother to govern whilst at the same time supervising and contradicting her. He admired her profoundly and his public eulogies of her were quite sincere, yet he had not the sense to take advantage of her long experience. He interfered and played at being king, a game he thoroughly enjoyed, yet of which he tired as quickly as of the jokes of Chicot, his very wise fool whom he would dismiss only to send for the pictures he liked to cut out or his collection of old Italian coins; or else he would change over to studying philosophy and theology and grammatical oddities or to holding discussions on history, politics, or the best literature, in all of which subjects he excelled. Then all of a sudden this cultured man would for days on end shut himself up with his ministers, working at his statutes, edicts and regulations, proud of being mockingly nicknamed *Roi de la Basoche* (King of the legal fraternity). He knew that he was doing good and useful work and the documents are in existence to prove that it was the truth.

Suddenly the man of law would have enough of it. He put on women's clothes again, took his pleasures with handsome boys, left them to sleep with Queen Louise, of whom he was still fond, and whose love for this extraordinary husband never waned. From the conjugal bed he would go to his oratory, pray with genuine fervour and make penance. He visited churches, retired to monasteries, followed the processions, disciplined himself, then returned to his amusements, his balls, and his work. The constant instability of this neurapathic son, in whom there was something of a great king and even of genius, gave his mother's life with him an atmosphere of continued uncertainty. He played the king too often for her to be the queen who really governed. She was a kind of Prime Minister to an affectionate despot who never ceased to disconcert her. In view of the nation's peril the best thing was to take leave of him. Was not Anjou even crazier than his brother? And the French people almost as much so? In spite of being nearly in her sixties, Madame Catherine left for Angers. She would fetch François back and afterwards, in the course of another journey, she would try to bring her people back to national unity, which they were determined to destroy.

Since the end of 1577 Henri de Guise had become the ally of Philip II. He was in constant touch with Don Juan of Austria, who requested him to recruit troops on behalf of Spain for the Low Countries. Philip II needed the head of the French Catholics in order to counteract the activities in Flanders of the French Protestants. In December 1577 Don Juan de Vargas Mexia was appointed Spanish ambassador at Paris, with orders to enter into close contact with Henri de Guise and to organize a diversion against Elizabeth I of England. The liaison man between the ambassador of the Catholic King and the Duc de Guise was Beaton, Archbishop of Glasgow, the representative of the imprisoned Queen of Scotland. In view of this new Spanish threat it was essential for Catherine de Medici to unite the French Royalists, whether Catholic or Protestant. This was the reason why it was necessary to get back her son Anjou and to draw closer to her son-in-law Navarre. After the precarious truce of the previous spring the enmity between Henri III and his brother had again become acute.

Having seen and duly lectured the fugitive at Bourgueil Madame Catherine thought that she had beaten him. But in reality Monsieur, who was a great liar, had made his mother promises that he fully intended to break. Catherine hoped to end the matter by marrying him to the Queen of England, and was above all else anxious, in order to avoid a conflict with Spain, to prevent him from accepting the advances of the Flemish. She suggested giving him a southern kingdom which was to include the marquisate of Saluzzo, Provence, the Comtat Venaissin. This we know through a letter from Henri III to Villeroy, dated at Saint-Germain-en-Laye, July 2, 1578. Taking advantage of the love—probably an incestuous one—between Marguerite and François, she charged her daughter to turn his mind away from the affairs of the Low Countries. But her efforts were in vain. At the end of July the Duc d'Anjou left secretly for

Flanders. In order to avoid a break with Spain it was necessary officially to disown him. The English marriage seemed to the Queen Mother the best means of ridding herself of her son. She exchanged a long correspondence on this subject with Elizabeth I and Monsieur. She flattered the former and advised the latter with a wealth of seductive phrases, visibly delighted at carrying on this matrimonial scheme, the prospects of which were as brilliant as its execution was difficult.

On August 2nd she left for the south and arrived at Bordeaux on September 18th. Thirteen years later, travelling once again in the cause of French peace, she was delighted to find herself in the setting in which she had dreamed of it prior to Bayonne. This time, she felt sure, she would be successful; The Treaty of Bergerac and the edict of Poitiers should provide sufficient ground for all reasonable Frenchmen to rally round her policy, which in the end would still triumph over the madmen. Was not the King of Navarre as anxious for peace as she was? In spite of being on bad terms with her husband, Margot was too intelligent not to plead her mother's cause with him. Catherine had taken her with her to the south, as well, as her Chancellor, Pibrac, the Cardinal de Bourbon and the Duc de Montpensier. Since Anjou was playing the fool in Flanders and his brother the eccentric in Paris, Madame Catherine's best chances of success lay with the Navarrese Royal couple, however little she may have cared for them. Henri was politically-minded; Margot needed to be restored to his graces and her help could be counted upon. When wisdom had triumphed in the south, peace could be restored in the north. Catherine was convinced that with France reconciled, Philip II would hesitate to declare war merely for the sake of punishing Monsieur, posing as the liberator of the oppressed Flemish people.

In order to impress her southern subjects favourably Madame Catherine, in spite of the financial stringency, made this journey in pomp and luxury. Owing to the deliberate absence of the King of Navarre she was disappointed by her official entry into Bordeaux. To this disappointment was added her anxiety with regard to the unpredictability of Henri III. This betrayed itself in the letter she wrote on the very day of her arrival in the capital of Guyenne to Pomponne de Bellièvre, the man of confidence she had left behind with Henri III who liked him, remembering how during his exile in Poland he had left all matters of State in his charge. She had taken the other members of the Council with her—Saint-Sulpice, Paul de Foix, Jean de Monluc, the Secretary of State, Pinart. 'I would infinitely regret', she ended her letter, 'the trouble I have taken to come here if I were obliged to return like a disabled ship, and if God does me the grace of doing as I wish, I hope that this realm will benefit by my work and that it may remain peaceful. . . . '

My work . . . the peace of France. . . . Nothing could express better than the moving simplicity of those words the efforts made by the good housewife and mistress of the Kingdom of the Lilies who for eighteen years and more had been working indefatigably to give it the peace that it needed, but which it refused, preferring to continue its religious and civil struggles with increasing fury. It was in the interests of that peace that Catherine had made her own mistakes and errors, some of which were criminal. During the course of this journey she wrote Henri III long letters, incomparable reports on practical politics enabling us to follow her work of national reconciliation from day to day. As she wrote one day to Henri III: 'You are the king of all and should love them all, settling their private quarrels but not partaking of them; love your servants, but their partialities are not yours.' The Nuncio Salviati had judged her very correctly when he had written that Catherine was very jealous of her authority or of anyone who claimed to be her rival in power. But it should properly be added that she identified that personal power with the State, of which she was the impassioned servant, in order to restore its greatness, strength and unity. Giovanni Michele had noted that the Queen Mother believed in the prophecy of Nostradamus, to which the latter had certainly given her the key:

> *Au chef du monde le grand Chyren sera*
> *Plus outre après aymé, criant, redouté:*
> *Son bruit et los les cieux surpassera,*
> *Et du seul titre victeur fort contenté.*

Chyren was the anagram of Henri, who would ascend the greatest throne on earth, who would be loved and feared and whose fame and glory would arise to heaven—Henri the Victorious. Madame Catherine was sufficiently well versed in astrology to have remembered carefully this seventieth quatrain of the sixth century of the prophet of Salon. She did not forget that according to the stars three of her sons would become kings and that the Valois would disappear without leaving any legitimate male descendants. Henri was the third of them to bear the crown, the third and last to reign. The first Prince of the Blood was her son-in-law, the Navarrese.

In 1575, the Venetian ambassador already made no mistake about it; he was struck by the interest that the Queen Mother showed in Margot's marriage, by her overtures to the Cardinal de Bourbon and her kindness to the Duc de Montpensier. It was clear that she was already looking to the future on the Bourbon side. 'Her aim is always to remain the mistress and to safeguard her authority, even in the event of the Royal succession passing to her son-in-law, as if she believed that she would never die, and assured, as she said, that having the King on her side she would lose nothing of her power and her reputation, even if the whole kingdom were to be against her.' *Prudentia fato major*, as she was fond of saying. The *fatum* was the religious division in France, which favoured the enemy both at home and abroad—Huguenots, Leaguers, even Politicals (these, in spite of their sound attitude, because they had unfortunately put Monsieur at their head) the Pope and his theocratic aims, Elizabeth I and her tendency to intervene in favour of the Protestants, the German Lutheran princes, the Emperor, always thinking of the Three Bishoprics, and especially Philip II, the principal adversary who in alliance with the Leaguers was continuing to aspire to hegemony over France.

Catherine de Medici needed the alliance with the King of Navarre. Their first meeting, as she wrote to Henri III, took place on October 2, 1578, 'in a house standing all by itself, called Castéras, between Saint-Macaire and La Réole'. Both son-in-law and mother-in-law were equally anxious for peace. They were both politically-minded and too masterful and intelligent not to know that they had a common interest in it. Margot understood the situation immediately and when points of disagreement arose she intervened in order to arrange matters. As for instance in the case of an interview with the Marshal de Biron, Henri de Navarre's interim Governor of Guyenne, and to whom, as they were on bad terms, he refused to hand over this post. They finally reached agreement on the matter of holding conferences in order to put the edict of Poitiers into execution. The discussions between Catherine's councillors and those of her son-in-law were successful. Commissioners were appointed, five on either side. On October 11th the Queen Mother arrived at Agen, where the consuls gave both her and her daughter a magnificent reception. On the 15th, before leaving, she held a reception at the bishop's palace for the Catholic aristocracy of Guyenne. The speech she made to them is a masterpiece of political perspicacity.

What did she aim to do? To establish peace well and securely, in order to restore the kingdom to its ancient dignity and splendour, so

that it would not in the future fall back into the ruin and desolation
which it had known for too long, owing to the division and party
strife which had reduced it to so miserable a condition. The Queen
Mother thanked her faithful nobility in the name of the King, of
whom she drew a heroic portrait: 'His valour is known to you all; you
have seen him, arms in hand.' This reference to Jarnac and Moncontour was intended to win the approval of the belligerent noblemen. The Queen showered similarly fine compliments on them. It
was now no longer a question of war but of peace, and the King was
asking them to place those brave hearts of theirs at the service of the
State, which was their own. This was followed by an apologia on
behalf of the King of Navarre and Queen Marguerite, whom she had
'lovingly brought up and taught to honour and acknowledge the
King, her brother'. She herself, Catherine de Medici, like the gentlemen of Guyenne, was merely a subject of Henri III. She flattered
them, as on the day after Saint Quentin she had flattered the proud
bourgeois of Paris. It was necessary that they should place the
service they owed to the King before every other consideration. Her
daughter, the Queen of Navarre, would be led by the grace of God to
conduct herself with such wisdom that they could bestow their full
trust in her.

The eloquence of this old champion of French peace was not
merely rhetorical at those moments when, forgetting to be clever,
she spoke from her heart, which was never moved except on such
rare occasions, for France. It was a touching appeal and its sincerity
strikes a rare note in the minds of those used to the lies of history:
'There remains, therefore, nothing more to do than to secure peace
and to carry out everything necessary in order that it may be entirely
preserved; to which end I am determined to spare no means in my
power, nor my own life, considering myself very fortunate to be
enabled to devote it to so good a work, so necessary and so profitable
to this realm.'

This speech was rounded off by her very long letter to Henri III
dated from Agen on October 11th and 15th and from Moissac on the
17th. She told him of her struggles and work, of the imaginary and
unreasonable obstacles she was having to encounter, and which she
could only 'overcome with much patience and various ways of dealing
with one or the other'. Neither by day nor by night did she lose an
hour's opportunity to be of service. Today in Agenois, tomorrow in
Quercy. She would omit nothing that had to be said or done in the
King's service. If only she had money! . . . fifty or sixty thousand

livres that she could pay out secretly. The essential point was, however, that her daughter had told her that Henri de Navarre did firmly want peace. On the other hand she realized that her journey had prevented the resumption of civil war and 'it was to be feared that this time things would have been done that I do not doubt nobody could have imagined and which would have brought about the danger of the ruin of your State'.

In order to counteract this she remained in frequent contact with the Béarnais. She corresponded with Montmorency-Damville, softening him little by little in preparation for the meeting she was to have with him at Toulouse, where he received her and also Margot on October 28th. Great celebrations were held there amidst popular acclamation, and Damville was most friendly. Reassured as far as he was concerned, the Queen Mother was preparing for an assembly which both Protestants and Catholics were to attend. She was making her preparations with Turenne, representing the King of Navarre, who was ill, and she worked at them arduously. Above all Catherine wanted to put an end to the recourse of the French Huguenots to the German Reiters, who ravaged the kingdom. On November 20, 1578, she was at Auch, where she again met her son-in-law. Whilst the two courts of France and Navarre were entertaining one another with feasts and balls the Catholics captured La Réole. As a reprisal the Béarnais, with a few horsemen, occupied Fleurance, city of the King of France, in the night of November 22nd to 23th. Catherine thought that the war was flaring up again. She managed to settle this incident ten days later but without dissipating the reciprocal distrust that had arisen from it, and which affected the negotiations. On December 15th, the two courts were installed at Nérac. The days passed in entertainments and things advanced no further. From December 22, 1578, until February 2, 1579, Madame Catherine resided at the Abbey of Paravis, near Port-Sainte-Marie, about three leagues to the north of Nérac, on the Garonne. There she held almost continuous discussions with, on the one hand, her son-in-law and the Huguenots, and on the other Biron and the Catholics, but her conciliatory efforts appeared to be in vain. The King of Navarre adopted an attitude of reserve towards his mother-in-law and quarrelled with Biron. Yet in the end Catherine's patience won and on February 3rd the Nérac conferences opened.

The remonstrances of the Huguenot ministers, the letters of the Queen Mother to Henri III, the diary of Damville's secretary, and an anonymous account of 'what happened at the conference of Nérac', have given us detailed information on this major episode in Catherine's political life. Neither verbal complaints nor presentation of petitions were lacking to keep the Queen aware of the situation. The claims of the Huguenots seemed excessive to her, especially those regarding the garrisoned towns, which they refused to surrender to the King, though they demanded that he should, nevertheless, pay the wages of the garrisons. Catherine presided over the discussions in the flexible manner at which she excelled. The representatives of the parties involved occasionally went at it so hard that in spite of her self-control she would lose patience, but in the end she always succeeded in calming their passions. Once she gave the assembled deputies a real discourse, which was approved by all those who heard it. She ended it by saying that 'as mother of the King she wanted also to show herself as the mother of the people, and that she had devoted herself to contenting all her subjects, leaving aside everything that might lead to the renewal of the troubles', adding that she would ask two or three of the delegates to come and discuss with her the questions that remained unsolved on the very next morning, 'not in writing nor by articles but verbally, step by step, in order to settle matters more quickly'.

The Queen had private interviews with her son-in-law and made an ally of him. She was indefatigable, rising sometimes at five o'clock in the morning, hearing Mass at six, holding council from seven to eleven and from one to five. It happened that Monluc and Foix, worn out, had to take to their beds. Everyone was astounded by Madame Catherine's powers of endurance; she hesitated at nothing, saw everybody herself, argued and would not give in. When she felt that she had made as many concessions as possible, she did not refrain from speaking quite brutally. One day she vehemently accused the Protestant ministers of being defiant and ill-willed. She declared that 'they were hindering peace, they, who themselves did not go to war but were causing the deaths of the noblest Frenchmen, and that they should be made to go and be placed in the vanguard, like the Swiss; that the gentlemen were quite wrong to believe that they could do themselves any good by listening to them, for they would fall between two stools, their bottoms on the ground'.

What enchantingly frank words! Catherine knew what war was like; she had seen it, at Rouen and Le Havre. She was rightly indignant at the belligerence of the Genevese clerics, who wanted no part of it for themselves. How well and truly she put them in their place! And they gave way to her. On February 16th the Queen held a session from seven until midday, together with the King of Navarre and the deputies. She let them know that the conditions she had accepted were her last word. The agreement of Nérac was signed on the 28th; the Protestants obtained, but only for six months, three strongholds in Guyenne and eleven in Languedoc. As for the choice of delegates charged with carrying out the agreement, the Queen Mother insisted that they should without differentiation be either Catholics or Huguenots. She appointed the Protestant Ussac governor of Le Réole, restored to the King. On March 8th she left for Agen, remaining there until the end of the month. She re-assembled the nobility of Guyenne once again and addressed them, justifying the Nérac agreement on the grounds of the need of civil and religious peace, reminding them that the King would not hesitate to take up arms if the honour of God, the good of the State, and the protection of his Catholic subjects were to make it necessary. 'But he has learnt by experience, as each one of us has also been able to see, that fighting has brought nothing but evil.'

Experience.... Catherine accepted no laws but those of experience. Neither ideologies nor fanaticisms could prevail against realities. Everyone had been able to see this for themselves. Experience condemned war; the only fruitful policy was sacrifice in the cause of peace.

But such sacrifices would have to be agreed upon with full understanding of the situation and within the limitations of what was possible. The Queen Mother resumed her journey at the beginning of April 1579 by way of Toulouse and Castelnaudary, where she parted from her daughter with, for her, a rather surprising show of emotion, as her letters bear witness. At the latter place she presided over the meeting of the States of Languedoc, and ensured that they voted the subsidies necessary to carry out the clauses of Nérac for the period of one year. On May 15th she arrived at Narbonne from Carcassonne. Travelling on through Béziers, Pézenas and Agde, without stopping at Montpelier, on account of the plague there, she arrived at Beaucaire. But whilst going through Montpelier she had by sheer will-power made the Huguenots see reason, 'who', she wrote to Henri III, 'are so accustomed to harassing the Catholics'. Although she congratulated herself on this success she feared for the future. Writing to the Duchesse d'Uzès, she said: 'I saw all the Huguenots of Languedoc; I am so tormented by the quarrels of Provence that my mind is full of annoyance. And God, who is still helping me, has so highly favoured me that I was successful here as well as in Guyenne; and here there is no lack of birds of prey. . . . I do not know whether they will be better in Dauphiné. If it is true, as the proverb says, that the sting is in the tail, I greatly fear that I shall find it here; but I always have my hope in God.'

She also had all her good humour. She was pleased that Queen Margot's marriage had been patched up again.

Her naturalness, her courage, her trust in God and in the right-eousness of her cause shine through her correspondence of this period. In spite of her anxieties she was always at work, always hoping. She did not forget that Machiavelli had written: 'Men may abet Fortune but may not oppose it; weave its weft, follow its threads, but not destroy them. I do not think that for this reason they should give up hope. They ignore what the end may be, but as it only works by dark and roundabout ways, they always have hope. Such hope should uphold them, whatever reverses they may meet with and whatever deeds they are obliged to endure.' After Guyenne she had pacified Languedoc. She had won over Henri de Navarre and Montmorency-Damville to the King. During the ten months that she had been away she had once again worked well for France. Henri III clearly understood how valuable her services had been. On May 19th he wrote to Du Ferrier: 'As for the Queen my mother, she is at present in Provence, where I hope that she will restore peace and unity to my subjects as she has done in Guyenne and Languedoc and that in passing through Dauphiné she may do the same there. By these means she will go on implanting in the hearts of all my subjects the remembrance of, and immortal gratitude for, the benefits she has conferred on them, making them obliged eternally to pray to God with me for her prosperity and her health.'

In that month of May 1579 Henri III was in one of his best moods. For the time being he was ruling as a king. For the past two years his councils had been working at the grand ordinance which was to rectify and complete those of Orleans and Moulins, as well as the various edicts of administration and police supervision promulgated since the States-General of 1560. In the 363 articles of the Grand Ordinance of May 1579 there was nothing important or useful to the good advancement of public and private business that escaped the royal attention, from the freedom of trade in grain to the halving of apprenticeship fees, in the edict of November 1577; from the rulings laid down for the ecclesiastical orders to the prohibition applied to foreigners to found banks without a security of 15,000 écus. Henri III,

Roi de la Basoche, desired that all the laws of France should be codified, as he stated in article 207 of his Ordinance. This idea was so dear to him that later he ordered Barnabé Brisson, Advocate-General of the Paris Parliament, to take it up. Brisson's work did not appear until 1587, under the title, Code Henri III, and could not be promulgated owing to the misfortunes of the times. But Catherine de Medici could find a proof in it that the advice she had given her son had not been neglected. Henri III, however, lacked the power of concentration required in order to carry out such a great piece of legislation relatively quickly.

The indefatigable Madame Catherine, on the contrary, had not only been concerning herself with the south during those ten months of uninterrupted activity. She had not ceased to pass on her instructions and to collaborate in the government of the kingdom, both with regard to policy at home and abroad and in its administration. Whether it was a question of tax relief in Brittany, or of the succession in Portugal—to which she claimed to have a right as the descendant of a Countess of Boulogne, Mathilde, who three centuries earlier had been Queen of that country—or the confused affairs of the Low Countries, she neglected nothing but spoke, wrote and acted. She sought information and spied. She desired to be informed of everything in order to foresee and forestall. She constantly pretended to refer to Henri III when in reality she was controlling him. She was still the expert rider, the cunning huntress, who knew how to mount and guide the recalcitrant steed, to catch the elusive game. All her letters to her son are exquisite examples of ingeniousness; in appearance the servant, in fact she remained the mistress.

There are many references in her correspondence to her ailments, but she overcame those as she did her political problems. She left a preference for comfort to others. 'You have the chair and I the mule', she wrote from Carcassonne on May 8, 1579, to her gossip, Madame d'Uzès, 'for I prefer to go a long way.' A long way and slowly, on mule-back—'a little mule for me to ride on as much as I like.'

She liked riding throughout France—on her mule the old Queen went from town to town and village to village, like a doctor, in order to bring her people a cure for their many ills, which crushed them by their own fault, by their madly obstinate insistence on fighting one another.

A real Jacquerie had broken out in Provence, in the region of Trans, where the Razas, insurgent peasants, had captured and destroyed the castle after murdering their lord, Claude de Villeneuve. It was indispensable that the Queen Mother should be present in the locality. At the beginning of June 1579 she installed herself at Marseilles, where she was received by Henri II's bastard, the Grand Prior of Malta, Henri d'Angoulême, Governor of Provence. Shortly afterwards she received very alarming news from the Dauphiné, where the Marshal de Bellegarde had rebelled against the King, in agreement with Savoy and Spain, as well as with Lesdiguières and the Huguenots. As she dared not enter into a war which would have provoked the twofold intervention of Emmanuel-Philibert and Philip II against France, the Queen Mother opened negotiations in the hope of reconciling Bellegarde and Lesdiguières with the throne. She referred to her ties with the Court of Savoy and her dear memories of the Duchess Marguerite, who had died five years earlier. To the various Italian Governments, Venice and the Holy See, she described the matter as a purely local quarrel, which could be settled with as little trouble as those of Guyenne and Languedoc. She was unable to obtain an interview with Lesdiguières, but on the other hand she did see the Duke of Savoy, at Grenoble, in August. Emmanuel-Philibert was in agreement with his sister-in-law in compelling Bellegarde to attend a conference which opened at Montluel, in her presence, on October 15, 1579.

It was very hard work, for Bellegarde was strengthened by the *fait accompli* and Catherine de Medici feared a war with Savoy and Spain. The Marshal was offered the Government of Saluzzo, in exchange for which the rebel was to admit his guilt, repent, beg for Royal clemency, and swear a new oath of fidelity! The Queen Mother's correspondence dwelt on these delicate negotiations and expressed her gratitude towards Emmanuel-Philibert, who had ended by openly taking her side against Bellegarde. On October 20th she returned to Lyons from Montluel, 'having mended matters regarding the Marquisate of Saluzzo', she wrote to the Duc de Montmorency, 'in such manner that the honour and good of the service of the King, my son, is preserved there, so much so that I hope that the fruit of my labours (which I shall never regret for the sake of the satisfaction of the King, my said lord and son, and the good of the kingdom) will be of great utility to the said kingdom'. She announced her intention of returning to Paris.

Matters were not in fact as settled as she imagined. The Marshal de Bellegarde continued to conspire with Lesdiguières with the intention of arranging to obtain the support of the King of Navarre.

In his capital Carmagnola he affected the behaviour of a sovereign prince. He died on December 20, 1579—so opportunely for Catherine that she was later, as usual, accused of having poisoned him. The diplomatic documents and the correspondence of the period invalidate this accusation, which was hawked around by Brantôme, Davila, Le Laboureur and Girard. According to the Venetian Lippomano the Marshal died of gallstones, and he was known to have suffered from a bladder disease. On December 14th Emmanuel-Philibert had already informed his ambassador to France that Bellegarde was dying. He took a week to die and his son Caesar never for a moment suspected that his death was an unnatural one; he was intent on succeeding his father, which he did not do, as the King gave the succession to one of his favourites. Later on the Marshal de Retz was sent to Piedmont in order to re-affirm France's interests there, after the death of the Duke of Savoy in 1580.

This affair, involving both the Dauphiné and Savoy, was complicated for the Queen Mother by the negotiations she had to conduct with her son-in-law Navarre regarding the return of the strongholds mentioned in the Nérac agreements. A new prank played by Monsieur le Prince—who had inherited from his father the art of throwing himself into adventures that could have no issue—required her attention at the same time. Monsieur le Prince was holding La Fère in rebellion. After having spent only ten days in Paris, from November 30th until December 9th, the old Governess of France, called in to help by her son Henri III, was obliged to leave again for Picardy. She succeeded in keeping down the new insurrection of the Reformationists around Condé, but failed to compel the latter to evacuate Le Fère, where he remained until May 22, 1580, on which date he crossed the Rhine to ask the German Lutheran princes for help. Madame Catherine had returned to Paris on December 27, 1579.

She remained in peace there during the whole of the first quarter of 1580. Her correspondence shows that at that moment she was chiefly concerned with her plans for the marriage of Elizabeth I of England and Monsieur, and in keeping up French interests at the Court of Ivan the Terrible in Muscovy, as well as those of the Kings of Denmark, Poland and Sweden, as she wrote on March 5, 1580, from Saint-Germain-en-Laye to Charles de Danzay, ambassador to Copenhagen. Nor did she lose sight of the Portuguese succession or of the situation in the Low Countries, in which with the greatest rashness in the world Monsieur persisted in involving himself. On account of the Spanish danger this situation in the Low Countries was her greatest anxiety. It was there that Monsieur was liable to destroy all the work of pacification she had undertaken her long journey to accomplish, the importance of which the Parisians had so well understood that on her return in the preceding November they had gone out to welcome her.

Nevertheless, Protestants and Catholics were once more beginning to come to grips in various parts of the kingdom. The Queen Mother soon realized that, contrary to what had previously been generally the case, in this re-emergence of civil disputes religion was much less important than politics, both at home and abroad. The demands of John Casimir, who provided the Reiters for the French parties that were fighting one another, made matters no easier. The Count Palatine was so much of a war contractor that he was thought capable of being just as willing to sell his human war material to his Protestant co-religionists as to their Catholic enemies. Henri III still owed him three million livres, and so long as this enormous indemnity, which would have to be settled before French territory was evacuated, was not paid up, John Casimir had an excuse to threaten the King and to make promises of assistance both to the Guises and the King of Navarre, Monsieur le Prince and the Duc d'Anjou.

In order to pacify this dreadful creditor to some extent, Madame Catherine appealed to the good offices of her son-in-law Charles III of Lorraine. The Politicals were becoming restless and Monsieur no longer concealed his ill-will towards his mother. At mid-April the Queen went to visit him at Bourgueil. He realized that his mother's intention was to deprive him of the support of the Politicals and the Reformationists. The latter were only waiting for a chance to break the Nérac agreements, in order to retain the strongholds. On the pretext of interference and ill-treatment by the Catholics, but in reality because the war-minded gentry of Gascony, Guyenne and Languedoc were unemployed owing to the peace that had been concluded, the strong-armed men of the Religion forced the hand of Henri de Navarre, who in the middle of April ordered hostilities to be resumed. Contemporary opinion imagined that the love affairs of Queen Margot and her ladies, the King of Navarre and his gentlemen, Henri III and his Mignons, had exasperated those Southerners, quick in seeking vengeance for their insults. That was why this very short Seventh War, this rising of the Huguenots in the spring of 1580, was known as the Lovers' War.

Once again the tapestry of the Penelope of French peace had been torn up by the Protestants. Catherine gave vent to her indignation in her letters to Henri de Navarre, 'of whom, being issued from so noble a race', she would never have believed that he wished 'to be the leader and general of brigands, robbers, and evil-doers of the kingdom'. The whole letter that she wrote to him from Chenonceaux on April 21, 1580, is pathetic, appealing to the King of Navarre's sense of responsibility, telling him that she was willing to forgive this lapse: 'These mistakes are no sooner made than penitence for them comes as promptly as repentance of them; but all that, after this blow has fallen, is no longer anything. I ask you to believe me and to restore matters once again as reason would have them be.'

As reason would have them be. . . . The Béarnais, at twenty-seven, clever though he was, did not yet have the wisdom of Henri IV. He liked going to war, a remedy for the boredom of inaction which the amorous adventures of the young gallant that he was did not supply. Nothing, not even the lure of pretty girls, was as satisfying as sword-play. The Navarrese forgot his promises at Nérac and gave himself up to the pleasures of war. The old Queen knew only too well, alas, what the consequences would be, but her son-in-law did not agree with her.

Fortunately the majority of the Huguenots did not follow the King of Navarre in this escapade. La Rochelle disapproved of it and the Bas-Languedoc refused to become involved. Nevertheless, on the night of May 28 to 29, 1580, the Béarnais made a surprise attack on Cahors. He spent four days of unbroken combat in capturing it and showed himself to be a fighter whom nothing and nobody would stop. The audacity and tenacity of the victor of Cahors were greatly admired, but gained him no adherents, nonetheless. The peasant insurrection in the Dauphiné, Condé's resistance at La Fère, remained isolated incidents. The troops sent by the King to the various points at which war had again broken out were everywhere victorious. Catherine refrained from exploiting these successes, for if the war spread it would merely benefit the Guises, the allies of Spain, and Spain proper. The Duc d'Anjou was invited to act as mediator and gladly accepted in the hope that his good offices would win his mother's gratitude and her help in the matter of the Low Countries.

These really excited him. He had taken Cambrai on August 22nd and the States-General of the Low Countries had offered to recognize him as their king. Catherine, on learning of the Treaty that

Monsieur had signed with them on September 19, 1580, at Plessies-lez-Tours, involving the question of a French alliance, needed immediate peace at home in order to face the more and more pressing danger of a Spanish war. Accompanied by Bellièvre and Villeroy, real guardian angels, the future king of the Low Countries went to Périgord at the begining of October to meet Henri de Navarre. On November 26th the Treaty of Fleix ended this somewhat ridiculous Lovers' War, born of an impulse of the King of Navarre's. Bergerac and Nérac were confirmed at Fleix. The Protestants gained the advantage of being allowed to retain the strongholds for six years. Catherine never hesitated to pay a high price for the greatest of goods —the peace of the country. Her letters expressed her joy, of which she informed all her correspondents. She was so pleased that she believed that the Duc d'Anjou would become a skilled politician. On December 23rd she sent him a long letter from Blois which was a real memorandum, of the same kind as those that she had drawn up for Henri III. As usual she was anxious about Spain and did not hide from herself the fact that the Queen of England and the princes of Germany, Protestants though they were, offered no security against the Catholic King. She was very well informed on the policy and activities of the latter—'I pray you also, my son, to consider which are the minds that the Spaniards have won over in this kingdom, by the continuation and interaction of our divisions, which every day are becoming more dangerous owing to the unbridled licence which is growing and increasing before our eyes, to our very great regret, but without agreeing that, as some say, one could allay them by starting a foreign war; on the contrary one must believe that as in that case such factions would have better means of doing harm and accomplishing their designs nothing would be more dangerous and damaging to the King's business.'

What lucidity! Catherine de Medici's foreign policy was justified by events. In spite of Henri IV's victories the Spanish intervention, when it did occur, prolonged the French civil wars for another ten years. What would have happened under Henri III, when the King had no army capable of beating those of Spain? Essentially a realist, the Queen Mother knew only too well that the King was in no condition to make war on Philip II, 'his constabulary being in so bad a state'. She was against the Flemish adventure because she did not possess the military means with which to back an anti-Spanish policy: 'What could you do for the States of the Low Countries that are calling on you? This State being ruined, and the King without means to assist you, you would bring them nothing but charges and expenses, and would be in danger of being dismissed and sent away with more shame and vituperation than they are now expending to bring you to them with honour.'

There is no greater self-deception than to indulge in a policy of prestige and splendour. The Governess of France remained the Florentine shopkeeper, carefully weighing up the profits and losses of an enterprise which might appear seductive to thoughtless minds. She concluded that it was an unsound proposition and wisdom counselled giving it up. The essential thing was to pacify France and bring the country back to unity. Let us listen to Madame Catherine, always so reasonable and prudent: 'The King must and wishes to establish the affairs of his kingdom, to be assured of the loyalty of his subjects, and to provide himself with foreign friends and money, before embarking on a foreign war; nor does he wish to undertake anything lightly, whereof he might repent. . . .'

Monsieur would not listen. His mother knew the military strength at the disposal of Alessandro Farnese. He was—and how much worse this made matters!—a man of genius, as great a politician and administrator as a great captain, and to whom the major work of Leon Van der Essen paid the brilliant tribute worthy of this bastard grandson of Charles V and a simple artisan's daughter, Jeanne Van der Gheynst, the beautiful Flemish girl. The Duke of Parma's forces numbered roughly 10,000 men, including 3,000 cavalry, and they were the redoutable veterans of the Spanish victories in the Low Countries. In spite of his impatient desire to return to Flanders the Duc d'Anjou was obliged to spend the entire winter in the south, whilst Catherine piled new attentions on Elizabeth of England in the attempt to persuade her to marry her son. The Spanish threat in the Low Countries, the arrival of the Jesuits in Ireland, England and Scotland, the crusade against her launched by Gregory XIII, inclined Elizabeth to exercise particular care towards France. During his visit to her in August 1579 she had liked the Duc d'Anjou; she had nicknamed him her 'Frog' and this clumsy jest seemed a good omen to Madame Catherine. Like his three elder brothers, of whom Nostradamus had predicted that they would bear the sceptre, the youngest of her sons would also become a king. But soon she was compelled to realize that the opposition of the English Parliament and of public opinion to a Papist marriage was stronger than Elizabeth's wish to marry Monsieur.

Catherine took care, nevertheless, to encourage it and in her correspondence we find her cajoling her good sister as if she had been the most beautiful of young princesses and not a sexually abnormal old maid of forty-seven. Knowing the Florentine Queen's taste for Italian comedy it is easy to imagine the pleasure she took in dishing out these gross flatteries. Elizabeth's diplomatic correspondence shows that she was not taken in by this game and that as a good Englishwoman the last thing she wanted was a French Prince in the Low Countries. Before there was any question of an engagement the Duc d'Anjou would have to renounce his ambitions there. Catherine was no less suspicious of her putative daughter-in-law than Elizabeth was of her future mother-in-law. Both of them were highly cunning. Catherine's letters to Villeroy and Bellièvre during January and February 1581 leave us in no doubt that an English alliance which such a marriage would have made possible and efficacious was the aim of the Queen Mother: 'This marriage', she wrote to them from Blois on February 19th, 'will succeed and give much benefit, not only to this realm and that of England, but also to all Christendom'.

Equally tired of Elizabeth's indecision and his mother's advice, in April 1581 Monsieur decided to follow his own inclinations and to leave for Cambrai, arranging to avoid meeting both the Queen Mother and the King. But the Governess was not going to allow him to shake off her tutelage so easily. She stayed with Monsieur at Alençon from May 12th to 15th, in order to prevent him from leaving for the Low Countries, but her sermons were in vain. Her son's resistance irritated the Queen, who made him violent scenes which only succeeded in making him cling more obstinately than ever to his plans. So Catherine, whose political methods were always so careful, found herself more and more thwarted by Monsieur's unreasonable pigheadedness. Her family were forever putting the most dangerous obstacles in her way, and of all her children the Duc d'Anjou was the least docile. A further meeting with him at Mantes, at the beginning of July, was no more successful. Catherine saw that the danger was growing and was deeply depressed by the uselessness of her efforts. The torments she was suffering in the cause of unity were becoming unbearable. Catherine told Du Ferrier of her sorrow, her perplexity, how badly she needed to be helped by the grace of God, for which she prayed daily. But she did not take refuge in prayer and cease to act; she prayed in order to be able to fight on with more strength. She saw Henri III, who, exasperated once again by his brother, was prepared to use force in order to prevent him from going to Cambrai. Her two sons loathed one another and would not recoil from fighting. That would be the worst of all catastrophes—the king and the heir to the crown plunging into war against one another. It would mean the destruction of all her work at Beaulieu and Bergerac, Nérac and Fleix, four years of effort wasted and this time with the certainty of a Spanish invasion, with England's approval, since Flanders was involved. This must be avoided at any price. Catherine resorted to her usual procedure when a problem arose that appeared to be insoluble. As Charles IX did of Genlis, so Henri III would officially disavow Monsieur, whilst helping him in secret.

Catherine would greatly have preferred Monsieur to give up Flanders. On August 7th, at La Fère, she sermonized him again, with no further success. To guard against all eventualities a barrage of French troops was placed between the Spaniards and the Duc d'Anjou's men, when he entered Cambrai on August 18, 1581, and captured Cateau-Cambrésis on September 7th. The Queen Mother was torn between two feelings—her joy at this partial reversal of the defeats of Henri II, and her fear of a Spanish reprisal. On August 23rd she had written to Du Ferrier: 'I am in great anxiety regarding the result of the journey on which my son has embarked.' She reassured herself with the thought that Phillp II, who had just annexed Portugal after a military walk-over, would carefully refrain from endangering this striking success by a conflict with France, which would clearly not be without risks.

On the other hand this Spanish victory over Portugal and her overseas Empire made it necessary for England to draw closer to France. Elizabeth wanted the alliance before her marriage to Monsieur. Catherine, who remembered Hampton Court, pointed out to Walsingham, when she received him at the Tuileries on August 30th, 'that one could make use of several arguments and pretexts to break treaties based only on ink and paper'. Once her son was the husband of the Queen of England, war against Spain might become possible, but not before. Elizabeth I was sufficiently attracted by Monsieur to give way, or that, at least, was what Catherine hoped. When the Duc d'Anjou visited England a few months later the Queen received him most cordially, kissing him on the mouth and giving him a ring. But she did not for that reason overlook her political interests and continued to postpone her final reply, which was to depend on official French intervention in the Low Countries. Monsieur remained with Elizabeth, like a fiancé, from November 1581 until February 1582.

When he left for Flanders the Virgin Queen wept, telling him to regard her as from that moment as his wife, which caused her ministers, Cecil, Walsingham and Sussex, to protest.

From Catherine de Medici's point of view the thing that mattered was that England appeared at last to be taking sides against Spain; a fleet under the command of Leicester, Elizabeth's favourite, was sent to Zeeland, to support the Flemish. But in the end this English marriage did appear to her to be chimerical. Faithful to her usual method of bearing several possibilities in view, she allowed it to be uggested to Philip II that a marriage between the Duc d'Anjou and one of the Infantas might enable the situation in the Low Countries to be settled. It seems that Catherine thought that her claim to the Portuguese throne might prove a useful counter in this matter; a claim to which she attached a great deal of importance. With her usual optimism she even occasionally imagined that Philip II would take note of it and would give her Portugal in exchange for her renunciation of all French plans with regard to Flanders.

Matters turned out differently. The Catholic King, by annexing Portugal without regard to anyone else's rights, had presented Catherine de Medici with a *fait accompli*, with the result that in order to affirm her rights she would be forced to declare war on him, a War of Succession to the Portuguese throne, which might prove to be a very hazardous undertaking. When Sebastian, King of Portugal, was defeated and killed in Morocco, at the battle of Alcazar-Kebir on August 4, 1578, he was succeeded by the Cardinal Henry, who was sixty-seven. As the son of the Empress, *née* Isabella of Portugal, Philip II had contested the proclamation of the Cardinal King. He did not take seriously either the claims of Ranucco, son of Alessandro Farnese or those of Emmanuel-Philibert of Savoy, and even less those of Catherine de Medici. Catherine, a keen student of archives and genealogies, revelled in this problem of succession, which went back to the marriage of Mahaut, Countess of Boulogne and Alphonso of Portugal, in 1235.[1] She cared little for the fact that Mahaut had been repudiated by her husband for, she claimed, as there had been children of that marriage, the children of Alphonso III's second marriage, to Beatrice de Guzman, natural daughter of Alphonso X of Castille, had no right to the succession. Had Alphonso of Portugal not declared himself Count of Boulogne, and used the seal of the Counts of Boulogne until such time as he became defender and procurator of the Kingdom of Portugal, after the deposition of his

[1] Genealogical table, B.N. *Manuscrits, fonds Français*, No. 16106. Highly interesting.

brother, Don Sancho II? Was not the prior claim to the succession of the House of Boulogne obvious?

The arguments brought forward by the daughter of Madeleine de la Tour d'Auvergne, Countess of Boulogne, were approvingly recounted in his *Relatio* of 1582 by the Venetian ambassador, Lorenzo Priuli. Was he himself really convinced by them? It seems doubtful. In this claim of Catherine's he saw above all a political move against Philip II, made 'with the sole aim of seeing whether she could bring the Catholic King to make a bundle of all their current problems, those of Portugal and those of Flanders, and by means of a marriage come to some arrangement regarding them'. However that may have been Madame Catherine made a personal issue of her Portuguese succession. Her authority had been considerably enhanced by her journey of pacification. The Venetians report that on her return the government was at her orders, her ministers assistants rather than councillors. In the Council chamber the Queen, the King and a confidential secretary formed a separate group. Catherine directed everything, gave the orders. In his gratitude for what she had done, Henri III was for the moment submissive to her, but this submission was to last only a short time. This explains why this prince, whose dominant characteristic was a much more deeply-seated mistrust than his mother's (she was mistrustful only through necessity but not by nature) allowed her without in any way opposing it, to embark on a chase after her fabulous Portuguese heritage, which she very soon pursued with passion.

From the end of 1578 the Queen Mother's correspondence is full of allusions to, or accounts of, the developments in this matter of the Portuguese succession. It is marked by a very odd desire to obliterate her humble origins. In face of the Queen of Portugal, who would still have dared to recall the Florentine shopkeeper? The death of Cardinal Henry on January 31, 1580, had given France the opportunity to reply to the Portuguese requests for help against Philip II, who was preparing to invade their country. For lack of money and troops such assistance remained merely theoretical. France proclaimed the dignity, splendour and freedom of Portugal and promised her aid, comfort, and goodwill. In fact nothing was done and the Duke of Alba was able to conquer Portugal without difficulty. Fear of Spain was the stronger.

Without in any way giving up her claims Catherine resigned herself, as she had done with regard to the Low Countries, to underhand intervention. The Pretender to the Portuguese throne, Don Antonio (he was the natural son of a brother of the Cardinal-King), had retired to one of the Azores, the island of Terceira. The French Government allowed him to raise troops and ships in France. When Spain complained, the Queen Mother replied that it was a private matter between herself and her son-in-law. Her long letter of January 24, 1581, to the ambassador Saint-Gouart, expressed her point of view—the Catholic King had entered Portugal by force, 'to the prejudice', she said, 'of the rights I was claiming there, which I had placed before the courts of justice, where I was requested to prove my said rights. . . . ' She was going to law, but Philip II had resorted to force. She was justified in supporting Don Antonio, who was a plaintiff like herself, against a pretender who had acceded before the case had been judged.

Catherine had a taste for judicial discussions, and although the King of Spain had occupied Portugal she did not give up her case. Since Philip took up arms Catherine was justified in supporting the pretender who was fighting him. This is the background to her intervention in the Azores. Her letters show how careful she was to base herself on her legal rights. 'Monsieur de Mauvissière', she wrote on July 21, 1581, to her ambassador to Elizabeth I, 'you will see from the superscription of the letter I have written to Don Antonio that I do not call him King of Portugal . . . that the reason why I have not done so is not to deprive him of his title but only in order not to prejudice my own rights also; that if I were to do otherwise the King of Spain might say that by calling Don Antonio king I was not persisting in my rights and claims, on which we are well agreed, my said cousin and myself.'

Portugal was her legitimate heritage. Don Antonio, having taken refuge in England, was a subject of Catherine de Medici and not of Philip II, who had established himself in Lisbon by the most scandalous misuse of power, and was a mere usurper. To all Spanish protests the Queen Mother replied by referring to the law. Why should Philip II not accept a happy compromise between might and right by marrying one of his daughters, Catherine's granddaughters, to the Duc d'Anjou, their uncle? This was what the Queen wanted, as Mariéjol saw very clearly: 'Her personal claims and her matrimonial plans were very closely linked. In her mind the Infanta's dowry—a territoral dowry—was to be the price of her giving up these claims. As she was too intelligent to suppose that Philip II would relinquish Portugal to his son-in-law it would be necessary for such compensation to be looked for in the direction of the Low Countries, and this the Spaniards understood.'

It seemed to Catherine that a direct threat was necessary in order to make them understand it all the better. In October 1581 she raised a very large sum, for her privy purse, sufficient to pay half the wages of 10,000 French infantry, as well as 4,000 Germans. She took up Antonio's cause, he meanwhile having arrived in France from England. The idea had come to her that if, with the help of the English, Philip II could be defeated by sea she would claim Brazil as the price of her intervention. She had always been interested in colonial affairs. Although she was a Queen she remembered that she was the daughter of merchants, and much as the impertinent remarks to which this gave rise annoyed her, Madame Catherine had an understanding of economic matters, of the interdependence of politics and economics, an understanding which was exceptional among the sovereigns of her day and would even have been unique, had Philip II not also shared it. She was magnificent and practical at one and the same time. She was impressed by the advantages that Spain derived from her overseas wealth. Even when her husband was still alive she was attracted by what today is known as exoticism. The scenes from Brazilian life performed on October 1, 1550, at Rouen had not found a bored spectator in Catherine. The physician Nicot had offered her snuff, the tobacco which was called the Queen's herb. She had supported Coligny's plans for a Calvinist exodus to America. In the spring of 1568 she had vehemently taken sides against the Cardinal of Lorraine and supported the French Protestants in Florida. She quarrelled with Elizabeth I—and very bitterly—on each occasion when English pirates captured French ships. The sea and the colonies were always of great importance to Catherine—yesterday, Florida; today, Brazil.[1]

An expedition against the Azores was planned to take place at the end of the autumn of 1580. For lack of money weeks and months passed before Brissac, in command of the troops, and Philippo Strozzi, head of the fleet, could leave. Catherine begged in vain for funds, from Henri III, the City of Paris, the bishops. She lamented yet she still did not despair of a change of mind on Elizabeth's part which would lead to Monsieur's marriage in spite of public opinion and the English ministers of the Crown. Philip II's spies kept him extremely well-informed. All useful information was reported to the

[1] Regarding all this, cf. in the admirable *Histoire de la Marine française* by Charles de La Roncière, *Le Secret de la Reine* (Catherine de Medici's own Colonial policy).

ambassador, Tassis, by great noblemen and ecclesiastics. Miguel Vaez, General-Intendant to Don Antonio of Portugal and a former Spanish bankrupt, was the Catholic King's best spy. He controlled a whole string of informers recruited among the unfortunate prince's confidants. Being thus furnished with first-hand evidence, Tassis bitterly reproached Henri III, who replied to him that he knew nothing of the business and that he had better address himself to his mother, whereupon she pretended to be highly astonished at the situation. Philip II was carefully preparing his counter-offensive. A fleet under the command of Santa-Cruz received orders to sail to the Azores.[1] Spain was fully conversant with the French plan to occupy Madeira recapture the Azores and the Islands of Cap Verde, and to follow this up with an expedition to Brazil of which Strozzi was appointed Viceroy. When Antonio had recovered the throne of Portugal, Brazil would become French. The final choice of the realistic Florentine shopkeeper had fallen on the American Empire and its vast wealth in preference to Portugal, ruined by the Moroccan disaster and the Spanish invasion.

Philip II organized troubles in France. Renieri, the Florentine envoy, informed his government of them: 'Those people who are aroused are many, but neutrals are few and I will give you an opinion which will be confirmed as correct, that the said passions are so violent that as concerns the business of the Crown and especially that of Monsieur, brother of the King, many people express the sorrow that they feel.' Renieri showed that many Frenchmen were no more than Spaniards, only endeavouring to serve the interests of Philip II. The gold from the galleons allowed a large number of consciences to be bought. Without doubt the masterpiece was to arrange for Vaez to accompany Don Antonio when he embarked with Strozzi's fleet on June 16, 1582. Nothing was allowed to escape Philip II's watchful eye, and he was informed of all the intrigues at the French Court. The most serious of these was that since the last months of 1582 Henri III's Mignons were waging a regular campaign against the Queen Mother.

The Mignons killed in duels, like Quélus, Maugiron, Livarot, Schomberg; assassinated, like Saint-Mesgrin or Bussy d'Amboise;

---

[1] Documents that were in the *Archives nationales, fonds Simancas*, κ 1560 and 1573. Forneron published the most important of them (*Histoire de Philippe II*, Vol. III, Chapter IV, in particular III and IV). Cf. also H. Léonardon: *Essai sur la Politique française et l'Intervention de Catherine de Médicis dans la Question de la Succession de Portugal*, 1578–83.) *Positions des Thèses de l'Ecole des Chartes*, 1889.) Cf. also Maurice Maindron: *L'Expédition des Açores*, one of this authority's last works, Paris, 1910.

dismissed, like Saint-Luc or d'O, were mostly cut-throats or play-boys, who took little interest in politics. But in order to pit the King's party against Monsieur's, Henri III wanted politically-minded Mignons. The two most famous of these were Arques, whom he created Duc de Joyeuse, and La Valette, Duc d'Epernon. The King persuaded the Duc de Mayenne to sell him his admiral's commission to the advantage of Joyeuse. As for the Duc d'Epernon, he was appointed Colonel-General of the French infantry in succession to Strozzi, when the latter was named as Viceroy of Brazil, as yet unconquered. Finally, Birague delivered up the seals to Cheverny. Henri III replaced Catherine's men by his own, accusing her of showing too much favour to Anjou.

The hatred between the two brothers was the first obstacle in the way of that unity which the Queen Mother longed for. With the King's party against Monsieur's and Catherine little by little forced into the role, which she found both ridiculous and hateful, of Dowager Queen, it could not have been made clearer both to the foreigner and the factions that the French State, split from top to bottom, was incapable of carrying out the mission of uni-fication on which the public welfare depended. The King built up his clan under the influence of Joyeuse and d'Epernon. Joyeuse became a member of the Royal Family on his marriage to Queen Louise's sister, whilst her brother, the Duc de Mercoeur, suc-ceeded the Duc de Montpensier in the government of Brittany. Epernon received that of the Three Archbishoprics, Joyeuse that of Normandy, Bernard Nogaret de la Valette, Epernon's brother, that of Saluzzo.

Henri III thus made clear his determination to hold the State through his creatures. His mother knew only too well that owing to his morbid changeability and weakness of character the contrary was inevitable and that his creatures would dominate the King. For that very reason the State was falling into the hands of feudalists, all the more dangerous as, being newcomers, their greed for gain and high offices was excessive. By force of circumstances the Queen Mother also grew to be looked upon as the head of a party, a head without followers. It seems that the key to her obstinacy over Portugal and her Brazilian plans was to be found in this situation—she needed a brilliant success that would provide her with supporters. She could depend on Philippo Strozzi. The commander of the fleet that was to sail to the Azores was a new Jason, setting out for the capture of a Golden Fleece without which the Florentine Queen would have no hope of reconquering power. Madame Catherine placed her hopes of good fortune and glory, which she knew to be irremediably threatened by the political Mignons, in the Argonauts voyaging towards the Azores archipelago.

At the same time she endeavoured to draw the King of Navarre and the Marshal de Montmorency into her game, for both of them were also in danger from the political Mignons. Epernon had the ambition to become Governor of Guyenne; Joyeuse was demanding Languedoc for his father and had had the archbishopric of Narbonne conferred on one of his brothers. The Queen Mother worked for a reconciliation between Navarre and Montmorency, but failed, for the Navarrese and the Marshal knew that her credit had fallen too low to wish to involve themselves with her. She met her son-in-law at the end of March 1582 at the castle of La Mothe-Saint-Héray, near Melle, in Poitou. She indiscreetly intervened in his love affair with one of Margot's maids-of-honour, Françoise de Montmorency, La Fosseuse. Henri allowed Margot and her mother to return to Paris without him and went back to Gascony. Once again Catherine's domestic problems destroyed her political plans. The quarrel regarding La Fosseuse became envenomed; the Queen heaped reproaches on her son-in-law, telling him quite bluntly what she thought of his conduct towards Margot: 'This is not the way to treat women of good standing and of such a House, to insult them on account of a public whore.' Meanwhile Montmorency took good care not to enter into any engagement whatever with her.

Madame Catherine was losing everything at one and the same time. Would the Duc d'Anjou, whose States-General of the Low Countries had recently proclaimed their sovereignty, be more favourably inclined towards her? In her every-penetrating and subtle mind the old Queen refused to separate the affairs, on the surface very disparate, of the Low Countries and Portugal. The military threat in the north alone was capable of lowering Philip II's strength in the south. If she were able to marry Monsieur to one of the Infantas, the Catholic King, with a daughter who was queen of the Low Countries, might perhaps surrender Portugal. But in these calculations Catherine was deluding herself—she underestimated Philip II's uncompromising and totalitarian imperialism which would never release her Portuguese inheritance for the pleasure of seeing one of his daughters reigning at Brussels. Great politician thought she was, Madame Catherine sometimes reasoned like a woman, emotionally rather than logically, and her son-in-law was well aware of it. As he wrote to Tassis on March 19, 1582, the Queen of France's plan was a crazy one.

Catherine herself regarded it as highly ingenious. She explained it in great detail to Henri III. Her aim was to re-establish the unity of the Kingdom of France. The Queen Mother was ceaselessly working to preserve that kingdom intact for Henri III, to give it back to him as it had been under Charles IX, with the exception of the strongholds in Savoy, which had been promised to Emmanuel-Philibert. On this responsibility her mind was perfectly clear and she viewed it in an objectively historical light: 'I have preserved and guarded it, [the French realm] from being divided into several parts: God granted it to me that I might see it entirely obedient to yourself, and whatever evil and hatred towards myself this may have occasioned this never came from people of position nor your good servants but from those whom I prevented from carrying out their own plans, for in the end those of their servants who remained were obliged to tell the truth and that I had preserved everything for you and the king your brother, as I should. I know that in doing this I did so for myself and partly in satisfaction of the obligation I bore towards the kings your father and grandfather, by preserving what they themselves ruled over and if not the whole at least in part as great as they left it. That is why I have never feared nor ever shall fear to say and do what I think able to serve to maintain everything as nearly as possible according to their intentions. . . . '

A superb apologia and so fully justified. In spite of everything, apart from Henri III's gifts in Savoy, the France of 1582 was the France of Cateau-Cambrésis. In spite of twenty years of appalling civil wars and the exhaustion of the State, neither Spain, England nor the Empire had been able to disrupt French continuity. Although ruined and bleeding the nation had remained whole. The *sine qua non* condition for its recovery had been safeguarded and saved. If Henri III and Monsieur were to become reconciled such a recovery could easily be made: 'That this kingdom, which is still so weak that it is like a sick man whom the slightest relapse might cause to die, may be preserved and restored to its previous state; thus any war, against whomever it might be, would plunge it into great and obvious ruin.'

The clarity of her language expressed that of her thoughts. Concerning Philip II and the Infanta's marriage the Queen Mother's delusion was a sentimental one, but when it came to the respective

situations of France and Spain her intellect worked realistically. If
Monsieur were able to maintain his position in Flanders, and if the
Azores could be retained, then, Catherine reckoned, the King of
Spain 'will in good earnest wish to negotiate, and in view of his age
common sense requires of him not to leave to his children, who may
be said to be still in swaddling-clothes, a war begun against such a
powerful enemy as you would be to them'. In the Queen's view
Flanders and Portugal were complementary means of bringing
pressure to bear on Philip II. And in this, history bore her out, for
the Portuguese never agreed to the annexation of their country nor
the Low Countries to the Spanish domination. The Catholic King
was weakened by the necessity to maintain himself there by force.
Yet he remained sufficiently strong to be able to deal terrible and
perhaps mortal blows to France were he compelled to go to war with
her. The dates of the Treaties of the Pyrenees in 1659, of Aix-le-
Chapelle in 1668, of Nymeghan in 1679, strikingly vindicate Catherine de Medici's foreign policy. It took nearly a century after Le
Cateau-Cambrésis and Henri IV, Louis XIII and Richelieu,
Mazarin, and finally Louis XIV, to overcome Spanish hegemony.
This shows sufficiently clearly what a war with Philip II would have
entailed at the time of Henri III; France might no doubt have borne
it more easily than was the view of Catherine de Medici, who had no
knowledge of the weaknesses inherent in the vast Spanish organization, as later revealed by the archives. In the end, however, even had
it cost Spain more dearly, it would have been as disastrous for France
as it had already proved to be under Henri II and would have been
under Charles IX. From 1560–80 the foreign policy of the Governess
of France followed the same lines because she was faced with the
same situation.

For the reasons she had explained to Henri III the Queen Mother
thought that the King of Spain would not engage himself very
completely in the Azores. But in thinking that her adversary would
not make a great effort to retain the Portuguese islands she was wrong.
She was counting on taking him by surprise, but this was not to be
the case, for the Spaniard was too well informed. His espionage
service was far better than Catherine's, who was mistaken about the
seriousness of her son-in-law's ailments. The bureaucrat of the
Escorial was one of those valetudinarians who survive much stronger
men. He was only eight years younger than his mother-in-law and
his career was to be as long as hers. He did not die until he was
seventy-one and she, who in 1581 had been expecting her son-in-law

to give up the ghost at any moment, by the time of his death had herself been dead for nine years. Her mistake was that of an energetic traveller regarding a feeble recluse who never left his study. In the same way Elizabeth I's affectations caused Catherine to overlook her genius with the contempt for a simpering old maid of a woman who knew no other passions than the passion for power.

She thought that she would succeed in this sudden attack on the Azores. Far more clearly than his mother, Henri III—whose intelligence, when he temporarily shook off his various manias, was really infallible—foresaw Philip's probable reactions, both in Flanders and the Portuguese islands. Nevertheless, as it concerned a matter of succession, Catherine appeared to him justified in proceeding against her son-in-law, even by means of war, since the latter had been the first to take up arms by invading Portugal, the reason for her claim. This matter did not concern France but solely Madame Catherine, heiress of Mahaut de Boulogne.

The heiress had carefully prepared the means with which to claim her inheritance. As Catherine wrote to de la Mauvissière, when Philippo Strozzi sailed from Belle-Isle on June 16, 1582, he was in command of fifty-five good ships. Exactly a month later Catherine de Medici's fleet arrived at the island of San Miquel in the Azores. The attack failed. The Marquis of Santa Cruz, one of the victors of Lepanto, met him with forty vessels and 7,000 men. The naval battle of July 26, 1582, was a disaster for France—Strozzi killed and 1,200 prisoners in the hands of the Spaniards, who garotted the officers and hanged the sailors, treating them as pirates, since no state of war had been proclaimed between the Very Catholic King and His Catholic Majesty. A second expedition was prepared, for Catherine wanted her revenge and the insolent delight of the Spaniards had wounded Henri III's pride, a pride that in this neurotic was so curiously blended with indifference. By the spring of 1583 a new French fleet made the Azores, but Santa Cruz, who disposed of 12,000 men and a hundred or so galleons, beat the French in the island of Terceira. This land victory complemented the naval victory of the preceding year. In both cases the annihilating counter-blow had been made possible by the superiorty of the Spanish information services over the French. The Queen Mother learned of this second defeat by intercepting Philip II's diplomatic courier in France. She temporarily renounced Portugal and turned to Flanders. As the Emperor's ambassador, Busbecq, wrote, 'she decided to take the stronghold of Cambrai as a pledge for her claims to Portugal'.

Since February 19, 1582, the Duc d'Anjou, who had become Duc de Brabant, was playing the king at Antwerp, but he was a king without power. The conspiracy of Salcedo proved to the new Duc de Brabant that the Spanish political police was the best in the world. Salcedo, an adventurer related to the Lorraine princes, had offered Monsieur his services, as an enemy of the Guises and of Spain, in order to avenge his father, a victim of the Cardinal de Lorraine. In fact, as a good double agent he was in the pay of those whom he was supposed to be fighting. William of Orange, to whom Salcedo's story had appeared suspicious, ordered an investigation of him, which proved instructive. The character in question had in the past been condemned, by default, to be boiled alive for arson and forgery. Arrested in Bruges, on the very day of the first French defeat in the Azores, he made a complete confession, from which it emerged that he had been employed by Henri de Guise to spy on Strozzi, and that a conspiracy had been planned against the Duc de Brabant. Calais was to be delivered up to Alessandro Farnese, and the Leaguers were to rise in the north of France, in alliance with the Savoyards in the south-east and the Spaniards in the south-west. Henri III was to be taken prisoner and Philip II would become master of France. To what extent was Salcedo telling the truth in his confession? This cannot be verified, since the records of his trial were destroyed after he had been quartered in Paris, on October 25, 1582. At the last moment, just before the four horses began to tear him apart, he retracted it under the promise of being strangled instead. The fact that Henri III and his mother witnessed his torture emphasized the exceptional importance they attached to the case; nor did this aspect of it escape Van Dyke in the remarkable pages he wrote on Salcedo's conspiracy. It is likely that Salcedo was a second La Renaudie, this time in the service of the Guises, and charged with organizing a tumult in Flanders in the course of which the Prince of Orange and the Duke of Brabant were to be assassinated. Catherine, remembering Amboise and Fontainebleau, determined to support Monsieur; Salcedo's revelations left her in no doubt that the Leaguers had settled on the Low Countries as their point of attack for the destruction of the Valois monarchy, by first eliminating the heir to the Crown and afterwards the King himself. The latter feared the power of the Guises, who were becoming more and more dangerous. His continued enmity towards his brother enabled him to see matters more clearly than Madame Catherine, who, in spite of all her grievances against him, still felt for her youngest son the natural affection of a mother. Like Jean Bodin, Henri III thought that Monsieur was incapable of bringing so difficult an enterprise to a successful issue, whilst the Queen imagined that she would be able to provide for everything.

Owing to his blunders, his inconsistencies and pretentiousness, the Duke of Brabant soon made himself unpopular. It was remembered how he had won Cambrai by trickery; he had taken advantage of being the guest of the governor, Inchi, to have the town occupied by French troops. He was wrongly accused of having instigated an attack on William of Orange and serious troubles in Antwerp had resulted from this. Papers found on the would-be murderer after he had been killed proved that he was a Spanish agent. These accusations and riots had severely strained relations between the Duke of Brabant and his subjects. The prince, whose nature was very revengeful, was anxious to punish the people of Antwerp and by a show of strength to tighten his hold over them, whilst they remained extremely jealous of their freedoms and rights. Thanks to the heavy reinforcements he received, under the command of the Duke of Montpensier and the Marshal de Biron (around 10,000 men) he thought himself entitled to behave, no longer as a liberator, but as a conqueror.

He conceived the plan of taking Antwerp by surprise, as he had Cambrai, and to follow this up with a series of attacks on Bruges, Dunkirk and Ostend. Fervaques incited him in this design and it is also possible that the Queen Mother approved of it as a compensation for her setback in the Azores. This is what her contemporaries claimed and Pierre Matthieu agreed with them. Biron and Montpensier were strongly against it. It is not impossible that Catherine de Medici may have believed that such a surprise attack might succeed. However that may be it was planned to take place on January 16, 1583.

The assault succeeded at Dunkirk, Dixmude, and Dendermonde, but failed completely at Ostend, Nieuport and Bruges. The following day Monsieur in person led the attack on Antwerp, which he had just left. One of the gates was stormed and the town occupied. The people of Antwerp fought back with such fury that the French, to whom it seemed that the Matins of Paris were recurring, were soon routed, leaving behind twelve or fifteen hundred killed and several hundred prisoners, including Fervaques. The fugitives were pursued by armed peasants. Monsieur did not halt until he reached the outskirts of Malines. The canal gates had been opened and stranglings were followed by drownings. The survivors were rallied by the Duke of Montpensier. This catastrophe became known to history as the

Folly of Antwerp and through it France lost any further chance of conquering the Low Countries. The impotent fury of the French was laughed at everywhere. Alessandro Farnese, whose diplomatic ability—inherited from his mother, the second great Marguerite of Austria—Philip II's natural sister—was no whit inferior to his brilliant military leadership, at once assumed the role of pacificator. Whilst the Protestants remained uncompromising the Flemish Catholics were drawing closer to Spain. Catherine had immediately disavowed her son and repudiated all official French responsibility for the Folly of Antwerp. But the blow had fallen, nonetheless; the Flemish Catholics preferred the Duke of Parma and the Catholic King to Monsieur and the Very Christian King. Yet again one of her children had dragged Madame Catherine into an adventure that ended deplorably, and the advantage she had hoped to gain by it as compensation for the Azores disaster escaped her.

But as we know, she never allowed herself to be discouraged. Bellièvre negotiated very cleverly with the States-General of the Low Countries. Catherine had taken matters in hand, as is shown by her letter of January 30, 1583, to the Prince of Orange, in addition to Mirambeau's mission to him. She maintained that intriguers and adventurers had forced the Duc de Brabant's hand. Orange could not be taken in by such a daring claim, but he needed the support of France against Spain and he upheld Bellièvre in his negotiations which on March 18th led to the agreement of Termonde. Monsieur was allowed to keep Dunkirk and the Antwerp prisoners were released; in return the French were to evacuate the other occupied towns, and their troops were to be disbanded. Monsieur was discouraged by his mother's annoyance and his brother's enmity. His health was declining more and more rapidly and he left Dunkirk, of which Spain regained possession on June 18, 1583. But with his usual changeability the fugitive Duc de Brabant refused to give up his Flemish aspirations altogether and also to make an act of submission to Henri III. The disagreements between the King and his legitimate successor caused their mother the greatest anguish, which was aggravated by the double setbacks she had suffered in the Azores and the Low Countries, in consequence of which the Spanish marriage, by which François de Valois might have gained a crown, became as chimerical as the English one.

But on the contrary the Spanish threat to France was becoming a terrifying reality. Although the Low Countries had been pacified, thanks to Farnese, it was a certainty that Philip II would demand a heavy price from France for Catherine's personal intervention in the Azores. The old Queen realized this so clearly that she felt the loss of Dunkirk as a very heavy blow. She revealed her despair in a letter dated July 25, 1583, to Castelnau de La Mauvissière. Monsieur's incompetence was now as clear as daylight and he must at any price be deprived of the means of carrying out his deplorable plans which would have no other result than war with Spain. Thenceforward Catherine's restricted aims were to give up Flanders and to save Cambrai. In order that they should succeed it was necessary that Monsieur should cease to play at being Duc de Brabant, the ludicrous sovereign of a phantom State, and re-affirm his obedience to Henri III. Once her domestic peace was re-established it would be possible to restore political unity. On July 11th Madame Catherine had a meeting with François at Chaulnes, in order to induce him to return to the French Court. Henri III was demanding that he should do so, quite rightly taking the view that his brother's enterprises were ruining the kingdom.

Monsieur chose to make no reply to the King's request. From Chaulnes he went to Nesles, and from there to La Fère, where his mother again visited him, on August 19th. She lectured him on the necessity of being reconciled with Henri III, and on the defence of Cambrai. The young Prince finally went there, remaining in that town from the beginning of September until the beginning of October 1583. After a few weeks spent at Laon, he installed himself on November 9th at Château-Thierry, which formed part of his appanges. He was feeling more and more unwell and his mother's insistence was exacerbating him; as he could not prevent her from visiting him, he opposed her by the force of inertia. Yet he kept in touch with the Huguenots in the Low Countries and tried to obtain the help of those in France. At that time Philip II was making approaches to Henri de Navarre. Owing to Monsieur's illness, which was incurable (haemophtisis, fever, nocturnal sweating, all the symptoms of advanced tuberculosis, the illness from which Charles IX had died) it was clear that the Béarnais would be the next King of France. Nor, knowing himself already to be the successor to the Crown of Lilies, did he hesitate to keep Henri III informed of the proposals made to him by the Catholic King.

Duplessis-Mornay gave Henri III detailed evidence on the Spanish plans to raise the Calvinists in the south, by promising the King of Navarre subsidies and the opportunity to enlarge his States at the expense of the King of France. Duplessis-Mornay was accompanied by Maximilien de Béthune, the future Duc de Sully. The King of Navarre's confidential advisers were among those Royalist Protestants who preserved intact the tradition of national policy championed by Catherine de Medici, a policy that was slipping from the now feeble hands of the Queen Mother and which Henri de Navarre had taken over. As Henri III understood the situation quite clearly, he offered the sum of 100,000 écus to his cousin and his servants as a token of gratitude. Duplessis-Mornay replied that neither his master nor he desired any reward as they had only wished to prove that one could be at one and the same time a good Huguenot and a good Frenchman. Duplessis-Mornay's letters to Henri de Navarre show that thenceforward the latter was acting as heir-presumptive to the Crown. The Béarnais had taken over the policy of Catherine.

Duplessis-Mornay, who wrote to him as his councillor—and a sovereign's councillor is always his confidant—made this policy very clear: 'Remember that from this moment the whole of France and even Europe will have their eyes fixed on Your Majesty. It will be for you, Sire, to direct your life and your acts in such wise that not only will the public find in them nothing to criticize, but even everything to praise. I mean, Sire, that the King should find in them obeisance to himself; the princes, fraternity; the Parliaments, a love of justice; the nobility, magnanimity; the people, a care for their relief; the clergy, moderation; your enemies, clemency and ease of accommodation; and all of them, in general, an open nature, free from perfidy, dissimulation, vengefulness and animosity, virtues, in truth, that you have not acquired but which are natural to you. . . . It is suitable, now, that you should make love to France. . . .'

Make love to France—a magnificent phrase. A task for a man, a warrior, and a hero. In spite of her genius, her will to serve, and her patriotism, Catherine de Medici was only a woman. However brave she had shown herself to be in the trenches of Rouen and Havre, she was only a diplomat. With all her courage she was no heroine and preferred compromise to sacrifice. Only for a short time did she ever become a lioness; her normal temperament was that of the fox. She loved France passionately, but she could not make love to her. The unity for which Catherine strove so hard could not be won by cunning, but had to be mastered by the force of the warrior who would take to his bed a France that had been conquered in order to be saved.

Henri III was no more able than his mother to save France. Catherine nevertheless made this salvation possible. She took all the necessary measures for the defence of Cambrésis. Her correspondence from the end of the summer of 1583 until the end of the spring of 1584 enables us to follow them, and forms one of the most valuable sources of evidence in proof of her political clearsightedness. The Queen Mother's instructions to La Mauvissière and Bellièvre are as precise as they are detailed. England and Navarre were the two poles between which she operated in order to contain the Spanish threat. Bellièvre was sent from the Low Countries to Béarn. Catherine's relations with her son-in-law were particularly difficult in view of a fantastic domestic situation which once again developed to impede her policy. Her contemporaries have dealt at great length with this affair, which became a scandal and which concerned the quarrel between Henri III and his sister Marguerite. This is what happened.[1]

Margot's affection for her brother François was a perpetual source of conflict between her and Henri III, who according to the Venetian ambassadors was even more afraid of seeing him become King of the Low Countries than of Philip II remaining in occupation of them. In addition, the Queen of Navarre detested the political Mignons, Epernon and Joyeuse, who slandered her, all the more easily as her many love affairs were the talk of the Court and the town. They told Henri III that she was trying to prevent her husband from drawing closer to him. Monsieur's disaster in Flanders deprived Margot of all support against the King; Catherine, mortified by her own Portuguese failure, avoided contradicting her son, whose opinions had been right regarding the deplorable business of the succession to the Countess of Boulogne, and refrained from supporting her daughter. Guillaume Du Vair, in his *Anecdotes* and Varillas in *L'Histoire d'Henri III* expatiated on the love affair between Queen Margot and de Champvallon, favourite of François d'Anjou. Endless gossip kept Henri III informed of his sister's amorous adventures. He wrote a report about them to Joyeuse, and the courier carrying it was killed. The King, convinced that Marguerite was responsible for his murder in order

---

[1] Cf. the correspondence of Busbecq, the Emperor's ambassador, which leaves us in no doubt regarding the violent scenes between Henri III and Margot. Cf. also Ph. Lauzun, *Itinéraires de Marguerite de Valois*; the article by Baguenault de Puchesse on the *Renvoi par Henri III de Marguerite de Valois* (*Revue des Questions Historiques*, October 1, 1901); and the books by Merki and Mariéjol on Queen Margot, as well as the article by Amand Garnier, *Un Scandale princier au XVIe siècle*, in the *Revue du XVIe siècle*, Vol. 1, 1913.

to obtain possession of this too compromising document, and once more falling a victim to his neurosis, impulsively decided to avenge himself. According to Busbecq, he insulted the Queen of Navarre with indescribable violence in front of the entire Court, at the ball of August 7, 1583, at which she was doing the honours in place of Queen Louise, who was then holidaying at Bourbon-Lancy.

On comparing all the original documents it appears that Busbecq was reporting gossip, and that the scene between Henri III and his sister was not witnessed by the entire Court, since balls never took place when the King was not in residence. The documents confirm that Henri III was in retreat in the Bois de Boulogne, and that the Queen Mother was close by (her letter of August 8, 1583, to the Marshal de Matignon, was addressed to him from Passy). The scandal must have occurred privately; the Mignons and a few ladies may have been present and there had possibly been dancing after supper. Nevertheless everyone was talking about a scene during the course of a ball and the news spread through Paris so that fifteen days later Busbecq thought it his duty to inform the Viennese Court of it. The Queen of Navarre had been driven out on the 8th, and if Busbecq is to be believed Henri III had told his sister to relieve the Court of her infectious presence. Champvallon, whose house was searched, had fled. Margot was treated like a public prostitute and her litter was searched at Palaiseau by the King's archers as she was travelling towards her States.

The memoirs of the period are full of picturesque and often contradictory details of these incidents, as ridiculous as they were unpleasant, in which public opinion, always greedy for scandal, delighted, whilst Catherine, as her letters reveal, was trying to repair the damage done by her double failure—her Portuguese caprice (this correct and charming description of it was the Tuscan ambassador's), and Monsieur's expedition to Flanders. At that moment she fell ill, 'beset by melancholy passions', as her doctor, Renaud Vigor, wrote to Henri III. She was given appocene laxatives which, by causing incredible vomitting, gave her relief. The quack did not suspect that the technical terms he used expressed the profound disgust of the Queen Mother at her children's shameful behaviour at a moment when it was a matter of extricating themselves with the least possible damage from an extremely difficult political situation. She knew her son-in-law well enough to be certain that he would use his wife's expulsion as a pretext for making new political demands on Henri III concerning affairs in Guyenne, which had still not been settled. Margot had written to her mother, begging her to defend her against the accusation that she was pregnant by a casual lover. She was expecting to die and demanded that after her death an autopsy should be held.

Such were the anxieties with which her children's quarrels burdened Catherine de Medici. The King of Navarre refused to receive his dishonoured wife, protesting to Henri III and demanding explanations and proofs. When his anger passed away, Henri III had enough intelligence to realize the political consequences of the scandal he had so incautiously started. Henri de Navarre's good offices were necessary in order to bring the pacification of the south to a successful issue. The Queen immediately took steps to appease him, charging Bellièvre with making good Henri III's mistake. She wrote to him on September 6, 1583, without hiding from him how difficult his task would be.

Not realizing that her son Anjou was so ill, she went on with the marriage plans she was making for him. Her principle, conforming to the method of Roman diplomacy, was never to give up and even less to break off any negotiations so long as her partner in them had not taken the initiative in breaking them off. In spite of Philip II's obvious ill-will and bad faith, on September 6th she wrote to the Sieur de la Motte-Longlée, her representative in Spain, that she was hoping to have more time to devote to the negotiations for the marriage with one of the Infantas. Meanwhile she was using every effort to deter her son-in-law Navarre from the reprisals he was threatening to take, both against a wife, whose indecent behaviour was legendary in France and all Europe, and his brother-in-law, responsible for the scene which had made it public knowledge. She was in correspondence with Bellièvre, whom the Béarnais had received kindly, at the end of October 1583. It was nevertheless necessary to negotiate with him until the middle of April 1584 before the King and Queen of Navarre were reconciled. Her son-in-law's deliberate procrastination did not exhaust Madame Catherine's patience; to what tests had he not already put it!

Nor did the Queen Mother neglect Cambrésis for Navarre. She renounced the Low Countries solely in order to concentrate resistance on Cambrai. Her aim was still to bring Anjou and his brother together again. The latter could not have been less inclined to be reconciled with him. A letter from Catherine to Villeroy, written from Château-Thierry, where she was staying with Monsieur, on January 2, 1584, informs us that Henri III was thinking of depriving the former 'of all the advantages and prerogatives bestowed on him by himself and the late King, his brother, in granting him his appanage'. On January 25th, having a week earlier returned to Saint-Germain-en-Laye, she wrote to Castelnau de la Mauvissière: 'I made a long journey to visit my son the Duc d'Anjou, which I hope will have served always to maintain the good friendship between the King, Monsieur my son, and him, and will remove the opinions that certain malicious persons put into his head.'

In spite of the political Mignons, his mother's authority over Henri III was still sufficiently great to cause him finally to give up his intentions of depriving Monsieur of his prerogatives. The King even agreed to see him, and invited him in affectionate terms to stay with him for the pre-Lenten carnival festivities. The Duc d'Anjou had until then refused to give way to his mother's pleading and to return to Court. Sulky, melancholy, and ill, as Nevers said in his *Mémoires*, the loser of Antwerp imagined that there was a conspiracy against him. He was threatening to sell Cambrai to Spain, which greatly alarmed Catherine de Medici, who wrote to Bellièvre on November 22, 1583, saying that she doing everything possible to deter the prince from this harmful plan.

The Queen Mother's feelings were disturbed by the thought that this city, which circumstances had allowed to be united with France, should fall to the foreigner. Whenever she spoke of her country's soil the most moving phrase came naturally to her mind. And now one of her own sons was considering selling the conquered city! This made it appear to the Queen all the more necessary to keep a watch on him, and for this reason Monsieur's acceptance of his brother's invitation filled her with the greatest delight. The States-General of the Low Countries had again approached him with a request to contain Spain. It is possible that when he agreed to return to Court Monsieur had a political afterthought and hoped to interest Henri III in another attempted intervention. Like all consumptives he was making the most splendid plans for the future, whilst his state of health became worse and worse. On February 12, 1584, he arrived at his mother's, who was at that moment herself ill and in bed, at her Hôtel des Repenties in the Rue de Grenelle-Saint-Honoré, the famous Hôtel de la Reine of which she was very fond, because it was surrounded by a large garden and was also conveniently near the Louvre.

Ill though she was, she got up in order to bring the two brothers together; made them become reconciled and embrace one another, whilst the King expressed himself as satisfied. 'I praise God with all my heart', she wrote on February 23rd to Liverdis, ambassador to the Swiss Catholics, 'to see them on such good terms, which can only be for the great good and prosperity of the affairs of the realm,' and on March 11th, to Bellièvre 'I need not also tell you of the pleasure I had in seeing my son return to the arms of the King, in the way . . . that he has done. I never knew a greater joy since the death of the King, my lord, and I am sure that had you seen the behaviour of them both you would have wept, like me, for joy.' She added, in her invincible optimism still not realizing the degree to which the Duc d'Anjou's disease was ravaging him, that 'he has returned to Château-Thierry, where his tertiary fever has since recurred, but in those parts it is a common illness from which nobody dies, but which is a long one. I pray to God that he may soon be cured of it'.

She received worse news, left for Château-Thierry on March 19th, found the patient improved, was reassured and on the spot wrote a letter to Villeroy on the business of Cambrai and Flanders. She thought him convalescent and left. At the beginning of April she went to Montceaux-en-Brie for a few days' rest. Her journey had done her good, but as soon as she returned to Saint-Maur-des-Fossés she fell ill again, which did not, however, slow down her activities. The reconciliation between the King of Navarre and Margot complemented that of Henri III and Monsieur. Madame Catherine was so happy that she wrote to Bellièvre in her letter of April 25th: 'After God you have given me back my health, by having through your prudence and good management, carried out so good and important a task for our whole House and honour, as to have re-united my daughter with her husband.'

Had her struggle for unity at last attained its end? Was the domestic unity that had been achieved a precedent for a return to national unity? The Queen Mother was certain of it. Nonetheless, she wrote to Bellièvre on April 29th that 'it is something to which I am so accustomed, never to have an unspoilt joy'. As his illness relentlessly progressed, the Duke d'Anjou was going through one crisis after another; with sad simplicity Catherine's letters reveal her maternal suffering stage by stage. Separated from her youngest son, she was re-living the days passed ten years previously at the bedside of Charles IX, the alternating moments of hope and despair which precede the death of a consumptive. However much she was in love with politics, Madame Catherine remained a loving and cruelly tried mother. Reading her letters, how can one doubt it, and not despise the stupid calumnies of the libellers and the chroniclers? On May 23rd she had again left for Château-Thierry. Her hopes revived and she informed Bellièvre of them: 'I saw him last evening and found him in good condition, considering his illness, and at night he is still better, which gives me hope that according to the doctors he will recover and that God will take pity on me, who have lost so many, and that He may grant me that I should see no more die; which is what I beg of Him and that He may allow me to go, according to my age.'

A touching and gentle reproach. . . . Jules Gassot was right to call her that good Mother Catherine. In these intimate notes we see her as she really was at bottom—a bourgeoise who did not dress up her emotions; the kingdom was her household and with her passion for politics she combined a permanent desire to see her brood well set-up.

François died on the following June 10th, 'at the castle of Château-Thierry', reported l'Estoile, 'of a haemorrhage accompanied by a slow fever which had shrunken him little by little until he was all dried up and emaciated'. He was thirty years old. His mother, who had not expected such a sudden end, was at Saint-Maur. This is how she informed Bellièvre of this new loss: 'You can imagine what it must be like to see myself so unhappy at living so long that I see everyone dying before me; even although I know that one must bow to God's will, that all belongs to Him and that He does but lend us for so long as it pleases Him the children he gives us; yet human nature cannot so easily resign itself so that one does not realize the loss that one has suffered, and I, it seems to me, have all the more reason to complain of my misfortune as I see myself deprived of all save one who remains to me, although he be, thank God, very healthy, so that if he were to have children, as I hope to God he will have, it would be a great consolation to me and for all this realm, for besides my own grief I should also feel that one it would have if this race were to end, for the obligation that I have and no great consolation remaining to me except to see those who remain of the King my lord on good terms together, they being now only two.'

Henri and Marguerite. Being the only two left, would their reconciliation not now take place? Her mother appealed to Marguerite. 'I would pray you to say to the Queen of Navarre, my daughter', she wrote to Bellièvre, 'that she be not a cause of increasing my sorrow, and that she be willing to recognize the King, her brother, as she should, and do nothing to offend him. . . .' Let Marguerite become the link between Henri III and the future Henri IV, and if thus the Royal Family were reunited after so many cruel quarrels, the efforts of the Governess of France would not have been wasted.

On such unity the unity of the kingdom might be re-built after twenty-five years of divisions. The princes and the great had set the people the example of such divisions, although the old Queen could pride herself on having incessantly fought against them. Even when she had aroused opposition she had done so deliberately in order to weaken the forces of division. The facts and documents are there to prove that even when her methods varied her aim remained immutable. The Florentine Queen could say with Machiavelli that 'those who do not know how to change their methods when the times demand it, no doubt prosper so long as they march hand in hand with Fortune, but are lost, should the latter alter and they fail to follow this goddess in her blind changes'.

Would Fortune pause, this time, to give France that unity for which Catherine de Medici longed so much, and to achieve which she had struggled so hard? Henri III had accepted his mother's policy of an alliance with the King of Navarre, and sent the Duke d'Epernon to him with this intention, dealing with and treating him as the heir-presumptive. In consequence he invited him to become a Catholic again. But alas, another nine years were to elapse before the Béarnais, in spite of his political genius, having become Henri IV, resigned himself to giving up his mother's religion for that of his kingdom.

Nine years that were lost to France.

PART IV

THE SOLITUDE OF EVENING

CHAPTER ONE

THE VICTORY OF VIOLENCE
(June 1584—September 1588)

❧❀❧

The death of Monsieur raised two political problems of extreme importance. At home the King of Navarre became the heir-presumptive to the Crown, since Henri III, now married for nine years, still had no children and it was almost a certainty that he would have no direct descendants. Abroad, by the will of the late Duc de Brabant, the King of France was left the succession to his realm, of which the only part still remaining to him was the Cambrésis. As the acceptance of this legacy might constitute a *casus belli* with Spain, it was necessary to find some means of retaining Cambrai without annexing it. The Portuguese succession provided an example. Henri III renounced Cambrai and his brother's rights in the Low Countries. The Queen Mother inherited the Cambrésis in her own right.

This was arranged within a few days. Immediately on the death of Monsieur the consuls of Cambrai had sworn an oath of fidelity to Catherine de Medici, requesting her aid and protecion. On June 18, 1584, Alessandro Farnese protested on this score to the Court of France. In spite of this, three days later, the Queen Mother went a step further. She notified the people of Cambrai of her pleasure and her intention of protecting them, their lives, goods and rights. She took care to emphasize that she did so in response to a free appeal from the consuls and people of Cambrai. She expressed her joy at their unanimity, thanked them for the oath of loyalty they had sworn and for wishing to live and die under her protection. Jean de Monluc, Sieur de Balagny, Governor of Cambrai, son of the late bishop of Valence, belonged to the inner circle of Madame Catherine's servitors, but events were soon to show that her confidence in him was misplaced. The documents prove that the Queen Mother immediately took all necessary steps to hold the Cambrésis, but that Balagny was hastening to betray her, negotiating with Spain with the intention of becoming the successor to the prince-archbishops of Cambrai under Spanish sovereignty. Catherine believed him to be faithful to her and had charged the Cardinal de Retz to organize in conjunction with him this new possession, which to some degree compensated her for her set-back in Portugal. Shrewdly as usual, the Queen in accordance with the Capet tradition represented herself as a protectress and not a conqueror, and avoided referring to herself as the sovereign. It was always more important to her to hold power in fact rather than in name, as had been the case during her Regency, whilst Charles IX was still a minor. Her letters make this abundantly clear. The situation was therefore as follows—the Cambresians remained autonomous under the protection of the Queen of France; Balagny had no other official designation than a military one. A diplomatic agent was appointed to represent France in dealing with the Prince of Parma as regarded the business of Cambrésis.

This agent, by the name of Blatier, Lord of Belloy, enjoyed Catherine's particular confidence and enabled her to keep watch on Balagny, whose ambitions she had soon discovered. They were shared by his wife, Renée de Clermont, sister of Bussy d'Amboise. In reading the Queen Mother's numerous letters dealing with Cambrai, nearly all of them addressed to the faithful Retz, one is struck by the degree to which she left the initiative to her representatives, by the care she took to be discreet in the wielding of her authority, which nevertheless gave her the greatest satisfaction. She invariably associated the King's name with her own, knowing as she did that by refraining from arousing his touchiness she would gain a free hand, and wherever she wished to have it. As she wrote to Retz on September 4, 1584, her method of dealing with Cambrai was to maintain everything whilst making no innovations. Thus, with her customary patience, on December 15th she achieved the truce of Bures, signed by the Prince of Parma as Lieutenant-Governor and Captain-General of the Low Countries, and Blatier, as agent of the Very Christian King. This was a major success, for both sides agreed that for one year, as from January 1, 1585, there would be no more fighting in Flanders between the French and the Spaniards.

As protectress of Cambrai Catherine de Medici had succeeded in six months in the pacification of the northern frontier. In a thorny and dangerous situation she now had a year of at least relative peace ahead of her. She intended to put that time to good use by carrying out another and equally difficult task, that of religious pacification, by converting to Catholicism the future King of France, Henri de

Navarre, head of the French Protestants and regarded as a public enemy by the Leaguers, whose power was growing from day to day. Although they did not hate the Béarnais, the French Catholics as a whole would not allow that the King of France might be a heretic. Their apprehensions were only too well justified by the principle, of *cujus regio ejus religio* observed throughout Europe; a Huguenot King would mean a Huguenot France and bring Catholic France under a rule similar to those of England under Henry VIII and the Lutheran States of the Empire.

The very failure of Catherine de Medici's policy of two religions under one prince left no hope that once the Calvinists became masters of the State they would accept that, owing to the King of Navarre's personal tolerance, that State should remain Catholic. To discuss whether a Protestant sovereign might have been able to reign over a Catholic country in the sixteenth century is an anachronism. It would have been contrary both to the spirit and the customs of the period if in the sixteenth century a sovereign had tolerated a minority that did not belong to his own religion. Henri IV had to resort to force—which Catherine always lacked—to push through the edict of Nantes, which still did not put an end to the Protestant Wars. To achieve this it was necessary to attain to the peace of Alès (the edict of Grace) in 1629, by the victory of Louis XIII and Richelieu over the people of la Rochelle. A sovereign who did not belong to the same religion as almost the whole of his people—one must incessantly return to the fact that the official Huguenots only comprised about one-sixteenth of the population of the kingdom, and that the *sympathisants*, thanks to whom they appeared to include larger numbers, would never have tolerated the yoke of the preachers—a Calvinist King in Catholic France is a chimera. The conflict between the Salic Law and the heresy of the heir to the Crown was insoluble otherwise than by the heir's renunciation of his heresy. Given the dual fanaticism of the Leaguers and the Huguenots, the family tradition of Jeanne d'Albret's son, the general resistance of a Catholic country to a Protestant monarchy, the problem could only be resolved by tragedy. Henri III's and his mother's political acuteness never doubted this for a moment. They were immediately and completely in agreement on the need for Epernon's mission to the Béarnais. And religious and civil peace would depend on the success of this mission.

In her letter to Bellièvre of July 4, 1584, from Montceaux-en-Brie, Madame Catherine expressed her anxiety regarding her daughter Marguerite, who loathed the Duc d'Epernon. She asked Bellièvre to ensure that the Queen of Navarre made the envoy of the King of France welcome. The diplomat and her husband concurred, and Marguerite agreed to receive Epernon kindly when he arrived at the Court of Nérac on August 4th. The Béarnais was too intelligent and well-balanced not to realize that as the heir-presumptive his wisest course would be to become a Catholic. But he was not merely a heretic—he had relapsed, having abjured the Reformation on Saint Bartholomew, and having subsequently re-joined it. He now considered that a second abjuration would be contrary to his honour. Owing to an oversight, to which even the ablest party leaders are not immune, he imagined that his forces were stronger than in fact they were and he did not despair of imposing himself as a conqueror on Catholic France, although resolved, as far as he was concerned, to respect its traditions and beliefs. His entourage thought the same, as is proved by Philippe Canaye de Fresne's account of the discussions brought about by Epernon's visit. Arnault Du Ferrier, who had become Chancellor of Navarre, claimed that the sincerity of Henri's conversion would be universally suspect, but it would have been easy to reply to this argument that such suspicion would only be found among the Huguenots and the Leaguers and that most of the French people would, on the contrary, be happy to see the Blood of France submit to the true faith.

The King of Navarre did not think of such an answer. He thought that it would be possible for him to become the Protestant sovereign of a Catholic nation and Du Ferrier also believed this. Their mistake lay in thinking that France was weary to the point of accepting such an innovation, compared to which the policy of compassion desired by Catherine de Medici was a mild one, and in not realizing that even that policy had been impotent. They believed that the time had come for religious peace: 'All France is famished for that time to arrive. The two factions, seemingly so incompatible, finding themselves thus reunited by clemency, will themselves throw off all hatred and rancour and will renounce all seditious leagues.' Thus Ferrier reasoned, in complete ignorance of the true state of mind of the French people, even those least inclined to join the League. His master agreed with him. Political realism was on the side of Catherine and Henri III, whom the events bore out.

The old Queen and her son saw the situation as a whole. The Béarnais and his Chancellor saw it through the prisms of their own generosity, curiously associated with their party interests. This association alone explains their illusions (similar to those of all their contemporaries excepting Catherine de Medici and Henri III after the death of his mother), that one could serve France and the dynasty even in rebelling against the State when, having fallen into unworthy hands, it had to be set free from them. Parties as such did exist in the sixteenth century and with what factional fury! Yet our conception of the term today was foreign to the men of that time. Whether on one side or the other they all appeared to be sincerely convinced of their own devotion to the public welfare. It was a case of protecting the king against his enemies or of tearing him from them. They believed themselves to be and called themselves his protectors even when they held the king in their power. Those who wished to destroy that power considered and called themselves liberators.

A Son of France, Henri de Navarre regarded himself at one and the same time as the appointed protector of a weak prince such as his cousin Valois and an equally appointed liberator of the throne which Henri de Guise was obviously intending to seize. His followers were no less convinced of this. That was why certain isolated Catholics served under his standard in the hope of his conversion; such as Antoine de Roquelaure, whom, in his report, Philippe Canaye de Fresne shows opposing the minister Marmet, a fanatic filled with revengeful anger against the butchers of Saint Bartholomew, and Du Ferrier, who thought that the time had come when religious peace could be attained through mutual concessions.

Nothing could be more false than to imagine that with the exception of certain adventurers the men of the sixteenth century lived on the party to which they belonged. This is another example of making the serious historical error of attributing to our ancestors the feelings and habits of our own time, parallel and antinomian to the political illusion that would project on to our period the ways of the past. These two illusions are the running sores of history written by men of literature. The men of the sixteenth century never believed that the State should belong to the strongest of them, but were solely concerned with justice and the public welfare. They formed parties in order to serve the State and to save it, to save and serve the king, the State's natural pilot. Henri de Navarre and Du Ferrier had understood that after twenty-five years of civil wars the monarchy had itself become a party and the King, surrounded by his Mignons, a party leader. The Salic Law, according to which the heretical Bourbon was the incontestable heir to the Lily throne, legitimized his determination to become the King of all the French without abjuring his religion. It would ensure the victory of his party in the cause of national salvation.

The Catholics, reasoning similarly, but in the opposite sense, discovered in this law the certainty of their defeat. Since the Valois had produced no heir in the direct line the Crown had become a stake which each side claimed. As Henri III's cousin to the twenty-second degree his brother-in-law was incontestably a Prince of the Blood. But for too many years the mystique of the Blood of France had been soiled by the powder and smoke of fratricidal struggles and no longer retained its immaculate purity. Catherine de Medici and Henri III understood this, and that Navarre's conversion was ineluctable in order to avoid a new War of Religion, even more terrible than the former ones, and in which the fundamental laws of the kingdom themselves would be at stake.

Catherine and her son had too deep a respect for the dynastic tradition to admit the possibility of a mortal blow being dealt to that tradition by the refusal of the French people to accept the legitimate heir as their king. There was only one possible solution, namely that the legitimate heir should return to the traditional religion. But the King of Navarre was not yet willing to accept this solution. He was, however, too prudent to bar the way to reconciliation entirely. He was prepared 'to be guided by a free and legitimate council, in which the controversies concerning matters of religion would be well debated and decided'. He did not see that there was any urgency in the matter. He suggested a middle path which Catherine, more realistic in this case than her son-in-law, knew to be inefficacious and which, in spite of her predilection for compromise, she did not dwell upon. He would remain a Calvinist, but offered his alliance to Henri III against the Leaguers. He thought that Henri, although not in the best of health, was in no mortal danger. The King was thirty-three and his successor had plenty of time to wait. The propagandists of the Guises deliberately exaggerated Henri III's ill-health, claiming that he was decrepit and on the edge of the grave. How long would he survive? And in any case, cried the Lorraine supporters, it would come to the same thing, for he was also on the verge of madness. According to them the kingdom was likely to find itself under a second Charles VI, and handed over to an heretical regent.

Here was a splendid theme for the Guisards, the Jesuits, the curés of Paris and the big cities to embroider their arguments on. The Protestant atrocities in England and the Low Countries allowed one to foresee what would become of unhappy France under an heretical king! Remember Mary Stuart, Queen Dowager of France, in Elizabeth I's prisons! And Scotland under the Presbyterian terror, and martyred Ireland! The paper war was in favour of the Lorraines and the Catholic zealots. Too many proven facts could be brought up against an heretical monarchy. Even the implacable war, in France itself, between the political police of England and Spain provided both parties with information, which made the cruellest repressions possible. All well-informed people knew this to be the case. Had not the King of Navarre sent Jacques de Ségur-Pardaillan on a mission to the German Lutheran princes? For some time past Catherine de Medici had been having this person watched, as she informed her ambassador in England, Castelnau de La Mauvissière, in her letter of November 25, 1583. She knew that Ségur-Pardaillan accompanied by Soffroy de Calignon, was Henri de Navarre's agent in Germany, the Low Countries and the Empire. Mauvissière had obtained copies of documents for her, for which she thanked him on December 17th. She was also watching another gentleman in the service of her son-in-law—the Sieur de Chassincourt. She was very well informed.

On June 28, 1584, she wrote to Danzay, ambassador at Copenhagen, that Ségur-Pardaillan was dealing, in Germany, with a plan for a league between Lutherans and Calvinists, in order to 'trouble Christianity, and if it were possible, to re-light the fire which has been put out in this realm'. The Guisards also had an excellent espionage service which collaborated very closely with that of Spain. They even published a libel at Frankfort, entitled *Le Boute-Feu des Calvinistes*, containing all the useful documents with regard to the mission of Ségur-Pardaillan. The King of Navarre's plans were all defensive, but he was accused of offensive ones and was violently denounced for his duplicity. The Leaguers represented themselves as the defenders of an innocent people whom the most perfidious of princes was planning to massacre, making use of his position as heir-presumptive to murder the Catholics. Contrary to the King of Navarre's opinion, there was no time to be lost in order that he should by abjuration put an end to the more and more rapid development of the spirit of the League. It grew even more quickly as the result of the accusation that was carefully spread around after the failure of Epernon's mission, that there was a criminal connivance between the Queen Mother, Henri III and Henri de Navarre.

Catherine and her son were too clearsighted to make any mistake about it; they knew that their real enemy was Henri de Guise and not Henri de Navarre. The alliance the latter had offered them would only have been of advantage had he been converted at the same time. Remaining a heretic the Bourbon was compromising the Valois, instead of serving him. The Duc de Guise did not fail to stress such a shameful rapprochement. The influence of the leader of the Catholic zealots had continued to grow ever since the peace of Fleix. Public opinion was affected by the campaign of libels in favour of a restoration of the Carolingian dynasty, as embodied in his person. In the situation of the Very Christian King the Protestant danger was only a secondary one. Henri III's own policy was more and more based on the Guisard danger, aggravated by the ambitions of Monsieur, which had deprived his brother of a natural ally. To Madame Catherine's despair, force of circumstances had transformed Henri III into a party leader. The legend that the Mignons were his bed-fellows is based on historical fact—Henri III was turning away more and more from his mother's policy of national unity, which led to nothing but failure, and surrounding himself with his own men, of whom he could be absolutely certain, the Viziers, whom Catherine de Medici hated and whom the populace mocked. The Joyeuses and the Epernons may or may not have had all the vices attributed to them by polemical literature; that is a question of mere historical gossip. As regards political history the matter is clear, for being unable to enlist the support of the Protestants in view of the French people's implacable hostility towards them; being unable to turn to the Politicals, of whom his brother François was the leader and obliged by that very fact to forego the services of such influential or able men as the three Montmorencys, a Crillon, a Pibrac, a Pithou and a Pasquier, the King had been forced to create a new aristocracy for the defence of his own party.

Forneron saw very clearly that it was in Poland and Venice that Henri III discovered the advantages of a political aristocracy united to the State. In France the State, which had fallen into tatters, in theory had only one head—the King. If the King had at his disposal men who were exclusively his own, he would thereby be able to strengthen the State. In order to provide himself with his own servants he created dukes, for the legislators of the Council were his mother's creatures. He even—which for a King of France was without precedent—surrounded himself with a personal bodyguard, hired bravos, forty-five in number, under the command of Honorat de Montpezat, Lord of Lanugnac, the Man of Prey, as he was so well named by Maxime Formont. Since Monsieur had his followers, Navarre had his, and Guise also, the King would be a gang-leader, too, among the other gang-leaders. He would substitute a policy of violence for the negotating and conciliatory policy of his mother, the policy of conferences and treaties, for those signatures that she loved. In this instance that reader of Machiavelli did not learn his lesson: 'In order to retain power in a State by stern means it is necessary, a sage has said, that the repressive strength should be in proportion to that which is repressed. Such authority by means of violence can be maintained provided that this proportion exists; but if the oppressed can command more real strength than the oppressor, then its overthrow must be feared from day to day.' Leaguers on the one hand and Huguenots on the other were actually stronger than the King of France, who had no army and imagined that he could replace it by a Palace guard. Catherine understood this and remained true to her policy of compromise.

But to Henri III this seemed mere self-deception on her part. What had this woman, whose genius he admired, succeeded in obtaining after twenty-five years of unswerving loyalty to a policy of arbitration? The King of France had never been so unpopular; he was insulted and harassed as if he had been the leader of some despicable party. The threat that he might be succeeded by an heretical sovereign inclined the most peaceable Frenchmen towards the Guisards. The King's person was no longer sacred, but insulted and threatened. Henri III accepted the challenge; let violence be met with violence. He would resort to the cunning which was his mother's instrument in the cause of peace in order the better to prepare his onslaught. He and his Dukes would beat the factions whom Madame Catherine and her legislators had never been able to subdue.

Let the old Governess of France amuse herself in her solitude by writing futile diplomatic screeds! The King remembered Jarnac and Montcontour. He could now no longer fight but he would use his strong-armed men, since Navarre and Guise had the soldiers. The two of them were dividing France between them under the contemptible sceptre of Henri III. The King of Navarre was master in the south. Partly on his own authority and partly through his relatives and allies, the Lorraine prince controlled Champagne, Burgundy, the Lyonnais, Brittany, Normandy and Picardy. In June 1583 Guise and his brother Mayenne held a secret meeting at the Nuncio's in Paris where with Albert of Bavaria they came to an agreement to invade England, free Mary Stuart, and reconquer

Scotland. The relations between the Lorraine and Philip II were becoming closer and closer. Their intermediaries were the Spanish ambassador and the Jesuits, whose delegate was Father Allen. As usual Philip hesitated, suspicious of the ambitions of the Lorraines, fearing to see Henri de Guise King of France and with England in his power should Mary Stuart wrest the Crown from Elizabeth. As long as the Duke was merely pretender to the throne of France he remained the Catholic King's prisoner, being in the latter's pay. Since the end of 1581 the name of the son of the victor of Calais figured on the list of those receiving Spanish subsidies in secret, at first under the surname of Hercules and later of Mucio.[1]

The sums he received were considerable; Henri de Guise was treated as an agent and paid very highly so that the docility and devotion required of him had to match the expense involved. From September 1582 to December 1586 he received 452,000 écus-gold, spread over seven different payments, after which he was constantly demanding further subsidies, arguing about his retainer and bombarding the Spanish offices with his complaints. The sympathy and collusion between the English and the Calvinists never came anywhere near the slavery of the Guises and the Leaguers to Spain. Even by the Treaty of Hampton Court the Protestants had only given temporary and territorial pledges in order to obtain help in men and money. It remained for the League to stimulate partisan hatred to the greatest heights of evil by becoming a real French province of Spain. In reading the minutes in the archives recording this Hispano-Leaguer collusion, Coligny emerges as a Frenchman who still retained a small degree of freedom of movement when compared to Henri de Guise and his brothers, the humble pensioners of the Catholic King. The regularity with which they were paid proves how well organized were the Escorial's methods of corruption. Philip II possessed galleons that were constantly being replenished by the Peruvian and Mexican mines and could afford to maintain his propaganda to a degree of handsomeness that his old rival, Elizabeth I, was never able to attain. As for Catherine de Medici and Henri III, they were too poor to compete either with the English Queen or the Spaniard. They could only afford to hire spies, but not traitors. At all times treachery has cost far more than espionage. In spite of his

---

[1] Henri Forneron, *Histoire de Philippe II*, Vol. III, p. 221, note 2. All the original documents were in the *Fonds Simanca* of the *Archives nationales* (K. 1560–63 and 1573), but have now been restored to the archives of that town, from which Napoleon I had removed them. Cf. *supra*, note at the bottom of p. 197.

munificence Philip II carefully controlled his accounts, argued and haggled.

In what shame was the noble blood of the Guises thus steeped! And Duke Henri, possessing such high virtues, had descended to such a trade! He had put his finger in the machine in order to pay his personal debts, which towards 1580 had reached three million livres, and his whole body soon followed it. Philip III supervised his accountancy and just as much a watchful bureaucrat as he was an enlightened art patron, a meticulous writer, a collector of rare books and precious manuscripts, demanded receipts which were carefully filed away in his cabinets. The most heartbreaking of the papers signed by the King of Paris was perhaps the following: 'We, Henri de Lorraine, Duc de Guise, peer and Grand Maître of France, confess that for ourselves, and in the name and on behalf of all those included in our common League, we have received by the hands of Gabriel de Allegria, the sum of 50,000 écus-pistoles of gold.'

Such infamous receipts prove to what an extent the Duc de Guise and his partisans were in the power of the Catholic King. As it was impossible, owing to his impecuniosity, for the Very Christian King to fight him on this ground, did it not seem more reasonable in the end to resort to violence than to continue the Florentine Queen's perpetual efforts at arbitration? How could one negotiate with men who depended to this extent on Spain? On December 31, 1584, at Joinville, the League transformed itself into one sole Hispano-Guisard alliance, under the pretext of 'the sole tuition, defence, and preservation of the Catholic religion and the complete extirpation of heresy in France and the Low Countries'. The Protestant Bourbons were to be excluded from the succession to the throne and their uncle, the Cardinal, was recognized as successor to the Crown of France. Philip II, that devoted son-in-law, did not forget his mother-in-law—the Lorraine Princes pledged themselves to return Cambrai and guarantee Flanders to the Catholic King in return for a monthly payment of 50,000 écus.

Meanwhile the League was being organized in Paris. From the beginning the frankly revolutionary character of this scheme was clear. The common enemy of the Spaniards, the League Princes of Joinville and the Parisian Leaguers was Protestantism and the King of France, whom they regarded as its ally. Their agreement with one another soon followed. Catherine de Medici, who was following matters closely, knew that the Duc de Guise was establishing garrisons in the towns of Champagne, and that the Cardinal de Bourbon was beginning to take on the part of heir to the throne. He left the Court for his diocese of Rouen and installed himself at his castle of Gaillon under the pretext of being obliged to make a Lenten retreat. On March 16, 1585, the Queen Mother wrote somewhat dryly to Henri de Guise: 'My nephew, I am as much annoyed as astonished by the news that is going round and the information we have of some new troubles of which it is said that you are the cause. . . .' She sent Louis d'Angennes, Sieur de Maintenon, to see him, with instructions from the King, presenting herself as an intermediary between them. Henri III detested Guise, against whom she, however, had no prejudice. On the contrary, her genuine and old friendship for his mother made her indulgent towards that prince, who was born in the same year as Charles IX and had grown up under her eyes as an intimate friend of her own children. And also, as Duke Charles III was her son-in-law, the House of Lorraine was related to her. We know that she was always greatly influenced by family ties. Charles III's behaviour towards his mother-in-law and brother-in-law was always perfectly correct and even friendly. His elder daughter, Catherine, was called after her grandmother and lived with her. The old Queen also liked his son, the Marquis of Pont-à-Mousson. She had only one other grandson, the bastard of Charles IX and Marie Touchet, Charles d'Angoulême, the future Count of Auvergne, whom she called her cousin and cared for equally.

One should never overlook the importance of the very bourgeois family attachments of Catherine de Medici. If this were forgotten it would be impossible to understand her attitude with regard to the Lorraines after the struggle between Guise and Henri III had become unforgivable. This was the reason for Michelet's misreading of the situation when he accused the Queen Mother of betraying her son in favour of the Guises and found her attitude 'absurd, unbelievable' since 'she had never loved anyone but Henri III. But she loved one thing still more, power and intrigue.' The truth was quite different and quite naturally so—Madame Catherine now had only one son and one daughter and for this reason her grandchildren took an ever greater place in her affections. She never saw the Infants of Spain, but the daughters and the son of Duchess Claude lived with her or near her, and they were Lorraines. Her letter to the Duc de Guise was a circular one; on the same day Catherine wrote an almost exactly similar one to the Cardinal de Guise and the Duc de Mayenne. She was informed of the Spanish machinations. The Joinville plot had been revealed to the King and his mother by Galmet,

Sieur de Villefallier, the father-in-law of Péricart, Henri de Guise's secretary.[1] We know through Villeroy the anxiety that Catherine was feeling on the subject: 'It is being said', he wrote on March 30, 1585, 'that this enterprise has been authorized by the Pope and is supported by Spanish deniers. Some people are also of the opinion that the other Catholic princes are of the Party and League, and even the Venetians are accused of it. The Huguenots are rallying and also beginning to raise levees in Germany. . . . The Queen, mother of His Majesty, although very indisposed, is having herself taken to meet them at Epernay, for their gathering is taking place in the town of Châlons in Champagne, in order to endeavour to put out this fire before it spreads any further.'

The Governess of France, eternally the pilgrim of peace, this time was going to meet the Lorraine princes as yesterday she went to meet her son-in-law Navarre and Condé the day before. During twenty-five years she had never allowed herself to become discouraged. Villeroy describes her perfectly in one line: 'Although very indisposed, she is having herself taken to meet them.' Neither old age nor illness would stop her from doing so. She was always determined to arrive in time and on March 28th she was at Epernay. She did not find the Duc de Guise there as he had left for Picardy. On March 31st the Cardinal de Bourbon published the manifesto of Péronne, in which, although it abused Henri III, advances were made to his mother: 'Let us all very humbly beg the Queen Mother of the King, our very honoured Lady (without whose wisdom and foresight the kingdom would fall to pieces and be lost) for the faithful witness she can bear of our great services, especially as regards ourselves, Cardinal de Bourbon, who have always honoured, served, and assisted her in her most important affairs, without sparing our goods, life, friends and relatives, in order with her to strengthen the party of the King and the Catholic religion, not to abandon us but to use thereto all the credit that her struggles and hard labours might have faithlessly ravished from her, with the King, her son.'

This was an appeal for her mediation. The Leaguers were aware of the suffering Henri III's new policy was causing Catherine de Medici. Before taking action against Henri de Navarre they wished to win over the aged princess, around whom the solitude of her life's evening was deepening. How precious her experience and her genius would

[1] Villefallier's evidence (to which Catherine refers in her letter of April 4, 1585, to Bellièvre) is in the Manuscripts of the B.N. (*Fonds français* No. 3247, fo. 71, and No. 3420, fo. 31).

be to them! They feared that Henri III would ally himself with his brother-in-law Navarre against them. But they also knew that the King's financial distress made it impossible for him to embark on any large-scale activity against them and that he himself had requested his mother to go to Epernay. He had even more openly revealed his weakness by sending the Bishop of Auxerre, Philippe de Lenoncourt, and the Marshal de Retz on a mission to the Cardinal de Bourbon.

Mayenne had taken Dijon; at Châlons, Guise was affecting to treat the Cardinal as the appointed successor to Henri III, and on this assumption had requested him to sign the manifesto of Péronne. He purposely did not hasten to meet the Queen Mother, who, becoming impatient, spent a few days at Château-Thierry, and on returning to Epernay on Easter Day, April 9th, in gracious terms (she signed her letter 'Your good aunt') invited the Duc de Guise to negotiate with her: 'I promise myself', she told him, 'that for your part you will bring to it all the kind affection that you owe to us.' That same evening (Châlons was only eight lieues from Epernay) Henri de Guise was with her. Although she was very ill she dictated a long account of their interview for the King, to which she added a few lines in her own hand.

This document, drawn up only a few minutes after the interview, is basic. It reveals that the Duke was no more easy in his mind than the King with regard to the consequences of a new civil war. Catherine had found her nephew very melancholy: 'and in conversation he wept, showing himself very sad'. She had 'very amply remonstrated with him' as she 'deemed suitable'. She was struck by his obstinacy in refusing to tell her the reasons for the rising that he was planning. 'I told him that it was more likely for the purpose of destroying and weakening our religion than for the extirpation of heresy.' Madame Catherine's clearsightedness was in contrast to the blindness of the Lorraine Prince: 'Our experience has been that peace has weakened the Huguenots more than war,' but she tried in vain to make him understand this. She pressed home the point that had always caused her the greatest anxiety as Governess of France, that 'this kingdom would be incontinently full of foreigners and (that) we would all be in danger of being thrown out by them'. Tight-lipped and silent, the prisoner of Spain could not oppose a word to those arguments, those strong reasons, as the Queen called them. And she added, 'I could get nothing out of him.' The postscript, in her own hand, contains a confession by Guise: 'He could do nothing', so he said, 'by himself.'

The Spanish handcuffs had, in fact, been well riveted on him. Catherine's convincing arguments were useless; in order not to give way to the temptation to become a Frenchman again the victor of Dormans left. For Catherine weeks were to pass in anxious waiting; everyone knew, as Busbecq wrote, that on her negotiations depended 'the conclusion of peace or war with the Guises'.

There is an abundance of documents regarding this waiting period. They include letters from the Queen Mother to her son, to Villeroy, Bruslart, Bellièvre; replies from Henri III; letters from Lansac and Pinart, whom Catherine had with her at Epernay; letters from the Archbishop of Lyons, Pierre d'Espinac, who provided the liaison between the Court and the Lorraine Princes; articles presented to the King by the princes, officers of the Crown, noblemen, gentlemen, towns, communities and other Catholics of the kingdom; the correspondence of the Duke of Guise and the reports of ambassadors.[1] This period lasted until May 12th. On that day a conference was held at a country house at Sarry, belonging to the Bishop of Châlons. From May 28th the Epernay interviews were resumed, but it was an unusually laborious business. Catherine was used to patience and defended the territory of royal sovereignty foot by foot. This sovereignty—since the King was no longer anything more than a party leader—was now fictitious, but as her correspondence shows, the Queen Mother did not despair of re-establishing it: 'To reduce them as far as I am able', she wrote to Bruslart of the Leaguers, 'and if possible to a reasonable degree, under the King's good pleasure.'

But whatever she thought, this was no longer possible. The demands of the Leaguers went on increasing—the castle of Rouen, the town and castle of Dieppe, for the Cardinal; Nantes, Saint-Malo, Dinan, for the Duc de Mercoeur; Metz in Lorraine and fortresses in Champagne, for the Duc de Guise; Chalon-sur-Saône and Dijon for his brother Mayenne; Rheims for his brother the Cardinal; towns in Picardy for Aumale, and in Dauphiné for Elbeuf, his other brothers —rich spoils. Compared to their successors the Guises at the time of Amboise had been moderates. Catherine, who was ill, finally lost courage. In order to avoid a disastrous war she capitulated. She left Epernay on June 27th, beaten. On July 1st she was at Nemours where she was to sign the Royal capitulation to the feudalists of the League, by the Treaty of July 7, 1585.

[1] The letters of Henri de Guise are in the *Fonds français* of the manuscripts in the Nationale, and were in the former *Fonds Béthune*.

For the first time in her life Catherine de Medici capitulated without having tried to make good by force of arms the breakdown of her
negotiations. Her preference for compromise did not include surrender. She had never given way except in the matter of method, and
had always upheld the principle of arbitration by Royal sovereignty.
At Nemours the King was no longer the arbitrator who agreed to
personal sacrifices in order to establish peace between the contending
parties—he was himself a partisan, obliged to submit to an enemy
stronger than himself. On July 7, 1585 the factionalists did not come
to an agreement but dictated one. The Queen Mother was compelled
in person to repudiate her policy of French unity and religious freedom. Without having lost a battle she surrendered cities and fortresses and proscribed those of her subjects whom she had hitherto
constantly protected against the fanaticism of their enemies—the
Huguenots, whose excesses she had as firmly repressed as she had
energetically defended their rights. It was a genuine abdication in
favour of Henri de Guise.

Those of her contemporaries who were not feudally subject to the
Catholic party immediately realized the extent of this defeat without
a war: 'The worst part of it', Pierre de L'Estoile remarked with good
sense, 'was that the King went on foot and the League on horseback,
and that without doubt he bore the penitent's sack on his back
whilst they wore the armour.' Nothing was truer. At Nemours Henri
III was stripped to his shirt and defenceless whilst Henri de Guise
was in warmail. As she returned to Saint-Maur-des-Fossés Madame
Catherine had leisure to taste the full bitterness of the worst humiliation of her long career. Her signature on the Treaty preceded those
of the Cardinal de Bourbon and the three Lorraines, the Cardinal
and the Duc de Guise, and Duke Charles III, her son-in-law. The
sole prerogative that remained to her was to have been the first to
sign it. She knew only too well, alas, that after twenty-five years of
struggle she had put her name to her own failure and that in her
attempt for the last time, and in vain, to safeguard peace she had
delivered over France, defeated because unarmed, to war. The Protestants, reduced to desperation, could not do otherwise than take
up arms under the King of Navarre, whom she had hoped to gain as
her ally but who was now inevitably her enemy, to whom nothing
was left but to conquer or to die, whilst the King of France, fallen
into servitude thanks to the League, would himself have to wage war
against his legitimate heir.

But Catherine de Medici, who never gave up hope, nevertheless had a glimpse of salvation. On May 31st, although she had already given way on everything, she wrote to Bellièvre: 'As I hold, there is no means of ever seeing our repose in this realm well-assured unless the said King of Navarre become a Catholic.' Her hope was to be realized, but not until after long years of ruin, blood, and tears. Catherine was to live long enough to suffer her share of them which was so heavy that thenceforward she would no longer be able to conquer her destiny. Whatever she did, she was obliged to submit to her fate. *Fata viam invenient.* Virgil's words did not apply to her alone. Henry IV was to be the destined victor, for whom she had prepared the way in spite of herself, and who was to carry her hopes to fulfilment. As Governess of France she was only the interim Queen, but an intermediary without whom—three and a half centuries later we know this to be true— all would have been irremediably lost and France would have been dismembered as Poland was, two centuries later.

At Nemours, in fact, she, the constant adversary of the great feudalists, had laid the State wide open to the Duc de Guise; as Commander-in-Chief of the King's armies he was able to levy troops, confer ranks, and had become master of the palace. In spite of its enmity towards the Huguenots the Paris Parliament immediately understood that the defence of the Catholic religion was merely a pretext for taking over power. Even in Rome they realized it. Pastor and Henri de l'Epinois rightly emphasized the cautious reserve of the Holy See regarding the purely political ends pursued by the Guisards under the pretext of defending the faith. The Parliament resisted and it was necessary to hold a Royal session for the registration of the edict proscribing the Reformationists, on July 18, 1585. The King of Navarre clearly understood that the outlawing of his party amounted to an abrogation of the Salic Law. On July 21st he wrote to Henri III, reminding him of all the offers of peace he had made him and pointing out that his quarrel with the Guises should be fought out by themselves, fact to face, without the King of France taking part in it. Henri III's advisers considered that as the Treaty of Nemours inevitably involved war with the Protestants it behoved the sovereign to assume this responsibility. Henri III knew himself to have been too heavily despoiled by the Leaguers to be able to do so. He obtained pecuniary assistance from the Parisians, which enabled him to raise three armies—one for Guyenne, a second for the defence of the Eastern frontier and the third for Paris. The latter would be his own; the others would be commanded by the Lorraine Princes in association with Epernon and Joyeuse. Lucid as ever in spite of his impotence he did not conceal the fact that he was making this war on his Calvinist subjects against his will: 'I very much fear', he said, 'that in thinking to destroy the pulpit we may place the Mass in great danger.' As Cavriana wrote to the Grand Duke of Tuscany, at Nemours the Queen Mother had laid one plaster on top of another without curing the ailment.

The greatest evil was that there were two States against the State—the League and the Reformation against the Very Christian Monarchy. And everyone could see that the weakest of these three States was the Royal one. Henri III knew very well that political wisdom required the alliance with Navarre but that such wisdom would remain of no practical value without the King's conversion. He attempted a final move in order to obtain it, but his envoys, Philippe de Lenoncourt and Nicolas Bruslart de Sillery failed, as the Duke of Epernon had done before them. Henri of Navarre had written his mother-in-law several letters, very dignified and noble in tone, declaring that he could not accept a peace made without him and against him. Reminding her of their relationship, according to which he was the appointed successor of Henri III: 'I hold myself obliged to oppose the ruin of the Crown and House of France with all my power, against those who would undertake it.' His Blood gave him the right to do so, but his Faith destroyed that right. The choice between two alternatives (either to fight or to renounce) was the essential reason for the Treaty of Nemours. But such alternatives only existed as the result of the weakness of the Royal State, which, had it been strong, could have solved this tragic problem by bringing about the submission of the heir to the throne to the French State religion at the request and order of the King, and in the case of an obstinate refusal by summoning the States-General in conformity with the fundamental laws of the kingdom, the primary electoral principle regaining its rights in face of such a refusal by the legitimate successor to accept the Sacrament of Rheims.

Catherine saw matters clearly. Referring to the bull of excommunication against the Béarnais published by Sixtus V, on September 14, 1585, she wrote from Montceaux to Villeroy: 'In all this I see harm only for the King, for if I saw that he had the means to be strong as I wish that he were I would not give a button for all these practices and dealings, for there would be neither pope nor king and even less his subjects who would not consider themselves very happy, the former to please him and the latter to obey him.' And she added, 'I would be sweet to all of them, popes and kings, to gain the means to possess such forces as would enable me to command and not to obey them.' The old Gallican Queen was indignant at the insolence of the Pontiff, intervening in French politics. But she knew only too well that her anger was in vain: 'I expect that we shall always have to endure what they want us to do, since we are the weakest.' She was ready to leave for Rome; two days later she wrote to Villeroy that the time was no longer, alas, when 'the King could have dealt with it as reason and duty commanded; but this is not God's will and we must be patient until it please Him to appease His ire against us and this poor kingdom'.

It was a cry of distress and a deeply moving one! This resigned Catherine was not her usual self. She had no illusions regarding her impotence, but would she give up? Certainly not. The Duc de Nevers, brother-in-law of the Duc de Guise, was a Leaguer but he did not approve of the Royalist ambitions of the victor of Dormans. From the beginning of June until the beginning of July he had been living in Rome. When he returned, Henri III thought that he had betrayed him in favour of Philip II. But the Queen Mother knew of Nevers' scruples and set about reconciling the King with him. A large part of her correspondence, during the second half of that year 1585 was given over to this matter. She saw Nevers as a possible ally on the side of the Leaguers. He belonged to the House of Mantua and links with Italy were still dear to the Florentine Queen. In these delicate negotiations Cavriana served as her intermediary. On December 18, 1585, Henri III agreed to write to the Duc de Nevers. In the Queen Mother's mind, their relations having thus been re-established would provide an easy means of contact with Sixtus V, for she knew that he was suspicious of the Lorraine Princes and Spain, having discovered that although their means were religious their ends, were political and that they were aiming to gain possession of France.[1] Nevertheless, in granting them on September 9th the bull excommunicating the King of Navarre and declaring him deprived of his rights to the Crown of France, he had provided them with the most efficient of weapons against Henri III, who did not want to set himself against the Salic Law. His respect for this fundamental law of the kingdom forbade him to accept the bull. He refused to publish it, and the Parliament to register it. By doing so he made himself appear as the apparent friend of the League but in fact the ally of the Hugue-

[1] With regard to all this cf. J. de Hübner: *Sixte Quint*, and L'Epinois, *La Ligue et les Papes*. The essay of Eugène Saulnier on *Le Rôle Politique du Cardinal de Bourbon* is important.

nots, and in consequence drew the hostility of both camps upon himself.

On October 11, 1585, the King of Navarre had ordered Duplessis-Mornay to address protests to the Sorbonne, the nobility, the Tiers, and the City of Paris. He declared that he was not persisting in belonging to the reformed religion out of ill-will and on the contrary demanded a council in which he might explain himself. It was necessary to call a meeting of the States-General to remedy the public ills. He also protested to the Holy See. He wrote to Catherine de Medici: 'I shall see the day, Madame, when the King and you will realize, perhaps too late, into whose hands you have placed your arms.' They realized it as well as he did, for they had never had the slightest illusions regarding the League. Beaten by force of circumstances there was nothing else left for them to do, and the Queen Mother's letters repeatedly admit this. Montmorency, foreseeing the inevitable rupture between the signatories to the Treaty of Nemours, as early as August 25, 1585, warned the Nuncio Frangipani that if the Catholics rallied round the King of Navarre they would most certainly bring him to re-enter the bosom of the Church. He declared his intention to collaborate in such an aim, for one year of civil war would do the Catholic religion more harm than ten years of a compromise peace. Catherine's traditional policy was thus supported by Montmorency. In his address to the French people of the following October 1st the Marshal reminded them that his attitude was a similar one to that of his father, the Constable—namely to live in peace whilst awaiting the Council and to respect the fundamental laws of the kingdom and the rights of the Princes of the Blood. By these means the King's own freedom would be assured. Montmorency was above all a royalist, and in the person of a prince who was still a heretic, although no one could state that he would remain one forever, he acclaimed the true protector of the State. Henri de Navarre 'alone, since the King was surrounded by enemies, could and should lift up the barrier around which all good Frenchmen would rally'.

By a cruel irony of fate, when Montmorency pronounced himself in favour of the Béarnais whom she was finding herself compelled to fight, he was carrying out the very line of thought of the Queen Mother, as expressed in the memorandum that he had received from her at the end of the preceding month of May. In this, Catherine exhorted him to work for peace: 'As war upholds the League, peace destroys it.' The fall of Epernon would inevitably follow on an alliance between Henri III and his cousin: 'The union is so strong that it can better lay down the law than receive it.' At that moment the Queen Mother, following the line of Machiavelli and Guicciardini, in whose views feelings and ideas should always give way to reality, still believed that the King of Navarre would quickly agree to become a convert. Montmorency's help was indispensable to her: 'It is for you to decide what you wish to become. If the whole thing is settled without you, you will get no thanks for it and if it (the request presented to him) is dragged out, you will have no excuses either to God or your country.'

God.... his country.... Madame Catherine used these words quite naturally, like the word, union. Her present tragedy lay in the fact that owing to the helplessness of the disarmed King, the nation, under the pretext of it being in the service of God, was being delivered over to the factions, and that at Nemours she herself had surrendered all that remained of the Royal prestige. *Stat magni nominis umbra*. The future Henri IV and Montmorency looked to this shadow for their justification. Guise knew it so well that he offered the Marshal his alliance and informed Philip II of it. Thus, he said, he could lay down the law to the King. But on the contrary, Montmorency, a politician, volunteered to raise the Royal standard up again. Herein lay the essence of the contrast between the Politicals and the Leaguers—to serve the King or to dominate him.

Catherine, the captive of the Leaguers, now found the defenders of her own policy ranged against her in the other party. Meanwhile she saw how her son, unbalanced still further by despair, was once again falling back into his ridiculous mummeries—an oratory, draped in black, bones dangling on the walls, lit only by the light of candles, in which the King on every Friday practised his devotions in the company of two Capuchins and a few intimates, flagellating himself. The Nuncio, who was very indignant at this decadent asceticism, which was another side of the morbid frivolity of Henri III's private life, asked the Pope to order the King's confessor, Father Edmond Auger, 'to see to it that these devotions do not prevent the King from fulfilling his principal duty'. Sixtus V's good sense did not allow that a sovereign should indulge in such mad pietistic practices.

The Royal degenerate could not succeed in overcoming the crisis brought about by the surrender of Nemours. He was still lucid and still impotent and had neither troops nor money, whilst the Mignons finished emptying his coffers to the bottom. Catherine then thought that the Pope might furnish him with some subsidies. The Cardinal d'Este had been refused her request that the King might be authorized to sell certain ecclesiastical properties against a return of 100,000 écus. The Bishop of Paris, Pierre de Gondi, one of the Queen Mother's Italians, was luckier, and successfully pleaded her cause. On December 31, 1585, Catherine expressed her gratitude to him, as well as to Sixtus V and the Cardinal d'Este. The three letters are amusing to read, written by the, on this occasion, ultramontane pen of the Gallican Queen, assuring the Pope that the King and herself would more and more endeavour, by their deportment, to prove to His Holiness and all the world 'their firm and sincere intentions as regarded the honour and service of God and the restoration of his Church'. She remained his daughter in Jesus Christ.

Catherine de Medici never found it repugnant to lower herself to those who were stronger than she was. But she had never until then been obliged to do so by pretending to such a degree to possess ideas and feelings that were the very opposite of her real ones. The Leaguers were not taken in; they were watching her very closely, and with good reason. Madame Catherine's correspondence during the first six months of 1586—incomplete as it is, to the despair of the historian, for the gaps in it are irreparable—nevertheless reveals to us that she was once again actively taking part in politics. On April 14th Cavriana informed the Grand Duke of Tuscany of it. Henri III, who had become a complete religious maniac, was no longer dealing with anything. His mother had won the admiration of the Florentine ambassador, by her health, which in spite of a few attacks of gout was once again good, and her energy, always equal to the difficulties of the day. She was negotiating with Scotland, Tuscany, Venice, Mantua, Rome, and Spain. The Cardinal d'Este had succeeded in obtaining Sixtus V's agreement to the recall of the French ambassador, Jean de Vivonne, Marquess of Pisani, on account of Henri III's refusal to accept the Nuncio, Frangipani, in July 1585. Cavriana had succeeded in reconciling Henri III with the Duc de Nevers, their official reconciliation taking place on June 24, 1586. To this, Catherine attached very great importance, for Nevers was her chosen intermediary with the League. She needed him all the more since her son-in-law, Charles III of Lorraine, had completely gone over to the Guises in the fear of seeing his Duchy ravaged by the troops of the League. She was secretly working to divide the Leaguers and to draw closer to the Reformationists.

Since September 1585 there had been fighting in the south-west.

After being beaten outside Angers, which he had reached, Monsieur le Prince had been forced to fly to England. After a few lucky attacks in Limousin, Quercy, and Périgord, Mayenne and Matignon had fallen out. Even after Condé's return to La Rochelle the King of Navarre took care not to pass over to the offensive, preferring to establish himself solidly in Poitou. Owing to the misunderstandings between the Holy See, Spain, and the League, who had no common interests but only a common enemy—himself, the Béarnais whom they all detested, time was on his side. Apart from this common hatred of the King of Navarre, these temporary allies had divergent aims. Sixtus V's only interest was the extirpation of heresy; Philip II wanted complete anarchy in France; thanks to the Leaguers the Duc de Guise was aiming to become King of Paris and then of France. The Béarnais held his ground, keeping in constant correspondence with the Royalists scattered among the clergy, the nobility, the Tiers, the Parliaments and the towns. 'They have surrounded me like a hunted animal', he said of the Leaguers, 'and think to catch me in their net. But I shall pass through it, or over their stomachs.'

Joyeuse, in charge of operations in Languedoc, and Epernon in Provence and Dauphiné, were incontestably devoted to the King. The nobility was forming a Royalist group around them. Henri III would only have had to recapture the ardour of Jarnac to attempt to re-establish his position with a genuine chance of success. *Una salus victis nullam sperare salutem. . . .* But the humanist who bore the Crown was a broken man who had forgotten Aeneas's sublime exhortation. Had he taken over the supreme command he might have negotiated with the German Lutheran princes, who were then still neutral, and with the King of Navarre, who wanted to stop the war. For the moment he apparently had a fairly strong force. But instead he was preparing to go to Pougues and to Bourbon-Lancy to take the waters, and from there to Lyons. Jacques-Auguste de Thou described this Caesar of the Low-Empire, the laughingstock of the people of Lyons, surrounded by his bedfellow Mignons (the political Mignons were with the armies) and his pet pugdogs, playing with his cups-and-balls, and the scissors with which he cut out miniatures from manuscripts, which he amused himself by sticking on to the walls of his oratories. Such were the pastimes of this unfortunate prince. We understand his neurosis, but his contemporaries did not. They thought that he was a responsible adult whilst in fact he was a mentally sick man, in whom genuine political genius lay side by side with infantilism. In consequence they came to hate him as much as they despised him. The fiscal edicts succeeded one another, quite incoherently, arousing unanimous protests but bringing in nothing. Posters appeared against this most despised of monarchs, who in the end withdrew the edicts. Catherine was gradually regaining the sphere of influence she had lost, explaining that there was nothing left to do except to reach agreement with Navarre. As Cavriana said, the kingdom was vanishing away. The Eighth War was beginning.

The future Henri IV, legitimate heir to the throne, was from the point of view of political wisdom the natural bulwark of a State that was out of joint and falling into ruin day by day. On July 23rd Madame Catherine and her son left Paris. She went to Chenonceaux and from there was going to Poitou, 'in the attempt', l'Estoile reported, 'to reach some agreement with the King of Navarre', whilst Henri III travelled to Pougues, whence he planned to go on to Bourbon-Lancy, Moulins and Lyons. In theory the King was supposed to be visiting his States whilst his mother would begin negotiations with his brother-in-law Navarre: 'I am constantly pursuing my design for the re-uniting of all my subjects to our religion', he wrote to Hurault de Maisse, French ambassador to Venice; 'up to the present I have done everything I could do to this end and will tell you that I have requested the Queen, my Dame and mother, to go to Chenonceaux and to Champigny, the house of my cousin the Duc de Montpensier, to give occasion to the King of Navarre to get in touch with her, in order to make him aware of my intention; to which she was very agreeable, as one who has always desired and procured the salvation and peace of this kingdom.'

At Chenonceaux, where she resided from August 14th until October 23, 1586, the Queen Mother prepared for an interview with her son-in-law. She charged the Abbot of Gadaigne, one of her most faithful Italians, with several missions to the King of Navarre. We have numerous letters on this subject, which show her in constant touch with Birague, Villeroy, and Bellièvre. It was an important and delicate matter, which took nearly four months to come to term. Only on November 28th was the Queen Mother able to write to François de Balzac d'Entragues, Governor of Orleans: 'I have agreed with my son, the King of Navarre, that on the fourth or fifth of the month of December next we will see one another and meet near here, to look into the said means of a good peace and general repose of this kingdom.' She had been staying at Saint-Maixent since November 16th and spent the entire second half of the month there, holding

her Court, giving receptions, concerning herself with the government of Poitou, happy to be able to exercise in all freedom the power
that was so dear to her. Not wishing to travel away from his States,
Henri de Navarre requested her to come to Cognac, where she arrived
on December 8th.

Their conferences took place at the castle of Saint-Brice, between
Cognac and Jarnac, where the Béarnais had his headquarters. But
in this environment, which reminded her of the youthful valour of
Henri III, brilliant horseman and victor of the Huguenots, Madame
Catherine tried in vain to reach agreement with her son-in-law. She
gave the King a detailed report on their interviews at Saint-Brice,
which began on December 13, 1586, and other evidence supplemented her account of them. It is very interesting to note to what an
extent the two antagonists competed in feinting with one another,
passing from compliments to threats and returning to compliments.
Her son-in-law having said that Henri III had made war on him like
a wolf, and she like a lion, she asked him if she had not always been
his good mother; to which the Béarnais replied that that had been so
in his youth but he realized that she had changed a great deal during
the past six years. At one moment she reproached him for having
kept her on tenterhooks for six months. He answered gaily that he
had not prevented her from sleeping in her bed, but that for six
months she had been preventing him from sleeping in his. He knew
her too well to doubt for an instant that she was anything but happy
in the distress of which she complained: 'That distress pleases you
and nourishes you', he told her, 'and if you were tranquil you would
not live very long.'

Such was their tone. Their strength was equally matched, a
strength inseparable from cunning. Neither the one nor the other
could win. And from this sprang their quick irritability, with which
they mutually reproached one another. Embittered irony led to
sarcasm; the Béarnais even forgot himself so far as to be rude,
reminding his mother-in-law of her age, which was damaging her
memory. Nevertheless he did not want to burn his bridges any more
than she did. They met again, this time at Cognac, on December
16th and 17th. When she received the Viscount de Turenne, the
King of Navarre's envoy, Catherine returned to the necessity for
the conversion of the legitimate heir. She proposed that the Reformed
religion should be suspended for a year, whilst waiting for the States-
General to be summoned. Her son-in-law's refusal of this proposal
seemed so serious to the Queen Mother that she thought it necessary

to inform Henri III of it immediately. He, in his Louvre, was in the hands of the Leaguers, masters of Paris. In reading his replies one can judge to what degree he was powerless.

No longer hoping to establish public and universal peace in his country Henri III declared himself ready to assure 'the public welfare'. What lay behind this bold statement? First of all, a tribute to Catherine de Medici: 'You were truly a very good and helpful mother to wend your way to where you are without considering your age, the rigours of the weather and the badness of the roads, nor the displeasure of our separation and apartness.' The King once again proclaimed that peace would not be possible unless Henri de Navarre agreed 'to submit himself to the Catholic religion and bring to it those of his opinion.' The obstinacy of this prince and his followers in remaining Protestants made war inevitable. The Government, in fact, would no longer tolerate two religions. Since gentleness had failed, it would resort to force. Henri III declared this before the princes, the knights of his Orders and other noblemen and members of his Council. He called upon his Catholic subjects, to their unity and devotion against the Huguenots, to 'clean up my kingdom', as he cried, with an ardour worthy of the League. This declaration was made for two reasons: 'One, so that my resolution to prepare ourselves in good earnest for war shall ring in the ears of the Huguenots . . . and the other, in order to efface the impression that certain people are trying to give to my people and subjects and principally through the cities, regarding my intentions concerning the reunion of those of the Catholic religion, based both upon the conduct of your negotiations and the behaviour of the said King of Navarre with respect to you, before and since the truce.'

Henri de Navarre had agreed to this truce, the result of the conferences of Saint-Brice, because it enabled him to gain the necessary time to await the arrival of the reinforcements from Germany. On January 11, 1587, at Friedelsheim, Pardaillan-Ségur signed a Treaty with the King of Denmark for the despatching of Swiss and German troops to join up with those of the Palatinate ruler Johann-Casimir and to invade Lorraine and Champagne. The King of Navarre was pitting the Swiss and Germans of the Lutheran princes against the Spaniards and Italians of the League. Both sides were delivering up their country to foreign mercenaries. In order to repel the German invasion, Catherine and her son, possessing no royal army, were reduced to having recourse to the Spanish invasion. But in the minds of the King of Navarre and the Huguenots this invasion that they were bringing about was merely the response to their own outlawry.

There was no longer a king in France except nominally. Between the two Henri's—Lorraine and Navarre—Henri III was not even able to drag matters out, as his mother had hoped. The King of Paris held him captive and dragged him into combat against the King of Navarre. Henri III might accuse his Bourbon cousin of allowing himself to be 'carried away by his passions, the enemies of his soul's salvation, his country, and his own honour, greatness, and duty', but those noble words and pathetic adjurations were merely a mask for his own submission to the Leaguers, who were forcing him to go to war against his natural ally and legitimate heir. He knew this so well that he wrote to his mother: 'Madame, I do not know how you may honestly enter into negotiation and treaty with the King of Navarre and his followers, after what has been said and taken place between you and them on the matter of Religion.' The ridiculous monarch was at that moment envisaging a prolongation of the truce of one or two years, during which the Protestants would be in fact tolerated, until the decision of the States-General. The edict imposed by the Treaty of Nemours was unworkable and it was merely a matter of suspending its application. The true thoughts of Henri III and Catherine de Medici were expressed thus: 'To base the said cessation of armed warfare on a truce, from the desire that we have to give our subjects a suspension of the ills they are suffering on account of the war and to find a means whereby to reunite them all to our religion, by another path than that of arms, which is the cause of so many calamities and afflictions.'

Henri III did not conceal from himself any of the difficulties of the situation. The Catholics were keeping a close watch on him, the Protestants defying him. Nevertheless, the essential thing was not 'in any way to abandon or give up the said negotiation'. What he was asking his mother to do was to win the heart of the King of Navarre: to reconcile Henri and Marguerite. It would be 'hard to swallow', but how great are the resources of maternal diplomacy! In his distress the King was imploring the Governess of France for help. It was no longer a question of discarding her; in her lay his only hope: 'Madame, here is truly everything that I have discussed and thought over in these matters, that I wished thus to present to you as a whole and place before the consideration of your judgement and best opinion, in order that you may to the best advantage profit therefrom in my service, as I beg you to do....'

Discouraged, the old Queen had left Cognac for Niort where she remained from January 15 until February 19, 1587. Her letters reveal how she regained hope, according to her customary and always reviving optimism. She sent emissaries to her son-in-law, notably Nicolas Bruslart de Sillery. She proposed to him that he should be instructed by theologians with a view to his possible conversion. Hostilities, in the form of surprise attacks and small operations, were developing throughout Poitou. It was clear that the Protestants wanted war no less than the Catholics. 'You said', Catherine wrote to Bellièvre on February 14th, 'that heaven, the earth, and the abyss were all set against this poor realm.'

Madame Catherine placed matters in God's hands. In those intimate notes to her dear counsellor, which she signed '*la bien vôtre*' the diligent reader of *Il Principe* recognized that no human salvation remained possible. The Crown had never been in worse state. Guise and Navarre both knew it and were determined to fight one another. The victor would pass over the inert body of Henri III and would become King of France. The Béarnais as well as the Lorraine had become a civil war hero. Catherine de Medici saw that her policy was in ruins, and in this her instinct did not deceive her. Faced with this irreparable disaster it was necessary to win over Navarre, in whom rested the Blood of France, to her side. At any price she must see him and in her memoranda and instructions sent out to her agents in February 1587 we can read that she conceded him everything. Thus she obtained his promise of an interview with him near Fontenay-le-Comte, at Marans, on the last day of the month.

She was already at Fontenay on the 20th. The correspondence that was exchanged between herself and the Bourbon Calvinist proves that he had promised to meet her at the ford of Velluire, two and a half leagues from Fontenay, and afterwards to hold a conference at Marans. At the last moment, pretexting the risk of an ambush, he defaulted. The rumour was also spread that the Queen Mother was to be kidnapped, but she refused to change her plans, for, as she wrote to Henri III, she was not deceived by 'these artifices'. Did the King of Navarre fear that he would be obliged, under the accusation of obvious bad faith, to renounce going to war? To Catherine's bitter disillusionment he refrained from keeping the agreed appointment. There was a succession of bad news. She learned that Mary Stuart had been beheaded at Fotheringay on February 18th. In view of the information she had been receiving from England since the death sentence had been passed on this beautiful, heroic and touching princess, this did not surprise her. She immediately understood the meaning of this atrocious challenge to the Catholic monarchies on the part of the Reformation—the decapitation of a vanquished queen. Only the weakness of France had made it possible: 'That is what', she wrote to Bellièvre on March 14th, 'our misfortunes and troubles in the kingdom have brought us to.' And she also saw how this deed would encourage regicide: 'It only requires a beginning to give much boldness to those who desire to reign. . . .'

Her son-in-law sent her the Vicomte de Turenne, carrying a plea-to-bar, saying that his master neither would nor could discuss a peace treaty for two months, the period necessary to convoke the deputies of the churches. Unfortunately there is no letter from Catherine extant referring to her interview with Turenne. This regrettable lack of documentation merely allows us to imagine the indignation of the Queen Mother, faced with the King of Navarre's determination to go to war, which had thus been so brutally revealed to her.

Madame Catherine travelled via Niort, Saint-Maixent, and Lusignan to Chenonceaux, where she arrived on March 13, 1587. She was as much shocked as distressed by the fury of the parties, implacably determined to make war on one another: 'Henceforward it will only be a question of doing as much harm on every side as possible; from which nothing else can result but more misery and desolation in this poor realm,' she wrote on March 7th to the Marshal de Matignon. After only one day's rest at Chenonceaux she left for Paris, which she was not to leave again for any length of time except for a journey to Champagne towards the end of July of the following year, 1588. She knew that it was essential that she remain there with her son, more bewildered than ever and forced into a war that he was no more able to direct than to bear. Her correspondence tells us nothing about the progress made by the Parisian League, prior to the negotiations she attempted to open in May and June 1587 with the Guises, at Rheims, where she remained for three weeks. At the same time she was negotiating there with the Duc de Bouillon, who was allied to Henri de Navarre, and the Duc de Guise. Not having been able to obtain peace from her son-in-law, perhaps she might obtain it from the head of the Leaguers? As she had done in the case of the former negotiations she kept Henri III informed of all the details of the situation and this time we have her letters—those of May 24, 25, 29, 30 and June 3, 1587.

Would the north grant her the truce which the south had refused her? Henri de Guise, who was very well informed regarding her relations with 'those of Sedan', as he wrote to the Spanish ambassador, Bernardo de Mendoza, suspected the Queen Mother of wanting to give the Huguenots 'a means of joining up with the foreign forces' and accused her of a plan to 'allow the foreigners to enter so that, coming into Paris after so much ruination, they would force the Catholics to ask for a shameful peace'. Catherine wrote to her son: 'Reason still remains on our side.' But reason that was not based on armaments was impotent to control the passions that had been unleashed. Although she herself was ill, the brave old woman worried, not about her own health, but the King's. She took great care of herself and did not give ground to the Lorraine intrigues. Villeroy deplored the blindness of the Guises, who refused to come to any agreement and constantly increased their demands, claiming the right to retain the towns of Picardy in which they had established garrisons. Their tactics were the same as those of the King of Navarre—to play for time whilst they awaited the arrival of the Spanish reinforcements, as their enemy was awaiting the German.

Catherine still imagined that matters could be arranged. On June 16th she wrote to the Duc de Nevers that she had found Monsieur de Guise willing to treat. She understood very well, nevertheless, that the League movement would be keener than its hesitant chief to make war on behalf of the King of Spain. The least evil would be for the King of France to take part in this war which he could no longer either avoid or postpone. By his presence, at least, he would block the road to power of the King of Paris. Henri III had at last placed himself at the head of the troops ordered into combat south of the Loire. His mother personally took charge of the defence of the Paris region. She gave it her full attention—armaments, levees of men and money, stockpiling provisions—her letters show how she was ordering and supervising the preparations for war in August, September, and October 1587. As usual, active participation in politics restored Madame Catherine's good humour. She thought to re-live again the days of Jarnac and Moncontour, and created for herself a new image of her heroic son; in her letters she saluted the just cause, the holy resolution, of Henri III. As for herself, she was weighed down by financial burdens. Her letter to her son from Paris on October 26, 1587, reveals to us how the Zamets, the Gondis, the Mario Bandinis, were profiteering by the situation. They lent money at usurers' rates and 'by taking as their sureties' the conveyance of the revenues forced out of the towns and the clergy by the Government.

But if the affairs of the farmers of the revenue prospered, those of the King became catastrophic. On October 20, 1587, Joyeuse was beaten and killed at Coutras. The King of Navarre destroyed the Catholic army, 2,500 horsemen and 5,000 foot soldiery strong, whilst only himself losing forty men. Whilst the political Mignon was eliminated at Coutras, at Vimory, on October 26th, and at Auneau, on November 24th the King of Paris defeated the Germans with whom the King of Navarre was preparing to link up. Of the three Henri's, Henri of France alone suffered a double and irreparable defeat—only his troops were wiped out. The Huguenots and the Leaguers exulted over their respective victories. Nothing remained of Henri III's plan—my enemies will avenge me on my enemies. On the contrary, his two enemies were stronger than ever. He was only able to rid himself of the vanquished of Vimory and Auneau by paying them very dearly—400,000 écus, but this did not deter the Lorraine Princes from pursuing them, once they were in the Marquisate of Pont-à-Mousson. No notice was any longer taken of the signature of the King of France. No one but the King of Navarre was now able to stand up to the King of Paris.

The King of Paris now addressed the King of France as a conqueror. He spared him no affront, whether it was a matter of demanding strongholds, the dismissal of the La Valette brothers, the publication of the decrees of the Council of Trent, the establishment of the Inquisition, or the outlawry of all heretical subjects. Her son held Catherine de Medici responsible for these Lorraine insolences. Henri III had become so accustomed to his mother's diplomatic victories that Henri de Guise's contempt for the promises he had given her seemed in the King's eyes a sign that the Governess of France's time was over. He made her aware of it, and in such unveiled terms that Catherine confessed her sorrow to Bellièvre, charged to negotiate in her place at Soissons. The King believed that there could no longer be any other outcome but violence. He forbade Guise to enter Paris, a challenge that the King of Paris took up. In order to prove that he was the master of his capital and that Henri III in his Louvre no longer represented the legitimate authority he ignored his orders and on May 9, 1588, entered Paris to the delirious acclamations of its people.

But their rapturous enthusiasm scared him, for he was too intelligent not to realize that his prestige was based on his revolt against the despised Valois and almost solely on this revolt. He desired and was determined to be the King of Paris, but not king of the mob.

This great feudalist feared the democratic Leaguers howling in the streets, whose excesses were increasing day by day. He did not share the fanaticism of his sister Catherine, widow of the Duc de Montpensier. The curés of the League—Boucher, Lincestre, Pigonat and others of their kind—on whom the Duchess showered gold and who placed her portrait on their altars beside that of the Holy Virgin, disgusted this intelligent nobleman, who did not share his sister's fanaticism. She delighted in mob risings, even provoked them, having no understanding of the dangers of this Parisian revolution which she encouraged and with which she collaborated. On hearing of the scandal created by the King and his bed-Mignons at the fair of Saint Germain in the preceding February Guise did not doubt that he had lost his senses completely. The hour had come to depose him but this should be done by the great leaders and only by them. In a Paris in revolt this was not the propitious moment to do so; it was necessary to wait. Furthermore, nothing could be accomplished without the consent of Philip II, who would make no decision until the Invincible Armada was in sight of the British Isles, had avenged Mary Stuart, punished Elizabeth I, and by exterminating the English heretics had defeated the Reformation in Europe.

The balance of forces did not yet allow Henri de Guise to seize power. The Armada had not as yet even left Cadiz, and therefore a recourse to violence must be postponed. An obvious ally was available—the Queen Mother. Instead of marching on the Louvre, Henri de Guise went to see her, having been in correspondence with her whilst Bellièvre was negotiating. He was aware of the fact that she wished to see him, having been greatly vexed at being kept away from the Soissons interviews. The Town Clerk of Bar-sur-Seine, Jacques Carorguy, a member of the Political party, has left *Mémoires* full of first-hand information about those days during which Guise preferred to temporize instead of attempting a *coup de force*. He recorded that Catherine had advised the Duc de Guise to meet her as quickly as possible, 'all the more as she desired to inform him that the King had not approved the League and association they had made together, which was also forbidden by law and ordinance'.

Guise attended the Queen Mother, who although ill and bedridden immediately rose to receive the Duke, who asked her to conduct him to the King. She was shaken by this request, since Henri III's annoyance with the Duke was such that anything might be feared from such a meeting. On the other hand the Duc de Guise was too proud to suffer any insult. Both of them had shown similar courage on the battlefield. The appalling scandal of a duel before the throne was no impossibility, and the Duke even alluded to it himself. 'I have a sword with which to avenge myself against him who might offend me or wish to offend me.' Whilst she was in conversation with him the Queen sent L'Aubespine to the Louvre to prepare the King to receive the Lorraine Prince. At one moment Henri III thought of having him killed by Ornano and his Corsicans, but promptly gave up this idea . . . for in such a case the Parisians would immediately hurl themselves on the Royal Palace and there were not enough troops to resist them. In order to safeguard his dignity he prayed Catherine, through Queen Louise, to conduct the Duc de Guise to the Louvre. Catherine entered her sedan chair, the Duke walking beside her.

Before her son she assumed responsibility for the interview, which was brief and passed without incident. A second audience was accorded for the following day, in the course of which the Duc de Guise requested permission to call the Archbishop of Lyons, Pierre d'Espinac, to Paris; an able and useful intermediary between the Court and the League. More and more perturbed by the attitude of the Parisians the King sent an order to return to Paris from Rouen to the Duc d' Epernon. This was not calculated to please Catherine. We know through Miron how deeply she had been mortified by Epernon's 'insolences and unendurable contempt, which had reduced her to such extremity that whatever might result she was resolved on his ruin, making use of the present occasion'. The recall of d'Epernon was to throw Catherine into the Lorraine camp. In future she would support Guise and endeavour to reconcile him with the King. Such a reconciliation, as we know today, was impossible. Nevertheless Catherine had succeeded in bringing off such exceptional and subtle combinations that in this extremity, alluded to by Miron, the Lorraine card may have seemed to her the least weak one she could play. Whether it was so or not she did play it. She lost; and this was to be her end. This time and finally violence was to defeat cunning. The Day of the Barricades was to provide the partisans of violence with their most effective means of persuading Henri III to throw off his mother's tutelage. The cruelty of this defection was all the greater since on that day Madame Catherine had saved her son's life, and during the following weeks succeeded in preventing the King of Paris from taking advantage of the King of France's flight to assume power.

What had happened? In the afternoon of May 10, 1588, the Queen Mother, accompanied by Bellièvre, had visited the Duc de Guise. She was unable to persuade him to become reconciled to the King, who was to receive him on the following day. She had a very long interview with the Archbishop of Lyons. All this was a waste of time for her and the King, but time gained for the League and Guise. The latter showed the greatest respect to Catherine. Whilst he was with her he met Henri III, who affected to ignore him, and he then returned to the Louvre. This third visit was received in silence; it appeared that the King had decided to have no more dealings with the Duke. It was then learned that Epernon's orders had been countermanded, for Henri III had no desire for a battle in Paris and preferred to leave the city himself. In order to safeguard his departure, he ordered the French Guard and the 4,000 men of the Swiss Guard—his last remaining loyal troops—to enter the capital at dawn on May 12th. The proof that in doing so his intentions were peaceable lies in the fact that the Swiss were forbidden to use their arms. His Capetian repugnance to causing French blood to flow was stronger than any temptation to provoke a trial of strength by taking advantage of the undeniable military superiority enjoyed for a few hours by the King as the result of the entry of the Swiss soldiery into Paris.[1]

Catherine knew only too well that in such days of tumult musket-shots were likely to fly off at their own volition. Immediately on the arrival of the Swiss she sent Bellièvre to Guise, who affirmed his own good intentions towards the King. Swayed by her own wishful thinking she believed him, and encouraged her son to refuse to enter into combat. L'Estoile is definite on this point: 'The King replaced his sword in its scabbard, forbidding all his men on pain of death even to half-draw their own swords, hoping that by temporizing, gentleness and soft words the fury of the rebels would be calmed and that foolish people would thus be gradually disarmed.'

The mob-leaders took advantage of it. The Duc de Guise was obliged to intervene personally to stop the massacre of the Swiss, who had been surprised on their march to the Louvre, where, after suffering heavy casualties, they took refuge. On May 13th, a Friday —and both Catherine and Henri III were superstitiously aware of it

[1] The most complete modern account of the Day of the Barricades is that of Paul Robiquet: *Paris et la Ligue au Temps d'Henri III* (*Histoire municipale de Paris*, Vol. II.) There are very numerous contemporary accounts, of which one of the most interesting is *L'Histoire de la Journée des Barricades*, by Un Bourgeois de Paris, and *L'Historie de la Ligue*, Anon, published by Charles Valois (Vol. I).

—the League prepared to attack the Louvre. Accompanied by Pinart, the Queen Mother went to implore Guise to put an end to the rioting. In the view of the Lorraine Prince abdication was the only means by which the King could save his life. Now convinced that if Henri III could not flee in time the Leaguers would kill him, Catherine spent the morning going to and fro between the Duc de Guise's residence and the Louvre. All the documents agree in proving that by so doing she was risking her own life each time she went from the Marais to the Louvre, since she was obliged to go on foot, in the midst of the barricades and amongst a population drunk with hatred, 'mad bulls', as Guise described them to her, admitting that he was incapable of appeasing them.

With the same calm courage the Amazon of Rouen and Le Havre was reborn in that woman, nearly seventy years old, ill, deserted, and witnessing the collapse of her thirty years' life-work. Only one thought remained to her—to save the life of her child, that big sick child over whom she had watched for so long, ever since he had been king in name, with never a reproach, but of whom she had never been able to make a man. Here she was, now, stumbling over chains, sacks, casks and barrels, piled-up paving-stones, commanding that a passage should be cleared for her. Such contempt for danger could not leave the French unmoved—their admiration for her was greater than their hostility. In this Paris in revolt Madame Catherine passed and re-passed. She knew that they were expecting the King's abdication. She pretended to be sure of herself, like an ambassadress between the King of Paris and the King of France, and showed 'a smiling and confident face, surprised at nothing'. She was covering-up the King's escape and no one, Guise least of all, dreamed of it. Whilst she held him in discussion, thus retarding the giving of the signal for the assault on the Louvre, the King had time to leave the Tuileries through a little gate in the gardens, take to horse, and to flee. It was five o'clock in the evening. Only at six o'clock did the Duc de Guise learn that Henri III had escaped. The Queen was still with him. 'Madame', he cried, 'now I am dead! Whilst Your Majesty keeps me occupied here the King leaves, to my perdition!' And indeed he had gone for that reason. Meanwhile he left it to his mother to maintain the Royal Government in Paris. This most difficult task had been left to an old woman, alone in the midst of her enemies.

Impavidam ferient ruinae. Catherine de Medici's strength of character rose to the situation in the most natural way in the world, perhaps the most tragic situation in all her long life, and yet the most fruitful in sudden changes of fortune. Henri III had been forced to such sudden flight that Queen Louise was unable to accompany him. The gentle and gracious princess was a Lorraine; Catherine had always been in perfect accord with her and now she would be precious to her in keeping up the family tie with the Guises. Whilst Henri III was no longer anything but the King of Chartres the two Queens of France, in Paris, would maintain the State there. Madame Catherine would not leave the side of her daughter-in-law, a better protector to her than any guards, for a single day. A cousin of the Guises, Louise was loved by the Parisian masses. A fragile and charming rampart in whose shelter the Queen Mother organized her defence; a diplomatic defence in conducting which she was at her ease, as her correspondence after May 14, 1587, very clearly shows.

The common enemy of Catherine and the Lorraines was the Duc d'Epernon.[1] It was certain that Henri III, left to himself, would once again fall under the tutelage of the most powerful of the political Mignons, who possessed the stuff of statesmanship. Catherine was resolved to take immediate advantage of the circumstances in order to remove or defeat this Admiral of France and Lieutenant-General of Normandy, this obstacle to her personal power. As early as May 20th she assumed the offensive in a letter to Henri III—although a veiled offensive. The Queen declared herself to be only the inter-mediary between the League, which was demanding the dismissal of the La Valettes, and the King, who was supporting them. The sacrifice of Epernon would make peace possible between the League and Henri III. If the Duc de Guise were to become the sole Coun-cillor the danger of a *coup d'Etat* would diminish.

Was Catherine the dupe of the King of Paris? Certainly not. She had her own plans. There was no doubt that Henri III would leave no issue, but Catherine had a grandson; a grandson in the female line, the Marquis of Pont-à-Mousson, the son of Claude de Valois and Charles III of Lorraine. Attached as she was to the legislative tradition the Queen Mother assuredly did not underestimate the strength of the Salic Law. She had done everything to ensure the legitimate succession to the throne of her son-in-law Navarre. But after Coutras the heretical victor had the whole of Catholic France against him with the exception of the isolated Politicals. The King of Paris was being swept along to the throne according to the almost unanimous wishes of the Catholic population. Since Bourbon and Guise were both of them against the King it seemed an alternative

[1] On Epernon, cf. the authoritative book by Léo Mouton: *Un Demi-Roi*.

solution to have the latter adopt his Lorraine nephew as his heir, thus combining both policy and family interests. The Marquis of Pont-à-Mousson represented the elder branch of Lorraine. Queen Louise, her sisters, the Duc de Mercoeur, her brother, were naturally in favour of this plan. It might not be impossible to win over Henri de Guise through the prospect of a regency; Catherine was old, Henri IIII in ill-health. It might prove a tempting outlook to this ambitious man and one that could be achieved in the near future.

If anyone were to be deceived it would be he and not the Queen. Catherine thought that she still had many years before her and Henri III was healthier than he seemed. (Her letters prove that she believed this to be the case.) The young Lorraine heir to the Crown of France would serve his Royal apprenticeship under his grand-mother's guidance. It seemed to Catherine, enjoying this dream of the future, as if there might still remain some fine political occasions in store for her.[1]

But for the moment it was necessary first to eliminate the viceroy, the odious Epernon, whose strong personality, she knew, would never give way to her own, although she imagined that she would be able to dominate Henri de Guise. Her friendly reception by the Parisian authorities inclined her to think that the Leaguers were capable of once more becoming loyal to the King. Her immediate plan, therefore, was to remain on good terms with the League whilst ensuring the dismissal of Epernon and his brother. To this she constantly returned in her letters to Henri III; this time she was wholeheartedly adhering to the policy to which she had submitted at Nemours. How could this not have been a deliberate plan? The very contradiction between her resistance to the League in 1585 and her collaboration with it after the Day of the Barricades appears to indicate Catherine de Medici's reversion to the Machiavellism she had practised before the death of Monsieur—to an alliance with the stronger party in order that it should not destroy her. But Henri III was resisting the exorbitant claims of the League, which was demanding an even more drastic version of the Treaty of Nemours—(the Paris municipality even dared to demand the destruction of the Bastille). Catherine,

---

[1] Mariéjol, at the end of his *Catherine de Médicis*, joined issue with those historians who took this plan seriously, particularly with Davillé (*Les Prétentions de Charles III de Lorraine à la Couronne de France*). Without discounting the force of Mariéjol's arguments we continue to believe that Catherine did have such a plan. In her mind it was a case not of a change of the dynasty but of its prolongation, to the advantage of a child whom she regarded as a Valois. To her, blood was of greater account than male primogeniture. She was an Italian and did not share the French belief in the Salic Law.

then, revealed her inmost thoughts to Bellièvre: 'I know quite well', she wrote to him on June 2, 1588, 'that, feeling as he does, it is bitter medicine for him to swallow, but it is even harder to be lost, and praise is given to those who know how to give way in time to save themselves. I am preaching to the preacher: but forgive me, for never have I found myself in such trouble nor with so little light as to know how to free myself from it successfully.'[1]

The Spanish danger was coming closer; the Armada had sailed for England and the Duke of Parma was pacifying the Low Countries. The League was in the service of Spain. Peace had to be made at any price or else the threatening catastrophe would no longer be delayed. This was Catherine's view, for she never doubted that Philip II would be victorious over Elizabeth I and Protestantism. The wreck of the Armada was to prove her wrong. At Chartres, Henri III, better advised than she was of the extreme riskiness of the Spanish enterprise and England's ability to defend herself, was counting on Philip's defeat (and events were to prove him right). He said so to Elizabeth's ambassador. That was why, on July 15, 1588, he agreed to the Treaty of Rouen—a treaty that he was certain would never be implemented. It included the extermination of the heretics, the dismissal of Epernon, the bestowal of the Lieutenant-Generalcy of the realm on Guise, with Metz, Boulogne, Angoulême as strongholds, and the granting of the Marquisate of Saluzzo to the Duke of Savoy. The League was to obtain everything.

With one of those frequent flashes of genius that from time to time pierced through his inaction, Henri III had placed his stake on the destruction of the Armada, which the news from Flanders had shown to be a crazy adventure. The English were confident that they would destroy it and thus for a very long time make it impossible for Spain to take the offensive against France and by that very fact to assist the League. Henri III accepted a treaty which he hoped, and which he was even certain, never to have to endure. This, as we can appreciate, was the reason behind the jovial cynicism with which he received Henri de Guise at Chartres: 'My Cousin, let us drink to our good friends, the Huguenots!' 'It is well said, Sire.' 'And to our good barriacaders of Paris. Let us not forget them!'

He forgot them so little that as soon as the news of the Spanish

---

[1] Regarding the Queen Mother's role after the King's flight, cf. the *tirage à part* by Baguenault de Puchesse: *Les Négociations de Catherine de Médicis à Paris, après la Journée des Barricades* (Comptes rendus de l'Académie des Sciences morales et politiques, Vol. LIX, meeting of March 14, 1903).

naval disaster, received only at the beginning of September, was confirmed, on his return to Blois he immediately broke off his connection with his mother's political activities by dismissing the ministers and Secretaries-of-State who had supported her—Cheverny, the Chancellor,[1] Bellièvre, Superintendent of Finances, Bruslart, Pinart, and Villeroy. Their dismissal was brutal and its significance clear—Catherine was disavowed. The King appointed leading parliamentarians who had not hitherto been members of his Councils and who would owe him everything: Montholon, Keeper of the Seals, was to be the successor of Cheverny at the Chancellery; Beaulieu-Ruzé and Revol, Secretaries-of-State. He camouflaged this Palace revolution by also appointing to the Council well-known Guisards: Pierre d'Espinac, Claude La Châtre. Contemporary commentators were mistaken; in their records Aubigné, Pierre Matthieu, Palma-Cayet reflected the prevailing but erroneous opinion according to which Henri III was ridding himself of the legislators who were on the side of the King of Navarre.

Catherine had been with her son since August 7th, when she had joined him at Chartres. The dreadful truth was quite clear to her; Henri III, by the dismissal of the ministers, had deprived her of all power. On September 20th she sent a note to Bellièvre in which she said: 'I would be very sorry were you to take that which I tell you in any other sense than to regret the harm that has been done to me, to teach the King that one should truly love and honour one's mother as God commands, but not to give her so much authority and credence that she may prevent one from doing as one wills; for those who have done so I believe did it to no other end than that, when they wanted to persuade him of something that I did not think to prevent by my prayers, and not considering my remonstrances of great weight, to go beyond that which he would have persuaded.'

Her tone was bitter but without acrimony, expressing lassitude and disgust. Madame Catherine knew that she was no longer anything but a supernumerary. The elections to the States-General held at Blois on September 15th gave the League a triumphant majority.[2]

[1] He had succeeded Birague, who died a poor man, although an Italian and therefore a blood-sucker of the French in public opinion, on November 23, 1583. Birague had spent but not amassed money. Mazarin, a high-living robber as well as a man of genius, did both. Birague was an honest man and a legislator.

[2] With reference to the States of Blois in 1588, cf. Picot, *Histoire des Etats Généraux*, Vol. III. Picot was in every respect mistaken with regard to the reasons for the Palace revolution of September 8th. One of the best sources is the *Journal d'Estienne Bernard*, deputy of the Tiers état of Burgundy, contained in Vol. XIV of the *Etats généraux* by Mayer.

In the hour when her new allies were winning throughout the country the Queen ceased to be Governess of France. How should she have failed to realize that her son had disguised himself as a Leaguer in order to change his policy?—the fox among the wolves. Disgraced though he still remained, Epernon had won. Henri III had always been like that; he needed someone else to govern for him. Since Catherine had been repudiated the greatest of the Mignons would inevitably exercise power in her stead; how soon, Madame Catherine did not know, for this would depend on the time her son would take to avenge himself on Henri de Guise. One thing only she knew for certain—that the King would avenge himself. Why, otherwise, would he have removed from the government her of whom the Archbishop of Lyons had said that 'infinite regard is due to her because she achieves what she sets out to do and holds nothing dearer than the good of her son and his own authority'? And Pierre d'Espinac added: 'Let not the King think that one leans more on her than on him, and it will be sound policy to keep her in perfect intelligence.' Sound policy, sadly thought Catherine, now discarded. The King had changed his policy. 'The day of the dagger will come,' as Felipe de Cavriana had written as early as July 1st.

Was Catherine aware of this prophecy by the Mantuan doctor who had become the Florentine ambassador? It is possible. She was also aware that François d'O, the partisan of violence, was encouraging the King to do away with Henri de Guise. The legate Morosini had spoken to her of it and she feared the worst, which she no longer had any means of preventing. On August 9th Bernardo de Mendoza was already informed of what was being prepared and wrote prophetically to Philip II: 'The only and real danger for the Duc de Guise would be to be attacked and killed in the King's chamber.'

Nothing would any longer stop Henri III from taking the path of violence, for he had only freed himself of his mother in order to be free to avenge himself.[1] And what in his eyes legitimized his revenge was that in satisfying a personal enmity the King of France was

[1] The following two essays should be consulted with reference to the last negotiations of the Queen Mother: *Catherine de Médicis, le duc de Guise et le traité de Nemours*, by Count Edouard de Barthélemy, in Vol. XXVII (1880) of *La Revue des Questions historiques*; and, in the October 1884 number of the same review, *La Conférence de Saint-Brice*, by Guy de Brémond d'Ars. The remarkable book by Edouard Frémy: *Essai sur les Diplomates du Temps de la Ligue* (Paris, 1873) contains two chapters of prime importance on *La Diplomatie pendant la Journée des Barricades* (Chapter VI) and on *Les Négociations à l'Interieur et à l'Exterieur sous le gouvernement municipal de la Ligue jusqu'au Siège de Paris* (Chapter VII). Cf. the book by P. Richard on Pierre d'Espinac.

identifying this with the exercise of his sovereign justice. In having Henri de Guise put to death he was punishing a felon, a rebel and a traitor. But he did not see that the remedy would be worse than the evil. Catherine, on the contrary, was not deceived. This was the cause of her anguish, all the deeper because from that time onward she knew herself to be impotent.

CHAPTER TWO

A DEAD GOAT
(September 1588—January 1589)

-ᢒ⦿⧉ᡣ-

Madame Catherine endeavoured to conceal her displeasure from Henri III as best she could, thought no one else failed to notice it. All she said to him was that he had made great changes in his ministry. We know, through Mendoza, of the ironic reply to her made by the King. His irony was the more cruel since all the men in question had been utterly devoted to his mother: 'I made them because the Chancellor had made an arrangement with the contractors: Bellièvre was a Huguenot; Villeroy, conceited, wanting to be the only one to enjoy the Royal confidence; Bruslart, a nullity; Pinart, a greedy rascal, who would sell his mother and father for money.' He was too intelligent to misjudge the merits of these great administrators. He detested them firstly because they were the enemies of Epernon, and secondly because they were the servants of Catherine. The papal legate, Morosini, did not conceal his anxiety from the King, at seeing him thus dismiss men whose superior abilities and experience he praised. It may be assumed that in doing so Morosini was pleading on behalf of Catherine, all the more as he stressed the risks of possible revenge on the part of the dismissed ministers. The King goodhumouredly replied to the legate in the tones he had used towards his mother. He did not, he said, think them so ill-natured. And he added, mockingly: 'They are all rich and no doubt will want to enjoy in peace the great wealth they acquired in my service.' He continued by declaring that he wanted to learn from the Pope how to make himself obeyed and feared by all, that he was thirty-seven years old, wanted no more associates, and intended henceforward to apply himself uninterruptedly to the government of the kingdom. The allusion to Catherine de Medici was emphasized: 'In order to see whether, by governing it myself, according to my own ideas, I shall arrive at a better result.' For the

rest, he had only acted in advance of the wishes of the States-
General. The latter were supposed to have demanded the dismissal
of the councillors, who had entered into a thousand arrangements
from which the realm had suffered greatly, and of which the people
had bitterly complained.[1] A born orator, Henri—it was obvious—
was enchanted to find himself so eloquent.

Nevertheless he was considerate towards his mother. He always
treated her with the greatest respect, even pretending to consult her.
Catherine was not taken in by these purely formal attentions, seeing
only too clearly how, in his decisions, her son was pursuing his will
to abolish a diarchy that weighed on his mind. In the matter of the
Marquisate of Saluzzo, for instance, the few letters from the Queen
Mother to the Duc and Duchesse de Savoy prove, by their very
banality, that Catherine was no longer consulted. She lamented and
moaned, like a good mother and a good grandmother depressed by a
family quarrel. One can imagine how she champed at the bit. On
October 16, 1588, the day of the opening of the States-General, the
flowers strewn over her by Henri III seemed to the impassive old
Princess like a funerary tribute. Her son paid her homage as
The Mother of the State and the Realm, but alas! this was now all
past. Henri III's entire discourse revealed a surprising determination to rule alone. All his hearers marvelled at it; on the scene of the
monarchy the King was taking the place of the Queen Mother, who
kept silence. And we know that the eloquence of that prince was
worthy of the greatest models of Antiquity.

Henri was playing at exercising authority whilst his mother knew
that he was quite incapable of shouldering its responsibilities except
in words; eloquent and enthusiastic words, of which he knew the
secret. She also knew him to be vindictive and the veiled threats his
discourse contained were directed at the Lorraines: 'Certain of the
great in my kingdom have formed leagues and associations; with my
usual kindness I will as regards this tread the entire past underfoot; but
under my authority no other leagues will be suffered to exist, and as
from now I declare that all those who in future depart from this or
meddle in such without my accord, will be attainted and convicted
of the crime of *lèse-majesté*.'

Since Henri III no longer asked her advice, Madame Catherine,
discarded from the government, occupied herself with her personal
affairs, including the marriage of her granddaughter, Christin o

[1] Documentation in the Archives of the Vatican, *Lettres des Nonces et autres de France*,
in particular in this connection, Vol. XXVII.

Lorraine, with Ferdinand de Medici, Grand Duke of Tuscany since the mysterious death of his brother Francis. The contract was signed in her presence at Blois, on October 24, 1588. The Queen provided the fiancée's dowry, consisting of all her Florentine property and 2,000 écus in gold. The marriage did not take place until five months later, after the death of Catherine on January 5, 1589.

It had been necessary to overcome a good deal of opposition to bring about this match, especially on the part of the Duc de Savoy, who had hoped to marry his daughter Christine to his cousin Nemours, but this last diplomatic success only gave Catherine slight pleasure. She was more and more weary and disgusted with everything. With Ovid she could say:

Hic quoque substiterat post taedia longa laborum.

She was continually ill and her exceptional powers of resistance were being undermined by her gout, her rheumatism, and her catarrh. Towards the middle of December she nearly died of pneumonia. Neglect was added to illness and her solitude was all the more heavy for Catherine, exhausted as she was, to bear, as her intelligence and genius remained unimpaired and tortured her with the memories of her former glory. Sometimes Henri III told her of his growing anxieties, without, however, asking her for advice. Then her courage would revive and she would tell him what she thought to be possible; that he should retire to Lyons to escape from the tyranny of the Guisards, who were masters of the States-General. She agreed with the King's ministers that if the Lorraine prince were suddenly arrested, this might intimidate the Leaguers. Henri III did not contradict her, for he was anxious above all that she should remain unaware of his plan to execute Guise.

'To imprison the Guisard', he told his close collaborators, on whom he could rely not to inform his mother of his intentions, 'would be to net a wild boar, who might prove stronger than our ropes; when he is killed he will give us no more trouble, for a dead man does not go to war.' The tragedy was imminent, but for his part, the Duc de Guise did not believe it: 'I am not afraid of that one', he replied to those who warned him to be on his guard, 'I know him well and he is too much of a coward.' His contempt was as disastrous as it was unjustified and his blindness was fatal to him. That Henri, so magnificently strong, did not guess at the inner resources of energy of the other Henri, depraved and weak though he might be.

Madame Catherine's extremely serious attack of pneumonia facilitated the King's revenge, since he was confident that the plan he was preparing against his proud and imprudent enemy would never be known to her, whose death was expected from day to day. By the time the Queen was convalescent everything was ready: only the occasion was waited upon. In Henri III's view, which was in accordance with the ideas of the century on reasons of State. this was to be the execution of a criminal guilty of *lèse-majesté*, by extraordinary means since it was impossible to bring him to trial and torture according to the usual procedure of justice. It had been the same with Coligny and the King had not forgotten it. His hesitation, on which all the evidence agrees, was not due to any doubts on the score of his right to such a procedure, but to the difficulties of carrying it out and the consequences that were likely to ensue from it. He kept the matter secret from his mother solely because he knew how strongly she was opposed to such terrible deeds of violence (she remembered the morrow of the death of the Admiral) and feared that at the last moment she might warn the Lorraine Prince of the trap. When all was ready he even arranged, with a refinement of cunning, to be present with the Duke, on the Thursday morning, December 22nd, in Catherine's chamber, where she had been taking medicines, and showering all manner of kindnesses and consideration on his redoutable and detested rival.

The next morning, the day before Christmas Eve, Henri de Guise was murdered by the Forty-five. Henri III informed his mother of the *fait accompli*. Then he spoke—never imagining that this appalling news would kill her. On the contrary, he was radiantly happy.

The old Queen, sequestrated in her chamber, inevitably heard the tumult raised by the murder (murder, not assassination, Louis XVIII always royally insisted, when the tragedy of Blois was mentioned to him) the King's apartments being just above her own. Exhausted by her emphysaemia, she had purged herself, and fearing to catch cold on the stairs of the castle, in spite of her anxiety she dared not move, although she could guess only too well what might be happening in her son's study. Cavriana was with her, and the Florentine diplomat has left us his personal account of what occurred when Henri III arrived to visit his mother. The ambassador went forward to meet the King, who asked him how the Queen was feeling. 'I answered him that she was well and that she had only taken some slight medicine. Going towards her then, with the most confident mien and the calmest manner in the world, he said to her: 'Good morning, Madame, I beg you to forgive me, Monsieur de Guise is dead, and no more will be spoken of. I had him killed in order to forestall the same plan that he had formed towards myself. I could no longer tolerate his insolence. . . .' And still satisfied with himself, whilst Madame Catherine remained reprovingly silent, he gave her his reasons in detail—he had even forgiven the Barricades, but faced with new threats from Henri de Guise he had resigned himself to this execution. He desired to relieve his people, and hold the States, but only on condition that the latter spoke as subjects and not as sovereigns.

His mother listened to Henri III without interruption and he continued in these terms: 'I intend now to be king and no longer a captive and a slave, as I have been from May 13th until this hour, when I once again begin to be king and master.' He ended by declaring that he would wage war against the Huguenots with ardour, for he intended to extirpate heresy from his realm. According to Cavriana, Henri III left without his mother having replied a word to him. 'Without weakening,' he reports, 'and on the same firm tone the King went away, seeming not in any way disturbed, neither visually nor mentally, which to me, being present, appeared really marvellous. And I left, full of thought, reflecting on how sweet must be revenge, in order thus to revivify a mind, and light up a face.'

Cavriana was the only witness of Henri III's visit to the Queen Mother, and the fact that he did not report anything that she may have said inclines one to believe that she made no reply. According to other Italian records she did speak a few words, but the various accounts of them differ. The Papal legate, Morosini, informed the Curia that when Catherine cried out: 'But you will lose the kingdom!' the King had replied: 'Come what may! I am avenged!' Giovanni Mocenigo, the Venetian ambassador, who was very much in Catherine's intimacy, and in whom she often confided, complaining notably of Sixtus Quintus—'a certain man who understands nothing of affairs of State'—attributed other words to her: 'My son, I am pleased to hear it, so long as it be for the good of the State. . . . At least I ardently desire it.'

Catherine may well have spoken the words reported by the legate and the Venetian, but not to Henri III. She was stunned by this new blow. Did her son, who had always been so weak and changeable a character, imagine that he could make war at one and the same time on both the Guisards and the Reformationists? Had he gone mad? We know from Cavriana, who recorded it on December 31, 1588, that she was staggered: 'Although very prudent and very experienced in matters of this world, nevertheless she does not know what remedy to apply to so many present ills, nor to the ills to come.' The anonymous author of *L'Histoire de la Ligue* states that on Christmas Day the Queen Mother gave an interview to an Italian capuchin, Bernardo d'Osimo, which appears correctly to express her mind: 'Ah! Unfortunate! Ah! Unfortunate! What has he done? Pray for him, who needs it more than ever, for I can see him hastening to his ruin, and I fear that he will lose his body, his soul, and the kingdom.'

December 25th. On Christmas Eve Madame Catherine learned of the second murder, that of the Cardinal de Guise, killed by six soldiers recruited by one of the Forty-five, Michel de Gast. So her son's madness was increasing! And she herself was ill, immobilized. She questioned her advisers, and received permission to leave her chamber at the end of a week. It is likely that the King visited her either once more or several times. Owing to the lack of direct documentation we are obliged to reconstitute these interviews according to the accounts of them given by the chroniclers and historians of the period. It is the misfortune of Clio that the larger part of the life of the past has vanished, together with those spoken words which were not recorded and preserved in writing. And so we are reduced to mere conjecture with regard to the conversations between Henri III and his mother during the week between Christmas and New Year's Day, those days of anguish and dismay, to know of which would have been so deeply interesting.

We can only imagine Catherine facing her son, now sobered up by the consequences of his revenge. The news from Paris was terrible; the town had risen. Morosini had warned Henri III, who had given the order to kill a prince of the Church, that he would be excommunicated. It would have been natural for Catherine to have thought of renewing her alliance with the King of Navarre. And this probably explains her visit on January 1st to the Cardinal de Bourbon. To the imprisoned Cardinal she brought the promise of safe-conduct. A Leaguer and a Bourbon, the old prelate had always been on excellent terms with her. Might he not be brought in to serve as intermediary between Henri III and the Guisards? Pasquier has reported the scene: 'Then both of them began to make fountains of their eyes. And suddenly afterwards that poor lady returned to her chamber without supping. . . .' In spite of the dual fountains of tears her attempt had ended in utter failure. The Cardinal had reproached the Queen for her deceits, her fine words, her illusory guarantees, her thousand false promises, without which the Lorraine brothers would not have been killed, nor he himself have been a prisoner.

The defeat of this final hope was the end of Madame Catherine. And what injustice—to accuse her of having collaborated in the tragedy which was killing her! She returned home broken. The cruelty of fate was too strong for her. Nothing was left to her but to disappear from a scene on which she no longer had any part to play. Like Machiavelli, she had sacrificed everything for her country only, like him, to fail in everything. And although history has proved that she had only apparently failed, to the Queen, under the rubble and the ruins, her failure could not but appear to have been final.

When in defiance of her doctors she had gone out on that icy day she had deliberately undertaken that dangerous visit to the Cardinal de Bourbon. Despair rendered her incapable of fighting against her illness, which recurred. Morosini, who was very well informed about the seriousness of her infection, which she had not been able to shake off for a fortnight, knew that this relapse would be fatal.

He informed Rome of the fact: 'She has a very great fever', he wrote on January 4th, 'and although the doctors say that it is merely a feverish cold and there is no danger, the advanced age of the patient and her relapse are causing great anxiety.'

Madame Catherine no longer resisted; at last the great fighter admitted that she was finally beaten. In spite of fever and suffocation she remained lucid. In this evening solitude, when she was wrapped in suffering, how should she not have remembered her past, arising before her eyes that were closed to the dreadful present? It was a present peopled by bloody ghosts who brought with them those of other days who had also uselessly shed their blood. Blood and tears and all those ruins . . . did nothing remain then but ruins? Was no human consolation allowed to this old woman, her lungs and her mind threatened with the death she had so often defied, the dangers she had so often mastered? There were servants in her chamber, her beloved Italians. But where were the French? Why were they not there? And her son? He could spare her only a few moments, for with his ministers he was trying to organize his defence against Paris, against the provinces, the Pope, the King of Navarre, the Guises and Spain—all of them. He could no longer rely on anyone. Below his

own, his mother's chamber only contained a dying woman; Madame
Catherine was dying and leaving him disarmed. Never had he had
such need of her whom he had so harshly repudiated.

Dreams and ghosts . . . the implacable procession of memories and
the torture they brought with them. Yet some of them were happy
ones. They did not come from the political heavens, black with
thunder-clouds. They came from that heaven and those gods that
had illumined the too infrequent occasions when the Medici
Princess could again become a humanist, in love with pure science
and luminous beauty, as she had always been, by nature and tradition. How much she had loved the Court, the feasts, the castles and
theatrical performances! She had even included entertainments and
luxury in her policies. From her Florentine ancestors she had inherited a taste for the refinements of civilization, with its painters,
Clouet especially; its sculptors, particularly Germain Pilon; her
enameller, Léonard Limousin; her potter, Bernard Palissy; her
tapestry worker, Nicolas Houel. How greatly she had enjoyed giving
them her orders, interesting herself in their work both as a keen
collector and a generous Maecenas! With her goldsmiths she designed
jewels; with her architects and gardeners, mansions, palaces, and
parks.[1]

In the company of scholars she chose the admirable books and
rare manuscripts in her library. Erudite herself, interested in mathematics, astronomy, astrology, stones, plants and animals, she devoted
all her spare time to reading and study. Agreeable as she found them,
the balls, receptions and banquets did not induce rest. They were
still part of her political activities, of her Royal labours, premeditated
and carefully organized occasions, on which her mind was allowed
no relaxation. Her male and female dwarfs, whom it amused her to
marry with one another in order to create future generations of
little monsters to the astonishment of the seers at her Court, were
never able to distract her mind for long, any more than her fools.

[1] In his remarkable work, *Construction de Paris*, (Paris, 1938) M. René Héron de Ville-
fosse devotes a whole chapter to Catherine de Médici's influence on the architecture of
the capital (*L'Italianisme vainqueur*, pp. 102–40.) For an entire century, from Médici to
Mazarin, the Italian influence predominated in the arts; e.g. the Hôtel de Soissons,
Hôtel de Scipion Sardini, the Luxembourg and the Palais Cardinal, the whole series of
Dômes until the Invalides of the Grand Roi and with Sainte-Geneviève under Louis
XVI, by way of the Sorbonne, the Val de Grâce, the Collège des Quatre Nations, the
chapel of the Hôpital général, the churches of L'Assomption and La Visitation. Spain
reigned over literature. She dominated over religious policy through the works of Saint
Ignatius de Loyola and the Jesuits, and mystical theology through the influence of Saint
Teresa of Avila, and Saint John of the Cross and Carmel.

She had too many anxieties to be able freely to enjoy such trivial amusements. Anxiety and solicitude were her portion and chained her to her heavy task. She was never free except at short intervals amidst her musicians and poets, when it amused her to submit her short verses and those of her son Charles to Ronsard or Jodelle, to Baïf or Belleau.

She was even in the fresh air of her country seats, at Montceaux, Chenonceaux, Saint-Maur. She decided that the Tuileries should be a park, dedicated to the Muses, in the heart of her capital. Close by she built a veritable palace, her own home.[1] Whenever possible she was at Saint-Maur, where she lived a farmer's life. In spite of her royal love of splendour, Madame Catherine, now dying in solitude at that castle of Blois where she had never felt really at home, had remained a bourgeoise and a countrywoman. Although she built palaces, and very competently collaborated with architects like Primatice, Philibert de L'Orme, Pierre Lescot, Chambigues and Jean Bullant, she never overlooked what was useful as well as magnificent. A keen gardener, she watched over the watering of her kitchen gardens, over the fountains and conduits that provided the fertilizing water. She planted vineyards, kept silkworms, aviaries, and animal preserves. Why was Catherine not allowed to die at Chenonceaux, where she had created all this; Chenonceaux, the home, Henri III said, where she found greater happiness and pleasure than anywhere else.

Were Chenonceaux and Touraine perhaps so dear to her, Chenonceaux, that she decided would be more sumptuous than Fontainebleau itself, because she had won it from Diane de Poitiers, the rival whom she had first had to endure but whom she later vanquished? The Lady of the Crescent had ordered Philibert de l'Orme to build the five-arched bridge over the Cher, above which rose the two floors of the gallery, like a bow stretched five times over the controlled course of the river below. The Bow and the Crescent—was not the Bow Catherine's? This jealously-loved property, which had been built for Catherine Bohier, a minister's wife, and beautified for a king's mistress, was the emblem of Catherine's victory. The inner vision is heightened by fever. Madame Catherine could now see in her mind's eye the waving masses of foliage, the waters, like tarnished mirrors, almost as calm as a pond, the portico with caryatides by

[1] Later the Hôtel de Soissons, on the site of the convent of the Filles pénitentes. This masterpiece was destroyed in 1755 owing to the vandalism of the municipality of Paris, in order to build the Halle aux blés.

Jean Goujon, the gateway and the motto encased in gold of the General of Finances, son-in-law of Briçonnet: '*S'il vient à point, il me souviendra.*'

What had now come to term for the sovereign, heavy with years, sadness and disillusionment, with deceitful glory, who knew that the end of the Valois was decreed by fate, was Death, the liberator, whom she accepted. At last she welcomed the Victory of Death, which she had never feared but had always beaten back because her task had been unfulfilled, constantly disrupted and taken up again, a tapestry of Penelope, but a Penelope who now no longer awaited a Ulysses. It had come to term because, had she lived, Catherine de Medici could have accomplished nothing more. Nothing now remained to her but memories.

In that hour when one no longer lies to oneself any more than one lies to God the Queen remembered her mistakes, her faults, her failures and her sins, due not to pride but to weakness. She also remembered what the libellers had called her crimes, for which her conscience reproached her not at all, since they were only executions for the public good, in the service of the State. During thirty entire years she had performed this service like a good woman, a good housewife, a good mother, a good mistress of the kingdom. An incompetent husband had left her a most imperilled inheritance; had she maintained it intact before and against all comers? The future was to answer that question but Catherine was not to know the answer. The Queen from Florence who with so much intelligence and ability had placed the methods she, with Machiavelli and Guicciardini, had been taught to use by the revolutions and civil wars of Italy, at the service of the shaken and almost crumbling Capetian tradition, handed on to her son a France that had not been dismembered during those thirty years in spite of having to endure the attacks of both the factions and the foreigner. But deprived of his mother, what would he do with it?

The dying woman's agony suddenly became sharper. Only her hated son-in-law, whose genius, however, she was too perspicuous to underestimate, would save this heritage. By force of circumstance the Navarrese would replace the Florentine Queen, whose alliance he had rejected, at the side of the Valois, who was to become no more than a petty Italian princelet. The stage was too small for them to remain upon it together: the stage that by her son's command she had been obliged to vacate some months previously. This act of will, the only one that her too well-loved Henri had shown, was an act of

ingratitude, and was accompanied by the mad presumption he showed
in committing murders that were neither useful nor profitable. Henri
had not learned the lessons of the deaths of François de Guise and
Coligny as Catherine de Medici had done. Her horror at the sight
of the murdered bodies of the Duke and the Cardinal included both
prescience and understanding. The fate of the Valois had not
ceased to forge a chain of murder.

No refuge remained save in God. Superstitious and yet sceptical
with regard to the subtleties of dogma and ritual ceremonies, Madame
Catherine was always a believer, untroubled with regard to the
essence of Catholicism, peacefully observant both of faith and practice. As for all the disputes regarding the mysteries and the sacraments, that was a matter for the theologians. God was the supreme
judge and the Queen placed herself in His infinite mercy. She knew
that her hour was near. On Thursday morning, January 5, 1589,
she dictated to her notaries and scriveners, Pierre Favin and Jean
Chesneau, a very long testament, which proves that she retained her
full and complete consciousness. The text of this testament is at
first sight surprising, for it is entirely personal, religious, and private,
containing nothing political. The Queen Mother was vanishing without a word on the subject of the most dominating passion of her life.
She died as a simple Christian woman, solely preoccupied with her
spiritual salvation and her dependents. She 'wills and orders that her
body be interred in the church of Saint-Denis-en-France'. She had
considered this matter a long time ago and all preparations had been
made. She had ordered a chapel to be constructed in the form of a
rotunda, adjacent to the abbey, based on the plans of Primatio, Pierre
Lescot, Jean Bullant and Baptiste Androuet du Cerceau.

At the time of her death this chapel was not yet completed, and as
if incompleteness were to follow Catherine de Medici to her grave,
the work was never either continued nor resumed. This chapel of the
Valois, also known as Notre-Dame-de-la-Rotonde, gradually fell
into ruins and was ultimately demolished in 1719. According to certain authors the stones from it were used to build the Naumachie in
the Parc Monceau. Thus all that remained of Catherine's wish to have
her chapel in Saint-Denis was this graceful colonnade, so called
because of the resemblance of its circular form to the naumachy
erected by the Emperor Domitian on the banks of the Tiber, bearing
a warlike name in the peaceful and charming gardens designed by
Carmontelle for the Folie de Chartres, for the pleasure of the future

Philippe-Egalité. Was there some posthumous irony attached to the fate of the Queen, whose dream of the Portuguese succession had foundered at the Azores, in this peaceable representation of a naval battle on the site of a hamlet with the same name as her property in Brie? This naumachy, last vestige of an unfinished chapel . . . history does contain such unexpected meetings and unknown twists and turns.

Her tomb survived the chapel. After the demolition of the latter it was re-erected in the Abbey of Saint-Denis. Whilst she still lived Catherine had been able to contemplate this masterpiece by Germain Pilon and its magnificence must have delighted the daughter of the Medici. As Jean Juste had done for Louis XII and Anne de Bretagne, Philibert de L'Orme and Pierre Bontemps for François I and Claude de France, Germain Pilon, in completing the unequalled trilogy in stone of the Royalty of the French Renaissance, decided that Henri II and Catherine who lay beneath the mausoleum, should be represented in prayer, as conquerors of death, on the pedestal above it. The recumbent sovereigns are watched over by four bronze Virtues— Prudence, Temperance, Justice and Strength—whilst their transparent marble covering allows their forms to be seen, as in the case of pagan statues.

Did such paganism in the necropolis of the Kings of France appear to Madame Catherine to be out of place? Between 1580 and 1582 she ordered another group. The recumbent marble figures on a bronze base were now dressed in coronation robes. Those praying on the tomb of Saint-Denis were of bronze, in Court dress—Henri II, his right hand on his chest, his left hand outstreched; Catherine with her hands clasped. The King's face is melancholy. The meditative expression of the Queen's agrees with all we can imagine of her that is not in contradiction to her subtle and secret genius. With prodigious intuition the stone-mason's son has depicted in Catherine's case the bitterness that was normally unrevealed but that was hidden beneath her deepest hopes and which only a few passages in her letters have revealed to the historian.

Although she willed and ordered that she be buried beside Henri II at Saint-Denis, the Queen, 'with regard to her obsequies and funeral leaves this to the will of the King her son and others, her testamentary executors'. She was interested in the place where she would rest, but not in the pomp and vanity of the funeral ceremony. She dictated a list of pious foundations, alms and bequests. Her principal heiress, to whom almost all her property was to revert, was

'Madame Chrétienne or Christine, born in 1566, Princesse de Lorraine, her granddaughter.' Queen Louise was to have her dear Chenonceaux. Her natural grandson, Charles de Valois, was to inherit her properties in the maternal line—the comtés of Clermont and Auvergne, the baronies of La Tour and La Chaise, and the comté of Lauraguais. Then followed the bequests to all those who had served her faithfully—ladies, lords, chaplains, officers and servants. The remainder, which she did not define precisely, was to go to 'the King, her son, whom she appoints and institutes as her sole heir'. She forgot nothing, and even ordered that 'all and each of her possessions that will be the property of and belong to the said King, as the inheritance of the said Lady in virtue of the present testament or otherwise by intestacy, should pass to him as to a private individual, without being stated to form part of a whole and annexed to the Crown of France, and this, in the most conclusive manner in which it may be done, either by form of codicil, donation as the result of death, or otherwise'.

Or otherwise. . . . Madame Catherine had taken her precautions. Nothing was to go to the couple who would succeed to the throne, Henri and Marguerite de Navarre, nothing that was the private property of their mother, who did not renounce her grudge against them even if—God alone knew it—she forgave them. The wording of the document leaves no room for doubt: the old dying woman took care to disinherit the Gascon and Margot. She was certainly predestined to become a Balzac heroine.

'The said Lady, the testatrix, has declared her inability to sign, on account of her weakness.' Who did sign her will? Henri III, Queen Louise, the Princess Christine, the Keeper of the Seals, Dupuy, the First President of Brittany, Du Riz, who were her testamentary executors. The notaries countersigned it. Thus all was in order; she had made, spoken, and named the present testament, had read and re-read it. The text mentions this deliberately.

This had taken place before noon. It was known that Catherine was doomed but her imminent passing was not expected. It was hoped that she could live a few days longer still. It was the eve of Epiphany. At one o'clock she received the Last Sacraments, deeply repentant of her sins in the sight of God. If one may believe her contemporaries, her end was hastened by learning the name of her confessor. He was one of Henri III's almoners, Julien de Saint Germain, Abbot of Charlieu. Catherine de Medici's astrologers had predicted that she would die near to Saint Germain. When she heard that name she cried out: 'I am dead!' Was there any truth in this picturesque anecdote? We do not know, but the fact remains that as soon as the Sacrament had been administered to her the Queen Mother gave up the ghost, at half past one in the afternoon.

Her entourage mourned her deeply, for she had been the best of mistresses, loved and venerated. The King, the Queen, the Princess Christine, were also deeply moved by her end, realizing all that they were losing with her, who had dominated a third of her century. At the beginning of her illness, three weeks previously, Morosini had written that 'if she should die one would have reason to fear that the affairs of the realm would suffer greatly from her death'. The legate knew Henri III's incapacity to carry out a big plan and that his intelligence was permanently undermined by his weaknesses. Although she had been cast aside, in the face of danger Madame Catherine would have been recalled. Everyone had become so used to seeing her always at her combat post that this sudden end was unimaginable. When she had fallen ill public prayers had been said for her recovery. It was thought that once she recovered, although a septuagenarian, she would still be strong enough to live for another fifteen years. Morosini immediately took the measure of the seriousness of her death. 'Only this great blow remained to be delivered', he wrote, 'to complete the disasters of this unfortunate kingdom, against which we can observe God's wrath so fully unleashed that we may fear great ruin.'

In his *Sonnets à la Reine mère du Roi*, the Court poet, Jodelle, had anticipated Morosini's view. An impartial history must approve his splendid lyrical praise:

> *C'était grand bien (encor que la crainte ou contrainte*
> *T'ait pu, même à bon droit, tel vouloir ébranler)*
> *Que tu voudrais toujours entre nous rappeler*
> *La Paix, bannie hélas! par ardeur sainte ou feinte,*
>
> *Que tu as sans rien t'épargner, et sans crainte*
> *D'aucun hasard, voulu peiner, fonder, aller*
> *Deçà dela, mander, desseigner et parler*
> *Tant bien, pour par raison rendre l'ardeur éteinte.*

C'est grand bien, nonobstant tant de sang, tant d'horreurs,
Juste amende, payée à Dieu pour nos erreurs,
D'avoir enfin pourtant étouffé la grand'flamme,

Et même désigné la place fraîche, avoir
Tout fermé, tout couvert; mais c'est tout de pouvoir
Qu'un mal caché, couvert, ne se sauve et renflamme.

As he said in another sonnet:

Quand je te vois sur toi porter toute la France...

.   .   .   .   .   .

Quand je vois que sur toi toute l'Europe a l'oeil,
Quand je te vois porter souvent un double deuil
Du temps et de Henri, quand je vois qu'on te charge,

T'aboyant des deux parts, je te plains fort dans moi...

Yes, Catherine de Medici was to be pitied. She had worn her widow's weeds and the mourning of a misunderstood queen and she died forgotten, misjudged, and cast aside. The poet's intuition had here penetrated to the deeper truths of a soul that was full of suffering, a soul to which only her courage brought the comfort of hope constantly reborn, which only the rebellion of her favourite son could finally destroy. At that moment her physical resistance also gave way. This was her whole *raison d'être* although Lucretius disdained it:

Noctes atque dies niti praestante labore
Ad summas emergere opes, rerumque potiri...

Nothing of it remained....
Why go on living if she were no longer to reign?

'The Queen's body was dissected on the King's orders and it was found that the lung was attacked, blood had flowed into the brain, with an abscess on the left side. The body was embalmed, placed in a lead coffin and enclosed in a wooden one. In order to satisfy the people, who came running from all quarters to see the Queen, her body was transferred from the ordinary chamber to the audience chamber, dressed in the most beautiful golden clothes in the palace. Many ladies in mourning watched by the body, around which a quantity of lights were burning and Franciscan Fathers sang psalms over it all night.[1]

Her funeral, which took place in the Church of Saint-Sauveur at Blois on February 4, 1589, was a regal one, for Henri III decided that it should be given in all the splendour authorized by ceremonial. The Patriarch and Archbishop of Bourges, Primate of Aquitania, Regnault de Beaune, gave an admirable funeral oration. As Paris was in the hands of the Leaguers it was impossible for the burial to take place in Saint-Denis, and the coffin was provisionally placed in the crypt of Saint-Sauveur. As, according to Pasquier, she had been badly embalmed, the grave had to be dug in the soil beneath the church, during the night, on account of the body's dissolution. Whilst the Parisians were demanding that Catherine de Medici's corpse should be thrown into the common sewers, Pierre de L'Estoile described in the following terms the impression her death had made on the moderates: 'On Saturday January 7th the news reached Paris of the death of the Queen, mother of the King. . . . She was seventy-one years old.[2] and for so corpulent a woman as she was, carried her years well. She ate well and fed well, but did not have a very good grasp of public matters, although during the thirty years since her husband's death she had had to deal with as many great and important affairs as any queen in the world. She died indebted to the extent of 800,000 écus, being prodigal and therefore more generous than any prince or princess in Christendom; this she had inherited from those of her House.' L'Estoile was well-informed and knew that the Queen's death had been hastened by her visit to the Cardinal de Bourbon and the reproaches that she had received from him. 'She did not recover from it but died on January 5, 1589, which was the eve of the Feast of Kings, a date fatal to those of her House; for Alessandro de Medici was killed on that day and Lorenzo de Medici and others, as the history of Florence proves.'

The chronicler, who had no illusions left on the score of human vanities, after recalling the fury of the people of Paris against the

[1] Archives of the Vatican, *op. cit.* January 15, 1589.
[2] The chronicler was mistaken. Born on April 13, 1519, on January 5, 1589, Catherine was not yet seventy.

Queen Mother, concluded: 'As for Blois, where she was adored and venerated like the Juno of the Court, no sooner had she drawn her last breath than nowhere did they pay more notice to her than to a dead goat.'

A 'dead goat' buried in a provincial church. Even after her death misfortune continued to pursue Catherine de Medici. Henri IV, who had most certainly not forgiven her for deliberately leaving him out of her testament, carefully omitted to carry out the clause relating to her burial in the chapel of Saint-Denis. Yet he and Margot were not the only members of the Royal Family not to have been mentioned in her will. The legitimized daughter of Henri II, Diane de France, did not appear in it, either. Catherine had liked her and we do not know for what reason or motive the old Queen excluded this noble and great princess, whose bastardy Henri II had annulled, from her succession. We may be allowed to suppose that it was from revenge against the Montmorencys, who had not supported her in her last conflicts.

The widow, since 1579, of the Marshal François de Montmorency, Madame Diane, Duchesse d'Angoulême and Châtellerault, beautiful, intelligent, and good, was devoted to the Blood of France. She served the cause of French unity, rallied around the King, with a devotion that was as able as it was wholehearted. It was she who after the death of the Queen Mother was the intermediary in bringing together Henri III and the King of Navarre. The affection which she bore both these princes favoured her message of peace. Catherine's policy was resuscitated by this admirable Daughter of France, Italian on her mother's side, as the Florentine Queen had been French on hers. In Diane de Montmorency a love of France and an Italian pliability were once again united, and by the time she was fifty years of age she had acquired a deep knowledge of life and men. The qualities that Catherine de Medici had been unable to transmit to any of her children—will-power, the feeling and the knowledge that her personal interests, her passions and desires, must be sacrificed to the national interest—were by an irony of fate to re-appear in the daughter borne to her husband by his first mistress, the humble Piedmontese. The Duchesse de Châtellerault refrained from remembering that in spite of the services she had rendered her during the past ten years, Catherine when on her death-bed had passed her over. As soon as Henri IV had disappeared in his turn the daughter of Henri II caused the forgotten lady of Saint-Sauveur de Blois to be interred in the Dionysian chapel, beside her husband.

1610. Madame Catherine had slept for twenty-one years, almost forgotten, in the soil of France; that soil which she had so dearly loved, served, and defended; that soil which she had saved. Like a naked babe, like a dead goat. When she arrived and when she departed she was the unnoticed one. The morning of her life was spent in humility, her evening in solitude. Between these two periods, when her effacement was equally unjust, had stretched the span of a life which had gradually become greater as her task became greater. It was a hard and ungrateful task which she did not complete. This incompleteness was the cause of perpetual suffering to the great artist she had been, born in Florence at the very moment when Leonardo da Vinci was dying near Amboise, and applying her own artistic genius to politics.

No suffering that is accepted, borne and offered, fails to bear fruit. Hers led to the salvation of the kingdom. By maintaining intact its principles and its frontiers Catherine de Medici, a great King of France, ensured the victory of the Blood of the Capets in the person of Henri IV and the restoration of the nation.

Nogent-le-Rotrou, June 1934–December 1939.
Orry-la-Ville, September 1958–November 1959.

INDEX